AND   ENT
                                           AGE
                                           RS:
                                           or of
                                           rown

The Development of Language and Language Researchers: *Essays in Honor of Roger Brown*

Edited by

FRANK S. KESSEL
University of Houston

LEA LAWRENCE ERLBAUM ASSOCIATES, PUBLISHERS
1988   Hillsdale, New Jersey   Hove and London

Lawrence Erlbaum Associates, Inc., Publishers
365 Broadway
Hillsdale, New Jersey 07642

Library of Congress Cataloging-in-Publication Data
The Development of language and language researchers.

Includes bibliographies and indexes.
1. Language acquisition.   2. Linguistics.   3. Brown,
Roger William, 1925–   . I. Brown, Roger William,
1925–   . II. Kessel, Frank S.
P118.D445   1988   401′.9   87-24548
ISBN 0-89859-906-7
ISBN 0-8058-0063-8 (pbk.)

Printed in the United States of America
10   9   8   7   6   5   4   3   2

Contents

Roger Brown

On Words and People:
An Introduction
to this Collection

Frank Kessel
University of Houston

> *Why does the writing make us chase the writer? Why can't we leave well*
> *alone? Why aren't the books enough? Flaubert wanted them to be: few*
> *writers believed more in the objectivity of the written text and the insig-*
> *nificance of the writer's personality; yet still we disobediently pursue.*
> —Julian Barnes (*Flaubert's Parrot*)

Disobedient pursuit of the writer-on-language-development provided the proximate beginnings of this celebratory collection, a pursuit that was itself launched
during a dinner that took place, in the Spring of 1980, in the elegant dining room
of a particular Boston hotel with Parisian parentage. Somewhere between the
entrée and dessert I turned to my generous-hearted host and said, "You know,
SRCD is in Boston next year. Wouldn't it be great to gather some members of
the Harvard language-acquisition group and get them to think about how their
ideas originally took shape and have since developed?" To which my host gently
replied, "Yes . . . that's a fine idea . . . I'll even be pleased to come and listen
from the back of the room." Which wasn't altogether the answer I had hoped
for.

Thus began a lengthy tale, during the first phase of which this ever-gentle
refusal to participate in any way in the projected gathering remained rock-steady,
as firm, in fact, as my conviction that a 1981 Boston meeting on language
acquisition without Roger Brown would be akin to a gathering to herald the joys
of *Rigoletto* and *La Traviata* held in Milan in 1881 without Giuseppe Verdi!
Strengthened in such a conviction by inside-members-of-the-Harvard-group now
party to the plot, I-the-outsider persisted; and we, having engaged in rather
devious and disobedient pursuit over many months, prevailed. Thus, when the

1

Society for Research in Child Development did convene in Boston in early April 1981 we were delighted to have Roger with us . . . on the podium at the front of a crowded room! From which spot—as "Co-chair" of a symposium on "The Development of Language and Language Researchers: Whatever Happened to Linguistic Theory?"—in miniature character essays of gem-like quality he proceeded to introduce Dan Slobin, Melissa Bowerman, Michael Maratsos, Steven Pinker and Courtney Cazden as speakers (in that order) and George Miller as discussant.

Soon—perhaps as soon as during the immediately following lunch—the evident success (in several senses) of the symposium led to the idea of expanding the cast and collecting their contributions in a *Festschrift*. We thus entered the phase of bringing this volume into being. After some consultation with Roger—happily no longer at the back of the room—I extended invitations to people who had studied with him to compose chapters that focused on any area of language development of interest to them and that included—again, in a manner they felt most appropriate—at least a thread of "intellectual biography," i.e., a consideration of how their ideas had taken shape during their Harvard days and how they had subsequently evolved.

Enthusiastic acceptances of such invitations in hand, and the goal of getting the collection into Roger's hands for his 60th birthday having been declared, I gladly undertook the role of editorial organizer. And though we patently did not achieve that birthday goal[1]—and though in a small number of instances I reluctantly had to give a rather more literal meaning to "chasing the writer"!—I remain more than glad of the opportunity to help bring together contributions of such quality and contributors of such commitment. Almost without exception they responded cheerfully and graciously to my extended editorial organizing, suggesting, and cajoling. For that I, the "outsider," extend most sincere thanks to them.

Regarding the organization and substance of these chapters, I need only note that—as in the original group of five—the contributors represent, in a rough way, different cohorts of students who had worked with Roger. That Cazden, a member of one of the earlier Harvard groupings, spoke last at the SRCD Symposium reflects the fact that the range of substantive interests Roger's students felt free to pursue makes uninformative, if not misleading, a strict "cohort chronology." Hence the loose and largely implicit organization of this collection—since none of the chapter categories and labels Roger and I could construct seemed especially more "natural" than any others, in the end I thought it best to allow the reader relative freedom in discerning a meaningful structure of ideas and themes.

That said, certain substantive features of the language development story

---

[1]In truth, the party alluded to in Roger's Afterword—held in Boston in April, 1985—was more a celebration of his 60th birthday than of the at-that-point-incomplete book.

seem to me to resonate and relate to one another in various of these chapters—Slobin tells of its beginnings, and Bowerman, de Villiers, Hanlon and Wanner pick up in some ways some of his threads; Pinker and Maratsos form something of a natural pair in considering in contemporary terms issues presaged in earlier (1960s) writings, as do Bellugi and Petitto, Cromer and Tager-Flusberg. (The specific content of their discussions seemed to call for a reversal of cohort chronology for the first of these pairs.) A more "social" theme is then variously sounded by Berko Gleason, Cazden, Hakuta and Coleman (chronology here preserved), a somewhat more "literary" theme by Rubin and by Winner and Gardner. And Rosch provides an apposite closing in considering coherence in cognitive categories and in the kind of intellectual history to which Roger Brown has made his signal contribution.

It is also worth noting that, given this range of contributions, it made little sense to even try to retain as a single focal point for the volume what was one of the original symposium's stated organizing issues, *viz.*, the shifting and problematical link between linguistic theory and language acquisition research. This is, of course, not to suggest that the issue has, in the interim, somehow been resolved. Indeed, several of the chapters—most notably Bowerman's and de Villiers'—can be read with profit from that perspective. (See also Maratsos' Historical Addendum.) This is, indeed, but one of several fundamental matters pertaining to language and language development addressed, in various ways and to varying degrees of depth, in these chapters. And while the ideal introduction to such a collection would analyse and even synthesize the discussion of such matters, I can defensibly make no claim to having the competence to perform that task. If, after all, Roger himself issues such a disclaimer in his Afterword. . . . ! The contributors, in any event, can and do speak admirably for themselves.

But, to complete the story of this volume's genesis, how—someone somewhere may well be wondering—did I-the-outsider come to the editorial role? The more distant beginnings for the collection were laid in the fall of 1967 when I arrived from Cape Town at the University of Minnesota accompanied by a crate of books that included Bellugi and Brown's (1964) *Monograph* (purchased—the inside front cover now reveals—in June '66); Brown's (1965) *Social Psychology* (purchased in October '66); and several annual reports from the Harvard Center for Cognitive Studies containing heavily underlined accounts of the ideas on language and language acquisition of Brown, McNeill, Slobin and others.[2] Whereupon, in that first Minnesota semester, I took a course on "Advanced Language Development" taught by John Flavell and built around Brown's (1965) language chapters, Chomsky (1965), Smith and Miller (1966), and a

[2]How I would happen to have such material in hand is a tale—to be told elsewhere perhaps—that says much about the quality of psychology, *and* psychologists, I had been fortunate enough to encounter at the University of Cape Town.

variety of unpublished papers by Brown, Bellugi, Cazden and others.[3] Relatively soon thereafter, having heard much more about Chomsky's "revolution" from Jim Jenkins and others in the Human Learning Center[4] and having made a brief summer stop for preprints at MIT, I found myself planning and conducting dissertation research focused, in part, on the soon-to-be-published studies of "late" language acquisition by Carol Chomsky (1969). And not long after that research was published (Kessel, 1970) I received, in the early Spring of 1971, an unsolicited note from Roger Brown saying something simple and sincere about the *Monograph*. On the verge of embarking on a professionally wayward path— but hoping to stay informed about language and other developmental research—I replied with gratitude and received from Roger, in turn, a draft copy of Stage I for *A First Language* (1973). I could not, then, have left North American academic life with a finer and more strengthening experience of "simple" intellectual fellowship and collegiality.

To speak of Roger's generosity of scholarly spirit brings me easily and appropriately back to this collection, for such a spirit is attested to in various ways by each and every contributor. For my part, having returned to the academic fold and having finally made personal and musical contact with Roger,[5] I conceived of the SRCD symposium partly in the context of a rekindled interest in post-positivist philosophy of science (Kessel, 1969). Thus, in introducing that gathering I suggested—in fairly high-falutin' fashion—that there is growing recognition of the place of historical, sociological, psychobiographical and personal-stylistic considerations in any worthwhile account of the individual and collective workings of scientific thought and imagination and of scientific change (e.g., Toulmin, 1972). Given my belief then—still largely intact now—that psychology too seldoms reflects that recognition, the original symposium, and hence this volume, were partly conceived in the spirit of making one kind of modest beginning in examining, for example, questions of research-group dynamics—How does a group begin and coalesce, what ideas and basic thematic commitments (Holton,

---

[3]If memory serves, this was the first time the new wave of ideas on language development were considered in a course in the Institute of Child Development. As a further sociological sign of the times the formal appointment of a "language person" (Michael Maratsos) was only made several years later.

[4]Not unlike this one in spirit, a volume of essays by "Minnesota cohorts" on *The Cognitive Psychology Revolution Reconsidered* is presently being prepared in Jim Jenkins' honor.

[5]This occurred when Roger visited Houston to participate in the second Houston Symposium (Brown, 1981). Appropriately attuned to this biographical note (see his Afterword), one finds the following operatic touch to the Preface of *Social Psychology*: "I have had great pleasure from the writing of this book over the past three-and-one-half years; partly because I enjoyed the work but also because the Boston FM stations provided a sustaining flow of Bellini, Verdi, Puccini, and Wagner. My first acknowledgement of help is to them" (Brown, 1965, p. vii). Note too, in the Appendix "Autobiography" his "perfect springtime" of study of emotional meanings in music ("perfect" despite the intellectualistic expectations of music educators!).

1978) do its members share; how do their ideas grow and their influence spread? From such a perspective, then, this group of Harvard language researchers can be seen as having provided beginning notes on their intellectual biographies for future scrutiny by the historian, philosopher and, even, ethnographer of science.

What such scrutiny might yield would, again in the ideal introduction, be worth considering. But, again, I must demur, knowing well that my more recent excursions into the history and philosophy of psychology[6] are no defense against doing dilettantish damage here.[7] I do, however, want to offer a couple of closing, broad observations on Roger Brown's significance and scientific style, and the significance of that style.

About Roger's significance to the 20th-century study of language development little need be said. This volume serves as true testimony to that. It is perhaps only worth adding that, as a close corollary, he can be seen to have significantly strengthened—in his ever-gentle and graceful way—one of the major streams of the cognitive psychology revolution whose late-1950s and early-1960s headwaters lay largely in Cambridge.[8] And to speak of his "gentle and graceful way" is not merely to speak of the person. It is to speak also of the quality—both the substantive and stylistic quality—of his work *and* of the subtle blend between the person and the work.

Much deserves to be said on these matters. For present purposes, however, I am content to draw attention to the manifold ways in which the contributors to this collection underline the meaning and significance of Roger's keen-eyed and open-minded breadth, his care and commitment to the spoken and written word, his intellectual-cum-personal modesty.[9] Such qualities, I suggest, are not merely manifested in his substantive writings and in small but revealing ways in his

---

[6]Bronfenbrenner, Kessel, Kessen, and White (1986); Kessel (1983, 1985); Kessel and Bevan (1985).

[7]Not the least of reasons for making this disclaimer is the emerging work on "the ethnography of science" with which I am only obliquely familiar. The most penetrating conceptual consideration of the context and potential reach of such writing comes, naturally, from Clifford Geertz (1983). For all sorts of reasons—humor high among them—the best single illustration of an earlier "sociology of science" comes, equally naturally, from Robert Merton (1985).

[8]Reviewing the recent history of cognitive psychology Bill Bevan and I suggested that it has been comprised of two overlapping, yet discernibly different, major tributaries, each with somewhat different intellectual affinities, origins and styles, and each running its own somewhat independent course from the 1950s to the present. Roger, together with Jerry Bruner, can be seen as representing the stream that uses the metaphor of information processing in an informal fashion and more readily blends with developmental, social and personality psychology, with anthropology and sociology. (The second stream—George Miller as prototype—has been more formal and mathematically inclined, runs closest to traditional areas and methods of experimental psychology, and has blended more readily with computer science and AI.)

[9]Not surprisingly, Roger has consistently voiced the Flaubertian view that the personal parts of this story be kept to a minimum.

introductions to the writings,[10] but are also intrinsically and organically central to them.

In the end, then, contemplating such a suggestion in light of our need to acknowledge a plurality of modes of knowing—even in "the sciences"—I am put in mind of Barbara McClintock's naturalist "feeling for the organism" (Gould, 1984; Keller, 1983). And contemplating the corresponding need to cultivate conversations between "the social sciences" and "the arts and humanities" in the light of this collection and Roger's work and autobiography,[11] I am reminded of another true writer (albeit *not* a "novelist of social protest"!)

> He took events as they came along . . . and, sifting them through his odd, playful mind, came out with conclusions and observations that were sensible to the point of genius. He was not a man for profundities or large abstractions; he stayed with the detail of everyday living, . . . but he remained calm through it all, . . . without ever lapsing into frivolity or foolishness. He never raised his voice, in or out of print. . . . His soft-spoken eloquence was heard. Humor pervaded what he wrote; the touch remained light; he ran counter to the century's fashion. . . . For that matter, he sometimes seemed unaware of the very intellectual and literary fashions he was resisting. This most companionable of writers kept to himself in his personal life: a private man. . . . Renowned as his writing was for its simplicity and its clarity, his mind constantly took surprising turns. . . . E. B. White did serve as a model . . . for many, if not most of our country's writers. Other writers took their

---

[10]The appended "Third Person Autobiography" contains numerous delicate delights: "He concluded that, while thinking in terms of S & R obviously enabled some people to be very creative, it did not do so for him." "He could not see why a text in social psychology should look like a text in chemistry or physics." "The whole venture had been a vast fishing expedition. It did leave him knowing what things something reliable could be written about and what things one might as well remain silent about." To which collection should be added, for example, this:

> An interest in the speech of children, one that goes beyond the usual extra-scientific interest in all aspects of the development of one's children, is scarcely normal and needs to be accounted for. . . . What made children's language interesting to us, and makes it so still, are certain mysteries. Probably there is some dominating mystery behind any program of research that stretches over a period of years. It is a good thing to confess to these since they give direction to a path that may otherwise seem erratic. We know the mystery must be there because the pellet-sized presumed truths laid down by a succession of research reports cannot alone account for the researcher's labors" (Brown, 1970, pp. 1–2).

This last is a lovely example of a body of work and writing—"introductory" and otherwise—whose singular characteristic, for me, is its freedom from scientistic cant and, as significant, from anti-scientistic sloganeering. . . . Temperate sense and sensibility. . . . Asked about the Bellugi "delegation from Africa" tale and about the minimal mention of "methodology" in his work, Roger disarmingly and laughingly says, "Oh, I never could understand that [design and statistics] stuff"!

[11]A more complete, presumably "first-person" autobiography will appear in a forthcoming volume in the series *History of Psychology in Autobiography* (edited by Gardner Lindzey and published by Stanford University Press).

bearings from him, and learned from him a respect for craft and discipline and the language (*The New Yorker*, 1985, p. 31).

With these essays on language development we others are delighted to honor, as standard-bearer indeed of simplicity and clarity, of seriousness and humor, of soft-spoken eloquence, Roger Brown.

REFERENCES

Barnes, J. (1984). *Flaubert's parrot*. London: Jonathan Cape.

Bellugi, U., & Brown, R. (Eds.). (1964). The acquisition of language. *Monographs of the Society for Research in Child Development, 29* (Serial No. 92).

Bronfenbrenner, U., Kessel, F., Kessen, W., & White, S. (1986). Toward a critical social history of developmental psychology: A propaedeutic discussion. *American Psychologist, 41,* 1218–1230.

Brown, R. (1965). *Social psychology*. New York: The Free Press.

Brown, R. (1970). *Psycholinguistics: Selected papers*. New York: The Free Press.

Brown, R. (1973). *A first language*. Cambridge, MA: Harvard University Press.

Brown, R. (1981). Cognitive categories. In R. A. Kasschau & C. N. Cofer (Eds.), *Psychology's second century: Enduring issues*. New York: Praeger.

Chomsky, C. (1969). *The acquisition of syntax in children from 5 to 10*. Cambridge, MA: M.I.T. Press.·

Chomsky, N. (1965). *Aspects of the theory of syntax*. Cambridge, MA: M.I.T. Press.

Geertz, C. (1983). The way we think now: Toward an ethnography of modern thought. In C. Geertz, *Local knowledge: Further essays in interpretive anthropology* (pp. 147–163). New York: Basic Books.

Gould, S. J. (1984). Triumph of a naturalist. Review of E. F. Keller, *A feeling for the organism*. *The New York Review of Books*, March 29.

Holton, G. (1978). *The scientific imagination: Case studies*. New York: Cambridge University Press.

Keller, E. F. (1983). *A feeling for the organism: The life and work of Barbara McClintock*. New York: W. H. Freeman.

Kessel, F. S. (1969). The philosophy of science as proclaimed and science as practiced: "Identity" or "dualism"? *American Psychologist, 24,* 999–1005.

Kessel, F. S. (1970). The role of syntax in children's comprehension from ages six to twelve. *Monographs of the Society for Research in Child Development, 35,* (serial No. 139).

Kessel, F. S. (1983). On cultural construction and reconstruction in psychology: Voices in conversation. In F. S. Kessel & A. W. Siegel (Eds.), *The child and other cultural inventions* (pp. 224–259). New York: Praeger.

Kessel, F. S. (1985, August). The reconstruction of cognitive psychology: Now and then. Invited address, American Psychological Association Convention, Los Angeles.

Kessel, F. S., & Bevan, W. (1985). Notes towards a history of cognitive psychology. In C. W. Buxton (Ed.), *Points of view in the modern history of psychology* (pp. 259–294). New York: Academic Press.

Merton, R. K. (1985). *On the shoulders of giants: A Shandean postscript*. (The Vicennial Edition). New York: Harcourt Brace Jovanovich.

The New Yorker. (1985). The Talk of the Town, Oct. 14, pp. 31–32.

Smith, F., & Miller, G. A. (Eds.). (1966). *The genesis of language*. Cambridge, MA: The M.I.T. Press.

Toulmin, S. (1972). *Human understanding*. Oxford: Oxford University Press.

1 From the Garden of Eden to the Tower of Babel

Dan I. Slobin
University of California, Berkeley

This essay is a frankly autobiographical excursion, setting forth a bit of my odyssey from the "Garden of Eden" studies of the language development of Adam and Eve at Harvard to the "Tower of Babel" of crosslinguistic studies of acquisition carried out at Berkeley. I hope it is of some interest as a partial documentation of the intellectual world in which the modern study of child language began to develop. My involvement in that development began as a graduate student at Harvard in 1962, when Roger Brown gathered a small group of people to embark on a new endeavor, armed with the technological advances of portable tape recorders and transformational grammar. Ursula Bellugi and Colin Fraser were to be visiting two little children to record their speech, and the research group was to be involved in following the progress of these children as they constructed the grammar of English. In the following self-indulgence of autobiography, I try to reconstruct something of the atmosphere and the goals of our meetings at the Center for Cognitive Studies over two decades ago.

THE GARDEN OF EDEN

The children, of course, were "Adam" and "Eve" (later to be joined by "Sarah," following Roger's sequential Biblical naming scheme). The Center for Cognitive Studies, in addition to Brown's project, included George Miller's beginning research on the psycholinguistics of sentence processing—the first attempts to bring transformational grammar into the laboratory, and Jerry Bruner's grafting of Piaget and Vygotsky onto American roots. Eric Lenneberg

9

was lecturing on biological foundations of language. And at the other end of "Mass. Ave.," Noam Chomsky was lecturing at MIT on new approaches to the study of grammar, with implications for the study of mind. The task for the day, in George Miller's terms, was to rescue that four-letter word, *mind*, from the status of taboo term in American psychology.

Roger has described our discussions of the speech transcripts of Adam, Eve, and Sarah in his monumental book, *A First Language*, published in 1973. Going back to 1962–63, he says in that book:

> During the first year of the project a group of students of the psychology of language met each week to discuss the state of the children's construction process as of that date. The regular participants were: Jean Berko-Gleason, Ursula Bellugi, Colin Fraser, Samuel Anderson, David McNeill, Dan Slobin, Courtney Cazden, Richard Cromer, and Gordon Finley. We had wonderfully stimulating, light-hearted discussions. Anyone in developmental psycholinguistics looking over the membership of this seminar will realize how bounteous that year was (Brown, 1973, pp. 52–53).

He goes on to say:

> Long before the end of the first year the children got way ahead of the seminar. Their records were far too rich to be analyzed in a two-hour session. It became clear that a fine-grained analysis was a big job and had to be undertaken by one person. Even then only a fraction of the data could be examined. Still I was determined to make the effort because I had not set out to create an immense archive that no one would use.

The result, so far, has been the detailed analysis of the first two stages of development in *A First Language*, and detailed, unpublished analyses of later stages—a warning to anyone who would take on such research lightly (but also an inspiration to those who would take it on seriously). (As an aside, let me mention that Roger certainly did not create "an immense archive that no one would ever use." I can't think of any researcher who has been so generous with his data, and I've lost track of the dissertations and papers that have explored various aspects of the speech of these three children and their parents.)

In preparing these retrospective observations, I have spent some time going over my notes from those meetings of the first year of the project. Two things stand out: the extent to which our guiding questions were shaped by transformational grammar, and the ways in which research directions of future years kept appearing in the margins of our discussions.

But first of all, what is evident in those notes is a sense of wonder, the wonder that comes from looking at something for the first time, without knowing what you may find. In thinking back on that feeling, the closest intellectual and aesthetic experience I can compare it to is the amazement I felt in an introductory zoology lab when I cut open my first mouse and saw all its organs lying neatly in place. We had not listened to extensive tape recordings of child speech before, but had read diary studies. New dimensions were raised by the addition of full, unedited auditory records. For example, in my notes from the second week of our research meetings, in October 1962, I find the surprised observation:

> *Much* repetition. This must be an important aspect of language learning. Often with rising inflection, as if making sure of pronunciation and meaning.

But much of what is in those notes is now familiar. And the fact that the findings of those first years now seem familiar attests to the *cumulative* nature of child language study. We *have* learned something about the acquisition of English, and similar patterns have repeated themselves in enough children, in enough studies, to give us a feeling of secure knowledge. The wonder is still there—but it is no longer the wonder of novelty. As our knowledge of children's accomplishments grows, we are faced with deeper problems and unsolved puzzles.

In those years of 1962–63, we were clearly oriented to current questions of transformational grammar. Our only guides were Chomsky's little 1957 book, *Syntactic Structures,* along with ongoing lectures at MIT; and we used Nelson Francis' (1958) book, *The Structure of American English,* as a back-up for structural definitions of linguistic categories. We paid close attention to the auxiliary system and to word-order patterns, because these had played a central role in *Syntactic Structures.* We kept track of sentence types—affirmative, negative, and questions—in which uses of auxiliaries and word order would vary. Linguistic growth was assessed in terms of things to be added to childish sentences to make them adult-like: the additions of omitted functors (inflections, prepositions, articles, and the like) and transformational operations. We did not categorize utterances in terms of communicative intent—that is, in terms of semantics or speech acts or extended discourse skills—and so we did not look for growth in terms of additions or enrichment of such abilities. Our central concern was with syntax and morphology, with some later interest in prosody. We worried about such questions as whether child grammar was finite state or transformational, and whether syntactic "kernels" were the first sentence forms to appear in child speech.

By the first month we decided that Adam's early sentences were not transformationally derived in the adult sense, because of the absence of the elements *be, have, -ing, will, can,* and *do.* We found that contractions such as *can't* and *don't,* which we thought to be transformations, had to be described in different terms in the children's grammars, because the corresponding full forms, such as *cannot* and *do not,* and the affirmative *can* and *do,* were not yet present in their speech. It was already necessary to think of the growth of grammar in the *child's* terms, rather than to read backward from adult grammar. And already, at that point, it was evident to us that transformational grammar could not help us to describe the ways in which a child *constructs* a grammar. I find a marginal note from 1963:

> The problem is that of the child's *discovery procedure,* which Chomsky doesn't discuss much.

This problem, of course, remains with us. What we did have from Chomsky was a redefinition of linguistic behavior in terms of *rules.* He has stated this Leitmotiv in many ways through the years. In my notes from a 1963 lecture of his, I underlined:

> *Language is rule-governed rather than memory-produced behavior.*

And so we looked for evidence for rules in regularities of speech, drawing our categories from transformational grammar. In that first year we found evidence for such syntactic operations as inversions for questions, fronting of question words, use of auxiliaries to carry negation and tense, formation of tag questions, and similar phenomena. What is of interest to me now is that such findings are still important for theories of language acquisition, even though the particular linguistic model that inspired them has been replaced by so many revisions and alternates.

But these findings are well known in the literature. More interesting to me in those old notes are the hints of things to come. And here I would like to discuss first issues of method and then issues of theory. In the introduction to *A First Language,* Brown says:

> In the seminar small experiments or near-experiments were often suggested and tried by the main investigators. The results were sometimes useful but never conclusive; the difficulties of experimentation with small children are considerable, and we put the transcription schedule first (p. 53).

Experimentation, of course, would require larger numbers of children and more careful controls. But what surprised me in reading through the notes was the broad range of techniques that we devised and attempted. We studied imitation, comprehension, production, and judgments of grammaticality. There were elicited imitations of systematically distorted sentences. There were comprehension tests of singular/plural, active/passive, past/present, locative prepositions, and possessives. To study production there were Berko tests with nonsense words. New words were taught in one context, and we tracked their appearance in other contexts. For example, Adam was taught that he could *pim* a piece of paper— that is, crumple it—and later he spontaneously said *I pimming,* giving us conclusive evidence of the productivity of the progressive at that stage. We devised mini training experiments, in which the child was to change verbs from one form to another. And so forth. It was evident that experimentation and the study of naturalistic data would have to go hand-in-hand in the study of child language.

In terms of theory, it was also evident in our asides that grammatical development was embedded in processes of thought and social interaction, and that general cognitive principles were at play. Since those days—in the late 60s and 70s—a variety of social and cognitive factors have been added to our initial study of grammar. In fact, extralinguistic variables have attracted so much recent attention that the linguistic variables themselves have often been ignored or even redefined out of existence. I can think of seven popular terms that have both enriched and obscured the study of the acquisition of linguistic structure in recent years: *semantics, context, input, pragmatics, discourse, cognition,* and *strategies.* These terms reflect three intersecting groups of variables that lie outside of linguistic structure per se but must play their roles in the acquisition of that structure. The current problem of our field, as I see it, is to attend to these three sets of issues without losing sight of language itself.

First, theoreticians of semantics and contextual factors emphasize that early messages are supported by situational as well as linguistic information—in both comprehension and production. The observers of Adam, Eve, and Sarah certainly kept contextual notes, but because our interest was focused on syntax and morphology, these notes were used primarily for disambiguation. The "rich interpretation" of Lois Bloom came several years later, but we did wonder, from time to time, what the children were intending to say; and we did test their comprehension of linguistic structures in situations lacking contextual cues, since we were aware of the role of context in supporting comprehension in natural settings.

A second group of modern researchers—theoreticians of input, pragmatics, and discourse—emphasize that much of meaning is carried by the structure and content of social interaction. We attended to mother–child interaction, but not as a problem in its own right. For example, in regard to input, I find the following observation in the third week of our meetings:

We constantly run up against the problem of individual differences in the tutor.

This issue lay dormant until the 70s. In the early 60s we were looking for universals, and individual differences were a nuisance. We were concerned with mother–child interaction, but we saw it as a source of linguistic training. We attended to mothers' expansions of child speech and children's imitations of mothers' speech. Conversation was a source of knowledge, not a skill to be studied in its own right at that time. Yet we did pay attention to sequences of interchanges and the linguistic skills required to ask and respond to questions.

A third group of modern theoreticians attend to cognition and language-processing strategies, arguing that syntax is a reflection of more broadly-based structures and processes. Attempts are made to replace grammar with a set of semantic structures and on-line processing of temporally-patterned sequences.

We were concerned with such factors as asides, though they did not play a central role in the theorizing of the early 60s. For example, in regard to semantics and cognition, I find a remark in Roger's discussions of the eighth week of Adam's speech samples:

> Is appearance of a form—e.g., past—solely linguistically (structurally, acoustically) determined, or also semantically?

An anticipation, then, of the development of theories later in the decade of "cognitive prerequisites" for the emergence of linguistic forms in child speech.

In regard to language processing, we paid attention to the child's emerging sense of grammaticality, as evidenced in self-corrections and vacillations in use of inflections. The group, at one point, discussed whether the sense of norms emerging in grammar had parallels in the development of other social norms, such as etiquette.

But we were not yet ready to explain language in terms of other cognitive systems, or to reduce grammar to processing capacities, or to seek the roots of grammar in nonlinguistic processes of thought or social interaction. These were later developments, which many of us have since approached, but with caution, remembering our lessons about the special nature of syntax among the systems of human cognition. By and large, those of us who came out of Roger's workshop have remained fascinated with the central puzzle of the child's discovery and shaping of linguistic structure, while grappling more and more with the major extralinguistic issues which have come to prominence.

In my own case, this fascination soon became embedded in a lifelong fascination with other languages. I find a marginal question in my notes from 1963:

> Can anything important about grammatical development be learned by comparing the acquisition of various native tongues?

I have spent the years since then trying to show how this question can be answered in the affirmative. This is not the place to summarize those attempts. (See Aksu-Koç & Slobin, 1985; Ammon & Slobin, 1979; Johnston & Slobin, 1979; Slobin, 1966, 1973, 1977, 1981, 1982, 1985, 1986; Slobin & Bever, 1982; Slobin & Talay, 1984) Rather, I would like to explore a new approach developing at Berkeley and elsewhere—an approach that looks for the ways in which individual children, acquiring different sorts of languages, seem to begin with similar notions about the meanings and functions of grammatical categories. This approach attempts to bring together the insights of the three directions mentioned above—semantic, pragmatic, and cognitive—in accounting for children's early uses of grammatical morphemes.

THE TOWER OF BABEL

Briefly stated, our approach at Berkeley has been to select matched pairs or sets of languages that vary in the ways in which they express particular semantic or pragmatic notions. The world provides countless "natural experiments," presenting children with different kinds of problems to solve. Such diversity makes it possible to control variables that are confounded in any given single language.

For example, languages differ in *where* particular kinds of grammatical markers are placed, and in how much acoustic substance is allotted to various markers. In the Harvard studies we had found that English locative prepositions— words like *in, on,* and *under*—were omitted in early child speech. Was this because of the difficulty of encoding locative notions, or the low acoustic salience of prepositions, or a serial position effect in immediate memory disfavoring medial material like prepositions? By comparing languages in which locative notions are encoded in varying positions, it has become evident that both conceptual and perceptual factors are important (Johnston & Slobin, 1979). Such notions are grammatically expressed earlier in languages where they are encoded in more salient positions for perception and short-term memory—that is, when they appear as noun suffixes or as postpositions following nouns. At the same time, across languages, there is a common order of emergence of locative notions, regardless of how they are expressed grammatically. The earliest notions to be encoded—by prefixes or suffixes, prepositions or postpositions—are simple topological notions of proximity, containment, and support—'in', 'on', 'under', 'next to'. Locative relations embodying notions of perspective, such as 'back' and 'front', are always later. And so on. That is, conceptual development provides the content for linguistic expression, while linguistic discovery procedures are necessary for working out the mapping of content according to conventions of particular languages.

Our work at Berkeley over the past 15 years or so has been to chart out the course of acquisition of basic notions and their means of expression in a broad spectrum of different types of languages. It is evident that along the way to discovering the full adult system of grammar, the child reveals crosslinguistically standard ways of organizing and simplifying systems of syntax and morphology. Children create grammars in which clearly identifiable surface forms map onto basic semantic categories. Much of the earlier work dealt with children's use of word-order principles and their construction of morphological paradigms. Most recently, we have begun to see ways in which the emergence of grammatical categories arises from ways in which children view the world and interact with people. As an example of this approach, consider what we are beginning to learn about how children organize the uses of grammatical morphemes before they have fully mastered them according to some adult-like criterion.

The Harvard School contributed a criterion of a child's mastery of a grammatical form: 90% correct usage in obligatory contexts for that form. This was based on notions of formal grammar prevalent in the 60s (and since), according to which one could specify linguistic contexts for grammatical morphemes. Until the child reached a point of near-perfect use of a form in its specified context, it was assumed that fluctuations in use of the form simply reflected incomplete mastery, presumably due to performance factors operating within a theory of incremental learning. Presence or absence of a form was not considered to be motivated in ways that were linguistically or psychologically interesting. More recently, however, it has become evident that the absence of a grammatical form in an "obligatory" context can reveal the child's own definition of the contexts that call for use of the form in question. Crosslinguistically, it appears that children begin with common notions of the semantic–pragmatic categories that are most salient for grammatical expression.

This first became evident to me in examining children's early grammatical marking of agents and objects in ergative and accusative languages (Slobin, 1981). Gvozdev (1949) noted, long ago, a significant restriction in his child's first uses of the Russian accusative inflection on nouns. Rather than inflecting every direct object, his son at first applied the accusative only to nouns that were the objects of verbs of direct, physical manipulation, such as 'give', 'carry', 'put', and 'throw', omitting the accusative for less manipulative verbs such as 'read' and 'see'. The child was thus below the 90% criterion for use of this grammatical morpheme, yet he was clearly using the morpheme consistently. He was orienting to what I have called the "Manipulative Activity Scene" (Slobin, 1985), using the accusative to grammaticize highly transitive events (Hopper & Thompson, 1980). Since Russian is an accusative language, this early grammaticization was recruited to the object noun as the locus for grammatical expression of the Manipulative Activity Scene.

More recently, Schieffelin (1979, 1985) has investigated acquisition of an ergative language, Kaluli, of New Guinea. In such languages, *agents* of transitive verbs, rather than patients, receive grammatical marking. Schieffelin found that early use of the ergative inflection on nouns in Kaluli was limited to agents in the Manipulative Activity Scene—that is, the inflection appeared only on subjects of verbs such as 'give', 'grab', 'take', and 'hit', and was omitted on subjects of verbs such as 'see', 'say', and 'call'. (It was also not overgeneralized to subjects of *in*transitive verbs, such as 'run' and 'fall'). Again, 90% mastery was not demonstrated, but children's restrictions of usage were motivated, following the same criterion for restriction as in Russian. Furthermore, the ergative at first appeared only in sentences that were affirmative and in the past tense. Apparently children determine that an event is truly manipulative only if it has actually occurred and has been carried to completion.

The Berkeley School has sought both cognitive and pragmatic reasons for children's definitions of the scope of application of grammatical morphemes below the 90% criterion. In highly inflectional languages, such as Hungarian and

Turkish, case inflections can even appear on single words. In an early study of the acquisition of Hungarian—another accusative language—MacWhinney (1973) found that 44% of single nouns occurred in the accusative in the speech of one child. Even before the presence of an obligatory grammatical frame, these nouns expressed a clear pragmatic function. Accusative forms were not used for naming objects but referred specifically to things that the child wanted to have or to build—obviously nouns that would be the objects of highly transitive, manipulative verbs—whereas nouns in the nominative were used for naming.

These uses of accusative inflections are involved in particular kinds of speech acts—what Nancy Budwig (1986) has called expressions of "the child's desire to control or claim an object to carry out an action." The Manipulative Activity Scene thus includes both a characterization of a prototypical event type (highly transitive) and the expression of a prototypical action frame (control/claim object). This action frame serves as the locus of organization for other grammatical morphemes as well.

Deutsch and Budwig (1983) re-examined possessive constructions in Brown's original transcripts of Adam and Eve. Brown had noted apparently random use of uninflected names and possessive pronouns to indicate possession (e.g., "Play with Eve broom"; "That my bottle"). The nominal and pronominal possessive forms were used with a fairly equal distribution for a period of several months. However, in terms of a functional analysis, the two forms regularly occurred in different pragmatic contexts. The pronominal forms were used in the "volitional" action frame described above, while the nominal forms were used in "indicative" action frames in which the child simply indicated possession in situations where the fact of possession was not in question. For example, when an adult wanted Adam to give up a toy car that he was playing with, the child asserted control by saying "my car"; whereas when he was noting a comparison between a picture in a book and his own possession, he said, "Just like Adam horsie shirt." Budwig (unpublished dissertation draft) points out that Adam and Eve (as well as some of the children studied by Susan Ervin-Tripp and Wick Miller at Berkeley) have apparently grammaticized a distinction that is not marked in adult English:

> It should be noted that the distinction drawn by the children is also not one that the caregivers used with the children. That is, the children are not picking up on a contrast that they hear as part of their interactions with caregivers who themselves often employ nominal and pronominal forms (cf. Deutsch & Budwig, 1983). The distinction that the children make then seems to be of their own creation, one motivated by the pragmatic perspective that the child takes on such utterances.

Budwig (1986) has gone on to find that nominal and pronominal forms contrast in similar fashion when they are used as subjects. Pronominal subjects occur with verbs expressing desires and intentions, as in the following examples from the Berkeley data: "I want it Mommy." "I like something else for me." "I need toast after breakfast." Nominal subjects describe objects belonging to an individual, often in a contrastive framework: "Laura has a green car." "Carol has a life belt." Nominal forms also tend to be followed by action verbs: "Carol do it." "Sally read." Budwig characterizes the use of nominal subjects as "instances in which the perspective on the self taken by the child was one of describing, and the self is viewed from a referential perspective." Again, we have something like a more dynamic, affectively loaded use of pronouns, along with a less dynamic, information-giving use of nouns.

If we look back at the one-word stage, we find intriguing hints that English pronouns, and Hungarian nouns in the accusative, are used to express the volitional function. In English, Gopnik (1980) has found frequent early use of *my, mine,* and *mines* when the child wanted to claim an object. This finding is similar to MacWhinney's report of early use of accusative nouns in Hungarian. (The accusative is not productive at this point, but it is important to note that nouns in the accusative form contrast with those in the nominative, in that only the latter are used for naming objects—a precursor of the indicative function.) It is probably a crosslinguistic regularity that children, early on, seek expression of the volitional and indicative functions, drawing upon salient grammatical morphemes offered by the language. Eventually, from such a starting point, children will organize systems of pronouns and case inflections; but, to begin with, all of these various forms seem to express particular, child-oriented speech functions.

Children's use of verb tenses casts further light on the distinction between these two functions. Recall that Kaluli sentences with ergative subject nouns tend to be in the past tense, suggesting that the use of nouns is involved in the descriptive function. The volitional function is future–oriented, and I would expect that volitional utterances in child Kaluli are expressed with ergative subject pronouns and non–past verbs. Budwig presents suggestive supportive evidence from the Berkeley English data. Sentences with nominal subjects and process verbs refer to past or ongoing events, such as "Carol do it"; "Sally read"; and "Laura finish hers too." By contrast, sentences with pronominal subjects have stative verbs of desire or intention in regard to future events, such as "I want something else a bag"; "I want play puzzle"; and "I like something for me." Budwig suggests that this split reflects "a distinction between using language to *Describe vs. Plan (in the performative sense) happenings.*"

A related distinction has been elaborated in depth by Julie Gerhardt (1983) in a Berkeley dissertation on the language of 3- and 4-year-olds. Gerhardt has discovered a clear distinction between the use of *will* and *gonna* in the future-oriented utterances of the children she studied. *Will* is used to carry out acts of what Gerhardt calls *Undertaking,* while *gonna* expresses acts of *Planning.* In Undertaking, the child commits herself to carry out part of an ongoing, cooperative endeavor in the immediate future, whereas Planning is related to more distant future events, such as description of end-states or narrating possible future events. Undertaking is clearly volitional, while Planning is more descriptive. Again, we see children organizing the grammatical means provided by the language to express particular pragmatic functions.

In another Berkeley dissertation, Savasir (1984) has investigated the development of tense, person, and voice morphemes in Turkish. He has found an early grammatical distinction between the expression of intentions and the consequences of intentions. The first passives in 2-year-olds occur in limited contexts: A first-person active is followed by a third-person passive. In a typical example, a child attempts to open a box, announcing her intention in the future tense: 'I'll open the box'. When her attempt fails, she reports this failure in a negated third-person present tense in the passive: ''It isn't being opened'. The passive is, at first, limited to this peculiar conjunction of grammatical morphemes. Savasir (1984) suggests: ''It would seem that the earliest occurrences of the passive in the present tense are used to report those instances in which the child's intentions or plans are inhibited due to a resistance from an object'' (p. 38). The passive thus allows the child to ''view the verb as an 'attribute' of its grammatical object'' (p. 38), thereby shifting attention from his or her own action to the resisting object. Thus we have a shift from a volitional to a descriptive mode, with an early narrow restriction of the function of the passive in Turkish.

This finding is similar to Antinucci and Miller's (1976) study of Italian child language, also carried out at Berkeley. They found that Italian 2-year-olds, in past-tense utterances, make the past participle agree with the *object* in number and gender, although such agreement is not part of the adult language. For example, a boy says *Ho presa la campana* 'I took+FEM.SG the+FEM.SG bell+FEM.SG' rather than *Ho preso la campana,* with the appropriate neutral form of the participle, *preso.* The Italian children seem to be attributing the past participle to the object, just as the early Turkish passives allow for attribution of the verb to the object. These verb morphemes, then, seem to adapt the verb to function in a description of the affected object, shifting attention from the active perspective of the volitional mode.

These studies, and others carried out elsewhere, reflect a growing interest in the prototypical semantic and pragmatic functions that seem to underlie the initial organization of grammatical morphemes crosslinguistically. This approach seeks to fill in the picture of development from the first uses of grammatical morphemes to the 90% stage of mastery studied at Harvard. Many pieces, theoretical and empirical, remain to be filled in at every step of the way. We are still working on the same puzzle as Roger Brown's 1962–63 seminar. We have found a few more of the pieces scattered around the globe, and are trying to find additional ways to fit them into the puzzle.

1988 POSTSCRIPT

This essay was completed in 1984. In the several years since then, the tradition that I have called ''The Berkeley School'' has continued to explore cognitive and pragmatic bases of children's acquisition and use of grammatical constructions, with special attention to discourse.

Julie Gerhardt (Gee) and Iskender Savasir have written a series of papers in which they explore the discursive purposes served by a range of forms expressing tense, aspect, and modality in English (Gee, 1985; Gee-Gerhardt, 1986; Gerhardt, in press; Gee & Savasir, 1985, 1986). The essence of this approach ''is to show how a distributional analysis characterizing the use of a particular grammatical construction in the speech of . . . children, also counts as the description of a distinctly organized social practice—brought about, in part, through the use of this grammatical construction'' (Gerhardt & Savasir, 1986, p. 502). They show, for example, how the use of the simple present in 3-year-olds is not simply a matter of grammatical tense, but implicitly refers to *norms,* thereby ''structuring . . . ongoing activities in terms of an impersonal motivation or a conformance to a normative way of acting'' (p. 530). Thus when a child says, ''I'm *puttin'* my shoes back on'' she is commenting on an ongoing activity, whereas when she says, ''And you *put* them like that'' she is giving instructions with regard to a norm.

Nancy Budwig (1986), in her recent dissertation, characterizes her approach as part of ''a major shift in paradigm'' in the following terms: ''Rather than starting one's analysis with some a priori definition of what constitutes an obligatory context for the employment of forms, focus is placed on revealing the child's own definition of appropriate contexts of use'' (p. 1). Continuing her work on grammatical expressions of agency and control, she has found that some 2-year-olds encode the Manipulative Activity Scene by the differential use of *I* and *my* as subject pronouns. These children use *my* in utterances in which the subject is a prototypical agent, with a highly kinetic verb and a direct effect—either to report a completed volitional act, such as ''My blew the candles out,'' or to announce such an act, as in ''My take it home.'' Thus *my* tends to co-occur with verbs that are either past-tense and perfective, or future-intentional. When *I* is used as subject pronoun, the utterances are low in agentivity, expressing experiential states, such as ''I like peas,'' in response to an adult question. Budwig concludes that semantic and pragmatic factors function jointly to determine such idiosyncratic pronominal uses (1985, p. 34): ''The uses of *my* . . . appear in utterances that function as Control Acts: that is as directives, requests, challenges, protests and disputes over control of objects and enactment of activities. . . . In contrast, utterances ranking low in transitivity involving the use of *I* involve no such attempt to bring about a change.'' Thus we see that particular *semantic/pragmatic constellations* play a key role in directing the early uses of grammatical forms. Such constellations include speech act dimensions in combination with markings of grammatical function, case, person, and tense-aspect-modality.

The interaction of form and function in discourse is also being explored over a wide age range (from 3 to adult) in a series of studies initiated by Michael Bamberg's (1985) dissertation on narrative development. As he puts it (p. 251): ''The underlying implication of such studies of form-function relationships is the assumption that there are discourse motivating factors that rule the use of the investigated forms, and at the same time guide the development of the constituted form-function relationship.'' Bamberg has shown that German children's uses of both tense-aspect forms and referring expressions (nouns and pronouns) reflect successive stages of narrative organization. This work is continuing in a broad crosslinguistic format, in which children working on the Tower of Babel learn to construct narratives in English, German, Hebrew, Icelandic, Spanish, Turkish, and American Sign Language (Berman & Slobin, 1987).

A quarter-century from Adam and Eve, we are still trying to interpret the Book of Genesis.

REFERENCES

Antinucci, F., & Miller, R. (1976). How children talk about what happened. *Journal of Child Language, 3,* 167–189.

Aksu-Koç, A. A., & Slobin, D. I. (1985). The acquisition of Turkish. In D. I. Slobin (Ed.), *The crosslinguistic study of language acquisition,* Vol. 1. Hillsdale, NJ: Lawrence Erlbaum Associates.

Ammon, M. S., & Slobin, D. I. (1979). A cross-linguistic study of the processing of causative sentences. *Cognition, 7,* 3–17.

Bamberg, M. G. W. (1985). *Form and function in the construction of narratives: Developmental perspectives.* Doctoral dissertation, University of California, Berkeley.

Berman, R. A., & Slobin, D. I. (1987). Five ways of learning how to talk about events: A crosslinguistic study of children's narratives. Berkeley Cognitive Science Report No. 46 (Institute of Cognitive Studies, University of California, Berkeley).

Brown, R. (1973). *A first language.* Cambridge, MA: Harvard University Press.

Budwig, N. (1985). Me, my, and 'name': Children's early systematizations of forms, meanings and functions in talk about the self. *Papers and Reports on Child Language Development, 24,* 30–37.

Budwig, N. A. (1986). *Agentivity and control in early child language.* Doctoral dissertation, University of California, Berkeley.

Chomsky, N. (1957). *Syntactic structures.* The Hague: Mouton.

Deutsch, W., & Budwig, N. (1983). Form and function in the development of possessives. *Papers and Reports on Child Language Development* (Stanford University, Department of Linguistics), *22,* 36–42.

Francis, W. N. (1958). *The structure of American English.* New York: Ronald Press.

Gee (Gerhardt), J. (1985). An interpretive approach to the study of modality: What child language can tell the linguist. *Studies in Language, 9,* 197–229.

Gee-Gerhardt, J. (1986). Beyond semantics: A discourse analysis of the verb inflections in distinct narrative-like and communicative formats in the speech of a 2 year old. *Proceedings of the Second Annual Meeting of the Pacific Linguistics Conference.*

Gerhardt, J. B. (1983). *Tout se tient: Towards an analysis of activity-types to explicate the interrelation between modality and future reference in child discourse.* Doctoral dissertation, University of California, Berkeley.

Gerhardt, J. (in press). From discourse to semantics: The development of the verb morphology and forms of self-reference in the speech of a 2 year old. In K. Nelson (Ed.), *Narratives in the crib.*

Gee (Gerhardt), J., & Savasir, I. (1985). On the use of *will* and *gonna:* Toward a description of activity-types for child language. *Discourse Processes, 8,* 143–175.

Gerhardt (Gee), J., & Savasir, I. (1986). The use of the simple present in the speech of two three-year-olds: Normativity not subjectivity. *Language in Society, 15,* 501–536.

Gopnik, A. (1980). *The development of non-nominal expressions in one to two year old children.* Doctoral dissertation, Oxford University.

Gvozdev, A. N. (1949). *Formirovanie u rebenka grammatičeskogo stroja russkogo jazyka.* Moscow: Izd-vo Akademii Pedagogičeskix Nauk RSFSR.

Hopper, P., & Thompson, S. (1980). Transitivity in grammar and discourse. *Language, 56,* 251–299.

Johnston, J. R., & Slobin, D. I. (1979). The development of locative expressions in English, Italian, Serbo-Crotian, and Turkish. *Journal of Child Language, 6,* 529–545.

MacWhinney, B. (1973). *How Hungarian children learn to speak.* Doctoral dissertation, University of California, Berkeley.

Savasir, I. (1984). *How many futures?* Masters dissertation, University of California, Department of Psychology.

Schieffelin, B. B. (1979). *How Kaluli children learn what to say, what to do, and how to feel: An ethnographic study of the development of communicative competence.* Doctoral dissertation, Columbia University. (To be published by Cambridge University Press.)

Schieffelin, B. B. (1985). Acquisition of Kaluli. In D. I. Slobin (Ed.), *The crosslinguistic study of language acquisition,* Vol. 1. Hillsdale, NJ: Lawrence Erlbaum Associates.

Slobin, D. I. (1966). The acquisition of Russian as a native language. In F. Smith & G. A. Miller (Eds.), *The genesis of language: A psycholinguistic approach.* Cambridge, MA: MIT Press.

Slobin, D. I. (1973). Cognitive prerequisites for the development of grammar. In C. A. Ferguson &

D. I. Slobin (Eds.), *Studies of child language development*. New York: Holt, Rinehart, & Winston.

Slobin, D. I. (1977). Language change in childhood and in history. In J. Macnamara (Ed.), *Language learning and thought*. New York: Academic Press.

Slobin, D. I. (1981). The origins of grammatical encoding of events. In W. Deutsch (Ed.), *The child's construction of language*. London: Academic Press.

Slobin, D. I. (1982). Universal and particular in the acquisition of language. In E. Wanner & L. R. Gleitman (Eds.), *Language acquisition: The state of the art*. Cambridge, MA: Cambridge University Press.

Slobin, D. I. (1985). Crosslinguistic evidence for the Language-Making Capacity. In D. I. Slobin (Ed.), *The crosslinguistic study of language acquisition* (Vol. 2). Hillsdale, NJ: Lawrence Erlbaum Associates.

Slobin, D. I. (1986). The acquisition and use of relative clauses in Turkic and Indo-European languages. In D. I. Slobin & K. Zimmer (Eds.), *Studies in Turkish linguistics*. Amsterdam: John Benjamins.

Slobin, D. I., & Bever, T. G. (1982). Children use canonical sentence schemas: A crosslinguistic study of word order and inflections. *Cognition, 12*, 229–265.

Slobin, D. I., & Talay, A. (1984). Development of pragmatic use of subject pronouns in Turkish child language. In A. Aksu Koç & E. Erguvanlı Taylan (Eds.), *Proceedings of the Turkish Linguistics Conference: August 9–10 1984*. Istanbul: Boğaziçi University Publications No. 400.

2 Inducing the Latent Structure of Language

Melissa Bowerman
Max Planck Institute for Psycholinguistics

> *Every child processes the speech to which he is exposed so as to induce from it a latent structure. This latent rule structure is so general that a child can spin out its implications all his life long. It is both semantic and syntactic. The discovery of latent structure is the greatest of the processes involved in language acquisition, and the most difficult to understand.*
> —Brown & Bellugi, 1964, pp. 314–315

When I arrived at Harvard in the fall of 1964, I was not aware that there was such a field of study as child language development, much less that Harvard was perhaps the ideal place at that time to pursue it. And yet, ironically, I was already much interested in the problem.

During my last undergraduate year at Stanford, I had shamelessly neglected my psychology major to follow every course on language offered by Joseph Greenberg, who had recently joined the anthropology faculty. Descriptive linguistics, language and culture, languages of Africa—all were fascinating. I do not recall that children figured at all in this coursework. The problem of acquisition came to my attention by what seems like a chance event: my presence at a casual conversation in which a speech pathologist described a child in her clinic who, despite apparently normal intelligence, had not progressed beyond the most rudimentary syntax. Until that moment I believe I had scarcely thought about how children learn to talk. Suddenly, the fact that they do seemed remarkable. The tale of the boy with so little language made salient to me for the first time the phenomenon I later came to know as "productivity": the ability of normal

23

children—and of course adults—to go beyond what they have heard to produce novel but appropriate utterances.

As this interest took root I was trying to decide what kind of graduate program to follow. Absurd as it now seems, I was not sure that language acquisition could be pursued in an academic setting. Psychology did not seem very promising. I could not even remember having read anything about language development in my psychology courses. In retrospect I see that I had dutifully underlined paragraphs in my child psychology text, published in 1961, on the size of children's vocabularies, the length of their sentences, and the proportions of nouns, verbs, and adjectives in their speech at successive stages of development. This information seems to have made no impression, and I was unaware of more recent and meatier research like Jean Berko's study of wugs, Roger Brown's ideas about "the original word game" and about part-of-speech as a guide to the intended referent, and Martin Braine's hypotheses about the child's own "pivot grammar."

I made a few inquiries about speech pathology. Perhaps I could learn something about children's language in such a program, but training to help children with communicative disorders seemed a roundabout way to satisfy what was basically an interest in *normal* language acquisition. In the end I applied to graduate programs in anthropology. The anthropological approach to language in general was the most congenial one I knew (Stanford did not have a linguistics department at that time), and there were other anthropological topics that interested me as well. I thought that I might eventually get at child language through anthropology.

This goal seemed far away in the fall of 1964. Australopithecus, classical Mayan civilization, and kinship systems were the subject matters closest at hand. "But if you are interested in child language," said a new acquaintance, "you probably know that there's someone in the Social Relations department who is working on that. His name is Roger Brown." Surprised, I went to see Roger. As he described his Adam, Eve, and Sarah project, I recognized immediately that his research was directed at just the problem I had been groping to formulate for myself—how children induce the underlying structural regularities of their language.

To study with Roger I would have to change departments, and to do this he would have to agree to sponsor me. Would he? "Can you do phonetic transcriptions?" he inquired. "Well . . . I think so," I replied, with more optimism than my experience warranted. "I'm taking phonetics and phonemics." "Fine," said Roger. "I'm looking for someone to do phonetic transcriptions of the Sarah tapes." And so, after one semester my career as an anthropologist was over. I was to be a psychologist after all.

Was there something special about the approach to child language that Roger passed on to his students and colleagues, something that has stuck with us and put a distinctive mark on our way of formulating questions, carrying out research, or evaluating evidence? Frank Kessel evidently thought so when he organized a symposium—and subsequently this book—around our Harvard experiences and subsequent development. I think he is right. In my own case I see clearly that the large questions about language acquisition that I came to appreciate during my graduate studies are to a remarkable extent still the ones that preoccupy me today. And many of these concerns, in various combinations and sometimes in new guises, lurk in the work of the colleagues who came before, during, and after my time at Harvard. In this chapter I want to first outline some of the themes that were especially important to me and then describe how they all seem to have converged and become bound up together in the problem that has intrigued me the most over the last decade: children's "late" or "reorganizational" speech errors.

LINGUISTICS AND THE CHILD'S
INTERNALIZED RULE SYSTEM

Transformational grammar was in the air when I arrived in Cambridge. Chomsky's new ideas had begun to revolutionize the way psychologists would look at language, and nowhere was this change felt earlier or more intensely than at Harvard.

The claim with the most immediate impact for the study of language acquisition was that knowledge of a language is neither a repertoire of sentences nor a set of conditioned responses. Rather, according to Chomsky (1965), "a child who has learned a language has developed an internal representation of a system of rules" (p. 25). The child does this by observation of the speech he or she hears, with the help, argued Chomsky, of an innate theory specifying the form of a possible human language.

If the child's task is one of rule construction, then the psycholinguist's, in part, is to determine the rules that children have formulated at successive stages of development. Psychologists began to treat children like speakers of an unknown, exotic language, and to try to write sets of rules that would account for their utterances (Braine, 1963; Brown & Fraser, 1963; Brown, Fraser, & Bellugi, 1964; Miller & Ervin, 1964). Grammar writing was intended as more than a formal exercise. According to Chomsky (1968), "the linguist constructing a grammar for a language is in effect *proposing a hypothesis* concerning the [speaker's] internalized system" (p. 23, emphasis added). Similarly, the scholar writing a grammar for a child was making a very explicit proposal about the current state of the child's developing linguistic knowledge.

The enterprise of writing grammars for children flourished and became more sophisticated in the late 1960s and early 1970s (e.g., Bloom, 1970; Bowerman, 1973a; Brown, 1973; Brown, Cazden, & Bellugi, 1968). In related efforts, Roger and others looked into whether linguistics offered a guide to the relative difficulty of different language forms for children. In particular, they tested the hypothesis that the order in which related forms are acquired is predicted by the derivational history of these forms in grammars for adult language (e.g., Brown & Hanlon, 1970).

This period was relatively short-lived. By the mid-1970s attempts to write grammars for children had all but died out, and derivational complexity had been found to make as many wrong predictions about order of acquisition as right ones. Many new topics were springing up to claim the attention that researchers had earlier lavished on the learning of syntactic rules, e.g., the role of meaning in language development, cognitive prerequisites, mother–child interactions, and the pragmatic uses to which children put language. New generations of child language scholars emerged who had never taken a linguistics course. "Whatever happened to linguistic theory?" asked Frank Kessel in the original title of his symposium.

The declining role of linguistics in the study of child language was not an isolated trend, but was embedded in a larger historical process in which psycho-linguistics more generally was developing its own research traditions and loosening its ties with linguistics. Psycholinguists had met with many disappointments in their efforts to predict processes of sentence comprehension on the basis of linguistic descriptions of the structures involved. The relationship between competence, as studied by linguists, and actual performance, as studied by psycho-linguists, seemed at best to be "more abstract" than had originally been thought (e.g., Fodor & Garrett, 1966); at worst, linguists and psycholinguists might be studying quite different things.

Throughout this period I found that a lingering effect of my early Harvard experience was a certain immunity to skepticism about the relevance of linguistics for the study of language use and language acquisition. I had taken very seriously Chomsky's claim that a grammar for a language was supposed to be a hypothesis about the speaker's internalized rule system. If psycholinguists and linguists could not get together, perhaps it was not because they were studying different topics or because the relationship between competence and performance is so indirect, but because linguistic models did not yet provide adequate representations of what speakers know about language (see Bresnan, 1978; Brown, 1970, pp. 156–157), or because we did not yet know which behaviors yield the best clues to speakers' linguistic knowledge.

It also seemed to me that if linguistics appeared less relevant to the study of language acquisition than it had earlier, perhaps it was because researchers were now often looking at everything about child language except at the acquisition of specifically linguistic structures and operations. Dan Slobin drew attention to this neglect with pointed irony in his paper title, "The role of language in language acquisition" (1979). The grammatical puzzles that confronted us in the 1960s had not yet been solved, although their complexity was often underestimated as attention focused on successively earlier stages of development. One of Roger's most important legacies to his students, I think, has been an abiding interest in the acquisition problems posed by syntax and morphology, and a ready skepticism of hypotheses about language development that do not do them justice.

PSYCHOLOGICAL REALITY

An interest in linguistics does not necessarily mean adherence to a particular theory of grammar, and it is perhaps significant that most of the psycholinguists who have worked in proximity to Roger have not committed themselves to a particular theoretical framework.[1] Where does this reluctance to embrace a single party line come from?

In part, I think, it derives from the influence of Roger's general approach to doing psychology. Rubin's (this volume) succinct summary of what he learned from Roger applies to me and others as well: "Find a phenomenon that is interesting for reasons other than the latest fad in psychology. . . . Be aware of—but do not be guided by—current theories, the latest statistics, or the research method you just mastered for your last project; rather, let the phenomenon itself determine which theories, statistics, and methods you should use." In addition, the tendency of Roger's students and associates to avoid commitment to a specific grammatical theory may reflect the deep respect Roger conveyed to us for the problem of *psychological reality*—determining whether hypothesized linguistic constructs correspond to the structures and operations that function in the minds of individual speakers.

Psychological reality of course concerns all psycholinguists. But Roger's perspective on this problem was not that of mainstream psycholinguistics. In the 1960s, investigators usually started with proposals by linguists about the constituent structure or transformational history of sentences and then tested whether these constructs play a role in sentence comprehension. Roger typically worked the other way around. Starting with relatively few theoretical preconceptions about children's grammars, he tried to infer the structure of their linguistic knowledge by looking at the distribution of forms and construction patterns in their spontaneous speech. The focus was not on the actual process of producing the utterances, but on the way the child's linguistic information must have been organized in order to give rise to the obtained sample.

For the investigator who tries to infer a grammar from speech samples, the problem of psychological reality is driven home at innumerable points by the *indeterminacy* of the data, i.e., its compatibility with more than one description

---

[1]I point this out in part to distinguish between linguistics as it has been applied to the study of language acquisition by students and associates of Roger's and the recent upswing in the use of linguistics by investigators more specifically guided by developments in Chomsky's theoretical approach, e.g., Berwick & Weinberg (1984); Otsu (1981); papers in Tavakolian (1981); Wexler & Culicover (1980).

(see Brown, 1973, p. 56; Brown & Fraser, 1963; Brown, Fraser, & Bellugi, 1964). The description to be preferred, of course, is the one that corresponds to the way the speaker's linguistic knowledge is structured, the one that determines the kinds of novel utterances he can produce or understand, how he construes their meanings, and what his intuitions are about grammatical well-formedness. But which description is this? The choice of theoretical framework in this way of thinking is not a matter of a priori commitment, no matter how appealing a model may be by standards of linguistic argumentation. It should be motivated by characteristics of the speaker's speech and other relevant empirical information. Alternative theoretical descriptions can be taken as *hypotheses* about how a speaker's grammatical information may be organized, and all available data should be exploited for clues that will help in deciding among them.

CATEGORIZATION

Roger's sensitivity to the problem of indeterminacy, and his efforts to make principled choices among alternative structural descriptions, seems to me to have been a natural outgrowth of his long-time interest in *categorization*. In particular, the ambiguity of spontaneous speech data for the would-be grammar writer was a new instantiation of a more general psychological problem that had intrigued Roger in other contexts: the susceptibility of any array of stimuli to *multiple categorizations*.

Categorization is the process by which people reduce the infinitely varied world of experience to manageable proportions by regarding discriminably different things as equivalent. This process was already an important topic among cognitively-minded psychologists at Harvard well before Roger took up the study of grammar acquisition. Bruner, Goodnow, and Austin's influential book on concept formation, *A Study in Thinking*, was published in 1956, with an eloquent appendix by Roger on the role of categorization in language. Roger's *Words and Things* and "How shall a thing be called?," both with extended discussions of categorization, followed in 1958. The climate in which these studies originated persisted at least up through my early years in graduate school. Roger's students therefore teethed not only on generative grammar, but also on the problem of how people render dissimilar things as "the same."

In deciding between alternative structural descriptions of a child's spontaneous speech data, the psycholinguist attempts to classify the utterances according to the categories that are functional in the child's linguistic rule system. This task is analogous to the one faced by the child, who must classify the linguistic input in ways that accurately predict what novel sentences are possible and under what circumstances they can be uttered.

No acquisitional task puts greater demand on children's skill at categorizing than learning to talk. The forms of language are themselves categories, and these forms are linked to a vast network of categorical distinctions in meaning and discourse function. For example, the form that marks plurality in English is a category comprising three distinct allomorphs, /s/, /z/, and /əz/. Parts of speech like "noun" and "verb" are formal categories that encompass sets of words that share the same privileges of occurrence. Grammatical functions like "subject of the sentence" are categories of relationships defined by the similarities in the way constituents performing these roles in particular sentences behave; e.g., one of the hallmarks of subjects in English is that they control verb agreement.

With respect to categories of meaning, the plural picks out a property of "more than one-ness" that can be shared by entities otherwise as different as apples and appointments. Basic word order in English indicates notions like "who did what to whom," which classify as equivalent in critical respects such diverse events as Mommy feeding the baby, Johnny pushing his wagon, and the dog biting the mailman. The suffix -ing signals "progressivity," an aspectual property that can be imputed to activities as disparate as "jumping" and "suffering."

Children are never exposed directly to the categories of language. They must infer these from instances of the categories encountered one-at-a-time in individual sentences distributed across time. What is a child to make of -ing on hearing sentences like "Are you jumping?" and "Mommy's cooking dinner"? That the event is "in progress" is one possible interpretation, but the child might also reasonably hypothesize that -ing signals present time, or that the actor enjoys what he is doing, or that the speaker feels affectionate toward the listener (as in uses of the diminutive to children), or that the event is incomplete (an aspectual distinction, imperfectivity, which is related to but not identical with progressivity; see Comrie, 1978).

Further, what can the child assume about the kinds of words to which -ing can be applied? Any word? All predicates (hence, *wanting, needing, noisying,* and *hotting* as well as *jumping* and *cooking*)? Words for activities under voluntary control? (This correctly rules out *needing, hotting,* and the like, but it also eliminates the perfectly good *sneezing* and *sweating*.)

What ideas does a child develop about how to order words on hearing sentences like "Grandma's eating a cookie" and "Daddy kissed Johnny"? That the name of the one who eats or who kisses should come before the word for eating or kissing? More generally, that the name of the person who performs an action should come before the name for the action? Or, at a still higher level of abstraction, that the word for any entity who "does" something goes in first position?

These examples, although brief, illustrate the problem of multiple categorization. The items in any array of objects, events, relationships, etc. exhibit many properties according to which the items can be grouped or differentiated. By selectively attending to similarities in certain properties and allowing other properties to vary, we arrive at one classification scheme. Change the emphasis and another scheme emerges. No one scheme is inherently the "right" way to classify a given domain, although it may be the one needed for a particular purpose, such as using a linguistic form appropriately.

The language-learning child, then, is faced with a formidable concept-attainment task. Which properties of situations or of language forms will best predict the distribution of -*ing* in the speech she hears, or the potential of a noun phrase to be placed preverbally or to govern verb agreement, or whether a certain verb can be passivized? The similarities in meaning, form, or structural configuration to which the child is sensitive will determine how she extends newly learned elements and operations to novel utterances. Since different theoretical frameworks make different assumptions about which categories of form and meaning are basic to the structure of language, the investigator in search of the best model for capturing a child's internalized grammar must continually ask about the makeup and scope of the child's linguistically relevant categories.

WHERE DO CHILDREN'S MEANING CATEGORIES COME FROM?

From an interest in what categories of meaning children attach to linguistic forms, it is only a small step to the question of *why* they adopt these meanings and not others. In particular, does nonlinguistic experience play the critical role in the way children come to classify the elements of their world? Or does language itself direct their attention to bases for classifying that they otherwise might not hit upon?

Roger raised this question repeatedly in his publications, starting with "A study in language and cognition" with Eric Lenneberg (Brown & Lenneberg, 1954). Although much stimulated by Whorf's arguments that language shapes cognitive development, he did not conceive the problem in all-or-none terms. Certain concepts, he suggested, are surely formed without assistance from language. This is especially likely to be true for such apparent universals as "conceptions of space, time, causality, and the enduring object" (Brown, 1958b, p. 195). But other concepts are more plausibly formed through observation of how fluent speakers use language, with novel words or other morphemes serving as a "lure to cognition" (Brown, 1958b, p. 206). The most compelling reason for making this assumption, argued Brown (1965), is the existence of crosslinguistic differences in categorization:

> If reality were to impose itself on the child's mind one would expect it to have imposed itself in that same form on all the languages of the world. The ubiquity of linguistic non-equivalence suggests that reality can be variously construed, and, therefore, that the child's manipulations and observations are not alone likely to yield the stock of conceptions that prevail in his society. The requirement that a child learn to make correct referential use of a morpheme or a meaningful construct

is sufficient to cause the child to form the governing concept if the world has not already imposed it upon him. (p. 317)

The hypothesis that children's categorization of reality is guided by language interested many researchers in the 1950s and 1960s (e.g., Carroll, 1958; Fishman, 1960; Hoijer, 1954). However, by the 1970s the intellectual tide was turning against this idea in favor of the priority of nonlinguistic cognitive development. Explicit attempts to test the Whorfian hypothesis had yielded mixed or disappointing results (e.g., Carroll & Casagrande, 1958; Maclay, 1958; see Lenneberg, 1962, for some critical evaluations). Interest was growing in the work of Piaget, who emphasized how much cognitive development takes place in the prelinguistic period. Rosch and Mervis (1976) found that children can group objects at the "basic object" level even before they learn the names for them. Crosslinguistic work began to suggest that certain domains, most notably color, are conceptualized more uniformly across cultures than had previously been supposed (Berlin & Kay, 1969; Heider, 1972). As notions of universality and cognitive priority came to predominate, interest in the possible concept-shaping role of language fell off dramatically.

My graduate school experiences proved deeply influential in the way I thought about these issues. The idea that nonlinguistic cognitive development might make an important contribution to language acquisition intrigued me, but at the same time I had become thoroughly sensitized to the problems posed by crosslinguistic differences in the categorization of meaning.

At first I worked primarily on the role of cognition. While writing my dissertation I had become interested in the possible cognitive underpinnings of early syntax. As a psychologist interested in learning, I was unwilling to accept without argument Chomsky's claim that (among other things) relational grammatical notions such as "subject of the sentence" are innately known to children. Moreover, in looking over the data I had collected from Finnish and American children, I could find no evidence for the psychological reality of these constructs. But the cross-language semantic uniformity of the early sentences was impressive, and, as Roger pointed out (Brown, 1973), the meanings they expressed seemed to be ones that children might plausibly formulate during the sensorimotor period without assistance from language.

On the basis of these findings, I suggested that children's earliest syntactic rules operate on relational categories derived from nonlinguistic cognitive development, such as "agent," "action," and "location," to specify the order in which words performing these relational roles should be combined. I hypothesized further that, after additional experience with language, children begin to notice[2] that words in different semantic roles often behave similarly with respect

---

[2]Terms like *notice, realize,* and *recognize* imply conscious awareness. However, for lack of more precise terms I use them in this chapter to refer to learning processes that are assumed to be entirely unconscious—i.e., that the child has no ability to reflect on or talk about.

to ordering, transformational possibilities, etc. On the basis of these similarities they eventually abstract away from a meaning-based syntactic system to a system of purely formal grammatical relations (Bowerman, 1973a,b).

My interest in the cognitive bases for early syntax proved to part of a more general movement toward grounding explanations of language acquisition in children's prelinguistic perceptions and conceptions of the world (e.g., Bloom, 1970, 1973; Clark, 1973; Macnamara, 1972; Nelson, 1974; Schlesinger, 1971; Slobin, 1973). As the approach took hold during the 1970s, however, I began to feel that the cognitive solutions being forwarded for specific problems of lexical and grammatical development were often oversimplified and probably at times simply wrong.

First and most simply, the approach often led to incorrect predictions about the way children initially extend patterns of word combination or inflection. For example, in testing the hypothesis that children's early word combinations are based on rules like "agent precedes action" against postdissertation data that I had collected from my two daughters, I could find little evidence for the psychological reality of categories like "agent." Instead, it looked as if quite a lot of initial sentence construction was based on children's learning about the combinatorial potential of *individual predicates* (verbs and adjectives). This stage apparently could be quickly succeeded by productive combination with predicates of diverse semantic types, without evidence for an intervening stage in which the child relies on relational categories of meaning like "agent" or "action" (Bowerman, 1976).

Second and more generally—and here is where my early exposure to linguistic relativity was telling—I felt that the new, ostensibly "semantic" approach to child grammar often betrayed an inadequate appreciation for the way in which meaning is woven into the structure of language (Bowerman, 1983a, 1985a,b). To many researchers, semantics could apparently be directly equated with nonlinguistic cognition. On the one hand there are the "meanings" encoded by language, and these are provided by nonlinguistic cognitive development. On the other hand there are the forms of language, and these are provided by the linguistic input. The child's task, according to this view, is simply to find the forms that are appropriate to the meanings, and match them up.

As Roger's student, I had read Whorf attentively, and also the more moderate Sapir, who was Whorf's teacher. Even if one rejects Whorf's linguistic determinism, and regardless of his unquestionable circularities of reasoning and enthusiastic excesses, I believe that anyone who has studied these authors closely, and given more than passing thought to crosslinguistic differences, cannot accept the view that language is simply an overlay on nonlinguistic thought. What is missing from this approach is acknowledgment of a system of *semantic organization*—a level of structure in which, from among all the possible ways the human cognitive apparatus can categorize experiences, a language selects and combines certain options and not others.

I have already mentioned the categorical nature of language. Let me pursue this further in order to point out some important differences between non-linguistic thought and the way language structures meaning (see Bowerman, 1983a, 1985a, 1985b; Schlesinger, 1977; and Slobin, 1979, for more extended discussions).

Nonlinguistic perceptions are finely graded: People are capable of making very delicate distinctions in what they experience and think about, and they can detect and respond to any number of similarities and differences among objects, events, relationships, etc. But language works on the basis of *categorical* opposi-tions.[3] For example, an object in contact with a surface may be "contained" within a concave curvature of that surface to varying degrees (picture a button resting against the palm of a gradually closing hand). But English speakers must decide categorically if the object is "on" or "in" the entity whose surface it is; continuously graded expressions reflecting changes in *degree* of containment (e.g., gradual alterations of the vowel in the frame / __n/ from /ɔ/ to /ɪ/) are not characteristic of ordinary language (see also Brown, 1958b, pp. 211–212; New-port, 1982; and Talmy, 1983).

Speakers not only must learn to make categorical distinctions among events, relationships, etc. that vary along a continuum, but they also must learn to do so on the basis of oppositions in meaning that often differ markedly from one language to another. For example, Spanish speakers, unlike English speakers, do not have to worry about the breakdown of the "on-to-in" continuum unless they want to be very explicit; for most purposes a single preposition, *en,* will suffice to encode the entire range of spatial relations that English obligatorily splits into *on* versus *in.* On the other hand, Dutch speakers must attend not only to whether there is containment but also, when there is not, to details of the *kind* of contact that obtains between the located object and the surface of the reference object.

Roughly, if the surface offers relatively horizontal support, the located object is *op* ("on") it, e.g., an apple *op* the table. However, if the surface is not horizontal, the spatial relationship is described as *op* only if the located object is firmly attached over a wide area of its own surface, e.g., a sticker *op* the refrigerator, a bandaid or pimple *op* the chin, a poster glued *op* the wall. If the located object is attached by a more restricted point, the spatial relationship is called *aan* (corresponding also to "on"), e.g., a framed picture *aan* the wall, a button *aan* a sweater, a coat *aan* a hook. Children learning English and Spanish are presumably as capable as those learning Dutch of noticing differences in the

---

[3]Perception is also sometimes categorical, e.g., for hue and certain continua of speech sounds there is less sensitivity to distinctions located at some points on the continuum than to distinctions of comparable magnitude located at other points (see Bornstein, 1979, and Newport, 1982, for discus-sion). But even when this is the case, human perceivers are capable of making far finer discrimina-tions than are needed for distinguishing the forms that make up the contrast sets of natural languages. That is, languages do not even begin to take advantage of the degree of resolution offered by nonlinguistic perception.

way an apple is in contact with a table, a bandaid with the skin, and a picture with a wall. But only those learning Dutch must learn how to make *categorical decisions* on the basis of a to-be-identified subset of these differences in order to make appropriate spatial reference.

To take a second example, consider the conceptual domain of *animacy*. The animacy of referents figures importantly in the structure of many unrelated languages, and it is plausible to assume that this is because animacy has high nonlinguistic significance to human beings. However, even if children come prepared to think that animacy may be important in the structure of language, they must still learn how distinctions in animacy are locally defined.

On the basis of crosslinguistic comparisons, animacy can be described as a hierarchy rather than a dichotomy (I am relying here on Comrie, 1981, chapter 9). Its principle components, from highest to lowest in degree of perceived animacy, are human > animal > inanimate; further subdivisions within components are sometimes also made, e.g., between adult and child humans, between higher and lower animals, or between inanimate entities that are capable of spontaneous movement, like wind and lightning, and those that are not. Different languages make cuts in this hierarchy in different ways (and sometimes in more than one way for different purposes). For example, to control the distinction between *who* and *what* in English, children must make a split between humans on the one hand and animals and inanimate entities on the other. If asked *WHO did you see downtown?*, they must learn to respond with phrases like *Mary* or *a lot of strange people*, but not **a horse* or **a new building*. Conversely, if asked *WHAT did you see downtown?*, they can say either *a horse* or *a building*, but not **Mary*. In Russian, the comparable distinction is between *kto* and *čto*. Here, however, the relevant split is positioned further down the hierarchy between animals and inanimate objects, thus throwing *Mary* and *a horse* into the same category and distinguishing them from *a building*.

In addition to learning where to make semantic cuts, children must learn how the categories defined by these cuts interact with other, often logically independent meaning distinctions to form complex conceptual bundles. For example, in Hausa a speaker's selection from among the deictic terms comparable to English *this* and *that* requires simultaneous attention to both *degree of distance* from the speaker (a two-way split) and *whether the referent has previously been mentioned* (Welmers, 1973, as summarized by Anderson & Keenan, 1985):

a. wánnàn "this (i.e., close to speaker) (new)"
b. wáncàn "that (i.e., far from speaker) (new)"
c. wànnán "this (previously mentioned)"
d. wàncán "that (previously mentioned)"

In the deictic system of Kwakwa'la, in contrast, the dimension of distance from speaker (this time a *three-way* split) is combined with the dimension of *visibility to the speaker* (visible vs. not visible) for a total of six terms ("close to speaker-visible," "close to speaker-invisible," etc.) (Boas, 1947, as summarized by Anderson & Keenan, 1985). And in many languages of New Guinea and Australia, distance from speaker is combined with still another dimension, *height* of referent relative to speaker, for a complex set of contrasts between forms meaning, e.g., "this (near) higher," "that (far) higher," "yonder (remote) higher," "this (vs. that/yonder) lower," "that same level" (Murane, 1974, as summarized by Anderson & Keenan, 1985; see also Denny, 1978, on Eskimo).

To summarize, nonlinguistic cognition, no matter how powerful, does not directly provide children with the categories of meaning they need to become fluent speakers of their language, nor with information about how these categories work together to determine the choice among alternative forms. Some distinctions are no doubt so salient for humans that the contrasting categories they define are accorded separate lexical, morphological, or syntactic treatment in the structure of every language. Others may be so unimportant that no language obligatorily honors them. But in between are vast stretches of "semantic space" in which the partitioning is not predetermined by the structure of human cognition (Bowerman, 1985b).

In consequence, an important part of the child's "induction of latent structure" must be to work out the distinctions in meaning that correlate with contrasts in form in the language being learned. How children perform this task— how they apply their general nonlinguistic understanding of the world to solving the delicate and finely articulated semantic categorization puzzles posed by their language—preoccupied Roger already 30 years ago. And despite major changes in psychologists' conceptions of the structure of semantic categories (from "criterial attributes" to "prototypes," see Brown, 1976), Roger's earliest writings on the subject are still as relevant today as when they were first published.

APPROACHES TO DATA

This outline of some major ideas to which Roger's students and colleagues were exposed during the years in which he was working on language acquisition would not be complete without a least a small discussion of methods of approaching language data. In particular, I want to highlight two interrelated themes: the stress Roger placed on obtaining a deep familiarity with the body of data one intends to analyze, and the value he attached to allowing the data themselves to reveal interesting directions for analysis.

These themes figured prominantly in Roger's direction of my dissertation. I had long been interested in how crosslinguistic comparisons could be used to distinguish between what is universal and what is language-specific in the acquisition of language. Since little information was then available on the acquisition of languages other than English, I began to collect data from children learning Finnish, a language historically unrelated to English with a much richer inflectional system and freer word order.

Before going far, I had to submit a thesis prospectus outlining what I intended to do. An ad hoc interdepartmental committee would evaluate the prospectus and question me; if they accepted it I could proceed. Roger counseled me on how to compose my prospectus.

"Many people feel that the only proper way to do scientific research is to test hypotheses," he pointed out. "I don't hold this view myself. In fact, I think that often the most interesting things we find are things we weren't looking for ahead of time, and this is likely to be true in the case of your Finnish data. But to satisfy everyone on your committee, be sure to include some hypotheses and show how you will test them." (Of course, I am paraphrasing wildly in trying to reconstruct these remarks.)

Intrigued by the conspiratorial tone of this advice, I duly included hypotheses. But I had little confidence in them, nor did I much care whether they were confirmed. However the answers turned out, I would learn things about language acquisition from the data that I could not learn from English data alone. More than hypotheses, I needed the sensitivity to detect patterns in the data that I did not know in advance to look for, and the confidence to pursue them.

Roger's faith in the power of careful observation to start off a fruitful chain of questioning and analysis was immensely inspiring. But sensitivity and confidence did not come immediately. Early on, I felt overwhelmed by my masses of undigested data. Page after page of transcripts, pile after pile of note cards—how would I ever find my way beyond all this detail?

Roger was unperturbed. "Be patient," he advised. "You've spent all your time so far collecting and transcribing tapes. Now the more interesting part begins, when you begin to find out what you've got. As you get better acquainted with your data, you will start to have ideas about it." I was unconvinced, but the prediction proved sound. With increasing familiarity, what had seemed a morass of unrelated details began to resolve itself into coherent patterns, and I started to think of new lines of analysis I wanted to pursue.

Getting intimately acquainted with a body of child language data does take time and patience, and the sometimes prolonged uncertainty about possible outcomes can be unsettling. Particularly in this era of computer technology and competition for funds, the temptation may be great to decide on analyses for which coding categories can be set up ahead of time so that the raw data can be processed by assistants and machine. Of course, there are many analyses for which this approach is appropriate. But much is lost when it is done routinely. To a human eye that has not been blinkered by a strong set of starting assumptions about what to look for, utterances that at first glance seemed totally unrelated begin to connect up. Abstract patterns emerge that no coding scheme thought up ahead of time would have been able to reveal; hypotheses come out of the data. This is one of the most important lessons I learned from Roger.

LATE ERRORS

In the preceding sections I have outlined the ideas and attitudes that impressed me most deeply during my graduate study: (1) the potential of linguistics to suggest hypotheses about how linguistic knowledge is organized in the minds of speakers; (2) a concern for establishing the psychological reality of linguistic descriptions, and a preference for studying this by looking at patterns of generalization in spontaneous speech data rather than, for instance, at comprehension; (3) an interest in categorization, and especially in the existence of multiple, equally valid ways to classify any single array; (4) curiosity about where the meaning categories that children attach to linguistic forms come from—nonlinguistic cognitive development, experience with the input language, or both?; and (5) the conviction that careful observation and thorough familiarity with one's data can suggest fruitful lines of investigation that are likely to be missed if one only follows plans of analysis that are set up ahead of time.

These themes are broad, and they did not a priori define any specific directions for my research beyond graduate school. Yet in looking back, I find it striking and hardly coincidental that children's late speech errors—the problem to which I have returned most persistently over the last decade—manages neatly to implicate them all!

To begin with the last-mentioned theme, I did not go out looking for late errors; they seemed to come to me. In the early 1970s I had begun to take notes and tapes on the language development of my two daughters, Christy and Eva. Major milestones in the speech of English-speaking children were well known at that time, and I was not expecting to find anything qualitatively new. My intention was to learn more about the relational categories on which productivity in early word combination is based. To do this I needed a data base that was rich and detailed enough to allow me to analyze the history of every word before, during, and beyond the time it started to enter into combination with other words.

My notes included both conventional utterances and those that deviated in various ways from the standard English input that the children were receiving. Some deviations I was expecting from my knowledge of the literature, e.g., inflectional overregularizations and WH-questions like *What Daddy ate?*. Others did not correspond to any error genres that I had read about. At first I perceived each of these unexpected errors as essentially unique. And some remained so— isolated oddities about which little can be said. Over time, however, other novel deviations began to look familiar. One instance might be widely separated in time from the next and the exact words and context might differ, but after several exemplars I started to recognize "errors of the same kind" when they came along again. Some examples are shown in Table 2.1.

Errors have long held a special fascination for students of language acquisition, and rightly so. As long as children speak in the way adults around them speak, we cannot be certain whether they are *constructing* their utterances or

TABLE 2.1
Examples of Late Errors
(C=Christy, E=Eva, M=Mother; age in years, months)

A. 1. E 5;0 Can I fill some salt into the bear? (=fill the bear
    [a salt shaker] with some salt.)

  2. C 4;9 She's gonna pinch it on my foot. (=pinch my foot with
    it. Protesting as E approaches with a toy.)

  3. E 4;5 I'm going to cover a screen over me. (=cover myself
    with a screen.)

  4. E 2;11 E: Pour, pour, pour. Mommy, I poured you. (waving
        empty container near M)
    M: You poured me?
    E: Yeah, with water. (= I poured water on you.)

  5. E 4;11 (M asks at breakfast if E is going to finish her toast)
    I don't want it because I spilled it of orange juice.
    (= spilled orange juice on it.)

B. 6. C 2;9 I come it closer so it won't fall. (=make it come/bring.
    Pulling a bowl closer to her as she sits on counter.)

  7. C 2;11 I'm gonna sharp this pencil. (= make sharp/sharpen.)

  8. C 3;1 (M and C playing with broken music box cow)
    M: The cow would like to sing but he can't.
    C: I'm singing him. (=making him sing. Pulling string
       that used to make cow play.)

  9. E 3;7 I'm gonna put the washrag in and disappear something
    under the washrag. (=make something disappear. Playing
    in tub.)

 10. E 5;0 I want to sleep with it 'cause they'll stay me warmer.
    (=make me stay/keep. Protesting when M tries to take
    her pants off at bedtime.)

C. 11. C 3;8 I pulled it unstapled. (After pulling a stapled booklet
    apart.)

 12. C 3;10 Untie it off. (Wants M to untie piece of yarn and take
    it off tricycle handle.)

 13. E 2;0 I'm going to turn it open. (Later:) I can't turn it
    open. (Trying to rotate lid of Kentucky Fried chicken
    barrel until it comes off.)

 14. E 3;9 A gorilla captured my fingers. I'll capture his whole
    head off. His hands too. (Playing with rubber band
    around fingers.)

D. 15. C 3;9 This is pooey that's coming out of here. (In tub, show-
    ing water spouting out of holes in cup.) And this is how
    to make it uncome. (Blocking holes with hand.)

 16. C 4;5 (C has asked why pliers are on table)
    M: I've been using them for straightening the wire.
    C: And unstraighting it? (=unstraightening; bending.)

 17. C 5;1 He tippitoed to the graveyard and unburied her. (Telling
    ghost story.)

 18. E 3;10 (M grabs E in a game)
    M: I have to capture you.
    E: Uncapture me! (=release; trying to pull loose.)

 19. E 3;11 How do you unsqueeze it? (=reverse squeezing; coming
    to M with clip earring hanging from ear.)

(continued...)

TABLE 2.1
Examples of Late Errors
(C=Christy, E=Eva, M=Mother; age in years, months)

(continued)

E. 20.	C 3;6	I don't want to go to bed yet. Don't let me go to bed. (=don't make me go to bed.)
21.	E 2;9	I want to sit in my place. Always you let me sit in your place! (=make me sit; protesting to M.)
22.	C 3;6	But usually puppets make--let people put their hands in. (After M had called dolls with toilet paper roll bodies 'puppets'; disagreeing with the name.)
23.	C 3;9	Make me watch it! (=let me watch it. Begging to be allowed to watch a TV program.)

simply repeating what they have heard. But departures from conventionality signal children's own efforts to find patterns in what they are hearing: "The clearest evidence that a very young child can give that he is working out the latent structure of language is, paradoxically enough, the production of an unlawful utterance" (Brown, 1965, p. 297). A recurrent error is a challenge—an invitation for the investigator to discover the latent structure that the child has discovered.

For errors like *breaked* and *foots* we do not have to look far: The regular inflectional morphology of English is as salient to the parent as it is to the linguist, and when the child smooths out an irregular form it is clear that she has perceived the larger pattern to which it is an exception. Many of the errors I was recording posed more of a puzzle, however. It was not always obvious that the child was responding to a structural pattern of English, and, even where this seemed likely, it was not necessarily clear how to characterize the regularity. A further problem was that the onset of the errors was routinely preceded by a long period—sometimes even a year or more—during which the child used the pertinent words or construction patterns correctly. How to account for this delay?

It is well known that children use irregular forms like *broke* and *feet* correctly before they begin to make errors like *breaked* and *foots*. The accepted explanation for this sequence attributes the early correct usage to the child's rote memorization of both regular and irregular forms as "unanalyzed units." Errors occur later when the child comes to realize that the forms are composed conceptually (and segmentally, in the case of regular forms) of two units, and begins to extend the regular combinatorial pattern to forms that are exceptions to it. This explanation is plausible enough for *breaked* and *foots,* but it cannot be applied in a straightforward way to errors that do not involve inflectional or derivational morphology (e.g., A–C, E in Table 2.1). Moreover, the correct usage preceding the errors is not limited to a few fixed phrases that might plausibly have been memorized, but rather is flexible and varied in a way we normally associate with full productivity.

I began to read what linguists had said about the words and construction patterns involved in the errors. Opinions often differed. But the ways in which they differed sometimes offered clues to why children at first seem to have fully mastered these forms and yet later start to make errors.

Linguistic Approaches to Partial Regularity as Hypotheses about Speakers' Knowledge

With the perspective of hindsight, it is possible to summarize a number of late errors as overregularizations, not of morphology but of the relationships obtaining between predicates and the syntactic frames in which they can appear. Table 2.2 shows examples of the patterns that are relevant for error types A–C in Table 2.1.

Patterns like these pose particular difficulties for the construction of comprehensive models of grammar. They are neither fish nor fowl. On the one hand they display regularities of a kind that has often been associated with syntactic rules. Linguists have therefore proposed transformational operations for deriving structures of one kind from structures of the other kind, or both from a common ancestor. For example, Hall (1965) suggested deriving *spray the wall with paint* (for instance) by optional transformation from a structure similar to *spray paint on the wall.* Many generative semanticists (e.g., Lakoff, 1970, McCawley,

TABLE 2.2
Sentence Patterns of English Relevant to Error Types A-C in Table 2.1

A. 1a. Spray/spatter paint on the wall.
   b. Spray/spatter the wall with paint.

   2a. Load hay into the wagon.
   b. Load the wagon with hay.

   3a. Spread/smear butter on the bread.
   b. Spread/smear the bread with butter.

   4a. Drain/empty the water from the bucket.
   b. Drain/empty the bucket of (its) water.

B. 5a. The stick broke/cracked.
   b. John broke/cracked the stick.

   6a. The door opened.
   b. George opened the door.

   7a. The milk is warm.
   b. Mom warmed the milk.

C. 8a. Dad chopped (on) the tree, which made it fall down.
   b. Dad made the tree fall down by chopping (on) it.
   c. Dad chopped the tree down.

   9a. Mary wiped the table, which made it clean/become clean.
   b. Mary cleaned the table by wiping it.
   c. Mary wiped the table clean.

   10a. Jim kicked the door, which made it close.
   b. Jim closed the door by kicking it.
   c. Jim kicked the door closed.

1971) advocated deriving constructions containing transitive causative verbs like *to break* (something) from underlying structures containing a predicate like CAUSE plus an intransitive predicate, as suggested by the paraphrase "cause (something) to break/become broken." And Fillmore (1971) and Talmy (1976) argued that sentences like *Dad chopped the tree down* and *Mary wiped the table clean* should be derived from underlying structures consisting of two propositions, one specifying a causing event and the other a resulting change of location or state, as suggested by paraphrases like *Dad chopped (on) the tree, which caused the tree to fall down* and *Mary wiped the table, which caused the table to become clean.*

On the other hand, however, patterns like those in Table 2.2 are riddled with lexical exceptions and semantic idiosyncrasies that confound straightforward solutions through syntactic rules. Many predicted constructions do not occur. For example, *Pour paint on the floor* is similar both syntactically and semantically to *Spray paint on the wall*, but there is no construction *Pour the floor with paint* analogous to *Spray the wall with paint*. Similarly, *Fill the wagon with hay* is similar to *Load the wagon with hay*, but *Load hay into the wagon* does not have a counterpart in *Fill hay into the wagon*. Further, although we can say both *The stick broke* and *John broke the stick*, we cannot operate on *The rabbit disappeared* to derive *The magician disappeared the rabbit.* Finally, we balk at *Wipe the table dirty/wet* (e.g., with a dirty or wet rag), *Comb your hair untangled*, and *Untie the ribbon off your braid*, even though the two-proposition structures that would be hypothesized to underlie them are fully comparable to those hypothesized to underlie acceptable constructions like *Wipe the table clean, Comb your hair smooth*, and *Tie the ribbon on your braid.*

Even when anticipated constructions do exist, their meanings often differ from what would be predicted on the basis of general rule (Aronoff, 1976; Jackendoff, 1975). For instance, corresponding to the intransitive verb *to bleed* there is a causative transitive verb *to bleed* (someone/something). However, it does not simply mean "to cause to bleed"—notice the oddity of *I bled my toe when I stubbed it.* Its use is restricted to certain medical and metaphorical contexts.

Because of such gaps and semantic irregularities, linguists have in recent years increasingly rejected the syntactic approach to patterns like those shown in Table 2.2 in favor of treatment within the lexicon, traditionally the repository in a grammar for whatever information is not predictable by general rule. Instead of deriving certain constructions in which a predicate appears from other, more "basic" constructions, the analyst simply lists, in the lexical entry posited for that predicate, all the syntactic frames in which it can occur (e.g., Jackendoff, 1975). Alternatively, each predicate is given as many separate lexical entries as there are syntactic frames associated with it. Phrases like *chop down* and *wipe clean* can simply be listed in the lexicon as two-part verbs (Chomsky, 1962). The meaning that a predicate expresses in a certain frame can also be presented in full in the lexical entry, which makes accounting for semantic idiosyncracies unproblematic.[4]

In principle, the grammar could now be considered complete: It is capable of generating the well-formed sentences of the language, and—in contrast to the "general rule" approach—it will not generate unacceptable constructions like *The magician disappeared the rabbit. But to capture speakers' intuitions that some patterns of syntactic frame alternation are shared by more than one predicate, the lexicon can also be furnished with *lexical redundancy rules,* which state generalizations across existing lexical entries. Unlike syntactic rules, redundancy rules are conceived of as normally passive; that is, speakers do not, by hypothesis, call on them in routine sentence production or comprehension, but instead retrieve the information they need directly from the listings stored in their mental lexicon. However, some linguists (e.g., Jackendoff, 1975) suggest that lexical redundancy rules might at times be used creatively to generate syntactic frames for novel predicates.

The two approaches just discussed—the listing of syntactic frames in the lexical entri(es) for a predicate versus derivation by general syntactic rule—constitute sharply contrasting hypotheses about the organization of speakers' linguistic knowledge. However, *both* approaches characterize possible states of knowledge that are compatible with behaving like a fluent speaker most of the time. The speaker who has learned only the set of syntactic frames in which each predicate in his lexicon can appear will produce only acceptable pairings of predicate and frame, but can produce these quite freely with a variety of noun arguments. The speaker who has formulated very general rules that relate classes of predicates will also be capable of producing all acceptable frames for a given predicate; his only fault will be that he sometimes also produces predicate/frame pairings that fluent speakers find ill-formed, even though these pairings conform to a larger semantic/syntactic pattern.

Notice that the first description is a good characterization of how young children behave before errors in a particular lexico-syntactic domain set in. The second description, in contrast, fits older children, after the onset of errors. This suggests that both accounts may be correct, but for speakers at *different stages of linguistic development.* That is, young children may initially rely heavily on information specific to particular predicates in determining what kinds of con-

---

[4]This approach has recently been favored not only on grounds of descriptive adequacy but also because it has been hypothesized to provide a solution to the so-called "no negative evidence" problem. Children receive little feedback about what is not an acceptable sentence of their language. This means that if they should formulate grammatical rules that are overly general—i.e., that generate all acceptable utterances of a certain type and err only in generating some unacceptable ones as well—it is unclear what would eventually lead them to correct these rules (Braine, 1971). This logical puzzle has led several linguists to hypothesize that children approach the acquisition task very conservatively, never formulating rules that would lead to errors that could not be eradicated on the basis of positive evidence alone (e.g., Baker, 1979).

structions the predicates can appear in and what they will mean in those constructions. Later, after a repertoire of predicates-cum-frames has been acquired, the child reorganizes, extracting from sets of individual predicates more general information about what kinds of frames are likely to be associated with predicates of various types. Usage continues to be mostly correct, but overregularizations like those under A–C in Table 2.1 now sometimes occur (Bowerman, 1974, 1982a,b).

How speakers eventually cut back on overly productive rules—e.g., begin to behave as if they have passive lexical redundancy rules that are at most used only to create new frames for *novel* predicates, not for well-known predicates—is an important further question, but it need not concern us here (see Bowerman, 1982a, 1983b for discussion). For present purposes it is enough to note that although the earlier state of knowledge is sufficient to the demands of normal adult usage, the later state of knowledge reflects deeper generalizations about regularities in the linguistic input. Although the child mostly continues to talk as before, his underlying categories have covertly broadened: Privileges of occurrence that earlier were tied to individual predicates are now seen as applicable to whole classes of predicates.

Finding the Semantic Correlates
of Grammatical Generalizations

The class of predicates to which a particular syntactic or morphological generalization applies is often not arbitrary, but semantically coherent. For example, the syntactic alternation exemplified by *spray paint on the wall* versus *spray the wall with paint* is not open to an arbitrary set of verbs with both direct and oblique objects, but is limited to (a subset of) verbs belonging to a restricted semantic class: those specifying an action in which the entity named by one of the postverb noun phrases is moved (actually or metaphorically) toward or away from the entity named by the other postverb noun phrase.[5] A second example: Not all verbs of English can be prefixed with reversative *un-*. As Whorf (1956) pointed out, *un*-able verbs constitute a "covert" semantic category, all sharing "a covering, enclosing, and surface-attaching meaning. . . . Hence we say 'uncover, uncoil, undress, unfasten, unlock, unroll, untangle, untie, unwind,' but not 'unbreak, undry, unhang, unheat, unlift, unmelt, unopen, unpress, unspill' " (p. 71).

When a grammatical generalization is productive in adult speech, it is essential for children to learn the semantic constraints on the class of words to which it

---

[5]More precisely, these NPs perform the semantic case roles termed Figure and Ground by Talmy (1976) (Fillmore's 1977 Patient and Goal/Source and Jackendoff's 1972 Theme and Goal/Source; see Bowerman, 1982b, for discussion of this construction pattern and how children learn its semantic correlates).

applies if they are to attain adult-like fluency. Even when a pattern is not really productive, children often reveal their appreciation of its semantic correlates by (eventually) confining their overgeneralizations to lexical items of the appropriate semantic class (Bowerman, 1982b).

How do children arrive at the semantic correlates of syntactic or morphological generalizations? According to the hypothesis discussed earlier (pp. 31–32), that language merely maps onto meanings that are formulated independently of language, children should come to appreciate the category of meaning associated with a particular grammatical generalization independently of learning the generalization itself. In other words, they should *not* learn the category as a direct consequence of learning the generalization, e.g., by noticing that there is an abstract meaning shared by all the forms to which the generalization applies in adult speech.

This hypothesis does not find support in the data on children's late over-regularizations of the types shown under A–D in Table 2.1. In general, the pattern of development leading up to and following the onset of errors of a given type suggests that identifying the semantic correlates of late-learned regularities is typically part and parcel of determining the way the regularity itself works in adult speech (Bowerman, 1982b). For example, learning the semantic category associated with *un*-prefixation is a drawn-out process, at least for some children. At first they may freely attach *un*- to any verb to create a novel verb meaning "to stop or reverse the action/process specified by the base verb" (e.g., 15–16 under D in Table 2.1). Gradually, however, they narrow down its use to precisely those verbs that share the "covering, enclosing, and surface-attaching meaning" described by Whorf, even though some of these verbs happen not to allow *un*-prefixation in adult English (e.g., 17–19 in Table 2.1).

Meaning Categories Not Displayed in the Input

Late errors provide evidence that children can and do work out categories of meaning to fit the syntactic and morphological patterns they have discovered in their language.[6] But although children are considerably more willing to accept guidance in semantic categorization from the input language than is predicted by the hypothesis that linguistic forms map only onto preestablished meanings, they also demonstrate that they are not completely dependent on language. Their

---

[6]Further evidence for learners' sensitivity to the semantic organization of their language comes from crosslinguistic comparisons: Even when languages differ strikingly in the way they partition certain conceptual domains, children may show language-appropriate categorization schemes from their first productive use of the relevant forms (Bowerman, 1985b). In this case it is *error-free* learning rather than errors that reveals children's ability to construct categories of meaning by observing the distribution of linguistic forms.

speech also shows the influence of their own spontaneous ideas about what is similar to what.

One source of evidence for children's spontaneous meaning categories is their initial under- or overextension of morphemes or construction patterns, relative to the semantic range of these forms in adult speech, e.g., *doggie* for all four-legged creatures (Clark, 1973, 1977), or the accusative case ending only for the direct objects of verbs naming actions of seizing, manipulation, or transfer (Slobin, 1985). Certain late errors provide further evidence.

For example, E in Table 2.1 shows instances of a recurrent late error in my data in which the child substitutes either *make* for *let* or *let* for *make* in periphrastic causative constructions. In adult English, *make* is used when the relationship of the causer to the caused event is "active," i.e., the causer does something to bring the event about. *Let,* in contrast, is used for "permissive" causation, in which the causer refrains from doing something that would prevent the event from taking place. (Compare *John made Mary sing* and *John let Mary sing.*) At first, my subjects respected this distinction completely, always choosing correctly between *make* and *let* according to the intended meaning. Later, however, they began to make substitution errors occasionally, which suggests that the meanings, although still distinguished, had grown similar enough in the mental lexicon that the child's search for a word to express one meaning now could activate the word for the other meaning as well (Bowerman, 1978).

Recurrent substitution errors like the *let/make* confusions display a hidden logic. They do not take place on the basis of all conceivable similarities between referent entities or events, but instead reflect meaning categories that are linguistically "sensible"—i.e., that play a role in the grammatical structure of some languages, even if not in the language that the child happens to be learning (Bowerman, 1983a, 1985b). For example, the abstract category that results when the distinction between "active" and "permissive" causation is blurred is not needed for learning English. But it is precisely the right one for Georgian and many other languages, which construct causative sentences with verb affixes or other forms that range in meaning over both active and permissive causation (i.e., that can mean either *let* or *make,* according to context; Comrie, 1981, p. 164). If my subjects had happened to be learning such a language, their ability to conceptualize active and permissive causation as similar would have assisted them in acquiring the grammar of causatives. Since they were learning English, however, it led to errors.

In summary, late errors and evidence of other kinds show that *both* the semantic structure of the linguistic input *and* children's nonlinguistic predispositions for categorizing contribute to the language learner's organization of meaning. Working out how the two sources of structure interact as children construct the semantic system of their local language remains one of the most complex and challenging problems confronting child language researchers today.

CONCLUSION

This chapter opened with a quote: "Every child processes the speech to which he is exposed so as to induce from it a latent structure . . . " This passage has always appealed to me, for it captures with utmost simplicity and profundity the central mystery of language acquisition. Late errors have fascinated me in part, I think, because they provide a slow-motion view of the induction of latent structure. Acquisition is drawn out over time, as the child discovers successively deeper layers of regularity in the input.

The various themes I have outlined in this chapter all contribute to understanding late errors and, through them, the larger problem of how children ferret out the patterns of their language. As I have thought back over the last 20 years in preparation for writing this chapter, I have been struck by how persistently the themes I became interested in through Roger have stayed with me. So often when I thought I was looking at a new problem, I have discovered that it was really one of the old problems again, simply in a different disguise. Those early questions were extraordinarily rich, and they will continue to challenge and inspire students of language acquisition for a long time to come.

ACKNOWLEDGMENTS

I am grateful to Jane Edwards and Lee Ann Weeks for their comments on an earlier draft of this chapter.

REFERENCES

Anderson, S. R., & Keenan, E. L. (1985). Deixis. In T. Shopen (Ed.), *Language typology and syntactic description, Vol. III: Grammatical categories and the lexicon.* Cambridge, England: Cambridge University Press.

Aronoff, M. (1976). *Word formation in generative grammar.* Cambridge, MA: MIT Press.

Baker, C. L. (1979). Syntactic theory and the projection problem. *Linguistic Inquiry, 10,* 533–581.

Berlin, B., & Kay, P. (1969). *Basic color terms.* Berkeley: University of California Press.

Berwick, R. C., & Weinberg, A. S. (1984). *The grammatical basis of linguistic performance: Language use and acquisition.* Cambridge, MA: MIT Press.

Bloom, L. (1970). *Language development: Form and function in emerging grammars.* Cambridge, MA: MIT Press.

Bloom, L. (1973). *One word at a time: The use of single word utterances before syntax.* The Hague: Mouton.

Boas, F. (1947). Kwakiutl grammar, with a glossary of the suffixes. Edited by H. B. Yampolsky. *Transactions of the American Philosophical Society, 37,* 203–377.

Bornstein, M. H. (1979). Perceptual development: Stability and change in feature perception. In M. H. Bornstein & W. Kessen (Eds.), *Psychological development in infancy.* Hillsdale, NJ: Lawrence Erlbaum Associates.

Bowerman, M. (1973a). *Early syntactic development: A cross-linguistic study, with special reference to Finnish.* Cambridge, England: Cambridge University Press.

Bowerman, M. (1973b). Structural relationships in children's utterances: Syntactic or semantic? In T. M. Moore (Ed.), *Cognitive development and the acquisition of language.* New York: Academic Press.

Bowerman, M. (1974). Learning the structure of causative verbs: A study in the relationship of cognitive, semantic, and syntactic development. *Papers and Reports on Child Language Development* (Stanford University Department of Linguistics), *8,* 142–178.

Bowerman, M. (1976). Semantic factors in the acquisition of rules for word use and sentence construction. In D. Morehead & A. Morehead (Eds.), *Directions in normal and deficient child language.* Baltimore: University Park Press.

Bowerman, M. (1978). Systematizing semantic knowledge: Changes over time in the child's organization of word meaning. *Child Development, 49,* 977–987.

Bowerman, M. (1982a). Evaluating competing linguistic models with language acquisition data: Implications of developmental errors with causative verbs. *Quaderni di Semantica, 3,* 5–66.

Bowerman, M. (1982b). Reorganizational processes in lexical and syntactic development. In E. Wanner & L. R. Gleitman (Eds.), *Language acquisition: The state of the art.* Cambridge, England: Cambridge University Press.

Bowerman, M. (1982c). Starting to talk worse: Clues to language acquisition from children's late speech errors. In S. Strauss (Ed.), *U-shaped behavioral growth.* New York: Academic Press.

Bowerman, M. (1983a). Hidden meanings: The role of covert conceptual structures in children's development of language. In D. R. Rogers & J. A. Sloboda (Eds.), *The acquisition of symbolic skills.* New York: Plenum Press.

Bowerman, M. (1983b). How do children avoid constructing an overly general grammar in the absence of feedback about what is not a sentence? *Papers and Reports on Child Language Development* (Stanford University Department of Linguistics), *22.*

Bowerman, M. (1985a). Beyond communicative adequacy: From piecemeal knowledge to an integrated system in the child's acquisition of language. In K. Nelson (Ed.), *Children's language* (Vol. 5). Hillsdale, NJ: Lawrence Erlbaum Associates.

Bowerman, M. (1985b). What shapes children's grammars? In D. I. Slobin (Ed.), *The crosslinguistic study of language acquisition.* Hillsdale, NJ: Lawrence Erlbaum Associates.

Braine, M. D. S. (1963). The ontogeny of English phrase structure: The first phase. *Language, 39,* 1–14.

Braine, M. D. S. (1971). On two types of models of the internalization of grammars. In D. I. Slobin (Ed.), *The ontogenesis of grammar.* New York: Academic Press.

Bresnan, J. W. (1978). Toward a realistic model of transformational grammar. In M. Halle, J. W. Bresnan, & G. A. Miller (Eds.), *Linguistic theory and psychological reality.* Cambridge, MA: MIT Press.

Brown, R. (1958a). How shall a thing be called? *Psychological Review, 65,* 14–21.

Brown, R. (1958b). *Words and things.* New York: The Free Press.

Brown, R. (1965). *Social psychology.* New York: The Free Press.

Brown, R. (1970). *Psycholinguistics: Selected papers by Roger Brown.* New York: The Free Press.

Brown, R. (1973). *A first language: The early stages.* Cambridge, MA: Harvard University Press.

Brown, R. (1976). In memorial tribute to Eric Lenneberg. *Cognition, 4,* 125–153.

Brown, R., & Bellugi, U. (1964). Three processes in the child's acquisition of syntax. In E. H. Lenneberg (Ed.), *New directions in the study of language.* Cambridge, MA: MIT Press.

Brown, R., Cazden, C., & Bellugi, U. (1968). The child's grammar from I to III. In J. P. Hill (Ed.), *Minnesota Symposium on Child Development* (Vol. 2). Minneapolis: University of Minnesota Press.

Brown, R., & Fraser, C. (1963). The acquisition of syntax. In C. N. Cofer & B. S. Musgrave (Eds.), *Verbal behavior and learning.* New York: McGraw–Hill.

Brown, R., Fraser, C., & Bellugi, U. (1964). Explorations in grammar evaluation. In U. Bellugi &

R. Brown (Ed.), The acquisition of language. *Monographs of the Society for Research in Child Development, 29* (1), Serial No. 92.

Brown, R., & Hanlon, C. (1970). Derivational complexity and order of acquisition in child speech. In J. R. Hayes (Ed.), *Cognition and the development of language.* New York: Wiley.

Brown, R., & Lenneberg, E. H. (1954). A study in language and cognition. *Journal of Abnormal and Social Psychology, 49,* 454–462.

Bruner, J. S., Goodnow, J. J., & Austin, G. A. (1956). *A study of thinking.* New York: Wiley.

Carroll, J. B. (1958). Some psychological effects of language structure. In P. Hoch & J. Zubin (Eds.), *Psychopathology of communication.* New York: Grune & Stratton.

Carroll, J. B., & Casagrande, J. B. (1958). The function of language classifications in behavior. In E. C. Maccoby, T. M. Newcomb, & E. L. Hartley, *Readings in social psychology.* New York: Holt, Rinehart, & Winston.

Chomsky, N. (1962). A transformational approach to syntax. In A. A. Hill (Ed.), *Proceedings of the Third Texas Conference on Problems of Linguistic Analysis in English.* Austin: University of Texas Press.

Chomsky, N. (1965). *Aspects of the theory of syntax.* Cambridge, MA: MIT Press.

Chomsky, N. (1968). *Language and mind.* New York: Harcourt, Brace, & World.

Clark, E. V. (1973). What's in a word? On the child's acquisition of semantics in his first language. In T. M. Moore (Ed.), *Cognitive development and the acquisition of language.* New York: Academic Press.

Clark, E. V. (1977). Universal categories: On the semantics of classifiers and children's early word meanings. In A. Juilland (Ed.), *Linguistic studies presented to Joseph Greenberg.* Saratoga, CA: Anma Libri.

Comrie, B. (1978). *Aspect.* Cambridge, England: Cambridge University Press.

Comrie, B. (1981). *Language universals and linguistic typology.* Chicago: University of Chicago Press.

Denny, J. P. (1978). Locating the universals in lexical systems for spatial deixis. In D. Farkas, W. M. Jacobsen, & K. W. Todrys (Eds.), *Papers from the parasession on the lexicon, Chicago Linguistic Society.* Chicago: University of Chicago Press.

Fillmore, C. (1971). Some problems for case grammar. In R. J. O'Brien (Ed.), *Georgetown University Round Table on Languages and Linguistics, No. 24.* Washington DC: Georgetown University Press.

Fillmore, C. (1977). The case for case reopened. In P. Cole & J. Saddock (Eds.), *Syntax and semantics. Vol. 8: Grammatical relations.* New York: Academic Press.

Fishman, J. A. (1960). A systematization of the Whorfian hypothesis. *Behavioral Science, 5,* 323–339.

Fodor, J., & Garrett, M. (1966). Some reflections on competence and performance. In J. Lyons & R. J. Wales (Eds.), *Psycholinguistics papers.* Edinburgh: Edinburgh University Press.

Hall, B. (1965). *Subject and object in modern English.* Doctoral dissertation, MIT (published under B. Partee [same title], New York: Garland, 1979).

Heider, E. R. (1972). Universals in color naming and memory. *Journal of Experimental Psychology, 93,* 10–20.

Hoijer, H. (1954). The Sapir–Whorf hypothesis. In H. Hoijer (Ed.), *Language in culture.* Chicago: University of Chicago Press.

Jackendoff, R. S. (1972). *Semantic interpretation in generative grammar.* Cambridge, MA: MIT Press.

Jackendoff, R. S. (1975). Morphological and semantic regularities in the lexicon. *Language, 51,* 639–671.

Lakoff, G. (1970). *Irregularity in syntax.* New York: Holt, Rinehart, & Winston.

Lenneberg, E. H. (1962). The relationship of language to the formation of concepts. *Synthese, 14,* 103–109.

Maclay, H. (1958). An experimental study of language and nonlinguistic behavior. *Southwest Journal of Anthropology, 14,* 220–229.

Macnamara, J. (1972). Cognitive basis of language learning in infants. *Psychological Review, 79,* 1–13.

McCawley, J. D. (1971). Prelexical syntax. In R. J. O'Brien (Ed.), *Georgetown University Round Table on Languages and Linguistics, No. 24.* Washington, DC: Georgetown University Press.

Miller, W., & Ervin, S. (1964). The development of grammar in child language. In U. Bellugi & R. Brown (Eds.), The acquisition of language. *Monographs of the Society for Research in Child Development, 29* (1), Serial No. 92.

Murane, E. (1974). *Daga Grammar.* Norman, University of Oklahoma, Summer Institute of Linguistics.

Nelson, K. (1974). Concept, word, and sentence: Interrelations in acquisition and development. *Psychological Review, 81,* 267–285.

Newport, E. L. (1982). Task specificity in language learning? Evidence from speech perception and American Sign Language. In E. Wanner & L. R. Gleitman (Eds.), *Language acquisition: The state of the art.* Cambridge, England: Cambridge University Press.

Otsu, Y. (1981). *Universal grammar and syntactic development.* Unpublished doctoral dissertation, MIT.

Rosch, E., & Mervis, C. B. (1976). Children's sorting: A reinterpretation based on the nature of abstraction in natural categories. *Developmental Psychology.*

Schlesinger, I. M. (1971). The production of utterances and language acquisition. In D. I. Slobin (Ed.), *The ontogenesis of grammar.* New York: Academic Press.

Schlesinger, I. M. (1977). The role of cognitive development and linguistic input in language development. *Journal of Child Language, 4,* 153–169.

Slobin, D. I. (1973). Cognitive prerequisites for the development of grammar. In C. A. Ferguson & D. I. Slobin (Eds.), *Studies of child language development.* New York: Holt, Rinehart, & Winston.

Slobin, D. I. (1979). *The role of language in language acquisition.* Unpublished manuscript, University of California at Berkeley.

Slobin, D. I. (1985). Crosslinguistic evidence for the language-making capacity. In D. I. Slobin (Ed.), *The crosslinguistic study of language acquisition.* Hillsdale, NJ: Lawrence Erlbaum Associates.

Talmy, L. (1976). Semantic causative types. In M. Shibatani (Ed.), *Syntax and semantics, Vol. 6: The grammar of causative constructions.* New York: Academic Press.

Talmy, L. (1983). How language structures space. In H. L. Pick, Jr. & L. P. Accredolo (Eds.), *Spatial orientation: Theory, research, and application.* New York: Plenum Press.

Tavakolian, S. L. (Ed.) (1981). *Language acquisition and linguistic theory.* Cambridge, MA: MIT Press.

Welmers, W. E. (1973). *African language structures.* Berkeley: University of California Press.

Wexler, K., & Culicover, P. W. (1980). *Formal principles of language acquisition.* Cambridge, MA: MIT Press.

Whorf, B. L. (1956). *Language, thought, and reality* (J. B. Carroll, Ed.). Cambridge, MA: MIT Press; and New York: Wiley.

3 Faith, Doubt, and Meaning

Jill de Villiers
Smith College

I entered Harvard in the Fall of 1970, knowing everything. After 4 years of graduate school and 10 years of teaching, I now know much less. In this chapter, I intend to trace the loss of my knowledge, acknowledging some of the individuals who, through their searching questions, passed on their doubts to me.

As an undergraduate I had discovered in Behaviorism an organizing framework for psychology, but I had decided that the unknown element in the prediction and control of human behavior was language—words seemed to have unaccountable control over our actions. Although my goal was to understand how self-control developed in children through language, I found myself employed by Roger Brown as a research assistant. As for Chomsky, I knew his work only as maligning my true hero, B. F. Skinner, and I was continually advising my fellow students to read *Verbal Behavior* rather than just the more famous review (Chomsky, 1959). Michael Maratsos, then several years ahead of me in wisdom but not in tact, suggested that I had better learn some linguistics if I was to continue working with Roger Brown, and that probably delayed my education by another year. This was the early 1970s, and the proliferating tree diagrams, increasingly remote from observable speech, were distasteful to one of my persuasion. Roger Brown was working on the final drafts of "A First Language," a project clearly beyond my grasp at the time, the pages populated with individuals whose contribution to the field I had yet to recognize. I needed to start at the beginning: What do we mean by "word"? How can we tell if two creatures share the same meanings? By what means can we test syntactic distinctions? Discussion of these and similar questions must have flourished in the early 1960s when the project began, but new graduate students have to get to the roots all over again. By a stroke of luck, David Premack was visiting at Harvard that year, and those questions were very much alive and well in his work. Although my enthusiasm might well have been tempered had I actually met the chimpanzee, for a while that Sarah was much closer to my interests than Roger Brown's subject of the same name.

In part, the differences in taste and approach went along party lines: Peter de Villiers and I had entered the Experimental Psychology Program at Harvard, unlike the famous graduate students who just preceded us: Courtney Cazden, Melissa Bowerman, Ursula Bellugi, and Michael Maratsos. Fiercely empiricist, we believed experiments provided answers, and when we took Roger Brown's seminar, he encouraged us to perform experiments with a vengeance that first year. To our delight, we not only had data to play with, but the data showed that everyone else had been wrong—Piaget was wrong, Bruner was wrong, Gleitman was wrong, Chomsky—oh, Chomsky couldn't have been more wrong. In attempting to write up these empirical efforts, I found myself in need of the vocabulary and concepts that I had earlier shunned. In teaching linguistics still, I overdo the justification for every new term, for every hidden structure. My students yawn, offering no resistance. I feel as one who has given up a religion, to find herself in the company of those who have never questioned their atheism.

Three questions from Roger Brown's work at that time continue to hold my attention and govern the direction of my research and reflections about the field, though in each case my conception of the issue has undergone a shift. The three are as follows: (1) What is the relationship between syntactic theory and the course of language acquisition? (2) When can the competence–performance distinction be invoked for child language? (3) Are syntax, semantics, and pragmatics separable components in child language?

A fourth major question is notably absent, namely, the question of how much of language is innate and how much is learned. In my experience, Roger Brown assumed a comfortable agnosticism on that question, unwilling to be swayed by the minor triumphs of either side of the argument. My own reading of the literature has been less comfortable, and a full account is still in progress, too much of a tangent for the present volume.

FAITH: SYNTACTIC THEORY AND LANGUAGE ACQUISITION

The relationship between linguistics and language acquisition has not been consistently defined. There are several levels on which the relationship could hold, and theorists have a striking tendency to shift levels when things do not work out as hoped. Here are some of the ways that the relationship has been described:

1. Syntactic theory defines the endpoint of acquisition, the adult grammar. One cannot study development without having a detailed specification of the goal, and this is what syntactic theory supplies (Chomsky, 1965).

2. Once that goal has been identified, one can study the problem of arriving at it in a finite time as a problem in learnability. If it is impossible to search the hypothesis space containing all possible grammars, how must the infant be equipped to reduce the hypotheses among which it must search? (Chomsky, 1965; Pinker, 1979; Wexler & Culicover, 1980).

3. Syntactic theory defines constraints on possible grammars, and children's language will be sensitive to those constraints (Otsu, 1981; Roeper, 1982a,b).

4. By studying children's earliest grammars, we can gain information about the hypotheses that they are predisposed to select about language (Hyams, 1983; McNeill, 1970).

5. The steps in a linguistic derivation coincide with the steps a child takes in learning the structure (Bellugi, 1967; McNeill, 1970; Valian, Winzemer, & Erreich, 1981).

6. Syntactic theory defines certain constructions as exceptional, or more complex to characterize, than others. Children will have difficulty learning, or make characteristic errors with, those constructions. (Chomsky, 1969; Lust, 1977).

The hypotheses are ordered, roughly, by the degree to which they have something to say about the process of language acquisition. The first statement says only that development will be towards that goal but is noncommittal about the path, or intermediate grammars. The second adopts a similarly neutral stance about whether any light will be shed on the nature of language learning by studying the way young children talk. That is probably why it was more congenial to Steve Pinker than it was to us in the earlier period—we had our own data to which we were accountable, whereas at the time he was freer to theorize! The third position does predict something of the form of child grammars, namely that they will be obedient to the same structural constraints that are universally true of adult grammars. The fourth hypothesis also permits the possibility that data from child language can be used to study the child's choice between rival hypotheses, or to examine the initial setting on the parameters (Chomsky, 1981; Roeper, 1982a) that make up natural languages. Although the fifth position has an old-fashioned ring to it, harkening back to the derivational complexity theories of the 1960s in both adult and child psycholinguistics, it has some modern counterparts in which the particulars of derivations, movement rules, and so forth find parallels in the errors that young children make on their way to the adult form. The sixth position, perhaps the most neutral in terms of syntactic theory, essentially argues that children, like linguists, will have difficulty dealing with some forms in arriving at a coherent and maximally simple grammar.

In *A First Language,* very few of these accounts find mention because the early stages of language acquisition seemed to have more to do with the child's cognitive growth than with syntactic theory. It was in turning to the later stages of language development that we all had difficulty in finding a syntactic theory to put our faith in. This was particularly true for us as psychologists trying to make sense of the data on child language itself. The strongest predictions, position 5, seemed to fail everywhere they were tried (e.g., Maratsos, 1978). There were quite a few cases of success of hypotheses like 6, in which syntactic theory predicted a difference in difficulty, and children showed such a difference (e.g., Brown, 1973; Brown & Hanlon, 1970; 14 morphemes), though the examples were hardly united by an all-embracing theory. Indeed, the particular linguistic theories that had given rise to the predictions had shifted. We were happy to find consistencies among children, even (or sometimes especially) if those consistencies contradicted the predictions of prevailing linguistic theory (e.g., de Villiers, Tager-Flusberg, & Hakuta, 1977). In the mid-1970s we were linguistically lost at sea, able only to take potshots at passing theories. Around that time, I attended a large lecture by Chomsky at MIT on "psychological reality and linguistic theory." I needed to hear it, but I had to leave after 5 minutes with an acute attack of food poisoning. I was gratified later to learn that my cohorts, Steve Pinker and Kenji Hakuta, had believed my hasty exit to be theoretically rather than intestinally motivated. As I lay looking at the endless swimming corridors of MIT's Building 5, is it any wonder that pragmatics seemed to offer a brighter alternative?

It should be evident that linguistic theories are most attractive to me if they predict what young children should say, or do. However, there is a credibility gap between those researchers who have their training and investment in linguistics, and those who originate in psychology. We approach the same data with different perspectives and at times are unwilling to accept the extra assumptions necessary to make an argument work, if they are grounded in a different field from our own. Take one example from the work on "universal constraints." The constraint known as c-command (Reinhart, 1976) specifies how NPs are to be coindexed in a phrase structure. The node A on a tree structure is said to c-command a second node, B, if the first branching node that dominates A also

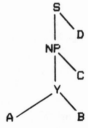

FIG. 3.1.   The node A c-commands only node B.

dominates B, and neither A nor B dominates the other (see Fig. 3.1). The constraint says that a lexical NP must c-command an empty node if it is coindexed with it; hence it is important in anaphora, constructions with "traces" of moved elements, and so on. In particular, the constraint specifies that for a sentence like (1) John told Bill to mow the lawn, it is possible to coindex "Bill" with the null subject of "mow." However, in the sentence (2) John phoned Bill after mowing the lawn, "Bill" does not c-command the null subject of mow, but "John" does. If children's language is obedient to the same universal constraint, then children should not misinterpret the second sentence to mean that Bill mowed the lawn. Goodluck (1981) reports the results of her experiments on this issue with 4-to-6-year-old children and concludes that they do show c-command at this stage. So did no children violate the preceding prediction? Well, only 45% of the 4-year-olds did. How then did Goodluck reach the conclusion that those children obey c-command?; by arguing that they didn't yet have the appropriate phrase structure for sentences like (2), in that they misattached the participial phrase to the VP rather than the S-node, proven by "assuming that the c-command condition constrains children's grammars" (p. 154). A parallel argument was made by Otsu (1981, described in Roeper, 1982b) in an experiment on whether children obey another putative universal constraint, in this case, A-over-A. Once again, young children misunderstood certain complex sentences in a way that could be construed as a violation of the universal constraint. Nevertheless, Otsu argued that the failure was in the children's phrase structure grammars for the constructions in question; they were actually NOT violating the constraint if one allowed them to have the wrong tree structures. In that case, the children's language was said to have flatter tree structures than the corresponding adult forms; in Goodluck's case, the tree structures of the children's language were held to be more embedded than the adult form. Both theorists may be right; perhaps my religious preparation has been sorely inadequate. In pointing out my doubts, I do not wish to malign the enterprise as a whole. In fact, the growing literature on how linguistic theory can explain children's comprehension of complex sentences is a fascinating and healthy development (e.g., Otsu, 1981; Phinney, 1981; Tavakolian, 1981). However, instead of preaching among the converted, the movement could use some input from those still outside the faith.

DOUBT: COMPETENCE AND PERFORMANCE

In principle, the distinction between underlying knowledge and performance on a task seems valuable for both adults and children. Unfortunately, when the knowledge is in the process of being acquired, the distinction is harder to draw. The only evidence from which to reach conclusions about underlying knowledge comes from performance, and the hard lesson is that performance in young children is inconsistent. In a paper early in our career, we pointed out the discrepancies among estimates of when an English-speaking child might be said to understand that word order carries basic sentential meaning (de Villiers & de Villiers, 1974). Should it be when the child first uses order consistently in speaking his or her own sentences? Maybe, but then there is the problem that the categories subject and object are not well motivated linguistically in young children's speech. Perhaps they only know how to order particular words, or particular meanings? So should one instead take the point at which the contrast in meaning is first understood? For example, take an act-out comprehension task and request the child to act out "Bear kiss cat" versus "cat kiss bear." I remember the first such experiment we did, in which we caught buses and subways carrying a large bookbag full of squeaky toys to visit toddlers throughout suburban Boston. We had made several dozen mimeoed scoresheets with the scoring categories already devised for each sentence: Did the child make the bear kiss the cat, or the cat kiss the bear? The first 18-month-old we tested very deliberately kissed first the bear and then the cat, making a mockery of our preconceptions. In general, children were a little older and more developed before they could reliably use word order as a cue in comprehension, and, of course, even then they would misinterpret a passive sentence. A linguist would be likely to use judgment, of correct and deviant sentences, as the acid test of competence. But then children would not be called competent for a couple of years after they succeed on comprehension tests. If one is to expect not only judgment but corrections of word order, then the diploma must be delayed even longer. The hope that the diverse performances would somehow magically converge on the same estimate seemed doomed in that case. We were unwilling to use the first estimate as the right one, with the delays simply due to extra-linguistic skills, such as memory span or attention. Why? Because the earliest estimate may also be spurious, may mean that the task provides additional clues, or that the child's biases coincide with the right response. There are several instances of that phenomenon in the literature (e.g., Clark, 1977). A review of the pitfalls and advantages of various performance measures can be found in de Villiers and de Villiers (1982).

Nevertheless, it may be possible to use the technique of "converging methodology" not so much to arrive at an estimate of when a child knows something, but to check that linguistic complexity makes the same predictions regardless of the performance chosen. In the series of studies on coordination (Tager-Flusberg, de Villiers, & Hakuta, 1982), we found several performances consistent with the notion that young children's grammar contains rules for the conjunction of like constituents and rejects sentences that would involve the conjunction of nonconstituents (e.g., SV + SVO, SVO + SO). Unfortunately, the picture of children's grammar for relative clause constructions remains more complex, with performance measures less often converging on the same ordering of difficulty (see de Villiers & de Villiers, 1986 for a review). All of which leads to the problem: Under what circumstances can the competence–performance distinction be invoked to account for discrepancies between theory and observation, or between observation of one performance and another? At a recent conference (University of Massachussetts, 1984) a linguist, perplexed by the mismatch between syntactic theory and some data collected from young children by Larry Solan, made the serious suggestion that such data should best be shelved. Several of the audience were sympathetic to that suggestion, because for them data from child language could be used in support (oh, how nice, that'll brighten up Introductory Linguistics next semester) but not to refute linguistic theory. But Roger Brown, and the rest of us, need to account for child language, and our shelves are already full.

The solution generally adopted in the field at present may be something we shall have to live with for some time, so let me try to articulate it. Here is how to test a portion of syntactic theory against child language data:

1. Select a performance, carefully controlling as many extraneous variables as you can imagine in advance—behavioral biases, real-world knowledge, preferences, memory span limitations, etc.

2. Design the stimuli (or the eliciting conditions) to be as semantically varied as the real linguistic distinction and as functionally appropriate as the real linguistic distinction (see Hamburger & Crain, 1982).

3. Test the child in optimal circumstances.

4. Use your intuition during the test to ferret out unanticipated strategies, boredom, silliness, etc.

5. If all these conditions have been satisfied, score the data as conservatively as possible and use the most conservative statistical procedures.

6. Carry out individual analyses and group statistics (e.g., Bridges, 1980).

7. If the data are consistent with the predictions, ask whether there is an alternative linguistic or nonlinguistic account that would also predict the result.

If the data are not consistent with the theory but consistent across and within subjects, develop an alternative account (this is definitely more impressive if done in advance) and go back to 1., choosing another task to replicate the result.

8. Ask what ramifications an alternative account would have, not just for that distinction but for the rest of the child's developing grammar.

9. If the alternative account is highly unlikely as an account of adult grammar, demonstrate at what stage and how the child makes the transition (see Gleitman & Wanner, 1982).

10. If all else fails, either shelve the data or drop back a level (p. 53) in your beliefs about the connections between linguistic theory and language acquisition.

There are those who would argue that certain principles within linguistic theory are so powerful, and support for them is so strong from adult data, that child language data could never be held up in refutation. Such theorists have two possible aces up their sleeves: Deny that child language can ever be revealing about adult linguistics or argue that the child's competence is being masked by unspecified performance factors. Whereas the first argument is one that we might unwillingly accept, to go our separate ways, the second is one that should inspire psychologists interested in the representation and use of knowledge to construct an appropriately specific model.

MEANING: SYNTAX, SEMANTICS, PRAGMATICS

In Chomsky's (1965) standard transformational account of adult language, the grammar was modular in form: phonology, syntax, and semantics were separable components each having their own specifiable rules. Obviously, information was exchanged between the components, but they were largely described independently. As for pragmatics, linguistics being concerned as it is with idealization, with abstraction away from the particulars of performance, why should linguists be interested in the effects of contexts of use? Such concerns were left to the psychologist, or educator, or sociologist. Yet philosophers of language (Austin, 1962; Searle, 1969) had made some headway on a systematic account of language as communication, and it was inevitable that students of child language would feel that pull as syntactic theory seemed less and less applicable. For the study of child language is inescapably tied to contexts of use, and that fact had become increasingly evident within the discipline over the 20 years or so of its modern revival. In a chapter written in 1978, we tried to capture the roots and the parallels of the movement towards first semantic accounts and then pragmatic accounts of child language. For both, the initial dissatisfaction was that the prevailing account of child language failed to capture some aspect of the child's knowledge; in other words, it underrepresented what children knew (for semantics, see Bloom, 1970; for pragmatics, see Antinucci & Parisi, 1973). A second advantage of broadening the account was the possibility of cross-linguistic similarities: Ignoring the particulars of syntactic form, young children everywhere seemed to have the same things to talk about (e.g., Brown, 1973). Third, an increased interest in the very beginning of language in infancy had reached something of an impasse over the issue of the "holophrase" (McNeill, 1970). Did babies really intend whole sentences by their first words? Introducing semantic and pragmatic accounts of early language provided a continuity to the account of development (Bruner, 1975; Dore, 1975). Nevertheless, the advantages attached to the broader approach brought with them some costs that were recognized more slowly. Syntax is about forms, and forms we can describe, and justify by distributional or other analyses. Semantics and pragmatics are about meanings and intentions and are only supposed to be indirectly reflected in forms. How do we know that the baby means what we would mean? How do we read intentions in behavior? Roger Brown educated his students about these concerns, and several of us have worried about them ever since (e.g., Bowerman, 1973, 1976; de Villiers, 1980; de Villiers & de Villiers, 1978a; Maratsos, 1979). Rather ironically, the solution most widely practiced and accepted to the problem of divining the child's intentions, or the psychologically real semantic/pragmatic categories, is to use linguistic forms as a guide. If the child does not treat members of a purported semantic class, such as "agent," equivalently in his language, then it is not linguistically real for him. The status such a category might have for him psychologically is beside the point. As several have pointed out, semantics is about aspects of meaning that have linguistic consequences (e.g., Schlesinger, 1974), rather than about conceptual distinctions in general.

Apart from the theoretical and methodological issues for early child language, what have been the other ramifications of paying attention to semantics and pragmatics? One very general concern is the description of children's syntactic rules, and the extent to which such descriptions can be made without reference to semantic classes. Once that idea had gained currency for Stage I speech (Brown, 1973), it was quite natural to ask whether older children's rules were formulated with respect to syntactic categories (subject, verb, object, auxiliary, etc.) or semantic or lexical categories. Several accounts exist in which at an earlier point in development, children's rules are held to be less abstract in their formulation than the corresponding rules in adult grammar (verb inflections, see Bloom, Lifter, & Hafitz, 1980; the passive voice, see Maratsos, Kuczaj, Fox, & Chalkley, 1979; auxiliary placement, see Kuczaj & Brannick, 1979). However, the rules at issue may escape formulation at a semantic level also and may instead reflect the child's propensity to acquire syntactic information with reference to particular lexical items (Bresnan, 1978; Pinker, 1982). Alternatively, Valian (1986) has pointed out that child language data may look less abstract because the content of young children's communications is more limited. There may be little evidence for a distinction between "verb" and "action," or between "subject" and "agent," because children do not yet know the abstract vocabulary on which such distinctions depend. What is the difference between the accounts? On the account by which children's rules are first formulated with respect to semantic classes, a reorganization is entailed before the child's grammar becomes like an adult's (on most accounts). If the description is abstract from the start, the child's existing categories are simply filled out by new vocabulary without changing their nature. In practice, data to distinguish decisively between these alternatives are in short supply, though the issue lies at the heart of many recent controversies in language acquisition. At the very least, we can no longer make the methodological assumption that the vocabulary and semantic variety of our language tests is irrelevant for the testing of syntactic knowledge (see caution 2. aforementioned).

Theories of syntax acquisition remain less influenced by pragmatic accounts, with some notable exceptions (Bates & MacWhinney, 1982; Bloom, 1970;

Bloom & Lahey, 1978). Bates (1976) argued that syntax and semantics derive ultimately from pragmatics in ontogenesis. If that is so, one would at least expect preschool children to show some pragmatic limitations on syntactic rules. We thought we found a good example in 1979, after studying the early negative sentences produced by our son, Nicholas. In our just-completed review of the literature on negation in 1978(b), we had concluded that evidence for an early stage in which children formulate the rule for negation as "NEG + S" was very limited (Bellugi, 1967). We shared Bloom's (1970) conclusion that most examples of sentences with an external "no" were probably instead anaphoric negations, with the "no" referring to an earlier proposition. In apparent defiance of our conclusion, our son then proceeded to produce dozens of examples of non-anaphoric "NO + S" sentences. However, a careful examination of the contexts of use revealed that he had two rules for negatives: one for denials, which were well formed, and one for rejections, which had initial "no." Hence, his syntactic formulation made reference to the pragmatic intent of the utterance, and so, in retrospect, did Adam's and Eve's (de Villiers & de Villiers, 1979). Furthermore, the source for their syntactic hypotheses was evident in the styles of negation used by their respective parents. Far from being a "universal first stage in negation" (McNeill, 1970), the rule is apparently adopted by some children who hear certain kinds of input about negation. On making this discovery, which we thought was rather neat, I met Roger Brown in the corridor and gave him a potted version of what we had found. His reaction floored me, and yet I am sympathetic to the tradition from which it stems. He said, "Well, well, so it wasn't so interesting after all."

Finally, there is the claim that because syntactic forms must have evolved in the service of some communicative function children will do better, learn faster, under circumstances in which the form is functionally appropriate. Such an argument has been used to account for children's learning of passives (I. Brown, 1976; de Villiers, 1980), for relative clauses (Hamburger & Crain, 1982; Tager-Flusberg, 1982), and for coordinations (Tager-Flusberg et al., 1982). The generalization seems valid, but I am haunted by one of Roger Brown's favorite counterexamples, the tag question. Tag questions in English serve no more elaborate function than their counterpart in French; yet in English the rules fill a chapter (Akmajian & Heny, 1976), whereas in French one has the single form "n'est-ce pas?" English children learn them anyway, at an absurdly tender age, for no apparent reason except that they can. Disappointed that Nicholas had never produced a tag by age 3½, I decided to "teach" him the form one rainy afternoon. It took about six examples for him to "learn" it, and he persisted in playing the game long after I got bored. He heard from me only full-formed examples like "It's raining, isn't it?" and "You're a boy, aren't you," but when we sat down to dinner and I said "Mm, good soup," he added "isn't it?" I called for his father, showing the politeness typical of intimate family, "Come get your soup!" and Nicholas said "Won't you?" Such anecdotes reveal to me how much children know about syntax and remind me how little we know about the motivation for learning it (Brown & Hanlon, 1970).

CONCLUSION

Faith (in theories of syntax) still eludes me; of doubts (about how we assess children's knowledge) I have plenty; I continue to search for meaning (in child language).

REFERENCES

Akmájian, A., & Heny, F. (1976). *Introduction to the principles of transformational syntax.* Cambridge, MA: MIT Press.

Antinucci, F., & Parisi, D. (1973). Early language acquisition: A model and some data. In C. Ferguson & D. Slobin (Eds.), *Studies of child language development.* New York: Holt, Rinehart, & Winston.

Austin, J. L. (1962). *How to do things with words.* Oxford: Oxford University Press.

Bates, E. (1976). *Language and context.* New York: Academic Press.

Bates, E., & MacWhinney, B. (1982). Functionalist approaches to grammar. In E. Wanner & L. Gleitman (Eds.), *Language acquisition: The state of the art.* New York: Cambridge University Press.

Bellugi, U. (1967). *The acquisition of negation.* Unpublished doctoral dissertation, Harvard University.

Bloom, L. M. (1970). *Language development: Form and function in emerging grammars.* Cambridge, MA: MIT Press.

Bloom, L. M., & Lahey, M. (1978). *Language development and language disorders.* New York: Wiley.

Bloom, L. M., Lifter, K., & Hafitz, J. (1980). Semantics of verbs and the development of verb inflections in child language. *Language, 56,* 386–412.

Bowerman, M. F. (1973). Structural relationships in children's utterances: Syntactic or semantic? In T. E. Moore (Ed.), *Cognitive development and the acquisition of language.* New York: Academic Press.

Bowerman, M. F. (1976). Semantic factors in the acquisition of rules for word use and sentence construction. In D. Morehead & A. Morehead (Eds.), *Directions in normal and deficient child language.* Baltimore: University Park Press.

Bresnan, J. (1978). A realistic transformational grammar. In M. Halle, J. Bresnan, & G. Miller (Eds.), *Linguistic theory and psychological reality.* Cambridge, MA: MIT Press.

Bridges, A. (1980). SVO comprehension strategies reconsidered: The evidence of individual patterns of response. *Journal of Child Language, 7,* 89–104.

Brown, I. (1976). Role of referent concreteness in the acquisition of passive sentence comprehension through abstract modeling. *Journal of Experimental Child Psychology, 22,* 185–199.

Brown, R. W. (1973). *A first language—the early stages.* Harvard University Press.

Brown, R. W., & Hanlon, C. (1970). Derivational complexity and order of acquisition in child speech. In J. R. Hayes (Ed.), *Cognition and the development of language.* New York: Wiley.

Bruner, J. S. (1975). The ontogenesis of speech acts. *Journal of Child Language, 2,* 1–19.

Chomsky, C. (1969). *The acquisition of syntax in children from 5 to 10.* Cambridge, MA: MIT Press.

Chomsky, N. (1959). Review of Skinner, *Verbal Behavior. Language, 35,* 26–58.

Chomsky, N. (1965). *Aspects of the theory of syntax.* Cambridge, MA: MIT Press.

Chomsky, N. (1981). *Lectures on government and binding.* Dordrecht, Holland: Foris.

Clark, E. (1977). Strategies and the mapping problem in first language acquisition. In J. Mac-Namara (Ed.), *Language learning and thought.* New York: Academic Press.

de Villiers, J. G. (1980). The process of rule learning in child speech: A new look. In K. E. Nelson (Ed.), *Children's language* (Vol. 2). Gardner Press.

de Villiers, J. G. (1982). Functional categories in early language. In D. Bricker (Ed.), *Intervention with at-risk and handicapped infants.* Baltimore: University Park Press.

de Villiers, J. G., & de Villiers, P. A. (1974). Competence and performance in child language: Are children really competent to judge? *Journal of Child Language, 1,* 11–22.

de Villiers, J. G., & de Villiers, P. A. (1978a). Semantics and syntax in the first two years: The output of form and function and the form and function of the output. In F. Minifie & L. L. Lloyd (Eds.), *Communicative and cognitive abilities: Early behavioral assessment.* Baltimore: University Park Press.

de Villiers, J. G., & de Villiers, P. A. (1978b). *Language acquisition.* Cambridge, MA: Harvard University Press.

de Villiers, J. G., & de Villiers, P. A. (1982). Language development. In R. Vasta (Ed.), *Strategies and techniques of child study.* New York: Academic Press.

de Villiers, J. G., & de Villiers, P. A. (1986). The acquisition of English. In D. Slobin (Ed.), *The cross-linguistic study of language acquisition.* Hillsdale, NJ: Lawrence Erlbaum Associates.

de Villiers, J. G., Tager-Flusberg, H. B., & Hakuta, K. (1977). Deciding among theories of the development of coordination in child speech. *Papers and Reports on Child Language Development* (Stanford University), *13,* 118–125.

de Villiers, P. A., & de Villiers, J. G. (1979). Form and function in the development of sentence negation. *Papers and Reports on Child Language Development,* (Standford University), *17,* 56–64.

Dore, J. (1975). Holophrases, speech acts and language universals. *Journal of Child Language, 2,* 21–40.

Gleitman, L., & Wanner, E. (1982). Language acquisition: The state of the state of the art. In E. Wanner & L. Gleitman (Eds.), *Language acquisition: The state of the art.* New York: Cambridge University Press.

Goodluck, H. (1981). Children's grammar of complement-subject interpretation. In S. L. Tavakolian (Ed.), *Language acquisition and linguistic theory.* Cambridge, MA: MIT Press.

Greenfield, P. M., & Dent, C. H. (1982). Pragmatic factors in children's phrasal coordination. *Journal of Child Language, 9,* 425–444.

Hamburger, H., & Crain, S. (1982). Relative acquisition. In S. Kuczaj (Ed.), *Language development: Syntax and semantics.* New York: Lawrence Erlbaum Associates.

Hyams, N. (1983). *The acquisition of parameterized grammars.* Unpublished doctoral dissertation, CUNY.

Kuczaj, S. A. II., & Brannick, N. (1979). Children's use of the Wh question modal auxiliary placement rule. *Journal of Experimental Child Psychology, 28,* 43–67.

Lust, B. (1977). Conjunction reduction in child language. *Journal of Child Language, 4,* 257–287.

Maratsos, M. P. (1978). New models in linguistics and language acquisition. In M. Halle, J. Bresnan, & G. Miller (Eds.), *Linguistic theory and psychological reality.* Cambridge, MA: MIT Press.

Maratsos, M. P. (1979). How to get from words to sentences. In D. Aaronson & R. Rieber (Eds.), *Perspectives in psycholinguistics.* Hillsdale, NJ: Lawrence Erlbaum Associates.

Maratsos, M. P., Kuczaj, S. A., II, Fox, D. M., & Chalkley, M. A. (1979). Some empirical studies in the acquisition of transformational relations. In W. Collins (Ed.), *Children's language and communication; The Minnesota symposia on child psychology (Vol. 12).* Hillsdale, NJ: Lawrence Erlbaum Associates.

McNeill, D. (1970). *The acquisition of language.* New York: Harper & Row.

Otsu, Y. (1981). *Universal grammar and syntactic development in children.* Unpublished doctoral dissertation, MIT.

Phinney, M. (1981). *Syntactic constraints and the acquisition of embedded sentential complements.* Unpublished doctoral dissertation, University of Massachussetts, Amherst.

Pinker, S. (1979). Formal models of language learning. *Cognition, 7,* 217–283.

Pinker, S. (1982). A theory of the acquisition of lexical-interpretive grammars. In J. Bresnan (Ed.), *The mental representation of grammatical relations.* Cambridge, MA: MIT Press.

Reinhart, T. (1976). *The syntactic domain of anaphora.* Unpublished doctoral dissertation, MIT.

Roeper, T. (1982a). The role of universals in the acquisition of gerunds. In E. Wanner & L. Gleitman (Eds.), *Language acquisition: The state of the art.* New York: Cambridge University Press.

Roeper, T. (1982b). On the importance of syntax and the logical use of evidence in language acquisition. In S. A. Kuczaj (Ed.), *Language development. Volume 1: Syntax and semantics.* Hillsdale, NJ: Lawrence Erlbaum Associates.

Schlesinger, I. M. (1974). Relational concepts underlying language. In R. L. Schiefelbusch & L. L. Lloyd (Eds.), *Language perspectives-acquisition, retardation and intervention.* Baltimore: University Park Press.

Searle, J. (1969). *Speech acts.* Cambridge: Cambridge University Press.

Tager-Flusberg, H. (1982). The development of relative clauses in child speech. *Papers and Reports on Child and Language Development, 21,* 104–111.

Tager-Flusberg, H., de Villiers, J. G., & Hakuta, K. (1982). The development of sentence coordination. In S. Kuczaj (Ed.), *Language development, Vol. 1: Syntax and semantics.* Hillsdale, NJ: Lawrence Erlbaum Associates.

Tavakolian, S. L. (1981). *Language acquisition and linguistic theory.* Cambridge, MA: MIT Press.

Valian, V. (1986). Syntactic categories in the speech of young children. *Developmental Psychology, 22,* 562–579.

Valian, V., Winzemer, J., & Erreich, A. (1981). A "Little Linguist" model of syntax learning. In S. L. Tavakolian (Ed.), *Language acquisition and linguistic theory.* Cambridge, MA: MIT Press.

Wexler, K., & Culicover, P. W. (1980). *Formal principles of language acquisition.* Cambridge, MA: MIT Press.

4 The Emergence of Set-Relational Quantifiers in Early Childhood

Camille Hanlon
Connecticut College

Among my most treasured "flashbulb" memories is one associated with my first encounter with Roger Brown. It was a hot summer day in Minneapolis, a little over 20 years ago. The setting was a classroom at the Institute for Child Development and Roger was giving a lecture on language development for a group of mostly graduate students. Early in the session the excited shouts and squeals from the children's playground outside threatened to drown out the lecture altogether. Finally, in a dramatic showdown, Roger confronted the problem head-on. Half turning toward the open window, he scowled fiercely and uttered a *sotto voce* "shut-up." Then, grinning impishly at the class, he resumed his lecture in a stentorian voice. It seems symbolic to me that Roger's instinctive choice in this episode was to adapt his approach to fit the children's voices. At the same time, he displayed the classic ambivalence of the serious scientist toward inconvenient input.

The occasion for this class was a 1964 Summer Institute on Cognitive Development, sponsored by the Social Science Research Council and attended by graduate and postgraduate students from all over the country. I had just finished my graduate work at Stanford and was on my way to a teaching job at the University of Iowa. The intellectual exchange at this institute was informal but intense, and I have many other happy, though less symbolic, memories of this time.

Later on, in 1967 and 1968, I spent a year as a postdoctoral research fellow working with Roger's group at Harvard.[1] I saw this time as an unparalleled

---

[1]That work was principally with Roger himself and resulted in the Brown and Hanlon (1970) chapter. Those collaborating with him at the time on other areas of research included Ursula Bellugi,

opportunity to learn how to make science out of the puzzling phenomena of children's language acquisition, a study then in its infancy. My undergraduate and graduate interests in biology and epistemology had long sat uneasily with my schooling in the experimental tradition of psychology, and I found it especially challenging to work with linguistic theory on naturalistic data in the early, exploratory phase of this research.

On the present occasion I am delighted to play a role in honoring Roger Brown's important contributions to psychology. However, my connection with his work has been relatively minor, so it must be clear that Roger's pedagogical responsibilities for any blunders in this research are negligible. Readers should see this study primarily as an illustration of the widespread influence that Roger's writings have had on a generation of psychologists. Many of these, like myself, began reading his work as undergraduates in the fifties, when it was, together with Piaget's early books, the hottest underground psychology around. It was what you read for pleasure when your verbal learning class was cancelled. Through this reading my longstanding interest in children's learning of words and their meanings was transformed into the serious possibility of a research career. It meant that someone out there was actually applying the methods of modern psychology to the most interesting developmental questions, and doing it with style. As you can see from the discussion that follows, my debt to Roger's work is clear in the matter of problem choice and research strategy. As for style, some things are inimitable.

SET-RELATIONAL QUANTIFIERS

In this account I describe some studies of children's use of English set-relational quantifiers. These are words like *all, some, no, none, each, every, any, another, other, both, either,* and *neither* as they are used to quantify nominals. The goal of this research has been to take a particular lexical semantic domain, set-relational quantification, and explore its acquisition by children learning American English as a first language. In this work I have had the competent and cheerful help of several undergraduate research assistants: Terry Carpino, Kate Tweedie Erslev, Hal Flagg, Miriam Kalamian, Nadie Lowe, and Beverly Sweny.[2]

For the developmental endpoint of the acquisition process, we needed a

Melissa Bowerman, Courtney Cazden, Howard Gardner, Robert Krauss, Eleanor Rosch, and Klaus Scherer.

[2]Warm thanks to Roger Brown for the generous sharing of his data, and the children, teachers, and administrators of the Connecticut College Children's School and Pine Point School of Stonington, Connecticut for their friendly assistance. The research was supported by U. S. National Institute of Mental Health Small Grant MH-27638.

working model of the organization of adult lexical semantic knowledge in this domain. It turns out that no work has been published on the full range of lexical contrasts in set-relational reference, either for English alone or across languages. So, as the first step in our work, we did our own descriptive analysis of these lexical contrasts as they are used in adult English. Our working model includes contrasts of four general kinds. The first dimension of contrast consists of three levels of generality in reference. The generic level refers to members of the general class named, as in the sentence "*Some* of these trees are evergreen." The specific level refers to a specific set, as in "*Some* trees are evergreen." And at the nonspecific level, the potential reference set is left unspecified, as in "We may plant *some* evergreen trees." Not every quantifier may be used at every level; lexical gaps appear within the general pattern, and morphological and syntactic variations occur across levels. Table 4.1 lists the forms to be found at each level of generality of reference, with examples of each type of use. The meaning of each quantifier word can also be described in terms of a characteristic transformation of a supposed reference set into an actual one. For example, the meaning of the word *some* can be described as "Take an indefinite portion of the potential set referred to by the quantified nominal." Transformational descriptions for the full set of terms we studied can be found in Table 4.2. One subset of these terms, *both, either,* and *neither,* can be used only when the potential or suppositional set size is two. Another subset of terms, *each* and *every,* is restricted to the case of distributive predication. That is, the relevant predicates outside the quantified nominal must be interpreted as describing the members of the set individually, taken one at a time. It is the difference in meaning between the sentence, "*All* of the children in the class sang a song," and "*Each* of the children in the class sang a song."

These terms are among the most frequent words used in everyday conversation, and they occur no matter what the topic of conversation. This means that young children are likely to hear all of these words in the speech around them from an early age. Nonetheless, the terms seem to enter children's spoken vocabulary at widely varying times throughout the period of early childhood. Thus, we thought that the order in which children acquire these terms in appropriate reference might be predicted on the basis of independently established principles of cognitive development in relation to our a priori semantic analysis. The first of these principles is that cognitive development proceeds from simple to more complex forms of knowledge. Using our model of adult quantifier knowledge, we were able to predict a partial ordering of our terms based on cumulative semantic complexity. We predicted that the forms for which the reference set is identical to the suppositional set would emerge earlier than corresponding forms requiring an extra transformation of some type to derive the reference set from the suppositional set. For example, at the specific reference set level, *all* is predicted to be mastered before *some, none, any, another,* and *other.* And *both* should be acquired earlier than *either* and *neither.* In a parallel

TABLE 4.1
English Set-Relational Quantifiers as They Occur
at Three Levels of Generality in Reference

Quantifier	Example of Use
Generic Level	
all	Mommy, why do all animals have tails?
no	No wolves talk like that.
some	Some animals wake up in the morning time.
any	They don't want any cranky little girls that are tired.
each	Each person is a world apart.
every	What every little girls plays with--wet, soggy tea bags.
Specific Level	
all	Drinking all my grape juice.
none	I don't want to share none of my books.
some	You can't have some of my candles.
any	Do you know any of the kids?
(the) *other*	You marry de other cat, Miss Cat.
another	Have another of these.
each	Dey not go...each one is gonna have a flat tire.
every	Every people...every man's gonna drive de car.
both	Hold it all the way like that, with both fingers.
either	Some are on either side, see?
neither	Neither pen is mine.
Nonspecific Level	
no	No children are in it.
some	I going make some groceries.
any	I don't have any toys in here.
another	Hey, let's do another page.

way, forms with an extra restriction on their usage (and thus presumably an additional component of meaning) should come later than their matched unrestricted forms. Therefore, *each* and *every* should emerge later than their unrestricted equivalent *all* because these forms are used appropriately only when distributive predication is intended. The predictions I have described so far are listed in the left-most column of Table 4.3, Parts C and D.

Predictions about the developmental order of levels of generality in reference are based on different contrasts across levels. We predicted that the specific suppositional set forms would be mastered later than the nonspecific set forms.

TABLE 4.2
Definitions for English Set-Relational Quantifiers Expressed
as Transformations of Suppositional into Actual Reference Sets

Quantifier	Definition
all	The actual reference set is identical to the potential reference set.
no, none	The actual reference set is null or empty.
some	The actual reference set is an indefinite portion of the potential reference set.
any	The actual reference set is an indefinite portion of the potential reference set, with an equal chance or selection across all members or portions of the potential reference set.
another	The actual reference set is an indefinite new member of the potential reference set.
(the) *other*	The actual reference set is that portion of the potential reference set remaining after a specific subset has been subtracted.
each	The actual reference set is identical to the potential reference set. Also, the relevant predicates outside the nominal must be applied distributively; that is, the predicates must be interpreted as describing the members individually, or taken one at a time.
every	The actual reference set is identical to the potential reference set. Also the predicates outside the nominal are applied to set members distributively, with stress on the exhaustiveness of the process.
both	The actual reference set is identical to the potential reference set. Further, the potential reference set is a previously specified set of two.
either	The actual reference set is one member of the potential reference set, with an equal chance of selection across set members. Further, the potential reference set is a previously specified set of two.
neither	The actual reference set is null or empty. Further, the potential reference set is a previously specified set of two.

This prediction is based on that aspect of the model that calls for the cognizance of a specific suppositional set as a reference set for the specific forms but not for the nonspecific forms (e.g., I want *some* hats vs. I want *some* of these hats). The prediction that the generic forms are acquired later than the specific forms is not strictly grounded in semantic complexity. It is based instead on the well-documented trend in language development during early childhood toward more remote (Cromer, 1968) and general (Brown, 1957) reference. That is, the generic forms, unlike the specific forms, require a cognizance of the entire set or class characterized by the predicates of the quantified nominal, and this level of conceptualization seems at least one step more advanced than that required for the specific forms (e.g., *Some* of these trees are evergreen vs. *Some* trees are

TABLE 4.3
Semantic Complexity Predictions Tested for Order of Emergence
in Production of Set-Relational Quantifiers (Brown Longitudinal Data)

A. Nonspecific forms before specific forms, e.g., *some hats* (with nonspecific reference) before *some of the hats:*

	Adam +	Adam ?	Adam -	Sarah +	Sarah ?	Sarah -	Eve +	Eve ?	Eve -
some	X			X			X		
another	X			X			X		
none	X			X			X		
any	X			X			X		

B. Specific forms before generic forms e.g., *some of the hats* before *some hats* (with generic reference):

	Adam +	Adam ?	Adam -	Sarah +	Sarah ?	Sarah -	Eve +	Eve ?	Eve -
all	X			X			X		
some	X			X			X		
none	X				X			X	
any		X			X			X	
each	X				X			X	
every	X				X			X	

C. Specific *all* and *both* before other equivalent specific forms:

	Adam +	Adam ?	Adam -	Sarah +	Sarah ?	Sarah -	Eve +	Eve ?	Eve -
all < some			X	X			X		
all < none	X			X			X		
all < any	X			X			X		
all < another	X			X			X		
all < other	X			X			X		
both < either	X			X			X		
both < neither	X			X			X		

D. Specific *all* before specific *each* and *every:*

	Adam +	Adam ?	Adam -	Sarah +	Sarah ?	Sarah -	Eve +	Eve ?	Eve -
all < each	X			X			X		
all < every	X			X			X		

Note: The symbol (+) means predictions confirmed; (-) means they were disconfirmed; and (?) indicates they were untestable.

evergreen). It is also true that grammatical complexity is not equivalent across the three levels of generality in reference, being greatest at the specific level. So the prediction of specific after nonspecific forms can also be made on the basis of grammatical complexity, but for specific and generic forms our conceptual model and grammatical complexity lead to opposite predictions.

Let me summarize the major predictions, then, as they are outlined in Table 4.3. Nonspecific forms will come before their specific equivalents, and specific forms will come before their generic equivalents. Forms with identical suppositional and reference sets will be acquired earlier than transformational forms that are their semantic equivalent in other ways. The distributive forms *each* and *every* will be mastered later than their unrestricted equivalent form *all*.

We choose to look first at the primary forms of semantic knowledge—comprehension and production. We obtained and analyzed the data in ways that are appropriate to a first study of the domain, that is, a combination of specific hypothesis testing and frankly exploratory work. Practical considerations led us to use comprehension and production data from different children, so I present the results separately. There was no compelling rationale for predicting a different order of acquisition in comprehension and production, and whenever possible, hypotheses about the developmental sequence are tested with both indices of semantic knowledge. Our hypotheses about the order of acquisition in speech production were tested with the data from Roger Brown's longitudinal study of Adam, Eve, and Sarah (1973). These three children's mother–child conversations were sampled systematically throughout most of early childhood. Counts of the quantifier forms were made from the verbatim transcripts. The criterion for the point of emergence for each quantifier was the time at which the form had occurred in three different phrase contexts across samples. Table 4.3 shows the results of the hypothesis-testing with these children's productive frequencies. All of the doubtful cases were occasioned by the children's not having reached the criterion of productivity for either form in the comparison by the time the study ended. In general, then, we were heartened by the modest success of our predictions for these data.

We tested *comprehension* of the terms at the specific level with a sample of 75 children ranging in age from 3 to 7 years, and 10 adults. There were two parallel tests of elicited comprehension, one called "Letters" and one called "Cookies." The children were tested individually in two sessions. One task was administered at each session. The two sessions usually occurred within the same week for a given child. In both tasks the children were given a series of trials with a small set of identical objects. On each trial the child was given an instruction using the quantifier word for that trial. The sentence context was consistent across quantifier words for each task. So for the task called *Cookies,* a child on a particular trial might be given a set of two plastic cookies and instructed to "Give him (The Cookie Monster) *either* of the cookies." For *Letters,* instead of feeding the Cookie Monster, the children learned to be letter carriers by putting letters in a series of postboxes. The sentence contexts for each task are given in Table 4.4. Each quantifier was tested on three different trials per task, each quantifier appearing once in random order within each third of the trial series. The object placement responses were highly consistent for adults and conformed to our expectations based on the model. These responses were used as the standard in scoring the children's responses as correct. They are listed in Table 4.5. The 3-year-olds received a short form of the test, using the quantifiers *all, some, none, any,* and *both.*

Overall, we had complete data on both tasks for 70 of the 75 children, 61 with the long form of the test. The percentages of these older children passing each quantifier comprehension test with 2 out of 3 trials correct on each task are

TABLE 4.4
Sentence Contexts for the Quantifiers Used in the Comprehension Tasks

Task	Instruction
Letters	

"Put $\left\{\begin{array}{l} all \\ none \\ some \\ any \\ both \\ either \\ neither \\ each \end{array}\right\}$ of the letters in a box."

"This is a special letter. Now

put $\left\{\begin{array}{l} (the)\ other \\ another \\ all \end{array}\right\}$ of the   letters in a box."

Cookies

"Give him $\left\{\begin{array}{l} all \\ none \\ some \\ any \\ both \\ either \\ neither \\ each \end{array}\right\}$ of the cookies

"This is a special cookie. Now

give him $\left\{\begin{array}{l} (the)\ other \\ another \\ all\ of\ the \end{array}\right\}$ of the cookies."

Note: For all trials except those with *both*, *either*, and *neither*, sets of four identical objects are presented. Fpr trials with these quantifiers, two objects are used. For the trials with *the other*, *another*, and an additional control set with *all*, the "special" object instructions are used. On these trials the "special" object is one of the four identical objects presented. It is placed slightly apart from the others, and so designated.

shown in Table 4.6. We tested our hypotheses about the order of comprehension by using an index of individual deviation from the predicted order (Loevinger's H_{ii}, 1947). The results for the full sample of children with complete data (70) are shown in Table 4.7. There were no subjects in the sample whose data were contrary to the predictions. So our model permitted us to predict the order of acquisition of these terms in children's conversational production and the extent to which they were understood by children in another cross-sectional study.

What about frequency as a predictor? Although our terms were among the highest frequency words in spoken English, we were curious to see whether or not the variation in frequency of usage among the terms would also correlate with their order of emergence. We counted the total frequencies of the terms at the specific level in the parental speech of Adam, Eve, and Sarah, the three children in Brown's longitudinal study. Then we turned to the comprehension data.

TABLE 4.5
Object Placement Responses Scored as Correct for Each Quantifier
on the Elicited Comprehension Tests

Quantifier	Correct Response
all	Four objects
none	No objects
some	Two or three objects
any	One to four objects
other	Three residual objects, omitting object designated as "special"
another	Any one object from residual set of three
all (sp)	Four objects, including "special" object
each	Four objects placed distributively (Letters: each in a separate box Cookies: each fed or placed in bowl one by one)
both	Two objects
either	One object
neither	No object

Note: For *both, either,* and *neither,* the tester provided a set of two objects, for the remaining quantifiers, a set of four objects.

Because no subject deviated from the predicted order of acquisition on the comprehension tasks, we have taken the group percent passing each quantifier (2 out of 3 trials) as a reliable index of the general sequence of acquisition in the cross-sectional comprehension data. These are the respective percentages for each quantifier for each task that are shown in Table 4.6. Notice that they include only the data for the 4- through 7-year-olds, so that every child contributes a score on every measure. The correlation between the acquisition orders based on these results for the two tasks taken separately is high enough to justify averaging the task results into a single average order (Spearman rho = + .92, $p < .001$). This order for the quantifiers is really an average order of comprehension diffi-

TABLE 4.6
Percentage of 4-Through 7-Year-Old Subjects Passing Each
Quantifier Comprehension Test in Each Task
(Pass - 2 out of 3 trials correct, N = 61)

Quantifier	Task	
	Letters	Cookies
all	100	100
none	87	89
some	89	92
any	93	92
other	80	93
another	49	51
both	100	100
either	46	46
neither	31	43
each	31	3

TABLE 4.7
Test of Semantic Complexity Predictions for Order of Emergence
in Comprehension of Specific Set-Relational Quantifiers

	Interitem Homogeneity	
Prediction	Letters	Cookies
all < some	1.00	1.00
all < none	1.00	1.00
all < any	1.00	1.00
all < another	1.00	1.00
all < other	1.00	1.00
both < either	1.00	1.00
both < neither	1.00	1.00
all < each	1.00	1.00

Note: Cross-sectional data: seventy 3- to 7-year-olds and 10 adults (N = 80). Tables values are Loevinger's H_{ii}, where 1.00 represents the absence of any subjects in the sample passing the harder and failing the easier item.

culty from which we are inferring an order of acquisition, a thing that is routinely done in cross-sectional study. The parent frequencies did not vary with the developmental level of their children and were highly correlated with each other (Table 4.8). The parental frequency measures are strongly correlated with the comprehension test orders of difficulty (Table 4.9). The best summary measure is the correlation between the mean parental frequency order and the mean comprehension order. The Spearman coefficient for this relationship is .77, which is significant at the .005 level of probability.

Very few indices of parent behavior show such a strong relationship to children's development, short of the obvious effects neglect or abuse. Is it a matter, then, of threshold effects? These could operate on the exposure side, so that the children might just learn a word when they hear it the first time, with the most frequent words on the average heard earliest. We cannot rule out this possibility absolutely on the basis of the present data, but it seems unlikely given the general

TABLE 4.8
Intercorrelations Among the Rank Orders of Specific Quantifier
Frequencies for the Parents of Adam, Eve, and Sarah

Parental Frequency	Parental Frequency			
	Adam	Eve	Sarah	Mean
Adam		.81	.80	.98
Eve			.77	.81
Sarah				.88
Mean				

Note: The entries in this table are Spearman rank order correlation coefficients. N = 10 (the number of specific quantifiers). The range of probability values for the significance of these coefficients is .001 to .005.

TABLE 4.9
Correlations Between Parental Frequency Measures and
Comprehension Measures for English Set-Relational
Quantifiers Used in Specific Reference

Parental Frequency	Comprehension Task		
	Letters	Cookies	Mean
Adam	.61	.73	.65
Eve	.47 (NS)	.72	.56
Sarah	.82	.95	.88
Mean	.74	.83	.77

Note: The entries in this table are Spearman rank order
coefficients, with N = 10. All the correlations in the table
are significant at the .05 level of probability or better, with
the exception of the entry marked NS. The probability for this
cooficient is .08. The others range from .001 to .045. The
data for parental frequencies are longitudinal (3 subjects);
those for comprehension are cross-sectional (61 subjects).

frequency range for the set of quantifiers and their cross-topic and cross-listener generality. A more plausible possibility is that children learn the words gradually up to a point, so that differences in the level of comprehension of a set of related terms during acquisition can be accounted for in terms of relative frequency of exposure. But how does this account fit with the larger pattern of developmental findings on the acquisition of linguistic forms? The trend has been to stress children's tendency to assimilate their experience with a language to their current level of understanding of that language. The expectation has been that, for frequent forms at least, differences in linguistic or cognitive complexity rather than frequency of usage would determine their order of mastery. And the findings have been consistent in the main with this view. Studies with invented language materials (e.g., Mervis, 1976) have even shown that, when the variables of frequency and cognitive structure are experimentally separated, it is cognitive structure that determines ease of acquisition.

However, the language learning model on which these studies are based gives no clue as to why we should find a strong negative relationship between frequency of usage and structural complexity in the case of natural language itself. I would like to suggest that an important design feature of natural language involves assigning structurally more complex forms to rarer occasions of usage. The best documented case of this possibility is the inverse relationship between word length and frequency reported by George Kingsley Zipf (1935, 1949), who argued that it was a function of the principle of least effort. However, a case more closely related to our present finding is that of linguistic marking. Marking is a pervasive phenomenon at every level of the structure of natural languages (Greenberg, 1966). In lexical marking, sets of related contrasts are assigned distinctive forms in a way that matches the usual case with the structurally simpler form (Lyons, 1977). Both formally and semantically marked words tend to be more restricted in their distribution than are the corresponding unmarked terms. Because semantic marking can be described as the presence of an extra component of meaning in the semantic structure for a word, one can expect an inverse relationship between frequency and complexity. In fact, the relationship between semantic marking and distributional restriction can be seen clearly in our set of quantifiers. For example, *both* is marked with respect to *all* in that it bears the component of meaning "two," and it is correspondingly restricted in its appropriate reference to such sets.

Suppose, then, that there *is* a tendency for natural languages to provide the simplest forms for those things that are likely to be said more frequently. What are the implications of this possibility for the study of first language acquisition processes? It would certainly make the correlation of frequency and structural complexity the usual case in natural language studies (cf. Brown & Hanlon, 1970). However, the overall pattern of evidence would lead one to hypothesize that frequency might not be a direct determinant of the relative order of acquisition of linguistic forms in relation to the learning process for each child. Instead, it might serve as one of the variables that shape the language of the community as a whole. What might be the advantage in communication of the design feature that we suggest? In addition to minimizing the effort required in everyday language use for the fluent, it would place the novice in an early position of strength as an active conversant. This is just the role that would best explain the remarkable progress that the young child normally shows in acquiring a first language.

INTELLECTUAL PUZZLES AND A LEGACY

It seems appropriate to conclude this discussion by acknowledging my specific intellectual debt to Roger Brown in this work. Not only have I borrowed his data, but I am still puzzling over the relative influence of frequency and structural complexity, a theme that is a familiar subject to Brown readers. (Although I trust the present solution adds a new inductive twist to the argument.)

A not-so-obvious irony in all of this is the emergence of the ubiquitous transformational rule as a structural description in my work. Since I was not overly fond of such formulations when working on derivational complexity (Brown & Hanlon, 1970), I had thought to be entirely done with transformations when I returned to my own lexical semantic problems. You can imagine my dismay when they proved so useful in the case of set-relational quantifiers. (See the two other Hanlon papers listed in the References (1981, 1982) for a fuller discussion of the linguistic work.) This time, of course, the transformational rules are much more modest creatures, simple generalizations unencumbered with the intellectual baggage of a generative grammar. I believe that this difference reflects the relative state of the art in syntax and lexical semantics at the moment.

But why do transformational rules, despite all their problems, keep turning up in linguistic descriptions? Is there something about these formulations that capture an important aspect of human cognition? Could they be a linguistic expression of a generalized tendency to cognize entities and events in terms of certain ideal types and variations therefrom? This, the Gestalt notion of cognitive reference points (Wertheimer, 1938), has already proven useful in the study of other domains (Rosch, 1975). Or, in the case of set-relational quantifiers at least, could transformational generalizations be a simple result of the occasional usefulness of commenting succinctly upon the properties of sets and subsets of entities and events? These are just two of many possibilities.

It must be clear from the preceding discussion that I still have the liveliest curiosity about the relationships between formal descriptions of language structure and the processes of first-language acquisition. This curiosity stems from the belief that the answers to such questions can give us important insights into the nature of the human mind. For me, and for countless other scientists, this quest is Roger Brown's greatest intellectual legacy so far.

ACKNOWLEDGMENTS

Portions of this chapter have been reproduced from the published proceedings of the First and Second International Congresses for the Study of Child Language by permission of the following individuals and organizations: the volume editors, Philip Dale, David Ingram, Carolyn Johnson, Carol Thew; the publishers, University Park Press and University Park of America; and the International Association for the Study of Child Language.

REFERENCES

Brown, R. (1957). Linguistic determinism and the part of speech. *Journal of Abnormal and Social Psychology, 55,* 1–5.

Brown, R. (1973). *A first language: The early stages.* Cambridge, MA: Harvard University Press.

Brown, R., & Hanlon, C. (1970). Derivational complexity and order of emergence in child speech. In J. Hayes (Ed.), *Cognition and the development of language.* New York: Wiley.

Cromer, R. (1968). The development of temporal reference during the acquisition of language. Doctoral dissertation, Harvard University.

Greenberg, J. (1966). *Language universals.* The Hague: Mouton.

Hanlon, C. (1981). The emergence of set-relational quantifiers in early childhood. In P. Dale & D. Ingram (Eds.), *Child language: An international perspective.* Baltimore: University Park Press.

Hanlon, C. (1982). Frequency of usage, semantic complexity, and the acquisition of set-relational quantifiers in early childhood. In C. Johnson & C. Thew (Eds.), *Proceedings of the Second International Congress for the Study of Child Language.* Washington, DC: University Press of America.

Loevinger, J. (1947). A systematic approach to the construction and evaluation of tests of ability. *Psychological Monographs, 61*, No. 4 (Whole No. 285).

Lyons, J. (1977). *Semantics* (Vol. 1). Cambridge, England: Cambridge University Press.

Mervis, C. (1976). Acquisition of object categories. Doctoral dissertation, Cornell University.

Rosch, E. (1975). Cognitive reference points. *Cognitive Psychology, 7*, 532–547.

Wertheimer, M. (1938). Numbers and numerical concepts in primitive peoples. In W. D. Ellis (Ed.), *A source book of Gestalt psychology.* (pp. 265–273) New York: Harcourt Brace.

Zipf, G. (1935). *The psychobiology of language.* Cambridge. MA: Houghton–Mifflin.

Zipf, G. (1949). *Human behavior and the principle of least effort.* Cambridge, MA: Addison-Wesley.

5 The Parser's Architecture

Eric Wanner
Russell Sage Foundation

Whether wayward academic offspring should be cursed or celebrated, Roger Brown has certainly had his share. I am hardly alone among Roger's former students in straying from matters exclusively psycholinguistic or undertaking research on something other than language acquisition. Donald Olivier, Jeffrey Travers, and Volnay Steffler are three particularly brilliant examples of this divergence who jump easily to mind, and there were many others that I knew less well. Of course we, the wayward, surely figure that our existence is undeniable evidence of Roger Brown's intellectual breadth and good taste. But it is also true that Roger Brown is an extremely tolerant man.

I recall a moment when I must have taxed Roger's tolerance heavily but, as I remember it, he paid the tax without flinching. It was sometime during the dreary Cambridge winter of 1966. Roger and I were in the lunch line at William James Hall, pushing our trays together towards the gastronomic oblivion of those marginally sublethal salami sandwiches, when I announced to Roger with all the ignorant certainty criterial to third-year graduate students that I had decided not to do my thesis on child language acquisition. Too hard a problem, I argued. Because the child's grammatical knowledge and performance systems are both changing together during development, it may not be possible to figure out the nature of the acquisition system from developmental data. Better to study the steady state of the adult, pick apart performance and competence contributions to adult behavior, and then return to the puzzle of acquisition once we know more about just what is acquired.

Roger will be forgiven if he doesn't remember a word of this, particularly as I do not entirely recall his reply except that it was benign and did not deter me from my wayward path. Perhaps Roger would have made the counterarguments that returned me instantly to the fold if only the lunch line had been longer that day. Perhaps, the salami sandwiches intervened.

Certainly, history has shown that something in my graduate student logic must have been amiss. The study of child language has become a thriving industry whereas the study of adult performance is kept alive by a few obsessional types, myself only intermittently included. Worse still, the "easy" problem I picked instead of language acquisition remains unsolved to this day. That problem is the "parsing" problem: Simply put, how does the listener assign a syntactic analysis to the sentences of his language in the course of comprehension? In the mid-1960s, this problem seemed just about the right size. Enough linguistics had been done, or so it seemed, to specify a reasonably accurate picture of the language user's syntactic knowledge. The problem was to show how that knowledge is put to use during parsing. Admittedly, the linguist's picture of syntactic knowledge was a bit abstract and the framework of transformational grammar made for awkward incorporation in a mechanical parsing system. But that just left a few interesting subproblems for psycholinguists to solve: principally, to specify the grammar in a usable format and to determine the dimensions of the parsing system that puts the grammar to use. Once I learned about augmented transition network grammars from Thorne, Bratley, and Dewar, (1968) and Woods (1970), I thought we might have a solution to the format problem. But testing that conjecture unambiguously while at the same time testing hypotheses about the parameters of the parsing system has proved much more difficult that anyone imagined. In consequence, it is still too soon to cash that promise I made to Roger so long ago in the William James lunch line. Much as we might like to, those of us who study adult linguistic performance cannot yet tell those of you who study language acquisition just what it is that your little language learners are learning to do. Instead, we can only tell you something of our struggle in the last few years and suggest some implications for work in language acquisition. If this makes a modest birthday present, I will just have to count on Roger to give me many more opportunities to do better.

THE DIMENSIONS OF THE PARSING PROBLEM

There is general agreement about *what* the parsing system does. The question is *how* it does it. We know, on both psychological and linguistic grounds, that the language user must determine a proper bracketing of the input sentence into major phrases during comprehension. These phrases must be analyzed internally to the extent necessary to support semantic analysis of each phrasal referent; moreover, the grammatical role of each phrase (subject, object, etc.) must be identified in order to determine how the phrasal referent enters into the proposition(s) conveyed by the input sentence. Fodor, Bever, and Garrett (1974) distilled this dogma from the experimental and linguistic work of the 1960s, and although there may be some disagreement over the details of the phrase marker, its exact degree of precision, and the psychologically correct inventory of grammatical roles, these questions have usually been displaced by more heated controversies about the nature of the parsing mechanism. Because these controversies have clustered around a relatively small number of issues, it is now possible to factor the parsing problem into a few basic dimensions along which all parsing models can be compared. Four of these dimensions appear to me most important.

The first dimension of the comparison might be called the *horizontal* direction of parsing: Given the sentential string of input words arrayed linearly in time during speech, or in space across a printed page, in what direction does parsing proceed? Because the speech signal decays so rapidly in time and because the number of words that can be retained in human short-term memory is limited to something like Miller's (1956) magic number 7 ± 2, it is obvious enough that parsing must proceed generally from the beginning of a sentence toward the end (or from left to right across the page). This follows because there are many readily intelligible sentences longer that 7 ± 2 words. Hence, the psychological parsing system cannot be required to store the entire input string before attempting to fit phrase markers to it, as many early automated parsers did (e.g., Kay, 1965; Petrick, 1964). Instead, parsing must take place piecemeal and on the fly. But within the limits of human short-term memory, there are many variations on how this might be done. At one extreme, parsing might be attempted strictly word by word with all possible decisions about the analysis of each word made as soon as each word is identified. At the other extreme, parsing might be undertaken in chunks via a system that loads up short-term memory to the limit and parses all the words in that chunk before moving on to the next chunk. We still do not know just where the human parser lies between these two extremes.

The second dimension of comparison between parsers concerns the *vertical* direction of parsing. The parse three can be constructed from the bottom-up or from the top-down, or a bit of both. There is good reason to suspect that parsing is at least partially top-down because parsing does not grind to a halt whenever an unknown word or a nonsense word is introduced into a sentence, as in:

(1) The girl fripped the worthless frap.

We may not know what *frips* or *fraps* are when we hear this sentence, but we are in no doubt as to which word is functioning as a verb and which as a noun in sentence (1). Such knowledge would be beyond the ken of a strictly bottom-up parser that must make syntactic category decisions solely on the basis of dictionary information associated with the input word. Evidently, we can use our syntactic knowledge to impose a syntactic category on the input word that is appropriate to the partial phrase marker being developed. Only top-down parsing is capable of such impositions. However, strictly top-down parsing suffers from pathologies that language users do not, most notably the possibility of becoming infinitely hung up in the generation of left recursive structures derivable by repeated application of a rule like NP → NP S:

(2)

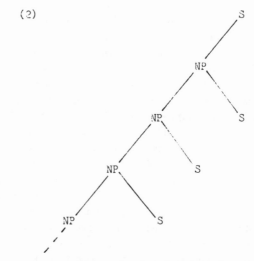

Such a parse tree might go on growing indefinitely before the first word of the sentence is ever analyzed. This left recursion pathology is the most dramatic symptom of a more general disease, which is top-down parsing's insensitivity to information available in the input string. Somehow, the psychological parsing system preserves the ability to formulate syntactic expectations and impose them on the input, but it does so without suffering the myopia of strictly top-down parsing. No one yet knows how.

The third dimension of disagreement about parsing concerns the distinction between parallel and serial processing. The grammar often permits more than one analysis of a sentence, and even more often, it permits more than one analysis of a local stretch of input that is only resolved somewhat later in the sentence. The question is whether these multiple analyses are all pursued simultaneously or whether instead the parser pursues them one at a time, wagering on one analysis and, if subsequently proven wrong, returning to try another. The evidence on this score is puzzling to say the least. On one hand, there are the infamous garden path effects that seem to suggest serial processing. A sentence like:

(3) The man who hunts ducks out before dawn.

is usually misanalyzed on first hearing with *ducks* as the object noun phrase of the verb *hunts*. Only when this analysis backfires later does the listener appear to retrace his steps and arrive at the alternate analysis in which *hunts* has no object and *ducks out* is the verb of the main clause. This is just the kind of error a serial processor would make.

But perhaps we should not trust our intuitions about garden path sentences. One reason for doubt is that experimental work has repeatedly shown that there are indeed local effects of multiple analysis paths. If an experimental subject is required both to comprehend a sentence and to perform an additional task (such as detecting a click), performance on the additional task is degraded in regions of the input sentence where miltiple analyses are possible (see Garrett, 1970, for a review of these experiments). This is just what we would expect of a parallel parsing system that pursues all possible analyses simultaneously whenever they arise and therefore requires more processing capacity in regions of syntactic ambiguity. To date, the conflict between the existence of garden path effects and the evidence for parallel processing has not been satisfactorily resolved.

The fourth dimension of the parsing problem concerns the division of parsing into stages. One of the great lessons of modern cognitive psychology is that sensory information processing (which appears to consciousness to be instantaneous) actually takes place in discrete stages that have a definite order and temporal extent. Does the same lesson apply also to parsing, which appears equally automatic and instantaneous? Is there, for instance, some kind of pre-processor in the parsing system that does some of the work before passing the partially processed input string on to another component of the system that finishes the job? The old click location results of Garret, Bever, and Fodor (1966) have sometimes been interpreted as intimations of such a preprocessor whose job it is to chunk stretches of the input into clause-sized units, thus displacing the location of the click to the clause boundary. But there is a problem with this idea, namely, how would such a preprocessor know where the clause boundaries are located without accomplishing a complete parse? Because click displacement to clause boundaries can occur *without* the kind of prosodic cues that a preprocessor might exploit, the explanation of the click phenomenon appears to require more work than any preprocessor could accomplish.

To summarize, this minireview of the dimensions of the parsing problem suggests only agnostic conclusions. There is very little a priori psychological evidence to justify locating the human parser at one position or another on any of these dimensions. To motivate such choices we have to look in more detail at particular parsing schemes and the predictions they support.

The ATN and the Sausage Machine (Again)

Several years back, I became involved in a discussion of the relative merits of two particular parsing models, the augmented transition network (or ATN) parser on which I had done previous work (see Wanner & Maratsos, 1978) and the Sausage Machine (or SM), a parsing scheme proposed by Frazier and Fodor (1978). This skirmish was carried out in the back pages of *Cognition,* which quite properly allotted only one salvo to each side (see Fodor & Frazier, 1980; and Wanner, 1980). Although both parsers now threaten to become antiques, I confess to the belief that there is still something to be learned from a comparison

TABLE 5.1
A Comparison of the ATN Parser and the Sausage Machine

	ATN	Sausage Machine
1. Horizontal direction of parsing:	1 word at a time	1 chunk at a time
2. Vertical direction of parsing:	top down	mixed: bottom-up and top-down
3. Serial vs. parallel processing:	serial	parallel
4. Number of stages	1-stage	2-stage

of the two proposals. Table 5.1 shows how these two parsing models stack up on the four dimensions sketched in the previous section.

As the table indicates, the ATN (or more accurately, the version of the ATN that we explored in the 1970s) embodied an extremely restrictive set of choices across the major parsing dimensions. In the ATN, parsing is accomplished one word at a time from left to right; the parse tree is processed from the top down. Grammatical alternatives are searched serially and the parser is limited to a single stage of operation. In retrospect, these choices may appear much too rigid to provide a psychologically plausible model of parsing. Thus, perhaps the most charitable way to view the early ATN is as a type of null hypothesis whose restrictive assumptions might be progressively relaxed as the data warrant. Certainly the general ATN framework set forth by Woods (1970), and generalized further by Kaplan (1973), permits such relaxations, but it is important to recognize that there are several benefits to a modeling strategy that begins with a highly restrictive set of initial assumptions.

The first is *computational tractability*. By limiting our ATN model to rigid, word by word, top-down, serial operation, we could relatively easily hand-simulate exactly how the parser would process any input sentence. This allowed us to formulate reasonably explicit predictions and detect when the parser went awry by providing a poor fit to human performance data.

The second advantage is *grammatical transparency*. The relationship between the traditional grammatical format and the grammatical format employed by the ATN is entirely straightforward. For every phrase structure rule in the grammar, there is a corresponding network in the ATN; and this network instructs the parser to test for the presence of the constituent on the left side of the rule by attempting to complete those transitions in the network that correspond to the sequence of constituents on the right side of the rule. So, for a simple grammar like:

(4)   S ――――――→ NP   VP

           VP ――――――→ V   NP

           NP ――――――→ DET   (ADJ)   N

We have an equally simple set of networds, such as:

(5)

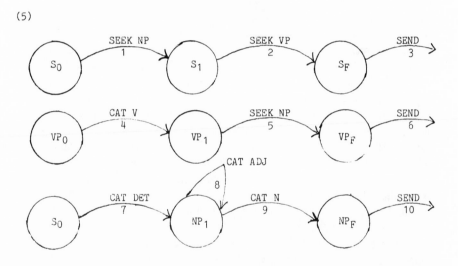

Beginning at state S_O and at the initial word in the input sentence, the parser attempts to reach state S_F by making a series of transitions, one at a time, through the network. Each transition is conditioned on the success of a test carried out against the input string. Transitions labeled CATegory require that the current input word be categorizable by the indicated syntactic category (DET, N, V, etc.). Transitions labeled SEEK require the discovery of an entire phrase of the indicated type (NP, VP, etc.) beginning at the current word in the sentence. To test for the presence of the phrase, the parser shifts to the subnetwork named by the SEEK and attempts to traverse that subnetwork. If successful, the parser then completes the original transition that instigated the SEEK. In this way, the ATN parser works its way from left to right through the sentence constructing the parse tree from the top down, as it goes, by adding a branch to the tree corresponding to every successful transition through the network.[1]

In sharp contrast to the ATN, the Sausage Machine embodies an extremely liberal set of choices across the four parsing dimensions listed in Table 5.1. Where the ATN operates one word at a time, the SM operates on chunks of the input sentence of about half a dozen words in length (roughly the limit of short-term memory). Where the ATN parses strictly top-down, the SM mixes bottom-up and top-down parsing. This mixture is accomplished in the SM by dividing parsing into two stages: a first stage, which assigns lexical and phrasal nodes from the bottom-up to words that appear within its limited "viewing window," and a second stage, which works from top-down to link together the phrasal packages supplied by the first stage. Frazier and Fodor (1978) also suggest that the SM operates in parallel: in their words, the goal of the SM is "to pursue all the (grammatically) legitimate hypotheses simultaneously" (p. 323).

It should be no surprise that Frazier and Fodor do not offer an account of the Sausage Machine that is either computationally coherent or grammatically transparent. The SM architecture is so complex that it is very difficult to say in what format the grammar would be employed. Among the unanswered questions are how much of the grammar is available to each stage of the parser? Do the two stages of the SM use the grammar in different forms? If so, what is the difference? Just as difficult are questions about the computational procedures employed by the SM. For instance, by what rules do the two stages interact with one another? How does the second stage recover from misanalyses in the partial parse provided by the first stage? And, how is parallel processing implemented?

These questions may seem excessively detailed and secondary, and to some extent they are. The primary question, after all, is whether the architectural liberalizations introduced by Frazier and Fodor provide a more psychologically accurate picture of parsing. Unfortuantely, however, the primary question cannot be answered without attention to such secondary questions. For, unless a parsing architecture is developed in some detail, it is simply impossible to know exactly how that architecture fits the data about human parsing. By way of demonstrating this bothersome but important point, I want to describe a rather surprising result that can be achieved by incorporating one of Frazier and Fodor's architectural innovations in the more computationally complete environment of the ATN. First, however, we need to introduce a small piece of data about the proclivities of the human parser.

---

[1]Readers unfamiliar with the ATN might verify this by applying network (5) to sentence (1) and verifying that (1) can be parsed via transitions 1(7,9,10)2(4,5(7,8,9,10)6)3. For a more complete description of the ATN showing how it builds trees, labels grammatical roles, and captures transformational generalizations, see Wanner and Maratsos (1978) and Kaplan (1973).

Parsing Strategies

In an extremely important and underrecognized paper published in 1973, the late John Kimball proposed that there are a number of tacit parsing strategies that the human listener uses unconsciously in order to resolve temporary syntactic ambiguities that arise during parsing. Two of these parsing strategies figured prominently in my discussions with Frazier and Fodor concerning the relative merits of the ATN and the SM. The first of these strategies Kimball labeled *Right Association* (or RA), and I will refer to it here as low right association. Kimball's name is somewhat misleading, because any left-to-right parser will always associate the new words it encounters with a right-hand branch of the one of constituents on the right-hand side of the developing parse tree. (This is so because branches in a parse tree never cross.) However, the developing parse tree often permits several such right attachments, and when it does Kimball's RA stipulates that the *lowest* attachment in the tree is the one to be tried first. For example, in a sentence such as,

(6) $(_{S_1}$ Tom said that $(_{S_2}$ Bill took the trash out yesterday.

listeners typically interpret the adverb *yesterday* as a temporal modifier of the complement clause $(_{S_2})$ *Bill took the trash out* rather than as modifier of the matrix clause $(_{S_1})$ *Tom said;* this, despite the fact that the grammar permits either interpretation. Similarly, the particle *up* is associated with the lowest VP in sentence (7) and the possessive *'s* is associated with the lowest NP in sentence (8):

(7) Tom $(_{VP_2}$ called the friend who $(_{VP_2}$ smashed his new car *up*.
(8) I met $(_{NP_1}$ the boy who was introduced to $(_{NP_2}$ Mary*'s* friend.

The second of Kimball's parsing strategies was more appropriately labeled *Minimal Attachment* (or MA). MA simply stipulates that the current word should be attached to the developing parse tree by introducing the fewest possible additional nodes. So, to take just one example, MA predicts that in an ambiguous sentence like

(9) We told the girl that everyone liked the story.

listeners will be biased toward the interpretation paraphrased by (10) rather than the equally possible interpretation paraphrased by (11);

(10) What we told the girl was that everyone liked the story
(11) What we told the girl that everyone liked was the story.

The existence of this interpretive bias has been confirmed by both comprehension tests and reaction time measurements (Wanner, Kaplan, & Shiner, 1975). We found that if you ask subjects who "everyone liked" in sentences such as (9), about 85% respond with the NP following the second verb (liked) and only

15% respond with the NP following the first verb (told). This distribution held quite consistently across our 16 test sentences despite broad variation in lexical content, suggesting that the observed bias was more a matter of a preferred syntactic structure than preferred semantic interpretation. Furthermore, the comprehension time required to arrive at the unpopular interpretation was significantly longer (by about 700 milliseconds) than the time required by the popular interpretation.

All this makes a good deal of sense if listeners are tacitly using a parsing strategy like Minimal Attachment. To see why, consider the developing parse tree for sentence (9) at the point at which *the girl* is to be parsed.

(12)

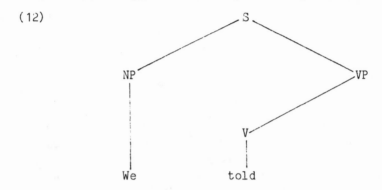

Here the grammar permits two options. Either the NP (*the girl*) can be directly attached to the VP node, as in:

(13)

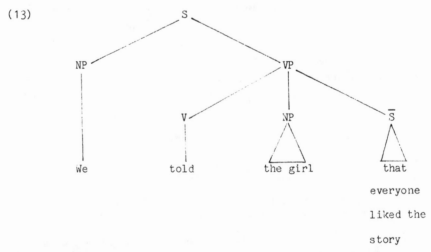

Or, the NP (*the girl*) can be indirectly attached to the VP as the head of a relative clause, as in:

(14)

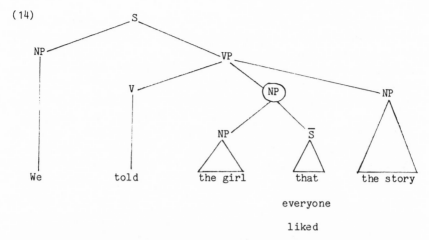

everyone

liked

But notice that this second attachment requires an additional NP node (circled) intervening between the VP and the NP node dominating *the girl*. For this reason, the Minimal Attachment strategy would cause the parser to attempt structure (13), instead of structure (14). Our comprehension data suggest that the human listener does much the same thing, at least 85% of the time; and in the 15% of the cases where Minimal Attachment is violated, comprehension takes longer, just as would be predicted if the less popular interpretation requires the construction of an extra node in the parse tree.

What is particularly interesting about the RA and MA strategies is that, taken together, they suggest that the human parser is predisposed to choose among multiple syntactic alternatives in favor of the minimally computable parse tree. Minimal attachment says, in effect, "introduce the fewest number of possible constituents when building the parse tree." Low right association says, in effect, "make sure that each new constituent which is introduced is as broad as possible in the sense that it dominates as much of the input string as possible." Together, MA and RA will result in the flattest, widest possible trees—trees with the fewest possible nonterminal nodes, each with the widest possible coverage over the input string. Such trees will necessarily exhibit the minimal node-to-terminal node ratio that, as Miller and Chomsky (1963) showed, will require the fewest possible computational steps for a parser of any kind.

In just this sense then, the MA and RA strategies conform to a *principle of least effort,* and functionally this principle might be offered as an explanation of sorts for why the human parser has gravitated towards the MA and RA strategies. But this explanation leaves entirely open just how minimal attachment and low right association are represented in the parser. On the one hand, they might simply be *described* as some type of ordering over the operations of the parser such that MA and RA are implemented. On the other hand, MA and RA might be *explained* if they arise as an automatic consequence of the architecture of the parser. It was

Frazier and Fodor's (1978) original, and very interesting, contention that the architecture of the Sausage Machine provides just such an explanation for MA and RA. And they argued further that the existence of these architectural explanations was important evidence that the human parser more nearly resembles the relaxed dimensions of the SM than the rigid specifications of the ATN.

In the following section, I review their case one more time, not in order to repeat old arguments (although some repetition is necessary) but to show that the conclusion may be quite different, and more interesting, than any of us previously anticipated. For, whereas Frazier and Fodor offered two entirely separate architectural innovations to account for the two parsing strategies, it now appears that the two strategies can be subsumed under a single explanatory principle.

Architectural Explanations

According to Frazier and Fodor's original paper, low right association was caused entirely by what they called the "short-sightedness" of the first stage of the SM, whose view of the sentence is limited to about six words. As evidence for their claim, consider a sentence like

(15) Joe bought the book for Susan.

Here, the prepositional phrase *for Susan* appears equally attachable as the PP complement of the NP *the book for Susan* or as the indirect object PP of the VP *bought the book for Susan*. There is no strong preference for the lower (or NP) attachment, as Kimball's RA strategy would predict. However, if the preceding NP is lengthened, as in

(16) Joe bought the book that I had been trying to obtain for Susan.

then the lower (or NP) attachment is preferred. Most listeners hear *for Susan* in (16) as part of the relative clause attached to the NP rather than as the indirect object attached to the VP. As Frazier and Fodor put it, RA appears to set in only "at some distance" in these examples. This is explicable in the Sausage Machine architecture if *for Susan* is attached to the parse tree by the first stage of the parser, which can only "see" the previous six words of the sentence. Within this limited window, only the relative clause will be visable in sentence (16); the first stage of the SM will have lost access to the higher VP entirely. On this account, there is no need to independently describe RA anywhere in the Sausage Machine because RA is merely an automatic consequence of the "short-sightedness of the first stage of the parser." Put simply, the parser makes the lowest possible attachment because that is the only attachment within view for the first stage of the SM.

The problem with this account, however, is that there are clear cases where the preference for low right attachment occurs quite strongly even when the two attachment sites fall within a span of six words (see Wanner, 1980). To repeat this demonstration, consider the following set of sentences, which represents a progressive shortening of sentence (6):

(17) (a) Tom said that Bill took the trash out yesterday.
      (b) Tom said that Bill took it out yesterday.
      (c) Tom said that Bill took it yesterday.
      (d) Tom said that Bill died yesterday.
      (e) Tom said Bill died yesterday.

Notice that as these sentences shrink, the preference for low right attachment does not diminish. The adverb *yesterday* seems to modify *Bill's* action in the complement sentence rather than *Tom's* action in the matrix sentence in all the sentences of (17). This holds despite the fact that in the (d) and (e) versions the *entire* sentence is six words or less—which means the entire sentence, along with both possible attachment sites, must fall within the limited purview of the SM parser.

In their reply, Fodor and Frazier (1980) acknowledge that SM architecture provides an inadequate explanation of low right attachment. In consequence, the chief motivation disappears for the claim that the human parser is organized in two stages with a memory-limited first stage. Fodor and Frazier (1980) do point out many cases where there appears to be some tendency (albeit unassessed experimentally) to make near attachments rather than remote ones. However, this tendency would be true of *any parser whatsoever* that has limited memory capacity for storing the developing parse tree. And because we know that human short-term memory is severely limited, it is not surprising that the human parser shows some preference for local attachment. But this preference does not require an architectural division into stages for its explanation.

Turning now to the Sausage Machine explanation of the minimal attachment, we have a somewhat happier story to tell, happier even than Frazier and Fodor (1978) anticipated. The architectural property of the Sausage Machine originally put forward to explain minimal attachment is a particular brand of parallel processing that works as follows: Suppose the parser pursues multiple attachment possibilities whenever the grammar permits them. But suppose also that these multiple parallel processes are pursued in horse-race fashion so that, as soon as one attachment succeeds, the race is over and all other attachment possibilities are abandoned. It is not difficult to see that this type of parallel parsing will, no matter what the details of the parsing process, result in minimal attachments. As Frazier and Fodor (1978) put it, "We need only suppose that the structural hypothesis which the parser pursues is the first one that it recognizes. Establishing the legitimacy of the minimal attachment of a constituent will take less time than establishing the legitimacy of a long chain of linking nodes" (p. 322).

At first glance, this proposal may appear to face severe difficulties characteristic of parallel processing schemes. For openers, how does it account for syntactic preferences other than minimal attachment? Unlike serial processors that naturally exhibit preferences by means of the order in which analyses are attempted, the race model will consider all analyses simultaneously and favor only those analyses that can be minimally attached. How then could it account for other preferences characteristic of the human parser—for instance, low right association? To study such questions, I formulated a version of the Frazier–Fodor race model inside ATN architecture and discovered something rather surprising: The race model automatically accounts for low right association as well as for minimal attachment.

To see this, consider an ATN that exhibits the following limited parallelism: At each state, all transitions leaving that state are attempted simultaneously. If any of these transitions invoke subnetworks via SEEK operations, these derivative transitions will also be attempted in the usual way. But as soon as any one of these analysis paths successfully analyzes the current input word and attaches it to the parse tree, all other analyses are abandoned. Control then passes to the state at the end of the analysis path that won the race and the same limited parallelism resumes at that state.

Assuming transition time is constant, this limited-parallel ATN will exhibit the minimal attachment preference because the minimal attachment will always have the analysis path with fewest transitions, and this analysis path will always win the race to attach the current word to the parse tree. To work through an example of this, consider how the ATN of Figure 5.1 would apply to sentence (9), which is repeated here:

(9) We told the girl that everyone liked the story.

The ATN processor will reach state VP_1 having analyzed *we* via transitions 1(11,16) and *told* via transitions 2(5). At this point the ATN grammar offers several different analysis paths for the next word *the*. But it is quite easy to verify that the shortest of these runs along the path from transition 6 to 12, which in turn leads to the minimal attachment of the NP *the girl* as the indirect object of the VP and the complement *that* clause as the direct object of the VP. The nonminimal attachment in which *the girl* functions as the head of the complex NP *the girl that everyone liked* is ruled out because more transitions are required to make the initial attachment of *the:* 6, 13, and 12.

None of this is particularly surprising because the limited parallel ATN was set up just in order to exhibit minimal attachment. What is much more interesting is that the same scheme automatically captures low right association. In general, the reason is this: In a top-down, left-to-right parser, like the ATN, the lowest right constituent is always the current constituent under construction. And in the ATN it will always require more transitions to close up the current constituent and make a higher attachment than it will to make an attachment inside the current constituent. To see an example, consider the application of the ATN in Fig. 5.1 to sentence (17e), which is repeated here:

(17e) Tom said Bill died yesterday.

Ignoring details, the parser will reach the analyses of the sentence final adverb *yesterday* along the path 1(17,16)2(5,7,8(19,20(1(17,16) 2(5,7,9,10). At this point, the parser can either analyze *yesterday* as the adverb modifier of the complement clause via transition 3; or the parser can close the complement clause via transitions 4 and 21, then close the VP of the main clause via transition 10, and finally attach *yesterday* as the adverbial modifier of the main clause via transition 3. Obviously, the higher attachment requires more transitions and will lose the race to the lower transition, thus exhibiting exactly the preference predicted by Kimball's principle of low right association.

This explanation of MA and RA in terms of limited parallelism has several

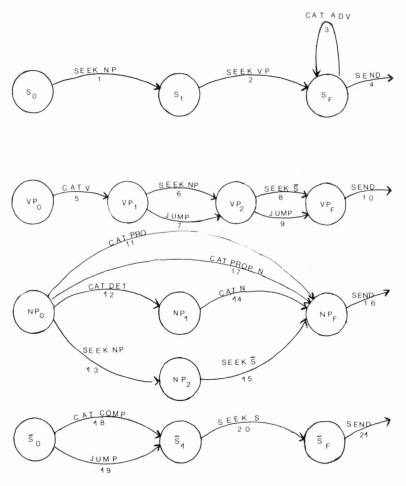

FIG. 5.1.   A simple ATN.

virtues that should be advertised by way of conclusion. First, of course, it gives you two for the price of one: Two parsing strategies fall out as the automatic consequence of one architectural claim. This is obviously a somewhat more satisfying result than the original Sausage Machine proposal, which required separate architectural postulates for each strategy. Furthermore, because MA and RA appear to fall together into a natural class of strategies designed to minimize computation, it is particularly satisfying to find that both members of the class have a common source.

Second, limited parallelism provides an automatic cure for the left recursion problems incurred by all top-down parsers discussed earlier. A recursive rule like NP → NP S will never be applied to infinite depth so long as there is a nonrecursive rule expanding the same nonterminal, such as NP → DET N, which will always win the horse race imposed by limited parallel architecture.

Third, limited parallelism may offer a solution to the puzzle posed by the coexistence of garden path effects and evidence for parallel processing noted earlier. This follows because limited parallel processing follows multiple grammatical paths wherever they exist but is also vulnerable to garden paths because the parser constantly wagers on the shortest analysis of each word. Thus, limited parallel parsers will be subject to misanalysis and back-up characteristic of garden paths but will also do more work wherever the grammar permits more possible analyses of the input sentence.

Finally, what about the old battle between the ATN and the Sausage Machine. Does the success of limited parallelism point toward either parser as a better psychological model of parsing? At this point, I think not. The old ATN assumption of exclusively serial operation appears to be too restrictive. To that extent, the original ATN was clearly wrong. But neither is there any evidence for the division of parsing into stages. To that extent the Sausage Machine appears to have been wrong. But beyond these negative conclusions, note that it was only within the more explicit framework of the ATN that it became possible to appreciate the explanatory power of the limited parallel processing scheme proposed by Frazier and Fodor. Therefore, if there is a moral here, it may be one of style more than substance: Only if we keep our modeling style reasonably precise will we be able to locate where on the major dimensions of parsing the psychological parser lies.

Is Parsing Architecture Innate?

As confessed in the opening pages of this chapter, I once thought the study of adult linguistic ability would supply the answer to the first-order question about language acquisition: Namely, what is acquired. Having been in the business awhile, I now deem it wiser to think more in terms of supplying questions than answers.

For instance, suppose we take it as true that adults employ parsing strategies such as MA and RA, which appear to be selected in order to minimize computation. The logical next question is just when and where this selection occurs in the course of language acquisition. There are really only two possibilities: ontogeny or phylogeny. Either children learn parsing strategies that economize computation by performing some kind of induction over their own parsing histories, or they come innately equipped with parsing mechanisms that automatically bias them toward minimally computable solutions. There are at least two reasons to suspect the latter alternative may be more correct.

First, notice that MA and RA are not the kind of principles that are obviously obtainable by learning. They do not lead, on the average, to the correct parse (the one intended by the speaker) but only to the most easily computed parse, which may or may not be correct. There is no reason to suspect, therefore, that MA and RA would be reinforced by experience. (Unless of course, speakers tend to produce sentences with minimally computable phrase-markers, which seems unlikely.)

Second, the discovery that limited-parallel parsing automatically implements both RA and MA strongly suggests that these strategies derive directly from the nature of the human parsing mechanism. Certainly, it is difficult to imagine how experience could lead the child toward this particular, not to say peculiar, method of parsing. But, in this case, the proof of the innateness hypothesis need not be left to the imagination for it leads directly to a testable proposition about children's parsing: If RA and MA result from limited-parallel parsing and if limited-parallel parsing is part of an innate architecture, then whenever RA and MA emerge in development, they should emerge together. Note that the innateness hypothesis does not require the appearance of RA and MA in the cradle. The data about parsing among toddlers are understandably murky, and it might well be that parallel-processing capacity matures late. However, when and if this capacity does emerge, RA and MA should show up together as an automatic result. Given the superficial differences between the two strategies, it would be rather surprising (and therefore interesting) if this hypothesis proved to be true.

At any rate, that is the hypothesis I'm stuck with and what I need to find is someone who knows enough about child language acquisition to tell me how to test it. So, I'm thinking of hanging around the William James lunch line to see if anyone comes along.

REFERENCES

Fodor, J. A., Bever, T. G., & Garrett, M. (1974). *The psychology of language.* New York: McGraw–Hill.

Fodor, J. A., & Frazier, L. (1980). Is the human sentence parsing mechanism an ATN? *Cognition, 8,* 417–459.

Frazier, L., & Fodor, J. A. (1978). The sausage machine: A new two-stage parsing model. *Cognition, 6,* 291–325.

Garrett, M. F. (1970). Does ambiguity complicate the perception of sentences? In Flores D'Arcais & W. T. M. Levelt, *Advances in psycholinguistics.* Amsterdam–London: North-Holland.

Garrett, M. F., Bever, T., & Fodor, J. (1966). The active use of grammar in speech perception. *Perception and Psychophysics, 1,* 30–32.

Kaplan, R. (1973). A general syntactic processor. In R. Rustin, *Natural language processing.* Englewood Cliffs, NJ: Prentice–Hall.

Kay, M. (1965). Experiments with a powerful parser. Santa Monica: The Rand Corporation, RM-5452-PR.

Kimball, J. P. (1973). Seven principles of surface structure parsing in natural language. *Cognition, 2,* 15–47.

Miller, G. A. (1956). The magical number seven plus or minus two. *Psychological Review, 63,* 81–97.

Miller, G. A., & Chomsky, N. (1963). Finitary models of language users. In R. D. Luce, R. Bush, & E. Galanter (Eds.), *Handbook of mathematical psychology* (Vol. 2). New York: Wiley.

Petrick, S. R. (1964). *A recognition procedure for transformational grammars.* AFCRL, Bedford, MA.

Thorne, J., Bratley, P., & Dewar, H. (1968). The syntactic analysis of English by machine. In D. Mitchie (Ed.), *Machine intelligence* (3). New York: Elsevier.

Wanner, E. (1980). The ATN and the sausage machine: Which one is baloney? *Cognition, 8,* 209–225.

Wanner, E., Kaplan, R., & Shiner, S. (1975). *Garden paths in relative clauses.* Unpublished manuscript.

Wanner, E., & Maratsos, M. (1978). An ATN approach to comprehension. In M. Halle, J. Bresnan, & G. A. Miller, *Linguistic theory and psychological reality.* Cambridge, MA: MIT Press.

Woods, W. (1970). Transition network grammars for natural language analysis. *Communications of the ACM, 13,* 591–606.

6 Learnability Theory and the Acquisition of a First Language

Steven Pinker
Massachusetts Institute of Technology

It takes a lot of gall for a psycholinguist who would have been too young to serve as a subject in the first modern study of language development (Berko, 1958) to record his autobiographical reflections on the development of the field. But when I was originally asked to do so (Kessel & Brown, 1981), it was as a representative of the "younger generation" of graduates of the Harvard psycholinguistics program. Youthful gall being what it is, I will proceed nonetheless, hoping the reader will indulge me in the following recounting of my own history and rewriting of that of developmental psycholinguistics.

A TALE OF TWO ORTHODOXIES

Several of the contributors to this volume write of their professional development in the context of a turning away from an entrenched orthodoxy. The orthodoxy, in caricature, went something like this: "Language is an innate, species-specific ability. In language development we see the child using formal syntactic categories and rules from the earliest stages, and despite meager and degenerate input, the child coins transformations until he or she has acquired a full standard transformational grammar." Tales of disenchantment with this orthodoxy also figure prominently in many papers, monographs, and textbooks in language acquisition published during the last 15 years.

It is commonplace in the history of science for reactions to orthodoxies to become orthodoxies of their own, and it was an orthodoxy of quite a different kind that entrenched itself in developmental psycholinguistics through most of 1970s and 1980s. The newer orthodoxy, also in caricature, goes something like

97

this: "Language development is just one aspect of cognitive development. Through rich social interactions between mother and child, including a simplified speech register, nonlinguistic precursors of language develop into semantically based communicative strategies." It seems to me that this orthodoxy is far more entrenched than the earlier one ever was, possibly because it was the one I personally encountered. Not having experienced the 1960s zeitgeist firsthand, I do not have the impression that nativism and formalism were ever widely held by developmental psycholinguists. To be sure, nativist claims can be found in the writings of a small number of authors, such as McNeill, Fodor, Lenneberg, and Miller. Transformational-generative characterizations of early speech were perhaps more widespread, but even there the number of prominent examples is small. But whatever formalist and nativist sympathies existed seem to have been almost unanimously abandoned. The newer views found expression at about the same time that language acquisition developed the trappings of an autonomous discipline, such as its own journals, societies, graduate programs, conferences, and textbooks. And Anglo–American developmental psychology has never been fertile ground for nativism, formalism, or faculty psychology to begin with.

My own professional development began with an unanticipated reaction against this new orthodoxy. I arrived at Harvard in 1976 to engage in graduate study in cognitive psychology, which at the time was not unlike Humphrey Bogart moving to Casablanca for its therapeutic waters. The closest things I found were Jill de Villiers's seminar on language acquisition, and Reid Hastie's seminar on reasoning. In the de Villiers seminar there was much lively discussion about the new orthodoxy, much of which took the form "obviously, you don't need *x* to learn a language," or "obviously, you can't do *without x* in learning a language." But what was most obvious of all, at least to me, was that none of us had the foggiest idea of what you did or didn't need in order to learn a language, even in principle. The descriptions of the language acquisition process were vague and metaphorical, with little attention paid to the structure of the languages that children invariably succeeded at acquiring. In fact, it seemed that all the favorite debating questions—about innateness, input, precursors, semantics versus syntax—were entirely unanswerable until someone could point to explicit computational models of the information processing that goes on in the mind of a child when he or she hears English or Japanese sentences and thereby draws conclusions about the English or Japanese language. Developmental psycholinguistics seemed to stand in stark contrast to other subspecialties of cognitive science, such as the study of sentence parsing, visual recognition, mental imagery, long-term memory, or problem solving, where mathematical models and computer simulations had focused debate on the relative plausibility of putative mental mechanisms that were at least demonstrably sufficient to carry out the task at hand.

At about that time, Hastie, whose philosophy of graduate education was "whatever doesn't kill you makes you stronger," assigned his seminar an article in *Information and Control* by E. M. Gold entitled "Language identification in the limit." The article, totally incomprehensible to anyone unfamiliar with the lingo of automata theory, outlined a set of theorems delineating what combinations of input and learning strategies were necessary and sufficient for a learner to acquire various kinds of languages according to various criteria of successful learning. Having taken an undergraduate course on the theory of computation as an undergraduate, I understood enough to conclude that the article was potentially of great importance to human language acquisition research. For here were explicit models of language learning, with clear commitments as to their "innate" learning strategy and the input they required, and formal demonstrations of whether or not they actually succeeded at acquiring language.

Hastie also provided me with a draft of J. R. Anderson's forthcoming book *Language, Memory, and Thought.* In it Anderson alluded to a number of computer simulations of language acquisition, including his own. Again, I was excited to find explicit models of language learning whose properties were laid out in sufficient detail so that questions about the adequacy of the model could be answered unambiguously. Michael Cohen, a fellow graduate student interested in mathematical psychology, gave me a copy of a technical report by Kenneth Wexler, Peter Culicover, and Henry Hamburger, describing the first versions of a mathematical model of the acquisition of transformational grammars (see Pinker, 1981b; Wexler & Culicover, 1980). This was added to my collection of explicit language acquisition models, which can loosely be referred to as "learnability" approaches to language acquisition. At the time, virtually all these models were unknown to the psycholinguistic community.

Several problems with the new orthodoxy became crystal clear when I examined that literature. First, it was not as easy to reject theories positing innate, language-specific learning mechanisms as developmental psycholinguists had conjectured. In the learnability literatures, it was apparent that a learning model's success in acquiring a significant portion of a language in a psychologically plausible way was in direct proportion to the number and richness of task-specific constraints built into the model. Learning a language on the basis of a sample of sentences perceived in concrete situations is an exquisitely complex problem, but one that our species manages to compute with astonishing ease. Nativist acquisition models could begin to account for this fact; there was no nonnativist model that came close. However, unlike the nativist proposals discussed in the 1960s, the neonativist arguments of learnability theory come with a recipe for how to falsify them: Devise an explicit computational model that can acquire a natural language in a realistic way, without using mechanisms that are tailor made for natural language acquisition; for example, a model that uses a single set of mechanisms to learn to speak English, to program computers in LISP, to ride a bicycle, and to recognize faces.

Second, claims about the importance of the special speech register directed at young children appeared to be at best grossly premature. Psycholinguists had written as if there was something inherent in the learning problem that made short, simple, redundant, here-and-now sentences optimal for learning. On the contrary, the learning models I examined were all over the map as far as their sensitivity to the properties of "Motherese" were concerned. In fact, Wexler and Culicover's model would do far *worse* with simple inputs, because certain flaws in the child's hypothesized transformational rules would only reveal themselves in detectable errors when they interacted in facing complex inputs. In any case, in the absence of explicit learning models, claims about the role of various input properties on language acquisition cannot be made in confidence.

Third, allowing the child access to the meaning of parental sentences from their perceptual or discourse contexts does not by itself solve any of the learning problems pointed out by nativists in the 1960s. Once the child has inferred a sentence meaning, he or she is still faced with the task of mapping it onto the input word string in such a way as to coin correct new grammatical rules for the language. Doing so requires certain innate assumptions about how syntax maps onto semantics, assumptions that are not necessarily less complex or task specific than putative innate assumptions about syntax itself.

My fourth discovery was of a more sociological nature. By and large, developmental psycholinguistics was not concerned with language acquisition. This sounds paradoxical—what *is* developmental psycholinguistics, if not the study of language acquisition? Well, if language acquisition is the study of the AC-QUISITION (i.e., creation of new knowledge contingent on environmental inputs) of LANGUAGE (i.e., adult linguistic abilities in all their complexity), then very few psychologists were studying the question. There were studies of the speech of children at one or more stages, and of their comprehension abilities, but virtually no one paid attention to the *learning* process itself (i.e., the process by which the child forms *new* rules), nor to the end state of acquisition (for example, the fact that at some time between birth and adulthood people acquire the ability to differentiate *John is too tough to complain* and *John is too tough to complain to,* to take a randomly chosen subtle and complex linguistic fact).[1] The field even took on a new name: Child Language. It was only by concluding that psychologists were uninterested in language acquisition that I could account for nonsequiturs in the literature such as the supposed refutations of theories of syntax, or of nativist conjectures about language acquisition, through appeals to the semantics of Stage I speech or the properties of "Motherese."

---

[1] I continue to find it puzzling that psychologists do not consider the facts of adult language as data that a theory of language acquisition must account for. Sometimes it is said that linguistic theories are based on judgments of grammaticality, which are unreliable, biased, nonreplicable, subject to individual differences, and so on. But I have seen enough linguistic theories refuted by embarrassing uncontroversial judgments, and enough psychological theories that float in limbo as their proponents and critics endlessly debate the soundness and replicability of their "supporting" experimental data, to eschew prejudging the utility of different kinds of evidence.

THE DEVELOPMENT OF A LANGUAGE
ACQUISITION THEORY

This all happened in 1976, possibly the low point in the last 25 years for the job prospects of incoming graduate students. "Publish or perish" applied to graduate students even more than to faculty. Although I had no intention of going on to do research in language acquisition, I had decided that a paper reviewing formal models of language acquisition for the benefit of psycholinguists might be publishable in the *Psychological Bulletin,* a journal of literature reviews.

The Harvard graduate program, it turned out, was a perfect environment for me to work on that paper. One thing that can be said for a program without a large-scale cohesive research program is that there is no party line either. In a field that inspires as much emotion as language acquisition, I was fortunate to be able to develop my ideas in an atmosphere that was both stimulating and tolerant. My fellow graduate students, Kenji Hakuta and Helen Tager-Flusberg, and my advisors Reid Hastie, Jill de Villiers, and Stephen Kosslyn, provided intellectual guidance and an indulgent, somewhat amused encouragement, a "playing-the-trombone-is-fine-as-long-as-you-don't-expect-to-make-a-living-from-it" attitude.

Roger Brown taught me in several courses and eventually was a reader on my doctoral dissertation (on mentally scanning three-dimensional visual space). My first substantive contact with him centered on a paper I wrote for his seminar, in which I ground various axes about developmental psycholinguistics and learnability theories. Although it is apparent to everyone that Professor Brown is an utterly undogmatic scholar and teacher, I still submitted the paper with trepidation. This was a decidedly antiestablishment piece and Professor Brown at least in some sense represented the establishment (I did calm myself somewhat with the thought that my chief grievances with the field were that it abandoned the issues and methods that Brown himself had initiated 15 years earlier). I was, to say the least, relieved when I received his list of comments, handwritten in pencil (like several generations of his graduate students, I count these among my most prized possessions). For the comments had a characteristic Brownian mixture of sympathetic encouragement, penetrating commentary, gentle criticism, and timeless suggestions on style. My favorite is the following: "Personally I think 'trivial' and 'nontrivial' are terms to avoid, in spite of their great popularity, because it turns out that they are guns that can be switched around."

Mercifully, the first two versions of the paper I submitted to the journal were rejected, but in my final year of graduate school, a completely new version, with extensive discussion of the relevance of formal models to psychological questions, was accepted for publication in *Cognition* (Pinker, 1979). At that point language acquisition models had turned into a consuming interest, but I was utterly in the dark about what step to take next. None of the existing approaches to language learning offered clear directions for a tractable research program on human acquisition mechanisms. The mathematical literature was useful in telling us what kinds of mechanisms could *not* learn languages and hence could not be used by humans, but it was far less helpful in determining the mechanisms that humans did use. Within the field of language acquisition, empirical research had turned away from the acquisition of grammar: conferences, journals, and edited volumes were filled instead with research on developmental pragmatics, sociolinguistics, nonlinguistic correlates of language use, children's and parents' speech registers, mother–child dialogue, and the like. The computer simulations I examined were not much more helpful; most acquired ad hoc collections of simplistic rules that were clearly not "upward compatible" with more realistic mechanisms of grammar. Any realistic model of language acquisition must be capable of acquiring mechanisms that handle the intricacies of language. But where could one start? The complexity and abstractness of grammatical transformations, just as it refuted simple models of learning, seemed to thwart just about any attempt at devising a language acquisition model. The Wexler–Culicover model was an exception, but it was also a unique tour de force. A large number of working assumptions, some of them tenuous, were needed for the work to proceed, and it took many years of work by three brilliant theorists to arrive at the final version of the proof. Although projects of similar scope were clearly crucial for progress in the field, I did not have the courage to commit myself for several years to exploring the implications of a fixed set of assumptions, to say nothing of the formal skills needed to produce noteworthy results. A final discouraging observation was that none of the learnability models made contact with detailed developmental data, nor did the developmental studies address any of the learning models.

With a postdoctoral fellowship at MIT in hand, I was ready to abandon language acquisition and turn full attention to my primary interest, visual imagery, but two developments made me change my mind. First, I discovered that theories of grammar had changed in encouraging ways. In the so-called "Standard Theory" of transformational grammar, sentences were derived with complex chains of transformational rules, which left few perceptible traces in the sentences for children to exploit during learning. But in the later theories of Chomsky (1981) and of Joan Bresnan (1982), the transformations thought to be empirically justifiable were far simpler, fewer in number, and less diverse than those in the Standard Theory. Furthermore, the grammar itself was factored into simpler, partially independent subcomponents, each of which could be acquired relatively autonomously. Finally, linguistic researchers were beginning to make good on their long-standing promise to separate the universal properties of grammar from the properties that varied parametrically among languages.

Gradually, a research program on language learning mechanisms could be envisioned. The task was to examine one subcomponent at a time, focus on the interlanguage and intralanguage variation in the rules belonging to that component, and find some type of information in parental speech that was diagnostic of which versions of those rules a language had opted for. A mechanism that looked for that information in the input and then outputted the language-specific rule revealed by that information could then be attributed to the child's language acquisition system. Naturally, there are also interactions among these inference procedures to map out, but the modularity of grammars within recent theories, and progress at delineating cross-linguistic parametric variation, made it clear how to begin.

At this time an increasing number of researchers became interested in language learnability. Conferences at Laguna Beach in 1979, and at Austin and MIT in 1980, were devoted to the topic, and I profited from the many examples of learning strategies that were discussed informally at those conferences. At MIT, Joan Bresnan ran a seminar on her theory of Lexical Functional Grammar, and for several weeks she and Jane Grimshaw encouraged me with constructive criticism as I struggled at the blackboard, trying to outline mechanisms for the acquisition of LFG rules. Soon afterwards (in the spring of 1980), I had amassed enough such mechanisms that I felt ready to write a chapter outlining a partially explicit theory of language acquisition (Pinker, 1982).

Although I continue to believe the tenets of the theory I outlined then, the paper clearly overestimated the formal coherence and empirical support of the theory as presented (not to mention its expressed optimism, since deflated, that developmental data could easily discriminate among competing linguistic theories). Although some of this could be attributed to youthful excesses, I realized that I was not getting any younger. With the dubious luxury of an academic job (actually, three jobs), I spent a good part of my waking life during the next 3 years examining the literature on language acquisition, gathering new data, and trying to make the acquisition mechanisms more cohesive, explicit, and linguistically and psychologically realistic. A new and improved version of the theory, consisting of mechanisms designed to acquire phrase structure, inflection, complementation, auxiliaries, and the lexicon, is outlined in Pinker (1984).[2]

Two sources of information helped in that effort. One was a room in William James Hall directly across from the office I occupied during my year as an assistant professor at Harvard. That room contained the original transcripts from Adam, Eve, and Sarah, numerous unpublished concordances and distributional

---

[2]It has often struck me how fortunate I was to come of age during the Sloan Foundation's program in support of Cognitive Science during the late 1970s and early 1980s. Many events that were critical in my intellectual development would ordinarily have been closed off to researchers so early in their careers had it not been for the foundation's generous level of support for interdisciplinary work during that time: attending the three conferences on learnability in 1979–1980 (and subsequent conferences at Stanford in 1981 and the University of Western Ontario in 1982); my postdoctoral fellowship at MIT, with colleagues both from linguistics and psycholinguistics; and access to interdisciplinary audiences across the country through technical report and speaker series.

analyses, and Brown's grammars for each of the three children at each of five stages of development. These are the "15 weighty manuscripts that not more than half a dozen people in the world have the *knowledge*, the *patience*, and the *interest* to read; nay, not so many as half-a-dozen" (Brown, 1973). Either I belong to a very select group or I have come across my first sharp disagreement with Roger, because I found the grammars fascinating reading and a gold mine of information.

The other source of information was the body of experiments and detailed analyses of children's grammatical development that appeared in journals and unpublished presentations but that were rarely cited in textbooks or any of the numerous polemics on language acquisition. I soon discovered that the literature on children's language was more informative in constraining theories of learning than I had believed (and than many linguists apparently still believe). In particular, I continually found myself referring to the prescient work of many of the contributors to this volume (among others), who had a knack for choosing empirical issues that would turn out to be relevant when, thanks to developments in linguistics and learnability theory, it would be possible to develop explicit language-learning algorithms. Although I cannot review even a fraction of my retrospective interpretations of these studies, I can provide several examples pertaining to Roger Brown's inspiring study of the language development of Adam, Eve, and Sarah.

The Relevance to Learnability of Data from the Harvard Child Language Project

As the first modern large-scale study of language development, Brown's Harvard Child Language Project explored largely uncharted waters. The discoveries that came from it are so numerous, and so many have been transformed into today's "common knowledge," that it would be impossible to enumerate them. But some of those discoveries hold a special interest to a learnability theorist, for, although they were made in the process of addressing some question that was particularly relevant at the time, today they take on a special new or additional significance only partly related to the original question. In the rest of this chapter I summarize some of the ways in which data from the project can constrain learnability models; the interested reader is referred to Pinker (1984) for a more detailed presentation and for related analyses.

Negative Evidence

A phenomenon reported as a side attraction in Brown and Hanlon (1970) may be one of the most important discoveries in the history of psychology. Brown and Hanlon sought to test B. F. Skinner's claim that language development was propelled by parents reinforcing the child's utterances that are grammatical and punishing or extinguishing those that are ungrammatical. The authors examined whether the environmental contingencies that Skinner required—reward contingent on the well-formedness of the child's most recent utterance—even existed. Two results emerged. First, the number of approving or disapproving responses to children's utterances was unrelated to the well-formedness of the utterances; rather, they were related to the utterances' truth values. Second, the number of comprehending replies versus nonsequiturs to children's questions and negations was also unrelated to the well-formedness of the those utterances. Thus, children's environments seem to lack at least two of the possible examples of the contingencies of reinforcement that Skinner's account presupposed (parental approval, and the consequences in parental behavior of successful comprehension). Anecdotal reports from other investigators such as Braine and Mac-Neill suggest further that when overt corrections are offered to children, they are ignored or misconstrued.

Today there is such a consensus that Skinner's account is a nonstarter that Brown and Hanlon's analysis may seem like overkill. But students of reinforcement theory have long pointed out that reinforcement in general has two components: an informational component, where reinforcement serves to inform the organism that stimuli or responses must be divided into classes, and a hedonic component, where the reinforcer has some motivational or drive-related significance (e.g., pleasure or pain). Regardless of the relevance of reinforcement, with its conflation of these components, an implication of Brown and Hanlon's discovery is that there is probably no information available to the child as to the grammaticality of his or her utterances.[3]

---

[3]Brown and Hanlon's discovery has held up extremely well during the last 15 years, despite attacks from two sources. Many theorists, who clearly have not read the paper, point out that overt corrections of the child's utterances are not the only possible form of negative evidence, and that failures of parents to comprehend ungrammatical utterances could provide the same information. In a thoughtful discussion, Brown and Hanlon raised and then convincingly rejected that possibility, both on theoretical and empirical grounds. More recently, Hirsh-Pasek, Treiman, and Schneiderman (1984) replicated Brown and Hanlon but also found that mothers had a proportionally stronger tendency to repeat their children's utterances that were ungrammatical compared with those that were grammatical. This was true only of 2-year-olds; for their three older age groups, no such contingency could be found. Although Hirsh-Pasek et al. are circumspect about whether children use this information, even their modest conclusion that "mothers do give subtle cues as to which utterances are grammatically correct and which incorrect" is too strong. First, the statistics they cited overstate the across-subject reliability of the effect. Their t-statistic was significant only in a one-tailed test, though a two-tailed test seems more appropriate (there is no antecedent theory dictating whether it is ungrammatical or grammatical responses that should elicit more repetitions). And their contingency table used utterance tokens (pooled from different mothers) rather than mothers as the unit of analysis, leaving it unclear whether the contingency was significant across the population of mothers or only for some mothers. Furthermore, the information value of repetitions is small: if a 2-year-old's utterance was repeated by a parent, there was a .50 probability that it was ungrammatical; if it was not repeated, the probability was .34. Worse, this asymmetry reverses at some unspecified point between 2 and 3 years, and as far as one can see from the data, it may even be backwards for the mothers of some 2-year-olds. Given these facts, there are many reasons to doubt that a learning mechanism

E. M. Gold first pointed out the profound consequences of such a discovery. Gold's major proof was that a learner with access to information both about which strings were grammatical in the target language and about which were ungrammatical can acquire any language with a grammar whatsoever (under certain assumptions about the success criterion and other aspects of the learning scenario). However, a learner with access only to the sentences of a target language could not learn any class of languages that included all the finite languages plus at least one infinite language—which would render most mathematically "interesting" classes of languages, such as the phrase structure and the unrestricted transformational languages, unlearnable. The reason is simple: If the learner hypothesizes too large a language, nothing in the environment will ever tell him that he or she is wrong.

Gold's theorems do not directly pertain to the class of natural languages, which as far as we know does not contain *any* finite language, let alone all of them. Nonetheless, basically the same problem arises in most efforts at accounting for the child's acquisition of natural languages. Any time a child overgeneralizes, he or she is generating too large a language, and there is nothing in the world that strictly speaking informs the child of the error. Thus, learning theorists are faced with the profound problem of explaining how children succeed at language acquisition given their lack of access to "negative evidence." In the following sections I outline the three principal solutions that have been proposed.

The Smallest Language First Strategy (see Baker, 1979; Berwick & Weinberg, 1984; Pinker, 1982).   For every case in which Rule A generates a subset of the sentences generated by Rule B, the child would first hypothesize A, then abandon it for B only if a sentence generated by B but not by A was encountered in the input. The child would have no need for negative evidence because he or she would never guess too large a language. The problem with using this solution for the acquisition of any particular domain of rules is that it predicts that children should never produce both errors and correct structures in that domain. For some domains that is true (Maratsos & Chalkley, 1981), but for others it is patently false (Pinker, 1986).

Indirect Negative Evidence (Chomsky, 1981).   The child could note the absence of a given form in the input after some elapsed time and conclude that the missing form was ungrammatical. An as-yet unsolved problem for this strategy is

---

sensitive to this information could be of much help to children in general. Contrast this with the facts of *positive* evidence (i.e., evidence that a string of words *is* in the language): From what we know of the properties of parental speech, we can predict that when parents utter a string to their children, the child can assume that the string is a well-formed grammatical sentence or phrase with a probability greater than .99, at all ages, for all children.

that an infinite number of grammatical sentences are missing from any finite sample of input. For the child not to reject these spuriously, he or she must have some way of assessing whether a given construction had had ample opportunities to appear in the input, or of predicting the circumstances under which a sentence would *have to* occur if it was grammatical.

Uniqueness (Pinker, 1984; Wexler, 1979; Wexler & Culicover, 1980).   There may be some constructions that are constrained to appear in only one form in a language, at least as the default case. The appearance of one version of such a construction in the input could be taken as evidence that some other form was ungrammatical and should be expunged from the grammar. That way errors can be eliminated in the absence of corrections or other negative evidence. For example, if the child assumed that every verb has at most one past tense form, then the appearance of *brought* in the input could preempt *bringed,* which would never appear. If an exceptional verb could appear in both versions (e.g., *dived/dove*), each would be heard in the input and the child could thereby realize that both were admissible. A counterintuitive but probably unavoidable consequence of this hypothesis is that the child must record whether items in the grammar and lexicon were witnessed in the input or generated internally by a productive rule. Otherwise, he or she would not know whether to keep both forms, expunge one, or expunge the other.

No one knows which of these solutions is correct; my own theory uses Uniqueness and (less often) Smallest-First. But any learning theory must address this central problem.

The "Semantic Look" of Stage I Speech

Close to half of Brown's *A First Language* is devoted to arguing that children's first word combinations universally express a small number of semantic relations, such as "agent–action," "action–object," "entity–location," and "possessor–possessed." In fact, listing the semantic relations and the order of the two terms they are composed of provides the best description of children's "Stage I" speech. This conclusion was an alternative to earlier formulations by Brown and others that attributed to the child adult-like grammatical categories like noun and verb or distributionally defined categories such as "pivot" and "open."

If one accepts Brown's characterization of Stage I speech, one is faced with the problem of accounting for the child's transition from a purely semantic grammar to the adult grammar, in which there are rules couched in purely formal terms such as *subject* and *noun.* One approach is to deny that there is any transition at all, arguing that adults, too, have a grammar specifying the order and composition of elements defined by the semantic properties and roles of their referents, such as "attribute" or "agent." Although originally Brown's Stage I grammar gave comfort to "semantophiles" in their pointless debate with "syn-

tactophiles'' over whether syntax or semantics was in some sense more important, I think even a cursory examination of adult linguistic abilities shows that
adult competence involves rules that dictate purely formal, syntactic properties
of sentence elements (and also, of course, rules that dictate how meanings are
expressed in sentences). Adult grammatical subjects are not restricted to agents
or experiencers; they can refer to any entity or type of semantic relation whatsoever. Furthermore, to take just one example of the partial autonomy of syntax,
rules like passivization and raising work the same way whether a noun phrase
refers to a thing in the world with a determinate semantic role, or consists of
meaningless elements like *there: It is believed that there is a vase on the table; I
believe there to be a vase on the table; there is believed to be a vase on the table.*

An alternative approach is to conjecture that the child's semantic categories
and relations evolve into the adult's syntactic categories and relations through a
learning process analogous to classical concept identification. The child would
notice, for example, that a word referring to an experiencer appeared in the same
position that agents do in the ''agent–action'' schema and hence broaden the
inclusiveness of the first term of that relation so as to include experiencers. As an
increasingly heterogeneous set of subjects is encountered, the initial term will
become increasingly inclusive until it coincides with the adult subject class. The
problem with this hypothesis, aside from the fact that no one has explicitly
presented a theory of the necessary learning mechanisms, is that subjects do not
constitute a superset of agents; grammatical relations and semantic relations are
essentially independent types. Grammatical categories and relations are defined
formally in virtue of their being treated identically by a class of rules; they cannot
be defined by what they refer to (see, e.g., Maratsos & Chalkley, 1981; Pinker,
1984).

A third position is that the semantic rules are simply jettisoned at a matura-
tionally determined point, just as a tadpole turns into a frog (Chomsky, 1975;
Gleitman, 1981). This would, of course, rob Stage I speech of most of its interest
as far as the learning of the adult language was concerned (not that that is
relevant to its truth or falsehood, of course). However, there is also not much in
the way of independent evidence for it, and it is inherently unparsimonious (see
Pinker, 1984, chapter 2).

I have argued for a fourth alternative: that the ''semantic look'' of Stage I
speech is a manifestation of an important functional property of the language-
learning mechanism. Language acquisition theory has for a long time been at a
standstill because of the following problem. Chomsky and other linguists have
shown that language has a ''rich deductive structure'': given one fact about an
element in a language, many others are either invariably true or have a high
probability of being true. That is a good thing, because many of the properties of
language are so abstract that it is hard to see how they could be discovered
individually, especially when they only serve to render certain sentences ungrammatical and hence are undiscoverable in the absence of negative evidence.

Others are not abstract but must be found from an astronomically large set of logical possibilities. With an innate deductive structure, the child does not have to discover all the intricate and abstract properties of language; many of them are there to begin with or can be easily deduced. For example, the following properties of certain kinds of noun phrases mutually predict one another to various degrees: appearing as the first argument in the sentence; being absent in complements and understood as coreferring with a matrix argument; agreeing with the verb in person, number, or gender; coreferring with a reflexive element in the same clause; expressing the agent argument of an actional predicate; blocking extraction of a noun phrase embedded within it.[4] The elements participating in this "family resemblance structure" are those we call grammatical subjects. With an innate knowledge of these contingencies, as soon as a child has categorized a relation as an example of subjecthood, he or she can deduce that the universal properties of subjects apply; for the properties that are not universal but likely, he or she can selectively examine subjects in the input for the relevant properties, rather than wastefully examining all possible contingencies among elements and their properties.

The reason that Chomsky's arguments, though persuasive, have historically not led to many concrete theories of language acquisition is that deductions need premises, and it has never been clear what premises the child could begin with. If nouns and verbs and subjects and phrase structure are purely abstract relations, with no universal perceptual correlates such as fixed serial positions, phonological markers, or necessary semantic correlates, how was the neonate to know which elements in the input were nouns and verbs and subjects in order to begin the deductions? As Fodor put it (1966), it does no good to put the statement "there exist nouns" in the mind of the child; he or she must have some way of *finding* them in the input.

There is one solution, first explicitly argued for by Jane Grimshaw (1981), that I developed and exploited extensively (Pinker, 1982, 1984), and that others (e.g., Chomsky, 1981; Wexler & Culicover, 1980) have assumed versions of as well. According to this solution, the input to children contains certain identifiable constructions in which semantic entities and relations are each reliably expressed by one and only one type of grammatical device. For example, in "basic sentences" (see Keenan, 1976), agents of action predicates are universally expressed as subjects, and patients expressed as objects. Names for physical things are universally expressed as nouns (Macnamara, 1982); names for physical actions or changes of state are expressed as verbs. If a child has learned the meanings of individual words and can infer the semantic relations of a sentence from its context, he or she can tentatively use these syntax–semantics correspondences to classify agents in basic sentences as subjects, things as nouns, and so on. At that point, the innate deductions that involve subjects or nouns can

---

[4]This list is imprecise and is only intended to illustrate certain points about learning.

precede apace, and the child can obey the unlearnable, abstract, or obscure constraints that linguists have called attention to. Because semantic notions are only used to identify grammatical categories and relations, whereas the knowledge acquired is couched in a purely syntactic vocabulary, elements that do not obey the syntax–semantics correspondences (e.g., subjects of passives, and deverbal or abstract nouns) can be correctly classified by virtue of their behavior in previously learned phrase structures or inflectional paradigms.

This "semantic bootstrapping hypothesis" makes a set of subtle developmental predictions, one of which is that the first correctly classified words and arguments acquired by the child should obey the syntax–semantics correlations assumed to launch the learning process. That is, all things being equal, the first nouns of the child should be names for things, the first verbs should refer to actions or changes of state, the first subjects should refer to agents of actions, the first objects should refer to patients. The child would not actually have a semantic grammar, but he or she would pass through a phase in which syntax and semantics were in one-to-one correspondence. Validating these predictions is not a simple matter; for one thing, it requires the scientist to know how the child classifies his or her words and relations; for another, it is relevant only to the child's "first" acquisitions, because distributional mechanisms exist for learning exceptions to the correlations once the first exemplars are acquired. But in broad outline, the "semantic look" of Stage I speech is consistent with the predictions of the hypothesis. Readers who are interested in the hypothesis and its predictions are referred to Chapter 2 of Pinker (1984), where these issues are examined in (probably too much) detail.

Thus, if Brown is roughly correct about the nature of the child's first word combinations and I am roughly correct about the bootstrapping of the grammatical deduction process, Stage I speech would not be a blind alley in the road toward adult mastery of language. Rather, it would be a necessary first step in using innate knowledge to acquire an essentially formal system with circumscribed areas of semantic predictability.

Word Order in Early Speech

A major finding that emerged during the first investigations of children's acquisition of English was that most children are fairly fastidious at obeying English constituent order (Braine, 1976; Brown, 1973). For reasons I describe next, this is an important and nonobvious finding. Curiously, although Brown reported the dramatic fact that an overwhelming preponderance of English children's utterances were in adult-like orders, he presented neither the methodology nor the data behind this conclusion, and the entire discussion of word order in spontaneous speech takes up only two pages in the book. If I can be forgiven another exercise in amateur history, I conjecture that this lack of emphasis reflected two things: a bad taste left from the stark disconfirmation by Slobin and others of careless claims from the 1960s that children were universally predisposed to learn English-like grammar, and a lack of explicit attention, prior to the prominence of learnability approaches, to the problem of how the child fixes the parameters of variation differentiating languages.

It is well known that languages differ as to whether grammatical relations are encoded by a fixed order of their major constituents or by case and agreement markers affixed to constituents that can appear in many orders. Children must learn which class their language belongs to, and they can do so in one of two ways. If children follow the "Smallest Language First" strategy, they should assume that in the default circumstance languages have a fixed constituent order. They would back off from that prediction if alternative word orders were heard, indicating that the language did permit constituent order freedom. Fixed order in general would be the default (though not any *particular* fixed order such as that of English or any other language.)

Alternatively, the child could assume that the default case was constituent order freedom. This does raise a learnability problem: Strictly speaking, in the absence of negative evidence there is no input datum that could refute such a guess. Thus, an American child whose first hypothesis was that English had the word-order freedom of Warlpiri could order constituents freely all his or her life. However, conceivably there is a model invoking indirect negative evidence that could note the lack of such freedom in the speech of others; for example, the child could tabulate the relative frequencies of all pairwise constituent orders within a phrase, and if a given order was eventually exemplified with overwhelmingly greater frequency than its opposite, a word-order rule could be coined. This account is not without problems, but let us assume some such strategy is viable.

Consider the possible developmental predictions made by these accounts. The fixed order default strategy would acquire individual phrase structure rules corresponding to each phrasal order that had been heard in the input. If enough distinct orders were heard, he or she would then subject these rules to collapsing procedures that would yield abbreviated rules permitting order freedom (see chapter 3 of Pinker, 1984, for details). That means that, for fixed constituent order languages like English, the child's grammar should not generate constituent orders not permitted by the adult grammar; one should thus expect no overgeneralizations of constituent order by children learning languages like English. However, for free constituent order languages, it is possible that a child using these procedures could pass through a stage in which he or she had recorded phrase structure rules corresponding to some subset of adult constituent orders that had been heard or attended to but had not yet applied the collapsing procedures that generalized beyond that set of input orders. This could happen if the collapsing procedures required that their input rules reach a threshold of strength or permanence before they applied. If so, it is possible (though not necessary) that a child acquiring free constituent order languages would pass through a stage in which he or she would fail to exploit all the order possibilities permitted by the adult language, in other words, the child could undergenerate constituent orders.

The other strategy, free order default, makes very different predictions. When learning free constituent order languages, such a child would immediately hypothesize correct rules permitting constituent order freedom, and so should not undergenerate. On the other hand, for fixed constituent order languages, it is possible that a child could first pass through a stage in which the constituency of a phrase had been established, but the order comparisons had not yet surpassed the thresholds necessary for any fixed order to be added to the grammar. So with this strategy we are prepared for the possibility that a child learning fixed constituent orders might overgenerate and utter orders that the target language does not permit. The predictions are summarized in Table 6.1.

To decide between the theories, it is necessary to consider the developmental evidence corresponding to each column. As for fixed constituent order phrases, Brown (1973) noted "in all the 17 samples of Stage I English listed in Table 9 the violations of normal order are triflingly few: *Nose blow* (Hildegard), *Slide go* (Gia I), *Apple more* (Christy), *Paper write* (Adam), *Horse . . . see it* (Kendall I) *see Kendall* (when Kendall sees, in Kendall II), and perhpas 100 or so others. Of utterances in normal order there are many thousands." Bloom, Lightbown, and Hood (1975), Bowerman (1973), Slobin (1973), and Braine (1976) give other examples of adherence to adult word order in children acquiring fixed constituent order languages. Brown also cited three isolated reports of apparent word order freedom in Stage I speech, two of them unpublished, but in these cases it is difficult to determine the extent of the word-order freedom, and whether it was truly ruled out by the phrase structure of the target language (see Braine, 1976, and chapter 4 of Pinker, 1984).

Turning now to the second column in Table 6.1, one finds that there have indeed been reports of children acquiring free constituent order languages who use only a subset of the orders permissible. Brown summarized reports of undergeneration of word order from the acquisition of Korean, Russian, and Swedish, and Hakuta (1982) provides corroborating experimental data concerning the acquisition of Japanese. Such undergeneration is not universal (e.g., it has not been reported for Finnish, Bowerman, 1973, or Turkish, Slobin, 1982), but it need not be under either hypothesis.

TABLE 6.1
Type of Phrase

	Fixed Constituent Order	Free Constituent Order
Fixed order as default	no overgeneration	undergeneration possible
Free order as default	overgeneration possible	no undergeneration

Thus, Brown's data and his summary of those of others can be used to address the question of which default the child uses in approaching the crosslinguistic parameter of variation concerning constituent order freedom. The evidence as I construe his summary of it suggests that the child constrains order from the start and relaxes it as the evidence warrants. Further analyses may or may not bear out this conclusion but I hope the general point is clear that available developmental data may be used in principle to answer questions about defaults in learning mechanisms.

Acquisition of Closed-Class Morphemes

The examination of Stage I speech and the formulation of a grammar of semantic relations for it occupies one of the two major sections of *A First Language;* the other is devoted to an examination of development in Stage II, primarily the acquisition of closed-class morphemes in that stage. The section culminates with the conclusion that the order of acquisition of 14 closed-class morphemes in English is a function of the syntactic or semantic complexity of the morphemes (basically, the number of features encoded) or both, but not of their frequency in parental speech. These conclusions have withstood several attempts at replication (see, e.g., de Villiers & de Villiers, 1973; Pinker, 1981b).

Once again, it is tempting (though no doubt foolhardy) to reconstruct the intellectual context of the research question. My impression is that the study was seen as being relevant to the question of whether the path of language development was shaped by the child or by the environment (in Herbert Simon's metaphor, whether the complexity of the ant's path is in the ant or in the beach); the former option seen as consistent both with Piagetian and Chomskyan views, the latter more congenial to behaviorists and empiricist learning theorists. The potency of the complexity factor in morpheme acquisition suggested that the size of the mental representations underlying knowledge of the morphemes was the crucial causal factor in development, and not the degree of environmental "stamping in."

Today, with the virtual demise of classical learning theory as an explanation of language development, and with the formulation of explicit acquisition models, Brown's alternative independent variables do not divide the landscape in the same way. Frequency effects bear on whether learning mechanisms produce rules in all-or-none fashion or with graded strength values, but learning models of any kind, empiricist or nativist, can work in either way (see, e.g., Pinker, 1987, in press). Complexity effects, too, are compatible with learning models that disagree widely over the role attributed to environmental input.

Brown's analysis does cut a lot of ice nonetheless; at least it does in attempts at formulating algorithms for the acquisition of closed-class morphemes. Consider first what the child must acquire, then the circumstances under which he or she must acquire it. Knowledge of closed-class morphemes can be modeled by entries in the mental lexicon specific to each morpheme, listing the feature values that must be true of the clause in which the morpheme is found. For example, the lexical entry for the English 3rd person singular verb inflection (the *-s* in *Sam sings*), forcing number and person agreement between verb and subject, could look as follows:

-s: verb affix: present tense
                 imperfective aspect
                 singular subject
                 3rd person subject

An entry for a case marker encoding accusative case, definiteness, and animacy in some hypothetical language could look as follows:

-shig: noun affix: accusative case
                    definite
                    animate

Let us assume that a child has already isolated an inflection or other closed-class morpheme, has learned its syntactic categorization or that of its stem, and, in the case of verbs, knows the grammatical roles of their arguments (e.g., that a given verb's agent is a subject, its patient an object). Dan Slobin (1982) has pointed out the chief problem the child then faces in attempting to figure out the features encoded by that morpheme. Different languages grammaticize different aspects of an event, and when they do, they do so obligatorily. Thus, the child cannot encode the pragmatically salient elements in the situational or discourse context of an input sentence containing inflections and work on the assumption that the inflections are encoding only those notions. For example, whether or not an adult wishes to communicate the information that an event is present or past, or that the subject argument of a verb is singular or plural, the English language leaves him or her no choice. And the child not only cannot use the situation to determine which notions are encoded, he or she cannot use a priori knowledge either, because for all the child knows, it could be subject animacy or object number that an affix is encoding. In other words, in determining which notions are encoded in a language's morphology, the child is faced with a formidable search problem.

In the 1980 version of my acquisition theory I attempted to solve this problem as follows. Imagine a procedure that created a tentative entry for a morpheme containing *all* the features that are (a) consistent with the situation, (b) in accordance with certain formal and substantive constraints on features and how they are encoded in closed-class morphemes, and (c) drawn from a finite set of grammaticizable notions. For example, when the child hears a sentence like *the man crumples a newspaper* and simultaneously attends to the accompanying scene, he or she could consider any of the following features (and a number of others as well) as candidates to be added to the lexical entry for *-s:*

1. singular subject
2. masculine subject
3. 3rd person subject
4. animate subject
5. human subject
6. imperfective aspect
7. present tense
8. witnessed event
9. singular object
10. 3rd person object
11. inanimate object
12. nonhuman object
13. flat-flexible object

The child would append to the lexical entry of the morpheme *all* the potentially grammatically relevant features exemplified in the things and events expressed in the sentence. If any equation previously added to the morpheme's entry is inconsistent with the current input, the child would expunge it permanently. Because the number of possible features in an entry is finite under a reasonable set of assumptions (see Pinker, 1982, Appendix 1), the child will eventually converge on the correct equations for the morpheme to be learned. In the present example, the child would repeatedly add equations 1, 3, 6, and 7 to the lexical entry for -*s* any time a sentence with that morpheme is encountered and would, at one point or another, encounter inputs that contradict each equation in 2, 4, 5, and 8–13. For example, *See that mare? Every day she licks her colts* is cause to delete equations 2, 5, 9, 11, and 13; *the noise annoys me* is cause to delete 4, 5, 9, 10, 11, 12, and 13.

This model is counterintuitive in that it has the child entertain very complex hypotheses, in fact, an exhaustive list of all hypotheses consistent with an input (that is how the child would solve the problem of the lack of contextual cues as to which features are encoded obligatorily). It would be unwise to reject this model on intuitive grounds, however. There is not much reason to trust our intuitions in the domain of learnability: There are difficult computational problems to solve, and little guide as to what the correct solutions will look like. But this model can be rejected decisively by Brown's analyses. The model predicts that affixes that are sensitive to a full set of grammatical features (e.g., an affix that was used only on plural, masculine, animate, accusative nouns) would be learned more quickly than an affix that was sensitive only to one feature (e.g., number), because in the latter case it would take more time for the incorrectly hypothesized features to drop out. And Brown, of course, found the exact opposite to be true. Another prediction of the account, incidentally, is that children should first undergeneralize the use of their morphemes at the stage at which they have not driven out the incorrect equations (e.g., they might restrict a nominative case marker to nouns with animate singular globular definite proximal referents) and then gradually expand their usage until it matches that of adults. Slobin (1985) reports that children the world over do the opposite: They quite frequently overgeneralize the use of individual morphemes to words that do not allow them in the adult language, respecting one distinction encoded by that morpheme while ignoring a second distinction also encoded by it, for example, respecting case in their use of noun affixes but ignoring gender, or vice-versa.

Thus, an alternative model is needed. One modification that will accommodate Brown's and Slobin's data is to have the child hypothesize not *all* the features consistent with an input, but only *one* feature randomly selected from the possible set. On each sentence, a different feature would be hypothesized: If an existing feature is contradicted by a newly hypothesized one, both would be permanently expunged. Eventually, all and only the correct features would be appended to the affix. This would allow development to go from simple to complex and from general to specific, as mandated by the data. There are other problems it will not solve (seven, at last count; see chapter 5 of Pinker, 1984), but Brown's data make it clear that any model must engage in sampling rather than exhaustive hypothesization of candidate features for closed-class morphemes.

CONCLUSION

I have tried to show how four empirical discoveries growing out of Roger Brown's Harvard Child Language Project, though made in the quest for answers to questions that were especially pressing at the time, take on additional significance when used in the construction of explicit learning theories. The absence of parental approval or comprehension success contingent on the well-formedness of the child's prior utterance was originally relevant to the refutation of reinforcement theory but now is the best evidence we have on the profound question of the child's access to negative evidence. The semantic regularities in children's first word combinations were seen as relevant to the overall centrality of semantics and conceptual representation in linguistic competence but currently may be relevant to how the child finds tokens of abstract linguistic universals in the input. The adherence to rigid word order in the acquisition of English may have been taken as evidence that the English order had some universal cognitive or linguistic significance but now can be used to address the question of whether rigidity of constituent order in general is a default assumption on the part of the child. And Brown's Law of Cumulative Complexity in the acquisition of closed-class morphemes, although originally relevant to the respective roles of the environment versus the child, can be exploited to discriminate between exhaustive and sampling models of feature hypothesization.

This retrospective exploitation of the Harvard data in learnability theory brings two points home to me. The first concerns the limits of the explicit modeling approach to language acquisition that I extoll. Although my sympathies have usually been with formalistic approaches to research, the preceding examples make it clear to me that great science is often the product of an ineffable intuition or taste for which phenomena are important, a sense that transcends the details of questions posed by contemporary theories and models.

The second point is about optimism and the study of language acquisition. In my 1979 review attempting to alert researchers to the need for explicit modeling of the learning process, I quoted the following passage from an unpublished lecture from Brown (1977):

> Developmental psycholinguistics has enjoyed an enormous growth in research popularity. . . . All of which, strange to say, may come to nothing. There have been greater research enthusiasms than this in psychology: Clark Hull's principles of behavior, the study of the authoritarian personality, and, of course, dissonance theory. And in all these cases, very little advance in knowledge took place. . . . A danger in great research activity which we have not yet surmounted, but which we may surmount, is that a large quantity of frequently conflicting theory and data can become cognitively ugly and so repellent as to be swiftly deserted, its issues unresolved. (p. 28; my ellipses)

My use of this characteristically eloquent quotation was an attempt at consciousness raising, and it appears to have been met with a certain degree of success, judging by the number of occasions since my article appeared that I have seen the quote reproduced. But I have some regret that my ellipses may have given an impression that Brown's words were something other than guardedly optimistic. The passages I deleted were far more upbeat:

> I trust our case is more hopeful. We are still trying to put down roots that are both deep and extensive—we attempt to keep up with acoustic phonology, cognitive psychology, linguistics, philosophy, and social psychology. . . . But in the end, the thing I credit most for what successes the field has had and the thing I most count on is that we are somehow lucky in our subject matter: there are astonishing regularities in child speech and some are very near the surface; a little deeper, I feel sure, are real laws. (p. 28)

My experience with Brown's data many years after they were gathered has convinced me that his optimism is justified, and I hope that the kinds of analyses summarized in this chapter will eventually play at least a small role in making his prediction true.

ACKNOWLEDGMENTS

Preparation of this chapter was supported by NSF grant BNS 82-09540 and NIH grant HD 18381-01.

REFERENCES

Baker, C. L. (1979). Syntactic theory and the projection problem. *Linguistic Inquiry, 10,* 533–581.

Berko, J. (1958). The child's learning of English morphology. *Word, 14,* 150–177.

Berwick, R. C., & Weinberg, A. S. (1984). *The grammatical basis of linguistic performance.* Cambridge, MA: MIT Press.

Bloom, L., Lightbown, P., & Hood, L. (1975). Structure and variation in child language. *Monographs of the Society for Research in Child Development 40.*

Bowerman, M. (1973). *Early syntactic development: A cross-linguistic study with special reference to Finnish.* Cambridge, England: Cambridge University Press.

Braine, M. D. S. (1976). Children's first word combinations. *Monographs of the Society for Research in Child Development, 41.*

Bresnan, J. (1982). *The mental representation of grammatical relations.* Cambridge, MA: MIT Press.

Brown, R. (1973). *A first language: The early stages.* Cambridge, MA: Harvard University Press.

Brown, R. (1977, April). *Word from the language acquisition front.* Invited address at the meeting of the Eastern Psychological Association, Boston.

Brown, R., & Hanlon, C. (1970). Derivational complexity and order of acquisition in child speech. In J. R. Hayes (Ed.), *Cognition and the development of language.* New York: Wiley.

Chomsky, N. (1975). *Reflections on language.* New York: Random House.

Chomsky, N. (1981). *Lectures on government and binding.* Dordrecht, Netherlands: Foris Publications.

de Villiers, J. G., & de Villiers, P. A. (1973). A cross-sectional study of the acquisition of grammatical morphemes. *Journal of Psycholinguistic Research, 2,* 267–278.

Fodor, J. A. (1966). How to learn to talk: Some simple ways. In F. Smith & G. Miller (Eds.), *The genesis of language.* Cambridge, MA: MIT Press.

Gleitman, L. R. (1981). Maturational determinants of language growth. *Cognition, 10,* 103–114.

Grimshaw, J. (1981). Form, function, and the language acquisition device. In C. L. Baker & J. J. McCarthy (Eds.), *The logical problem of language acquisition.* Cambridge, MA: MIT Press.

Hakuta, K. (1982). Interaction between particles and word order in the comprehension and production of simple sentences in Japanese. *Developmental Psychology, 18,* 62–76.

Hirsh-Pasek, K., Treiman, R., & Schneiderman, M. (1984). Brown and Hanlon revisited: Mothers' sensitivity to ungrammatical forms. *Journal of Child Language, 11,* 81–88.

Keenan, E. O. (1976). Towards a universal definition of "subject". 'n C. Li (Ed.), *Subject and topic.* New York: Academic Press.

Kessel, F., & Brown, R., Chair. (1981, April 2–5). *The development of language and of language researchers: Whatever happened to linguistic theory?* Biennial Meeting of the Society for Research in Child Development, Boston.

Macnamara, J. (1982). *Names for things: A study of child language.* Cambridge, MA: Bradford Books/MIT Press.

Maratsos, M. P., & Chalkley, M. (1981). The internal language of children's syntax: the ontogenesis and representation of syntactic categories. In K. Nelson (Ed.), *Children's language* (Vol. 2). New York: Gardner Press.

Pinker, S. (1979). Formal models of language learning. *Cognition, 1,* 217–283.

Pinker, S. (1981a). What is a language, that a child may learn it, and a child, that he may learn a language? (Review of K. Wexler & P. Culicover, "Formal principles of language acquisition.") *Journal of Mathematical Psychology, 23,* 90–97.

Pinker, S. (1981b). On the acquisition of grammatical morphemes. *Journal of Child Language, 8,* 477–484.

Pinker, S. (1982). A theory of the acquisition of lexical interpretive grammars. In J. Bresnan (Ed.), *The mental representation of grammatical relations.* Cambridge, MA: MIT Press.

Pinker, S. (1984). *Language learnability and language development.* Cambridge, MA: Harvard University Press.

Pinker, S. (1986). Producitivity and conservatism in language acquisition. In A. Marras (Ed.), *Learning: Philosophical and foundational issues in concept and language acquisition.* Norwood, NJ: Ablex.

Pinker, S. (1987). The bootstrapping problem in language acquisition. In B. MacWhinney (Ed.), *Mechanisms of language acquisition.* Hillsdale, NJ: Lawrence Erlbaum Associates.

Pinker, S. (in press). Markedness and language development. In W. Demopoulous & R. May (Eds.), *Learnability and linguistic theory.* Dordrecht, Netherlands: Reidel.

Slobin, D. I. (1973). Cognitive prerequisites for the development of grammar. In C. Ferguson & D. I. Slobin (Ed.), *Studies of child language development.* New York: Holt, Rinehart, & Winston.

Slobin, D. I. (1982). Universal and particular in the acquisition of language. In E. Wanner & L. R. Gleitman (Eds.), *Language acquisition: The state of the art.* New York: Cambridge University Press.

Slobin, D. I. (1985). Crosslinguistic evidence for the language-making capacity. In D. I. Slobin (Ed.), *The crosslinguistic study of language acquisition, Volume 2: Theoretical issues.* Hillsdale, NJ: Lawrence Erlbaum Associates.

Wexler, K. (1979, June 4–8). *Untitled presentation at the Workshop on Learnability,* Laguna Beach, California.

Wexler, K., & Culicover, P. (1980) *Formal principles of language acquisition.* Cambridge, MA: MIT Press.

7 Crosslinguistic Analysis, Universals, and Language Acquisition

Michael Maratsos
University of Minnesota

One of the most important recent trends has been the search for universals—or universal gradients—among languages (e.g., Cole & Saddock, 1977; Comrie, 1981; Dixon, 1979; Li, 1976; Silverstein, 1973). Simultaneously, arguments from what languages are like in general, and what children's acquisition is like across different languages have increasingly shaped what we think about acquisition (Chomsky, 1965; Maratsos, 1983; Pinker, 1984; Slobin, 1986). Originally, for acquisition, much of the impetus for this came from Chomsky's work. If one is to claim that much of children's ability to acquire language is innate, one must identify what it is they know about languages before they begin. The most reasonable place to look for hypotheses concerning such knowledge is across languages: What is universal to languages provides likely candidates for what children might know innately. Or if one believes that children acquire language on the basis of universal cognitive abilities, much the same argument obtains: What kinds of cognitive or cognitive-seeming factors appear to shape languages universally? Such investigations provide at least candidates for cognitive properties central in organizing the acquisitional process (Slobin, 1973, for example).

In fact, a reading of the developing crosslinguistic literature gives one the feeling of a real linguistic bestiary. At the beginning of this century, anthropologists concluded on the basis of their initial look that languages could differ from one another in any number of ways (Bloomfield, 1933). Nor does much more turn out to be universal now (Bolinger, 1968). Th use of word order to determine semantic relations among nouns is certainly not (Hale, 1978). Nor, in fact,

121

is even the ready applicability of notions like subject and object (Li & Thompson, 1976).

The first purpose of this chapter might be called pedagogical: an introduction to some of the properties of language that may be universal with an aim towards seeing what really is universal versus what kinds of things are trends.

A second purpose is to derive some general conclusions or grounds for speculation about acquisition from this work. I conclude, for example, that only a few semantic properties universally provide bases for grammatical category analysis by the child acquiring language. These include the distinction between predicate and argument, the interpretation of concrete terms as first-order arguments, and the nuclear versus nonnuclear arguments of a predicate, along with certain basic processes and meanings of predication as a process.

Third, I develop the following idea about the relation of children's grammatical analysis to crosslinguistic trends. There are indeed susceptibilities to various clusters of grammatical processes going together; for example, agency often controls grammatical properties such as verb agreement, complement noun phrase coreference, and others. These susceptibilities exist for natural reasons and show up in the trend of the world's languages. At the same time, though often overwhelming, they show up as no more than trends. I argue that their potential role in shaping languages is thus very great; but that in the words of Ecclesiates paraphrased, "time and accident happeneth to all languages." Further, I suggest that children's flexibility in dealing with such accidents is very much greater than either nativists such as Grimshaw and Pinker (e.g., Pinker, 1984) or semantic pragmaticists such as Schlesinger and Bates and McWhinney (Bates & McWhinney, 1982; Schlesinger, 1974) have argued. I make this contention at some peril to my own beliefs, however: first, because I do believe some semantic-pragmatic analyses are so basic as to be the kinds of givens all analysts require; second, children are clearly expert at finding the relevance of other such analyses in languages. What I wish to distinguish is inevitability (which I take, for example, to be characteristic of the analysis of object words as first-order arguments of predicates) versus susceptibility (for example, the association of topichood with various clusters of grammatical properties). And among the latter kinds of properties I wish to distinguish those that seem to operate more strongly on the equilibrational processes that result in languages per se from those that result in a particular child's language acquisition.

The chapter thus divides into two sections: a survey of the crosslinguistic bestiary, and an acquisitional section divided into a number of subsections. (In an Addendum I provide some historical notes.) A prior introduction of vocabulary is needed, however, to provide an explicit and consistent grounding for the discussion. If it is to be possible to consider whether or not a language has subject and object, for example, it must be possible to talk about its grammatical combinations in a more neutral and general way.

AN INTRODUCTORY VOCABULARY

Predicates and Arguments Defined

The basic function of simple sentences in any language is to state some property of things or some relation between one or more of them. The sentence "John is happy" asserts happiness as a property of John, the sentence "John likes marigolds" asserts a relation of fond affect between John and marigolds, and the sentence "John is in the yard" asserts a locative relation of containment between John and the yard, such that the yard contains John.

In many such English sentences, the various forms of the verb *be* are grammatically central. But it is hard to say they carry much of the semantic weight of the sentence. Children commonly do without *be* early on ("he big") as do many languages ("he big" is a good sentence of Chinese). So the clear semantic weight of the sentences falls on terms like *John, happy, in,* and *marigolds.*

At a broad level, such basic content words fall into two major categories: *predicates,* i.e., words that denote relations or properties and arguments of the predicate, i.e., words or phrases that denote what entities are thus being described or related. Thus, if x refers to some property of y, or some relation between y and z, x is said to be a predicate of y or y and z.

Predications as Parts of Arguments: Specifiers Versus Heads

The uses of predications vary. In particular, every language has devices for including a predicate as part of an argument. There is, however, a crucial difference in whether the embedded predicate is a specifier within the argument or the head of the argument. For example, in the sentence, "he remembers the big dog," the main argument-predicate structure is "he – remembers – the big dog." In the sentence, "He remembers the dog is big," it is "he – remembers – the dog is big." In both, bigness is predicated of "the dog," and the predication is part of the second argument of "remembers." In "he – remembers – the big dog," however, what he remembers is the dog. *Big* is predicated of *dog* to specify or describe the dog; in "he – remembers – the dog is big," what he remembers is the bigness of the dog. Thus, in the second case, the predication "dog big" comprises the argument and, if anything, the predicate is the head of the argument.

Nuclear Versus Nonnuclear Arguments

The arguments of a simple sentence may, however, differ in centrality vis-a-vis the main predicate. For example, in the sentence, "John ate eggs near Mary," just *John* and *eggs* are considered nuclear arguments of *eat;* Mary is also considered an argument of *eat,* but a nonnuclear one.

The reason for this is often straightforward. Essentially, an argument is a nuclear argument of a predicate if its specific meaning is given by combination with the main predicate per se. Thus, in "John ate eggs near Mary," there are three major argument terms or phrases: *John, eggs,* and *Mary.* John is specifically described as being an eater, the eggs, as eaten, and Mary as providing a place of orientation for the location of the action. Clearly, John is given that role by the predicate *eat,* as is *eggs.* Contrastively, the fact that Mary is a location point for the event of eating is not given by the verb *eat* per se, but by the combination of the general actional meeting of *eat* with the specific locative meaning of *in.* If *because of* were used instead (e.g., John ate dinner because of Mary), *Mary* would not have the same argument role.

Similarly, there are syntactically main and nonmain predicates of various kinds. In "John sang for his mother," tensing, negation, and other central operations can only be performed vis-a-vis *sing,* not *for.* Thus, *sang* is the main predicate, whereas *for* is some kind of adjunct. Predicates such as *for* seem to attain greater main predicate status if there is no predicate with a higher status in the sentence, however. For example, in "It was for his mother," the tense marking clearly refers to the relation denoted by *for.* And some other predicates are so demoted in status that they do not appear as separate words; for example, in many languages, locative relations are suffixes on the noun.

Role Relations

Predicates typically denote different roles vis-a-vis one another for their arguments. Thus, in "John likes Mary," *like* is a two-argument predicate denoting a relation of positive affect between some animate being and some cause or source of the affect. Which argument is in which role is typically marked by some grammatical device. Some of the general semantic relations, such as agency, often have a standard set of marking devices in the language.

Pragmatic Variables

Givenness, specificity, focus, and discourse topic are instances here. Specificity is exemplified by contrasting "John wants a watch," where the most likely interpretation for *a watch* is nonspecific because no particular watch is meant, and "There's a watch that John wants," where *a watch* does refer to a specific watch. Givenness refers to something already available for reference in the conversation for speaker and listener. Thus, in "There's a watch John wants; the watch costs $300," *the watch* is specific and given, because of the prior reference to a specific watch. Generics, as in "elephants have long tusks," can be considered given as well (Chafe, 1976). In English, definite references are typically to arguments that are both specific and given.

Focus refers to some emphasis on an argument (or predicate) as a choice between alternatives, or contrast to alternatives. It is best exemplified in discourses. For example, "Who did Mary see yesterday?" "Mary saw *John.*" "Mary kissed Sam, didn't she?" "No, Mary kissed *Harold.*" The underlined arguments are focused.

A discourse topic is just that, what the discourse is about. Thus, in the following conversation, the underlined references to vase are to the main discourse topic: "What happened to your vase?" "Someone broke *it* at our party. We took *it* to the best repair shop in the city, but the fellow there said he couldn't fix *it*. *It's* a genuine Ming vase, too."

Grammatical Devices

Order.   Languages often mark predicate-argument role relations with some standard, or at least unmarked order. Thus, in English the standard order is to put agent arguments before the actional predicate, and patient (affected entity) arguments afterwards.

Morphological Marking.   Languages may also mark predicate-argument relations of various kinds with bound morphemes attached to the beginning, end, or middle of terms. Thus, whereas Turkish allows any order of agent, action, and patient, definite patients (more generally, definite grammatical objects) are marked with an inflection on the argument (Slobin, 1982). Some languages, like German, use combinations of morphology and order to mark relations.

Tone.   Basic role relations may also be marked with different tonal inflections. For example, Masai, a Nilo–Saharan language, marks the accusative case by a particular tone inflection (Keenan, 1976b). More generally, intonation patterns may mark a great variety of important variables. In English, for example, focus is often marked by stress and intonation pattern.

Agreement.   Often, aspects of an argument of a predicate are marked morphologically on its predicate. Thus, in English, third person singular of the initial argument is marked by -*s* on certain classes of predicates (e.g., *he sings*).

Reduced Reference, Omitted Reference, and Control of Coreference

One of the central phenomena of all languages is the presence of devices for referring in a reduced way to various parts of sentences, such that the speech context or the sentential context has to be used to fill in the reference. One form of reduced reference is the use of pronouns. *He*, for example, means "some male, the reference of which can be unambiguously analyzed from the speech or sentential context; most prominent singular male being discussed in this context."

Another form of reduced reference is complete reduction—that is, complete omission. Some omissions are simply vague. For example, if we say "John ate," it is necessarily true that he ate something, given the semantic nature of *eat*. But *eat* allows omission of any reference to the eaten thing argument when the reference is unknown or uninteresting. Another form, however, is completely controlled coreference; that is, nothing, or 0, in certain grammatical contexts, takes on as definite a meaning as a fuller reference would. Thus, "Mary will eat lobsters, and John will 0 also" does not mean "Mary will eat lobsters and John will do something also"; it means he will also eat lobsters. Similarly, consider the sentences (1) John$_i$ went to the restaurant and John$_i$ ordered lobsters, and (2) John$_i$ went to the restaurant and 0$_i$ ordered lobsters. Needless to say, in (2) the reference of the omitted first argument is very definite; it can only mean that John ordered lobsters. Unlike the 0 of "John ate 0" (that is, "John ate"), here it cannot mean some vague, unspecified reference.

0-reference is often strictly controlled in complement clauses as well. Thus, the sentence "John wants 0 to kiss Mary" can only mean John wants himself to be the one who kisses Mary. On the other hand, "John wants Mary to kiss 0" might mean he wants her to kiss someone, which might include him. But it certainly does not have to have *John* be the coreferent of 0.

Rules for the control of coreference differ from language to language. Many languages, for example, are far more liberal than English in allowing omission of contextually or sententially available coreference. But some set of such regulations for controlling possible reference of pronouns or omitted references are found in every language. Consequently, they play an important part in crosslinguistic studies.

With this vocabulary in mind, I now turn to a discussion of some important crosslinguistic patterns. I begin with form classes; that is, intrinsic formal categorizations of individual terms such as noun, verb, adjective, preposition. Then, I consider crosslinguistic similarities and differences in the organization of grammatical relations like subject and object.

CROSSLINGUISTIC PATTERNS

Form Classes

The Universality of Nouns; the Nonuniversality of Particular Predicate Classes. Lyons (1968) and other non-Chinese linguists who describe Chinese suggest that it does not have adjectives or prepositions, only verbs. Obviously, this does not mean that Chinese has no words that mean the same as English adjectives like *big* or *smart,* or no words that convey the meanings of *at* or *in.* So what does it mean? In the last year, I had an opportunity and some reason to study Chinese, and so I could find out.

At the very broad descriptive level of predicate versus argument as set out earlier, the different meanings conveyed by terms like *run, hit, want, big, smart,* or *at* are all predicates: terms that convey a relation among or property of, entities. What Chinese does is to treat all such terms similarly enough grammatically, such that the linguist assigns them all to a single syntactic class. Consider negation. In English, adjectives and prepositions must be negated with a form of *be* (e.g., "he isn't fond of ducks," "he isn't for her"). Verbs, and only main verbs, can take a preceding form of *do* to convey similar negative meaning (e.g., "he doesn't like her," "they don't favor her"). But in Chinese, all the different predicates previously mentioned are negated the same way: The negative particle is *bu* placed before them. In translation, one says "he no run," "he no hit ball," "he no want ball," "he no big," "he no at Beijing."

The same applies to tense and aspect. In English, adjectives and prepositions require these to be marked on a form of *be,* e.g., "he was fond of her," "he was for her," "he is being nasty to her." Verbs may be marked directly on the stem for the same properties: "he liked her," "he was acting badly to her." In Chinese there is a single central aspect marker—*le.* It can mark completion relative to the time of discourse, or coming into being of the relation, depending on the semantic nature of the predicate. But it can be marked similarly on all of the different meanings: In effect, one says, "he run-le," "he hit-le ball," "he want-le ball," "he big-le," "he at-le Beijing." Very simply, because of their common grammatical treatment, Chinese is considered to have a single category of major predicates to cover essentially the same semantic ground covered in English by three major classes: verbs, adjectives, and prepositions.

In addition to Chinese having only verbs as major predicates, many other languages from different languages groups, such as American Indian, Philippine, and African languages, are similarly described by linguists. Many of these, unlike Chinese, are richly inflected. But the basic grounds for collapsing the predicates into a single syntactic category are similar: They act similarly in properties such as agreement, tensing, negation, and the manner of arranging major arguments. In effect, in these other languages, one says, "he sicks" or "he happies" or "he doesn't happy" just as one says "he runs" or "he doesn't like it" in English. These predicates are typically called verbs by Indo–European linguists because the largest number refer to meanings covered by verbs in Indo–European languages. It would be more neutral simply to say that such languages have nouns and predicates.

Nouns, of course, are simply the class of terms whose chief designated function is to serve as the arguments of predicates. They always include, and center on, the terms referring to concrete objects (including animates and inanimates) in languages. Apparently, every language has just one such category.

Thus, the universal minimum complement of major form classes is two: a major argument category centered on concrete objects, and a major predicate category. Predicate categories may be subdivided into two or more major categories, such as verb and adjective, but the argument category retains a unity that makes it a singular class universally.

Subdivisions of Predicate Categories. Subdivisions Within Languages: Formal Versus Semantic Divisions.   Predicates within a language are virtually always subdivided in the language along certain dimensions. Even in Chinese, linguists speak of coverbs versus main verbs. There is also a difference in Chinese between stative and process verbs. For example, stative predicates can all take *hen* to denote high comparative degree, roughly the meaning denoted by *very*. One can say "he very sick" or "he very big." One can also say "he very want ball," because *want* is a stative.

This points out a difference between a true semantic subdivision among predicates and a formal one. In English, verbs may be stative (such as *want, like, know, belong*) or process (such as *hit* or *melt*). Because verbs may also apply in comparative degree, we can speak of them this way: for example, "he wants the ball a lot," or "he really wants the ball." But despite the obvious semantic similarity between "a lot" or "really" and "very," "very" is reserved for use with the formal adjective class. So one cannot say "he very wants the ball," as one in effect does in Chinese. Thus, English verbs are distinguished from adjectives by distributional differences in how they carry out many of the same combinatorial functions; that is, by differences in how combinations expressing the same semantic function are expressed (Maratsos & Chalkley, 1980).

Demotion of Predicates.   Earlier, I mentioned the phenomenon of syntactic demotion of predicates; that is, failing to retain syntactic properties common to main syntactic predicates in certain circumstances. This occurs universally in languages, and there are semantic gradients that tend to describe its likelihood across languages. Consider the main Chinese predicate *zai,* which basically means "at." When it is the only predicate of a sentence, it acts like other main predicates. Suppose, however, that one of its arguments is itself a predication; that is, suppose we are speaking of someone named John eating at Beijing. The semantic first argument of *zai* is what is located at the location designated by the second argument, e.g., "John zai Beijing" = 'located object—*zai*—location." Logically, then, "John ate at Beijing" should have the order "John ate—at—Beijing," because John's eating was located at Beijing. Instead, however, one says, "John zai Beijing ate." Furthermore, when *zai* is so placed, it cannot be given aspect with *-le* or be negated with *bu*. Thus, *zai* is syntactically demoted.

Across languages, there are definite semantic trends in the likely demotability of a predicate: predicates that denote tense, aspect, and negation are highly demotable, followed by locative relations, intransitive stative relations, transitive stative relations, and actional relations. This can be seen as being directly related to event relations, in particular to notions of salience. Again, however, when a language formalizes predicate divisions, the hierarchy becomes formalized.

Thus, in English, verbs, whether actional or not, are the least demoteable predicates, and prepositions, among the major form classes, are the most demoteable.

To conclude this section on form classes, note that among the world's languages the presence of a single chief argument category, centered on concrete object terms, is universal. All languages also have at least one major predicate category. But the number of predicate categories or subcategories may differ, as may the grounds for their differentiation. In particular, distinctions such as adjective versus verb are based on structural differentiations: differences in how the same semantic combinatorial function is carried out. Languages may differ in how many such formally distinguished predicate categories they contain.

Nuclear Grammatical Relations

Grammatical Subject Systems and Accusative Systems.   One of the major efforts of linguistics recently has been to evaluate the universality of categories such as subject and object (e.g., Anderson, 1976; Cole & Saddock, 1977; Comrie, 1981; Dixon, 1979; Li, 1976; Schachter, 1976), and to specify what such categories might mean (Keenan, 1976b). I cannot deal with this work completely here. But what is possible, and useful, is to begin with a brief summary of some such major subject-related properties.

All languages have intransitive sentences; that is, predications with only one nuclear argument. At least for intransitive predications, if there is a standard subject, it must be this argument. The following are semantic and grammatical properties that tend to obtain for such intransitive arguments.

1. Common syntactic ordering. Languages tend to have a standard ordering for the intransitive argument and the main predicate of a sentence. Thus, in English, despite their obvious semantic role dissimilarities, the following all have the same order: he — ran; he — was big; he — is here; he — laughed; he — was sad.

(This is not uninteresting; one might easily imagine that some language would have one order for intransitive arguments of actional predicates, for example, and a different order for intransitive arguments of nonactional predicates.)

2. Common morphological marking. In many languages, predicate-argument order used to signal semantic role-relations order is freer than in English. In some cases (e.g., Warlpiri; Hale, 1978), it is impossible to detect even tendencies to a central order. Generally, such freer order languages mark arguments morphologically to specify their semantic and grammatical roles. The only vestige of such a morphological system is in English in the nominative-objective pronoun marking system, e.g., *he–him, she–her, they–them.* The nominative forms (*she, he, they*) are used for all intransitive arguments of finite clauses regardless of

semantic role, e.g., she — ran, they — were big, he — is sad. In languages such as Russian or Turkish, the full noun stems themselves are marked for grammatical case which in turn signals grammatical relations.

3. Common tone. As mentioned earlier, some languages indicate role relations through tone and so give a common tone to the intransitive argument (e.g., Masai).

4. Control of agreement markers. Commonly the intransitive argument controls agreement markers, such as markers for number and person of the argument, or its animacy or definiteness on the main predicate, or on an auxiliary verb of the predicate (e.g., he see+s vs. they see+0; he is happy vs. they are happy).

5. Control of argument deletion in complements. If the intransitive argument of a complement is identical in reference to an argument of the matrix predicate, it can often be deleted (in infinitival or gerundial complements). Thus, *he wants 0 to go* = "he$_i$ wants that he$_i$ go."

6. Control of argument deletion across conjunctions. The intransitive argument can be deleted under identity across conjunction: He went home and 0 was quiet for his mother = "he$_i$ went home and he$_i$ was quiet for his mother."

7. Tendency to be specific, given, and definite. In English, it is possible for an intransitive argument to be completely nonspecific, nongiven, and indefinite, e.g., "No one came." Overwhelmingly, however, the intransitive argument is semantically specific, given, and definite in reference. In some languages, intransitive arguments must be given or definite (Keenan, 1976b).

Generally, such properties apply to the intransitive arguments regardless of whether they are agents. They can be passive experiencer of emotion, or located objects, e.g., "the vase had fallen off the table and so 0 was no longer upright" means the vase was no longer upright.

As noted already, such properties tend to be true of the intransitive arguments in given languages. English has hardly any morphology at all; Warlpiri has no standard predicate-argument order (Hale, 1978). Some languages may have no number–person agreement on predicates (e.g., Chinese). But across all languages, intransitive arguments tend to have such properties.

Now consider the case of sentences with two nuclear arguments. How will these tend to act vis-a-vis the grammatical properties characteristic of the intransitive subject?

The most familiar (and common) pattern is called the *accusative* pattern. Because English is a member of this class, the pattern is easily described: One argument of the two nuclear arguments is assigned grammatical properties similar to those of the intransitive subject. Furthermore, this tends to be the animate argument if one argument is naturally animate (e.g., for verbs like *see*, the seer is naturally animate). More particularly, if one of the arguments is an agent, this is in the unmarked or normal case assigned these grammatical properties. Even in such languages, the relevant properties need not hang together perfectly. For example, in Vietnamese, either agentive or patientlike can control complement coreference. Thus, one can say either "Mary want 0_i kiss John" ('Mary wants to kiss John') or "Mary$_i$ want John kiss 0_i" ('Mary wants John to kiss her') (Comrie, 1981). But on the whole, in accusative languages, the agent is marked like the intransitive argument. The transitive patient is thus the grammatically distinctive nuclear argument.

Ergative Systems: Control of "Subject" Properties by Patients.   This confluence of intransitive argument properties on the transitive agent is the most common case, but it falls short of universality. In some languages, some of the important intransitive argument properties are assigned not to the agent but to the patient of the transitive agent–patient verbs. Such languages are called ergative languages.

Pure Ergative Languages.   A very few recorded languages, such as Australian or Dyirbal or ancient Hurrian (Dixon, 1979), appear to be virtually pure ergative languages; that is virtually all the important properties typically assigned to the intransitive argument are assigned to the patient, and related arguments in transitive sentences. Such languages are never argument–predicate–(argument) languages, so that it cannot be judged whether or not the patient occupies the most usual word position of the intransitive subject. But the patient typically has the same morphological marking as the intransitive subject (called the absolutive marking). The transitive agent contrastively has a distinctive marking, usually called the ergative. Thus, the morphology is the mirror image of an accusative language. Agreement properties are also controlled by the transitive patient; the transitive patient tends to have the specificity, givenness, and definiteness properties of the intransitive subject. Finally, the transitive patient controls coreference in complements and conjuncts. Thus, in Dyirbal, the equivalent of "John wants to kiss Mary" would be said something like "John wants John kiss Mary" (actually, patients tend to precede agents; I am anglicizing these translations). The equivalent of "John$_i$ wants Mary to kiss him$_i$" would be said something like "John wants Mary to kiss 0_i," which definitely means Mary is to kiss John. Similarly, "John went home and his mother kissed 0_i" means his mother kissed John. "John$_i$ went home and 0_i kissed his mother" is not possible.

Interestingly enough, languages like Dyirbal always have what linguists call an antipassive (Dixon, 1979): These are special morphological markings on the noun or verb or both so that the transitive agent argument can acquire the grammatical properties of the intransitive subject. This is the mirror image of the passive of accusative languages.

Mixed Ergativity.   Unlike nearly pure accusative languages, which are quite common, nearly pure ergative languages like Dyirbal are extremely rare. Much more common are languages that are ergative for some grammatical properties under some grammatical circumstances, but not for all. Nor does it appear to be random which properties are more likely to be accusative rather than ergative. Long-range coreferental control operations like complement or conjunct omission under identity are virtually always accusative in pattern with conjunction being slightly more likely to be ergative (Anderson, 1976; Comrie, 1981). Ergativity is far more likely to be found in the morphological semantic role-marking properties of a language.

Moreover, even these are likely to be ergative only under some conditions. Georgian (in the U.S.S.R.), for example, is morphologically ergative in some combinations of aspect and tense but not in others. Within languages, first and second persons are much more likely to be marked accusatively, and third person sentences, to be marked ergatively (Silverstein, 1976).

Other Kinds of Nuclear Argument Systems

Ergative systems nevertheless resemble accusative systems in one way: It is worthwhile for the language learner to set up two major nuclear argument categories. In a pure ergative language, one can treat the transitive patient-like arguments similarly to the intransitive subject, and the agent-like argument differently. Even in mixed ergative languages, once one has analyzed which properties go which way, it is still worth having two major argument categories in terms of which to analyze the nuclear argument of transitive predications. These can be generatively assigned as matching intransitive subject behavior or not for each predicate after the conditions for each property marking are learned.

On the other hand, there are types of sentence organization in many languages for which a subject–object axis of some kind does not appear to be nearly as central in the language as a whole.

Topic-Oriented Systems. As mentioned before, another important variable is discourse topic. In many languages, this can control grammatical properties like those controlled by grammatical subject. For example, in Chinese, certain complement deletion properties are still controlled by traditional accusative-like grammatical subjects; that is, *I want to go* means "I want that I go," for example. On the other hand, Chinese has a distinct grammatical construction of discourse topic. It is found clearly in sentences like "elephant(s)-(topic marker), tusk very big," or "Beijing, Harry no go." Obviously, discourse topic in this sense is not confined to agents or patients. In fact, it need not be one of the nuclear or even oblique arguments of the main predicate at all (Li & Thompson, 1976). This discourse topic can control properties like those controlled by subjects. For example, in Chinese, it controls sentence-initial position, as in the preceding example. It can control omission across a number of sentences, e.g.,

"This table-(topic marker), 0 too expensive, I no like 0_i, no buy 0_i." It can also control 0-reference across some types of conjunction, e.g., "this person$_i$, people no like, so 0_i leave party." In such a sentence, 0 can only refer to the discourse topic. The sentence cannot mean "this person, people no like, so they leave party."

Chinese is thus a language in which both topic and accusative subjects have some relevance. There also appears to be languages in which *only* topic controls grammatical properties in important ways. Thus, in Lisu, Li and Thompson report that topic consistently controls a number of critical properties such as sentence-initial position and omission across clauses. Agent and patient arguments, contrastively, are not distinguished by grammatical order or morphology. (This is so except in the unusual case where neither is presupposed, that is, sentences equivalent to "someone ate something," in which case the agent is ordered before the patient.)

Other Types of Systems. Even greater drift off of the subject–object axis is apparently possible. Schachter (1976) remarks on Tagalog, a Philippine language, that its subject-like properties are split between what looks like accusative subject and something else that is often called topic, but in fact, is simply givenness. Briefly, in Tagalog, omission and definite coreference assignment in complements are controlled by the usual accusative agent-centered type of accusative argument; that is, one says, in effect, "I want 0_i to kiss Mary." But a couple of important properties often associated with subject are not accusatively controlled. Each sentence in Tagalog has to give at least one argument that is pragmatically given. If the sentence has a verb, the verb must have an agreement marker that marks the grammatical case (nominative, accusative, dative, or benefactive, typically) of this given argument. But the argument does not have to be the discourse topic or the agent even if the sentence obviously has one. For example, suppose someone asks, "Where's Maria?" Someone could answer "work (agreement with locative marker), her house (givenness marker)," or they could answer "work—agreement with agent, Maria—givenness marker or her house—locative marker"; that is, clearly Maria is the discourse topic, and also agent. But the givenness marker simply has to be assignable to one of the noun phrase arguments of the sentence; and the verb simply has to agree in the grammatical case with whichever one this is. Because givenness is part of discourse topic, this resembles control by discourse topic; but it is not.

This second property has to do with relativization. Briefly, Keenan and Comrie (Keenan, 1976b; Keenan & Comrie, 1979) have found across languages that, in general, there is a hierarchy of relativizability (omission ability of an argument in a relative clause): in some languages, just the subject and object; in some languages, just the subject, object, indirect object, and so on. (In English, virtually any grammatical relation can be.) In Tagalog, there is such a constraint;

it is just the givenness-marked noun phrase that can be relativized. As Schachter says, complement coreference control in Tagalog acts like a normal accusative language. But relativizability and agreement control on the verb, typical subject properties, are controlled by givenness (which does not mean discourse topic, agent, or patient, in particular).

Finally, there are well known languages (e.g., Dakota, (Chafe, 1976)) in which intransitive subjects are marked by one morphological marker, and transitive arguments are each marked by individual markers of their own. This may obtain for noun phrase stems, or just pronouns, or both, depending on the language. Presumably, control of complement coreference is accusative.

Discussion

Very clearly, one does not find universally across languages the kind of subject–object nuclear argument organization characteristic of accusative languages such as English. What every language appears to have in common is the existence of predicates that take one nuclear argument and predicates that take two. Beyond that, there are various properties that can converge or diverge in varying types of association, both within and across transitive and intransitive predications, properties such as discourse topichood, unmarked predicate topic, givenness, specificity, agentivity, marking agreement marking, undergoing strictly controlled 0-coreference, and control of relativizability.

There are more or less natural lines of association of properties. But example after example indicates that none of these corelations is universal. For the speaker of an accusative language like English, it is natural to think of things in a certain way: Grammatical properties like order or morphology or agreement will be associated with the argument the predication is about. More subtly, one can see how properties like relativizability and omission with completely defined 0-coreference would also be associated with being what the predication is about. For example, a relative clause specifies or modifies a head noun phrase. So it is no surprise that if anything in a language can be relativized within a clause, it is the argument that is the idealized topic of the clause predicate, that is, the subject. Similar arguments can be made as to why the complement subject is what is omitted with securely controlled definite coreference. This may occur because the argument that the predicate is about is typically specified and given. So even under omission because of redundancy, the argument will be most likely, in a metaphorical sense, to demand a definite coreference, rather than settling for a vaguer reference.

It is natural that such properties would gravitate towards the intransitive subject. For a predicate's only nuclear argument is obviously what the predicate is typically about. The transitive predicate contrastively is centrally about two arguments. But of the two of these, it is natural to see the agent or animate experiencer as what the predicate is more centrally about. A narrative, for example, is typically about what people do and feel, especially do. So the agent, or agent-like arguments, would tend to be given the various order-, morphological-, coreference demanding, or other properties characteristic of the intransitive subject. The intransitive subject and transitive agent each are the natural "subject" or discussion and so control similar properties. The fact that the grammatical direct object (the second nuclear argument) can most easily be placed in a similar property-controlling position, by the passive, follows from the fact that it is the other argument that the predicate is centrally about.

What do the crosslinguistic data indicate about this "natural" picture? They indicate that it probably has something to it. For the accusative pattern is quite common, perhaps the most common among the world's languages; or, at least, having a strong element of accusativity is. Nevertheless, the pattern is clearly not so natural as to be universal. I focus now on a few points that seem to stand out.

For one thing, we cannot simply reliably describe the grammatical subject as being what an ongoing discourse is about. This point is already obvious from previous examples. (For example, in "Where's the vase?" "Someone broke it, and we couldn't get it fixed," *it* refers to the vase that is clearly the discourse topic (or one of them), but *it* is grammatical object.) In languages with a true discourse topic as a prominent grammatical feature, this is even more obvious. As shown in the previous discussion, such languages may lack much control of subject-like grammatical properties by either of the nuclear arguments (e.g., Lisu). Also, when the true discourse topic is actually made grammatically prominent, it is clear it not only does not have to be the transitive agent (e.g., "this table-(topic marker), I no like0_i, we no buy0_j); it does not even have to be one of the nuclear arguments at all, e.g., "elephant, tusk very big" or "that field, people no can grow rice."

There is thus only one way of seeing the grammatical subject, whether intransitive subject or transitive agent-experiencer, as being connected to the idea of being what the discourse is about. This is to imagine an idealized equilibration or tabulation over all discourses, such that the subject of the predicate attains an idealized or unmarked status as the normal argument about which the predicate says something. It is as though the language had only one transitive and one intransitive sentence to say, and for the transitive predication, chose an animate agent as what that sentence was likely to be about. Less romantically, one might think of it as an idealization of statistical predicate-scope trends. But despite the unmarked status of subject as what the predicate is about having complex interactions with the grammar, it cannot actually be understood reasonably as an argument that a particular discourse is necessarily about, or the argument from the perspective of which or whom the predication is necessarily seen (see Kuno, 1976, for examples of the contrary). One must say this without denying what appears to be a kind of overall equilibratory effect this has on the forms of grammar across different languages. But it must be understood clearly nevertheless.

Second, the crosslinguistic data indicate that even when the intransitive subject does consistently control various clusters of grammatical properties, the transitive agent does not inevitably control the same or similiar properties. Again, this is not to deny an overall trend. Overall, the transitive agent nearly always controls properties such as controlled 0-coreference in complements and conjunctions, or other major scope operations. It usually also controls semantic role marking morphological properties, though less reliably. Even when it does not, the transitive agent-experiencer tends to retain or lose control systematically, according to various pragmatically explicable gradients, such as that first- and second-person agent animates are treated similarly versus third-person arguments (see Comrie, 1981, Dixon, 1979, Silverstein, 1976 for discussion).

Nevertheless, there do exist languages in which important role-marking morphological properties, and sometimes coreference-control operations, are given to the nonanimate-agent argument in varying degrees; and there even can exist languages, such as Dyirbal, with stable and consistent organization in which patients and related nuclear arguments consistently control intransitive subject properties of all the major kinds.

Third, the data indicate that even when an argument of the predicate of some type controls central grammatical properties, it is not necessarily even a nuclear argument that does so. Schachter's (1976) discussion of Philippine Tagalog shows how simple givenness per se, divorced from discourse topichood or nuclear argumenthood, may control some subject-typical properties. One is tempted to account for this as a historical accident; that is, givenness became detached rather randomly from its status as just one of the properties of the grammatical subject and came to control some subject-typical properties independently. But this is obviously not known, nor known, if true, to a child learning the language.

Thus, what we have as universal is the occurrence of one-and two-argument nuclear predications (period). These may—or may not—have various semantic and grammatical properties distributed on them in various ways. The statistical pattern of property convergence across languages is not random, but no single convergence of properties is universal.

Both the linguist and the psycholinguist can find much of interest—more or less overlapping interest—in these problems. The same might be said of the psychologist viewing the problem of language formation in a community as compared with viewing language acquisition in the individual child. What are overall susceptibilities in languages to various gradients or similarities may be more or less compelling as favored possibilities to individual children. Obviously, no one can solve this problem in an a priori fashion. Nevertheless, in the last section, I draw a few speculations or conclusions from this discussion of the crosslinguistic data.

SOME ACQUISITIONAL REFLECTIONS

The Universality of the Predicate-Argument Division

Travel abroad is supposed to have the effect of being broadening. Work in cross-cultural linguistics and acquisition (e.g., see discussions in Brown, 1973, Bowerman, 1973, Slobin, 1982) may consistently be said to have the same effect.

In fact, a crosslinguistic survey shows very little to be truly universal, though many things frequently recur. In regard to major sentence structure and the formal categories, two things may be said to be of central importance. First, all languages have at least two major form classes, one that contains the basic argument terms (nouns) and another that contains the predicate terms. Second, every language has main predicates that take either one nuclear argument (intransitives) or two (transitives). The first fact is relevant to the divisions of the major form classes; the second to the major grammatical relations.

It is clear that across the world's languages, for the form classes, the predicate-argument division is fundamental. If we go by our linguistic intuitions, when the basic two categories—the basic cells of grammatical combination—embryologically split, only one of them splits in a basic way, the predicate category. Every known language retains one and just one argument category of nouns, and the predicates may split into two or more major categories. What is familiar is that the category of nouns, which includes common nouns, proper names, and pronouns, hangs together in a reasonably similar way across languages. What is unfamiliar is that, in languages such as Chinese, terms as diverse in meaning as *hit, like, big, see, at, enough,* and *be* (class membership only), terms that seem so semantically diverse and automatically diverse in their entailments for grammatical division, are in fact treated syntactically in highly similar ways; that is, they are similar how they take nuclear arguments and are treated for major predicate operations such as aspect and negation operations. The treatment is so similar that the linguist feels justified in grouping these all together as verbs, despite subdivisions for various operations along semantic lines.

The fact that languages taken as a whole reflect a major predicate-argument split in their central form classes supports what authors like Braine (1976) and, more tentatively, Maratsos and Chalkley (1980) have generally claimed either as an analytic necessity (Braine, 1976) or useful tool (Maratsos & Chalkley, 1980): the utility of the hypothesis that children necessarily analyze along the dimension of predication. The crosslinguistic data actually display languages that take this split division as central to the basic categorial repertoire of the language in a direct way. This supports not just the theoretical utility but also the psychological reality of the distinction; that is, it is reasonable to propose that analysis in terms of predicate and argument is one of the automatic ways in which children analyze relations among parts of grammatical strings.

Given that any number of other properties and relations must also be analyzed in parallel to give the actual diverse categorial systems of languages, this may not seem like very much of an advance, of much significance. But, in fact, in conjunction with some other reasonable assumptions, the analysis can help make more sensible aspects of acquisition that seem peculiar at first glance, not to mention theories of acquisition (e.g., that in Maratsos & Chalkley, 1980).

For example, Maratsos and Chalkley (1980) employ predicate and argument as a terminologically neutral division but do not assume its psychological reality. This had an implicit consequence: It was not used as a defining factor when not necessary. Thus, in our discussion of predicate subdivisions such as verb versus adjective, this led to a concentration on the small marker combinations that distinguish these classes as defining properties; e.g., verbs take tense and aspect markers on the stem itself (*pushed, likes*) whereas adjectives do not (**pushies, fonds of*) but must instead use a form of *be* to be marked for similar semantic properties (*was pushy, is fond of*).

In fact, I do not think it is insignificant that a language such as Chinese, which has no formal division among stative and active terms or anything corresponding to verb–adjective throughout the grammar, also has very little morphology or small marker combinations; and these few are not used obligatorily as in English. Small marker combinations in general appear to be central in differentiating many formal categories such as verb versus adjective, or noun gender categories (e.g., German—MacWhinney, 1978; Maratsos & Chalkley, 1980).

But an analysis without predicate versus argument function has two major difficulties. First, it implies that the categories themselves have no distinguishing semantic properties at all, that their defining properties are purely distributional. Second, without predicate versus argument function, problems of major constituent structure cannot be dealt with because these can only be captured by appeal to properties such as what serves to predicate what properties or relations of what.

In fact, verbs and adjectives share an important combinatorial semantic property that serves to distinguish them from nouns. Their primary function is to serve as predicates of arguments, whereas nouns are terms whose primary function is to serve as arguments of predications. Thus, to be a predicate is a defining property of a verb. This is not enough to distinguish verbs from adjectives. This is much like saying that knives and guns both have as distinguishing properties that they are weapons; that is, instruments whose primary function is to harm living creatures. The fact that they carry out this function in different ways, and have different appearances, is what further distinguishes them from each other. In other words, verbs and adjectives have similar major functions but carry these out in combination with other elements in different ways (and have different appearances, if one thinks of what kinds of things can be added to stems as a type of appearance). Thus, the semantic property of being a predicate does not distinguish verbs from adjectives but nevertheless is a distinctive property of both classes.

In addition, it is likely earlier combinatorial properties that are definable with predicate-argument functions could well play a role in the earlier part of formal category organization, as well as whatever other intrinsic properties of arguments and predicates turn out to be relevant in a given language. For example, consider the following properties that might be analyzed at a point in acquisition when a child mostly analyzes sequences of two or three stressed major terms for combinations: Among other things, the child might register that terms such as *pretty* and *sick* take both argument + predicate and predicate + argument orders to express a given predicate-argument relation (the child might hear both *pretty girl* and *dress pretty* or *good boy, Paul good*). Contrastively, terms like *dance* or *read* either are analyzed as being in just one such order (argument + predicate for *dance* as in *mommy dance,* predicate + argument as in *read book*), or as taking different relations to their predicates depending on order (*I talk mommy*). For example, our daughter Jessica, for a period around 2; 11, seems to have analyzed such a property for some predicate terms, judging from errors like *sick Paul* (said a few times in succession), and (said in sequence) *grumpy mommy, grumpy daddy, daddy grumpy, no daddy grumpy;* that is, a major semantic-structural difference begins to emerge distinguishing adjectives (or future adjectives) from other major predicates.

Naturally, some of these hypothetical early encodings, which vary early on from child to child (Braine (1976)), must change partially over time. Thus, for what will become adjectives, the child must eventually determine that the predicate + argument order only occurs when the predicate modifies or specifies its argument as part of a larger predication (e.g., *read little book*), that there are language-particular restrictions on such orderings (thus the ungrammaticality of *sick Paul*), and so on. It is an open developmental question as to how such major constituent properties interact over time with other developing properties, such as differentiated ways of taking negation. Despite some empirical research (see Maratsos, 1982, 1983, for a review of developing verb categories), there is virtually no work concerning the progressions for categories such as adjectives and prepositions (vis-a-vis verbs). However, the important point here is that consistent adoption of the predicate-argument relation as one of the classificatory properties of terms opens up central possibilities in developmental analyses of category formation.

Suppose we accept the psychological reality of predicate-argument distinction. The crosslinguistic data suggest another important organizing point for acquisition. Across the world's languages, terms denoting concrete terms, whether proper names, pronouns, or common nouns (class-denoting terms), are all grouped into the primary argument category. Why might this be, and what developmental significance could it have? Do children, for example, automatically make the same basic analysis the crosslinguistic data suggest?

To discuss these problems even briefly, we need a clarification of what it means to say a term can be classified as a primary argument term, or a primary predicate term. This is not straightforward. Sometimes it is obvious which term in a sequence is actually acting as a predicate or an argument; sometimes it is not. For example, when a child says "mommy sick," it is likely the child sees *mommy* as an argument, and *sick* as the predicate term denoting a property of mommy. But it is possible to view nearly anything as having some property worth commenting on, or some relation to something else; and languages commonly treat terms as either arguments or predicates in predications. For example, in "I want eat," *eat,* which is normally a predicate term, is clearly the second argument of *want,* for it is what is wanted. Or, in an utterance like "Paul good girl," which meant "Paul is a good girl" (Jessica, 2;11), one can easily analyze *girl,* which is normally an argument term, as being a predicate of *Paul,* because *good girl* denotes a property predicated of him. Languages typically have devices for treating verbs as heads of arguments of other verbs, or devices for converting verbs into nouns. So what is meant by saying something is a primary argument term or primary predicate term? I do not want to go into this in great detail here but instead will try just to give an idea.

Suppose we ask whether something is a weapon. A gun clearly is a weapon, as is a knife. Is an ashtray or a fireplace poker? They can clearly be used as weapons. But, even if they have properties that allow them to be used that way, their primary or intended use is not to harm other creatures. To make sense of this, we have to say that a gun or knife is a weapon in a distinguishable *primary* sense: Its primary design or properties are such as to make it a weapon. An ashtray can be assigned use as a weapon, but its primary use is not that. By primary argument term or primary predicate term, I meant something analogous, though the conditions of alternative use are highly conventionalized in languages. A primary argument term (noun) is thus a term whose primary use is to serve as argument in a predication.

Presumably, the child must in part analyze terms as primary argument or predicate terms in order to use these as properties for representing grammatical strings and forming word class categories. The crosslinguistic data suggest that, by and large, languages consistently evolve one idea of what is a natural primary argument term, based on parallel perceptual and cognitive properties: Object terms are natural primary argument terms. This would follow from the fact that humans probably see properties and relations as obtaining of or between concrete objects. Thus, terms referring to concrete objects would be primary argument terms by natural affinity of grammatical function to conceptual analysis. Under specified conditions other terms can be treated like arguments (e.g., verbs, treated certain ways, can be heads of arguments, as in *I want to sing*); or other terms can even be assigned related forms as primary arguments (e.g., most English verbs can be treated as primary arguments when *-ing* is added, as in *I like loud singing*). But the natural coherence of concrete object terms as primary arguments is apparently so great, as to lead to their cohering together to comprise one universal argument category, unlike the varying degree of splitting that can occur in predicate categories.

It is thus natural hypothesis that the child makes initial classifications of terms into primary arguments and predicates on this basis as well; that is, the child initially classifies concrete object terms as primary arguments and thus forms the first major defining property for predicting what kind of term can be a primary argument (or noun). Note, however, that this is only a hypothesis, even if one supported by crosslinguistic patterns, because there is another way for the child to make such assignments. In principle, the child could work out probabilistically that various terms are typically used as arguments in clearly analyzable sequences, and other terms typically as predicates. Thus, *daddy* might have uses in which its classification as predicate or argument was ambiguous, but there would be more cases in which it was clearly serving as an argument term. Over the whole lexicon, concrete object terms could turn out to have just this overall property and so be assigned as primary argument terms on a probabilistic basis (with or without some help from their natural semantic affinity to primary argument status).

Given the universal association of primary argument status with concrete objecthood, it may seem unnecessary to consider this alternative developmental process too seriously. But the empirical data indicate that it must be entertained. Martin Braine (1976) noted that in children's early word combinations with terms like *more* + X and *no* + X, in which *more* and *no* serve as clear predicate terms, children do not limit the argument slot to concrete object terms (or nouns). They commonly say things like *no out*, or *more read*. Here, for example, are some combinations from my daughter Jessica's combinations in the first month (in which virtually all her combinations were of the form *no* + X or *more* + X): more pen, no pen, no night night, more coke, more clock, no go out, daddy book, more doggie (actually means, "give more coke to the doggie"), my mommy, my glasses, more popsicle?, more cook, more shoe, no change, no yuck ("diaper is not dirty"), more car, more change (being changed again), no on? (after being told she should give her brother's shoes back). Clearly, she thought anything could be an argument of *more* or *no* as long as it could be seen as recurring or having some negative relation (disappearance, rejection, nonexistence, to use Bloom's categories). In other words, although she did generally use what looked like a predicate + argument form (even the *daddy book* and *my* + X sequences can be so interpreted), there was no necessary association of argument status with concrete object status. This is, as Braine (1976) points out, quite common. Thus, it is not idle to wonder if the natural affinity of concrete object terms with argument status, which clearly emerges in both children and languages, is automatic. Indeed, these early predications seem to show the flexibility about the possible semantic diversity of argument of a predicate that is actually required by any natural language.

To summarize, the crosslinguistic data indicate that among the major word classes there is a basic predicate-argument split. I have argued that, with other analytic considerations, this supports the premise that the distinction of terms according to predicate and argument function in sentences, and classification of them as primary arguments or predicates, are central psychological processes. I also discussed how semantic-distributional differences in how predicates take their arguments may form important beginning, or partial, definitional properties for formal predicate subdivisions such as verb versus adjective. Finally, I noted that the universal finding that primary argument terms always include concrete object terms suggests that children, from the outset, use this natural affinity of concrete objecthood with primary argument status to classify terms and analyze sequences. I also noted, however, that such a classification could come about developmentally, and the data on the earliest combinations do not point to children, for example, obviously restricting argument uses to concrete terms. Thus, this particular strong universal presently only makes attribution of this automatically undertaken analysis to the child a plausible hypothesis.

The Major Grammatical Relations

The crosslinguistic data show that, across languages, the major universal relevant to the grammatical relations per se is probably the distinction of nuclear versus oblique argument; that is, some arguments of the predicate, its nuclear arguments, are more directly given their relational properties by the predicate. All languages have predicates with one and two nuclear arguments and predicates with two.

Throughout the world's languages, there is a trend, often a very strongly skewed one. First, for the transitive predicate, a particular one of the nuclear arguments is most likely to be treated grammatically like the nuclear argument of the intransitive in control of morphological properties ordering properties, omission and relativization control properties, and certain semantic properties (e.g., tendency to be given, specific, and definite.) Second, in the world's languages the animate agent is highly likely to fill this nuclear argument role, when a transitive predicate has such an argument. Earlier I discussed how this could follow naturally if transitive agents were, overall, analyzed as what the predicate tends to be more centrally about. But as the data indicate, this is a tendency and not a certainty, even though for some grammatical properties, a very powerful one.

What does this imply for acquisition? Unfortunately, as for form classes, any discussion is mostly speculative, because there are virtually no data. Obviously, the fact that various semantic properties continually appear in at least partial association with each other in languages indicates some kind of importance for them. The child must accordingly register these properties and their correlations in a given language. Because children can learn any known language, they must be able to represent all the correlational possibilities and discover those on which their language actually converges. This, at least, follows tautologically. The central question, then, is one of susceptibility or bias; that is, we can imagine that certain analyses are easier for children to make, or even innately specified. Nativists claim (not implausibly) that given the complexity of languages, children could not simply sort through all the data impartially.

On the other hand, I think our crosslinguistic acquisitional experience for years has been roughly this: The more an expectation was based on what the local language group prominently does, the more likely the contrary surprise. Thus, English is very much a word-order-based language, probably on the extreme end of the world's languages in this respect. Studying children acquiring English, we came to regard languages that use strict word order to express semantic role relation as naturally easier to learn. Nevertheless, children learning languages like Finnish (Bowerman, 1973) and especially Turkish (Slobin, 1982, 1986) show little difficulty in dealing with less strictly word-ordered systems for encoding the grammatical role relations. This is especially so if the language is self-consistent, like Turkish, in how alternative means are used. Similarly, noun gender systems like those of German, Russian, and Polish seem—to those whose major forms have been English—analytically peculiar. Yet, children learn central aspects of these languages by 3 or 4, or earlier (Maratsos, 1983, Smoczynska, 1986), again especially if the system contains few internal irregularities.

In a related vein, Schieffelin (in press) has given us our findings to date (that I know of, anyway) on acquisition in an ergative language. The language she studied, Kaluli, was a mixed ergative language. In particular, when they are in focused forms, transitive agents have a distinctive morphological marker (pronounced roughly "eh"). This marker is unlike that assigned to intransitive subjects, whether they are focused or not. On the other hand, transitive patients always take a marker like that of intransitive subjects. Thus, in Kaluli the transitive agent is sometimes marked distinctively differently from the intransitive subject. (Actually, transitive subjects in general are consistently marked this way; early in acquisition the arguments so marked are overwhelmingly agents).

As we have seen, the crosslinguistic data indicate a strong skew towards grouping together grammatically transitive agent with intransitive subject in grammatical treatment. Presumably, this stems from some overall natural cognitive affinity, such as unmarked topichood. Do children then reveal this susceptibility more or less strongly than languages as a whole? Schieffelin's interesting finding is in the negative. Her three subjects did not transfer the distinctive transitive agent marking to intransitive subjects of any kind, whether the subjects were intransitive agents, intransitive focused arguments, or intransitive patients. Naturally, this does not indicate that the notion of agency is unavailable across transitive and intransitive arguments. At least it should not, for there are certainly properties of language that require intransitive and transitive agents to be treated similarly, in opposition to intransitive or transitive subjects as a whole. In English, for example, intransitive and transitive subjects can be omitted in simple sentences only if they are agents to register an imperative (e.g., *Run! Eat Dinner!*). So Schieffelin's findings must simply mean that children do not find the natural affinity between transitive agents and intransitive subjects, or even between transitive agents and intransitive agents, so overwhelming that generalization of properties from one to the other is automatic.

Given this background, I speculate that acquisition of a language like Dyirbal, or Tagalog or Lisu, in which subject-related properties are not controlled consistently by agents rather than patients (in agent–patient predicates), provides no severe developmental problem to children. If this turns out to be so, how should we understand it?

The speculation follows directly from the predicate-argument framework already suggested, and from it being natural for children to use converging appearance in semantic-structural patterns to define formal categories (as outlined in Maratsos & Chalkley, 1980); that is, in that paper, we assumed that children naturally form a grammatical category on the grounds that they control semantic-distributional operations in similar fashion. We also assumed that it is natural for children to analyze how major semantic properties correlate with such convergent analyses. Thus, by this account, for Dyirbal the child finds that, among transitive predicates, one argument consistently shares the grammatical properties of intransitive subjects. This leads to the idea of transitive predicates being grouped together with intransitive subjects as a major grammatical category. It would not pose a special problem that in Dyirbal, for example, this group of transitive nuclear arguments consistently includes patients rather than agents among the transitive argument sets. If anything, major category formation might proceed more smoothly in a language like Dyirbal than in one in which major intransitive subject properties of agreement, morphological, and coreferential control are not consistently controlled by the same nuclear argument for a given predicate (that is, mixed ergative languages); though, of course, children can learn these also. Or similarly in Tagalog, it is the properties of givenness (supplemented by patienthood) that control the subject-like matrix of agreement and relativizability properties.

This kind of assumption of naturalness stands, I think, in strong contrast to theorists who appear to have been more strongly taken with the skewed association of semantic properties with formal categorization. Thus, Bates and Mac-Whinney (1982) briefly note languages such as Tagalog and conclude, I think properly, that accusative systems result from a basic underlying convergence of agentive and topic properties being conventionalized in the language (to rephrase their analysis slightly). But they go on to assume that there is thus a natural and generative spread around the agent–topic core as a controller of subject properties. Although this might make things easier for the learning of accusative languages, it would certainly make things difficult for Dyirbal, Tagalog, or even

Kaluli. My guess is that Dyirbal or Tagalog, for example, would not show the resulting expected developmental strain any more than Kaluli seems to.

Interestingly, the same skewed associations have also been incorporated into the theories of various nativist theorists, such as Pinker (1984), Grimshaw (1982), and Roeper (1982). These theorists acknowledge the formal nature of major formal categories (I realize this sounds tautological without appropriate historical context) but see semantic properties as triggers for innate category recognition. Pinker (1984) thus proposes that agents are innately registered as grammatical subjects, and their distributional properties are analyzed in order to analyze the formal structure of subject in the language. Aware of morphologically ergative languages, he separates morphological role marking from subject properties (a considerable loss of parsimony, it seems to me) but proposes the agent-centered analysis for other subject properties. Because Dyirbal, Lisu, Tagalog, and languages like them naturally have both intransitive and transitive agents, the proposal implies that they are unlearnable or are analyzed as having two or many grammatical subjects, so to speak. Naturally, such proposals can be revised to take into account children's learning, but it seems to me that only further loss of parsimony can result.

Of course, we do not know about the relative learnability of such languages. But I think it is a good guess that, being self-consistent, such languages would be shown by empirical study to be highly learnable unless other special features of the languages give difficulties (as such features apparently do, for example, in learning the basic relational marking system of Serbo–Croatian (Slobin, 1982)). This in turn would indicate the flexibility of children's use of convergence of major semantic-distributional properties as a basis for grammatical grouping, at least compared to the kind of inevitable semantic skewness many theorists have attributed to their acquisitional processes. Again, this is not to claim that use of such correlated properties centered around predicate-argument analysis is the exclusive basis for formal category analysis. But it is surely a natural one.

Crosslinguistic Work, Semantic Properties, and Innateness

On the whole, in my past work, I have taken a nonnativist orientation. As Keil (1981) correctly points out, however, on no general a priori grounds is either a nativist or nonnativist orientation per se preferable. Nevertheless, to me, on the whole, not assuming a nativist orientation is more likely to lead to attempts to understand exactly what something is. For example, if one is a nativist, grammatical categories such as verb simply exist: The data only offer cues about how to recognize them when relevant to the particular language. But, in a certain sense, they are no more definable in essential character than is redness. They simply exist as internal symbols useful in writing grammars, although these eventually connect to something like meaningful communication. This, at least, is a possible (though perhaps not necessary) epistemological outcome of the nativist position. On the other hand, if one is not a nativist, one must be prepared to specify what a verb is, such that the category is constructible from non-linguistically specifical elements of analysis. This in the end leads to more insight about what such categories are. Obviously, however, this can be no more than a personal attitude and has nothing directly to do with evidence.

In fact, the world's languages are ambiguous in their implications. From one point of view, very little is universal. What is universal—notions such as the basic split into argument and predicate, use of various devices to control role relations in at least some contexts, leaving out redundant elements under various specified conditions, conventionalization to a major degree, one- versus two-argument predications—at least in theory, is traceable to more basic properties of the cognitive apparatus. Beyond that, I think the trends in the grammatical structures of the world's languages very much favor a functionalist view of how languages come to be as they are. If anything, the fact that much of what is found is only trends, rather than universals, favors this view even more strongly. For example, there is at least a plausible functional connection between transitive agentivity and the status of being usual topic argument of a predicate. But the fact that this is only a statistically significant association rather than a universal feels more like something caused by a functional skew, rather than the kind of biologically determined properties characteristic of the relations of motor elements in, for example, walking. Or as another example, givenness and definiteness constantly recur in association with grammatical formal category definitions. Sometimes they control subject-like properties directly, as in Tagalog. Or they may form part of something like discourse topichood in languages like Chinese or Lisu. Or how they are expressed with arguments may be an important constituent property of form classes like noun in languages like English. Or for predicate classes, different ways of marking similar semantic combinations to mark aspect, tense, and negation of predicate relations are universally central in unifying major predicate classes (e.g., Chinese) and subdividing them (e.g., English). Properties such as specificity–definiteness–givenness, number, aspect, tense, negation all have natural cognitive affinities with the categories they are most centrally marked of in languages. So again, we could see in this a functionalist gradient.

On the other hand, I do not think it at all implausible to hypothesize, as some nativists do (e.g., Bickerton, 1984; Grimshaw, 1982; Pinker, 1984), that children are specially keyed to look for the manner of expression of such meanings, or to look for how such meanings control grammatical combinations, as a matter of innate endowment. Such a view does, however, run counter to the usual Chomskyan nativist argument, which attempts to show that language must be innate because it has so many properties having very little to do with anything else, linguistic or cognitive. But as Bickerton (1984) points out, if such properties are cognitively important, biologically programming the child to make them central in grammatical analysis would at least comprise an evolutionary picture in which innate biases have adaptive properties, a picture to which we are accustomed.

The strong functional trends in the crosslinguistic data tend to strengthen nonnativist claims. To repeat, for many reasons, I do not think they disprove such claims, not the least of which is the fact that the nativists are right on one count: Languages are enormously complex. If children do derive linguistic formulations from general data-processing procedures, or from such procedures combined with a few linguistically specific analytic biases or algorithms, very high general intelligence is called for in this type of task.

But it seems to me that if some of how we learn language is innate, the crosslinguistic data indicates that the innate elements specifically geared or emphasized for language are less likely to consist of actual formal categories, such as subject and object, and their specifications. Rather, they are more likely to consist of more basic analytic processes and biases that can emerge in various combinations. For, as we have seen, crosslinguistically surprisingly little is universal. Similarly, too, if there are strong biases in learning language stemming from a more functionalist bent per se, again I argue from such data that these biases too are far less automatic in their effects on language acquisition than many have concluded. Perhaps this amounts to a somewhat lame ending, but I believe that further acquaintance with these crosslinguistic acquisition data brings out simultaneously the remarkable language biases that do seem to recur, *and* the enormous flexibility with which they can be grouped by actual children in actual language communities. One can hope that studies on acquisition in languages like Lisu or Tagalog or Dyirbal will soon be forthcoming to shed further empirical light on this conclusion.

ADDENDUM: HISTORICAL NOTES

In the ideal contribution to this volume, one could write of how one's personal development in graduate school and how one's contact with Roger Brown led, in a straightforward way, to one's present contribution. But I did not think I could compose such a chapter, so I have made a separate historical note to fill in the picture.

Historically, the famous Harvard group revolves around the famous seminar and group of figures that participated, from 1962 on, in the early collection and analysis of naturalistic data from Adam, Eve, and Sarah. (Even earlier, of course, and famous in its own right, was the collaboration with Jean Berko.) The sociology of things was different by the time I arrived in 1971, I think. I only remember one grouping of people which occurred when I took Roger's regular annual class seminar. There were some interesting people in that seminar, too— Ron Kaplan, Susan Carey, Alfred Bloom—but it was not centered on any focal problem. Other than that, I remember little common meeting. The general pattern then was that all of us worked separately with Roger on our various problems, even as he worked on his own.

This is not to say exciting things were not going on, even aside from the Vietnam War and the resulting draft. (Even the Brown seminar was disrupted by the Harvard strike of 1969.) When I first came, for example, David McNeill was a visitor at Harvard. In fact, the seminar I took from him in my first semester introduced me to and aroused my interest in the study of language acquisition, although I had found some preliminary interest in Roger's two chapters in his book, *Social psychology,* which I had read as an undergraduate at Stanford.

I did not come into much contact with Brown himself until the second year. At that point, as Chairman of Social Relations, he had become embroiled in a problematic course on Marxism developed by others during these years and then dropped by the higher administration because it had rather literally no academic standards. As Chairman, Roger had to defend this at a public meeting during which he was hissed at, shouted down, and so on, and I particularly remember his plaintive comment in the *Harvard Crimson,* that it seemed to him inaccurate to have called him a fascist (the customary epithet of the times) because, like most academics, he was a wishy-washy leftist.

More significantly, as far as language acquisition is concerned, during this time Roger developed and began to carry out the plan of *A First Language,* a book that came to reflect, at one major level, general current conditions in linguistics and psycholinguistics. By 1967, perhaps the period of greatest synthesis in generative grammar was coming to an end. The theory was probably never as uncluttered as it looked from the outside, but compared to what was coming, the earlier period—around 1959–1965—seemed intellectually idyllic. At the end of this period the synthesis of form and meaning embodied in *Aspects of the Theory of Syntax* (Chomsky, 1965) had emerged.

In psycholinguistics itself, however, exceptions to the theory of derivational complexity had now begun to appear, and Fodor and Garrett's 1966 paper summarized many of these problems. Perhaps just as problematically, fissures had begun to emerge in linguistics itself. In 1966, George Lakoff and John Robert Ross extended to their logical end some of the arguments that had been used to justify syntactic deep structure, and they questioned whether there was any distinction at all between a semantic interpretive component and a syntactic generative component. Instead, they argued, syntactic arguments showed that the beginning level for syntactic derivation was the meaningful representation of the sentence itself, not a syntactic structure from which meaning can be read. There also arose, of course, Fillmore's (1968) case grammar, which also was more semantic in deep structure than Chomskyan theory.

Aside from seeing the conflicts directly (because Lakoff and Ross were both teachers of mine), I remember particularly vividly a meeting called by a professor of the school of education. What he wanted to know was how, given all these different emerging analyses, could one say what the syntactic complexity of a sentence was. The linguists who came all said that it depends on what grammatical model is chosen; no general answer was possible. Besides, the argument went—and still goes—in terms of judging the effect on the psychological complexity, removing an operation from the syntax usually entailed having its work done elsewhere, such as the semantic component. So, attempting to ferret out the complexity of the syntactic component by means of judging psychological complexity is filled with confounds.

I cannot say that at the time these linguistic disputes were very encouraging. Over the years I was in graduate school, it appeared somewhat unlikely that any particular formal linguistic model would turn out to say very much about what psychological operations were actually employed in comprehending and producing sentences. Or perhaps a model would, if only linguists could agree on one. But if linguists could call models with apparently very different psychological ramifications equivalent for their purposes (as Chomsky did in his replies to Lakoff, Ross, & Co.), this could only make the psychologist of language wonder how direct the relations would be between linguistic models and psychological models. In subsequent years, this issue has neither disappeared nor become particularly less intractable.

Nevertheless, for most psycholinguists interested in language acquisition, the central problem has remained one of trying to find empirical evidence for particular hypotheses about what a child's grammar is at some point, and how it develops. This has typically involved taking over some fairly well-developed adult model of linguistics, or segments thereof, to test against the data. As Roger remarks in *A First Language,* this at least holds out hope of leading eventually to a description of adult competence in some reasonably direct way.

As for me, I was quite interested in all these problems—at this time Roger, with Camille Hanlon, produced the paper on derivational complexity and acquisition (Brown & Hanlon, 1970)—but made little contribution to them. Towards the end of my graduate years I did some work on relative clause processing with Eric Wanner. At that time, he was just becoming interested in the nontransformational comprehension processes afforded by ATN models (Woods, 1970) and was responsible for casting this work into the theoretically useful form it took on (Wanner & Maratsos, 1978). But the bulk of my graduate work was concentrated on children's understanding of the definite and indefinite articles (*the* and *a*). I did considerable reading then about the problems of reference in general (this was also an important topic in the developing arguments in linguistics and has remained so) and gradually developed various experimental techniques to try to investigate children's knowledge. Roger had already made some tentative conclusions on the basis of the naturalistic data in *A First Language* and these appeared in the experimental data as well.

I suppose one could find continuity in many ways from those days, if one does not demand much directness of relation. The skepticism that naturally arose from seeing the fragmentation of linguistics has never left me and has led eventually to my attempt to analyze as securely as I could what categories—such as verb— actually are, such that they can be analyzed by children. Clearly, the problem of what children's categories are, and how they can be formed, was a central one in the psycholinguistic work being done around me at Harvard. And Roger (Brown, 1973) and Melissa Bowerman (1973) were among the earliest to begin to draw importantly on the crosslinguistic data to form important conclusions about the ontogenesis of the formal categories in children. But these did not become central problems for me until 6 or 7 years later. Perhaps, then, the present contribution usefully closes some kind of circle. Even as he drew his own conclusions, Roger always served, consciously I think, to bring ideas before others in a disinterested (old meaning) way for them to use. If this chapter on the peculiar specimens of languages to be found elsewhere (specimens that in fact no longer seem peculiar to me at all) serves some kind of similar function, then that is perhaps not a bad tribute to someone who deserves one as much as anyone I have known.

REFERENCES

Anderson, J. (1976). *Language, memory, and thought.* Hillsdale, NJ: Lawrence Erlbaum Associates.

Bates, E., & MacWhinney, B. (1982). A functionalist approach to grammatical development. In L. R. Gleitman & H. E. Wanner (Eds.), *Language acquisition: The state of the art.* Cambridge, MA: Harvard University Press.

Bickerton, D. (1984). The language bioprogram hypothesis. *The Behavioral and Brain Sciences, 7,* 173–190.

Bloomfield, L. (1933). *Language.* New York: Henry Holt.

Bolinger, D. (1968). *Aspects of language.* New York: Harcourt, Brace, & World.

Bowerman, M. (1973). *Early syntactic development: A cross-linguistic study with special reference to Finnish.* Cambridge, England: Cambridge University Press.

Braine, M. D. S. (1976). Children's first word combinations. *Monographs of the Society for Research in Child Development, 41,* 448–456.

Brown, R. (1973). *A first language: The early stages.* Cambridge, MA: Harvard University Press.

Brown, R., & Hanlon, C. (1970). Derivational complexity and order of acquisition in child speech. In J. R. Hayes (Ed.), *Cognition and the development of language,* (pp. 11–55). New York: Wiley.

Chafe, W. (1976). Givenness, contrastiveness, definiteness, subjects, topics, and point of view. In C. Li (Ed.), *Subject and topic* (Vol. 2, pp. 25–56). New York: Academic Press.

Chomsky, N. (1965). *Aspects of the theory of syntax.* Cambridge, MA: MIT Press.

Cole, P., & Saddock, J. M. (1977). Syntax and semantics: Grammatical relations. (Vol. 8). New York: Academic Press.

Comrie, B. (1981). *Language universals and linguistic typology: Syntax and morphology.* Chicago: The University of Chicago Press.

Dixon, R. M. W. (1979). Ergativity. *Language, 55,* 59–138.

Fillmore, C. J. (1968). The case for case. In E. Bach & R. T. Harms (Eds.), *Universals in linguistic theory.* New York: Holt, Rinehart, & Winston.

Fodor, J. A., & Garrett, M. (1966). Some reflections on competence and performance. In J. Lyons and R. J. Wales (Eds.), *Psycholinguistic Papers: The Proceedings of the 1966 Edinburgh Conference*. Edinburgh: Edinburgh University Press.

Grimshaw, J. (1982). Form, function, and the language acquisition devise. In C. L. Baker & J. McCarthy (Eds.), *The logical problem of language acquisition*. Cambridge, MA: MIT Press.

Hale, K. (1978). *On the position of Walbiri in a typology of the base*. Massachusetts Institute of Technology, mimeo.

Keenan, E. L. (1976a). Remarkable subjects in malagasy. In C. N. Li (Ed.), *Subject and topic* (Vol. 9, pp. 247–301). New York: Academic Press.

Keenan, E. L. (1976b). Towards a universal definition of "subject." In C. N. Li (Ed.), *Subject and topic* (Vol. 10, pp. 303–333). New York: Academic Press.

Keenan, E. L., & Comrie, B. (1979). Data on the noun phrase accessibility hierarchy. *Language, 55*, 333–351.

Keil, F. (1981). Constraints on knowledge and cognitive development. *Psychological Review, 88*, 197–227.

Kuno, S. (1976). Subject, theme, and the speaker's empathy—A reexamination of relativization phenomena. In C. N. Li (Ed.), *Subject and topic* (Vol. 13, pp. 417–444). New York: Academic Press.

Lakoff, G., & Ross, J. R. (1966). *Is deep structure necessary?* Unpublished manuscript, later circulated by Indiana University Linguistics Club, Bloomington, IN.

Li, C. N. (1976). *Subject and topic*. New York: Academic Press.

Li, C. N., & Thompson, S. A. (1976). A new typology of language. In C. N. Li, (Ed.), *Subject and topic* (Vol. 15, pp. 457–489). New York: Academic Press.

Lyons, J. (1968). *Introduction to theoretical linguistics*. Hillsdale, NJ: Lawrence Erlbaum Associates.

MacWhinney, B. (1978). The acquisition of morphophonology. *Monographs of the Society for Research in Child Development, 43*, (1-2, Serial No. 174).

Maratsos, M. (1982). The child's construction of grammatical categories. In L. R. Gleitman & H. E. Wanner (Eds.), *Language acquisition: The state of the art*. Cambridge, MA: Harvard University Press.

Maratsos, M. (1983). Some current issues in the study of the acquisition of grammar. In P. H. Mussen (Ed.), *Handbook of child psychology* (4th ed., Vol. 3), *Cognitive development*. New York: Wiley.

Maratsos, M., & Chalkley, M. A. (1980). The internal language of children's syntax: The ontogenesis and representation of syntactic categories. In K. Nelson (Ed.), *Children's language* (Vol. II). New York: Gardner Press.

Pinker, S. (1984). *Language learnability and language development*. Cambridge, MA: Harvard University Press.

Roeper, T. (1982). The role of universals in the acquisition of gerunds. In H. E. Wanner & L. R. Gleitman (Eds.), *Language acquisition: The state of the art*. Cambridge, MA: Harvard University Press.

Schachter, P. (1976). The subject Phillippine languages: Topic, actor, actor-topic, or none of the above. In C. N. Li (Ed.), *Subject and topic* (pp. 491–518). New York: Academic Press.

Schieffelin, B. (in press). *How Kaluli children learn what to say, what to do, and how to feel*. Cambridge, MA: Harvard University Press.

Schlesinger, I. (1974). Relational concepts underlying language. In R. Schiefelbusch & L. L. Lloyd (Eds.), *Language perspectives: Acquisition, retardation, and intervention*. Baltimore: University Park Press.

Silverstein, M. (1976). Hierarchy of features and ergativity. In R. M. W. Dixon (Ed.), *Grammatical categories in Australian languages*. Linguistic Series 22 (pp. 112–171). Canberra: Australian Institute of Aboriginal Studies.

Slobin, D. I. (1973). Cognitive prerequisites for the development of grammar. In C. A. Ferguson &

D. I. Slobin (Eds.), *Studies of child language development.* New York: Holt, Rinehart, & Winston.

Slobin, D. I. (1982). Universal and particular in the acquisition of language. In L. R. Gleitman & H. E. Wanner (Eds.), *Language acquisition: The state of the art.* Cambridge, MA: Harvard University Press.

Slobin, D. I. (1986). Crosslinguistic evidence for the language-making capacity. In D. I. Slobin (Ed.), *The crosslinguistic study of language acquisition.* Hillsdale, NJ: Lawrence Erlbaum Associates.

Smoczynska, M. (1986). The acquisition of Polish. In D. Slobin (Ed.), *Cross-linguistic studies in language acquisition.* Hillsdale, NJ: Lawrence Erlbaum Associates.

Wanner, E., & Maratsos, M. (1978). An ATN approach to comprehension. In M. Halle, J. Bresnan, & G. Miller (Eds.), *Linguistic theory and psychological reality.* Cambridge, MA: MIT Press.

Woods, W. (1970). Transition network grammars for natural language analysis. *Communications of the ACM, 3,* 591–606.

8 The Acquisition of a Spatial Language

Ursula Bellugi
The Salk Institute for Biological Studies
La Jolla, California

THE SIXTIES: A FIRST LANGUAGE

It was 1960, and I was about to meet Roger Brown for the first time in his office at MIT. We were to discuss the possibility of my editing the proceedings of a conference that would be held in October 1961 at Endicott House in Dedham, Massachusetts, sponsored by the Social Sciences Research Council. Roger Brown had recently begun studies of language development in children; I, in turn, had read several of his papers, as well as *Words and Things* (Brown, 1958), and had conjured up a mental image of the man who had written these wise, clear, and insightful works. I imagined an elderly scholar of 70 or so, relatively short, with a halo of white hair surrounding his head in unruly curls—a cross between Eric Erikson and Albert Einstein. Entering his office, I found instead an extremely tall, athletic-looking young man, and I hesitated, waiting for the eminent elder statesman of my imagination to appear. But when he spoke, the elegant sentences and wry intelligent humor soon made it apparent that, despite appearances, this was the wise scholar himself.

The Beginnings of Child Language

To my great pleasure, we agreed that I would attend the conference and help edit the proceedings. Roger said at the time that I might join with him and Colin Fraser in some research studies on child language for 3 months. It was an area that had long been of great interest to me, and so the connection began. Instead of 3 months, however, the collaboration continued for 8 years, and I have felt its influence ever since.

The first publication to come out of my apprenticeship with Roger was *The Acquisition of Language*, the report of the Dedham conference on First Language Acquisition (Bellugi & Brown, 1964). The conference brought together for the first time linguists representing the new transformational grammar (Noam Chomsky, Morris Halle, Robert Lees); and psychologists studying language acquisition (Roger Brown, Colin Fraser, Jean Berko, Sue Ervin), child development (Jerome Kagan and Paul Mussen), and the biological foundations of language (Eric Lenneberg and Hans-Lukas Teuber). As such, it was an important early event in the emerging wave of interest in language development.

Discussions at the conference were heated as well as interesting. The introduction to the slim volume stated:

> Linguistic development is a very old research topic, but there have been changes in the conception of the problem and in the methods used to study it; these provided the occasion for the conference. Quite recently, investigators in several parts of the United States have begun research on the acquisition of language as it is described by linguistic science. . . . The new work utilizes field methods from linguistics, experimental methods from psychology, naturalistic observation, and the study of deviant cases. . . . A great deal of the interest and tension of this conference emanated from the communication between psychologists working in studies of child speech and linguists who are in the process of developing new theories of the structure of language.

In the year that followed, Brown, Colin Fraser, and I began the longitudinal study of the development of English in two children, whom Roger named for the Garden of Eden: Adam and Eve; Sarah was added somewhat later. We interviewed 30 families for our studies and selected two children because their speech was exceptionally intelligible and because "they talked a lot." The principal techniques we used included tape recording the children's speech with their mothers, written transcripts on the scene, notes about important actions and objects of attention, and a distributional analysis of the speech of the child. And then, each week we met as a research seminar with other students of the psychology of language to discuss the current state of the construction process in one or the other of the children.

Those were exciting days, as Dan Slobin has testified in his chapter of this book. The lighthearted group of scholars, including Jean Berko-Gleason, Samuel Anderson, Colin Fraser, David McNeill, and Dan Slobin, sat around the large oak table in the conference room in William James Hall or in the Center for Cognitive Studies and discussed the problems raised by the children engaged in acquiring language. Later we were joined by Ed Klima from M.I.T., who raised important issues in theoretical linguistics that were relevant to child language.

The paper that reported on the three major phenomena that first struck us is called "Three Processes in the Child's Acquisition of Syntax." It was first published in 1964 and afterwards was reprinted so many times that I have quite lost count, somewhat like the brooms in the Sorcerer's Apprentice. The paper considers the processes of imitation and reduction that we noticed in Adam and Eve; it outlines the process of adult expansion of the child's utterances, which seemed to us ideally devised to provide the child with the grammatical regularities of sentence structures missing in his own speech; and, importantly, the article describes the process of "induction of the latent structure" of sentences by the child. Roger's beautiful last line expressed a thought that would later be widely repeated (Brown & Bellugi, 1964): "The very intricate simultaneous differentiation and integration that constitutes the evolution of the noun phrase is more reminiscent of the biological development of an embryo than it is of the acquisition of a conditioned reflex" (p. 149). For me, the "biological" association has remained a guiding force.

A No Boy

It seemed to me that the three children were far ahead of us, making progress at a rate that greatly exceeded our ability to catalogue and analyze, much less come to grips with, details of the current linguistic theory of comprehension, production, and underlying rule systems. I began to struggle to understand and work out a performance grammar for the development of the complex system of negation underlying Adam's utterances, that was later to become my thesis topic. In the middle of a session, Adam would open his eyes wide and provide me with special dialogues. In one case, Adam had just claimed that he had a watch, but he had never in fact had one, and what's more, couldn't tell time:

Me: "I thought you said you had a watch."
Adam: "I *do* have one," (with offended dignity), "What d'you think I am, a no boy with no watch?"
Me: "What kind of a boy?"
Adam: (Enunciating very clearly:) "*A no boy with no watch.*"

Examples like these gave us the sense of being in on the beginnings of a wonderful discovery: that the child is to some extent a "grammar explorer."

The Delegation from Africa

Roger Brown became justly famous throughout the United States and far beyond for his new work on language acquisition; work that promised to lead to a deeper understanding of the development of the child's mind. One day, a delegation of dignitaries from Africa arrived to visit him in his elegant Harvard office. They had heard, they said, about his exciting new techniques and equipment for the study of child language, and they wanted to establish a similar center in Africa. The visitors talked on at some length. Roger listened silently and politely, with a smile. Finally, they turned to him to hear what the great man had to say about technological advancements and the impact they had made on his progress in charting this new field. "I'll show you," he said, and without another word, got up, went into his inner office and returned, bearing tools in hand—a large, yellow, lined pad of paper and a sharpened pencil. "This," he said with a smile, "is the technology we use." And indeed it was. Paper, pencil, also a tape recorder, and Roger Brown's intellect. . .

At all times Roger Brown was our mentor, and we are much indebted to him for his intellectual breadth and depth and his originality. His research methods, elegance of style, and theoretical clarifications provided a stimulating and enriching environment for these early studies. He provided masterful leadership in integrating different theoretical approaches in psychology and linguistics, and he moved with astuteness and sensitivity among theory, data, and interpretation. He is an imaginative psychologist, using insights from the world around him as well as from established theory, developing novel methods of answering the searching questions he poses for himself.

A Writer's Pad

One of Roger's sterling qualities caused me problems long after I left his group. That quality still haunts me, because I naively thought I could emulate it. Working closely with him over a number of years, I often listened to Roger explain to visitors the intricate details of linguistic analyses that we were engaged in and frequently saw him bring out those large yellow pads of lined paper, covered from top to bottom in his rather scrawling, elongated handwriting. He always explained what we were doing simply and directly and wrote the same way— clear exposition, highly readable, well argued, with elegant turns of phrase. I decided then that I would follow directly in Roger's long strides with my own shorter footsteps. But when I tried to sit down by myself with lined pad and well-sharpened pencil, I ended up buried in mountains of crumpled, discarded yellow sheets. Unfortunately, a hundred papers, a couple of books, and more than two decades later—while Roger's prose remains polished, stylish, witty, and seemingly effortless—for me, writing remains a tortuous process!

THE SEVENTIES: LANGUAGE IN A DIFFERENT MODALITY

By organizing the Conference on First Language Acquisition, and coordinating the research program studying Adam, Eve, and Sarah, Roger Brown launched a new realm of investigation: how young children learn the complex underlying network of grammatical relations of spoken language; he worked out both the original questions and the ways of determining the answers to those questions.

After completing my time at Harvard in 1968 I moved to California, joining forces with Klima (but that is perhaps the basis for a different chapter). There, I found myself following in Roger's footsteps by entering another new realm of studies—the unexplored arena of communication in a silent language.

The Token

In 1969, Ed Klima and I took a trip to visit the "signing" chimp Washoe in Reno, Nevada. We became interested in the wily chimpanzee, who was presented to us the first evening in her filmy nightgown and stocking cap. We had never paid attention to a human signing, much less a chimpanzee, but we were duly impressed with what her trainers, the Gardners, reported that she was "saying." From that visit came a paper in 1970 with Jacob Bronowski, called "Language, Name, and Concept." One aspect of that paper was a comparison between the reported accomplishments of the chimpanzee in sign language and hearing children learning spoken language, because nothing was known at the time of deaf children learning sign language (surely a more appropriate comparison for Washoe.)

Then, unexpectedly, Jonas Salk asked if I would like to set up a small research section in the Salk Institute for Biological Studies. I was delighted and subsequently became the token nonbiologist in a setting at the time almost entirely devoted to molecular biology. In such a setting, Ed Klima and I thought about ways to set the problems we were studying in a broader framework: in a biological framework, in fact. The visit to Washoe seemed to point in an interesting direction.

A Loose Collection of Gestures

Thus, in 1970, we set about to study the acquisition of sign language by deaf children of deaf parents in order to compare and contrast it with what we then knew about the acquisition of spoken language (namely, English) by hearing children of hearing parents. We reasoned that examining what was common across the two language modalities might provide better clues to the biological foundations of the human capacity for language. This was a worthy and interesting aim, but at the start I had never met a deaf person, had no idea about what it was deaf people did when they gestured to one another, did not know a single sign, and was completely innocent of the many controversies surrounding the language and education of deaf people.

It soon became clear to us that one could not do good studies in the acquisition of some linguistic system if one had no knowledge of what systematic properties the adult system had, nor indeed if there were any such properties. Combing the available literature, we mainly found statements that were mutually contradictory and gave no clues that linguistic structure not derived from English would be found among the gesturing of deaf people. In different sources it was written that sign language is "a collection of vague and loosely defined pictorial gestures"; that it is pantomime; that sign language "has no grammar"; that it is "derived from English, a pidgin form of English on the hands with no structure of its own"; and (my favorite) that sign language is "much too concrete, too broken in pieces."

So, with no knowledge and no preconceptions about the hand waving that we saw, we began studying the sign language used by deaf people, setting aside acquisition studies for a time. It was a voyage of discovery that allowed us to ask what is fundamental to language as language, and what properties of language are determined by the mode in which it is produced and perceived. What kind of organization characterizes a language developed in the visual manual mode? How is that organization similar to and different from that of spoken languages? In a book published at the end of the 1970s (*The Signs of Language*, Klima & Bellugi, 1979), we give the results of the first decade of the research that blossomed from these questions.

In the preface we write:

> When we began these studies we did not envisage any of the research in this book. We started out to study the way in which young deaf children acquire the visual– gestural language of their deaf parents in order to compare language learning in a visual mode with language learning in an auditory mode. We soon found, however, that very little was known of the structure of what was being acquired by these deaf children; and so we turned our attention to the study of the adult language as well. . . The present book deals with the questions that we asked ourselves about this hitherto largely unknown communication system and the ways in which we attempted to determine its properties. We are now beginning to see how this language in a different modality may hold remarkably deep and unexpected clues to constraints on the possible form of language. (p. v)

It was in this respect that I was following Roger—I was looking at something for the first time, without knowing what would be found. In this gestural system we eventually discovered language in full flower, with myriad grammatical processes differently instantiated because of the rich dimensions of possibilities in the visual–spatial mode. Discovering the modulations of movement that constitute grammatical inflections in American Sign Language (ASL) enabled us to arrive at a sense of wonder for the second time, with heartfelt thanks to Roger for giving us the first.

Clues to Biological Foundations of Language

Until the studies in the 1970s, nearly everything learned about the human capacity for language had come from the study of spoken languages. Traditionally, it has been assumed that the complex organizational properties of language are intimately connected with the production and processing of vocally articulated sounds. There is, after all, good evidence that human beings have evolved for speech; indeed, even the major language mediating areas of the brain are intimately connected with the vocal–auditory channel (Lenneberg, 1967). It has even been argued that hearing and the development of speech are necessary precursors to cerebral specialization for language. Spoken languages have been found to manifest certain basic structural principles assumed to result from the fact that language is normally spoken and heard (Liberman, 1982).

The existence of signed languages allows us to ask fundamental questions about the determinants of language organization, presenting an interesting test case for questions of general principles of language. What kinds of structural properties would a language have if its transmission were not based on the vocal tract and the ear? How is language organized when its basic lexical units are produced by the hands moving in space and when the signal is organized spatially as well as temporally? Do these modality differences result in any deeper differences?

This is not the place to review the specific directions these initial questions have taken us, except to say that it has been—and continues to be—a voyage of unexpected discoveries. In a decade of studies, we examined historical change in signs, memory and processing for signs, slips of the hand, contrasts between independent signed languages, linguistic structure at different levels, acquisition of sign language by deaf children of deaf parents, poetry and wit in a language without sound, rate of speaking and signing, and many other aspects of sign language. We found that ASL, the primary gestural system passed down from one generation of deaf people to the next, is an autonomous language with its own mechanisms for relating visual form with meaning. ASL has evolved linguistic devices that are not derived from those of English or any other spoken language. It thus becomes clear that the human capacity for language is not limited to the vocal auditory modality, and that in the absence of hearing, an independent visual–gestural language had developed across generations. It is also clear that language is forged anew, in the hands and for the eyes, among generations of·deaf people, that there are different signed languages as well as different spoken languages, and that the two forms of language have independent histories.

We are now able to address important issues comparing the properties of signed and spoken languages (Bellugi & Studdert-Kennedy, 1980). And our program (as well as that of the Salk Institute) has broadened, but in ways we had not anticipated a decade ago. We now have a four-part program to examine properties of visual spatial languages: (a) the formal linguistic structure of American Sign Language as contrasted with Chinese and Italian Sign Language as well as with spoken languages; (b) a program of computer graphic modeling of language processes; (c) a program investigating brain organization for language; and (d) studies of the acquisition of sign language by deaf children of deaf parents. These acquisition studies have revealed—as we outline in this chapter—

that despite the dramatic differences in surface organization and in modality, in almost all respects the acquisition of spoken and signed languages takes a remarkably similar course.

As a preface to a discussion of the acquisition research, we begin with a brief description of the properties of a language in space. Like spoken languages, ASL exhibits formal structuring at two levels: the internal structure of the lexical units, and the grammatical scaffolding underlying sentences; that is, there is a sublexical level of structure internal to the sign (the equivalent of the phonological level in spoken languages) and a level of structure that specifies the ways complex signs are formed and are bound together into sentences. ASL shares underlying principles of organization with spoken languages (e.g., constrained systems of features, rules based on underlying forms, recursive grammatical processes). However, the instantiation of those principles occurs in formal devices arising out of the very different possibilities of the visual-gestural mode (Bellugi & Studdert-Kennedy, 1980). For example, unlike spoken languages, ASL displays a marked preference for layered (as opposed to linear) organization. The elements that distinguish signs (handshapes, movements, places of articulation) are in contrasting spatial arrangements and co-occur throughout the sign; grammatical mechanisms exploit the possibility of simultaneous and multidimensional articulation. In the lexical items, the morphological processes, the syntax and discourse structure of ASL, such multi-layering of linguistic elements is a pervasive structural characteristic (Bellugi, 1980; Poizner, Klima, Bellugi, & Livingston, 1983).

But perhaps the most significant distinguishing aspect of sign language, and one that we find crucial for understanding its acquisition, is the unique role of *space*. Spatial contrasts and spatial manipulations figure structurally at all levels. Some ways that space functions linguistically in ASL are represented in Fig. 8.1.

Lexical Use of Space.   Spatial locus minimally differentiates lexical signs, as in SUMMER,[1] UGLY, DRY made with the same handshape and movement at the forehead, nose, and chin (shown in the top row of the figure).

---

[1]We use the following notation in this chapter:

SIGN =   Words in capital letters represent English labels (glosses) for ASL signs. The gloss represents the meaning of the unmarked, unmodulated, basic form of a sign out of context.

SIGN[X] =   A sign form that has undergone derivational or inflectional change. The form or meaning may be specified.

*SIGN =   An asterisk preceding a sign form indicates that it is ungrammatical within adult ASL.

ᵢSIGNⱼ =   Subscripts from the alphabet are used to indicate spatial loci. Nouns, pronouns, and verbs of location are marked with a subscript to indicate the loci at which they are signed.

LEXICON

SUMMER   UGLY   DRY

Spatial Contrasts in the Lexicon

MORPHOLOGY

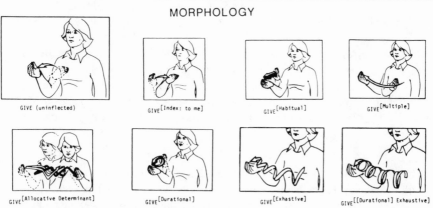

GIVE (uninflected)   GIVE[Index: to me]   GIVE[Habitual]   GIVE[Multiple]

GIVE[Allocative Determinant]   GIVE[Durational]   GIVE[Exhastive]   GIVE[[Durational] Exhaustive]

Layered Structure of Inflectional Processes

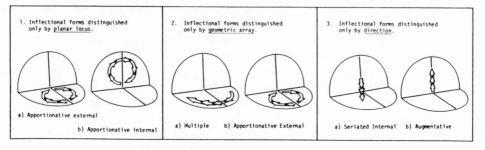

1. Inflectional forms distinguished only by planar locus.

a) Apportionative external
b) Apportionative internal

2. Inflectional forms distinguished only by geometric array.

a) Multiple   b) Apportionative External

3. Inflectional forms distinguished only by direction.

a) Seriated Internal   b) Augmentative

Dimensions of Patterning in Inflections

FIG. 8.1.   Spatial contrasts at lexical and morphological levels in ASL.

161

Morphological Use of Space.   Grammatical inflections in ASL are superimposed movement patterns co-occurring with the sign stem, using dimensions available to a visual–spatial language. Some sample inflections on a single sign GIVE are shown in the middle portion of the figure, including inflections for person, number, distributional aspect, temporal aspect, e.g., conveying the meanings "give to me," "give regularly," "give to them," "give to certain ones at different times," "give over time," "give to each," "give over time to each in turn."

Dimensions of Patterning.   In the kinds of distinctions that are morphologically marked, ASL is like many spoken languages; in the degree to which morphological marking is a favored form of patterning in the language, ASL is again similar to some spoken languages, but unlike English. In the *form* by which its lexical items are systematically modified in the sentences of the language, ASL has aspects that are unique. The lower portion of the figure shows some of the dimensions of patterning, specific to a visual–spatial language, used to build up morphological contrasts in American Sign Language: planes in signing space, different geometric contours (lines, arcs, circles), and directions of movement.

Syntactic Use of Space.   A most striking and distinctive use of space in ASL is its role in syntax and discourse, especially in pronominal reference, verb agreement, and anaphoric reference. In this language, person indexing and reindexing is accomplished primarily by manipulating points in a horizontal plane in the space in front of the signer's body. To refer to referents that are physically present in the discourse environment, a signer may point directly to self, when indicating first person, and directly to others, when referencing either second or third person. However, an abstract use of space occurs when reference is made to referents that are either physically or temporally distant.

Nominals introduced into the discourse are assigned to arbitrary and spatially distinct loci in a horizontal plane of signing space; signs with pronominal function are directed towards these points, and verb signs obligatorily move between such points in specifying grammatical relations (subject of the verb, object of the verb). Thus, a grammatical function served in many spoken languages by case marking or by linear ordering of words is fulfilled in ASL by essentially spatial mechanisms (Klima & Bellugi, 1979; Padden, 1983).

American Sign Language is markedly different in surface form from English, and from spoken languages in general. The inflectional and derivational devices of ASL, for example, make structured use of space and movement, nesting the basic sign stem in spatial patterns and complex dynamic contours of movement. ASL is unique in its use of space at all levels of linguistic organization. Although ASL is the most thoroughly analyzed of the signed languages of the world to date, other signed languages examined suggest that these characteristics may turn out to be general characteristics of primary signed languages.

In addition to the structured use of space in syntax, ASL is different from spoken language in the extent and degree of "motivatedness" between meaning and form. Characteristically, ASL lexical items themselves are often globally iconic, their form resembling some aspect of what they denote. At the morphological and syntactic levels also, there is often some congruence (motivatedness) between form and meaning. Spoken languages are not without such direct clues to meaning (reduplication processes and ideophones provide direct methods of reflecting meaning through form, for example). But in sign language such transparency is pervasive. ASL thus bears striking traces of its representational origins but, at the same time, is fully grammaticized.

THE EIGHTIES: THE ACQUISITION OF A SPATIAL LANGUAGE

One might have every reason to believe that such surface differences between signed and spoken language will influence the course of language acquisition. Given these differences, the task that the deaf child faces in learning sign language may be radically different from that faced by the hearing child for spoken language. For one thing, the mapping between meaning and form is more direct than in spoken language, and this might offer the child a more direct route into sign language at all levels. There are also differences in the channels used for production and perception of signed and spoken languages. Would the spatial, iconic aspects of ASL influence the course of acquisition? And how might the change in transmission system (from the ear to the eye, from the vocal apparatus to the hands) influence acquisition? In a language where the articulators are directly observable and, what's more, manipulable, the language learning situation takes on a different character. Do the special aspects of a language in a visual modality, and such differences in the character of the mother–child interaction, influence the course of the acquisition process?

Attempting to shed light on these questions, we have studied the acquisition of sign language by deaf children of deaf parents: monthly videotapes of mother–child interaction in the home, augmented by experimental interventions. We have undertaken longitudinal studies of 10 children between the ages of 1 and 8 years and have now charted the course of the acquisition of particular grammatical domains (e.g., pronominal reference, verb agreement, inflectional processes, derivational processes). We have also conducted cross-sectional studies with deaf children of deaf parents between the ages of 1 and 10 years old and have developed formal tests for each of the grammatical processes we have found in ASL (for phonological, lexical, inflectional, derivational, and compounding processes as well as syntax; Lillo-Martin, Bellugi, & Poizner, 1985). These tests have been normed with young deaf adults and are being used with deaf children of deaf parents as well as with other groups. This chapter sketches points from several doctoral theses that had their origins in intensive examination of the deaf children of deaf parents in our acquisition studies, including Petitto (1983a), Launer (1982), Supalla (1982), Meier (1982), and Loew (1984), across the same group of subjects. Here we focus primarily on how the spatial properties of ASL influence its acquisition in deaf children who are learning sign language as a native language. By examining the acquisition of specifically linguistic spatial mechanisms in ASL (as opposed to other types of more general spatial cognitive knowledge), important information about both the representation and the organization of space in development may be uncovered.

The Transition from Gesture to Symbol

The system of personal pronouns in ASL gives rise to a particularly striking issue in the connection between transparency and grammatical system in the acquisition of language; it also affords a dramatic example of the unexpected similarities between the acquisition of spoken and signed languages, despite striking differences in the form of the two types of language (Bellugi & Klima, 1982; Petitto, 1983a,b). Deixis in spoken languages is considered a verbal surrogate for pointing. In ASL, however, deixis *is* pointing. The pronominal signs in ASL are, in fact, the same as pointing gestures that hearing people use to supplement their words nonverbally. This directness of reference should lead to ease of acquisition of such forms by young deaf children learning ASL as compared with spoken languages.

The problems children have in learning terms that "shift" with speaker and addressee (such as *I* and *you*) is well known and well documented for spoken languages (Chiat, 1981, 1982; Clark, 1978). The hearing child's problems with the shifting nature of such arbitrary strings of sounds as *you* and *me* is readily understandable. In hearing children, problems with such deictic pronominal terms involving shifting reference are usually resolved by the age of 2;6 to 3;0. In contrast, we fully expected that, because of their transparent nature, the learning of the sign equivalents of pronominal reference in ASL would be early and error free ("trivial" is the way we expressed it). In ASL, the pronoun signs are exactly the same as the pointing gestures we would use to indicate self and addressee. Given such obvious gestures, directness of reference would seem inescapable. However, to our surprise, our early videotapes revealed that mothers, rather than use pronoun signs with their young deaf children, tended to employ name signs; moreover, their children did the same.

It was Laura Petitto who began to study this important aspect of the acquisition of ASL in depth. Laura formed a very special connection between Roger Brown and us; she completed her doctoral dissertation (Petitto, 1983a) with Roger and Courtney Cazden on this issue and did the research for it at our Salk

Institute laboratory with the deaf children in our acquisition studies. Her involvement in the study of pronominal reference surfaced very naturally; one day a deaf mother and child (age 1;11) were visiting and the child began signing YOU where she clearly meant herself. Her mother, embarrassed, signed "NO, NO, (YOU) MEAN (YOU)" taking the child's hand and making the pointing sign directly and forcibly on the child herself. In a language where the "speech organs" are directly visible, and moreover, manipulable, the form of mother to child correction is remarkably direct; yet astonishingly, the mother's corrections at this period had no effect whatever on the child's productions, and the child continued to walk around the lab blithely pointing *incorrectly* for reference to herself and others. Thus, the child was patently ignoring the transparency of the pointing gesture.

Petitto outlines the steps by which the deaf children attained mastery of the pronominal reference system in ASL in her contribution to this volume. She finds that deaf children display precisely the same progression—at the same ages—as do hearing children learning pronominal reference systems in spoken languages. Her results provide dramatic evidence of the transition from gesture to sign. It is a transition marked, first, by the emergence of a form used as a pointing gesture, then its absence over a period of several months, and finally the reemergence of the same form as a pronominal sign that is integrated into a linguistic system but marked by some systematic errors. Importantly, the errors and their resolution occur exactly on target with those observed in children learning spoken languages, at the same ages. It appears to make little difference, then, whether pronominal terms are symbolized by arbitrary streams of sound segments, as in spoken language, or by pointing signs that are indistinguishable in form from pointing gestures, as in sign language. These studies provide evidence for *discontinuity* in the transition from prelinguistic gesture to linguistic system, even when the form of the two are identical and share a single channel of expression. This is one form of evidence that the transition from gesture to sign requires a reorganization of the child's linguistic knowledge and suggests that the structure of a gesture *as a linguistic unit*, rather than the iconicity of its form, determines the course of acquisition. As we see in the following sections, our studies of how the morphology of ASL is acquired leads toward the same conclusion.

Acquiring a Multilayered Morphology

We turn now to another subsystem of ASL that involves spatial loci: the level of inflectional morphology by which verb signs are systematically modified to indicate grammatical categories such as agreement for person and number. Then we consider the acquisition of two different domains of derivational morphology, one of which is mimetically based.

The Spatial Marking for Verb Agreement.   For a specific subclass of verbs in ASL, "verb agreement" involves articulating the verb sign so that it moves from the position of the subject to the position of the object. Some verbs have obligatory agreement, some optionally undergo agreement, some can agree with only a single argument. The general mechanism is the same for all verbs that are indexible: movement between the spatial loci established for the noun arguments, either in accordance with actual loci for present referents or with abstract loci established in signing space (Klima & Bellugi, 1979; Lillo-Martin, in press-a; Padden, 1983). Thus, for a sign like GIVE, to sign a sentence such as "I give to you," the signer moves a flat grasping hand from in front of his own chest to the area in front of the addressee's chest; and to sign "you give to me," the movement of the verb is from addressee to signer.

Aside from the structural regularities that make this utterance part of a visual language (such as the form of the handshape, and the position of the utterance within a syntactic context), this sign resembles an iconic mime of giving, between "me," and "you." A priori, one might think, therefore, that such a form would be acquired relatively early, that the transparency in the form of the sign would facilitate its acquisition, regardless of the fact that in the adult language it is analyzed as a morphologically inflected form.

How do children acquire a morphological system that is grammaticized but that nevertheless displays a large amount of iconicity? Richard Meier (1981) analyzed the acquisition of such verb agreement both longitudinally and by experimental elicitation techniques. Working with three deaf children of deaf parents, ranging from 1;6 to 3;9, and 10 deaf children of deaf parents, ranging in age from 3;1 to 7;0, Meier mapped out three clear periods in their acquisition of verb agreement.

In the first stage of two to three signs (around the age of 2), signing children do not make use of the inflectional apparatus of ASL. Even when these children imitate, their imitations do not copy parental inflected utterances; they use instead the *uninflected* (or citation) form of the sign. Thus, signing children begin by analyzing uninflected forms out of the various patterns to which they are exposed and use only these forms. Furthermore, as Newport and Ashbrook (1977) showed, young deaf children at this stage tend to use sequential *order* of their uninflected signs, rather than spatial organization, to mark grammatical relations in their signing.

At the next stage, between the ages of 2 and 3, deaf children begin to produce inflected forms of the verb. Then, by 3 to 3½, in required contexts they master and consistently use the appropriate verb agreement system with present referents. In fact, they overgeneralize the system to nonindexible verbs (Meier, 1981, 1982). Figure 8.2 shows some young deaf children's overregularizations resulting in the production of forms that are ungrammatical in the adult language. Figure 8.2a shows overregularization of object markings to nonindexible verbs; 8.2b shows overregularization of plural markings on verbs to other grammatical categories.

*SPELL[X:'to me'] / SPELL   *SAY[X:'to you'] / SAY

*LIKE[X:'to it'] / LIKE

Over-regularizations of Object-Marking on Verbs

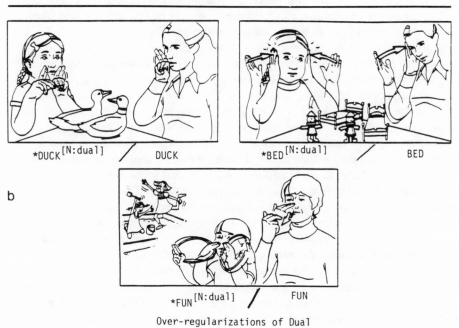

*DUCK[N:dual] / DUCK   *BED[N:dual] / BED

*FUN[N:dual] / FUN

Over-regularizations of Dual

FIG. 8.2. Deaf children's grammatical overregularizations.

Despite the difference in form of marking, the mastery of the inflections for verb agreement in ASL appears at the same age as mastery of comparable processes in spoken languages, as Meier argues. Moreover, the general pattern of acquisition—from no inflections, through consistent use of the inflectional system but with related overregularization, to complete mastery—is the same for ASL and for spoken languages. Thus, the iconicity of the ASL forms presented to the child again appears to have remarkably little effect on the acquisition process.

A Derivational Distinction.   In ASL there is a consistent formal relationship between verbs and their formally related deverbal nouns (e.g., SCISSORS and CUT; CAR and DRIVE), as first described by Supalla and Newport (1978). The members of such a pair share handshape, place of articulation, and movement shape, but the noun form is regularly differentiated from the verb form by frequency and manner of movement: whereas the verbs show a variety of movement characteristics, the related nouns are always *repeated, small,* and *restrained* in manner.

In our laboratory, Launer (1982) examined the development of this distinction in young deaf children's signing between the ages of 0;9 and 6;0, and again found consistent periods in the acquisition process. First, in children under 2 years, no formal marking whatever appears; such young deaf children use the same global form (handshape, place of articulation, approximate movement shape) throughout. Second, between the ages of 2 and 3, children sporadically mark nouns and verbs with appropriate features but do not do so systematically. They often use noncanonical or idiosyncratic markings, unrelated to the featural distinctions of the adult language. And third, between the ages of 3 and 5, children begin to mark systematically the full morphological distinctions between verbs and their related deverbal nouns; they even make overextensions of the formal markings to unpaired forms and to lexical innovations.

Figure 8.3 illustrates aspects of this developmental trend. Three-year-old deaf children correctly sign nouns and formally related verbs (e.g., the noun DOOR and the verb OPEN-DOOR in Fig. 8.3a) with the appropriate morphological markings. At this point, pairs with no distinctions—present in earlier signing— have virtually disappeared and most nouns and verbs are marked with some featural distinctions. The children are distinguishing nouns from verbs in earnest, even when they appear within a single sentence. For example, a child of 3;6 invented a story in which she had an imaginary car that she did not want to drive. "Here's the key," she signed to her mother, handing her an imaginary key; and then, "YOU DRIVE MY CAR," using the appropriate distinctions to systematically differentiate DRIVE and CAR (Fig. 8.3b). Finally, by 4 years of age, children even extend the morphological markers to nonexistent ASL forms, as shown in Fig. 8.3c. Based on the noun sign PICNIC, the child created a verb form nonexistent in ASL, clearly intending—in the context of her utterance—

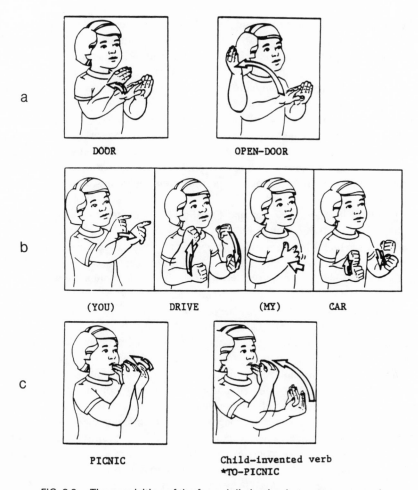

FIG. 8.3.   The acquisition of the formal distinction between nouns and verbs.

something like "to have a picnic." At this point, the children extend the morphological markers across all forms of a class, adding the nonmimetic markers characteristic of nouns (repeated, restrained, small), and they do so regardless of the iconicity of the image base of the signs.

Mimetically Based Verbs of Movement and Location.   In ASL there are constructions called "mimetic" and "analogue," used to portray the movement, shape, and location of objects. Newport (1981) and Supalla (1982) have argued that these verbs of motion and location are complex verbal stems constructed from the regular combination of a limited number of component morphemes. These component parts include classifiers for the semantic category of the object indicated by handshape (e.g., human vs. animate vs. vehicle), and movement morphemes indicated by movement path (e.g., straight vs. circular vs. arc), and manner (e.g., bounce vs. roll vs. random). Although these ASL verbs of motion are not analogue or mimetic representations of real world motions, many of them do (when viewed holistically) distinctly resemble their referent motions. If iconicity and the visual channel of ASL are facilitators in the acquisition of the language, here then is another ideal test case. Would such a system, which appears to portray a one-to-one mapping of meaning to form, be more easily acquired than a discrete system? Would children begin by viewing these verbs of motion as analogue representations, or mimes, and thus acquire them early?

Supalla (1982) and Newport and Supalla (1980) examined this question in studies of deaf children between the ages of 2;4 and 5;11. They used an elicitation task, in which films of moving objects were presented to the children, who were then asked to produce a sign utterance for the event just seen. The data on handshape and placement morphemes indicate that, even though the whole form is highly iconic, deaf children acquiring ASL *are* learning these component noniconic morphemes; moreover, they make systematic errors along the way. The following developmental pattern emerged: Until about 2;9, verbs of motion are either frozen single-morpheme stems or a small number of simple movements that do not appropriately combine morphemes. With increasing age, the child apparently begins to analyze internal morphemes, producing some correctly while omitting others, and the proportion of correctly combined morphemes increases. Sometimes the multiple morphemes are produced sequentially (e.g., a movement path and a manner morpheme) rather than simultaneously.

Their evidence suggests that young children do not acquire these mimetic forms early, despite their iconicity. Nor do they acquire them in analogue or holistic fashion; but rather, as the evidence across our range of acquisition studies also indicates, they do so by acquiring them morpheme by morpheme just as do hearing children acquiring spoken languages.

Summary of Acquisition of Morphology

Here we have examined some of the first morphological systems to be mastered by the signing child. Because of the transparency of ASL forms, we surmised that these would be systems profoundly influenced by iconicity. What we found, instead, was that their transparency at all levels appears to have little or no effect on acquisition. Indeed, Meier (1982) has argued that the young child may not be disposed to make use of the transparency of forms. Rather than focusing on iconicity, the deaf child, in an ordered and orderly fashion, analyzes morphological components of the system presented to him or her. The fact that the articulators in sign language are visible and manipulable could plausibly be thought to provide a special route to learning: Mothers do occasionally mold and shape young children's hands in signing. Our evidence suggests, however, that that practice is steadfastly and systematically ignored by signing children who firmly hold their ground, continuing their incorrect analysis and resulting errors, until they arrive at their own reorganization of the language system. The evidence so far suggests, then, that the course of acquisition of these morphological processes is remarkably like that for spoken languages.

THE INTEGRATION OF SYSTEMS: SPATIALLY ORGANIZED SYNTAX AND DISCOURSE

A Spatial Referential Framework

We have shown that, despite obvious differences in surface structure and modality, the time course of the acquisition of ASL is remarkably similar to that for spoken languages. We now turn to the acquisition of a domain in which the nature of the apparatus used in ASL may have its most striking effect: the means by which relations among signs are stipulated in sentences and in discourse. Languages have different ways of marking grammatical relations among their lexical items. In English, it is primarily the order of the lexical items that marks the basic grammatical relations; in other spoken languages, it is the morphology of case marking or verb agreement that signals these relations. ASL, by contrast, specifies relations among signs primarily through the manipulation of sign forms in space. In sign language, space itself carries linguistic meaning. And, the most striking and distinctive use of space in ASL is in its role in syntax and discourse, especially in nominal assignment, pronominal reference, verb agreement, anaphoric reference, and the referential spatial framework for discourse. In this section, we turn to some of the spatial cognitive, memorial, and linguistic requirements involved in a language whose syntax is essentially spatial; we then consider the consequences of these requirements for acquisition of such a language.

In English, the intended reference of lexical pronouns in children (and sometimes in adults as well) is often unclear. The spatial mechanisms used in ASL, by contrast, require that identity of referents be maintained across arbitrary points in space that are not lexical units. In ASL, then, the failure to maintain such identity results in strings that are ill formed, i.e., judged ungrammatical, rather than being simply unclear. Thus, the requirements of the grammatical system of such a visual–spatial language may reveal the problems the child has in organizing coherent and cohesive discourse.

As an illustration of the complexities involved in a spatially organized syntactic system, consider a brief account of the use of spatial loci for referential indexing, coreference, for verb agreement, and for the fixed and shifting spatial framework underlying sentences and discourse. Nominals introduced into ASL discourse may be assigned to arbitrary reference points in a horizontal plane of signing space. In signed discourse, pointing again to a specific locus clearly "refers back" to a previously established nominal, even with many other signs intervening. *Coreferential* nominals must be indexed to the same locus point, both within and across sentences. This *spatial indexing* in ASL allows explicit coreference and may reduce ambiguity. Further, because verb signs move between such points in specifying grammatical relations, the ASL system of *verb agreement* is also essentially spatialized; and classes of verbs bear obligatory markers for person (and number) via spatial indices (see Fig. 8.4a for an example sentence). The same signs in the same order, but with a reversal in direction of spatial endpoints of the verb, may indicate different grammatical relations. Moreover, because verb agreement may be given spatially, sentences whose signs are made in different temporal orders can still have the same meaning. These devices are diagrammed in Fig. 8.4b, an illustration of the spatial arrangement of an ASL sentence meaning "John encouraged him to urge her to permit each of them to take up the class." Overall, then, in *function* this system is like grammatical devices in spoken languages (Lillo-Martin, in press-b). However, in its *form*—marking connections between spatial points—spatially organized syntax in ASL bears the clear imprint of the mode in which the language evolved (Bellugi & Klima, 1982; Padden, 1983).

Spatial indexing permits a certain freedom of word order (in simple sentences, at any rate), while providing clear specification of grammatical relations by spatial means. The horizontal plane in front of the signer's torso is the locus for indices of definite reference (that is, if the speaker has already introduced a referent into the discourse). Different spaces may be used to contrast events, to indicate reference to time preceding the utterance, to express hypotheticals and counterfactuals. And it is also possible to embed one subspace within another subspace, as in embedding a past-time context within conditional subspace, illustrated in Fig. 8.4c.

Creating such a spatial referential framework for syntax and discourse is further complicated by interacting mechanisms. Whereas the referential system just described is a *fixed* system in which nominals remain associated with specific points in space until "erased," the spatial referential framework sometimes *shifts;* for example, third-person referents may be assigned to the locus in front of the signer's torso that otherwise denotes self-reference. When this shift occurs, the whole spatial plane rotates and previously established nominals are now associated with new points. In this system a fixed referential framework may be *implied* for the viewer, but it is not spatially fixed, thus adding complexity to the

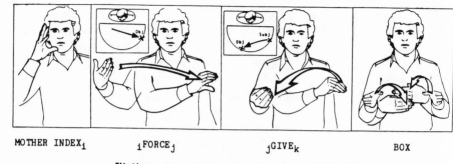

a

MOTHER INDEX_i   _iFORCE_j   _jGIVE_k   BOX

"Mother_i forced him_j to give him_k the box."

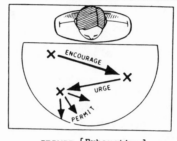

b

John ENCOURAGE_i   _iURGE_J   _jPERMIT_k[Exhaustive]   TAKE-UP   CLASS

"John encouraged him_i to urge her_j to permit each of them_k to take up the class."

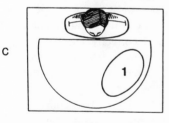

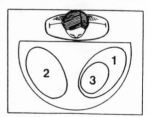

c

Spatial reference can be embeded, one subspace in another.

FIG. 8.4. Syntactic spatial mechanisms in ASL.

spatial cognitive requirements of the language. Little wonder, then, that Padden (1982) concludes as follows:

> An account of indexing in ASL as simply 'pointing' ignores the complex knowledge signers must have. The signer must not only determine which points in space to select (the same locus point cannot be used for different nominals) but must monitor their spatial positions thoughout the discourse for the purpose of subsequent pronominal reference. The interplay here between visuospatial memory and grammatical constraints is intriguing.

What of the young child in the process of acquiring a language whose syntax and discourse mechanisms are organized in these ways and, therefore, are intimately intertwined with spatial cognitive capacities? Complex uses of space in the service of linguistic contrasts involving syntax and discourse clearly have nonlinguistic spatial cognitive underpinnings. Consequently, in the course of investigating the acquisition of syntactic spatial mechanisms by deaf children, we are now examining the interplay between such acquisition and the development of the prerequisite underlying spatial cognition. This will allow us in the future to focus on the relationship between language and cognition in a powerful way. The issues underlying the development of spatial cognition were so important to our studies that we organized a conference around this theme that has resulted in a book (*Spatial Cognition: Brain Bases and Development,* in press). For the remainder of this chapter, we discuss some of our first findings in these domains in research that is still in progress.

A Deaf Child's Storytelling

In our laboratory Ruth Loew (1982, 1984) has completed a study of one deaf child's spontaneous narratives, examining in particular the acquisition of the systems underlying anaphoric reference. She finds the following stages in the child's development of signing.

At age 3;1, the child's storytelling is extremely difficult to understand, due in large part to unclear reference. Signs follow one another with no use of space and no syntactic indicators to communicate which characters performed which actions. Verbs are rarely indexed for nonpresent reference and, if they are, it is without explicitly associating nominals with the indices. It is important to note, nevertheless, that the same verbs are consistently and correctly indexed for present reference at this age. Thus, it is clear that the two systems (verb agreement and establishment of nominals) are functionally separate systems for the child. At this age, however, the child's formal mechanisms for conveying anaphoric reference beyond present contexts are minimal. The child does converse freely about matters outside the here and now and has no problems conceptualizing these; her problems clearly lie in conveying explicit information about such matters according to the spatialized grammatical mechanisms provided by the language.

At 3;6, the child begins to make use of indexing in storytelling; however, she still does not explicitly establish identities for loci. Furthermore, she tends to use one locus for several referents, stacking them up at one locus point, thus still leaving reference unclear and ambiguous (see Fig. 8.5a). (Petitto, 1980, describes another child's first use of abstract spatial loci, in which he "stacked" 11 characters in one location!)

At 4;4, the child uses several different loci in a single story but still does not generally establish identities for loci, nor does she maintain a referent-to-locus

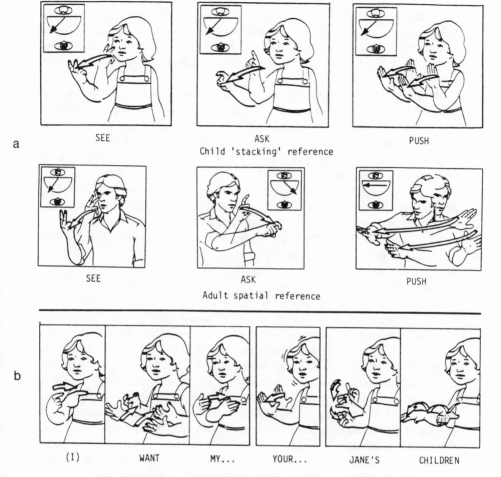

FIG. 8.5. Deaf children's errors in spatial indexing.

mapping. She seems to mark shifts in character spatially but does not maintain identities; she also distributes loci randomly.

By 4;9, the child reveals increased use of indexing and begins to use a designated locus for a referent consistently. Her storytelling is now qualitatively different from earlier stages and is much more adult like; the use of space is frequently incorrect, but by this age it is pervasive. The child has begun to integrate various aspects of spatial reference and addressee interaction; loci are now often formally established and consistently used. She attends closely to the addressee at role transitions and makes frequent self-corrections at such boundaries, suggesting that she is aware of the possibilities of confusion at these points. Figure 8.5b contains a particularly complex example where the child was recounting an imaginary story in which she (Jane) had 10 children, and another woman arrived to claim them as her own. Jane (in the role of the other woman) signed: "I WANT MY . . . YOUR . . . JANE'S CHILDREN." One can understand why in this situation she finally resorted to the use of her own name sign to clarify reference!

At a time when the child appears to have mastered the individual spatial components necessary to construct grammatically correct anaphoric reference in storytelling and the ability to cognitively comprehend and convey events about nonpresent referents (albeit in ungrammatical ways), she does not seem to be able to integrate these devices into a rule-governed linguistic system at the discourse level. Indeed, at the age of 4, deaf children begin to establish referents at distinct points in the horizontal plane of signing space, thereby differentiating referents at the sentence level, but they still fail to consistently maintain the identity of the previously established loci across stretches of discourse.

In summary, the deaf child's knowledge of the linguistic use of space in ASL must include information on the differentiation of signing space, explicit establishment of nominals at discrete spatial loci, consistent spatial identity of loci, and contrastive use of established loci in sentences and across sentences in discourse, in long-distance dependencies. Children appear to acquire these abilities over time, and it appears to be not until around ages 7 to 10 that the fully mature system can be integrated and mastered across sentences and discourse.

These findings raise several important questions. Central to these issues is the relationship between cognition and language. In a spatially organized language, the relationship between acquisition in such an alternative medium and the development of its nonlanguage spatial cognitive substrate is crucial. As Newport and Meier (1986) put it in their excellent review article, "It has sometimes been suggested that spatial representation is conceptually difficult for the child, and therefore is a cognitively complex medium in which to signal linguistic functions. On this view, the acquisition of morphological devices in ASL should occur somewhat later than the acquisition of formally similar devices in spoken languages, where spatial representation is not involved." In fact, the available evidence suggests that spatial representation itself does not constrain the acquisition process—the acquisition of phonological and morphological devices in ASL occurs on a strikingly similar timetable to the acquisition of spoken language devices that are formally similar in complexity. We are now comparing the acquisition of discourse functions (anaphoric reference and discourse organization) across hearing and deaf children in the same set of tasks as part of our ongoing research.

The Comprehension of Spatially Organized Syntax

In a series of studies, the spatially organized syntax has been broken down into component parts, to investigate the young child's processing and comprehension of separate aspects of linguistic structure (Lillo-Martin, Bellugi, & Poizner, 1985). A first step is to ask whether the child can understand what he or she is not yet producing. Can the young deaf signing child understand that nominals may be abstractly associated with arbitrary points in space, even when he or she is not producing such syntactic spatial mechanisms regularly in his or her own signing?

We examined this question with 68 deaf children of deaf parents between the ages of 1 and 10, using a formal language task devised to examine the association of nominals with spatial loci. The Nominal Establishment Test examines perception, comprehension, and memory for spatial loci associated with specific nominals. In the test, nominals are assigned to arbitrary loci in the horizontal plane of signing space that serves for definite reference. We ask two kinds of questions: where a certain nominal has been established (to which the child answers by pointing to a specific locus), and which nominal has been established at a certain locus (to which the child answers by signing the nominal). In associating loci with their nominal referents, the task assesses understanding of a key aspect of coreference structure in ASL syntax and discourse and has been used with deaf adults of different language background, and with left- and right-brain-lesioned deaf signers, as well as with deaf children (Poizner, Klima, & Bellugi, 1987; Lillo-Martin, Bellugi, Struxness, & O'Grady, 1985). Figure 8.6 presents a sample test item and results with 68 deaf children of deaf parents.

When we attempted to assess several 2-year-old deaf children, they were unable to deal with the task. When the deaf experimenter signed "Where's the doll?" (after previously associating an arbitrary locus with the sign DOLL), these children looked around the room as if looking for an actual doll; one ran to her bedroom to take one out. When asked "What is at point X?" (an arbitrary point in space previously associated with the sign BOY), they seemed nonplussed. Thus, 1-year-olds and most 2-year-olds fail the test; but importantly, already by the age of 3, deaf children perform well on the task, even with two and three nominals. This occurs despite the fact that such nominal establishment to spatial loci is not reported in deaf children's spontaneous signing before the age of 4½ (e.g., Loew, 1984). Such results suggest that the deaf child by the age of 3 does understand that in this language a nominal can be associated with an arbitrary point in abstract space; furthermore, he or she is adept at processing this aspect of language structure and can handle two and three nominals at a time in different spatial loci with ease and facility.

Our program of studies of acquisition of spatially organized syntax involves many more components, one of which is especially appropriate here, partly because we reused items from a test of comprehension developed more than 20 years ago in Roger Brown's Harvard laboratory (Fraser, Bellugi, & Brown, 1963). But now we are using such items to investigate grammatical relations signaled not by temporal order of words as in English but rather by the very different mechanisms of a signed language, where grammatical relations are signaled by spatial relationships of signs and points in space. With young children learning English, the pictures in Fig. 8.7 were used to test comprehension of the distinction between the sentences "the cat bites the dog" and "the dog bites the cat."

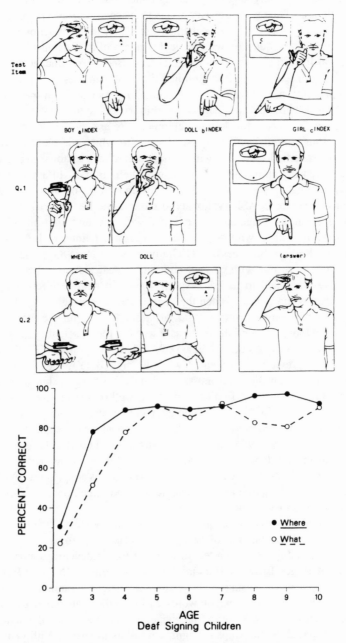

FIG. 8.6. Syntax: Comprehension of nominal establishment.

178

DOG (INDEX$_{3i}$)   CAT (INDEX $_{3j}$) $_{3i}$BITE$_{3j}$

'The dog bit the cat.'

DOG (INDEX$_{3i}$)   CAT (INDEX$_{3j}$) $_{3j}$BITE$_{3i}$

'The cat bit the dog.'

FIG. 8.7.   Spatial syntax: Test of verb agreement marking.

In the ASL version of the task, the equivalent contrast is signaled by spatial relations. In the ASL sentences illustrated in Fig. 8.7, only the direction of movement of the verb signals the different grammatical relations (the order of signs can vary and assignment to spatial loci is arbitrary). The spatial arrangements in the picture need not match the spatial arrangements established in the test item; in the example given, indeed they do not, thus adding spatial complexity as well.

These tests of comprehension of aspects of spatially organized syntax will help answer some questions about the deaf children's mastery of the complex linguistic system in a visual spatial language. We are generally finding that young deaf children can process aspects of the spatial syntax of the language in sentences distinguished only by different spatial endpoints of the verb (Lillo-Martin, Bellugi, Struxness, & O'Grady, 1985). We are currently investigating the comprehension of coreference in shifting spatial frameworks as well as contrasting narratives told by hearing and deaf children in order to examine discourse across language modalities.

THE SEPARATION BETWEEN SPATIAL COGNITION AND SPATIAL LANGUAGE

At the same time, we are tracking the developmental course for the acquisition of spatial cognitive underpinnings that are relevant to the mastery of the ASL linguistic system. Unlike his or her hearing counterpart, the young deaf child must acquire nonlanguage spatial capacities that may serve as prerequisites to the linguistic system. We are investigating the interrelationship and separability of these two domains in deaf children in a series of studies of nonlanguage visual–spatial processing. We investigate whether the acquisition of spatially organized syntax is yoked in particular ways to the development of its nonlanguage substrate; that is, to aspects of spatial cognition.

Our studies so far suggest that deaf children who have early exposure to processing spatial relationships in a linguistic system perform at the same level (and in some cases even show early enhancement) compared to norms for hearing children (Bellugi, O'Grady, Lillo-Martin, O'Grady, van Hoek, & Corina, in press; Reilly, McIntire, & Bellugi, in press). The studies suggest that exposure to a spatially organized linguistic system in no way impedes development of spatial cognition. In fact, results so far suggest that there may even be some *enhancement* of certain spatial cognitive abilities. These results are consistent with the studies of Neville, using correlations between electrophysiological measures and behavior, showing that in a spatial attention task, deaf signing subjects are superior to hearing subjects (Neville, in press). Perhaps, unexpectedly, the complex requirements for spatial processing in sign language may accelerate the development of particular visual–spatial capacities.

In a separate series of studies, we are investigating the effects of unilateral lesions to the left and the right hemisphere in deaf signers. Because ASL displays the complex linguistic structure found in spoken languages but conveys much of its structure by manipulating spatial relations, it exhibits properties for which each of the hemispheres of hearing people show a different predominant function. The study of brain-damaged deaf signers offers a particularly revealing vantage point for understanding the organization of the brain for language and spatial cognitive functions in deaf signers (Bellugi, Poizner, & Klima, 1983; Klima, Bellugi, & Poizner, 1985; Poizner, Klima, & Bellugi, 1987).

We found that on spatial tasks there were clear-cut differences in performance between left-hemisphere-damaged signers and right-hemisphere-damaged signers across a range of tasks. In nonlanguage spatial tasks, the right-hemisphere-damaged signers were severely impaired; they tended to show severe spatial disorganization, were unable to indicate perspective, and neglected the left side of space, reflecting the classic visuospatial impairments seen in hearing patients with right-hemisphere damage. These nonlanguage data suggest that the right hemisphere in deaf signers develops cerebral specialization for nonlanguage visuospatial functions.

On linguistic tasks and in analyses of ongoing signing, the two groups of patients were also markedly different. The signers with right-hemisphere damage were not aphasic. They exhibited fluent, grammatical, virtually error-free signing, with good range of grammatical forms, no agrammatism, and no signing deficits. This preserved signing existed in the face of marked deficits in the processing of nonlanguage spatial relations. The signers with left-hemisphere damage, in great contrast, were not impaired in nonlanguage visuospatial tasks but were very impaired in language functions. They showed distinct sign aphasias; one left-hemisphere-damaged signer even had impairment of spatially organized syntax.

These data show that in deaf adult signers it is the left hemisphere that is dominant for sign language, even though processing sign language involves processing spatial relations at all linguistic levels. Furthermore, there is a complementary specialization in the right hemisphere for visuospatial nonlanguage functions. Thus, in principle, there is a dissociation between spatial cognition and spatial language in adult deaf signers, reflected in the different functional specializations of the left and right hemispheres (Poizner, Kaplan, Bellugi, & Padden, 1984).

As opposed to its syntactic use, space in ASL also functions in a topographic way, i.e., the space within which signs are articulated can be used to describe the layout of objects in space. In such mapping, spatial relations among signs correspond in a topographic manner to actual spatial relations among the objects described. This distinction between the use of space to represent *syntactic* relations and to represent actual *spatial* relations allows us to examine different hemispheric involvement for the functionally distinct mental representations of space. Significantly, we find that even within signing itself these two opposing uses of space are mediated by opposite hemispheres: Syntactic representations are disrupted by left-hemisphere damage and topographic representations by right-hemisphere damage (Poizner, Klima, & Bellugi, 1987).

Language and spatial representation are attributes for which the two cerebral hemispheres in hearing people show different specializations, and we have extended this finding to deaf, signing adults also. The use of the two hands in sign language may provide clues to hemispheric specialization that one cannot obtain from speech because, in sign language, the hands themselves are the language articulators. The development of hand dominance in very young deaf signers affords a unique opportunity for marking the onset of cerebral specialization. Indeed, our preliminary studies suggest that hand dominance for sign language appears very early in some deaf children (perhaps as early as the first signs) and is much stronger than hand preference for nonlanguage activities in the same young children (Vaid, Bellugi, & Poizner, 1985). In these ways, then, the study of the acquisition process in sign language may provide additional clues to the biological foundations of language.

The study of the acquisition of American Sign Language in deaf children brings into focus some fundamental questions about the representation of language and the representation of space. In research over the past decade, we have been specifying the ways in which the formal properties of languages are shaped by their modalities of expression, sifting properties peculiar to a particular language mode from more general properties common to all languages and thus reflective of biological determinants of linguistic form. At all structural levels, the surface forms of a signed language are deeply influenced by the modality in which it develops, particularly in the pervasive use of spatial relations to express syntactic and discourse functions. Not only are there radical differences in the surface forms of signed and spoken languages, but there are also radical differences between visual and auditory processing. In addition, language in the visual modality offers possibilities for more direct entry into the system on the part of the child, and more direct instruction on the part of the parents. Yet, in our studies of the acquisition process we have found that deaf and hearing children show a strikingly similar course of development if exposed to a natural language at the critical time. These data thus dramatically underscore the biological substrate for the human capacity for creating linguistic systems.

The young deaf child is faced with the dual task in sign language of spatial perception, memory, and spatial transformations on the one hand, and processing grammatical structure on the other, all in one and the same visual event. In current studies, we are therefore investigating not only the development of a spatial language but also the development of spatial cognition, because in sign language the two are so intimately intertwined.

In general, our research demonstrates that, despite radical differences in language modality, deaf and hearing children follow a dramatically similar course of development, given natural language input at the critical time. Deaf children, as do their hearing counterparts, actively analyze components of the language system presented to them. Furthermore, the evidence suggests that even when the modality and the language offer possibilities that are explicit and therefore seem intuitively obvious, deaf children appear to ignore this directness and continue their systematic linguistic analyses. And after all, it is very exciting to find that children, when presented with this very different form of language, exhibit precisely the same kinds of processes of induction of latent structure that Roger Brown, myself, and others began to observe in Adam, Eve, and Sarah some 20 years ago.

ACKNOWLEDGMENTS

This research was supported in part by National Institutes of Health grants #NS15175, #NS19096, #HD13249, and National Science Foundation Grant #BNS 8309860 to the Salk Institute for Biological Studies. Illustrations were drawn by Frank A. Paul, copyright Ursula Bellugi, The Salk Institute. I wish to thank Edward S. Klima, Diane Lillo-Martin, and Howard Poizner for helpful comments on this chapter and the research on which it is based. Many researchers took part in the acquisition studies and in our lively discussions in sign language, including Leslie Jamison, Patricia Launer, Diane Lillo-Martin, Ruth Loew, Richard Meier, Elissa Newport, Lucinda and Maureen O'Grady, Carol Padden, Laura Petitto, Patricia Richey, Dennis Schemenauer, Ted Supalla, James Tucker, and Karen van Hoek, among others. We are very grateful to Dr. Henry Klopping and the staff of the California School for the Deaf in Fremont, California, as well as to the deaf children and their parents for their spirited participation in these studies.

REFERENCES

Bellugi, U. (1980). The structuring of language: Clues from the similarities between signed and spoken language. In U. Bellugi & M. Studdert-Kennedy (Eds.), *Signed and spoken language: Biological constraints on linguistic form*. Weinheim/Deerfield Beach, FL: Verlag Chemie.

Bellugi, U., & Brown, R. (Eds.). (1964). *The Acquisition of Language. Monographs of the Society for Research in Child Development, 29(1)*.

Bellugi, U., & Klima, E. S. (1982). The acquisition of three morphological systems in American Sign Language. Keynote address, *Papers and reports on child language development* (K1-35). Palo Alto, CA: Stanford University.

Bellugi, U., O'Grady, L., Lillo-Martin, D., O'Grady, M., van Hoek, K., & Corina, D. (in press). Enhancement of spatial cognition in deaf children. In V. Volterra & C. Erting (Eds.), *The transition from gesture to language*. New York: Springer-Verlag.

Bellugi, U., Poizner, H., & Klima, E. S. (1983). Brain organization for language: Clues from sign aphasia. *Human Neurobiology, 2*, 155–170.

Bellugi, U., & Studdert-Kennedy, M. (1980). *Signed and spoken language: Biological constraints on linguistic form*. Weinheim/Deerfield Beach, FL: Verlag Chemie.

Brown, R. (1958). *Words and things*, New York: The Free Press.

Brown, R., & Bellugi, U. (1964). Three processes in the child's acquisition of syntax. *Harvard Educational Review, 34*(2), 133–151.

Chiat, S. (1981). Context-specificity and generalization in the acquisition of preonominal distinctions. *Journal of Child Language, 8*, 75–91.

Chiat, S. (1982). If I were you and you were me: The analysis of pronouns in a pronoun-reversing child. *Journal of Child Language, 9*, 359–379.

Clark, E. V. (1978). From gesture to word: On the natural history of deixis in language acquisition. In J. S. Bruner & A. Garson (Eds.), *Human growth and development: Wolfson College lectures*. Oxford: Oxford University Press.

Fraser, C., Bellugi, U., & Brown, R. (1963). Control of grammar in imitation, comprehension, and production. *Journal of Verbal Learning and Verbal Behavior, 2*(2), 121–135.

Klima, E. S., & Bellugi, U. (1979). *The signs of language*. Cambridge, MA: Harvard University Press.

Klima, E. S., Bellugi, U., & Poizner, H. (1985). Sign language and brain organization. In V. Volterra & W. C. Stokoe (Eds.), *Proceedings of the Third International Symposium on Sign Language Research*, 72–78.

Launer, P. (1982). *Acquiring the distinction between related nouns and verbs in ASL*. Doctoral dissertation, City University of New York.

Lenneberg, E. (1967). *Biological foundations of language*. New York: Wiley.

Liberman, A. M. (1982). On finding that speech is special. *American Psychologist, 37*, 148–167.

Lillo-Martin, D. (in press-a). Effects of the acquisition of morphology on syntactic parameter setting. In *Proceedings of the North Eastern Linguistic Society*, Montreal.

Lillo-Martin, D. (in press-b). Null pronouns and verb agreement in American Sign Language. In S. Berman, J. Cohe, & J. McDonough (Eds.), *Proceedings of the North Eastern Linguistic Society, 15*, 302–318.

Lillo-Martin, D., Bellugi, U., & Poizner, H. (1985). *Tests for American Sign Language*. Manuscript, The Salk Institute for Biological Studies.

Lillo-Martin, D., Bellugi, U., Struxness, L., & O'Grady, M. (1985). The acquisition of spatially organized syntax. *Papers and Reports on Child Language Development*. Stanford University Press, *24*, 70–78.

Loew, R. C. (1982). Roles and reference. In F. Caccamise, M. Garretson, & U. Bellugi (Eds.), *Teaching American Sign Language as a second/foreign language* (pp. 40–58). Silver Spring, MD: National Association of the Deaf.

Loew, R. C. (1984). *Roles and reference in American Sign Language: A developmental perspective*. Doctoral dissertation, The University of Minnesota.

Meier, R. (1981). Icons and morphemes: Models of the acquisition of verb agreement in ASL. *Papers and Reports on Child Language Development, 20*, 92–99. Palo Alto, CA: Stanford University.

Meier, R. (1982). *Icons, analogues, and morphemes: The acquisition of verb agreement in American Sign Language*. Doctoral dissertation, University of California, San Diego.

Neville, H. (in press). Cerebral organization for spatial attention: Effects of early sensory and language experience. In J. Stiles-Davis, M. Kritchevsky, & U. Bellugi (Eds.), *Spatial cognition: Brain bases and development*. Hillsdale, NJ: Lawrence Erlbaum Associates.

Newport, E. L. (1981). Constraints on structures: Evidence from American Sign Language and language learning. In W. A. Collins (Ed.), *Aspects of the development of competence, Minnesota Symposium on child psychology* (Vol. 14, pp. 93–124). Hillsdale, NJ: Lawrence Erlbaum Associates.

Newport, E., & Ashbrook, E. (1977). The emergence of semantic relations in American Sign Language. *Papers and Reports on Child Language Development, 13*, 16–21. Palo Alto, CA: Stanford University Press.

Newport, E., & Meier, R. (1986). Acquisition of American Sign Language. In D. I. Slobin (Ed.), *The cross-linguistic study of language acquisition* (Vol. 2). Hillsdale, NJ: Lawrence Erlbaum Associates.

Newport, E., & Supalla, T. (1980). The structuring of language: Clues from the acquisition of signed and spoken language. In U. Bellugi & M. Studdert-Kennedy (Eds.), *Signed and spoken language: Biological constraints on linguistic form*. Weinheim/Deerfield Beach, FL: Verlag Chemie.

Padden, C. (1982). *Spatial syntax in American Sign Language*. Unpublished manuscript, The Salk Institute for Biological Studies, La Jolla, CA.

Padden, C. (1983). *Interaction of morphology and syntax in American Sign Language*. Unpublished doctoral dissertation, University of California, San Diego.

Petitto, L. (1980). *On the acquisition of anaphoric reference in American Sign Language*. Manuscript, The Salk Institute for Biological Studies, La Jolla, CA.

Petitto, L. (1983a). *From gesture to symbol: The relationship between form and meaning in the acquisition of personal pronouns in American Sign Language*. Doctoral dissertation, Harvard University.

Petitto, L. (1983b). From gesture to symbol: The relation between form and meaning in the acquisition of ASL. *Papers and Reports on Child Language Development, 22*, 100–107. Palo Alto, CA: Stanford University.

Poizner, H., Kaplan, E., Bellugi, U., & Padden, C. (1984). Visual–spatial processing in deaf brain-damaged signers. *Brain and Cognition, 3*, 281–306.

Poizner, H., Klima, E. S., & Bellugi, U. (1987). *What the hands reveal about the brain*. Cambridge: MIT Press/Bradford Books.

Poizner, H., Klima, E. S., Bellugi, U., & Livingston, R. (1983). Motion analysis of grammatical processes in a visual–gestural language. In *Motion: Representation and perception* (pp. 148–171). New York: Association for Computing Machinery.

Reilly, J., McIntire, M., & Bellugi, U. (in press). Faces: The relationship between language and affect. In V. Voterra & C. Erting (Eds.), *From gesture to language in hearing and deaf children*. New York: Springer-Verlag.

Supalla, T. (1982). *Structure and acquisition of verbs of motion and location in American Sign Language*. Doctoral dissertation, University of California, San Diego.

Supalla, T., & Newport, E. (1978). How many seats in a chair? The derivation of nouns and verbs in American Sign Language. In P. Siple (Ed.), *Understanding language through sign language research*. New York: Academic Press.

Vaid, J., Bellugi, U., & Poizner, H. (1985). *Hand dominance in a visual–gestural language*. Paper presented at Annual Meeting of the Body for the Advancement of Brain, Behavior, and Language Enterprises, Niagara Falls, Ontario.

9 "Language" in the Prelinguistic Child

Laura A. Petitto
McGill University

BEGINNINGS

My first exposure to studies of child language did not involve children at all. In 1974 I was living in a plantation-style, 37-room mansion on 13 acres of land in the Bronx with a very energetic (i.e., wild) male chimpanzee named Nim Chimpsky, attempting to raise him like a human child as part of a research project being conducted at Columbia University. The goal was to teach Nim American Sign Language (ASL), replicating and extending the pioneering work by Beatrice and Allen Gardner with their chimpanzee, Washoe. The project was headed by Herbert S. Terrace, who had been trained by B. F. Skinner and Thomas G. Bever, a former student of Noam Chomsky. Predictably, these men held radically different views about the nature of language; it was left to me to find a reconciliation of the behaviorist and mentalist perspectives that had eluded their mentors. Despite my relative inexperience, I was utterly convinced that I would achieve this goal. As embarrassing as it now seems, I thought I would reach across the evolutionary abyss and learn the structure of a chimpanzee's reality; I was going to do whatever was necessary in order to "talk to the animals."

Over a period of 3½ years I realized that there was something very wrong with Nim's "language." Although his signing compared very favorably with the reports of other signing apes, it became clear that his language was radically different from that of a child. I, and several other members of the project, began a painstaking attempt to understand the nature of this difference, pursuing two lines of inquiry. First, we began soliciting data from researchers studying hearing and deaf childrens' language acquisition in order to perform comparative analy-

187

ses. Second, we did a detailed analysis of thousands of hours of videotapes of Nim with his teachers. It was at this time that I first wrote to Roger Brown asking him for portions of his Adam, Eve, and Sarah transcripts and requesting unpublished information about their performance on his question-comprehension tasks. With extraordinary generosity Roger responded with a stack of transcripts and pages of detailed discussion of his findings. Both proved invaluable as we developed methods for analyzing the syntactic, semantic, pragmatic, and discourse characteristics of well over 20,000 of Nim's utterances.

With clinical precision the data analyses revealed that Nim's signing was markedly different from human language in numerous respects. Our conclusions, although disappointing, were unambiguous: Only a few of his 125 signs were ever used regularly (e.g., NIM, MORE, EAT, DRINK, GIVE), and these occurred only in fixed contexts (e.g., eating); of the full semantic range of expression afforded by language, Nim's primary semantic function was requesting (particularly food or other objects present); much of Nim's signing was an exact imitation of his teachers' signs; and his conversational use of signing was wholly inappropriate, as the incidence of signing that was simultaneous with that of his teachers was nothing like that seen in humans at any point in development. Finally, although Nim combined signs into sequences, his utterances lacked syntactic structure. (See Terrace, Petitto, Sanders, & Bever, 1979, 1980, for a detailed account of these findings.)

At this point, we were satisfied that the project had answered some basic questions. Nim's utterances lacked syntactic structure and seemed to be produced by various nonlinguistic response strategies. These conclusions presented new questions, however. First, why were the Nim data so inconsistent with the results from other ape sign language projects? Washoe had been said to have acquired a vocabulary of several hundred signs, which she creatively used to produce novel combinations and answer questions. This question had also occurred to my colleague, Mark Seidenberg, at the time a graduate student of Bever's. Seidenberg had been struck by the gross inconsistencies between the reported behavior of Washoe, who was said to sign, and that of Nim, who obviously could not. The resolution was to be found by performing careful analyses of the published reports on ape language, which led us to the conclusion that there never had been any clear evidence that apes such as Washoe had acquired language; what had occurred instead was the overintepretation of nonlinguistic behavior much like Nim's (Petitto & Seidenberg, 1979; Seidenberg & Petitto, 1979).

A second question proved more difficult to resolve. Although the Nim findings were important, they largely addressed what the ape could not do. However, they failed to explain *why* he (and the other apes) had not acquired language. I had an inchoate feeling that Nim was missing something fundamental, something more basic than simply an inability to string signs together into structured sequences. I began searching for a vocabulary in which to describe what this might be. I realized that chimpanzees presented a very curious paradox. It was clear that Nim exhibited a wide range of intelligent behaviors. He was able to solve complex problems involving same–different judgments based on physical identity (e.g., color, shape, size); he sorted objects along various dimensions and showed evidence of a powerful memory (e.g., he could remember where an object was hidden for several days and could lead "blind" caretakers to its location); he appeared to have achieved object permanence and other Piagetian sensorimotor milestones, and he performed well on serial ordering tasks. These findings were consistent with those from other studies indicating that apes are highly intelligent (e.g., Chevalier-Skolnikoff, 1976; Gillan, Premack, & Woodruff, 1981; Menzel, 1974; Premack, 1971, 1976; Van Lawick-Goodall, 1970; Woodruff & Premack, 1981).

At the same time, Nim exhibited this intelligence without the benefit of language. He did not represent any of his diverse experiences with symbols but would perform "on command" to obtain a small set of things that he valued (food, free-play, grooming). He would sign because he seemed to know that signing was valued by his caretakers and that specific movements of his hands (i.e., signing) would terminate a trial and release him from training sessions. Interestingly, he seemed to understand the pragmatic or instrumental function of signing, not the symbolic power of signs themselves. He did not reach out and designate objects, people, or events in the world around him. He did not use linguistic symbols to identify referents as belonging to some class or kind. Nim did not and could not *describe*. The dichotomy between Nim's cognitive capacities—which were considerable—and his linguistic capacities—which were not—had to be explained.

I then happened on Roger Brown's seminal book, *Words and Things* (1958). (Actually, Nim "happened" on Roger's book, and many others, as he tore up two shelves in Bever's office in order to gain access to a fossilized donut.) Few works have influenced me more and I finally began to feel that I had come closer to understanding the essential reason why Nim did not sign. Reading this book, I became aware of the special status of the human naming ability and how much more complex it is than the chimp behavior I had observed. The difference was profound and seemed to lie close to the core of the nature of meaning and reference. Somehow for Nim the power of the linguistic symbol had not been gained. For Nim, meaning seemed to have no role outside of the specific association between a form and its referent that had been explicitly taught to him. I had not succeeded in bringing him to the water fountain as Annie Sullivan had done for Helen Keller. For Nim, signs did not *refer;* he did not have words—signs, or names—for things.

Through Nim's failure, I recognized, in essence, part of what makes us distinctively human. I left the project in 1977 feeling that Chomsky was right: Language represents a species-specific distinct domain of knowledge, separate from other forms of knowledge. It also seemed likely that aspects of human language (in particular, syntax) could simply not be trained, regardless of the intelligence of the organism. I was also left with a deep interest in theoretical questions concerning the relationship between language and cognition, an interest in the nature of meaning and reference, and a passion for sign language, both as a language in its own right and as a tool for examining fundamental issues in cognitive science and, especially, language acquisition.

Immediately after leaving Nim I went off to work with Ursula Bellugi for a year at the Salk Institute for Biological Studies in La Jolla, California. There, Ursula, Ed Klima, and their team of researchers were conducting innovative research on the structure and grammar of American Sign Language (ASL). I began a linguistic analysis of the acquisition of ASL in profoundly deaf children, specifically, how they acquired knowledge of the morphological use of space in ASL (the linguistic unit most important in anaphoric referencing). This study left me with a feeling of amazement at the natural, effortless, and systematic way in which the children acquired sign language from their deaf parents. The contrast with Nim could not have been greater. I went on to conduct research on the grammar of ASL in William Stokoe's laboratory at Gallaudet College for the Deaf in Washington, D.C., and after 10 months I was off to Harvard.

When I arrived at Harvard in 1979, Roger Brown invited me to join him on the 12th floor of William James Hall, and there I began reading extensively in child language acquisition. It was not uncommon to find studies of child language in which there were no analyses of language data at all. Rather than focusing on formal descriptions of grammatical and semantic structures (as Brown had in his 1973 book), the new focus of research was on the "natural" way in which children's knowledge of a language is "built up" from non-linguistic factors and from their interactions with the environment. It was also common to find journal articles disavowing the claim by Chomsky (e.g., 1965, 1975) and others that language represented a distinct domain of knowledge. Rather, some viewed language as being just one of many behaviors resulting from the emergence of a general capacity to symbolize. Researchers holding this position have sought to demonstrate that infant gestural systems and other motoric activity serve as the prelinguistic foundation on which verbal language forms are "mapped" (e.g., Bruner, 1975; Clark, 1978; Greenfield & Smith, 1976; Lock, 1979; Zukow, Reilly, & Greenfield, 1980). Others have sought to demonstrate that the child's early gestural systems share important symbolic properties with linguistic forms (e.g., Bates, 1976; Bates, Benigni, Bretherton, Camaioni, & Volterra, 1979). Some claimed that grammatical structures were imparted to the child through the sentential and conversational (discourse) structure of parental speech and through the child's social interaction with adults (e.g., Snow, 1972; Keenan & Schiefflin, 1976, respectively). Other researchers, believing that the acquisition of grammatical structures was motivated exclusively by function (or pragmatic force), looked for the prelinguistic, gestural counterparts of such functions (Bates & MacWhinney, 1982). Thus, in the late

1970s it appeared that the focus in language acquisition research was moving away from studies of early language structures to studies involving nonlinguistic variables, with a special emphasis on the central role of prelinguistic gestures. (A recent paper by Golinkoff, 1983, corroborates this view.)

Given my previous research experiences, I found these accounts of language acquisition wholly unconvincing. Whether cognitive, social, or pragmatic factors play a role in language acquisition was not at issue; clearly, all parties agree that they play a major role. However, these accounts failed to respect a distinction between language and other forms of communication. The renewed emphasis on the role of the environmental input and the particular emphasis on gestural precursors to language acquisition failed to capture the properties of language that seemed distinct from other forms of knowledge. These accounts also failed to accommodate a logical point raised by Pinker (1979) and others, who argued that many possible grammars could be induced from the limited corpus of parental utterances that a child hears. Without some "built in" constraints on the process of induction, it does not appear that parental input alone can guide the child in selecting the specific syntactic rules of his or her grammar.

Since beginning my studies of child language acquisition, my goal has been to articulate what I have learned about the uniqueness of the human language capacity both from Nim and from deaf children acquiring ASL. The unifying theoretical focus of my research has been to examine the relationship between language and other forms of nonlinguistic, cognitive capacities in the language acquisition process. In pursuing this issue I have attempted to address a basic question: Is language the expression of a domain-specific mental capacity, or is it one of many expressions of a general capacity to engage in intelligent behavior?

In the remainder of this chapter, I present some evidence supporting the conclusion that language acquisition involves much more than the elaboration of prelinguistic knowledge. Language is a distinct formal system whose components and grammatical structure must be discovered in their own right. When data from both the nonlinguistic cognitive capacities of lower primates and innovative research on language acquisition in signing deaf children are considered, they strongly support the idea that language results from a biologically given, species-specific, distinct mental faculty.

ISSUES IN THE STUDY OF SIGN LANGUAGE

Structure of ASL. Intensive research on sign languages over the past 20 years has disproven three common myths about them: (1) that they are a crude mix of pantomine and concrete gestures, (2) that there is a single, universal sign language used by all deaf people, and (3) that they lack the grammatical organization characteristic of spoken languages. As a result of important and innovative studies by Stokoe (1960), Klima and Bellugi (1979), and others, the basic organizational structure and grammatical components of ASL, a naturally evolved language that is used by most deaf people in the United States and in parts of Canada, have been identified. Analyses of ASL have revealed that it exhibits formal organization at the same levels found in spoken languages, including a sublexical level of structuring internal to the sign (analogous to the phoneme level; Battison, 1978, Bellugi, 1980; Bellugi & Studdert-Kennedy, 1980; Bellugi & Klima, 1982; Klima & Bellugi, 1979; Stokoe, 1960), and a level that specifies the precise ways that signs must be bound to form signs and signs to form sentences (analogous to the morphological and syntactic levels; Klima & Bellugi, 1979; Marmor & Petitto, 1979; Padden, 1981, 1983; Supalla, 1982; Wilbur, 1979; Wilbur & Petitto, 1983).

The basic similarities between signed and spoken languages having been established, it is now possible to use sign language research to address deeper questions concerning human cognitive and linguistic capacities.

Sign Language and Language Acquisition.   Although signed and spoken languages share fundamental properties, they also differ in important respects. First, space and movement (including facial expressions) are the means for conveying morphological and syntactic information in signed languages, but not in spoken languages. The continuous, analogue properties of space and movement are used in ASL in systematic, rule-governed ways. These abstract spatial and movement units are analogous in function to discrete morphemes found in spoken language. The greater potential for nonarbitrary form-meaning correspondences afforded by the visual–gestural modality is exploited in sign languages. In particular, indexical signs point to their referents whereas the forms of iconic signs physically resemble aspects of their referents.

These modality differences allow us to address important issues in language acquisition. In particular, studies of ASL provide a way to resolve a major theoretical controversy concerning the role of prelinguistic gestures in the acquisition of linguistic symbols. Both deaf and hearing children rely on gestural communication prior to language. For the hearing child the transition from prelinguistic communication to spoken language involves a change in modality, whereas for the deaf child the transition to signed language does not; that is, for the deaf child gestures and symbols reside in the *same* modality. In evaluating the importance of prelinguistic gestures in early language acquisition, sign languages provide a unique methodological advantage, because, given a single modality and external articulators, certain developmental processes in language can be directly observed over time. In spoken language, of course, this is not the case; there appears to be an abrupt transition from the use of prelinguistic manual gestures to linguistic (spoken) communication: However, this could be an artifactual consequence of the shift in modality, rather than relfecting a deeper discontinuity between prelinguistic and linguistic knowledge. The basic question, then, is whether the acquisition of linguistic forms will (a) be facilitated by,

(b) be continuous with, or (c) share important symbolic properties with deaf children's knowledge of their extralinguistic communicative functions. In sum, this research provides a unique way to examine whether language derives from general cognitive capacities to think and learn, or whether it involves a domain-specific type of knowledge or faculty.

Objectives. The studies summarized in the following sections are concerned with the young child's transition from prelinguistic gestural communication to linguistic expression, as the strongest claims about the types of knowledge required for language acquisition have been made in regard to developments during this critical period. Findings from three studies are discussed: Study 1 examines the comprehension and production of personal pronouns whose linguistic forms in sign language correspond to their meanings in a one-to-one fashion. Studies 2 and 3 attempt to disambiguate the nature of prelinguistic communication, whether, for example, prelinguistic communicative forms can be used to perform linguistic functions such as naming, and whether children actually comprehend the communicative gestures they produce.

STUDY 1: ACQUISITION OF PERSONAL PRONOUNS

A recent study of the acquisition of personal pronouns in deaf children (Petitto, 1983a, 1983b, in press) provides a striking demonstration of unexpected similarities between the deaf and hearing children's acquisition of language. Three noteworthy features characterize the hearing child's acquisition of pronouns. First, they are acquired in a particular order. Beginning around 16–20 months children begin producing the pronoun me, followed by you around 22 months, and then third-person pronouns (e.g., Charney, 1978; Leopold, 1939-1949; Macnamara, 1982). Second, prior to this process children use proper nouns (e.g., "Jane do X" instead of "I do X"), rather than use the pronoun me. Third, around the time when you enters the child's lexicon some children—although not all—engage in systematic pronoun reversal errors. For example, mother might say to the child "Do you want to go to the store?" and the child would reply "Yes, you want go store." Similarly, the child may understand and produce me to refer to the adult rather than to herself; although it is uncommon for symmetrical you–me error pairs to co-occur. Some researchers have proposed that these children initially regard pronouns as having fixed or stable referents like names (i.e., you = child, or me = adult) rather than having changing or "unstable" referents that depend on the speaker role (Charney, 1978; Chiat, 1981, 1982; Clark, 1978).

Although the use of personal pronouns in ASL is constrained by the grammar of the language, they are not formed by arbitrary symbols. Rather, they are represented by pointing directly to the addressee (to intend YOU), or self (to intend I or ME). Thus, the formational aspects of these personal pronouns in

ASL resemble extralinguistic pointing gestures that commonly accompany speech and are used prelinguistically by hearing and deaf children. This provides a means for investigating the deaf child's transition from prelinguistic gestural to linguistic expression because gestures and linguistic units are virtually identical in form.

Given that the forms of personal pronouns in ASL are the same form as prelinguistic pointing gestures common to hearing and deaf children, the following questions arise: How does the deaf child move from the early, unconstrained, and communicative use of pointing gestures to the use of pronominal pointing constrained by the grammatical conventions of ASL? Is the acquisition of linguistically governed pointing facilitated by the child's knowledge of its extralinguistic communicative functions? Finally, given the seemingly transparent meaning of you and me pronouns in ASL, will deaf children learn these relations at an accelerated rate and in a relatively error-free manner?

The children in this study were two, third-generation profoundly and congenitally deaf girls. The children were learning ASL as a first language from their deaf parents; they were of normal intelligence and free of other neurological or physical handicaps. Two types of data were obtained: naturalistic data from ages 0;8 through 2;3 and experimental data from pronoun elicitation tasks for one child (age 1;11; for a detailed account of this study, see Petitto, 1983a).

The results indicated that, despite the transparency of the pointing gestures, deaf children acquire knowledge of personal pronouns over a period of time, displaying errors similar to those of hearing children. Although deaf children begin pointing communicatively at around 9 months, they do not use the pointing form to express YOU and ME until around 17–20 months, the range that hearing children first begin to use verbal pronouns systematically as well. Soon after ME has been established, deaf children gain productive control over the YOU pronoun (around 22–23 months), followed by third-person pronouns (see also Bellugi & Klima, 1981; Hoffmeister, 1978; Kantor, 1982; Petitto, 1983a,b). Like hearing children, they too use full proper nouns prior to the productive use of pronouns despite the fact that they use the pointing form in a rich, varied, and communicative fashion. Surprisingly, the children used the pointing form to refer to aspects of their caretaker's body but seemed to avoid the use of the pointing form to indicate the adult. For example, one child (age 1;11) used the pointing form to refer to a spot on her mother's bathing suit but did not use it to refer to her mother as YOU, not even in an experimental task specifically designed to elicit this and other pronouns. Although the phenomenon of "avoidance" has been noted previously in child language literature (e.g., Ferguson & Farwell, 1975), this case is especially intriguing because the children avoided a particular *function* of a form rather than the *form* itself. Further, like hearing children, the deaf children initially exhibited confusion over which pronouns were appropriate given a particular linguistic context, and they produced pronoun reversal errors (e.g., pointing to SECOND person as in YOU, but intending ME).

This study indicated, then, that despite differences between the modalities that might be relevant to acquisition, both deaf and hearing children showed remarkably similar performance in acquiring personal pronouns. The study provided evidence for a discontinuity in the child's transition from prelinguistic to linguistic communicative systems, even when they share a single channel of expression and the forms are transparent. This initial study also demonstrated how experimental research on sign language acquisition can provide a source of information bearing on theoretical issues in human cognition. The unique properties of sign languages (e.g., the fact that they make use of visual–gestural information expressed using external articulators, the hands) were exploited to provide a clear test of a current hypothesis concerning language learning; specifically, the notion that language is continuous with and directly elaborated out of prelinguistic gestures. The results clarified aspects of the acquisition process that were obscured by the nature of speech. In the next study I describe further research using this basic strategy to evaluate other aspects of the child's acquisition of language.

STUDY 2: GESTURAL PRODUCTION IN HEARING AND DEAF CHILDREN

One of the most compelling aspects of hearing infants' behavior is their spontaneous use of gestures well before the onset of speech. As young as 9 months, infants appear to use pointing, showing, and giving gestures in a wide variety of contexts, performing various communicative functions, including requesting and denoting. Equally interesting is the fact that infants will use these indexical gestures even when they are alone or when they are unaware that they are being observed by adults. Another class of gestures, nonindexical, manual ones, has also received a great deal of attention (e.g., see Bates, Bretherton, Shore, & McNew, 1983). For example, on noticing a hairbrush, most hearing children (around ages 12–13 months) will pick it up and make brushing motions, or, if presented with an empty cup, they will bring it up to their mouths as if to take a drink. Unlike indexical pointing gestures, which can refer to a potentially infinite class of referents, nonindexical, manual gestures appear to stand in a specific relation to particular referents; that is, a child can point to a variety of objects, using a single gesture, but the drinking behavior is only relevant to cups. Many researchers have concluded that these gestures assume an important role in the child's acquisition of language. Several different models have been proposed; all emphasize the relationship between gestures and a particular linguistic function, naming.

As previously noted in the discussion of pronoun acquisition, one view is that children's gestures and motoric activity are both the precursors of and prerequisites to language development. Knowledge of linguistic forms is said to be built up from this prelinguistic foundation in a direct and continuous manner (e.g., Bruner, 1975; Clark, 1978; Greenfield & Smith, 1976; Lock, 1979).

According to a second view, gesture and language are two examples of symbolic behavior resulting from the prior growth of a common underlying cognitive competence (Piaget, 1962; Werner & Kaplan, 1963). Bates (1976), Bates et al. (1979), and Bates, Camioni, & Volterra (1975) have presented the most articulate and thorough view of this position. They argue that the early pointing and giving gestures of children as young as 9 months old reflect important characteristics of language, specifically, the intention to communicate, shared reference with others, and the use of conventionalized behaviors. Each of these characteristics of linguistic communication is thought to be observed, in nascent form, in gestures. Moreover, Bates et al. (1983) assert that a particular linguistic function, naming, develops much earlier than previously thought.

Because Bates and her colleagues find that the functional properties of children's use of verbal naming are positively correlated with the functional properties of children's use of gestures (and with other cognitive measures), they conclude that verbal naming and gesturing must be generated by the same underlying cognitive "naming mechanism" (although the precise nature of this mechanism is not specified). On this view, the 13-month-old child's prelinguistic gestures with objects are not *pre*-linguistic at all. To the contrary, gestures of this type are said to be *names*. For them, naming is outside the linguistic system (and the "vocal channel") and exists as part of the child's general cognitive capacities to symbolize.

Interestingly, Bates et al. (1983) point out two ways in which children's use of gestures with objects differs from their verbal names for things: (a) "the contexts of symbol use" and (b) "the relationship between names and objects." With regard to (a) the young child's manual gestures are not used communicatively the way words are, but primarily in solitary or "private" cognition; that is, although children might pick up a cup on noticing it and hold it up to their mouths as if drinking from it, they do not use such gestures for common communicative functions. With regard to (b) the young child's gestures are object dependent, rather than arbitrary. Children rarely, if ever, produce empty-handed gestures (contrary to what might be expected if these are names); instead their gestures employ the associated object.

Although these differences might seem sufficient to undermine the claim that these gestures are names, Bates et al. minimize their importance, concluding that gestures function as verbal names because they meet the criterion specified in their definition of naming. Yet, in asserting that the young child's early gestures function like verbal names, they have defined names so broadly so as to include gestures. The conclusion that gestures function as names follows tautologically from their definition of naming and rests on their setting aside as unimportant the essential properties of names that do distinguish them from gestures.

A third position uses sign language research as the basis for a reinterpretation of the role of prelinguistic gestures in the hearing child's acquisition of spoken language. Bonvillian and his colleagues (Bonvillian, Orlansky, & Novack,

1983b; Bonvillian, Orlansky, Novack, Folven, & Holley-Wilcox, 1983a) studied the development of ASL in 12 hearing infants of deaf parents. Because these children used gestures "linguistically" from around 9 months of age, about 4 months earlier than hearing children are reported to use their first words, and because such gestures were not observed to occur prior to the linguistic use of signs, Bonvillian denies that prelinguistic gestures are a necessary prerequisite for the use of linguistic symbols. In effect, Bonvillian claims that children are capable of using linguistic symbols much earlier than studies of hearing children have suggested, with the usual delay in the transition from prelinguistic gestures to speech in the hearing child's acquisition of language due to a delay in the development of the speech articulatory apparatus. Because motor control over gesture production is achieved much earlier, signing children exhibit earlier use of language (as claimed by others: Caselli, 1983; McIntire, 1977; Prinz & Prinz, 1979; Schlesinger & Meadow, 1972).

Bonvillian's claims are undercut by serious problems of method and interpretation, and there are several reasons to question the validity of his finding that very young hearing children used gestures as signs. First, Bonvillian et al. did not establish any criteria to distinguish between the "linguistic" and "non-linguistic" use of gestures. Second, there were no criteria for establishing whether the children had mastered particular signs, attributions being base exclusively on the production of a "recognizable" sign. The children were credited with adult-like grammatical and semantic knowledge on the basis of the parent's and experimenters' judgments of the extent to which the children's behaviors resembled ASL signs. Attributions were made, then, on the basis of the *form* of the children's gestures, rather than how they were actually *used*, a procedure problematical on several counts and likely to lead to overattribution. First, the extent to which the children's gestures actually resembled ASL signs is unclear because, according to Bonvillian et al. (1983a) "the children frequently omitted some of the features [of ASL signs] and others were produced incorrectly" (p. 17). Second, the dangers involved in making attributions of linguistic competence merely on the basis of the form of the utterance alone are well known (Bloom & Lahey, 1978; Seidenberg & Petitto, 1979). Finally, Bonvillian et al. (1983a) incorrectly equates knowledge of a language with ability to *produce* linguistic forms and defines "language onset . . . as the acquisition of a productive sign vocabulary" (p. 11). If, however, "language onset" is not associated with the mere production of a vocabulary consisting of a few ill-formed gestures, without regard to the manner in which they are used, and if speech (or sign) is not equivalent to language, his strong claims regarding the precocious use of language among signing children cannot be sustained.

Are Gestures Names?

The research I summarize here raises two broad questions. The first concerns the validity of the claim that some gestures are isomorphic with linguistic names. As

I have already suggested, although both Bates and Bonvillian have noted correspondences between gestures and names, neither have established rigorous criteria to evaluate these two types of communication. The basic question of whether early gestures exhibit fundamental properties characteristic of names has been raised with respect to the behavior of signing apes such as Washoe and Nim. Signing apes are said to be able to name objects but, in the absence of any clear criteria by which to differentiate naming from other types of communication, the claim is difficult to evaluate. The same problem holds in evaluating the relationship between children's early gestures and names.

It is not my intention here to propose a general theory of naming (see, for example, Barwise & Perry, 1983; Frege, 1960; Macnamara, 1982, 1986). My goal instead is to identify briefly some basic characteristics of names that any comprehensive theory of naming must explain, and then to determine whether these characteristics also hold for children's early gestures. Such characteristics involve the three different aspects of names that follow.

Forms.   A critical characteristic of names is that they are physically distinct from the objects or actions to which they refer; that is, a behavior cannot simultaneously be a referent and its name. For example, the act of coughing cannot function as the noun cough. Names refer, designate, describe, and categorize classes of objects or actions, but they are not themselves the objects or actions in question. Thus, names are physically independent of that to which they refer. This implies that the use of names will not be tied to presence of the referent object or enactment of the referent action; speaking about a cough, for example, does not require enacting the actual behavior. An important empirical question, then, is whether children's early communicative gestures exhibit this independence of form and referent.[1]

Scope of Referring Relations.   Names refer to kinds of objects or actions, but the scope of this referring relation is of a particular type.[2] It can be roughly characterized as follows: (i) a single form is used consistently to designate a class of related referents or *kind;* (ii) the form itself must be consistent, rather than changing across occurrences; (iii) the form is not restricted to particular exemplars of a kind; (iv) if multiple forms are used to refer to a particular referent, each must independently meet conditions (i–iii).

(i) reflects the fact that names designate different types of referents. A name

---

[1]This point in no way excludes iconic signs in ASL.

[2]In this text when I speak of "names," I am referring only to common nouns. Whereas proper names refer to an individual, common nouns refer to a class of objects or actions. The strongest claims about the linguistic status of children's early gestures have been made with regard to this latter type of names.

can be used for a potentially infinite number of tokens of objects or actions, but the classes of objects or actions are themselves differentiable kinds. Thus, a book is a <u>book</u> and not a <u>picture,</u> even though books can have pictures in them and the word <u>book</u> does refer to a potentially infinite class.[3] Moreover, a pad of scratch paper is not a book (but a "pad"), even though it shares critical features of books (pages, binding, etc.). Although the number of tokens of the kind <u>book</u> is, in principle, infinite, the class itself is restricted (to all and only objects that are books).[4]

(ii) underlines the fact that names have stable forms, although these may undergo limited modification as the child's articulation improves. (iii) reflects the fact that, whereas names can be used to refer to particular objects or actions, their use is not restricted to individual objects or actions. Thus, <u>bear</u> cannot be exclusively used to refer to a particular exemplar of the class of bears; <u>run</u> cannot refer to a particular act of running.

In regard to (iv), it is obviously the case that several different names can refer to the same object or action; <u>canary, bird,</u> and <u>animal</u> could all be used for a particular small yellow organism that flies. However, if multiple names are used to index the same referent, each of the names must exhibit characteristics (i–iii). This issue is important because children often use several different gestures in the presence of a particular object (or several different objects); in order to evaluate such behavior, it is necessary to look at other uses of these gestures in order to determine whether they are themselves used systematically in the sense defined by (i–iii).

Gestures, such as pointing, could differ from names, then, by violating one or

---

[3]According to some theories (e.g., Macnamara, 1982), common nouns do not actually "refer" to objects. Rather, they refer to kinds, which specify sets of which it is either true or false of a particular object that it is a member of that set. The term *referring* is reserved for other linguistic expressions (proper nouns, indexicals, definite descriptions, and function expressions), which are used with respect to particular objects or individuals. On this view, "book" is not a referring expression because it does not itself refer to a particular book; "Roger Brown" is a referring expression because it picks out a particular individual. There are also several other accounts of naming, in which technical terms such as *refer* and *referring* are used in theory-dependent ways. For example, Barwise and Perry (1983) state that: "We think that, in fact, the ordinary English word REFERS captures rather well an important semantical notion. Through utterances people refer to people, things, times, and places, and the reference of these acts is relevant to the interpretation of the utterances" (page 21). These technical disputes, however, have no bearing on my analysis of childrens' gestures, and the data I discuss do not mediate between different theories of naming. In the text, the term "referring" is used in a theoretically neutral sense as a cover term for the two types of naming Macnamara has distinguished. Thus, I say that a word such as book "refers" to objects even though this usage is not sanctioned by some theories.

[4]This argument is not refuted by Wittgenstein's well-known observation that there cannot be necessary and sufficient conditions for class membership. The merits of his argument aside, it is nonetheless the case that names are used to differentiate among classes. Questions as to whether there can be strict criteria for class membership are separate from questions as to whether names for such classes are used systematically to differentiate among classes.

more of these conditions. For example, a single gesture could be used for objects or actions of different kinds; similarly, many different gestures could be used with reference to a single object or action even though none of these gestures is used with reference to a particular kind.

Functions.   In evaluating children's early communicative behavior, it is necessary to consider the semantic and communicative functions of names. Names serve several semantic functions including identifying, recognizing, describing, and categorizing referents as belonging to a known kind. In effect, to name an object is to assign it to a category; naming involves an implicit assertion that the referent has the properties thought to be true of members of the category.[5] If gestures are used as names, then, they should exhibit these referring, describing, recognizing, and categorizing functions.

In addition to their semantic functions, names are used for a very wide variety of communicative functions and are not used exclusively in "private cognition." Importantly, names are used to make requests, comment on the world, etc. It might be expected, then, that naming gestures would be used in similar ways. Moreover, names are generally used in combination with other linguistic forms. The extent to which children combine gestures with other gestures (and the relationship this shares with their capacity to combine words, if any) will be of special interest.

Finally, names are not restricted to imitated or routinized contexts. It has been noted in the literature that young children's gestures are "highly susceptible to imitation" (e.g., Bates et al., 1983; see also Piaget, 1962). Thus, prompted social gesturing such as Hi, Bye-Bye, one-time-only imitations of ongoing activities, and gestures learned and used only in the context of a game, cannot be considered to be names, unless independent evidence can be established that children understand these forms.

Clearly, naming is a complex linguistic function. In order to evaluate whether early gestures function as names, what is required is detailed evaluation of children's gestures along *all* of the dimensions specified previously: only then will we be able to make direct comparisons between the child's use of gestures and their use of verbal names.

---

[5]Clearly, names have important *grammatical* functions in language. Names belong to grammatical categories. These are important for syntax, because syntactic rules are defined over grammatical categories. Some common nouns take the plural form as well as the indefinite and definite articles, *a* and *the*, respectively. Such grammatical variations are accompanied by semantic variations as well (Macnamara, 1982, p. 5).

Rate of Acquisition

The second question addressed by this research is about differences between the acquisition of spoken and signed languages. Because both Bates and Bonvillian stress the close correspondence between gestures and names, their positions imply that deaf and hearing children's behavior should differ in important ways. For several reasons deaf children might be expected to acquire language more quickly than hearing children. The deaf child might also exhibit less differentiation between linguistic and nonlinguistic use of gesture because both occur in the same modality. Further, the deaf child's early gestures might be different or more elaborate because of exposure to sign language input.

Although the study of personal pronouns demonstrated the child's knowledge of the pronominal use of pointing was not simply elaborated from the child's prelinguistic use of this form—a finding that contradicts Bonvillian as well as Bruner and others—it could nonetheless be the case that indexical and other manual gestures do play an essential role in the acquisition of other linguistic functions, particularly naming. The studies that are described next addressed this possibility. Naturalistic and experimental evidence concerning children's production of gestures was obtained, bearing on four questions: (1) Are the hearing and deaf child's prelinguistic gestures fundamentally similar to verbal (and sign language) naming? (2) Does modality influence the acquisition of names? (3) Are signed languages easier to learn because many of the linguistic signs resemble conventional nonlinguistic gestures (i.e., will the iconicity of some ASL signs facilitate their acquisition by deaf children; what is the role of close form-meaning correspondences in the acquisition of linguistic forms in ASL?)? And (4) will the deaf child differentiate nonlinguistic gestures from signs even though both reside in the same visual–gestural mode?

This study focused on three hearing children—two acquiring spoken French and one acquiring English—and three deaf children of deaf parents—two acquiring Langue des Signes Québécoise (LSQ)[6] and one acquiring ASL. Monthly, 1-hour videotapes of the children and a parent were collected from ages 10 through 20 months. A controlled-elicitation procedure consisting of four tasks was used during each taping session, in order to elicit either indexical or nonindexical manual gestures. Detailed transcriptions of the videotapes were prepared, and the forms, functions, and contexts of hearing and deaf children's gestures were coded to determine their indexical, referential, symbolic, and linguistic status. The data were coded by two independent raters in order to determine whether prelinguistic gestures had the same lexical status as names and the extent to which they facilitated the acquisition process.

---

[6]LSQ is the native sign language used among French deaf persons in Canada, and especially in Quebec. It is fundamentally distinct from ASL (e.g., lexically, morphologically, syntactically, semantically).

Results

The overall gesture types, including their frequency and use, were strikingly similar for deaf and hearing children throughout development. Both deaf and hearing children produced indexical (pointing) and nonindexical manual gestures. Although indexical gestures occurred throughout the period under investigation, three distinct types of nonindexical manual gestures occurred within particular time periods: "natural" gestures (around 9 to 15 months, with a peak frequency around 12 months), instrumental gestures (around 12 to 18 months, with a peak frequency around 16 months), and iconic gestures (around 16 to 20 months). Most of the children's nonindexical gestures were produced with objects in hand (around 88% of approximately 3,500 nonindexical gestural tokens). Empty-handed gestures were produced less frequently (10% of all tokens). Of the empty-handed gestures that were produced, the natural and instrumental gesture types occurred most frequently. Empty-handed iconic gestures were exceedingly rare in both hearing and deaf children (around 2% of all tokens); iconic gesturing with objects in hand did not occur. Most of the children's gestures with objects were used in play (and "private cognition"), or in requests; the class of empty-handed gestures were used almost exclusively as requests.

There is little question that some of the children's gesturing was communicative. They appeared to use particular gestural forms (e.g., pointing) with the intent to denote objects in the environment, or to achieve an instrumental goal with regard to these objects. The purpose of the following analysis, then, is not to dispute the claim that prelinguistic gestures have communicative functions. Rather, it addresses the extent to which such gestures are isomorphic with linguistic symbols.

Indexical Gestures

The deaf and hearing children in this study exhibited the same usage of pointing gestures as observed in previous studies (see especially, Bates et al., 1975; Bruner, 1975; Clark, 1978; Petitto, 1983a,b) and is not discussed here at length. Indexical pointing was used in a rich, varied, and communicative manner beginning around 9 months. Between 12–18 months, children used pointing in combination with other pointing forms, natural gestures (such as reaching, grasping, and the open–close gesture described later), and words (or signs). Interestingly, the children *never* combined two nonindexical manual gestures, a finding that has also been observed by Volterra (1981), and one that would have provided important support for claims regarding the "syntax" of children's early gestures (e.g., Bruner, 1975).

What is noteworthy about children's early pointing is that they express themselves in a communicative, intentional, and even referential manner, yet we are still not justified in viewing the gestural means for expressing this intention as

202

linguistic. The child's use of pointing stands in a very different relationship than do linguistic units and their referents.[7] Although the pointing form indexed a particular object, it was not used to "stand for" a particular object or class of related objects. In fact, it is used with a large, and seemingly, unconstrained class of objects (recall the previous discussion about properties of names). Thus, despite children's rich communicative capacities, there is clearly something distinct about the linguistic means employed to represent or symbolize objects and events among them.

Nonindexical Manual Gestures

The three types of nonindexical manual gestures ("natural", instrumental, and iconic) are discussed according to their age (and peak frequency) of occurrence.

Ages 9 Through 12 Months. "Natural" gestures occurred during this period; one form, called the "open–close gesture," occurred frequently. Deaf children also produced babbling in sign language. These are discussed in turn.

(i) "Natural" Gestures. The children produced a range of gestures that were drawn from their natural activities. These are natural in the sense that they are unlearned and time-locked to ongoing activities. They are not abstract forms used to refer to or classify activities; rather, they are the actual enactment of an activity. These natural gestures include reaching, grasping, grabbing, waving hand(s), throwing, flapping arms, banging, mouthing objects, shaking objects, shaking head, pulling or turning head away, holding or raising hands above head, and pushing and pulling. These natural gestures neither have a "representational component" nor stand in a specific relation to specific objects; rather, they occur frequently across multiple contexts for a very wide variety of objects.

Often the children's gestures occurred as reactions to events rather than serving to encode the actions symbolically. In addition, children are highly adept at this age at imitating social and routinized gestures such as waving good bye,

---

[7]Some forms of pointing are lexical for deaf children beginning around 18 months (see discussion of personal pronouns in Study 1). There are other ways of discerning the young deaf child's knowledge regarding their use of pointing (i.e., when is pointing a gesture and when is it a sign?). Petitto (1981) observed that the acquisition of demonstrative and locative pronouns (this, that, and here, there, respectively) proceeds in the following manner. Deaf children progress from pointing *on* objects, often leaving the signing space to do so, to the grammatical use of pointing towards objects and locations within the linguistic constraints of the signer's signing space. Thus, the child's ability to bring the pointing form within the signing space without contacting the referent is an important aid in determining the shift from gesture to sign for these early deictic pointing gestures. Once the child's pointing conforms to the strict "phonological" spatial constraints of the language (and undergoes other changes such as occurring in combination with other lexical items in a systematic manner), it appears that the form has lexical status for the child.

clapping hands, smacking lips, playing peek-a-boo, and the like. Because these gestures occur across many contexts and are not referential, the young child will inevitably produce both appropriate and inappropriate pairings of actions and objects. Thus, sometimes the child mouths an object "appropriately" (e.g., a toy apple), but other times he or she mouths inappropriately (e.g., a mirror); sometimes he or she produces a banging motion with a hammer and sometimes he or she "hammers" with a sneaker; sometimes the child throws the ball, other times a cupful of milk.

The power of these gestures derives from the fact that adults freely attribute a variety of complex desires, intentions, and knowledge to children based on their interpretation of the context in which the gestures occur. Adults do not interpret children's gestures by how they were used in the past or whether there are consistent correlations between particular gestural forms and their referents. The children's gestures appeared across many contexts, with many different objects. Rather, the context itself was used as the basis for interpreting the gestures. Two types of context-based interpretations were noted by observing the adult's response to children's gestures over many trials. First, parents attribute a *single*, specific meaning to a child's gesture even if the child used a variety of *different* forms in the same context at different times. For example, during a single 1-hour taping session, while seated in his high chair, one 11-month-old hearing child performed the following actions at three different times: reached towards the floor, reached towards the ceiling, and banged on the top of his high chair with both hands. Each was interpreted by the mother as a request to get down. It is not that the mother was necessarily wrong—the child may have wanted to get down from his high chair—but there was nothing in the child's action that directly symbolized this information. And because these particular actions also occurred in many other contexts where getting down was not at issue, they did not stand in particular relation to a particular referent or class of related referents. Further, there was nothing about these forms in relation to this context that would permit a parent (or experimenter) to unequivocally rule out other interpretations, e.g., that the child was intending to convey instead, I want to get *up*, I want to move to the other side of the room, or I want a drink of water to be put on my high chair, etc. In fact, on one of the occasions just mentioned, the child attempted to get back into the high chair after mother had taken him down.

Conversely, the same mother in the same session attributed four different meanings to a waving/swatting motion of the child's right arm and hand (flat hand, spread fingers, path movement from eye level to waist with palm facing downward at endpoint): (1) as a request for more food, (2) as a command to approach the child, (3) as a command to move away from the child, and (4) as the good-bye gesture. Hence, a *single* gesture type is interpreted as having *multiple* meanings. In sum, "natural" gestures cannot be said to function in a manner similar to linguistic symbols.

(ii) Form and Function of the Open–Close Gesture: Are Signs Acquired Earlier? One ubiquitous gesture that begins during the 9- to 12-month period warrants special attention; both deaf and hearing children produced this type of gesture in nearly identical ways. It involved a repeated opening and closing of the fingers from an open or curved hand. At times, the children moved their arms up and down while opening and closing their hands; at other times the gesture occurred with the hands raised slightly above eye level. Occasionally, the children looked at their own hands while producing the form, but usually they looked at the object, event, or person that stimulated the occurrence of this behavior. Variations included the use of one hand rather than two, or producing the open–close hand gesture with bent elbows at waist level. Finally, during this period the form was very often accompanied by an interesting and amusing behavior: The young children tended to open and close their feet in conjunction with the opening and closing motions of their hand and fingers.

Detailed analysis of the longitudinal data revealed that this open–close gesture had no communicative function during this period. Instead, it appeared to be a general excitatory, motoric response to diverse stimuli, another example of a "natural" behavior that was part of the child's behavioral repertoire. Strong evidence for this claim comes from a close examination of the contexts in which the form occurred. The behavior did not occur in a systematic or principled fashion; there was no relation between the occurrence of the form and a specific referent or class of referents; nor was there a relationship between the form and a particular function, except as a behavioral indicator of the child's general excitement vis-a-vis some object or event that was occurring in her immediate environment.

As both deaf and hearing children produced it in a variety of contexts and for a wide variety of referents, it cannot be said that the open–close gesture was an early "sign." More importantly, the communicative function of this form could not be said to be a "natural" begging or requesting gesture to receive objects, as young hearing and deaf children would produce the form both before and after desirable objects were in hand.

Why, then, is this gesture worthy of special attention? I believe that this form has been the source of a great deal of confusion in the literature. The open–close hand gesture happens to resemble several actual signs in ASL. There is a close but entirely coincidental correspondence between global aspects of the form of a small class of signs in ASL and the open–close hand gesture: WANT, GIVE, GIVE-ME, GET, TAKE, COME, GO, UP, and DOWN (with raised or lowered arm(s), respectively), MILK, OPEN, BYE-BYE, HI, and WHICH (and others). Not surprisingly, these are some of the very signs that researchers have attributed to young children acquiring ASL based on their assessment of the context. In doing so, researchers have relaxed their criteria for what counts as a well-formed sign, enabling them to interpret the open–close gesture as various signs in ASL.

For example, one researcher (Caselli, 1983) claimed that a 10-month-old deaf infant had knowledge of the following signs: WANT, MILK, GIVE-ME, and even WHICH(!).[8] In thereby interpreting the reflexive gestures of the child as language, language researchers recapitulate the overinterpretations of parents. Both deaf parents and language researchers who study deaf children report that their deaf children are "signing" as early as 4 months. The basis of such overattributions should now be clear. With respect to deaf children, the temptation to attribute sign status to early gestures is greater than with hearing children because some of the gestures happen to look like signs in ASL. Interpreting the child's gestures as signs is especially compelling when these forms occur with the indexical point, yielding the illusion that the child has produced a "sentence." The mother walks into her hungry baby's room with a bottle of milk in her hand. The baby points at the bottle and in excitation produces a variety of gestures that may include (a) pointing, (b) reaching and grasping, and (c) open–close hand and foot gesturing. It is not difficult to see how the interpretation YOU GIVE-ME MILK could be derived. It may be that children have such thoughts. What I am contesting is that they have a gestural code for representing them. Thus, contrary to the claims by Bonvillian and others, deaf children possess gestures that function as communicative gestures and not linguistic symbols; deaf and hearing children's prelinguistic gestures are remarkably similar; and deaf children do not acquire signs earlier than hearing children acquire words.

Underscoring this conclusion, I recently asked a deaf researcher in my laboratory to transcribe a videotape of a *hearing* boy at ages 10 and 11 months. Only portions of the tape where the child was alone on the screen were viewed by the researcher. She was not told whether the child was hearing or deaf but was only instructed to write down any time she thought the child signed. This was not an ideal methodological procedure, but the results were interesting nonetheless. Based on the hearing child's natural repertoire of gestures (like reaching, grasping, banging), indexical pointing gestures, and the open–close hand gesture, she reported nearly a hundred "sign" utterances, including complex combinations of the type mentioned previously. This overattribution is, of course, reminiscent of a similar problem that occurred in the ape language projects (Seidenberg & Petitto, 1979). The signing apes also exhibited a rich class of natural actions and gestures such as those just reported for children (including reaching, grasping, grabbing, banging, throwing, mouthing, shaking, etc.). Unfortunately, these, too, were termed *signs*. In fact, behaviors of apes and infants (around ages 9 to 12 months) are strikingly similar across many dimensions. In neither case, how-

---

[8]I studied the same 10-month-old child (KATE from Study 1). I videotaped the session from which Caselli drew her conclusions. Analyses of the child's "signing" during this session by two deaf adults, the child's mother and myself, revealed that Kate did not demonstrate knowledge of the signs attributed to her by Caselli (e.g., WHICH, WANT, MILK, GIVE-ME).

ever, are these actions and gestures remotely similar to true linguistic symbols or the symbolization process. Indeed, the striking similarities between the "language" of apes and young children appears to be little else than similarities in the overinterpretation of nonlinguistic gestures by adult humans, parents and researchers alike.

(iii) Linguistically Relevant Sign "Babbling" in Deaf Children.   There is one important difference between deaf and hearing children's hand gesturing. At around 7 to 11 months of age deaf children engage in linguistically relevant sign babbling, in much the same way that hearing children begin to babble vocally. Although deaf children's production of unmodulated vocal babbling has been noted previously in the literature (e.g., Lenneberg, 1967), little attention has been given to their sign babbling. My analysis of the forms, use, and contexts in which sign babbling occurred for the deaf children suggests that these hand movements are not attempts to sign and are wholly unlike the forms and functions of their "natural" and indexical gestures. Rather, they are hand movements that specifically reflect the formational (phonological) features of ASL, especially hand configuration and movement parameters (Petitto, in preparation). Interestingly, deaf mothers consistently responded with *language* to their infants' sign babbling and *action* to their gestures.

Ages 12 Through 16 Months.   Beginning around 12 or 13 months the children's use of gestures became more focused on objects, events, and people in their environment. Two types of nonindexical gestures were observed: gestures with objects in hand and empty-handed instrumental gestures.

(i) Gestures with Objects: Are They Names?   By 13 months the children displayed a striking ability to produce a variety of nonindexical manual gestures with particular objects ("drinking" from an empty cup, "talking" on a toy phone). It is gestures of this kind that have been viewed as functioning in a manner similar to common nouns or names. This has led some researchers to assert that naming is "outside" the vocal (linguistic) channel and exists prior to the onset of vocal words as part of the child's general cognitive capacities (see especially, Bates et al., 1983).

At first, it might appear appropriate to regard such object-related gestures as *names* for things, albeit gestural in form. However, a close examination of the form, function, and content of these gestures suggests that even they do not have the same symbolic status as verbal names. First, not only must an object be present in order for children to produce these gestures, apparently it must be physically in their hands. For this reason alone we can reject entirely the claim that these gestures are symbolic in the same way as verbal/sign names. Second, the children gave no evidence of using these forms to identify and categorize objects as being a member of a known class. The gestures often did not appear to be communicative, the children failing to make eye contact with adults while producing them. Thus, the children seemed to be executing complex actions associated with the objects rather than providing names for things—an insight of Piaget's that I believe to be fundamentally correct. Further, these gestures appear to be indexical in the sense of Peirce (1932) because the motion of each gesture is actually part of its referent. In raising a comb to her head and combing her hair, the child cannot be regarded as explicitly symbolizing the comb. Nor are we justified in regarding this action as "standing for" the comb (or combing)—no more than we would want to label the child's inhaling of air the noun breath (or the verb breathe).

Nonetheless, Bates et al. (1983) argue that the child's solitary and "object-dependent" (non empty-handed) gestures should be considered as names because they *function* as names. Their argument is as follows. When the child gestures with a cup by bringing it to his or her mouth, he or she is in a sense representing knowledge of what is done with cups (the cup being that which holds liquid and is drunk from). On this view, the child is recognizing and categorizing the cup and identifying it as belonging to a known class, hence naming. This view predicts the following. If children's gestures reflect their knowledge of the functions of objects, thereby exhibiting a kind of gestural naming, then we should not observe children performing these actions with inappropriate objects; there should be little or no function violations. Just as we would expect a particular gestural *form* to stand in a systematic relation with a particular referent or a class of related referents, we would also expect the *function* of referents to stand in a principled relationship with a particular gestural form. Thus, to represent the "stirring" function we would expect the actual objects used to stir to be in some principled relationship to each other: Hence, we would expect a pairing between big and small spoons and the stirring gesture, but not spoons and pencils and the stirring gesture.

However, this is not what occurred. Young children routinely made object-related function violations. Function errors began around 13 months and continued until around 18–20 months, suggesting that object functions must be learned. Although the children would pick up a spoon, place it in an empty cup and "stir," they were also likely to pick up other objects that shared certain critical physical (but not functional) dimensions with spoons and use them as well (e.g., hammer, comb, mirror). Note that the children produced many of the words for objects *prior* to their learning the correct functions associated with the objects. Thus, it appears that the young children's gestures do not necessarily reflect their knowledge of the function of objects but rather more clearly reflect their knowledge of actions associated with them.

In summary, it appears that the most critical difference between manual gestures of the type just described and verbal/sign names were observed by Bates but dismissed: The children do not produce empty-handed manual gestures to stand for referents but produce such gestures—really actions—with the actual objects present and in hand. In addition, the meaning of the gestures can be understood without special knowledge about the relationship between symbolic forms and their referents; i.e., unlike words, there is a literal, physical resemblance between the action of the gesture and what it is ostensibly referring to. A third critical difference was that the children used objects in ways that did not always reflect their literal, intended functions. Finally, the range of communicative functions that these gestures serve is severely restricted. For example, the child does not use the brush gesture to describe (or comment about) someone brushing her hair; the child does not use the cup gesture to request a drink from mother. Children do *not* describe, request, or use gestures for the myriad of functions that words serve from their onset.

(ii) Instrumental Empty-Handed Gestures. Instrumental gestures account for nearly all the children's empty-handed nonindexical gestures throughout this period and beyond. Like natural gestures, their form is unlearned, context bound, and part of the child's natural behavioral repertoire (e.g., reaching, raising arms, open–close hand movements). Unlike natural gestures, the forms now appear to assume general meanings. For example, hearing and deaf children will reliably raise their arms to be picked up and reach (with open–close hand movements) to be given an object.[9] Further, like the natural gestures, instrumental gestures have a very powerful effect on adults, who respond with attention and/or desired actions.

Instrumental gestures differed from the children's first words and signs in important ways. The "give-me" gesture, for example, is literally the behavior used in the act of receiving (or taking), rather than a schematic representation of it (the child enacts rather than depicts). Moreover, the forms were used exclusively in requests; they were communicative "tools."

Ages 16 Through 20 Months. Beginning around 16 months the children were observed to produce a small class of iconic gestures; these gestures preserved partial information about actions that are associated with objects (e.g., "twisting" motions of the wrist as in opening a jar), but they are not literally the enactment of the designated activity (e.g., the child does not actually open a jar). In short, these gestures contain a representational component. If iconic forms are referential, communicative, and representational, why, then, are we not justified in viewing them as similar to linguistic names for things?

Briefly, the critical difference between the child's use of iconic gestures versus their early use of words is that they are used in reference to objects from different natural categories; that is, they do not pick out natural kinds (Macnamara, 1986). This is wholly unlike even the child's very first notions of word

---

[9]Highly routinized gestural games, social gestures (e.g., Hello and Bye waving), imitated forms, and one-time-only gestures were excluded from this analysis. The status of these gestures are relatively noncontroversial: Most researchers would not attribute lexical status to them.

meanings. Although children's early word meanings are not the same as adult's, they are constrained in systematic ways. For example, the child will not initially use a word such as table to refer to the same class of objects as the adult. The child's initial hypothesis as to the meaning of table is only partially correct; he or she will sometimes over or underextend the range of referents for a particular word. However, this process is not arbitrary. As Carey (1982) notes, "The child would never judge table to mean something like 'table and meal' because table is an object and mean is an event: a concept's including just a specific object and a specific event violates certain conceptual naturalness" (p. 381). Several other factors distinguish iconic gestures from words and signs. The use of iconic gestures is a relatively late development (around 16–20 months) compared with children's first words and signs (around 12 months). Importantly, iconic gestures typically do not occur until *after* the child has acquired the corresponding word or sign. Further, they occur with low frequency and nearly always to supplement a verbal/sign message during requests.

Finally, the deaf and hearing children's first signs and words (respectively) occurred around the same time, between 12 and 20 months; no child in this study began uttering words or signing prior to 12 months.

In sum, then, several findings characterize this second study. Beginning around 9 months, the children produced indexical and nonindexical manual gestures. A detailed analysis of the forms, functions, and contents of the children's early gestural forms and the parent's responses to them revealed that they appear to have radically different properties than words (or signs). Deaf children's gestures are not more elaborated and advanced than hearing children. Even though deaf children are being exposed to a language where both linguistic and gestural information are transmitted in a single channel and are produced with identical units (hands moving in space), the manner in which they acquire this system compels the surprising conclusion that they differentiate between linguistic and nonlinguistic uses of gesture; thus, these forms of expression appear to be constrained by distinct domains of knowledge. Finally, the modality of language transmission does not seem to facilitate the language acquisition process, nor does the child seem to be aided by the iconic (nonarbitrary) form of some signs. With the exception of sign babbling, the deaf children produced gestures that were nearly identical in form and function to those of hearing children, and they were not more advanced despite the fact that sign languages are constructed in such a way as to lend themselves to this unique type of iconic (nonarbitrary, pictorial), gestural elaboration.

STUDY 3: GESTURAL COMPREHENSION

The results of a third study are particularly revealing with regard to the linguistic status of children's early gestures. This experiment examined the comprehension of gestures among hearing and deaf children who had acquired significant spoken or sign vocabularies, respectively. Recall again the various positions arguing that there should be a close relationship between the child's vocabulary and the gestures he or she produces. Specifically, one view predicts that the child's earliest verbal or sign vocabulary should be preceded by corresponding gestural forms. A second predicts that the child should simultaneously possess gestural and spoken (or sign) forms for objects, people, or events in his or her world. And a third position predicts that the gestures of infants exposed to sign language should possess the properties typically associated with later words.

All three positions imply that children should comprehend the gestures that they themselves produce; that is, if knowledge of the semantic (and syntactic) role of lexical forms shares fundamental symbolic properties with gestural behavior, the speaking (or signing) child should already comprehend gestures by the time he or she can understand the corresponding spoken (or sign) name. Given the close relationship between gesture and sign in a sign language, related questions include: Will the deaf child exhibit greater mastery of gesture comprehension? Does the deaf child clearly differentiate between linguistic and nonlinguistic uses of gesture? Will the deaf child systematically misinterpret gestures as signs?

The children studied were acquiring spoken English or French and (deaf) children acquiring ASL. They were tested at 6-month intervals between 22–48 months, 3 deaf and 3 hearing per group per interval.

Four categories of stimuli were constructed consisting of three groups of gestures and one group of ASL signs:[10] (1) *Gestures Resembling Signs* included gestures that are nearly identical in form to actual ASL signs for a target object (e.g., the pantomime of ''brushing one's own hair'' is very similar to the sign BRUSH); (2) *Pure Gestures* are unambiguous pantomimes that do not correspond to ASL signs (e.g., the conventional pantomime for banana, a peeling activity, is unlike the ASL sign for BANANA or any other ASL sign); (3) *Ambiguous Sign/Pantomime Gestures* can be interpreted either as pantomime or as signs; however, the pantomime involves a different meaning than the sign (e.g., the movement in the ''tying a shoelace'' pantomime resembles the ASL sign NECKLACE, not SHOE); (4) *Pure Signs* are noniconic ASL signs that do not resemble conventional pantomime. There were six gestures in each group, comprising a total of 24 trials presented in random order.

Children were seen individually with a caretaker and were first permitted to play freely with each of the 24 test objects. They were then tested for their knowledge of both the names (verbal or sign) and the gestures associated with each test object. The children's comprehension of names (verbal or sign) was assessed for each test object using a matching object-to-picture identity game.

---

[10]The design of this study underwent several evolutions. Both Elizabeth Bates and Barbara O'Connell contributed to the original design of this study while I was working with them at The Salk Institute and UCSD in 1983; I wish to thank them for their support and important insights. Major modifications were made to the study's design subsequent to that time as a result of three pilots that I conducted in Montréal (see, Petitto, in preparation).

This condition was important as part of an extensive pretraining period to ensure that the children fully understood the experimental task. The children were then given a multiple-choice gestural comprehension task using the four groups of gestures. The critical questions were whether children at different ages would comprehend conventional, iconic gestures and would interpret ambiguous gestures as signs or pantomimes.

If knowledge of the semantic (and syntactic) role of lexical forms has its roots in prelinguistic gestural behavior, then children who can (a) comprehend and produce names for common objects (e.g., comb) and (b) produce a functionally appropriate gesture with the object (e.g., raising comb to hair and "combing") should be able to comprehend a gesture for that same object, particularly if the gesture is nearly identical in form to the one that they themselves produced for the same object.

The surprising finding of the study was that neither deaf nor hearing children comprehended highly iconic conventional gestures (groups 1–3) at an early age. This was true even for objects that they spontaneously named or had produced gestures with. Instead, children between 22 through around 28 months performed randomly on these groups. Even though many of the gestures used were the ones that the children themselves had produced moments before the trial, they did not comprehend them. In fact, both deaf and hearing children were unable to understand the meanings of the iconic gestures (even those that shared fundamental properties with ASL signs) until they were around 33–34 months, far too late for them to have contributed to their own early vocabulary learning. Further, the children's overall ability to comprehend gestures increased with age. As expected, deaf children were consistently better on group 4 (pure signs) throughout, whereas hearing children performed randomly on this group. Finally, for group 2 (ambiguous sign/pantomime gestures) it was only around age 40–48 months that a clear distinction emerged; deaf children favored a sign interpretation of the gestures and hearing children a gestural one.

The deaf and hearing children's failure to comprehend gestures, even when they had spontaneously produced similar gestures with the objects, raises important questions about the referential, linguistic status of the child's gesturing with objects. I contend that such gestures are not "functionally equivalent" to linguistic naming—these findings demonstrate the fundamental nonlinguistic nature of the children's object-linked gestures. Rather than being names for objects, these gestures appear to be part of the activity of using them; by age 22–28 months the children's use of gestures seems to reflect their knowledge of what one does with the objects that is, their functions. Interestingly, this functionally based knowledge appeared to be distinct from their knowledge and use of meaningful, linguistic symbols for representing objects. Both deaf and hearing children failed to perceive the iconicity inherent in the gestures presented to them. It appeared that the gestures were not meant to designate or categorize an object as belonging to a known class (i.e., they did not "stand for" the referent per se) but more closely resembled actions associated with them. Hence, when they observe the gesture in the task, they do not interpret them as names.

Finally, contrary to expectation, the deaf children's ability to comprehend gestures was not facilitated by the fact that gesture and sign share a single modality. Despite the close relationship between nonlinguistic and linguistic forms in ASL, deaf children's comprehension of nonlinguistic gestures was not advanced. Hence, we are provided with additional evidence for the distinct ways in which these children approach linguistic and nonlinguistic information even when they share a single channel.

GENERAL DISCUSSION

The three studies discussed in this chapter addressed two central theoretical questions in child language: What types of knowledge are involved in the acquisition process, and how does this knowledge change over time? Collectively, they provide evidence that the capacity to engage in prelinguistic gestural communication is distinct from the capacity to engage in linguistic expression.

In the first study, a radical discontinuity was observed between the deaf children's use of prelinguistic communicative pointing and the linguistic expression of YOU and ME pronouns, despite the fact that both forms were nearly identical. In the second study, detailed analyses of the forms, functions, and use of young children's prelinguistic gestures demonstrated that they differed from names in crucial ways. Finally, in the third study, hearing and deaf children (ages around 22–33 months) did not comprehend the conventional (iconic) gestures for objects that they themselves produced. The children's failure to comprehend these gestures calls into question the referential status of the gestures they produced for the same objects and provides additional evidence that the gestures the children produce do not have the same linguistic status as their names for the referents.

If these conclusions are correct, they suggest that the important issue is not the role of gesture in language acquisition, but rather why children gesture at all and why the use of gestures eventually declines. Children use gestures despite differing environments and cultures. The spontaneous onset of hearing and deaf children's gestures occurs around the same time (about 8–9 months) and begins to decline in frequency and type at around the same time (about 20–22 months). If this behavior does not represent the early expression of linguistic competence, why does it occur?

One possibility is that gestures are an early means to stimulate communicative interactions between the child and adults. Children's gestures generally attract adults' attention and response; adults respond by supplying linguistic information as, for example, when the child points and adults supply names or engage in a variety of other child-focused activities. Use of many gestures entails a highly social exchange between parents and their infants; this is most often seen in the rituals that parents and children engage in such as peek-a-boo, patty-cake, and the like. Social gestures are highly susceptible to imitation in the young child (e.g., hello, bye-bye). Gesturing with objects may also help the child learn general perceptual and cognitive information regarding proximal–distal, visual–spatial relations, weight and mass relations, and to acquire functional information about what one does with objects. Rather than providing the basis for *communicating about* objects through naming, the child *obtains* information by using gestures.

It is interesting that some early gestures—indexical points, as well as showing and giving actions—do seem to be used by children with communicative, instrumental, and referential intent. Why, then, are we not justified in assigning linguistic status to such gestures? These particular attributes of early gestural use have led some researchers to regard them as nascent linguistic markers (see especially, Bates, 1976; Bruner, 1975; Clark, 1978; Werner & Kaplan, 1963). However, these studies allow us to move beyond the initial observation that prelinguistic infants are social, intentional beings to a closer evalution of whether these properties—intentionality and the like—are sufficient to account for linguistic symbolization. It seems clear that it is fully possible for a child to be intentional, knowledgeable, communicative, and referential and yet not be engaging in a specifically linguistic act—as other distinctive properties of linguistic communication simply are not present. I am arguing that indexical pointing differs significantly from the way words are used to refer and that we are thus not justified in thinking of points to objects as names for those objects.

Why does the use of gestures decrease dramatically around 20–22 months? Shatz (1985) wonders whether the child's use of the early gestural system is only "an intermediary interaction device with just enough communicative features to carry out its function of eliciting interaction or whether it is continous with either later gestural accompaniments to speech or the development of a linguistic system in the gestural mode" (page, 17). She suggests that the gestural system might be an intermediary system encouraging communicative interaction and consequent linguistic input. Shatz further suggests that because hearing children's attention shifts around 20 months to interword relations during the multiword phase of language development, their production of gestures consequently drops dramatically (p. 18). My findings corroborate Shatz's general observation. The evidence from the acquisition of sign language in deaf children (as well as ape language studies) suggests that hearing and deaf children's inclination to use gestural communication is temporary and more important, distinct from later linguistic expression (see also Abrahamsen, Cavallo, & McCluer, 1985). The clearest evidence for this claim is found by observing how children approach the task of language learning where gestural and linguistic units are in the same mode. What is amazing is that, from the outset, deaf children tacitly seem to comb through the language input for units that are potentially significant to the target language, much the way hearing children first seem to extract phonemic features from a diffuse sound stream. Thus, regardless of the modality, children seem to isolate and separately analyze just those units—be they visual or aural—that will ultimately be significant to their language. This division between what is *in* their language and what is *outside* of it begins surprisingly early and is especially apparent when the language in question is externally articulated and resides in the same channel as gestures. The way deaf infants enter this process and begin differentiating among types of information within the single channel implies that a priori domain-specific—but not channel-specific—constraints must be at work during language acquisition.

It should be noted that, because many gestures are not universal, children must learn the specific gestures used in their culture. From around 13 months to 18–20 months, just before the extensive use of gesturing declines, children's gesturing with objects becomes more finely tuned to the specific functions associated with them, suggesting that learning which gestures belong to which objects must take place. Further, just as it is incorrect to assume that grammatical categories are "given" in the environment, it is incorrect to assume that knowledge of how to use gestures is directly apparent from relations given in the child's environment. Researchers who assert that perceptually salient information in the environment guides the child's use of gestures are implicitly ascribing an overly powerful theory of mind to the child. In trying to minimize the special status of language as a distinct domain of knowledge they have swung the other way, making claims about the child's general cognitive capacities that are equally implausible (see also Slobin, 1982). The environment provides the child with a potentially infinite number of ways to encode an object or event gesturally, which, in reality, cannot be exploited by the child. What, then, constrains the child's use of gestures? In maintaining that the 13-month-old's gestures are linguistic, researchers must provide an answer to this question. Finally, why do children favor linguistic rather than gestural means of encoding referents during times when, if the theory were correct, both systems are available to them? An explanation is not provided by asserting that "[gestures] remain too tied to their objects to move into flexible predicative relations", and "[gestures] are not used in communication [by the child], so that there is less pressure toward conventionalization and extension of use" (Bates et al., 1983). If anything, this argument describes the way in which gestures are distinct from linguistic expression. Further, it does not explain how deaf children differentiate between, and treat as distinct, gestural and linguistic information in cases where both gesture and sign are produced with identical forms.

The preceding analysis of the distinction between linguisitc and nonlinguistic domains of knowledge is further validated by considering again the gestures of apes. My intention here is to illuminate some potentially interesting behavioral similarities and dissimilarities between child and chimp in light of the preceding discussion. Perhaps the most common feature in research involving child and chimp signing is the researchers' propensity to overattribute linguistic meanings to their gestures. Leaving aside this methodological issue, there are other points of comparison. The behaviors of the young child—hearing and deaf—and chimp appear most similar in their general communicative and social interactions with people in their environment. By 12 months of age the cognitive abilities of both child and chimp are impressive: Both demonstrate possession of object perma-nence, both manipulate and handle objects, often in appropriate ways, both engage in social games (like patty-cake), and both explore the world around them. Both possess a set of natural gestures (including the open–close gesture) that are used across multiple contexts for multiple referents. Most importantly, both appear to be intentional beings and are able to use gestures to achieve instrumental ends. Both remember aspects of their daily routines and anticipate them; both recognize their caretakers; finally, both seek out and are part of social activities with adults.

The behaviors of hearing and deaf children and chimpanzees are very similar until around 12–13 months of age. At this point, hearing and deaf children effortlessly begin to experiment with their first names for things—one literally cannot stop them from naming—whereas the chimpanzee never takes this next step. Instead, into the chimpanzee's fifth year of life, and beyond, the training of simple vocabulary remains an extraordinarily arduous task. Teaching the chim-panzee the sign for CUP, for example, even with a cup physically present and in the chimpanzee's hands, can take literally thousands of trials, a fact well known among ape researchers, but little publicized. One noteworthy exception is a paper by Savage-Rumbaugh & Rumbaugh (1978), where they noted that their apes failed to learn six object names after 4 months of intensive training and over 3,000 trials. They concluded that "contrary to expectation, the subjects still demonstrated no reliable ability to name an object with a small lexigram symbol (page 273)". Moreover, it has been nearly impossible to teach apes (Nim and others) superordinate categories like *eating utensil* where there is no unique referent for the kind "utensil," only exemplars of the kind (e.g., forks and knives). Because apes do not grasp the special relationship between a sign and its referent (described as "scope of referring relations" in the discussion of names), it is little wonder that they do not combine signs syntactically; apes do not appear to understand that signs *refer*. They appear to know only that signs *effect*—cause some reaction or change in their environment. As my experience with Nim suggested, apes have knowledge about the pragmatic consequences of their hand gestures but not of the linguistic power of signs themselves.

A final observation about chimpanzees is that they do not use the indexical point to denote referents communicatively. Although it has been claimed that they do, this appears to be a misattribution, researchers having failed to dis-tinguish among the various types of pointing that human infants typically engage in (see Bates et al., 1975). Although apes do produce exploratory pointing to objects that are physically in hand, they do not point to a referent while moving eye gaze to and fro between the referent and the caretaker to establish joint visual regard. Interestingly, although chimpanzees will reach towards and beg for food (and other desirable objects), they will not point to the objects. Even after several years of training, the ape's use of the point differs markedly from that of a child. Chimpanzees simply do not spontaneously point to pick out and denote objects.

The developmental moment when the deaf or hearing child departs from the ape is when he or she begins to refer to and represent his or her world with linguistic symbols rather simply enacting actions with gestures. Moreover, around 18–22 months there appears to be a fundamental reorganization in children's knowledge manifested in strong discontinuities between linguistic and nonlinguistic knowledge systems (e.g., see Bowerman, 1982a, 1983b; Karmiloff-Smith, 1986). One particularly clear example of reorganization is seen in the acquisition of pronouns where the deaf child shifts from conceptualizing person-pointing as part of the class of deictic gestures to viewing such gestures as elements within the linguistic (lexical) system of ASL. Evidence from the other studies bearing on the issue of reorganization was seen in the very different ways children used gestures compared to linguistic symbols and in the children's failure to understand gestures as representing or naming objects. The cognitive or neurological basis for this reorganization is unclear and needs to be further investigated. However, the existence of the phenomenon cannot be doubted.

CONCLUSIONS

Language acquisition models that propose either a "direct mapping" from prelinguistic to linguistic expression, or a common underlying cognitive capacity that drives the symbolization process are not supported by the data from the studies described here. I do not suggest that there is no relationship between prelinguistic and linguistic knowledge, or that language acquisition is unrelated to cognitive development. I contend, however, that linguistic knowledge (concerning, for example, the relationship between form and meaning, and relations among forms) is not merely constructed out of the nonlinguistic materials at hand. In this sense, then, these studies compel the conclusion that central aspects of the language acquisition process are distinct from other forms of knowledge.

It is time once again to reintroduce specifically linguistic analyses in the field of "child language." Psychologists have recently shown antipathy to linguistics, perhaps because the field has become more complex. At times, linguists' controversies seem inscrutable to those of us on the sidelines. Further, the temptation to study gestures and other aspects of social interaction is great, because such external behaviors lend themselves to direct observation. However, an understanding of human language acquisition can only be achieved, I believe, with sophisticated and detailed analyses of the child's acquisition of linguistic phenomena per se. The challenge is to specify exactly what constitutes knowledge of *language* and how it evolves in ontogenesis. This requires an explicit theory of language, as part of a more general theory of language acquisition. Only a theory that considers the facts of language acquisition as well as the child's cognitive and developmental growth will succeed. Seen from this perspective, "learnability theory" is an important recent advance in theorizing, as it lays out a comprehensive program for what any adequate theory of language acquisition will necessarily have to specify (see especially the chapter in this text by Pinker and other important works on this topic: e.g., Pinker, 1979, 1984; Wexler & Culicover, 1980).

Roger Brown has always recognized the need for specific grammatical and semantic analyses in child language. This is clear not only from his published works, but also from the historical artifacts left behind in my office at Harvard. Looming behind my desk as I worked were seven wall-length shelves of the original audiotapes and phonetic transcriptions of Adam, Eve, and Sarah. Among the many artifacts (including Melissa Bowerman's notes from an anthropology class, Ursula Bellugi's Sage's shopping bag, a Lost-in-Space toy robot from 1967, and a five-pound box of sugar with a price of 89 cents) were hundreds of pages of Roger's notes. Writing by hand in pencil on yellow lined paper, he had carefully mapped out various grammars and semantic analyses for the three children. In the very late hours of a typical graduate student's day, I would find myself reading through these notes; I have learned tremendously from them as I have from Roger himself. If the present studies contribute to our understanding of child language, it is because they were inspired by his brilliant insights.

ACKNOWLEDGMENTS

I thank Mark Seidenberg for his important and insightful comments on earlier drafts of this chapter. I thank Frank Kessel and John Macnamara for their helpful comments on an earlier draft of this chapter. Special thanks to Fernande Charron and Robert Dufour for assisting in many aspects of this research. I thank my deaf research assistant, France Boulanger, for assisting with the transcription of videotapes. The data for Study 1 were reported in my Doctoral Dissertation (Harvard U.) and were collected at The Salk Institute for Biological Studies, La Jolla, California, in Ursula Bellugi's laboratory; I am very greatful for her generous support and guidance. This research was funded by a fellowship from the John D. and Catherine MacArthur Foundation's "San Diego Node" (Elizabeth Bates, Director), a NIH grant (#NS1151175) to U. Bellugi, and two grants from Canada: NSERC and F.C.A.R. (Québec).

REFERENCES

Abrahamsen, A., Cavallo, M. M., & McCluer, J. A. (1985). Is the sign advantage a robust phenomenon? From gesture to language in two modalities. *Merrill–Palmer Quarterly, 31.*
Barwise, J., & Perry, J. (1983). *Situations and attitudes.* Cambridge, MA: Bradford Book/M.I.T. Press.
Bates, E. (1976). *Language and context: Studies in the acquisition of pragmatics.* New York: Academic Press.

Bates, E., Benigni, L., Bretherton, I., Camaioni, L., & Volterra, V. (1979). *The emergence of symbols: Cognition and communication in infancy.* New York: Academic Press.

Bates, E., Bretherton, I., Shore, C., & McNew, S. (1983). Names gestures and objects: The role of context in the emergence of symbols. In K. Nelson (Ed.), *Children's language* (Vol. IV, pp. 59–123).

Bates, E., Camioni, L., & Volterra, V. (1975). The acquisition of performatives prior to speech. *Merrill–Palmer Quarterly, 21,* 205–26.

Bates, E., & MacWhinney, B. (1982). Functionalist approaches to grammar. In E. Wanner & L. Gleitman (Eds.), *Language acquisition: The state of the art.* Cambridge, England: Cambridge University Press.

Battison, R. (1978). *Lexical borrowing in American Sign Language.* Silver Spring: Linstok Press.

Bellugi, U. (1980). The structuring of language: Clues from the similarities between signed and spoken language. In U. Bellugi & M. Studdert-Kennedy (Eds.), (1980). *Signed and spoken language. Biological constraints on linguistic form* (pp. 115–140). Dahlem Konferenzen. Weinheim/Deerfield, FL: Verlag Chemie.

Bellugi, U., & Klima, E. (1981). From gesture to sign: Deixis in a visual–gestural language. In R. J. Jarvella & W. Klein (Eds.), *Speech, place and action: Studies of language in context.* Sussex: Wiley.

Bellugi, U., & Klima, E. (1982). The acquisition of three morphological systems in American Sign Language. In *Papers and Reports on Child Language Development* (Vol. 21, pp. 1–35). Stanford, CA: Stanford University.

Bloom, L., & Lahey, M. (1978). *Language development and language disorders.* Wiley.

Bonvillian, J. D., Orlansky, M. D., Novack, L. L., Folven, R. J., & Holley-Wilcox, P. (1983a). Language, cognitive, and cherological development: The first steps in sign language acquisition. In W. C. Stokoe & V. Volterra (Eds.), *Proceedings of the 3rd International Symposium on Sign Language Research.*

Bonvillian, J. D., Orlansky, M. D., & Novack, L. L. (1983b). Developmental milestones: Sign language acquisition and motor development. *Child Development.*

Bowerman, M. (1982a). Reorganizational processes in lexical and syntactic development. In E. Wanner & L. Gleitman (Eds.), *Language acquisition: The state of the art.* Cambridge, England: Cambridge University Press.

Bowerman, M. (1982b). Starting to talk worse: Clues to language acquisition from children's late speech errors. In S. Strauss (Ed.), *U-shaped behavioral growth.* New York: Academic Press.

Brown, R. (1958). *Words and things: An introduction to language.* New York: The Free Press.

Brown, R. (1973). *A first language: The early stages.* Cambridge, MA: Harvard University Press.

Bruner, J. S. (1973). The ontogenesis of speech acts. *Journal of Children Language, 2,* 1–19.

Carey, S. (1982). Semantic development: The state of the art. In E. Wanner & L. Gleitman (Eds.), *Language acquisition: The state of the art.* Cambridge, England: Cambridge University Press.

Caselli, M. C. (1983). Communication to language: Deaf children's and hearing children's development compared. *Sign Language Studies, 39,* 113–144.

Charney, R. (1978). *The development of personal pronouns.* Unpublished doctoral dissertation, University of Chicago.

Chevalier-Skolnikoff, S. (1976). The ontogeny of primate intelligence and its implications for communicative potential: A preliminary report. In S. Harnad, H. D. Steklis, & J. Lancaster (Eds.), *Origins and evolution of language and speech.* New York Academy of Sciences.

Chiat, S. (1981). Context-specificity and generalization in the acquisition of pronominal distinctions. *Journal of Child Language, 8,* 75–91.

Chiat, S. (1982). If I were you and you were me: The analysis of pronouns in a pronoun-reversing child. *Journal of Child Language, 9,* 359–379.

Chomsky, N. (1965). *Aspects of the theory of syntax.* Cambridge, MA: MIT Press.

Chomsky, N. (1975). *The logical structure of linguistic theory.* New York: Plenum Press.

Clark, E. V. (1978). From gesture to word: On the natural history of deixis in language acquisition.

In J. S. Bruner & A. Garton (Eds.), *Human growth and development: Wolfson College Lectures 1976*. Oxford: Clarendon Press.

Ferguson, C., & Farwell, C. (1975). Words and sounds in early language acquisition. *Language, 51*, 419–39.

Frege, G. (1960). On sense and reference. In Geach, Peter, & Black (Eds.), *Translations from the philosophical writings of Gottlob Frege* (pp. 56–78). Oxford: Basil Blackwell.

Gillan, D. J., Premack, D., & Woodruff, G. (1981). Reasoning in the chimpanzee: I. Analogical reasoning. *Journal of Experimental Psychology: Animal Behavior Processes, 7*, 1–17.

Golinkoff, R. M. (Ed.). (1983). *The transition from prelinguistic to linguistic communication*. Hillsdale, NJ: Lawrence Erlbaum Associates.

Greenfield, P., & Smith, J. (1976). *The structure of communication in early language development*. New York: Academic Press.

Hoffmeister, R. J. (1978). *The acquisition of American Sign Language by deaf children of deaf parents: The development of demonstrative pronouns, locatives, and personal pronouns*. Unpublished doctoral dissertation, University of Minnesota.

Kantor, R. (1982). *Communicative interaction in American Sign Language between deaf others and their deaf children: A psycholinguistic analysis*. Unpublished doctoral dissertation, Boston University.

Karmiloff-Smith, A. (1986). From meta-processes to conscious access: Evidence from children's metalinguistic and repair data. *Cognition, 23*, 95–147.

Keenan, E. O., & Schiefflin, B. (1976). Topic as a discourse notion. In C. Li (Ed.), *Subject and topic*. New York: Academic Press.

Klima, E., & Bellugi, U. (1979). *The signs of language*. Cambridge, MA: Harvard University Press.

Lenneberg, E. H. (1967). *Biological foundations of language*. New York: Wiley.

Leopold, W. F. (1939–1949). *Speech development of a bilingual child (4 vols.)* Evanston, IL: Northwestern University Press.

Lock, A. (Ed.). (1979). Action, gesture & symbol. New York: Academic Press.

Macnamara, J. (1982). *Names for things*. Cambridge, MA: MIT Press.

Macnamara, J. (1986). A border dispute. Cambridge, MA: MIT Press.

Marmor, G. S., & Petitto, L. A. (1979). Simultaneous communication in the classroom: How well is English grammar represented? *Sign Language Studies, 3*, 99–136.

McIntire, M. (1977). The acquisition of American Sign Language hand configurations. *Sign Language Studies, 16*.

Menzel, S. W. (1974). A group of chimpanzees in a one-acre field. In A. M. Schrier & F. Stollnitz (Eds.), *Behavior of nonhuman primates* (vol. 5). New York: Academic Press.

Padden, C. (1981). Some arguments for syntactic patterning in ASL. *Sign Language Studies, 32*, 239–259.

Padden, C. (1983). *Interaction of morphology and syntax in American Sign Language*. Unpublished doctoral dissertation, University of California, San Diego.

Peirce, C. (1932). *Collected papers*. C. Hartshorne & P. Weiss (Eds.). Cambridge, MA: Harvard University Press.

Petitto, L. A. (1981). *On the acquisition of anaphoric reference in American Sign Language*. The Salk Institute for Biological Studies, La Jolla, California.

Petitto, L. A. (1983a). *From gesture to symbol: The relationship between form and meaning in the acquisition of personal pronouns in American Sign Language*. Unpublished doctoral dissertation, Harvard University.

Petitto, L. A. (1983b). From gesture to symbol: The relationship between form and meaning in the acquisition of personal pronouns in American Sign Language. *Papers and Reports on Child Language Development, 22*, 100–107.

Petitto, L. A. (in press). On the autonomy of language and gesture: Evidence from the acquisition of personal pronouns in American Sign Language. *Cognition*.

Petitto, L. A., & Seidenberg, M. S. (1979). On the evidence for linguistic abilities in signing apes. *Brain and Language, 8,* 72–88.

Piaget, J. (1962). *Play, dreams and imitation.* New York: Norton.

Pinker, S. (1979). Formal models of language learning. *Cognition, 1,* 217–283.

Pinker, S. (1984). *Language learnability and language development.* Cambridge, MA: Harvard University Press.

Premack, D. (1971). Language in chimpanzee? *Science, 172,* 808–822.

Premack, D. (1976). *Intelligence in ape and man.* Hillsdale, NJ: Lawrence Erlbaum Associates.

Prinz, P. M., & Prinz, E. A. (1979). Simultaneous acquisition of ASL and spoken English in a hearing child of a deaf mother and hearing father: Phase I. Early lexical development. *Sign Language Studies, 25,* 283–296.

Savage-Rumbaugh, E. S., & Rumbaugh, D. M. (1978). Symbolization, language and chimpanzees: A theoretical reevaluation based on initial language acquisition processes in four young Pantroglodytes. *Brain and Language, 6,* 265–300.

Schlesinger, H. S., & Meadow, K. P. (1972). *Sound and sign: Childhood deafness and mental health.* Berkeley: University of California Press.

Seidenberg, M. S., & Petitto, L. A. (1979). Signing behavior in apes: A critical review. *Cognition, 7,* 177–215.

Shatz, M. (1985). An evolutionary perspective on plasticity in language development. *Merrill-Palmer Quarterly.*

Slobin, D. (1982). Universal and particular in the acquisition of language. In E. Wanner & L. Gleitman (Eds.), *Language acquisition: The state of the art.* Cambridge, England: Cambridge University Press.

Snow, C. E. (1972). Mothers' speech to children learning language. *Child Development, 43,* 549–65.

Stokoe, W. (1960). Sign language structure: An outline of the visual communication systems of the American Deaf. *Studies in Linguistics, Occasional Papers,* University of Buffalo.

Supalla, T. (1982). *Acquisition of morphology of American Sign Language verbs of motion and location.* Unpublished doctoral dissertation, University of California, San Diego.

Terrace, H. S., Petitto, L. A., Sanders, R. J., & Bever, T. G. (1979). Can an ape create a sentence? *Science, 206,* 891–902.

Terrace, H. S., Petitto, L. A., Sanders, R. J., & Bever, T. G. (1980). On the grammatical capacity of apes. In K. Nelson (Ed.), *Children's language* (Vol. 2, pp. 371–495). New York: Gardner Press.

Van Lawick-Goodall, J. (1970). Tool-using in primates and other vertebrates. In D. S. Lehrman, R. A. Hinde, & E. Shaw (Eds.), *Advances in the study of behavior* (Vol. 3). New York: Academic Press.

Volterra, V. (1981). Gestures, signs, and words at two years: When does communication become language? *Sign Language Studies, 33,* 351–362.

Werner, H., & Kaplan, B. (1963). *Symbol formation.* New York: Wiley.

Wexler, K., & Culicover, P. (1980). *Formal principles of language acquisition.* Cambridge, MA: MIT Press.

Wilbur, R. (1979). *American Sign Language and sign language system: Research and applications.* Baltimore: University Park Press.

Wilbur, R. B., & Petitto, L. A. (1983). Discourse structure of American Sign Language conversations. *Discourse Processes, 6:3,* 225–241.

Woodruff, G., & Premack, D. (1981). Primitive mathematical concepts in the chimpanzee: Proportionality and numerosity. *Nature, 293,* 568–570.

Zukow, P. G., Reilly, J., & Greenfield, P. M. (1980). Making the absent present: Facilitating the transition from sensorimotor to linguistic communication. In K. Nelson (Ed.), *Children's language* (Vol. 2). New York: Gardner Press.

10 The Cognition Hypothesis Revisited

Richard F. Cromer
Medical Research Council

Does the language we speak affect the way we think? Alternatively, are our thoughts independently arrived at and merely reflected in our language—with differing degrees of adequacy depending on the resources of the language we speak? The former position has usually been identified with Edward Sapir and Benjamin Lee Whorf and is often referred to as the Whorfian hypothesis. In recent use it has taken two basic forms. The "strong" form asserts that the language we speak determines what we think, whereas the "weak" form makes the claim that the language we speak merely predisposes us to think in certain ways. The opposing viewpoint, that particular thought processes are ontogenetically prior to and developmentally prerequisite for language development, has usually been associated with the Piagetian school. The fact that both views have been forcefully advocated and that evidence has been presented for each indicates the possibility that both views are somehow right even though they seem to be diametrically opposed.

When I arrived at Harvard as a graduate student in 1962, I was very much interested in these issues. In fact, as a result of my undergraduate studies in cultural anthropology at Tulane University, I leaned toward a Whorfian view that encompassed not only linguistic determinism but an associated linguistic relativity, that differences in the structures of different languages would result in cognitive differences in the speakers of those languages. Roger Brown was just setting up his study of language acquisition, and, because of my interest in the relation between language and thought, he hired me as a research assistant on the project. It was my job to accompany Ursula Bellugi and Colin Fraser as they visited and recorded Adam and Eve respectively on alternative weeks, and especially to note adult utterances directed at the child and the overall situational

223

contexts of all utterances. My other interest was in the concept of "time" and how it developed in the child.

Being involved in Brown's project gave me the ideal opportunity to combine these two interests and, in addition, to consider the language/thought controversy within a developmental perspective. Previous studies had examined cognitive abilities (such as memory for colors) in adult speakers of different languages. Here, by contrast, was the chance to examine the varying contributions of language and cognitive development to a particular aspect of conceptual acquisition in an individual child. Specifically, being involved in Brown's project made it possible for me to study the development of time concepts during the acquisition of language. And that became the subject of my dissertation.[1]

The conclusion of that study (Cromer, 1968) was somewhat the opposite of the Whorfian view with which I had begun. The concluding sentences of the dissertation were: "Approaches which do not take developing cognitive abilities into account cannot hope to explain these otherwise mysterious phenomena. Language acquisition is a complicated procedure and simple models will not suffice. . . . We must also look at cognitive processes and their development, and at the ways such processes direct language acquisition if we are to acquire new insights into that acquisition process" (p. 220). In 1968 that was neither an obvious nor a popular view. Influenced by the Chomskyan revolution in linguistics, most psychologists and developmental psycholinguists were not only concentrating on the acquisition of language structure but were also viewing that acquisition in primarily structural terms (e.g., Braine, 1963a, b). The alternative Genevan position was only just becoming known to those studying child language through statements by Piaget and Inhelder (1969) and Sinclair (Sinclair-de-Zwart, 1969). It was not until Lois Bloom's important and influential book appeared in 1970 that child language researchers began to take seriously the notion that the developing thought processes of the child might play an important part in language acquisition itself.

THE COGNITION HYPOTHESIS

From my thesis conclusions, the arguments from the Genevan psychologists, Bloom's data, and crosslinguistic evidence compiled even earlier by Dan Slobin (1966), it was then possible to develop the "cognition hypothesis of language acquisition." This hypothesis (Cromer, 1974) asserted (in terms meant to paral-

---

[1]The circumstances of my dissertation writing may be of interest, if only for the light shed on the quality of Roger Brown's commitment to his students. In early 1968, after six enjoyable years at Harvard, I had the rude awakening that I was no longer eligible to hold teaching assistantships and would have to go out and face the world. In panic, I took the data and thoughts I had been collecting for several years, all but locked myself inside William James Hall, and in 24 continuous days and nights wrote my 287 page thesis on the development of temporal reference during the acquisition of language. During this ordeal, almost daily Roger Brown would slip me 10 or 12 handwritten pages of suggestions for making the output from the night before coherent. This interest and attention saved my sanity and enabled me to obtain the PhD a month or so later.

lel the opposite Whorfian hypothesis): "We are able to use the linguistic structures that we do largely because through our cognitive abilities we are enabled to do so, not because language itself exists for all merely to imitate" (p. 234). However, it was clear even then that the relationship between language and thought was more complicated. In fact, the conclusion I reached in 1974 did not support the cognition hypothesis so stated but, instead, called for a "weak form." This "weak form" argued that linguistic development also depended on independent, language-specific abilities.

It now transpires that more recent findings may challenge even this weaker view. The purpose of this chapter, therefore, is to revisit and "update" the earlier position. First, I review a small part of the evidence that led to the cognition hypothesis. Then I note recent studies that lend support to that view by taking a more specific and differentiated approach to "cognition." At that point, the evidence that led to the necessity of positing the weak form of the cognition hypothesis is reviewed. Finally, I cite material from a variety of sources that may well undermine some aspects of even the weak cognition position. This includes evidence that language has an effect on cognition, and finally, evidence that in some cases language can be acquired even in the absence of claimed cognitive prerequisites. Greater specification and differentiation of what is meant by the term *language,* however, may help to highlight what part cognitive development does play in language acquisition.

EVIDENCE FOR THE COGNITION HYPOTHESIS

The Original Brown Evidence

My study of temporal reference during the acquisition of language provided evidence that the understanding of some particular temporal notions preceded the acquisition of linguistic forms usually used for their expression. The language data were examined in two ways. First, a description of particular linguistic forms was made regardless of what their assumed intended reference might be. Second, the ability to refer to a particular concept was traced regardless of the linguistic forms used by the child. This double search is necessary because linguistic forms do not stand in a one-to-one correspondance with the concepts they are usually thought to encode.

Because it was necessary to trace the development of time concepts over several years, and because Eve moved away after the first year of Roger Brown's longitudinal study, the data examined were those from Adam (from age 2;3 to 6;2) and from the third child added to the study, Sarah (from age 2;3 to 5;5). They had similar mean utterance lengths at similar chronological ages, and so only the ages and order of development are mentioned here. Although the speech protocols came from fortnightly recording sessions in the home, in order to see changes most clearly only the protocols from approximately 4-month intervals were examined.

The argument that particular conceptual understandings preceded the usual linguistic forms for their expression can be illustrated by referring to one of the concepts studied—the concept of hypotheticalness.

A true hypothetical was defined as predicating a future event on another event that is also in the future, with the hypothesized event being slightly later than the event on which it depends. Thus, in the utterance, "If it turns cold, I will take my heavy coat," the possibility of the weather turning cold is taken as a future event that, if it occurs, will result in the even later event of taking the heavy coat. This is, of course, only one kind of unactualized event; there are others that make different use of time reference. For example, in counterfactual statements such as "If you had cried out, I would have come to your aid," a possibility in past time that did not in fact occur is noted. Such hypothetical and counterfactual statements require complex cognitive abilities, including the ability to refer to "possibilities" as well as the ability to move one's viewpoint about in time. Tracing the development of the hypothetical concept and its expression in language revealed some evidence of conceptual growth preceding language.

A primitive type of *possibility* is found in the ability to pretend. In Adam and Sarah's language, pretending was present in such early utterances as:

I'll b'Bam Bam. (Sarah, 3:2)
This 'ill be the daddy. (Sarah, 3:2)
Dis could be the mother. (Adam, 4:0)

However, in these utterances and others like them at young ages, no true hypotheticalness is involved; the child is simply stating a convention to be used in playing. Nonlinguistic pretend play, of course, begins much earlier than these utterances (see Leslie, in press). At slightly later ages, some utterances begin to take on the character of possibility, as in, for example, Adam's: Maybe it's can . . . go dis way. (Adam, 3;2)

But it was only at age 4;6 that possibility emerged as a concept used regularly. On average, about half a dozen uses were recorded in each session from age 4;6 onwards. Here are just a few examples:

Someping might come out my pocket. (4;6)
This could be a hanging ceiling thing. (4;10)
Ursla, you could stay and eat with us. (4;10)
Mommy, she said maybe . . . she said we can see if I can keep the
whistle. (5;9)

At about the same time as *possibility* began to function, another type of concept appeared to emerge. This can be called *uncertainty of conditions*. It did not encode true hypotheticalness, even though the child made use of some of the same linguistic devices that were later employed in expressing that more complex concept. Uncertainty of conditions emerged in Adam at age 4;0. Early examples include:

Maybe that's my daddy. (4;0)
Maybe she left it for me. (4;6)
I wonder if Mommy has gone. (4;10)
See if the flowers would like to watch me. (4;10)

It remains to examine those utterances that in context have been interpreted as referring to true hypotheticalness. One instance occurred as early as age 3;2 in Adam:

You open it, de gas . . . de gas will come in.

Next, at age 4;0, the one instance of a possible "hypothetical" usage is actually an incomplete utterance:

If I put two of them . . .

It was not until age 4;6 and thereafter that hypotheticals appeared in regular use in Adam's speech. Some examples included:

Don't tear it again or I turn you into a puppet. (4;6)
And I'm gonna turn into a knight if you do dat. (4;6)
I(d) mind if a lion wakes me up. (4;10)
If you keep on going, it's gonna get bigger on this side and bigger on that side, right? (5;2)
Paul, you (can) put a top on it so the people wouldn't catch no cold in their car. (5;9)

In summary, it can be said that in Adam, except for one possible instance at age 3;2 (at the same age as one possible instance of "possibility" as well), true hypotheticals do not really emerge in quantity and regular use until age 4;6. Earlier references to pretending, possibility, and uncertainty of conditions have been noted. In Sarah all instances of "unactual" categories were infrequent, and it was not until 4;10 and 5;2 that the only instances of true hypotheticals were found in her utterances.

There is an important point to note in this short summary of the development of reference to "hypotheticalness": Such reference does not depend on the acquisition of some new linguistic form. It is expressable by the use of "if" and "or" and by means of various simple clauses preceding "so." The child has actually had the ability to utter the same linguistic forms at earlier ages but has done so only when those utterances have been used to express a different kind of meaning, for example, for expressing possibility or for determining uncertain conditions.

It may be, therefore, that some linguistic forms cannot be acquired until the child has developed the particular concepts they are used to express. Slobin

(1966), for example, noted that the hypothetical emerged late in children acquiring Russian as their native language, a seemingly odd finding because the hypothetical form is grammatically simple in Russian. Slobin concluded that it was the semantic and not the grammatical aspect that was difficult for the child. In the English examples from Adam and Sarah, an additional fact has been noted: In some cases, children actually possess the linguistic forms often used by adults to express particular concepts, but they use these forms only to encode the less developed concepts they have already acquired.

This review of the development of the concept of hypotheticalness during the acquisition of language illustrates the kind of data that led me to the view that cognitive development precedes and makes possible the acquisition of particular aspects of language. The original study (Cromer, 1968; see also 1974) included the development of a number of other time concepts that similarly supported this position. There were also other data from Brown's own study of Adam, Eve, and Sarah, showing that particular aspects of language acquisition depended on prior cognitive development.

Early Verb Modifications

In one of his many careful analyses of the data from Adam, Eve, and Sarah, Roger Brown (1973, pp. 317–318) studied not only the children's earliest verb modifications, but also the way these were understood by the parents. He found that after Stage I, children began to modify their verbs in three ways: marking the past with -ed or an irregular allomorph, adding the semiauxiliaries wanna, gonna, and hafta, and using a primitive progressive with -ing but no auxiliary. What was significant was that these three grammatical modifications encoded three of the four intentions that adults had attributed to the children when only the generic unmarked form of the verb was being uttered: reference to an immediate past, intentions or predications, and present temporary duration. Such a finding is interpretable as evidence that children may have developed those concepts before they had acquired the linguistic forms in which they are normally encoded.

The Genevan View

The examples cited previously from Roger Brown's developmental language data are a small but early part of the literature concerning the effects of cognitive development on language. The major theoretical impetus for this view came from the Genevan school. Piaget consistently held that the developing structures of the child's mental apparatus lay the foundations for linguistic development. In this view, early schemata that are built up during the sensori-motor period have structural properties that make language acquisition possible. Early cognitive developments are thus seen as prerequisites for language acquisition to occur.

It should be noted that the Genevan position on the relation between thought and language encompasses more than what has been mentioned here. Because the preceding view was held in relation to Chomsky's linguistic analyses, the emphasis was primarily on the relation between structural aspects of cognition and the structural aspects of language, i.e., syntax. But two aspects of the effects of cognition on language must be considered. First, there are mechanisms, processes, and cognitive structures that underlie our specific thoughts. Second, there are the "contents" of those thoughts that these underlying mechanisms make possible. Let us call the underlying level the *cognitive processes*. The Genevan position just considered was concerned with this level; in addition, a number of important cognitive processes and mechanisms that were not emphasized by Piaget would also be classified here—e.g., short-term memory capacity, sequencing and temporal ordering abilities, production span capacity, hierarchical planning ability, etc. (see reviews in Cromer, 1976, 1981, 1984). By contrast, let us call the contents of thought *concepts* or *cognitions;* these are the specific thoughts made possible by the underlying cognitive processes, but which are shaped in their details by many other factors.

This distinction will help us to classify more recent research on the language/thought controversy and, more importantly, to begin to see how "processes" and "concepts" may be differentially related to different subsystems of language. This is emphasized in the final section of this chapter. As the following examination of a few studies shows, some of the recent work on the cognition hypothesis of language acquisition has shifted from considering the process emphasis of Piaget's theory to specifying particular cognitive concepts and their effects on language.

RECENT STUDIES ON THE COGNITION HYPOTHESIS

Piagetian Research

Smolak and Levine (1984) studied 40 children between 12 and 36 months of age. Their object was to study the relation between emerging concepts and language. One main cognitive ability examined was the development of object permanence. Because Piaget had argued that nonlinguistic representation is a precursor of representational language, Smolak and Levine reasoned that success on a task involving invisible displacements should predate representational language, i.e., language used to refer to past events and absent objects. Object permanence was assessed through the administration of a graded series of invisible displacement tasks. Language was sampled during special play sessions that included a language "interview" (a series of questions designed to elicit references to past events and to absent objects).

The result of interest was that all 34 children who had representational language also successfully completed at least the multiscreen single invisible displacement task, whereas none of the six children who had not yet reached that level of cognitive ability gave any evidence of using representational language. In other words, Smolak and Levine's study suggests that the child must attain a particular stage of object concept development before a general language ability—the use of representational language—can occur.

McCune-Nicolich (1981) had made a similar claim for the importance of late sensori-motor period cognitive organization for particular language abilities. In this case, the claim was that a particular stage of object-concept development must be attained before the child is able to use "relational words." Although earlier studies had found only low correlations between language and sensori-motor measures, McCune-Nicolich believed that this was due to the fact that much of that research focused on the acquisition of "object words." By contrast, "relational words" develop and exist apart from specific content, because they encode consistent relational meanings regardless of the objects involved. Thus, for example, according to McCune-Nicolich (1981), a word like "more" supposedly "coded recurrence, whether a cookie was requested after one had been eaten, a second shoe was observed, or the child desired additional tickling" (p. 16). McCune-Nicolich argued that the use of relational words is based on the operative knowledge attained at the end of the sensori-motor period. Such words should therefore only appear after the attainment of sensori-motor knowledge. Furthermore, because operative intelligence is a universal aspect of cognition, the same categories of meaning should be observed in all children, even though varying lexical items would be used to encode them.

To assess this, McCune-Nicolich longitudinally observed five girls aged 1;2 to 1;6 at the beginning of the study. They were seen monthly in their homes for a 30-minute play session for a period of 7 to 11 months. Entry into stage 6 of the sensori-motor period was defined as being able to solve a single invisible displacement on at least two trials. The criterion for late stage 6 was immediate solution of random invisible displacements using three screens.

McCune-Nicolich's observations showed that although only 13 different relational word forms occurred, each child began to use 8 to 10 of these at some point during this period of single-word use. More importantly, contrary to her prediction and to earlier studies, some children used a number of relational words prior to the attainment of *late* stage 6 sensori-motor competence. Because all subjects were already in early stage 6 during the first observational session, McCune-Nicolich concluded that the operative sensori-motor knowledge at that point appears to be a sufficient cognitive foundation for the use of relational words.

More important than the precise point of emergence during stage 6 development, however, was the pattern of emergence of these words. The onset of their use was fairly abrupt. McCune-Nicolich reported that for each child more than half of the relational words first appeared within a two-session span. There was also no consistent order of emergence for particular words or meanings. Instead, the relational words tended to enter the child's lexicon as a group. These results seem to support the view that a certain level of cognitive development is necessary before the child can begin to use relational words. When that level of cognitive ability has developed, a number of these words begin to be used, and this is so regardless of their specific content.

However, other researchers have not found the simultaneous emergence of general types of words, and they argue that the semantic content of the child's early words should be related to specific developments in cognitive ability. Tomasello and Farrar (1984), for example, have suggested that McCune-Nicolich failed to make a distinction between relational words that signified visible displacements of objects (e.g., "up" and "move") and those that signified invisible displacements (e.g., "gone"). Furthermore, they argued that because "this is precisely the distinction between stage 5 and stage 6 object permanence behaviours, . . . it should be reflected in the cognitive structures underlying the child's early words" (p. 480). In other words, their view is that, contrary to McCune-Nicolich's predictions, relational words requiring only the understanding of visible displacements would be based on stage 5 object permanence development and should begin to appear at that time. By contrast, those relational words requiring the knowledge of invisible displacements will not appear until stage 6 of the sensori-motor period.

In the Tomasello and Farrar study, six 12-month-old children were observed weekly for a period of 6 months. All were initially in stage 5 of object permanence development. During the weekly visits, language samples were obtained; these were supplemented by diary records of the child's vocabulary kept by the mother. Cognitive testing was carried out at monthly intervals and consisted of modified versions of the object permanence and the means–ends subscales of the Uzgiris–Hunt infant assessment scale. The child was only credited with understanding a particular relational word when productive use was demonstrated in more than one context. Whether a word referred to a visible or an invisible displacement was decided through examination of the particular contexts in which the word occurred.

The results revealed that the children first began to use a variety of present-relational words during stage 5 object permanence—which requires an understanding of visible displacements of objects but not their invisible displacements as in stage 6. These included the use of "thank you" to refer to the transfer of objects, "uh-oh" in situations in which the child fell down or dropped or spilled something, "bye" in situations in which people who were in spatial proximity to the child began to move away, and "hi" to greet people within the visual field. Tomasello and Farrar note that words like "bye" and "hi" were never used by any child at this stage to refer to objects or persons already gone or to the existence or transformations of objects or persons outside the child's perceptual field. The child never used any words to refer to absent objects. Such absent-relational words first appeared during stage 6; these included "gone" for objects that were initially present and then disappeared, "find" and "more" for objects that were initially absent and then appeared, and "allgone" for objects that were initially absent and remained absent—as when a cup was found to be empty. Tomasello and Farrar (1984) concluded that "stage 5 object permanence does not suffice for the use of absent-relational words. These do not appear until stage 6, when children come to have an understanding of invisible-object transformations" (p. 486).

An additional finding of Tomasello and Farrar is important. They noted that, although one of the children in their study used an absent-relational word while still in stage 5 means–ends development, this child was at stage 6 on object permanence tasks. This is evidence of considerable specificity in the relationship between conceptual development and language development. Two experiments by Gopnik and Meltzoff (1984b) give additional support to this view. In one, thirty 18-month-old children underwent cognitive testing and their use of particular words was examined along lines similar to Tomasello and Farrar. The results showed a relation between success on particular cognitive tasks and the use of particular words relevant to those tasks. Children who did well on the object-concept tasks were the ones more likely to use disappearance words, whereas those children who did well in solving the difficult means–ends problems were more likely to use success/failure words. Significantly, there was no relation between the use of disappearance words and performance on the means–ends tasks, nor any between use of success/failure words and performance on the object-concept tasks. As Gopnik and Meltzoff (1984b) put it: "These results suggest specific relationships between *particular* linguistic attainments and *particular* cognitive skills. The use of disappearance words is closely related to progress in object-permanence, but not so closely related to progress in means–ends ability. Similarly, the use of success/failure words is more closely related to means–ends abilities than to object-permanence skills" (p. 13).

In a related study, Gopnik and Meltzoff (1984b) longitudinally followed for 6 months six children who were initially 16 to 19 months of age. During this period, their language and cognitive skills were investigated approximately every 2 weeks, using the same methods as in the cross-sectional study just noted. It was found that the gap between the first solution of the object-concept task and the first use of disappearance words was on average 18.7 days, whereas the gap between that same cognitive attainment and the first use of success/failure words was 59.7 days. Similarly, the gap between the first solution of the means–ends task and the first use of a success/failure word was on average 15.3 days, whereas the gap between that cognitive attainment and the first use of disappearance words was 55.8 days. Again, as in the cross-sectional study, there was evidence of a connection between the acquisition of disappearance words and the solution of the object-concept tasks, and of a connection between the acquisition of success/failure words and the use of insight to solve means–ends problems. More significantly, the results showed a dissociation between these two developments, underlining the specificity in the relation between cognitive development and language acquisition. Further, this suggests that cognitive development is more closely related to the content of early language, i.e., to the meanings children express, than to more general structural features of language (e.g., syntax).

Regarding the direction of the relation between cognition and language, as is seen in the next section, the results of these studies are open to various interpretations. One interpretation is that cognitive growth resulting in conceptual development makes particular acquisitions in the language system possible.

Non-Piagetian Research

Not all the research showing the effects of cognitive growth on language has been based on Piagetian concepts. Levine and Carey (1982), for example, studied the acquisition of the comprehension of the words "front" and "back" and their relation to the development of the concept of front–back orientation. They began their investigations with the Whorfian notion that in some cases learning a new word may precede and influence concept acquisition.

Thirty-six children ranging in age from 2;1 to 3;3 were tested. Two non-linguistic tasks were used to evaluate the children's concept of front–back orientation. For linguistic understanding, the child's knowledge of the words "front" and "back" was assessed. Although 3 children failed all the tasks, the remaining 33 children succeeded on at least one of the concept tasks. In fact, 30 of these 33 children obtained a score of at least 7 out of 9 correct on *both* tasks. By contrast, on the linguistic assessment only 5 children made no errors. Another 20 children scored in the range of 40 to 80% correct, and there were 8 children who scored in the range of 0 to 30% correct. In other words, whereas the linguistic knowledge of "front" and "back" ranged from virtually nonexistent in 8 children to perfect scores by 5 children, all the children performed at about the same high level on nonlinguistic tasks assessing their concept of front–back orientation, regardless of their linguistic level. Conversely, none of the children succeeded on the linguistic tests while failing on the concept tasks. Contrary to the hypothesis with which Levine and Carey began, the results suggest that the acquisition of the concept "front–back orientation" precedes the acquisition of the words "front" and "back."

Conclusion

So far, what has been reviewed supports the cognition hypothesis of language acquisition; the acquisition of particular cognitive skills (sensori-motor intelligence) or of specific concepts usually precedes the acquisition of particular linguistic abilities. But there is also a good deal of evidence that challenges this notion, and it is to this that the remainder of this chapter is devoted.

SHORTCOMINGS OF THE COGNITION HYPOTHESIS

My 1974 proposal of the cognition hypothesis did not put forward the form of that hypothesis alluded to in the previous section of this review. Instead, a "weak" form of that hypothesis was proposed. I had argued that cognitive principles were not *sufficient* to explain language acquisition and that some specifically linguistic development must also occur. The reasons for this are considered in this section. After reviewing those reasons and the related evidence, I examine the notion that language itself may in fact affect the development of some aspects of cognition. Finally, some evidence is presented that raises the question of whether particular cognitive processes are even *necessary* for language acquisition to occur.

Evidence that Nonlinguistic Cognitive Processes are Not Sufficient to Explain Language Acquisition

The arguments and evidence that something more is needed to account for language acquisition than the mere development and growth of cognitive processes were reviewed in the 1974 cognition hypothesis paper. One argument was based on the work with signing programs initiated with chimpanzees (Gardner & Gardner, 1969). Since 1974, such programs have been extended to other species (e.g., Herman, Richards, & Wolz, 1984, on bottlenosed dolphins; Patterson & Linden, 1981, on gorillas; and Schusterman & Krieger, 1984, on sea lions), but note that the same conclusions that follow also hold for those more recent studies. In the Gardner's chimpanzee, Washoe, for example, there was no indication that word order played any important part in the communication process; the Gardners have provided no evidence that signs produced in differing linear orders had different meanings. Furthermore, whereas children increase communicative content when they increase the length of their utterances, there was no evidence that Washoe's longer sign sequences served such a purpose. The chimp merely increased the number of signs used in proportion to the subjective importance of the message, but these were not structured in any meaningful way.

Comparing the first "sentences" of Washoe to the first utterances of the children in his longitudinal study, Roger Brown (1970) noted that the kinds of meanings expressed by children in their first sentences appeared to be extensions of sensori-motor intelligence. He reasoned that similar kinds of meanings might operate in other animals. Brown then carefully pointed out: "Grammatical relations are defined in purely formal terms, and while they may, in early child speech, be more or less perfectly coordinated with the semantic rules, the two are not the same" (p. 222); that is, the possession of sensori-motor intelligence does not explain how that intelligence is expressed in language. The fact that early grammar in children expresses the meanings that sensori-motor intelligence makes possible does not solve the problem of how those meanings are conveyed by a grammar. Thus, Washoe, in spite of possessing sensori-motor intelligence, might never necessarily acquire a grammatical language. (See Seidenberg & Petitto, 1979, for a critical review of the studies of signing behavior in apes.) More recently, Brown (1981) has argued that what the various ape studies have revealed is a rudimentary symbolic capacity; again, this is not the same thing as possessing a grammar.

A second argument that something more is needed to explain language acquisition than merely the possession of particular cognitive prerequisites comes from the observation of developmentally aphasic children. Following Premack's (1969) method of training chimpanzees to communicate with plastic symbols serving for objects and actions, and for communicating particular meaningful relations between them, Hughes (1974/75) was able to train developmentally aphasic children on the same functions using similar symbols. These children, although exhibiting normal intelligence on nonverbal tests, had been unable to acquire normal language. Their acquisition of communication functions in twice-weekly half-hour sessions in less than 10 weeks showed that their ability to understand and to communicate these meanings was not impaired. They could acquire this arbitrary system because it was learned as a linear set of signs associated with particular meanings and concepts, but they still remained unable to acquire the grammar of human language. Whatever the reasons for some aphasic children failing to acquire language, it is clear that their possession of conceptual understanding is not sufficient in itself to allow for the grammatical encoding of those concepts.

Although some developmentally aphasic children may have an impairment in the ability to encode material hierarchically (see Cromer, 1983), and although it could therefore be argued that these children do not possess all the cognitive prerequisites for grammatical language, a third line of evidence shows such prerequisites are not sufficient to explain the language acquisition process even in normal children with intact cognitive underpinnings. This evidence comes from the spontaneous productions of children acquiring language. For example, in the case of Adam, Eve, and Sarah, Bellugi (1967) traced the developmental stages of the linguistic expression of negation. Increasing linguistic sophistication was observed even when the same meaning was being encoded by the child. Bellugi has made such a case for another aspect of grammatical acquisition as well—the development of the expression of self reference (Bellugi, 1971; Bellugi-Klima, 1969). Children, in referring to themselves, progress through a number of stages, first using their own name instead of pronouns like ''I'' and ''me,'' and eventually reaching an adult-like stage where the pronoun depends on grammatical function rather than sentence position. Here not only has the reference of the pronoun not changed, but it is also difficult to see how broader cognitive constraints could account for this progression in linguistic forms because later stages sometimes represent a simplification of production.

Further evidence of language growth and change that is not dependent on cognitive or conceptual growth per se comes from following the development of language in children brought up bilingually. In an early paper, Slobin (1973), after reviewing data to support the argument that there are cognitive prerequisites for grammar, noted that at some point formal linguistic complexity also plays a role in acquisition. He pointed out, for example, that children learning Finnish lack yes/no questions at an age when children learning other languages have acquired them. The reason these are lacking in Finnish children is that yes/no questions are a particularly complex form in Finnish. He also underscored the role of formal linguistic factors in the acquisition of plurals and locatives in the now classic case of the child acquiring Serbo–Croation and Hungarian.

Slobin (1982) has continued these studies by comparing first-language acquisition in children acquiring diverse languages and has recently succinctly stated the overall point: "There is a long way between a *communicative intention* . . . and the *semantic structure* containing that particular array of notions which must be mapped onto a grammatical utterance in a specific language. . . . Each language poses the child with a different set of problems to solve in discovering the notions to be mapped and the means of mapping" (p. 137). Using the data collected by his Berkeley Crosslinguistic Acquisition Project, Slobin demonstrated acquisition differences in children learning to speak English, Italian, Serbo–Croatian, and Turkish. What Slobin's project shows in a variety of clear cases is that languages differ in what they must obligatorily encode and in the formal complexity with which that encoding is carried out, *and* that these differences play some role in language development. Thus, although the cognitive hypothesis may go some way in explaining why children in the course of language acquisition encode some concepts before others, it is certainly not sufficient on its own to describe the entire process of language acquisition.

Working to some extent from this evidence, Paul Harris (1982) has presented arguments against the cognition hypothesis. One of these concerns the acquisition of a second language. He reasons that if cognitive development largely determines the sequence of language acquisition, one should expect to find acquisition patterns in older children acquiring a second language markedly different from first-language acquisition; that is, many of the concepts not yet developed in the very young child will already be part of the competence of the older child. If the acquisition of particular linguistic forms is constrained by that competence, then language-acquisition patterns should differ. Harris notes, however, that reviews by McLaughlin (1977, 1978) indicate that first- and second-language acquisition in childhood follow remarkably similar paths.

There are theoretical reasons, too, why language acquisition is not easy to explain solely in terms of conceptual development. As Gleitman and Wanner (1982) have pointed out, of the many generalizations that children might draw from linguistic input, they somehow seem to draw the right ones. A current approach to this problem is that of "learnability theory" (see, e.g., Baker & McCarthy, 1981; Berwick & Weinberg, 1984; Wexler & Culicover, 1980), which is an attempt to restrict the class of human grammars in order to be learnable by the child under varying assumptions concerning the lack of particular types of feedback. Furthermore, widespread constraints on certain linguistic structures have been empirically observed across wide divergences in language. Although some of these linguistic universals may result from the operation of general cognitive constraints, it may be that others are specifically linguistic and cannot easily be explained in purely nonlinguistic, cognitive terms (see, e.g., Caplan & Chomsky, 1980). If this is the case, it may be necessary to postulate the existence of a specifically linguistic faculty in human beings that goes beyond what broader cognitive principles can account for in language acquisition.

The Effects of Language on Cognition

Another major reason why the cognition hypothesis of language acquisition may be inadequate rests on some recent evidence that language, for its part, may play a role in the formation of concepts. Earlier, I mentioned the studies by Gopnik and Meltzoff. In one (1984b), longitudinal findings were taken as evidence of the relation between *specific* cognitive attainments and the first uses of language encoding *specific,* associated concepts. More importantly, however, Gopnik and Meltzoff noted that the language developments and the related cognitive developments could occur in either order. On five occasions, the child achieved solution for the first time on the cognitive task before using the associated term for the first time, as would be consistent with a cognition hypothesis; but on two occasions, the child used the relevant word before solving the cognitive task. In the remaining five cases, the children first achieved the cognitive task solution and first used words encoding the related concepts in the very same session.

This pattern of results was interpreted by Gopnik and Melzoff (1984a) as evidence that concepts and language develop together. In other words, it is not the case that concepts develop before words, nor that words develop before concepts; rather, there exist transition periods during which conceptual ability and language are developing together. In the interaction between these two domains, language is seen as a contributing cause rather than as a simple consequence of cognitive development.

In a related study, Gopnik (1984) traced the developmental use of the word "gone" and the concepts it encoded in nine children who were either 12, 15, or 18 months old at the start of the study. She found that the children acquired the word "gone" when they were in the midst of developing the concept that it encoded. Conceptual and semantic development appeared to proceed simultaneously. Gopnik speculated that use of the word "gone" may have helped the child to develop the object concept. Schlesinger (1977) had earlier put forward a similar theoretical view: "On first dealing with a certain aspect of his surroundings the child may understand it only vaguely and imperfectly; the manner of talking about it then points the way for the child to gain a firmer grasp of the distinction in question'' (p. 166).

Shatz (1984) has been developing a theory compatible in some aspects with the view that language and cognitive development proceed in parallel and mutually influence one another. Shatz suggests that several areas of child development consist of ''bootstrapping operations,'' i.e., operations that allow children to use the competencies they already possess to attain still more complex competencies. In language acquisition, she argues, there is piecemeal organization and reorganization of an internally represented system. As part of this process, children incorporate bits of heard speech into their own system. They use terms that are not fully understood, but in the process of doing so their attention is drawn to particular regularities, this, in turn, contributing to cognitive growth.

The work that has so far been mentioned on the interactive effects of language and cognition has concentrated on the growth and change of specific concepts. Much of the earlier research—for example, Luria's (1959, 1961)—on the effects of language on cognition was, by contrast, concerned with ''cognitive processes'' such as memory and problem solving. (See Waters & Tinsley, 1982, for a review of some of these studies.) It is instructive to examine Premack's work on chimpanzees, keeping in mind this distinction between the effects of language on problem solving, broadly defined, and the formation of specific concepts.

Premack (1983, 1984; see also Premack & Premack, 1983) has compared the problem-solving abilities of chimpanzees that he has given language training using plastic symbols with chimpanzees that have not received such training. Premack reports that once the chimpanzee has been exposed to language training, it can solve particular kinds of problems that it could not solve otherwise. Premack (1983) is not claiming that he has been able to teach chimpanzees a syntactic system similar to human language. He is careful to point out that there was no evidence in his studies of any systematic appreciation of grammatical distinctions by the language-trained chimpanzees: ''While we find evidence for semantic distinctions, distinctions in the meanings of words, syntactic distinctions are not within the capacity of the chimpanzee. . . . [T]he evidence we have makes it clear that even the brightest ape can acquire not even so much as the weak grammatical system exhibited by very young children'' (p. 115). What one is concerned with, then, is the advantages an abstract system of representation confers on chimpanzees successfully trained to use it. Those that have acquired such a system are able to make same/different judgments, to match proportions of exemplars that are physically unlike, to solve analogies, and to complete incomplete representations of actions. Chimpanzees not language trained are unable to solve these tasks.

Basically, what do the Premack studies show? The ''language'' that Premack taught to the chimpanzees is not, of course, language in the human sense; it might be more accurate to call it a system of overt manipulable representations. But human language, whatever else it is, is also a system of manipulable representations. The issue, then, is this: Can such a system allow us to do certain kinds of tasks that we could not do without it? Premack's important experiments appear to show that the acquisition of a representational system allows for the development of particular types of problem-solving ability that would otherwise be impossible. Premack is careful to point out that this system does not instill some new kind of abstract capacity in the animal. Rather, if a species has an abstract code to begin with, Premack's type of training enhances the animal's ability to use that basic capacity, and thus to solve types of problems otherwise beyond its conceptual reach.

Focusing on young children, Blank (1974) has argued that language affects behavior and problem-solving ability on particular types of problems. Based on an earlier study by Blank and Bridger (1964), she argues that temporal discriminations, such as being able to differentiate between one and two successive flashes of light, are language dependent. Blank (1975) has also claimed that some aspects of language may be crucial in leading the child to use conceptual and problem-solving skills that would otherwise remain undeveloped. As an example (Blank, 1974) she contends that when children are confronted with words like "why" and "how" they can find no portrayable correlates for them. For example, if the child is asked "Why is the baby crying?," Blank claims that neither the observation of the named object nor the activity is sufficient for the child to grasp the meaning of the term *why*. Children are therefore forced to produce terms of this type before they comprehend them. They try out the term and from the adult's responses, they can learn when the use of this term is appropriate or inappropriate. Slowly children begin to learn how certain attributes are selected for the answer to their own "why" questions and begin to relate these to different types of "why" (whys of motivation, whys of cause, etc.). Blank's claim, then, is that when young children use "why," they are engaged in hypothesis testing to discern the meaning and use of "why." This in turn serves as an important impetus to further conceptual development.

Although studies by Luria, Premack, Blank, and others have demonstrated the enhancement of problem-solving abilities by language or language-like systems, it may be that human language does something more: Language may affect the actual concepts that are encoded. Blank's study of the acquisition of the word *why* comes close to this position, although she sees the use of why more as a problem-solving device that leads the child to acquire particular concepts including, of course, the meaning of why itself. By contrast, the claim that language may affect specific concepts is closer to the original Whorfian position for which little firm evidence has been found in most studies. But there may be exceptions.

The most important work for showing the effects of language on the development of particular concepts is Melissa Bowerman's. She claims that in some cases children gradually work out the categories of meaning implicit in the structure of language on the basis of experience with language itself (Bowerman, 1982). Some evidence for this position comes from the development of the use of the prefix "un-" that Bowerman studied longitudinally in her own two children over several years. The children progressed through several stages in their acquisition of the prefix, and Bowerman believes that it is the experience of language itself that leads to the construction of the most advanced concept underlying "un-." For example, the category of actions involving covering/enclosing/surface attachment—a category crucial to correct "un-" usage—has little nonlinguistic utility, and it is unlikely that children would otherwise form such a category. Bowerman hypothesizes instead that children come to appreciate the semantic correlates of "un-" and thus form what Whorf termed its cryptotype only on the basis of regularities observed in the linguistic forms used originally on a piecemeal basis.

Bowerman (1980) gives further examples of this process in the charming, idiosyncratic uses her children made of "hi" and "gidi." For example, Eva apparently constructed a concept to cover the use of "gidi" (possibly a rendition of "scuse me"), which involved the actual or anticipated physical displacement of objects. Bowerman suggests that the repeated exposure to a particular word (such as "hi" or "excuse me") "started her working on a concept she probably would not have formulated at that time in the absence of this specific kind of linguistic input" (p. 293).

Bowerman's position is an interesting one. It argues that, in some instances, children form concepts on the basis of language. This is not totally without problems, however. For example, in the case of forming a general concept based on a number of piecemeal uses of a syntactic structure, what purpose would the concept serve?; that is, if the child already produces correct syntactic structures on a piecemeal basis, what need is there of forming a crytotype to cover instances of productive use (such a description, of course, may help to account for productive "errors")? More importantly, is it really possible to write a "semantic" (conceptual) description for every syntactic structure? It is not possible to do this for gender, nor has it been possible to do so for the process/stative verb distinction. Indeed, it is doubtful that this can be done for *any* syntactic distinction or category. For example, it is well known that the past tense does not always refer to past time (see also Maratsos & Chalkley, 1980). Nevertheless, it may still be the case that for isolated parts of the language system, children do form concepts they would not otherwise form were it not for the linguistic regularities they observe in the input. Bowerman's careful observations are compelling evidence that this occurs, at least on occasion, for some parts of the language system.

There is some evidence, then, that language may play a part in the formation of concepts. It has also been hypothesized that the advent of a written form of language and the growth of literacy has had significant effects on thought processes (see Scribner & Cole, 1981). It is worth noting that language having specific effects on conceptual development is not strictly incompatible with a hypothesis that certain levels of cognitive development make particular aspects of language acquisition possible. But it does mean that an interactionist account of language and cognitive development would be more accurate. In their recent review of the various theories of the relation between language and thought Rice and Kemper (1984) characterize the Interaction Hypothesis as holding that linguistic expressions can alter the nature of children's cognitive development. In this section, evidence has been examined in support of that position.

There is, however, evidence of a different nature that is worrying for the cognition hypothesis even in this weaker interactionist form. Having argued earlier that nonlinguistic cognitive processes were not sufficient to explain language acquisition, I turn finally to evidence that nonlinguistic cognitive processes may not even be *necessary* for language acquisition to occur.

Evidence That Nonlinguistic Cognitive Processes May Not Be Necessary for Language Acquisition

The notion that language acquisition may in some important respects be independent of cognitive processes and content is not new. For example, the fact that language acquisition is relatively independent of IQ has often been taken as evidence in support of the idea that language is an independent faculty separate from other nonlinguistic cognitive abilities. Lenneberg, Nichols, and Rosenberger (1964), in their famous early study of 61 Down's syndrome children, found that on language imitation tests these children performed like younger normal children. It was the passing of particular motor milestones, and not the particular IQ level, that best predicted language development.

There is more recent evidence that the relationship between language acquisition and specific cognitive developments is not so close as has often been supposed. (See also Menyuk, 1975, for some early criticisms of interpretations of a direct relationship between the two.) For example, Miller and Chapman (1984) report data that show that mean length of utterance (MLU) is a better predictor of complex sentence acquisition in 3- to 6-year-olds than is nonverbally measured cognition. In fact, nonverbal cognition did account for additional variance—but in the *semantic* rather than in the syntactic component of the grammar. Other researchers have also found "language-internal" variables to be of greater potential explanatory value for language acquisition than general cognitive ones.

Even more interesting in this regard are rare cases in which the usual picture of development is disturbed. Curtiss and Yamada (1981), Yamada (1981), and Yamada and Curtiss (1981), for example, have presented case studies of hyperlinguistic children whose language abilities far outstrip the rest of their cognitive development.

Antony was studied by Curtiss and Yamada (1981) for 6 months from the time he was 6½ years of age. They report a Leiter IQ of 50 and a mental age of 2;9 when Antony was 5;2. Curtiss and Yamada gave Antony an array of nonlanguage cognitive tests. These included batteries of Piagetian measures (conservation, classification, seriation, etc.) and a variety of other measures including drawing, copying, nesting of objects, hierarchical construction, logical sequencing, auditory memory span, and many others. Antony's language was examined through the use of a specially designed battery called CYCLE (for the Curtiss Yamada Comprehensive Language Evaluation), given in both a receptive and spontaneous speech form.

Curtiss and Yamada report that on the nonlinguistic cognitive tests Antony scored below existing norms or below the 2-year-old level. On only one test, auditory (verbal) short-term memory, did Antony show normal, age-level performance. This poor performance contrasted sharply with his language. Whereas Antony performed poorly on the comprehension tests—due to such factors as attentional deficits—his best performances on these tests were on items examining syntactic structure. His worst performances, no better than the 2-year-old level, were on tests of lexical semantics or lexically encoded linguistic information. Antony also performed poorly on tests of inflectional morphology.

The pattern of results, then, seems to indicate that Antony does poorly on the semantic subcomponent of language and on those aspects of the grammar that are most dependent on specific meanings, i.e., inflectional morphology. His best comprehension performances are on syntactic items. In fact, in his *spontaneous speech,* Antony was highly advanced in his use of syntactic structures. He used 61 of the 68 different elements and structures Curtiss and Yamada analyzed, including infinitival and sentential complements, relative clauses, and other subordinate clauses. He also used a variety of morphological features that were consistent and well formed, although a number of his grammatical forms were inappropriately used. Curtiss and Yamada (1981) gave the following summary of Antony's performance: "His ability to use a wide range of syntactic devices . . . to encode his limited and confused thoughts, illustrates the discrepancy between Antony's grammatical knowledge and his conceptual/cognitive knowledge" (p. 75). They also pointed out that there were certain errors that he never made: "He did not place verb markers on nouns or vice-versa, did not use clausal connectors within VP's or NP's, nor use affixes as prefixes or vice-versa. His errors consisted exclusively of omissions and semantically inappropriate use. Antony appeared to have extracted purely syntactic and morphological constraints without the semantics which they normally encode" (p. 77).

This case illustrates how a conceptual deficit may affect the semantic subcomponent of the grammar while leaving the syntactic subcomponent free to develop. Because auditory short-term memory was the only cognitive test that Antony performed at an age-appropriate level, it appeared to be the only nonlinguistic cognitive process that might have been a necessary prerequisite for his developing syntax. Indeed, Yamada and Curtiss (1981) have reported another case study, of a young girl with Turner's syndrome, that also provides strong evidence of good syntactic development in spite of poor conceptual ability; again, the one nonlanguage area in which she excelled was on a test of auditory short-term memory. However, some doubt has been cast on even this "cognitive prerequisite" for syntactic acquisition by a third case study: Yamada (1981) has reported on the language and cognitive abilities of Marta, a hyperlinguistic, retarded adolescent who also evidenced advanced syntactic ability in spite of limited conceptual abilities. But unlike the other two cases, Marta also scored poorly on auditory short-term memory tasks.

Curtiss and Yamada's cases not only give evidence of a dissociation between language and cognition but also point out the need to differentiate language into its subcomponents. It was the syntactic (and phonological) component of the grammar that appeared to be relatively unaffected by conceptual and general cognitive deficiencies. These deficiencies affected primarily the semantic subcomponent. Curtiss and Yamada also noted several pragmatic deficits in Antony's speech and argued that semantic problems in presupposition and implicature often led to communication difficulties.

It appears then that syntax can be acquired even with severely impaired or limited conceptual and general cognitive development. There are still other cases revealing less impairment even in the semantic component than might be expected given the observed cognitive deficiencies. Rapin and Allen (1983), for example, used the label "semantic pragmatic syndrome without autism" for children who have very fluent expressive language. They described the utterances produced by such children as being "syntactically well-formed, phonologically intact, and, on the surface, 'good language.' On closer examination, however, one discovers that the language is often not really communicative" (p. 174). Children with this type of language show an impairment in the ability to encode meaning relevant to the conversational situation. It would be difficult to pinpoint the difficulty here as one of affecting the semantic component in the sense that Curtiss and Yamada reported for Antony.

The syndrome described by Rapin and Allen has usually been observed in some children with internal hydrocephaly who talk excessively but whose language, if they are mentally retarded, has been described as lacking in content. Hadenius, Hagberg, Hyttnäs-Bensch, and Sjögren (1962), for example, reported on six hydrocephalic children in which mental retardation was observed along with "a peculiar contrast between a good ability to learn words and talk, and not knowing what they are talking about" (p. 118). They described these children as loving to chatter but thinking illogically and therefore coined the term *cocktail-party syndrome* for the condition. Similarly, Ingram and Naughton (1962) described nine of 16 cerebral palsy patients with arrested hydrocephalus who fit this description. They referred to these children as "chatterboxes," "excessively talkative," or as "bletherers."

Several later studies have provided information on the "chatterbox syndrome." Swisher and Pinsker (1971) studied 11 children, ranging in age from 3;2 to 7;10, with spina bifida cystica and a history of hydrocephalus and who were considered by clinicians to be hyperverbal. Their language was compared to a control group matched for age, congenital physical handicap, and history of exposure to hospitalizations. Results showed that these children used significantly more words and initiated more speech than the control group. Utterances were also classified as being appropriate, inappropriate, or bizarre. Eight of the 11 hydrocephalic children used some language that was either inappropriate or bizarre, but only 2 of the control group children did so. Indeed, of those 8 hydrocephalic children, 6 produced both inappropriate and bizarre language whereas none of the control children did so.

Anderson and Spain (1977) reported a study at age six of 145 spina bifida children who had originally been observed when they were 3 years of age. They reported that 40% of these children showed the hyperverbal syndrome although only about half of that number exhibited it to any significant degree. The hyperverbal children were typically female and were poor intellectually, with considerably higher verbal than performance skills. Analysis of the children's spontaneous speech showed that they used quite complex syntax, but often inaccurately. They were described as having bizarre utterances with a tendency to change sentence in midflow, and to give more false starts to sentences and more incomplete sentences than a group of normal children matched for verbal ability on the WPPSI. They also produced a much higher rate of clichés, or adult-type phrases, although they rarely gave the impression of understanding their meaning. Commenting on the speech of one child with an IQ of 55 whose protocol they published, Anderson and Spain observed that he "clearly does not really understand what he is saying" (p. 130).

Finally, Tew (1979) compared 20 spina bifida children who had been classified as showing the cocktail-party syndrome with 29 spina bifida children who did not. One finding is particularly interesting: The children judged to be hyperverbal scored from 26 to 32 IQ points lower than the other spina bifida children on all three measures of IQ—verbal, performance, and full scale. These children, then, exhibit, in extreme form, fluent speech coupled with poor understanding and limited conceptual and general cognitive abilities.

More complete reports of these studies as well as other studies of hyperverbal children can be found in Cromer (in press). My initial investigations of hydrocephalic children who are hyperverbal indicate that they possess normal or near-normal syntactic *and* semantic abilities. It is difficult to pinpoint precisely the oddness of their language because, in a certain sense, their language is pragmatically appropriate. Indeed, they seem "expert" at social conversation. The language of some of these children gives the impression of being bright and educated rather than bizarre and inappropriate. As Rapin and Allen (1983) put it: "The low IQ scores of such children often come as a surprise because their skills for repetition, their good vocabulary, and their appropriate social interactions mask their inability to deal with abstract concepts" (p. 175).

CONCLUSION

The fact that some children can acquire syntactic competence in language while possessing such limited conceptual and general cognitive abilities poses a serious problem for the cognition hypothesis of language acquisition. The cognition hypothesis may have been useful in describing the usual pattern of association between language and cognition during normal development when I originally explored the issue empirically under Roger Brown's guidance and subsequently reviewed the related literature. But the decisive evidence emerging from this revisiting of the cognition hypothesis points to language as being made up of several subsystems—some of them more independent of conceptual understanding and general cognitive processes than many psychologists would have liked to believe.

At the beginning of this chapter, I raised the issue of whether the language we speak affects the way we think or whether the way we think affects our language. I originally leaned toward the Whorfian view, but the results of the studies I undertook with Roger Brown led me to the opposite conclusion. However, Roger made us all aware that there was something very special about language, and that we had better exercise a little caution in stating the conclusions that our investigations seem to point us towards. Language is a complex process and we cannot explain its acquisition merely by reducing it to its cognitive underpinnings. The contradictory findings on the language/thought controversy might well indicate that parts of both views are right.

REFERENCES

Anderson, E. M., & Spain, B. (1977). *The child with spina bifida.* London: Methuen.

Baker, C. L., & McCarthy, J. J. (Eds.). (1981). *The logical problem of language acquisition.* Cambridge, MA: MIT Press.

Bellugi, U. (1967). *The acquisition of the system of negation in children's speech.* Unpublished doctoral dissertation. Harvard University.

Bellugi, U. (1971). Simplification in children's language. In R. Huxley & E. Ingram (Eds.), *Language acquisition: Models and methods* (pp. 95–119). London and New York: Academic Press.

Bellugi-Klima, U. (1969). *Language acquisition.* Paper presented at the Wenner-Gren Foundation for Anthropological Research in the symposium on Cognitive Studies and Artificial Intelligence Research, Chicago.

Berwick, R. C., & Weinberg, A. S. (1984). *The grammatical basis of linguistic performance: Language use and acquisition.* Cambridge, MA: MIT Press.

Blank, M. (1974). Cognitive functions of language in the preschool years. *Developmental Psychology, 10,* 229–245.

Blank, M. (1975). Mastering the intangible through language. In D. Aaronson & R. W. Rieber (Eds.), *Developmental psycholinguistics and communication disorders. Annals of The New York Academy of Sciences* (Vol. 263, pp. 44–58).

Blank, M., & Bridger, W. H. (1964). Cross-modal transfer in nursery school children. *Journal of Comparative & Physiological Psychology, 58,* 277–282.

Bloom, L. (1970). *Language development: Form and function in emerging grammars.* Cambridge, MA: MIT Press.

Bowerman, M. (1980). The structure and origin of semantic categories in the language-learning child. In M. LeC. Foster & S. H. Brandes (Eds.), *Symbol as sense: New approaches to the analysis of meaning* (pp. 277–299). New York: Academic Press.

Bowerman, M. (1982). Reorganizational processes in lexical and syntactic development. In E. Wanner & L. R. Gleitman (Eds.), *Language acquisition: The state of the art* (pp. 319–346). Cambridge, England: Cambridge University Press.

Braine, M. D. S. (1963a). On learning the grammatical order of words. *Psychological Review, 70,* 323–348.

Braine, M. D. S. (1963b). The ontogeny of English phrase structure: The first phase. *Language, 39,* 1–13.

Brown, R. (1970). *Psycholinguistics: Selected papers by Roger Brown.* New York: The Free Press.

Brown, R. (1973). *A first language.* Cambridge, MA: Harvard University Press.

Brown, R. W. (1981). Symbolic and syntactic capacities. *Philosophical Transactions of The Royal Society of London,* Series B, 292 (No. 1057), 197–204.

Caplan, D., & Chomsky, N. (1980). Linguistic perspectives on language development. In D. Caplan (Ed.), *Biological studies of mental processes* (pp. 97–105). Cambridge, MA: The MIT Press.

Cromer, R. F. (1968). *The development of temporal reference during the acquisition of language.* Unpublished doctoral dissertation, Harvard University.

Cromer, R. F. (1974). The development of language and cognition: The cognition hypothesis. In B. Foss (Ed.), *New perspectives in child development* (pp. 184–252). Harmondsworth, Middlesex: Penguin Books.

Cromer, R. F. (1976). The cognitive hypothesis of language acquisition and its implications for child language deficiency. In D. M. Morehead & A. E. Morehead (Eds.), *Normal and deficient child language* (pp. 283–333). Baltimore: University Park Press.

Cromer, R. F. (1981). Reconceptualizing language acquisition and cognitive development. In R. L. Schiefelbusch & D. Bricker (Eds.), *Early language: Acquisition and intervention* (pp. 51–137). Baltimore: University Park Press.

Cromer, R. F. (1983). Hierarchical planning disability in the drawings and constructions of a special group of severely aphasic children. *Brain and Cognition, 2,* 144–164.

Cromer, R. F. (1984, January 3–6). Language and cognition in relation to handicap. Paper presented at the Spastics Society Medical Education and Information Unit conference, *Language development and communication problems of the handicapped,* Oxford.

Cromer, R. F. (in press). Differentiating language and cognition. In L. L. Lloyd & R. L. Schiefelbusch (Eds.), *Language perspectives II.* Austin, Texas: Pro-Ed.

Curtiss, S., & Yamada, J. (1981). Selectively intact grammatical development in a retarded child. *UCLA Working Papers in Cognitive Linguistics, 3,* 61–91.

Gardner, R. A., & Gardner, B. T. (1969). Teaching sign language to a chimpanzee. *Science, 165,* 664–672.

Gleitman, L. R., & Wanner, E. (1982). Language acquisition: The state of the state of the art. In E. Wanner & L. R. Gleitman (Eds.), *Language acquisition: The state of the art* (pp. 3–48). Cambridge, England: Cambridge University Press.

Gopnik, A. (1984). The acquisition of *gone* and the development of the object concept. *Journal of Child Language, 11,* 273–292.

Gopnik, A., & Meltzoff, A. N. (1984a). Semantic and cognitive development in 15- to 21-month-old children. *Journal of Child Language, 11,* 495–513.

Gopnik, A., & Meltzoff, A. N. (1984b, July). *Some specific relationships between cognitive and* semantic development: Disappearance words and the object concept and success/failure words and means–ends understanding. Paper presented at the Third International Congress for the Study of Child Language. Austin, Texas.

Hadenius, A-M., Hagberg, B., Hyttnäs-Bensch, K., & Sjögren, I. (1962). The natural prognosis of infantile hydrocephalus. *Acta Paediatrica, 51,* 117–118.

Harris, P. L. (1982). Cognitive prerequisites to language? *British Journal of Psychology, 73,* 187–195.

Herman, L. M., Richards, D. G., & Wolz, J. P. (1984). Comprehension of sentences by bottlenosed dolphins. *Cognition, 16,* 129–219.

Hughes, J. (1974/75). Acquisition of a non-vocal "language" by aphasic children. *Cognition, 3,* 41–55.

Ingram, T. T. S., & Naughton, J. A. (1962). Pediatric and psychological aspects of cerebral palsy associated with hydrocephalus. *Developmental Medicine and Child Neurology, 4,* 287–292.

Lenneberg, E. H., Nichols, I. A., & Rosenberger, E. F. (1964). Primitive stages of language development in mongolism. In D. McK. Rioch & E. A. Weinstein (Eds.), *Disorders of communication* (pp. 119–137) (Research publications of the Association for Research in Nervous and Mental Disease, Vol. XLII). Baltimore: Williams & Wilkins.

Levine, S. C., & Carey, S. (1982). Up front: The acquisition of a concept and a word. *Journal of Child Language, 9,* 645–657.

Luria, A. R. (1959). The directive function of speech in development and dissolution. *Word, 15,* 341–352.

Luria, A. R. (1961). *The role of speech in the regulation of normal and abnormal behavior.* New York: Pergamon Press.

McCune-Nicolich, L. (1981). The cognitive bases of relational words in the single word period. *Journal of Child Language, 8,* 15–34.

McLaughlin, B. (1977). Second language acquisition in childhood. *Psychological Bulletin, 84,* 438–459.

McLaughlin, B. (1978). *Second language acquisition in childhood.* Hillsdale, NJ: Lawrence Erlbaum Associates.

Maratsos, M. P., & Chalkley, M. A. (1980). The internal language of children's syntax: The ontogenesis and representation of syntactic categories. In K. E. Nelson (Ed.), *Children's language* (Vol. 2, pp. 127–214). New York: Gardner Press.

Menyuk, P. (1975). The language-impaired child: Linguistic or cognitive impairment? In D. Aaronson & R. W. Rieber (Eds.), *Developmental psycholinguistics and communication disorders. Annals of The New York Academy of Sciences* (Vol. 263, pp. 59–69).

Miller, J. F., & Chapman, R. S. (1984). Disorders of communication: Investigating the development of language of mentally retarded children. *American Journal of Mental Deficiency, 88,* 536–545.

Patterson, F., & Linden, E. (1981). *The education of Koko.* New York: Holt, Rinehart, & Winston.

Piaget, J., & Inhelder, B. (1969). The gaps in empiricism, In A. Koestler & J. R. Smythies (Eds.), *Beyond reductionism* (pp. 118–160). London: Hutchinson.

Premack, D. (1969) *A functional analysis of language.* Invited address before the American Psychological Association, Washington, DC.

Premack, D. (1983). The codes of man and beasts. *The Behavioral and Brain Sciences, 6,* 125–137.

Premack, D. (1984). Possible general effects of language training on the chimpanzee. *Human Development, 27,* 268–281.

Premack, D., & Premack, A. J. (1983). *The mind of an ape.* New York: W. W. Norton.

Rapin, I., & Allen, D. A. (1983). Developmental language disorders: Nosologic considerations. In U. Kirk (Ed.), *Neuropsychology of language, reading, and spelling* (pp. 155–184). New York: Academic Press.

Rice, M. L., & Kemper, S. (1984). *Child language and cognition.* Baltimore: University Park Press.

Schlesinger, I. M. (1977). The role of cognitive development and linguistic input in language acquisition. *Journal of Child Language, 4,* 153–169.

Schusterman, R. J., & Krieger, K. (1984). California sea lions are capable of semantic comprehension. *The Psychological Record, 34,* 3–23.

Scribner, S., & Cole, M. (1981). *The psychology of literacy.* Cambridge, MA: Harvard University Press.

Seidenberg, M. S., & Petitto, L. A. (1979). Signing behavior in apes: A critical review. *Cognition, 7,* 177–215.

Shatz, M. (1984, July 9–13). *Bootstrap operations in child language.* Plenary Address, at the Third International Congress for the Study of Child Language, Austin, Texas.

Sinclair-de-Zwart, H. (1969). Developmental psycholinguistics. In D. Elkind & J. H. Flavell (Eds.), *Studies in cognitive development* (pp. 315–336). New York: Oxford University Press.

Slobin, D. I. (1966). The acquisition of Russian as a native language. In F. Smith & G. A. Miller (Eds.), *The genesis of language* (pp. 129–148). Cambridge, MA: MIT Press.

Slobin, D. I. (1973). Cognitive prerequisites for the development of grammar. In C. A. Ferguson & D. I. Slobin (Eds.), *Studies of child language development* (pp. 175–208). New York: Holt, Rinehart, & Winston.

Slobin, D. I. (1982). Universal and particular in the acquisition of language. In E. Wanner & L. R. Gleitman (Eds.), *Language acquisition: The state of the art* (pp. 128–170). Cambridge, MA: Cambridge University Press.

Smolak, L., & Levine, M. P. (1984). The effects of differential criteria on the assessment of cognitive-linguistic relationships. *Child Development, 55,* 973–980.

Swisher, L. P., & Pinsker, E. J. (1971). The language characteristics of hyperverbal, hydrocephalic children. *Developmental Medicine and Child Neurology, 13,* 746–755.

Tew, B. (1979). The "cocktail party syndrome" in children with hydrocephalus and spina bifida. *British Journal of Disorders of Communication, 14,* 89–101.

Tomasello, M., & Farrar, M. J. (1984). Cognitive bases of lexical development: Object permanence and relational words. *Journal of Child Language, 11,* 477–493.

Waters, H. S., & Tinsley, V. S. (1982). The development of verbal self-regulation: Relationships between language, cognition, and behavior. In S. A. Kuczaj II (Ed.), *Language development* (Vol. 2). Hillsdale, NJ: Lawrence Erlbaum Associates.

Wexler, K., & Culicover, P. W. (1980). *Formal principles of language acquisition.* Cambridge, MA: MIT Press.

Yamada, J. (1981). Evidence for the independence of language and cognition: Case study of a "hyperlinguistic" adolescent. *UCLA Working Papers in Cognitive Linguistics, 3,* 121–160.

Yamada, J., & Curtiss, S. (1981). The relation between language and cognition in a case of Turner's syndrome. *UCLA Working Papers in Cognitive Linguistics, 3,* 93–115.

11 On the Nature of a Language Acquisition Disorder: The Example of Autism

Helen Tager-Flusberg
University of Massachusetts at Boston

INTRODUCTION

In the fall of 1972, my final year at University College London, I wrote an essay for my tutor in Psychology on recent trends in language development research and theory. My paper touched on many topics including the then-current "cognition hypothesis" of language acquisition and ending with a brief overview on disorders of language development. Lacking both extensive experience and background coursework, I found it easy to draw quite sweeping conclusions. And so I wrote with great confidence on the latter topic that children with language disorders could be classified as either delayed or deviant—a conclusion that did, incidentally, accurately reflect the current view in the literature. As I read over my paper before handing it in, I worried that I had not defined those terms *delay* or *deviant,* and the more I thought about them, the more problematic they became. The question of how to define language acquisition disorders and how they might be distinguished from cognitive disorders if, indeed, cognition and language are intimately related began to seem more complex than the simple multiple-choice response, delay or deviance, that I had offered. But I did not allow those worries to complicate or alter my completed paper—and luckily I do not recall my tutor's reactions to it!

The issue of how to define a disorder of language development stayed with me, and over the next decade my research interests turned more seriously towards language disorders. By this time I had moved on to graduate school at Harvard, where I was engaged in research on normal syntactic development in collaboration with Jill de Villiers and Kenji Hakuta, under the benevolent eye of our mentor, Roger Brown. When the moment arrived for deciding on a topic for

249

my dissertation, I felt the time had come to strike out on my own, and I returned to the issues I had written about in that early paper: What is the relationship between language and cognition, and how can one conceptualize the way in which language development in children with neurological or psychological deficits, retardation, or sensory handicap might differ from language development in normal children? Many studies later I still do not have the answers but I believe I have made some progress. In this chapter I discuss an alternative proposal on the nature of a language acquisition disorder, one that goes beyond the traditional ''delay or deviant'' approach and that may add to our theoretical conceptions of the normal language acquisition process.

The Autistic Syndrome

In choosing a population of language-disordered children who would be the focus of my dissertation, I selected the disorder known as autism—a rare pervasive developmental disorder in very young children, and one that includes among its core characteristics ''delayed and deviant language development'' (Rutter, 1978). Surely at the extreme I would find the essence of deviant language.

Autism is now viewed as a behavioral syndrome for which there is no single cause. The first signs that there is something wrong with an autistic child may appear as early as 5 or 6 months, when parents notice that their child is unresponsive to their approaches or demonstrations of affection, preferring to spend hours alone with just one or two toys for stimulation. In the case of other autistic children, parents will not report any major concerns until after the first birthday when their child, who had begun using a few words, might stop talking and responding to the speech of others. During the second year, the autistic child's preoccupation with certain special objects, their lack of interest in other people, and perhaps their rocking or banging become more prominent as their behavior appears more and more inappropriately infantile. Almost all children who are diagnosed autistic show these signs well before their third birthday. Throughout this early period they are most likely to be unresponsive to language, saying nothing with the exception, perhaps, of a few key words to express major needs.

As time goes on, the course of the disorder can take different routes. Some autistic children change very little, remaining mute, solitary, and infantile in their behavior. Others do change. They may become more interested in people: Early on they usually develop an obsessive attachment to just one or two individuals, and the quality of their later interpersonal relationships retains a peculiar quality so that one feels the autistic person, whereas in some ways quite sociable, still has no genuine interest in or understanding of his fellow humans. About half the children who are autistic do develop some functional language by middle childhood. Some remain at a very primitive stage whereas others develop language to quite an advanced level. Nevertheless, the autistic child's language development does not appear to follow a simple or typical path. Clinicians have described the peculiar intonation patterns, poor articulation, excessive echolalia, incorrect word order, reversal of the pronouns "I" and "you," and the rigid metaphorical content of autistic language. Yet, exactly what is atypical about the development of language in autistic children has not yet been elucidated, and numerous language researchers have noted the similarity of some of these so-called "autistic" features to what is seen in some normally developing children, and many retarded children, (cf. Bartak & Rutter, 1974; Prizant & Duchan, 1981; Tager-Flusberg, 1981a).

Psycholinguistic Research on Autism

Much of the most relevant psycholinguistic research on phonological, morphological, and syntactic aspects of language development in autistic children has been conducted by Bartolucci and his colleagues. Their research on phonological perception and production with a cross-sectional sample of 10 autistic children, matched on nonverbal intelligence to a similar number of retarded and normal children, showed that autistic children were no different from the control subjects either in their correct performance or in the error patterns they showed (Bartolucci & Pierce, 1977; Bartolucci, Pierce, Streiner, & Eppel, 1976; see also Boucher, 1976). In a later study using cross-sectional samples of spontaneous speech from the same subjects, Bartolucci, Pierce, and Streiner (1980) examined the percentage of morphemes supplied in obligatory contexts, scoring the same 14 morphemes that became so famous as a result of Brown's (1973) original work. The most impressive aspect of their data was the high proportion of use of almost all the morphemes by the normal and the disordered groups of children. There were a few morphemes, notably some verb endings such as present progressive and past tense and articles, that were less frequent in the speech of the autistic children. These results have recently been confirmed by Howlin (1984), using similar methods and scoring procedures. It is difficult to provide a simple interpretation of these findings: Bartolucci et al. offer a semantic explanation based on the autistic child's special difficulty with deictic linguistic categories. The morphemes that were found more difficult by the autistic children (which were incidentally still being supplied in more than 70% of their obligatory contexts) are not among the last ones acquired by normal children (cf. Brown, 1973; de Villiers & de Villiers, 1973a). But does such a difference constitute deviance, and if so what is the source of the deviance? The major problem in interpreting these data is that both studies relied on relatively small cross-sectional language samples that we know from normal language acquisition research are not especially powerful sources of evidence (Howlin, 1984). This is particularly critical because the number of obligatory contexts for each morpheme, specifically those not always supplied, was small, in some cases less than five. What is also lacking is any understanding of the developmental process: Did

Bartolucci's and Howlin's autistic subjects acquire these 14 morphemes in the same way as did Brown's Adam, Eve, and Sarah? Before one would consider morphological development deviant, we require more extensive longitudinal data collected at points where autistic children are not supplying most morphemes above the 90% level.

Several cross-sectional studies have examined the syntactic rules underlying the sentences produced by autistic children. The work by Cantwell and his colleagues (Cantwell, Baker, & Rutter, 1978; Cantwell, Howlin, & Rutter, 1977), as well as by Pierce and Bartolucci (1977), demonstrates that autistic children who have developed some productive language do not develop anomalous or idiosyncratic agrammatical linguistic systems. Rather, their speech is much like that of normal or retarded control children in that it is rule governed, syntactically complex, and shows similar variations in sentence length (MLU). Again though, the focus of these studies has been on the product of language acquisition rather than the developmental process, and so the possibility of learning about potential language-acquisition deficits is limited.

One aspect of Pierce and Bartolucci's data has received less attention than it deserves. Their normal, retarded, and autistic subjects were matched on nonverbal mental age and yet the syntactic levels evident in their speech were clearly not equivalent. The normal children used more complex transformational rules than either of the disordered groups, and the retarded children were somewhat more advanced than the autistic children. So whereas all the children developed appropriate rule-governed syntactic systems, the disordered children's language lagged behind their nonverbal cognitive abilities. This finding has been confirmed in other studies of retarded children where one often finds the same result in varying degrees (Dooley, 1976; Fowler, Gelman, & Gleitman, 1980; Miller, Chapman, & McKenzie, 1981). There is no clear explanation for this discrepancy between language and cognitive level in retarded or autistic children, though it may well be important for understanding the nature of language acquisition disorders.

Another aspect of autistic children's language that has been found to be especially deficient is comprehension beyond the one-word level. Bartak, Rutter, and Cox (1975, 1977) used standardized tests of language comprehension and production (the Reynell Scales) to compare autistic and developmental aphasic children at the same nonverbal mental age levels. The one area of language functioning that most clearly distinguished the two groups was comprehension, although the specific aspects of language contributing to their poor comprehension were not defined.

My decision on what to focus my first study on language in autistic children was heavily influenced by the literature I have reviewed here. Because there was too little time by my fourth year at Harvard (and practically speaking it was too difficult) to consider conducting a longutudinal study, I chose to investigate the comprehension deficits that were highlighted in the then-recently published work of Bartak and his colleagues.

My research was, quite naturally, rooted in the theories and methods of developmental psycholinguistics and strongly influenced by other research being done at Harvard and elsewhere in the mid-Seventies. Comprehension strategies were in vogue. Most existing research on the normal development of sentence comprehension was focusing on children's use of behavioral strategies, such as child as agent; semantic strategies such as animate agent or probable events; and syntactic strategies such as word order or the minimal distance principle (cf. Bever, 1970; Chapman, 1977; Chomsky, 1969; de Villiers & de Villiers, 1973b; Maratsos, 1974; Strohner & Nelson, 1974). These strategies represent an intermediate stage that are most evident in artificial experimental tasks, but they do not necessarily provide an explanation for how children learn to understand correctly complex syntactic rules. Nevertheless, they do provide insight into how children process sentences that are beyond their limited grammatical competence. So in my first set of experiments that formed part of my dissertation, I examined the use of comprehension strategies by autistic, developmental aphasic, and normal children, all matched on verbal intelligence, as assessed by the Peabody Picture Vocabulary Test. Because the data from the developmental aphasic children are not clearly interpretable, in this chapter I report only on the findings from the autistic children and normal 3- and 4-year-olds.

The first study (see Tager-Flusberg, 1981b) used an act-out procedure with active and passive sentences. Some of the sentences were semantically reversible (e.g., The boy touches the girl), and some were semantically biased either in the positive direction (e.g., The girl holds the baby) or in the negative direction (e.g., The hat wears the boy). Children were initially tested on their understanding of the lexical items included in the test sentences and then were trained on the act-out procedure. The task followed, with the experimenter verbally presenting 24 test sentences in random order. The main results from this study showed that autistic children were significantly worse than the 3-year-olds in their comprehension of the active and passive sentences, confirming Bartak et al.'s (1975) findings, and that their poor performance was primarily due to their inability to use the semantically based probable-event strategy.

A related second experiment was conducted based on test items that were first used by Sinclair and Bronckart (1972) with French-speaking children. Both reversible and semantically biased noun–verb–noun word sequences were presented to the autistic and normal subjects who had participated in the previous study. The word sequences were presented in all possible word orders. Again, the task for the children was to act out their interpretation of the "sentences" with toys. The results paralleled those obtained with the well-formed active and passive sentences. The autistic children had no trouble employing word-order restrictions in their interpretations; however, by and large, they ignored the semantic biases inherent in many of the test items. In contrast, most of the normal children were especially likely to use a probable-event strategy with these anomalous sentences, more so than with the active and passive sentences.

The results I obtained in these experiments were consistent with other findings reported in the literature for autistic children. As in production, their comprehension problems did not seem to lie in the area of syntax: My autistic children were not different from their matched normal controls in understanding reversible active and passives, or in using a word-order strategy. However, they were deficient in the use of the semantically based probable-event strategy. This latter finding fit well with some early cognitive research by Hermelin and O'Connor in England (1967). These researchers had found that autistic children were unlike normal or retarded children in that they failed to use semantic relatedness to facilitate recall of word lists. Their results were later replicated by Frith (1969), Fyffe and Prior (1978), and Wolff and Barlow (1979), thus establishing this failure to use meaning in memory tasks.

How should one interpret the nature of the semantic deficit that I and others had found in the related memory experiments? Menyuk (1976, 1978) had proposed that data like these suggested that autistic children were unable to form the conceptual categories that underlie the word or sentence meanings used in the cognitive studies. The first discussion I wrote on my comprehension results paralleled this hypothesis: I suggested that the autistic children did not use a probable-event strategy because they simply did not have the knowledge of the world inherent in the semantic biases that were built into the test sentences. But when Roger Brown read over my draft, he gently persuaded me to consider less radical alternatives. He pointed out that neither I nor any of the other researchers had tested our autistic subjects' underlying concepts or understanding of the world, and so one could not rule out that the children had the knowledge yet failed to use it. Of course he was right, and my final version of the thesis incorporated his wisdom.

A second question that I grappled with at that time was whether the autistic subjects' failure to use a probable-event strategy constituted deviant language acquisition. For the first time since I had written my undergraduate essay, when I had begun to worry about this issue, I explicitly discussed the problems in defining deviance, particularly in this context. The degree of deviance would, of course, depend on whether autistic children failed to form concepts and develop an understanding of relationships among things or people or whether they just failed to use that knowledge. One must also question whether the deviance is in language or in cognitive development. At that time I concluded that there were no clear answers to be offered, given the limited data available on autistic children.

These were the questions that guided some of the more recent research that I have been doing. After settling into postdoctoral academic life, I thought more about Roger's hunch that autistic children must have developed some basic conceptual knowledge or how could they get around in the world? How else would they know that they could sit on a new chair, write with a new pen, or spin the wheels on a new car? Such knowledge reflects some essential categorization abilities, the absence of which I and others (e.g., Fay & Schuler, 1980; Menyuk, 1978; Rimland, 1964; Simmons & Baltaxe, 1975) had proposed formed part of the deficit specific to the autistic syndrome. What was needed were studies investigating the representation of semantic knowledge in autistic children, and over the past few years I have been engaged in this work.

While I was at Harvard, Roger spent part of one seminar introducing us to the "new paradigm of reference" (Brown, 1975). We became well versed with the notion of prototypes and came to appreciate the importance of Rosch's work on the nature of concepts and conceptual representation. My recent research on the nature of semantic representation and organization in children with autism is based on the new paradigm. The experiments that I summarize here have focused on categorization of basic level and superordinate level concepts, and the extension of word meanings, employing examples that ranged in prototypicality from central to peripheral. I was primarily concerned with two issues: the role of prototypes both in autistic children's conceptual representations and in their generalizations of word meaning; and the psychological significance of the basic level of objects compared to superordinate or subordinate levels (cf. Rosch, 1973, 1975; Rosch & Mervis, 1975; Rosch, Mervis, Gray, Johnson, & Boyes-Braem, 1976).

Fourteen autistic children were matched on chronological age and verbal mental age to 14 retarded, nonautistic children. There was also a control group of 14 younger, normal children matched to the disordered children on verbal mental age (assessed by the Revised Peabody Picture Vocabulary Test). These subjects participated in both studies of semantic representation. The first set of experiments (Tager-Flusberg, 1985a) were designed to investigate conceptual representation, using a categorization task. In order to tap categorization, I employed a match-to-target procedure, in which the subject was shown a target and two choices. The subject's task was to select the choice that was "most like" the target. In order to ensure that the task of choosing on the basis of similarity was clearly understood, the subjects were given extensive nonverbal pretraining with reinforcement using shapes such as circles, squares, and triangles. The actual experiments used pictures of objects as stimuli.

In the first experiment, the children's ability to categorize at the basic level was tested. Three basic level concepts, CAR, CHAIR, and DOG were chosen, and for each there were five pictures that ranged in prototypicality. Prototypicality ratings were obtained for the pictures from adult judges, using Rosch's classic procedure (Rosch, 1975). On each trial one picture was designated the target, for example, a highly prototypical kitchen chair, and below it were placed two choices, one of which was another chair, for example, a rocker or an ottoman, and the other an example from either of the other categories, a dog or a car. All the combinations of stimuli were presented. The main findings from this experiment were that all the children from all three subject groups categorized basic level objects at near perfect levels. This was impressive considering that some of the examples for each category were quite unprototypical, and the children had probably not seen them before.

In a second experiment, the same match-to-target procedure was used to test the children's ability to categorize at the more abstract, superordinate level. As in the previous experiment, five examples varying in prototypicality were selected for each concept. Three biological concepts were included in one stimulus set: ANIMAL, VEGETABLE, and FRUIT; and three artifactual concepts made up a second stimulus set: FURNITURE, CLOTHING, and VEHICLE. The two sets were presented on separate days, always after the children had completed the basic level categorization experiment. The most significant aspect of the results was the similarity among the different groups of subjects. None of the groups performed as well on the superordinate concepts, supporting what we know from earlier literature (beginning with Brown, 1958) about the psychological significance of the basic level. Nevertheless, all but one of the retarded children and one of the autistic children showed some ability to categorize at higher than chance levels on at least one out of the six concepts included in this experiment. Looking at the error data, we again find similarities among the autistic, retarded, and normal children: There was a tendency, especially on the artifactual concepts (where there was a better range in prototypicality), to make significantly more errors on peripheral examples than on central examples. This error pattern suggests that, for all the children, prototypes played an important role in their representation of conceptual knowledge.

These two experiments on categorization suggest that autistic children are no different from retarded or normal children in the way they organize and represent concepts, indicating no specific cognitive deficit in this domain. But perhaps the deficit is linguistic, that is in representing word meanings that map onto such concepts. In order to test this hypothesis, I carried out a second set of experiments on the same subjects looking at their meanings for nouns labelling concrete objects (see Tager-Flusberg, 1985b). As in the previous experiments, I was interested in how similar autistic children were to matched retarded or normal children in the use of prototypes as the basis for word-meaning extension, for both basic level and superordinate level words (cf. Anglin, 1977; Bowerman, 1978; Kuczaj, 1982).

In the first experiment, designed to tap children's word comprehension, four nouns were chosen, two labelling basic level concepts (boat and bird) and two labelling superordinate level concepts (tool and food). To test children's understanding of these words, six pictures depicting examples of the word were drawn, with the examples ranging in prototypicality as rated by adult judges. To these positive examples, six picture foils were added, three of which were specially chosen because they were related in some way to the test word. For example, for the word "bird" the test stimuli included pictures of six different birds (cardinal, eagle, owl, rooster, penguin, and ostrich), three related foils (butterfly, bat, and nest), and three unrelated foils (brush, lightbulb, and box). Similar sets of stimuli were made up for all four test words. The pictures were mixed together, and children's understanding of the meanings of the words was tested by presenting each picture one at a time and asking "Is this a . . . (test word)?" A second experiment was conducted, also designed to test word meanings, but which did not require a yes/no response from the children. Similar sets of stimuli were created, this time including four examples, two related foils and two unrelated foils. The test words were fish, house, kitchen utensil, and musical instrument. In this experiment the eight pictures in each set created to test a particular word's meaning were set out in front of the child. The experimenter then asked the child to give her all the pictures of a . . . (test word). After the children had seen all the pictures for each experiment, they were asked to name them; thus, we also have word production data from the same children (Tager-Flusberg, 1985c).

The results from both experiments tell the same story so I present them together, omitting the details. The most striking aspect of the data is the consistent pattern of results obtained from all three subject groups. Both in terms of correct performance and error patterns, there were no differences among the autistic, retarded, and normal children in either experiment. On the highly prototypical examples of the words, children performed extremely well. On average, about 90% of the time children correctly selected prototypical pictures as examples of the words, and they were also correct in naming these pictures. Performance was significantly lower on the peripheral examples. Across the various words included, children correctly included peripheral examples on an average of 69% of the trials. This underextension of word meaning was found in all three groups of children. Children also had a harder time naming peripheral examples, and when they could name peripheral members of basic level concepts they were most likely to use a subordinate term, and not the basic level term. Thus, a cardinal was typically called a "bird" but a penguin never was; it was labelled more precisely as a penguin.

Children's performance on the foils demonstrated a predictable pattern of overextension of word meaning. Children in all three groups overextended meanings primarily to the related foils (on 40% of such examples) but hardly ever (7%) to the unrelated foils. These findings illustrate the fundamental similarity among the various groups of children in the way word meanings are represented. For all the children, prototypicality played an important role in determining the extension of the meaning of a word. Central examples were almost always included, but peripheral examples were often underextended. And pictures of objects that were in some way linked to the prototype, even if not a genuine example, were likely to be overextended. The findings underscore the results of the categorization experiments: Autistic children do not appear to be different from normal or retarded children in the way they acquire semantic knowledge, or in the organization and representation of word meanings and underlying concepts.

If autistic children are not deficient in developing and representing semantic knowledge (although they are clearly slower at doing so), what can account for the findings obtained by Hermelin and O'Connor (1967) in their memory experiments, and in my earlier sentence comprehension studies? Roger's original suggestion, that autistic children are not using their semantic knowledge or their knowledge of the world, is the obvious alternative in these experiments. I did check for this with the same children who participated in the categorization and word-meaning studies.

In a partial replication of Hermelin and O'Connor's original study, I gave the autistic, retarded, and normal subjects lists of words to recall (see Tager-Flusberg, 1986). One list contained 12 unrelated words, drawn from 12 different categories. The second list contained 12 related words, all names of animals. On separate days children heard these lists and had to recall as many of the words as possible. My findings confirmed the earlier studies: Normal and retarded children were able to recall significantly more words from the second list of related words. But the autistic children could not: Their recall of both lists was approximately the same, even though we know from the second categorization experiment that these same autistic children demonstrated their knowledge of the animal concept and understood the similarity among different examples of animals.

These studies on semantic functioning in autistic children demonstrate that autistic children are not genuinely deviant. On the contrary, the similarity among the autistic, retarded, and normal children, despite their differences in developmental history, early experiences, age, intellectual status, and neurological deficit, suggests that conceptual and lexical-semantic development are highly constrained processes that may be delayed but not deviant in children. Nevertheless, autistic children are different from other children in that they do not use their semantic knowledge. To what degree does this failure to use what they know extend to other aspects of linguistic functioning? Recent research on pragmatic performance in autistic children suggests that in this respect autistic children show certain consistent differences from control children. I conclude this section on language research with autistic children by describing one study that I have done on communicative competence in autistic children (cf. Tager-Flusberg, 1982).

We obtained about a 1-hour sample of spontaneous speech from eight children diagnosed autistic, who were engaged in play and discussion with a very familiar experimenter. The sample was transcribed in the traditional way, and the children's language level was determined by calculating MLU. The children ranged from late Stage I to early Stage V, and they showed similar correlated variation in their Peabody Scores. Eight normal control children were individually matched to the autistic subjects on the basis of MLU. The normal children were all 30 months old, and their spontaneous speech samples had been collected in very similar ways by Jill and Peter de Villiers. The analyses of the transcripts focused on how similar or different autistic and normal children at the same level of syntactic ability might be in the ways they could use language to engage in conversation.

We analyzed the children's responses to adult utterances examining in a variety of contexts (e.g., statements, questions) how well the child could maintain and expand on an established topic. In general, we found that autistic children, like their normal counterparts, understood the discourse requirement of responding in some way to what an adult says. Thus, overall, there were no real differences in the amount of responding to statements or questions that demanded a comment. But there were differences in how the autistic and normal children responded. Normal children typically expanded what the adult had said and offered some new information. Autistic children seemed to have little to say beyond what the adult had already expressed: They repeated more and offered significantly less new information to the conversation. They had greater difficulty responding to wh- questions that required them to provide specific information, but they were similar to the normal children in responding to simpler yes/no questions. More striking were the differences among the groups in their ability to maintain a topic through a series of conversational turns. Using the measure designed by Roger Brown (1980) called the mean length of episode or MLE, we found that normal children's MLEs were much longer than those of the autistic children. The general conclusions that we can draw both from this study and from other recent studies on autistic children's use of language in a social context (e.g., Ball, 1978; Mermelstein, 1983; Paccia-Cooper, Curcio, & Sacharko, 1981) is that even autistic children who have developed some relatively advanced syntactic skills cannot always use their language appropriately. This may be because they lack the interest or motivation, or because they lack the advanced understanding of both linguistic and nonlinguistic communication to offer much in a discourse context. They may know how to say it, but they basically have little to say.

The Nature of a Language Acquisition Disorder

What does this research on autism tell us about the nature of a language acquisition disorder? I began my work in this area looking for the essence of deviance: After all, clinical descriptions of the syndrome and texts on language disorders have pointed out how significantly deficient and atypical children with autism are in the area of language, compared with any other group of language-disordered children. One of the main conclusions that I have drawn from my own work in the area of autism is that the traditional dichotomy between delay and deviance is neither the most appropriate nor an accurate characterization of disorders of language development. In the final part of this chapter I set out an alternative conception of acquisition disorders, drawing on evidence from research on autism, and, where relevant, on selected research conducted with other populations of language-disordered children.

First consider the proposal that disorders of language acquisition can be characterized as "delay." In fact, *all* children who are language disordered as a result of neurological impairment, retardation, environmental factors, or cause unknown show delays in language acquisition. They begin speaking and understanding later than do normal children, and these delays in language and language-related processes (e.g., reading and writing) continue throughout childhood, relative to age-matched normal children. Delay is thus a part of the definition of language disorder, and not one alternative developmental path. One also frequently (though perhaps not always) finds that children who are significantly delayed in developing language do not reach the same endpoint as normal children (Lenneberg, 1967). Thus, they might not acquire as rich and varied a vocabulary, and they may never acquire complex rules of syntax such as those acquired by normal children in middle childhood (cf. Chomsky, 1969, for example). Lower endpoints have been studied primarily in retarded children and in some deaf children learning oral language, but little is known about the highest language levels reached by children with developmental aphasia (specific language impairment), or autism, for example. The actual endpoint reached by a child may well be correlated with the degree of delay and the age when the child began speaking.

The concept of "deviance" in language acquisition is more problematic than that of "delay." Unlike delay, which can be clearly defined by comparison to age-related norms, there is no unequivocal, objective definition of deviance. There exists in the retardation literature a lengthy debate and a volume of research on a related topic (see Weisz & Zigler, 1979; Zigler, 1969): To what extent can we characterize cognitive development in retarded children as delayed or deviant? Here, the same problems of definition exist, but the solution has been to compare cognitive development in retarded and normal children within some particular theoretical (typically Piagetian) framework. In this way one can predict a priori what would constitute deviance: for example, not following the cognitive stages in the same sequence as do normal children, or developing some atypical concepts. Having defined deviance in this way, the conclusion from this area of retardation research has been that there is no deviance in general cognitive development, only delay. Thus, retarded children follow the same cognitive stages that Piaget proposed for normal development in the same order, and their performance matches that of control children.

Research on language disorders should follow this example. Deviance must be defined within a particular theoretical framework. In fact, when research is conducted according to some specific linguistic or psycholinguistic perspective, we find that the language that does develop in, for example, retarded or autistic children cannot be characterized as deviant. For example, the research on syntactic development conducted by Pierce and Bartolucci (1977) used a transformational framework and found that the autistic, retarded, and normal control children all developed some transformational rules, and that there was nothing aberrant about the rules that generated their surface structure sentences. The same conclusions can be drawn from research on syntax that has been done with developmental aphasic children (Leonard, 1982), as well as with retarded children (Rosenberg, 1982).

With respect to morphological development, the data are not so clear-cut. Earlier, I reviewed the studies by Bartolucci et al. (1980) and Howlin (1984), which looked at morphological development in autistic children. I cautioned against drawing firm conclusions from these studies, primarily because the subjects had all virtually reached the endpoint in acquiring the 14 morphemes that were analyzed. The few differences among the autistic subjects in supplying articles and verb endings may suggest something atypical, but in light of the small cross-sectional sample sizes and the overall high levels of performance, we cannot claim to have discovered true deviance. Better data have been collected from both retarded children (e.g., Fowler, Gelman, & Gleitman, 1980; Kamhi & Johnston, 1982) and children with developmental aphasia (e.g., Johnston & Schery, 1976). These studies have also focused on Brown's 14 morphemes and found that they develop in these language-disordered children in the same order as they do in normal children. Whereas morphology may well develop in the same general order in normal children with a variety of linguistic handicaps, there is one curious difference in the handicapped children: Typically, their morphological development is not as advanced as would be predicted by either their nonverbal mental age or even their general linguistic stage of development. This discrepancy has been found in developmental aphasic children (Johnston & Schery, 1976), retarded children (Rosenberg, 1982), and autistic children (Bartolucci et al., 1980). We defer discussing the significance of this discrepancy to the end of the chapter.

The data on lexical-semantic and conceptual development in retarded and autistic children, described earlier, also suggests that such research, conducted within a cognitive theoretical framework developed initially by Rosch and her colleagues (e.g., Rosch et al., 1976), does not support the view of deviant semantic development. As in the studies on syntax and morphology, the similarities among the different groups of children are more striking than their differences. The same holds true for studies on phonological development.

In general, studies of language-disordered children, conducted within a well-articulated theoretical framework, have not uncovered areas of linguistic deviance. The more one looks for deviance, the more similar disordered children look like normal children. Hardly any of the studies cited here have been longitudinal in design, and therefore they tell us little about the developmental process of language acquisition. Instead, the focus of these studies has been on the product of language development; that is, the nature of the phonological or syntactic rules acquired, the representation of the lexicon, and so on. The lack of deviance in phonological, syntactic, or semantic-conceptual structure suggests that language and its underlying conceptual base are highly constrained systems.

The literature on language acquisition disorders contains investigations of children with a wide variety of known and unknown neurological deficits: children with different degrees of intellectual handicap, at different ages, various sensory and motor deficits, different early experiences and psychological traumas, as well as a variety of cognitive and social deficits. Yet, among all the studies of such children one cannot clearly point to examples of deviance within any aspect of the language system, as we have defined it here. Phonology, semantics, and syntax are all highly constrained systems, which, when they are acquired, are structured similarly in all children. These constraints inherent in linguistic systems are most clearly documented in children with acquisition disorders (cf. Curtiss, 1982).

The constraints that I have discussed here are concerned with the phonological, semantic, and syntactic products of language acquisition. To what extent is the developmental process for each of these systems similarly constrained? We cannot yet answer this question, first because we have no clearly stated developmental theory of how these aspects of language are acquired, and second because there are hardly any data from disordered children that address the issue of process. Despite the absence of theory and relevant research, language acquisition disorders can probably best be understood in terms of differences in the process of acquiring language.

Recent research on normal language acquisition has demonstrated the interrelationships among the various aspects of language in development. For example, phonological factors may partially determine the early words used by very young children (Schwartz & Leonard, 1979); semantic factors influence the acquisition of certain syntactic (de Villiers, 1980; Maratsos, Kuczaj, Fox, & Chalkley, 1979) and morphological rules (Bloom, Lifter, & Hafitz, 1980); and pragmatic functions and syntactic form influence one another in a variety of ways in development (de Villiers & de Villiers, 1981). These are just a few samples taken from current developmental psycholinguistic literature on how phonology, grammar, meaning, and function are intertwined in normal language development. In addition, there is a longer history of studies demonstrating the correlations among social-interactional, cognitive, environmental, and linguistic factors in normally developing children (see de Villiers & de Villiers, 1986, for a recent review). Development, in particular the development of language, is thus viewed as individual strands, representing the various component parts, that are braided together to form the whole system we call language.

What is the primary significance of these interrelationships? They clearly do not determine the products of language acquisition. Thus, the roots of syntactic rules do not lie in mother–infant interaction, input language, or human perception and cognition. Nevertheless, they do influence the developmental process in that, for example, nonsyntactic and nonlinguistic factors may facilitate the acquisition of syntactic rules, at least in those children who can take advantage of them. There is, too, large individual variation even among normal children in the pathways followed in developing language (Bates & Snow, 1984). The components may be braided in different styles. Thus, this variation may be related in part to the degree to which the language factors and the social, environmental, and cognitive factors are correlated within a particular child, but there is, to date, little empirical evidence to support this conjecture.

There is more evidence, much of which has been reviewed earlier in the chapter, in favor of the main proposal to be offered here on the nature of a language acquisition disorder. Children with disorders of language acquisition show disturbances in the interrelationships among language systems, and in some cases, among language, cognitive, and social factors; the braid is somewhat unravelled in such children. These disturbances in what are normally correlated aspects of language acquisition lead to asynchronies in development. In turn, the lack of developmental synchrony between, for example, language and cognition, or syntax and pragmatics, affects the process by which language is acquired, even though the product itself is constrained and similar in both normal and disordered children.

Autism presents us with a number of examples of asynchronies in language development. For example, cognitive development and language development are always discrepant: Language is significantly delayed relative to nonverbal mental age. This is true also in about half the mentally retarded population (Miller et al., 1981), and it has also been reported in other individual cases of atypical children (Curtiss, 1982). There is one case of a retarded child whose language, specifically syntax, was more advanced than would be predicted by her nonverbal mental age level (Yamada, 1981). Morphology is typically delayed relative to syntactic level or MLU in autistic, developmental aphasic, as well as retarded children (Bartolucci et al., 1980; Johnston & Schery, 1976; Rosenberg, 1982), illustrating a different kind of asynchrony in language development. My original experiments on sentence comprehension in autistic children highlighted the asynchrony in their use of semantic and syntactic knowledge (Tager-Flusberg, 1981b), and the study on discourse and communicative competence (Tager-Flusberg, 1982) shows the discrepancy between syntactic level and functional use of language found in almost all autistic children and supporting the generally accepted view that autism is characterized by social-interactional deficits that are not necessarily correlated with all aspects of language development. These are a few examples from the disorders literature that support the view that language acquisition disorders can be understood in terms of asynchrony. We must wait for future research to address the additional hypothesis that these asynchronies influence to some degree the process of language development in language-disordered children.

CONCLUSION

I began this chapter by describing what I had written in a paper 15 years ago. At that time I wrote that language acquisition disorders could be characterized as examples of delay or deviance. The work I have done since that time, influenced primarily by my teachers at Harvard, especially Roger Brown and Jill de Villiers, has taken me away from that simple choice. As I now have conceptualized language acquisition disorders, they are at once more similar to one another and more different. They are similar in that there is, almost always, delay and asynchrony; they are different in that the developmental asynchronies vary from child to child, and from one kind of disorder to another. To the extent that disruptions in the interrelationships among different systems of development affect the process of development, I am proposing that language, although it is an unchanging set of structured systems, may develop to some extent in quite unique ways in different children.

ACKNOWLEDGMENTS

Preparation of this chapter was supported by grants from the National Institute of Mental Health (5R01 MH 37074) and from the National Institute of Child Health and Human Development (1R01 HD 18833).

REFERENCES

Anglin, J. (1977). *Word, object and conceptual development*. New York: Norton.

Ball, J. (1978). *A pragmatic analysis of autistic children's language with respect to aphasic and normal language development*. Unpublished doctoral dissertation, Melbourne University.

Bartak, L., & Rutter, M. (1974). The use of personal pronouns by autistic children. *Journal of Autism and Childhood Schizophrenia, 4,* 217–222.

Bartak, L., Rutter, M., & Cox, A. (1975). A comparative study of infantile autism and specific developmental receptive language disorder: I. The children. *British Journal of Psychiatry, 126,* 127–145.

Bartak, L., Rutter, M., & Cox, A. (1977). A comparative study of infantile autism and specific developmental receptive language disorders: III. Discriminant function analysis. *Journal of Autism and Childhood Schizophrenia, 7,* 383–396.

Bartolucci, G., & Pierce, S. J. (1977). A preliminary comparison of phonological development in autistic, normal and mentally retarded subjects. *British Journal of Disorders of Communication, 12,* 137–147.

Bartolucci, G., Pierce, S. J., & Streiner, D. (1980). Cross-sectional studies of grammatical morphemes in autistic and mentally retarded children. *Journal of Autism and Developmental Disorders, 10,* 39–50.

Bartolucci, G., Pierce, S. J., Streiner, D., & Eppel, P. T. (1976). Phonological investigation of verbal autistic and mentally retarded subjects. *Journal of Autism and Childhood Schizophrenia, 6,* 303–316.

Bates, E., & Snow, C. E. (1984, March). *Individual differences in language development*. Workshop presented at the Stanford Child Language Research Forum.

264

Bever, T. G. (1970). The cognitive basis for linguistic structures. In J. R. Hayes (Ed.), *Cognition and the development of language* (pp. 279–362). New York: Wiley.

Bloom, L., Lifter, K., & Hafitz, J. (1980). Semantics of verbs and the development of verb inflection in child language. *Language, 56,* 386–412.

Boucher, J. (1976). Articulation in early childhood autism. *Journal of Autism and Childhood Schizophrenia, 6,* 297–302.

Bowerman, M. (1978). The acquisition of word meaning: An investigation into some current conflicts. In N. Waterson & C. Snow (Eds.), *The development of communication.* New York: Wiley.

Brown, R. (1958). *Words and things.* New York: Free Press.

Brown, R. (1973). *A first language.* Cambridge, MA: Harvard University Press.

Brown, R. (1975). *The new paradigm of reference.* Unpublished manuscript, Harvard University.

Brown, R. (1980). The maintenance of conversation. In D. R. Olson (Ed.), *The social foundations of language and thought* (pp. 187–210). New York: Norton.

Cantwell, D., Baker, L., & Rutter, M. (1978). A comparative study of infantile autism and specific developmental receptive language disorder: IV. Analysis of syntax and language function. *Journal of Child Psychology and Child Psychiatry, 19,* 351–362.

Cantwell, D., Howlin, P., & Rutter, M. (1977). The analysis of language level and language function: A methodological study. *British Journal of Disorders of Communication, 12,* 119–135.

Chapman, R. S. (1977). Comprehension strategies in children. In J. F. Kavanagh & W. Strange (Eds.), *Speech and language in the laboratory, school, and clinic.* Cambridge, MA: MIT Press.

Chomsky, C. (1969). *Acquisition of syntax in children from 5 to 10.* Cambridge, MA: MIT Press.

Curtiss, S. (1982). Developmental dissociation of language and cognition. In L. K. Obler & L. Menn (Eds.), *Exceptional language and linguistics* (pp. 285–312). New York: Academic Press.

de Villiers, J. G. (1980). The process of rule learning in child speech: A new look. In K. E. Nelson (Ed.), *Children's language* (Vol. 2). New York: Gardner Press.

de Villiers, J. G., & de Villiers, P. A. (1973a). A cross-sectional study of the acquisition of grammatical morphemes in child speech. *Journal of Psycholinguistic Research, 2,* 267–278.

de Villiers, J. G., & de Villiers, P. A. (1973b). Development of the use of word order in comprehension. *Journal of Psycholinguistic Research, 2,* 331–341.

de Villiers, J. G., & de Villiers, P. A. (1981). Semantics and syntax in the first two years: The output of form and function and the form and function of the input. In F. D. Minifie & L. L. Lloyd (Eds.), *Communicative and cognitive abilities: Early behavioral assessment* (pp. 309–348). Baltimore: University Park Press.

de Villiers, J. G., & de Villiers, P. A. (1986). The acquisition of English. In D. I. Slobin (Ed.), *Cross-linguistic study of language acquisition.* Hillsdale, NJ: Lawrence Erlbaum Associates.

Dooley, J. (1976). *Language acquisition and Down's syndrome: A study of early semantics and syntax.* Unpublished doctoral dissertation, Harvard University.

Fay, W. H., & Schuler, A. L. (1980). *Emerging language in autistic children.* Baltimore: University Park Press.

Fowler, A., Gelman, R., & Gleitman, L. (1980, October). *A comparison of normal and retardate language equated on MLU.* Paper presented at the 5th Annual Boston University Conference on Language Development.

Frith, U. A. (1969). Emphasis and meaning in recall in normal and autistic children. *Language and Speech, 12,* 29–38.

Fyffe, C., & Prior, M. (1978). Evidence for language recoding in autistic, retarded and normal children: A re-examination. *British Journal of Psychology, 69,* 393–402.

Hermelin, B., & O'Connor, N. (1967). Remembering of words by psychotic and subnormal children. *British Journal of Psychology, 58,* 213–218.

Howlin, P. (1984). The acquisition of grammatical morphemes in autistic children: A critique and replication of the findings of Bartolucci, Pierce, and Streiner, 1980. *Journal of Autism and Developmental Disorders, 14,* 127–136.

Johnston, J. R., & Schery, T. K. (1976). The use of grammatical morphemes by children with communication disorders. In D. M. Morehead & A. E. Morehead (Eds.), *Normal and deficient child language* (pp. 239–258). Baltimore: University Park Press.

Kamhi, A. G., & Johnston, J. R. (1982). Towards an understanding of retarded children's linguistic deficiencies. *Journal of Speech and Hearing Research, 25*, 435–445.

Kuczaj, S. A. (1982). Young children's overextensions of object words in comprehension and/or production: Support for a prototype theory of early object word meaning. *Foundations of Language, 3*, 93–105.

Lenneberg, E. (1967). *Biological foundations of language*. New York: Wiley.

Leonard, L. B. (1982). The nature of specific language impairment in children. In S. Rosenberg (Ed.), *Handbook of applied psycholinguistics* (pp. 295–327). Hillsdale, NJ: Lawrence Erlbaum Associates.

Maratsos, M. P. (1974). Children who get worse at understanding the passive: A replication of Bever. *Journal of Psycholinguistic Research, 3*, 65–74.

Maratsos, M. P., Kuczaj, S. A., Fox, D. E. C., & Chalkley, M. A. (1979). Some empirical studies in the acquisition of transformational relations: Passives, negatives and the past tense. In W. A. Collins (Ed.), *Children's language and communication*. Hillsdale, NJ: Lawrence Erlbaum Associates.

Menyuk, P. (1976, August). *Language of autistic children: What's wrong and why*. Paper presented at the International Symposium on Autism, St. Gallen, Switzerland.

Menyuk, P. (1978). Language: What's wrong and why. In M. Rutter & E. Schopler (Eds.), *Autism: A reappraisal of concepts and treatment* (pp. 105–116). New York: Plenum Press.

Mermelstein, R. (1983, October). *The relationship between syntactical and pragmatic development in autistic, retarded and normal children*. Paper presented at the Eighth Annual Boston University Conference on Language Development.

Miller, J., Chapman, R., & McKenzie, H. (1981, August). *Individual differences in the language acquisition of mentally retarded children*. Paper presented at the Second International Congress for the Study of Child Language, Vancouver.

Paccia-Cooper, J., Curcio, F., & Sacharko, G. (1981, October). *A comparison of discourse features in normal and autistic language*. Paper presented at the Sixth Annual Boston University Conference on Language Development.

Pierce, S. J., & Bartolucci, G. (1977). A syntactic investigation of verbal autistic, mentally retarded and normal children. *Journal of Autism and Childhood Schizophrenia, 7*, 121–134.

Prizant, B. M., & Duchan, J. F. (1981). The functions of immediate echolalia in autistic children. *Journal of Speech and Hearing Disorders, 46*, 241–249.

Rimland, B. (1964). *Infantile autism*. New York: Appleton-Century-Crofts.

Rosch, E. (1973). On the internal structure of perceptual and semantic categories. In T. E. Moore (Ed.), *Cognitive development and the acquisition of language*. New York: Academic Press.

Rosch, E. (1975). Cognitive representations of semantic categories. Journal of Experimental Psychology: General, 104, 192–233.

Rosch, E., & Mervis, C. B. (1975). Family resemblances: Studies in the internal structure of categories. *Cognitive Psychology, 7*, 573–605.

Rosch, E., Mervis, C. B., Gray, W. D., Johnson, D. M., & Boyes-Braem, P. (1976). Basic objects in natural categories. *Cognitive Psychology, 8*, 382–439.

Rosenberg, S. (1982). The language of the mentally retarded. In S. Rosenberg (Ed.), *Handbook of applied psycholinguistics* (pp. 329–392). Hillsdale, NJ: Lawrence Erlbaum Associates.

Rutter, M. (1978). Diagnosis and definition. In M. Rutter & E. Schopler (Eds.), *Autism: A reappraisal of concepts and treatment* (pp. 1–25). New York: Plenum Press.

Schwartz, R. G., & Leonard, L. B. (1979, October). *Do children pick and choose? An examination of phonological selection and avoidance in early lexical acquisition*. Paper presented at the Fourth Annual Boston University Conference on Language Development.

Simmons, J. Q., & Baltaxe, C. A. M. (1975). Language patterns of adolescent autistics. *Journal of Autism and Childhood Schizophrenia, 5,* 333–351.

Sinclair, H., & Bronckart, J. P. (1972). S.V.O. A linguistic universal? A study in developmental psycholinguistics. *Journal of Experimental Child Psychology, 14,* 329–348.

Strohner, H., & Nelson, K. E. (1974). The young child's development of sentence comprehension: Influence of event probability, nonverbal context, sentence form, and strategies. *Child Development, 45,* 567–576.

Tager-Flusberg, H. (1981a). On the nature of linguistic functioning in early infantile autism. *Journal of Autism and Developmental Disorders, 11,* 45–56.

Tager-Flusberg, H. (1981b). Sentence comprehension in autistic children. *Applied Psycholinguistics, 2,* 5–24.

Tager-Flusberg, H. (1982). Pragmatic development and its implications for social interaction in autistic children. In D. Park (Ed.), *Proceedings of International Symposium for Research in Autism.* Washington, DC: National Society for Autistic Children.

Tager-Flusberg, H. (1985a). Basic level and superordinate level categorization in autistic, mentally retarded, and normal children. *Journal of Experimental Child Psychology, 40,* 450–469.

Tager-Flusberg, H. (1985b). The conceptual basis for referential word meaning in children with autism. *Child Development, 56,* 1167–1178.

Tager-Flusberg, H. (1985c). Constraints on the representation of word meaning: Evidence from autistic and mentally retarded children. In M. Barrett & S. A. Kuczaj (Eds.), *The development of word meaning.* New York: Springer-Verlag.

Tager-Flusberg, H. (1986). The semantic deficit hypothesis of autistic children's language. *Australian Journal of Human Communication Disorders, 14,* 51–58.

Weisz, J. R., & Zigler, E. (1979). Cognitive development in retarded and nonretarded persons: Piagetian tests of the similar sequence hypothesis. *Psychological Bulletin, 86,* 831–851.

Wolff, S., & Barlow, A. (1979). Schizoid personality in childhood: A comparative study of schizoid, autistic and normal children. *Journal of Child Psychology and Psychiatry, 20,* 29–46.

Yamada, J. (1981). Evidence for the independence of language and cognition: Case study of a "hyperlinguistic" retarded adolescent. *UCLA Working Papers in Cognitive Linguistics, 3,* 120–160.

Zigler, E. (1969). Developmental versus difference theories of mental retardation and the problem of motivation. *American Journal of Mental Deficiency, 73,* 536–556.

12 Language and Socialization

Jean Berko Gleason
Boston University

Socialization is usually defined as the process whereby an individual takes on the behaviors, beliefs, and values that are appropriate to a particular society. This includes fairly general beliefs and behaviors shared by all members of a society, such as the conviction that marrying one's mother is wrong, as well as the more particularistic attributes of an individual's role at a given time; in the United States, for instance, even very young children are socialized to accept certain cleanliness and eating rituals, to sleep in beds, to believe that biting others, and lying to them, is wrong, and so on. Little boys are socialized to commit acts of aggression against other males of their own age–grade, but not against girls or adults of either sex, and girls are socialized to believe that it is important to be pretty. It is obviously important to know how it is that individuals take on the characteristics deemed appropriate in a given society, and socialization is a topic that is much discussed in developmental psychology; almost any textbook in the field outlines at least three major ways of explaining the process of socialization: psychoanalytic, learning theory, and cognitive-developmental approaches.

Although psychologists recognize that language is an important medium of cultural transmission, developmental psychological theories have neither emphasized nor made explicit the role that language plays in the socialization of children; it is rather as if the impact of language is so obvious as to make research on it unnecessary. And those of us who have spent our research careers studying the way that children acquire language have concentrated on linguistic systems while ignoring the cultural content of what children are acquiring along with phonology, morphology, syntax, and the lexicon. This chapter is an attempt to trace my own concern with this question, beginning with some historical notes

269

on the origins of that interest, and ending with a proposal about the role of language in socialization.

PSYCHOLINGUISTICS IN THE 1950s

My own interest in language acquisition dates from the first course I took with Roger Brown in 1952, while a senior at Radcliffe, majoring in history and literature. My senior honors thesis, which I was writing at the time under the direction of Claudio Guillén, was on George Borrow and the image of the Gypsy in nineteenth-century British literature. Harvard at the time had a department of Comparative Philology, rather than a Linguistics Department, with a strong emphasis on historical linguistics and broad offerings in languages, both ancient and modern. (When I say Harvard, I mean Radcliffe as well, because Radcliffe was an administrative entity that enabled women to study at Harvard.) Having already studied French and Spanish before coming to college, I took Sanskrit, German, and Norwegian at various points in my undergraduate career, in an attempt to satisfy a growing fascination with language.

The languages and the literature we read—*The Wild Duck* in Norwegian, for instance, and parts of the *Mahabharata* in Sanskrit—were absorbing, but they were not really what I was looking for. Quite by happenstance during my senior year I enrolled in a new course called the Psychology of Speech and Communication, taught by a young assistant professor named Roger Brown, who had recently arrived from the University of Michigan. The lectures were a revelation, beautifully organized and full of startling ideas: Language is a system, and the units that linguists describe have their psychological counterparts in the minds of speakers. It is possible to study the way human beings acquire, store, retrieve, comprehend, produce, or forget language. Obviously, this was the subject to study—after taking this course, I never had a second thought about what I wanted to do. Finishing my undergraduate studies, I went to the Radcliffe Graduate School, took a Master's degree in their new Department of Linguistics, and then petitioned Harvard to study for a joint Ph.D. in Linguistics and Psychology under the direction of Roger Brown. It was 1955.

My colleagues—Roger once called them littermates—in this new combined field of linguistics and psychology were Don Hildum and Eric Lenneberg, and we of this first cohort of Roger Brown's doctoral students were the only ones to attempt joint degrees, satisfying the requirements in both departments. Eric Lenneberg took Old High German to satisfy his historical linguistics requirement, whereas I followed the adventures of Roland and Olivier in Old French. I was happy to take Arabic to satisfy a non-Indo–European requirement, and happier still when Professor Whatmough, chairman of the Linguistics Department, said to me one day, "You can't make bricks without straw, Miss Berko; you shall have to have some Sanskrit."

I was able to reply, "But, Professor Whatmough, I've already had Sanskrit." One never knows how an early interest may later fit into the grand scheme of things. (Not only did the undergraduate work in Sanskrit stand me in good stead; the interest in Gypsies was also not wasted—in fact, it led ultimately to an invitation to Hungary, where for the past several years I have been working with Zita Réger of the Hungarian Academy of Sciences on how Gypsy children acquire Hungarian.)

In my fourth year of graduate school, I wrote my dissertation on how children acquire English morphology. The little creatures called *wugs* that I drew for the study have been following me around for the past 30 years. Roger Brown had left Harvard for MIT by this time, and I had a graduate fellowship to write my thesis from the American Association of University Women. My progress report to them says:

> On the first of November, [1957] I submitted my thesis prospectus to the committee on higher degrees in the Department of Social Relations and to the Department of Linguistics. A thesis conference was called, with Professor Whatmough, who is chairman of the Department of Linguistics, acting as chairman. The members of the thesis committee were Roger Brown, Associate Professor of Psychology at MIT; Jerome Bruner, Professor of Psychology at Harvard; Charles Ferguson, Lecturer in Arabic at Harvard; and Dr. Susan Ervin of the Harvard Graduate School of Education. Copies of the prospectus were also delivered to Dean Jones of the Graduate School, Professor Roman Jakobson, and Professor John Carroll of the School of Education.

Looking back at this list of distinguished faculty advisers, I realize the intellectual debt that I and everyone else in our field owe them. I worked closely with Roger Brown on the dissertation, which according to that same progress report:

> now covers three areas of English morphology: inflexion, derivation, and compounding. In inflexion we are attempting to establish the order of acquisition of English inflexional endings—for example, the various allomorphs of the plural, and the pretest I ran has given us a good idea of what this order will prove to be. In the other two areas we are seeing what types of formations the children can extend to new words and what kinds of knowledge they have of the compound words in their own vocabulary.

After the dissertation was completed, I began what has also become a 30-year research involvement by spending the summer working on aphasia with Harold Goodglass and an interdisciplinary group of linguists, neurologists, speech pathologists, and psychologists at the Veterans' Administration Hospital in Boston. Uriel Weinreich from Columbia's Department of Linguistics was a member of that group, and he was also the editor of *Word*. He asked for my morphology study and very promptly published it (1958).

The following fall (1958–1959), I began a postdoctoral fellowship with Roger Brown at MIT. We were in the Department of Economics, which is perhaps an indication of how odd and peripheral the study of children's language was in 1958. During those years we published a study called "Word association and the acquisition of grammar" (1960) and wrote a chapter on psycholinguistic research methods for Mussen's *Handbook of Research Methods in Child Development* (1960). It is difficult to believe we worked so hard because we were so interested in what we were doing and we had such a good time.

THE 1960s

During the next decade, various other forces diverted me from formal research in psycholinguistics. Not the least of them was motherhood and the production of my own set of child language subjects. Early in 1959 I married Andrew Gleason, a professor of mathematics at Harvard who is also the younger brother of the linguist Henry Allan Gleason, whose (1955) description of English we had used in devising many of our experiments; and for the next few years I had the opportunity to observe language development firsthand in our daughters, Katherine, Pam, and Cynthia, who were born in 1960, 1961, and 1963. I tried to stay current with the work of the day and was part of the lighthearted group cited elsewhere in this volume that met each week to discuss the latest Adam, Eve, and Sarah transcripts. When some years later I complained to Roger about the lacuna in my research career, he told me I had missed a decade of formalism. This is of course true: The wave of intense interest in the acquisition of syntax that inundated our field in the 1960s did not hit me, because I was already engulfed in domesticity.

THE 1970s AND 1980s

Although our early work was quite cognitive in its orientation, and this remains the major theoretical perspective shared by all of those who have been fortunate enough to work with Roger Brown, during the past 15 years or so I have found myself becoming increasingly interested in what Dell Hymes (1971) called communicative competence, particularly in the way that children acquire the social rules for language use. Early on we looked for invariance, for universals in the language acquired by all children. An interest in the social aspects, however, leads to questions about variability and individual and group differences, about the effect that the linguistic environment has on children, and about the ways in which children come to speak in various ways in different social contexts. Finally, one can ask even broader questions dealing with the role of language itself in children's relationship with society; if we do this from the perspective of what the child is attempting to accomplish through language, the topic is prag-matics, whereas if the interest is in society's agenda for the child, the topic is socialization.

Around 1970 I became interested in the question of how children learn styl-istic variation, particularly how they learn to talk in different ways to different people; this interest had been spurred by reading works on register, and by an interest in finding out when it is that children first begin to be able to talk in varied ways—most child language studies had reported the child's speech to only one person, usually the mother, as if that were the only way the child could speak. To find variation it seemed necessary to look at the same children either in different settings or speaking to several people with different addressee charac-teristics. Choosing the latter, I observed and recorded linguistic interaction in a number of families where the target child had the opportunity to speak to fathers, mothers, and younger siblings.

In the summer of 1971 the Linguistic Society met in Buffalo, and a number of us were invited to give papers. I reported the early evidence on variation I had found in a paper called "Code switching in children's language" (1973). While listening for variation in children's language, I had also been struck by the language parents use when speaking to children who already know the linguistic system, but who are not yet fully socialized: This was a very special register, which we called "the language of socialization." Whether at the dinner table or in the supermarket, the parents' speech was filled with instructions about how to behave, what to believe, what to say; simply quoting these parents led to a great deal of laughter in the audience, as people recognized themselves in this every-day language. After hearing the paper, Charles Ferguson gave me a list of researchers in various parts of the world who were also looking at parents' speech to children; it included names like Catherine Snow and many others who were later to take part in a conference on what was now called input language. The conference was held in Boston in 1974, and Snow and Ferguson edited the resulting book, *Talking to Children* (1977). In the intervening years, most of us have continued to work in this field—our research team, for instance, has stud-ied fathers' and mothers' speech to children both in the laboratory and at home. Roger Brown was at the Boston meeting, displaying a healthy skepticism about the possible role of input language in children's acquisition of language, but he later wrote an introduction to the book that provided a cohesive intellectual framework for all the individual papers.

The work on child-directed speech that began in the 1970s has had its impact on linguistic theory—so much so that Steven Pinker (this volume) claims that a faith in the importance of parental input language constitutes the new orthodoxy. Because the input work was begun partly in reaction to the Chomskyian view that children develop syntax through exposure to a corpus of complex and ill-formed adult-to-adult speech, it is not surprising that the syntax of parental input has been the leading subtopic of input study, whereas studies of input phonology, morphology, and lexicon have been far rarer. The actual *contents* of parents' speech to children, that is, the topics of discourse, have hardly been examined at all; when discourse has been investigated, it is more likely that the linguistic researcher has asked who set the topic (e.g., Howe, 1981), rather than what it was they talked about, or what psychological impact parental speech has on children. This concern is left to psychologists, who have largely ignored the topic as well. There have been some exceptions to this general rule, however; a child psychotherapist, the late Haim Ginott, for instance, included many insightful comments on parent–child verbal interaction in his book, *Between Parent and Child* (1968), but the conversations he cites are illustrative fabrications rather than actual discourse.

LANGUAGE AND SOCIALIZATION

Although the studies of specialized input to children have had an obvious impact on linguistics, they have not affected psychological theories of socialization in the slightest, so far as one can see. The major theories appear to rely on magical processes whereby children absorb their value systems, beliefs, and behaviors from the adults around them. Freudian theory, for instance, claims that with the resolution of the Oedipal conflict the child represses his love for his mother, identifies with his father, and thereupon *internalizes* what he believes is the father's moral system, thus gaining a superego; there is no hint in this theory as to how the child is supposed to have decided what the father's moral system is, but this internalization, or incorporation, according to psychoanalytic theory, is responsible for two major kinds of socialization: sex role socialization and the acquisition of moral values.

Learning theory assumes that the child is socialized by shaping by the parent; successive approximations of socialized-appearing behavior are rewarded, whereas negative reinforcement is applied to antisocial behavior. Parents' language is not examined for its content, but there is a general assumption that positive and negative reinforcement can be conveyed linguistically.

Social learning theory assumes that modeling and imitation account for socialized behavior; according to this view, children imitate appropriate models—for instance, they imitate their same-sex parent and thus come to behave appropriately. Or they can learn from observing others, such as from television and film personalities. Language as well as behavior can be imitated, but language plays no special role in effecting socialization.

Cognitive-developmental theory assumes that the child first arrives at some cognitive understanding of what it means to be, for instance, a girl or boy and then takes on the behaviors of girls or boys. Again, parental language plays no special role, except insofar as the child may notice and adopt the parent's style.

Thus, psychological theories emphasize identification, reward and punishment, imitation and modeling, and individual cognitive activity as major modes of socialization. Parents are described as nurturant or cold, as permissive or restrictive, but there is little mention of the actual use of language in conveying warmth or other traits and attitudes, except in rather oblique fashion: One may read, for instance, that some parents encourage independence, but we do not learn specifically how they do this, what is entailed in early independence training, or what the linguistic concomitants of any other socialization behaviors are.

If we try to consider the role of language in socialization, several different processes appear to be in operation; I note three: (1) the use of explicit instructions to the child about what to do, feel, think, etc.; (2) the use of explicit directions about what to say on various occasions; and (3) subtle but indirect socializing effects resulting from linguistic interaction: such things as interrupting some children more than others, praising or condemning some behaviors, etc.

The first is the most obvious: Language to children contains specific instructions about how to be socialized. A boy going to a birthday party need not have resolved his Oedipal complex, observed another child at a party, had a long history of reward and punishment surrounding birthdays, or come to a deep intellectual understanding of the significance of natal rituals. His parent is liable to tell him quite specifically ahead of time to eat nicely, give other children their turn at games, avoid fistfights, stay clean, even to have fun. There is an entire body of things that people explicitly tell children about how to think, to feel, to believe, to behave. Although this seems transparently obvious, the fact is that we do not know what that corpus of instructions contains, how it differs in different societies and social classes, to what extent males and females echo the same statements, and to what extent it differs to boys and girls. There does, however, appear to be a great deal of uniformity in what parents say to children, not simply in terms of the semantic content, but in the actual words used. At the dinner table, for instance, we have repeatedly heard parents say: "Sit up at the table" and "Don't talk with your mouth full." Recently, I asked an audience of about 200 people from all over the United States to say what they would tell a little girl of about 5 as they sent her off to the store several blocks away. Response was overwhelming and uniform: "Look both ways before you cross the street" and "Don't talk to strangers." Perhaps the fact that adults, whether they are parents or not, carry with them an explicit body of socializing statements that they can access when faced with real or imaginary children is more than an interesting epiphenomenon.

The skeptical reader may ask why we should believe that what parents say has any serious effect on children, because perhaps language is only a superficial manifestation of who and what we are, and perhaps children see through that veil to the real truth and become socialized in deeper, less accessible ways. I think we will have to prove that children are profoundly affected by their parents actual words, and that this might be easier to do than to show that, for instance, they have incorporated their fathers.

A second form of socialization that is carried by language pertains to language itself; speech to children contains a set of explicit devices for teaching them how to speak the right way. Our own work on politeness routines (Gleason, Perlmann, & Greif, 1984; Gleason & Weintraub, 1976; Greif & Gleason, 1980) has shown that however tangential "please" and "thank you" may be to the linguistic system, they are very central to the social system, and middle class American families are willing to expend a great deal of effort in making sure that their children produce appropriately polite linguistic markers. Parents' eagerness to teach their 6-month-old children the prelinguistic routine "bye bye" is one evidence of their desire to show that their baby is on its way to being a socialized person. Parents use various routines, usually including the word "say" (as in "Don't forget to say thank you") to socialize their children's language behavior all through the elementary years. Parents teach their children to use polite linguistic forms that are increasingly complex as children become more competent. For example, sitting at the dinner table children are told to produce sentences containing modals: e.g., "May I please have some more milk?," rather than the child's "More milk!" Parental language thus contains explicit instruction about both behavioral and linguistic socialization.

A third and more difficult to describe type of socialization through language can be found in much more subtle but nonetheless linguistic interchanges between parents and their children—such things as modeled differences in language, differences in interactive style, different emphases. Subtle linguistic forces undoubtedly impinge on children in important ways in the formation of their social and sex-role identities. For instance, Esther Greif (1980) showed in a small study that both mothers and fathers interrupted little girls more than they interrupted boys; others (West, 1979) have shown that later in life, at cocktail parties, for example, women are more likely than men to be interrupted. So this experience of being an interruptable person begins early in life and has some continuity. Surely, it also has an effect on the way that both men and women feel about women's relative importance. In the realm of social class, it also would appear that language contributes to the differences that exist between social groups. (Basil Bernstein, 1971 and elsewhere, has theorized that the use of restricted and elaborated code accounts for social class differences in cognition, but we do not have the data on exactly what social class differences exist in the speech of parents to very young children.) We certainly cannot adopt a cognitive-developmental view to explain the fact that by the time they arrive in kindergarten there are predictable differences between working-class and middle-class children; that is, one cannot claim that a working-class child first learns that he or she is working class and then adopts the behaviors appropriate to that class; nor are the demographic variables that are used to distinguish between classes directly responsible for observed differences in children—a parent's paycheck or level of education have no direct impact on children. Rather, subtle interactional factors shape and socialize children to think and act like members of their own groups. Until we have real data on what happens in many different households, we will not know how to account for social class and subcultural differences in children.

A MODEST PROPOSAL

Because subtle factors are notoriously difficult to delineate, let me return here to the observations about explicit parental statements to children about what they should be doing, feeling, thinking, and saying.

As noted earlier, we all seem to share a body of information that we pass on to children when given the chance; these culturally relevant statements are phrased in a quite formulaic way and do not necessarily reflect our own views so much as those afloat in society at large. We tell children that Disneyland is fun, that big boys don't cry, that they should be nice to their baby sister, that they should sit up at the table and say "please," that they should look both ways before crossing the street, and so on. What I suggest here is that these expressions do have an effect on children, and that in fact they constitute the nucleus of what is transmitted culturally, that they play a major role in socialization. Earlier, I mentioned the fact that psychoanalytic theory does not explain how children are able to divine what their parent's moral system is; now I suggest that young children, being literal minded, believe what their parents say in these rather formulaic pronouncements, and that is what they internalize. The superego, if that is the term to use, is liable to consist of memorized routinized pronouncements made by people to whom the child is attached. I add the emotional note of attachment here, because it is clear that all speakers do not carry equal weight with young children, even though children appear to internalize routinized speech of all types and to retain it permanently—consider the fact that you still know the words to "Rockabye baby" and "Patacake" after all these years, and that, depending on your age, you are liable to be able to recite the standard openings of radio or television shows heard only in childhood: "Jack Armstrong, all American boy. . . ;" "Look, up in the sky. . . ;" or "It's Howdy Doody time. . . ."

Obviously, Howdy Doody has not formed the conscience of a nation. But the capacity that makes the memorization of commercial messages so easy for children contributes to their ability to internalize socialization messages from significant people around them. Because the child is attached to parents, there is emotional impact to what parents say; and this is believed literally, because the child is literal minded. According to this view, parents' actual words become children's consciences; the voice of conscience repeats all those routinized phrases: Be nice to your baby brother. Look both ways before you cross the street. Big boys don't cry. Say goodbye. Say thank you. Obviously, this is not meant to say that one's adult conscience is limited to such simplistic content; rather, it implies that adults provide children with a starter set, so to speak, of socialization instructions that they can build on themselves in the ensuing years. It also implies that the initial set is sufficiently durable that it lasts into adulthood, where it becomes available to be passed on to the next generation of children.

If we are to do more than theorize about language and socialization, we will have to collect naturalistic data on parent–child linguistic interaction in many different settings. Some of the general questions to be answered are:

1. What, in any given culture, is the set of statements about behavior, thought, and feeling made to children?—what, in other words, are the child's marching orders?

2. Within a given family, is there consistency in what adults say, or do mothers and fathers say different things to children?

3. Across families within an identifiable social group, are the same things being said?

4. What kinds of social group differences can be identified?

5. What is the relative role of routines in the socialization of children in different societies? In our own, we know about politeness and a few others, such as Halloween, but some societies have many more formulaic kinds of language: proverbs, wise sayings, and many more ritualistic utterances in general. What is the content of those sayings?

6. How do we account for the linguistic consistencies and continuities over time in the socialization styles of different cultural groups? If adults are the bearers of certain kinds of linguistic interactional styles, where did we acquire them? For instance, is it possible that as children we learn a set of statements that we carry with us until we have children of our own, to whom we say the same things that were said to us 25 or 30 years earlier?

Although the answer to the last question might require a 25-year longitudinal study, I think it is possible in the short run to study the content of parents' speech to children, as well as the extent to which we can determine that specific parental statements are echoed by children at early ages, either in their play or in their monologues at night before going to sleep.

Parents' Speech.   In order to examine varied samples of parents' speech, we need naturalistic data, collected in such settings as breakfast, lunch, and dinner time conversations, bedtime situations, trips with children to stores, zoos, doctors' offices, etc. Families with children who are approximately 3–5 years old would be the most appropriate subjects.

Role Play.   One way of tapping the kinds of things that children have internalized is through role play. Children might, for instance, be given puppets and asked to act out scenarios similar to ones that they have already played in the real-life situations just described, except that they would be asked to take the part of the parent. Matches between what parents say in the real event and what children say when portraying the parent in the game could be noted. Or the experimenter might play the child and ask questions of the parent doll. The children's speech could then be analyzed for the explicit rules that preschoolers can verbalize.

Monologue.   Whereas children of this age tend to be beyond the typical age of presleep monologues, any that are produced could be analyzed for evidence of social rule practice. An example of this early internalization of parents' speech can be found in the work of Ruth Hirsch Weir (1970), who recorded the presleep monologues of her son, Anthony, when he was between 28 and 30 months old. Whereas Anthony's monologues are frequently cited as evidence that children practice linguistic structures, we also find Anthony echoing what appear to be other rules as well. Alone in his crib at night, Anthony says, among other things: "Don't go on the desk." "Don't touch mommy daddy's desk." "Don't take daddy's glasses." "Make it all gone." "That's the boy." and "Excuse me." These certainly sound like the voice of the parent echoing in the speech of the young child. Other archival records of child language studies might prove similarly illuminating.

Although these are only suggestions and examples, I think it is clearly time to include language in developmental psychological theory and recognize that research of this nature could help elucidate the role of parents' language in children's acquisition of social rules, and ultimately in their socialization.

CONCLUSION

This chapter has argued that developmental psychological theories have not recognized language as a major force in the socialization of children. During the past quarter century some psycholinguistic researchers have broadened their studies of language development in children to include the language spoken *to* children, but linguists' interests have almost invariably been in explaining how child directed speech may affect the acquisition of purely linguistic systems, and developmental psychologists have simply added "language development" as another chapter in their textbooks, alongside "cognitive development." The chapters on sex-role development, personality development, and socialization attribute these accomplishments to essentially nonverbal psychoanalytic, cognitive, and learning theory principles.

Yet, it becomes increasingly clear that in acquiring their language children also acquire the social systems that are embedded in language. Moreover, most adults produce a remarkably consistent set of socializing statements when talking to children, and children learn those statements in rote fashion, even to the extent of practicing them out loud when they are alone. If members of a given culture all carry with them a set of memorized messages, it is surely time to consider the *psychological* meaning and impact of those messages. This is not meant to imply or suggest that language is the sole, or even most important, medium of socialization. Children are often faced with conflicting messages from the behavioral and verbal realms and folk wisdom has long recognized this irony: "Do as I say, not as I do." A child with an aggressive parent, for instance, may learn early on to behave aggressively, despite being told "It isn't nice to hit people." That parental admonition may persist, however, as the voice of conscience and a source of guilt. Ultimately, perhaps a major source of cognitive dissonance for children lies in the fact that adults' own behavior is frequently at odds with the social rules they so consistently repeat. It is time for research in this area to concentrate on the cultural content of adults' speech to children, and on the psychological impact of that speech.

REFERENCES

Berko, J. (1958). The child's learning of English mophology. *Word, 14,* 150–177.

Berko, J., & Brown, R. (1960). Psycholinguistic research methods. In P. Mussen (Ed.), *Handbook of research methods in child development.* New York: Wiley.

Bernstein, B. (1971). *Class, codes and control. Vol. I: Theoretical studies toward a sociology of language.* Beverly Hills, CA: Sage Publications.

Brown, R., & Berko, J. (1960). Word association and the acquisition of grammar. *Child Development, 31,* 1–14.

Ginott, H. (1968). *Between parent and child.* New York: MacMillan.

Gleason, H. A. (1955). An introduction to descriptive linguistics. New York: Henry Holt.

Gleason, J. Berko. (1973). Code switching in children's language. In T. E. Moore (Ed.), *Cognitive development and the acquisition of language.* New York: Academic Press.

Gleason, J. Berko, Perlmann, R. Y., & Greif, E. B. (1984). What's the magic word: Learning language through routines. *Discourse Processes, 6,* 493–502.

Gleason, J. Berko, & Weintraub, S. (1976). The acquisition of routines in child language. *Language in Society, 5,* 129–136.

Greif, E. B. (1980). Sex differences in parent–child conversations. *Women's Studies International Quarterly, 3,* 253–258.

Greif, E. B., & Gleason, J. Berko. (1980). Hi, thanks and goodbye: More routine information. *Language in Society, 9,* 159–166.

Howe, C. (1981). *Acquiring language in a conversational context.* New York: Academic Press.

Hymes, D. (1971). Competence and performance in linguistic theory. In R. Huxley and D. Ingram (Eds.), *Language acquisition: Models and methods.* London: Academic Press.

Snow, C., & Ferguson, C. (Eds.). (1977). *Language acquisition and input.* Cambridge, England: Cambridge University Press.

Weir, R. H. (1970). *Language in the crib.* The Hague: Mouton.

West, C. (1979). Against our will: Male interruptions of females in cross-sex conversations. *Annals of the New York Academy of Sciences, 327,* 521–529.

13

Environmental Assistance Revisited: Variation and Functional Equivalence

Courtney B. Cazden
Harvard University

I came to language acquisition research in the early 1960s out of interest in two questions: what kinds of individual or cultural differences in children's language influence educational success, and how can educational contexts provide environmental assistance to language development. And so I focused on research on environmental assistance to that aspect of language then the object of most attention—grammar.

The results of both descriptive research on Adam, Eve, and Sarah's interactions with their parents (Brown, Cazden, & Bellugi, 1969) and experimental research on lower class black children's interactions with tutors (Cazden, 1965) were largely negative. To put the conclusions bluntly: Reinforcement did not exist, frequency did not correlate, and expansions did not help. It seemed at the end of the 1960s that, compared with the learning of vocabulary or the rules for language use, acquisition of grammar was relatively impervious to environmental differences.

Reactions to this state of affairs was mixed. For some, it stimulated continuing research on features of adult speech to children (e.g., Hirsh-Pasek, Treiman, & Schneiderman, 1984). Others, not only linguists, found that the implied exaltation of the power inherent in all children's minds helped solve other problems. In a historical essay on 50 years of one journal, the *Harvard Educational Review* (*HER*), where Brown and Bellugi's first article on Adam and Eve was published in 1964, a sociologist of communication (Schudson, 1981) suggested why ''language became a central concern of HER in the 1970's'':

> As educators have grown disheartened with the power of schools to affect students
> or change society, they have turned to a faith in the natural abilities of children to

achieve for themselves. This emphasis is most evident in research on the child's
capacity for learning language. . . .

That study of language touched on universal themes, revealed common human
elements, and illuminated the biological nature of learners and, perhaps, their
divine spark as well, was symbolized in Brown and Bellugi's decision to provide
the two children they studied with the names Adam and Eve. . . .

An understanding of language, then, seemed to offer a way through social
policy debacles and intellectual despair. A focus on language and the ability of the
preschool child to show the most remarkable capacity for rule-governed behavior
and the learning of exquisitely complex grammatical systems—regardless of
genes, family background, or the quality of schooling—offered hope for the liberal
position that the educational community had long tried to sustain. There was almost
a new theology of education arising out of the study of language. (pp. 20–21)

That new theology of education was appealing to me as to others, but the roles
of language in education still had to be understood. And so during the 1970s and
1980s I returned to my original concerns more directly, becoming a full-time
classroom teacher again for one year, and participating with students in research
on the demands that particular classroom speech events make on children's
communicative competence.[1]

More specifically, the new theology left us in a weak position to respond to
questions about children whose life experiences are different from those of the
white, middle-class families whom most of our research is still about. One recent
controversy, for example, argued in educational decision-making forums as well
as university seminars, arises from the world-wide phenomenon of immigrant
workers and refugees. It concerns not only the numbers but even the conceivable
existence of children who are less than normally proficient in either a first or
second language at the time of entry into school (cf. Cummins, 1979 vs. Edelsky
et al. 1983; Martin-Jones & Romaine, 1986). With a few exceptions (notably
Hymes, 1980, especially pp. vi–vii), linguists have been tempted to ignore the
possibility that, in particular sociocultural conditions, some environments may
not provide even the minimum necessary assistance.

Where are we now in our understanding of the critical environmental conditions for language acquisition? In this chapter I examine the evidence for one
intuitively appealing hypothesis that was suggested more than a decade ago by
Macnamara (1972) and since incorporated more formally into Pinker's (1979)
learnability theory—the hypothesis is: "that children learn syntax by inferring
the meanings of sentences from their non-linguistic contexts, then finding rules
to convert the meanings into sentences and vice-versa" (p. 243). Adopting

---

[1]Cazden (1976, 1979) report my personal experience as a classroom teacher. Analyses of children's language in classroom settings include Cazden, Cox, Dickinson, Steinberg, & Stone (1979)
and Cazden, Michaels, & Tabors (1985).Cazden (1986) reviews research on classroom discourse.

Pinker's terms, I refer to this as the "shared representation hypothesis." I first analyze the evidence for the hypothesis in the well-known set of studies of adult–child interaction in white, English-speaking families; then I raise questions about the implications of recent research in working-class and nonwestern cultures; and finally I end with a few words about similarities within the western world between adult–child interaction and classroom discourse.

THE SHARED REPRESENTATION HYPOTHESIS

Before looking at the evidence, it is important to be clear about what this hypothesis does and does not entail. First, it says nothing about how the child infers utterance meanings or figures out the grammatical rules, nor about how much "wired-in" structure constrains the child's hypotheses about either one. Second, it says nothing about the limits of the representation that is shared. Consider, for example, the important distinction between reference and sense (Frege) or reference and meaning (Vygotsky). For example, in any utterance that includes mention of Daddy, the adult will understand that word in its complex sense or meaning as a relational term. But to attain a shared representation of utterances likely to be spoken to the young child, the child need only understand its reference to a single man. In Vygotsky's view, such shared reference in early communication not only precedes shared meaning but is essential for its development (1962, p. 73; see also Wertsch, 1983).

What the shared representation hypothesis does entail is the assumption that critical input for language learning is not just the frequency of occurrence of particular structures in the child's environment (cf. Gleitman, Newport, & Gleitman, 1984, for their latest evidence on that alternative hypothesis), but the frequency of utterances that are interpretable by the child.

One major problem confronting the child in making that interpretation is what Pinker (1979) calls the *encoding problem:* "Barring telepathy, how does the child manage to encode a situation into just the structure that underlies the sentence that the adult is uttering?" (p. 272). His answer lists an interesting set of contributors: "I suggest that the primary role in syntax learning of cognitive development, "fine-tuning" of adult speech to children learning language, knowledge of the pragmatics of a situation, and perceptual strategies is to ensure that the child encodes a situation into the same representational structure that underlies the sentence that the adult is uttering concurrently" (p. 275). As Pinker points out, these contributory processes have been stressed by different researchers. But the interpretability of adult utterances should be evaluated by taking all of them into account at once, as the child can do. In that way, functional equivalencies for the child, across variation in adult syntactic form and communicative function, can be considered.

Before attempting that evaluation, I want to summarize the construct of functional equivalence in two theories—the Soviet psychological theory of activity as described by A. N. Leont'ev, and Merton's sociological theory of functional analysis. Both suggest ways of thinking about variation in adult–child interaction in relation to children's acquisition of language.

According to Leont'ev (1981), the structure of every human activity (which is energized by a motive) is composed of actions (which are directed by goals), and these actions in turn are composed of operations, selected and carried out automatically, out-of-awareness, depending on particular conditions. One feature of Leont'ev's theory is that any behavior can change in level from action to operation or vice-versa. So, for example, shifting gears starts as a goal-directed action for a beginner in the activity of learning to drive; later, the same behavior recedes to the level of an operation, activated automatically under certain driving conditions. A second feature is that alternative operations can be instrumental in realizing different actions, and, according to Leont'ev (1981), "one and the same action can be instrumental in realizing different activities" (p. 61). In other words, there is no one-to-one correspondence across levels.

To apply this theory to adult–child interaction, let us start with the largest unit, activities themselves. Most adult–child interaction is embedded in the ongoing activities of family life. Occasionally, there is some time out for adult–child interaction for its own sake, as in peek-a-boo games, book reading, etc. And, more familiar to researchers than to parents, there is the special research situation described by Brown (1980), in which an adult committee of Jill and Peter deVilliers and a child's mother have no other motive than to engage a 30-month-old child in conversation.

Within these activities, adults engage in various actions, both nonverbal and verbal, which express conscious intentions toward the child. The verbal actions can be categorized in ordinary speech–act terms: asking questions for information or requesting a display of knowledge (to serve [from Brown, 1980] "as a running check on the child's progress in building an apperceptive mass shared with his family" [p. 196]); directing the child where to attend, and what to do or say, etc.

At the lowest, least conscious level, actions are realized by operations that vary in "technical composition" (Zinchenko & Gordon, 1979, p. 75), depending on the conditions of the activity in which they are embedded. Familiar dimensions of variation of adult utterances include the degree of their semantic contingency on the previous utterance of the child, and the mean length of utterance (MLU) or syntactic complexity. In examining the evidence for the shared representation hypothesis, we can compare utterances that vary in technical composition (while fulfilling the external goals of the adult actions) for their ability to achieve (internally to the child) the shared representation assumed to be necessary for language growth.

The distinction between external and internal effects corresponds to Merton's (1957) distinction between manifest and latent functions: "Manifest functions are those objective consequences contributing to the adjustment or adaptation of the system which are intended and recognized by participants in the system; latent functions, correlatively, being those which are neither intended nor recognized'' (p. 51). Manifest functions are what parents know they are doing. As Bellugi (1967) wrote about Adam and his mother:

> The mother and child are concerned with daily activities, not grammatical instruction. Adam breaks something, looks for a nail to repair it with, finally throws pencils and nails around the room. He pulls his favorite animals in a toy wagon; fiddles with the television set; and tries to put together a puzzle. His mother is concerned primarily with modifying his behavior. She gives him information about the world around him and corrects facts. Neither of the two seems overtly concerned with the problems that we shall pursue so avidly: the acquisition of syntax. (p. 11)

As observers, we are concerned with the analysis of patterned ways of talking to children that can be shown to serve the latent function of the acquisition of grammar, as a precipitate (D. Hymes, personal communication) of the fulfillment of whatever manifest functions may be salient to the participants. The following chart summarizes the levels of activity theory applied to adult speech to children:

activities (distinguished by energizing motive	helping vs. playing vs. book reading etc.; dyadic vs. multiparty conversations, etc.
actions (distinguished by specific goals)	requests for information or display; directions to attend, do, or say, etc.
operations (distinguished by technical composition according to conditions)	semantic contingency, MLU, syntactic complexity, features of the Baby Talk register, etc.

Now to the evidence. One dimension of variation at the level of operations is that of semantic contingency. This dimension has been found to be a significant ingredient of environmental assistance in white, English-speaking families in two important correlational studies by Wells in England and Cross in Australia. Wells (1979, 1980) followed a sample of 128 children from four social class groups in Bristol from 15 months to 5½ years, and a representative subsample of 32 on into infant school. Cross (1977, 1978) carried out a set of ingeniously designed comparisons among children whose language development—or whose siblings' language development—was normal, accelerated, or delayed. In a synthesis of these and other studies, Wells and Robinson (1982) conclude that there are three critical environmental ingredients, at least for the youngest children: clear and intelligible adult speech; adult speech that is related to the topic presumed to be on the child's mind; and—less conclusively—the amount of such intelligible and topically related speech. Length and syntactic complexity do not turn up as significant variables, probably because they are adjusted, with insignificant variability, by the adult's shift to a Baby Talk register as a stylistic package (Cross, 1978, p. 208).

Topic-related speech, or semantically contingent speech as it is more often called by other researchers (e.g., Snow, 1983), can fulfill all the manifest speech act functions of questioning, directing, etc.; and it fulfills the latent shared representation function by adults following the topical lead of the child and speaking about what they presume to be on the child's mind. A case study of the frequency of semantically contingent speech is given in Moerk's reanalysis of the entire set of protocols for Eve, Brown's fastest learning child, whose MLU developed swiftly from 1.39 to 4.22 between 18 and 27 months. In an analysis of conversational topics, Moerk found that "Whereas the mother introduces a new topic less than 5 times per hour on the average, the child introduces new topics around 20 times." Moerk's (1983) discussion of this result, although expressed in more behaviorist terms, still fits Pinker's model:

> The import of these differences . . . for language acquisition generally can hardly be overemphasized. The mother, with few exceptions, deals with topics that are 'old,' i.e., they pertain to the preceding interactional context. The child therefore rarely encounters the task to abstract completely new content from the verbal input she receives. Since the mother employs mostly a theme proposed by the child and repeats it with minor and major linguistic variation, Eve's information processing capacity can be mainly centered upon the mastery of the linguistic form. (pp. 25,28)

Semantically contingent speech includes both expansions and extensions, which I tried experimentally to separate 20 years ago. Many reasons have been suggested for the failure to confirm the intuitively appealing hypothesis that expansions should be maximally helpful just because they encoded the meaning presumed to be on the child's mind. In designing the experiment, we conceptualized the contrasting input for the nonexpansion group as simply frequency of models of well-formed sentences. But, as we should have anticipated, in order to maintain a conversation without expansions in a reasonably natural way with young children, the adult tutors frequently spoke what we later called extensions, as close in topic relatedness as possible without being expansions of the child's previous utterance. In hindsight, an explanation of the inconclusive results is that expansions and extensions can be functionally equivalent with respect to semantic contingency. Combinations of the two in longer interactions that Cross (1978) calls *synergistic sequences* may be the most helpful of all, but they were outlawed in the experiment by the necessary separation of the two kinds of response.

Nelson, Denninger, Bonvillian, Kaplan, and Baker (1984) give a more differentiated set of semantic contingency categories and report that simple recasts (which include expansions) and topic continuations (which include extensions) at 22 months correlate positively with MLU and other child language measures at 27 months, whereas complex recasts and topic changes correlate negatively. Presumably, this pattern of correlations would be different at later ages. Because simple recasts by definition provide limited additions to the child's utterance— primarily closed class features—their assistance is inevitably limited; and children's advancing cognitive development makes increasingly complex recasts interpretable. In a more informal report, Nelson (1984) also suggests that recasts may enhance attention, whereas Cazden suggested that extensions should elicit more attention because their meaning is novel as well as contingent. Short of neurological indicators of utterance-to-utterance shifts in brain activity, how could we decide?

To say that semantically contingent adult speech seems a particularly good way of achieving a shared representation between adult and child says nothing about where in the course of daily family living—in what activity contexts— such interactions are most apt to occur. According to Wells, variation occurs not only among families but between boys and girls as well. At least in one of his subsamples, there were striking differences in the contexts of ''joint enterprise,'' a shared activity in which topic-related speech was most apt to occur: three times as many sequences with boys in contexts of play, and twice as many sequences with girls in contexts of helping (Wells, 1979). Whatever may be the consequences of this difference for other aspects of development, notably gender roles, contexts of play and helping seem to be functionally equivalent activity contexts with respect to interactions for language learning.

Activities can also vary in the nonverbal support they provide for adult–child communication. In activity theory terms, adult utterances (operations) that vary on such dimensions as MLU and systactic complexity can be equally interpretable depending on characteristics of the activity in which they occur. In terms of Pinker's list of contributors to shared representations, trade-offs are possible between the child's knowledge of the pragmatics of a situation and the fine-tuning of adult utterances. So, for example, Snow (1977a) reports that mother's speech is more complex in book-reading situations where pictorial clues can aid comprehension of both mother and child. And Brown's delightful analysis (1980) of ''the difference a game makes''—e.g., hide-and-seek—suggests that utterances that are not semantically contingent on the immediately preceding utterance can still be fully interpretable by both partners—and thus functional for the child's learning—in the special situation where shared understanding of a game structure can be presupposed.

The presence or absence of such functional equivalence with respect to one outcome—language learning—despite variation in activities, actions, or operations, across individual and cultural variation in children's lives, is exactly what we need to understand. But there is a major weakness with the research thus far: Achieving shared representations primarily by means of semantically contingent adult speech is the way we probably talk to children ourselves. At such a point in a research agenda, as Slobin (1982) has said about assertions of the "naturalness" of subject–verb–object word order, "when a theory of acquisition fits the local circumstances so well, it is time to look abroad" (p. 131). Fortunately, there is now research on adult–child interactions that has done just that.

Cross-Cultural Studies

At the end of the discussion of expansions in their first report, Brown and Bellugi (1964) remarked that, "It seems to us that a mother in expanding speech may be teaching more than grammar; she may be teaching something like a world-view" (p. 143). Because their focus was wholly on the child's acquisition of language, this important idea about child socialization into a culture was not developed. In more recent ethnographic research, the union of language acquisition and cultural socialization has been placed at center stage. This set of studies now includes descriptions of white and black working-class families (Heath, 1983; Miller, 1981) and families in three South Pacific cultures: Kaluli in Papua New Guinea (Schieffelin, 1979a,b), Western Samoa (Ochs, 1982), and the Kwara'ae in the Solomon Islands (Watson-Gegeo & Gegeo, in press-a,b). All provide vivid descriptions of children learning to talk in nonmiddle-class and nonwestern homes.

Consider first the work of Miller and Schieffelin (both former students of Lois Bloom). We find in their reports both similarities to, and differences from, our familiar accounts. For a similarity, those interested in game formats as a context for very early communication will be interested to know that Kaluli children play peek-a-boo (Schieffelin, 1979b, p. 87). About differences, Schieffelin (1979a) writes: "The Kaluli data call into question the universality of current theories of input language. For example, among the Kaluli there is the absence of a baby-talk lexicon, the prohibition of sound play, and the emphasis on triadic [instead of dyadic] interaction" (p. 320).

Within activities characterized by triadic interactions, both Miller from white working-class Baltimore and Schieffelin from the Kaluli report far more direct instruction in how to speak than has been reported before. Direct instruction can be defined as an imperative of a verb of speaking plus utterance X to be repeated: in English, *say, ask,* or *tell X;* in Kaluli, *X elema;* in Kwara'ae, X spoken in a special "invitational intonation contour" with or without the prefacing phrase *'uri.* Previously, direct instruction has been reported in middle-class families for naming—"That's an elephant, Can you say 'elephant'?"—often interpolated into book-reading events (Ninio & Bruner, 1978); and brief but socially important routines—"Say 'bye-bye'" or "Say 'thank you'" (Gleason & Weintraub, 1976). Both Miller and Schieffelin report extensive use of direct instruction to teach interpersonal uses of speech in encounters in which adults give children lines to say to a third party.

In Baltimore, Miller's three mothers taught appropriate compliance and assertiveness in what they know to be a harsh world. For example, when 5-year-old Kris took a doll from 2-year-old Amy, their Mother helped Amy to assert her claim by giving her appropriate lines to say (Miller, 1981, pp. 75 and 102):

Amy	*Mother*
My baby	Oh, what did she [Kris] do?
(A stands beside M)	(M takes doll from K and places it in her lap.)
	Tell her, say "keep off".
Keep off	
(A watches M wrap doll in blanket.)	
Keep off	
Keep off	
	Say "you hurt it."
You hurt it (A crying)	
Keep off (A swats at K)	
My baby (A moves closer to M)	

Among the Kaluli, parents use direct instruction to teach young children the basic cultural modality of assertion. Here is an extended *elema* sequence with Meli, one of Schieffelin's three subjects (1979a, pp. 126–127, with intonation notation deleted and columns reversed to place the child's speech on the left.)

Meli (24.3 mos.), Mother and Father at home. Cousin Mama (3¼ years) is outside; she had taken Meli's gourd. Note: All speech [with one exception-CBC] by either Mother or Father to Meli is further directed to Mama.

Meli	*Mother/Father*
	Mama! Elema.
Mama!	
	Yes, Mama! Elema. (softly) While sitting here, call out. Mama will hit you [if you go out]. While sitting here call out.
Mama!	

Meli	Mother/Father
	Bring the gourd! Elema.
Bring the gourd!	
	Quickly!
Bring!	
	Quickly!
Quickly!	
	Bring!
Bring!	
	Is it yours to take! Elema.
Is it yours to take!	
	Aren't you ashamed of yourself! Elema.
Aren't you ashamed of yourself!	
	Be ashamed! Elema.
(no response)	
	Mama! Elema.
(Mama sees marble on floor, picking it up)	
(Look at) this.	Marble, I took the marble. Elema.
(Meli is busy examining the marble and looses interest in what her mother is saying.)	

Ochs and Schieffelin go beyond descriptions of language acquisition and socialization in the particular cultures they have studied—Kaluli and Western Samoa—to hypothesize two contrasting orientations to children with more general applicability:

Two Orientations toward Children and Their Corresponding
Caregiver Speech Patterns (Ochs & Schieffelin, in press)

Adapt Situation to Child:	Adapt Child to Situation:
Simplified register features	Modelling of (unsimplified) utterances for child to
Baby Talk lexicon	repeat to third party (wide
Negotiation of meaning via expansion and paraphrase	range of speech acts, not simplified)
Cooperative proposition building between caregiver and child	Child directed to notice others
Utterances that respond to child-initiated verbal or non verbal act	Topics arise from range of situational circumstances to which caregiver wishes child to respond
Typical communicative situation: two-party	Typical communicative situation: multi-party

Adapting the situation to the child is the orientation characteristic of middle-class caregivers in the English-speaking world, and the one on which our language acquisition theory is currently based; adapting the child to the situation is characteristic, Ochs and Schieffelin suggest, of working-class American cultures as well as those they have studied in the South Pacific.

But Watson-Gegeo and Gegeo's work in Gegeo's native Kwara'ae community in the Solomon Islands shows that such a simple dichotomy is wrong. With specific reference to the Ochs and Schieffelin model, they (in press) write:

> Ochs and Schieffelin have suggested that societies can be contrasted according to two basic orientations toward child socialization. . . . The Kwara'ae are an interesting test case for the model in that they correspond to lower or working class peoples elsewhere—they are subsistent horticulturists, usually non-literate or with a minimum of Western schooling, and economically very poor. Yet they share characteristics with both orientations and interactional models described by Ochs and Schieffelin.
>
> More specifically, Kwara'ae caregivers use a simplified register and babytalk lexicon, negotiate meaning with the child via expansion and paraphrase, cooperatively build propositions with the infant, respond to child-initiated verbal and nonverbal acts, and engage in frequent two-party conversations with infants—all characteristic of the "adapt situation to child" orientation. Yet they also model utterances for the child to repeat to a third party, direct the child to notice others, orient it to topics of situational concern, and engage in frequent multi-party conversations with infants—all characteristic of the "adapt child to situation" orientation. Both sets of interactional strategies get equal billing in Kwara'ae caregiver–infant interactions.

The Kwara'ae case disconfirms the universality of the Ochs and Schieffelin model. But, confirming their cultural perspective, it argues for the importance of cultural systems that do not follow deterministically from socioeconomic class.

This set of ethnographic studies makes two important contributions to our understanding of environmental assistance. First, they describe the cultural system of beliefs and values that lie behind and give coherence to features of caretaker interactions that are separated in analysis. Second, they demonstrate how much variation is possible in those interactions at the level of activities, actions, and operations. At the most general level, all societies must be functionally equivalent in providing the young with experiences from which the language of the community can be learned. But those experiences can be organized, or choreographed, as Ochs and Schieffelin put it, in diverse ways.

Unfortunately, however, these studies are of limited use in testing Pinker's hypothesis. For example, do the Kaluli interactions disconfirm the hypothesis that shared representations are necessary, or do they only show that semantic contingency is not the only way to achieve it, or neither?

Consider again some of the utterances Meli is directed to say. I assume that rhetorical questions like "Is it yours to take?" and "Aren't you ashamed of yourself?," which Meli not only hears but speaks, are outside her grammatical system, even allowing for differences in the syntactic complexity of the original and the English translation. More importantly, such utterances almost certainly do not express a shared representational structure, because their function is to teach children not only how to speak but how to feel as well. Thus, both syntactically and conceptually, Meli's repetition of such utterances can be considered "performance before competence," to play on those familiar terms (Cazden, 1981, 1983). But utterances Meli is directed to say about the gourd are much more interpretable. "Bring the gourd" refers to an action in the immediate future, and "I took the marble" refers to an action just completed by Meli herself. The latter could even be considered semantically contingent, but on the child's actions rather than on her words. (I am indebted to Hilary Goldberg for this insight.) Of these categories of utterances, Schieffelin has emphasized the cultural importance of the first. But we do not know their relative frequency. And we still have no idea whether frequency only matters up to a certain level.

The studies are also limited in what they say about variability in children's language acquisition progress, even though Miller, Schieffelin, and Watson-Gegeo and Gegeo all provide some comparative information on their families. Of Miller's three mothers, one was a high school graduate, two had dropped out, and one of those could not read or write. But Miller does not discuss how the children's language environment varies with such differences in maternal education, nor the correlation between such differences and children's progress.

Schieffelin's three families vary on a tradition-modern continuum, with Meli's parents the most "modern": both baptised Christians, the father literate in three local languages, and the mother also learning to read. Schieffelin (1979a) mentions in passing that Meli's mother shared her literacy books with Meli, telling her the names of the pictures. But when Meli asked the names of objects around the house, the only village child to do so, her mother "found this activity boring and cooperated only for short periods of time" (p. 55)—an interesting case of culture in transition and contradiction. Schieffelin reports for herself that "Meli's language development during the study showed the most dramatic changes toward complexity" (p. 55) and reports for the village reactions that "Meli was acknowledged as having the most advanced language and social skills since she could use confrontational techniques spontaneously and appropriately at a relatively early age" (p. 139).

Watson-Gegeo and Gegeo (in press-b) provide a particularly rich qualitative description of five families who "share the same basic belief system, and are at the same socioeconomic level . . . [but] differ substantially in what they emphasize in childrearing, and in public evaluation made of their children's behavior." They summarize some of the interfamily differences: "In regard to [interactional] routines, we found that families differ in: their primary reasons for doing routines; the frequency with which particular routines occur; who is involved and how often; how completely the routine is carried out; the degree of creativity in presenting and extending the routine; and the balance of different kinds of routines used in a day'' (p. 65). But there is still insufficient information on the frequency of different categories of input and on children's relative progress.

Saying that these studies cannot be used to test the shared representation hypothesis is not intended as criticism. Any piece of research is designed to answer some questions and not others, and these were intended to answer questions about the manifest socialization functions of adult–child interactions, not the latent function of assistance to the acquisition of grammar. For the latter, more systematic cross-cultural comparison is necessary. Schieffelin (1979a) discusses the problems researchers faced in trying to use an earlier field manual (Slobin, 1967) designed for that purpose. But thanks to these recent studies, we are in a stronger position to try again, perhaps by a collaborative reanalysis of existing protocols. Some such systematic cross-cultural comparison of environmental assistance that is methodologically comparable to Slobin's crosslinguistic research on acquisition sequences seems an essential complement to cognitive science learnability research.

A Few Last Words About Education

Although this chapter (and book) are about young children's acquisition of language, I want to point out certain striking resemblances between features of adult–child interaction and classroom discourse in western-style education. Instead of environmental assistance to the child's acquisition of grammar, consider teaching as environmental assistance to students' acquisition of skills and knowledge. Instead of a shared representation of concretely present objects or events, consider the goal of teaching more complex concepts whose relation to firsthand experience may be quite remote. Instead of a semantically contingent utterance spoken in a dyadic relationship between mother and child, consider the semantically contingent utterances that teachers speak as the third part of the basic sequence of teacher Initiation–student Response–teacher Evaluation (IRE) (Mehan, 1979).

The third part of the IRE sequence frequently does more than simply indicate whether the preceding answer was right or wrong. By commenting on a selected aspect of that answer, the teacher response can be considered not just evaluation, but ''formulation.'' This is a category of utterance identified by ethnomethodologists Garfinkel and Sachs (1970): ''A member may treat some part of the conversation as an occasion to describe that conversation, to explain it, or characterize it, or explicate, or translate, or summarize, or furnish the gist of it, or take note of its accordance with rules, or remark on its departure from rules. That is to say, a member may use some part of a conversation to formulate the conversation'' (p. 350). Classroom discourse researchers Griffin and Mehan (1981) give a simple example from a primary grade reading lesson:

T. (writes 'tree' on paper attached to board). If you know what the word says, put up your hand. . . .

A. Tab

T. It does start with 't'. Matthew?

Griffin and Mehan (1979) comment: [The teacher's response "It does start with a 't' "] exemplifies a way of teaching called phonics; . . . By specifying, in fact by reifying, one of the possible interpretations of an utterance by a pupil, a teacher cooperates in the construction of that utterance as a learning of (or partial learning of, or steps toward learning) what is supposed to be learned (p. 196, 208).

In a very different educational context, high school science lessons, Lemke (1982) finds similar phenomena. Describing these third-part utterances as "retroactively contextualizing" or "retro" for short, he finds that teacher retros can recontextualize the immediately prior response either structurally or thematically. Structurally, for example, the teacher can reconstrue a student answer as only a bid to answer. Thematically, "a teacher can alter or enrich the content of a student answer by retroactively placing it in a wider thematic context relevant to the thematic aims of the lesson. This seems to occur regularly, and the brevity and lack of predication in student answers may reflect their implicit collaboration in this process" (p. 21).

Two members of Wells' child language research team, French and Woll (1981) were the first to refer to parental expansions as formulations in the same sense, although they did not suggest a connection to classroom discourse. But once similarities such as these are pointed out, others come to mind. For example, some classroom observers (e.g., Willes, 1983) comment with surprise when they hear teachers answer their own question if no student does. Isn't that reminiscent of Snow's description (1977b) of mothers' talk to infants? And when adults accept a young child's nonsequitur and weave a context around it, Brown (1980) comments that it "reminds one of a benevolent professor who accepts any student question or comment and then tries to make sense of it. At any cost, one does not wound but keeps things going" (p. 201).

There is even evidence in classroom research that the semantic contingency of a teacher's response varies across children wtihin a single classroom and correlates positively with academic achievement (e.g., Collins, 1986). But whether these correlations also indicate causality is as hard to determine in research on teaching as it is in research on the child's acquisition of grammar.

REFERENCES

Bellugi, U. (1967). *The acquisition of the system of negation in children's speech.* Unpublished doctoral dissertation, Harvard University.

Brown, R. (1980). The maintenance of conversation. In D. R. Olson (Ed.), *The social foundations of language and thought* (pp. 187–210). New York: W. W. Norton.

Brown, R., & Bellugi, U. (1964). Three processes in the child's acquisition of syntax. *Harvard Educational Review, 34,* 133–151.

Brown, R., Cazden, C. B., & Bellugi, U. (1969). The child's grammar from I to III. In J. P. Hill (Ed.), *Minnesota symposium on child psychology* (pp. 28–73). Minneapolis: University of Minneapolis Press.

Cazden, C. B. (1965). *Environmental assistance to the child's acquisition of grammar.* Unpublished doctoral dissertation, Harvard University.

Cazden, C. B. (1976). *How knowledge about language helps the classroom teacher—or does it: A personal account. The Urban Review, 9,* 74–90.

Cazden, C. B. (1979). Foreword. In H. Mehan, *Learning lessons* (pp. vii–xii). Cambridge, MA: Harvard University Press.

Cazden, C. B. (1981). Performance before competence: Assistance to child discourse in the zone of proximal development. *Quarterly Newsletter of the Laboratory of Comparative Human Cognition, 3*(1), 5–8.

Cazden, C. B. (1983). Peekaboo as an instructional model: Discourse development at school and at home. In B. Bain (Ed.), *The sociogenesis of language and human conduct: A multi-disciplinary book of readings* (pp. 33–58). New York: Plenum Press.

Cazden, C. B. (in press). Classroom discourse. In M. E. Wittrock (Ed.), *Handbook of research on teaching* (3rd ed.). New York: Macmillan.

Cazden, C. B., Cox, M., Dickinson, D., Steinberg, Z., & Stone, C. (1979). You all gonna halfta listen: Peer teaching in a primary classroom. In W. A. Collins (Ed.), *Children's language and communication* (pp. 183–231). Hillsdale, NJ: Lawrence Erlbaum Associates.

Cazden, C. B., Michaels, S., & Tabors, P. (1985). Self-repair in sharing time narratives: The intersection of metalinguistic awareness, speech even and narrative style: In S. W. Freedman (Ed.), *The acquisition of writing: revision and response* (pp. 51–64). Norwood, NJ: Ablex.

Collins, J. (1986). Differential treatment in reading. In J. Cook-Gumperz (Ed.), *The social construction of literacy.* Cambridge (Eng.): Cambridge University Press.

Cross, T. G. (1977). Mothers' speech adjustments: The contribution of selected child listener variables. In C. E. Snow & C. A. Ferguson (Eds.), *Talking to children: Language input and acquisition* (pp. 151–188). New York & Cambridge, England: Cambridge University Press.

Cross, T. G. (1978). Mothers' speech and its association with rate of linguistic development in young children. In N. Waterson & C. Snow (Eds.), *The development of communication* (pp. 199–216). New York: Wiley.

Cummins, J. (1979). Linguistic interdependence and the educational development of bilingual children. *Review of Educational Research, 49,* 222–251.

Edelsky, C., Altweger, B., Barkin, F., Flores, B., Hudelson, S. and Jilbert, K. (1983). Semilingualism and language deficit. *Applied Linguistics,* 4, 1–22.

French, P., & Woll, B. (1981). Context, meaning and strategy in parent–child conversation. In G. Wells (Ed.), *Learning through interaction: The study of language development* (pp. 157–182). New York & Cambridge (Eng.): Cambridge University Press.

Garfinkel, H., & Sacks, H. (1970). On formal structures of practical actions: In J. C. McKinney & E. A. Tiryakian (Eds.), *Theoretical sociology.* New York: Appleton-Century-Crofts.

Gleason, J. B., & Weintraub, S. (1976). The acquisition of routines in child language: "Trick or Treat." *Language in Society, 5,* 129–136.

Gleitman, L. R., Newport, E. L., & Gleitman, H. (1984). The current status of the motherese hypothesis. *Journal of Child Language, 11,* 43–79.

Griffin, P., & Mehan, H. (1981). Sense and ritual in classroom discourse. In F. Coulmas (Ed.), *Conversational routine: Explorations in standardized communication situations and prepatterned speech* (pp. 187–213). The Hague: Mouton.

Heath, S. B. (1983). *Ways with words: Language, life, and work in communities and classrooms.* New York & Cambridge, England: Cambridge University Press.

Hirsh-Pasek, K., Treiman, R., & Schneiderman, M. (1984). Brown & Hanlon revisited: Mothers sensitivity to ungrammatical forms. *Journal of Child Language, 11,* 81–88.

Hymes, D. (1980). *Language in education: Ethnolinguistic essays.* Washington, DC: Center for Applied Linguistics.

Lemke, J. L. (1982, April). *Classroom communication of science.* Final report of NSF/RISE (ED 22 346).

Leont'ev, A. A. (1979). The problem of activity in psychology. In J. V. Wertsch (Ed.), *The concept of activity in Soviet psychology* (pp. 37–71). Armonk, NY: M. E. Sharpe.

Macnamara, J. (1972). Cognitive basis of language learning in infants. *Psychological Review, 79,* 1–13.

Martin-Jones, M., & Romaine, S. (1986). Semilingualism. A half-baked theory of communicative competence. *Applied Linguistics, 7,* 26–38.

Mehan, H. Learning lessons. (1979). Cambridge, MA: Harvard University Press.

Merton, R. K. (1957). *Social theory and social structure.* New York: Free Press.

Miller, P. J. (1981). *Amy, Wendy, and Beth: A study of early language development in South Baltimore.* Austin: University of Texas Press.

Moerk, E. L. (1983). *The mother of Eve as a first language teacher.* Norwood, NJ: Ablex.

Nelson, K. E. (1984, Spring). *Language acquisition research: Recent searches for the "Right Stuff" in input and the child's mechanisms for analyzing it.* 52–61. American Psychological Association, Division 7 Newsletter.

Nelson, K. E., Denninger, M. M., Bonvillian, J. D., Kaplan, B. J., & Baker, N. (1984). Maternal input adjustments and non-adjustments as related to children's linguistic advances and to language acquisition theories. In A. D. Pellegrinin & T. D. Yawkey (Eds.), *The development of oral and written language in social contexts* (pp. 31–56). Norwood, NJ: Ablex.

Ninio, A., & Bruner, J. (1978). The achievement and antecedents of labeling. *Journal of Child Language, 5,* 1–15.

Ochs, E. (1982). Talking to children in Western Samoa. *Language in Society, 11,* 72–104.

Ochs, E., & Schieffelin, B. B. (in press). Language acquisition and socialization: Three developmental stories and their implications. In R. Shweder & R. LeVine (Eds.), *Culture and its acquisition.*

Pinker, S. (1979). Formal models of language learning. *Cognition, 7,* 217–283.

Schieffelin, B. B. (1979a). *How Kaluli children learn what to say, what to do, and how to feel: An ethnographic study of the development of communicative competence.* Unpublished doctoral dissertation, Columbia University.

Schieffelin, B. B. (1979b). *Getting it together: An ethnographic approach to the study of the development of communicative competence.* In E. Ochs & B. B. Schieffelin (Eds.), *Developmental pragmatics* (pp. 73–108). New York: Academic Press.

Schudson, M. A. (1981). A history of the *Harvard Educational Review.* In J. R. Snarey, T. Epstein, C. Sienkiewicz, & P. Zodhiates (Eds.), *Conflict and continuity: A history of ideas on social equality and human development* (pp. 1–23). Cambridge, MA: *Harvard Educational Review* (Reprint Series Number 15).

Slobin, D. I. (Ed.). (1967). *A field manual for cross-cultural study of the acquisition of communicative competence* (second draft). Berkeley: University of California.

Slobin, D. I. (1982). Universal and particular in the acquisition of language. In L. R. Gleitman & E. Wanner (Eds.), *Language acquisition: State of the art* (pp. 128–170). Cambridge, (Eng.): Cambridge University Press.

Snow, C. E. (1977a). Mothers' speech research: From input to interaction. In C. E. Snow & C. A. Ferguson (Eds.), *Talking to children: Language input and acquisition* (pp. 31–49). New York and Cambridge, Eng.: Cambridge University Press.

Snow, C. E. (1977b). The development of conversation between mothers and babies. *Journal of Child Language, 4*, 1–22.

Snow, C. E. (1983). Literacy and language: Relationships during the preschool years. *Harvard Educational Review, 53*, 165–189.

Vygotsky, L. S. (1962). *Thought and language.* Cambridge: MIT Press.

Watson-Gegeo, D. A., & Gegeo, D. W. (in press-a). The social world of Kwara'ae children: Acquisition of language and values. In J. Cook-Gumperz, W. Corsaro, & J. Streeck (Eds.), *Children's language and children's worlds.* The Hague: Mouton.

Watson-Gegeo, K., & Gegeo, D. W. (in press-b). Calling out and repeating: Two key routines in Kwara'ae children's language socialization. In E. Ochs & B. B. Schieffelin (Eds.), *Language acquisition and socialization across cultures.* New York and Cambridge, England: Cambridge University Press.

Wells, G. (1979). Variation in child language. In P. Fletcher & M. Garman (Eds.), *Studies in language acquisition* (pp. 377–395). Cambridge, (Eng.): Cambridge University Press.

Wells, G. (1980). Apprenticeship in meaning. In K. E. Nelson (Ed.), *Children's language,* (Vol. 2, pp. 45–126). New York: Gardner Press.

Wells, C. G., & Robinson, W. P. (1982). The role of adult speech in language development. In C. Fraser & K. F. Scherer (Eds.), *The social psychology of language* (pp. 11–76). Cambridge, (Eng.): Cambridge University Press.

Wertsch, J. V. (1983). The role of semiosis in L. S. Vygotsky's theory of human cognition. In B. Bain (Ed.), *The sociogenesis of language and human conduct* (pp. 17–31). New York: Plenum Press.

Willes, M. J. (1983). *Children into pupils: A study of language in early schooling.* London & Boston: Routledge & Kegan Paul.

Zinchenko, V. P., & Gordon, V. M. (1979). Methodological problems in the psychological analysis of activity. In J. V. Wertsch (Ed.), *The concept of activity in Soviet psychology* (pp. 72–133). Armonk, NY: M. E. Sharpe.

14 Why Bilinguals?

Kenji Hakuta
University of California, Santa Cruz

As a Sophomore at Harvard College in the fall of 1972, I was certain of my goal in life, but uncertain as to how to achieve it. I had just returned to school after a year off, which I spent performing odd jobs in Japan. Mostly, I spent the year taking advantage of my bilingual skills in English and Japanese. The goal that I envisioned for myself on completion of my Bachelor's degree was to go back to Japan and to go into the English-teaching business, of the Berlitz type. It was (and still is) a lucrative business in Japan. Having grown up in an entrepreneurial family environment, the conditions appeared right, both in terms of market demands and in terms of my skills and dispositions.

It was less clear to me how to build the necessary credentials to start a successful English-teaching enterprise in Japan. I tossed the idea around with my undergraduate advisor, John Marquand, who immediately convinced me that I should begin by unbinding ties with my previously declared major in government. Through mental routes that I cannot reconstruct any more, I wound up with the decision that the best "sales route" for an English-teaching program in Japan would be to claim that it is based on research on how children learn their native language. John Marquand suggested that I look into linguistics and into psychology and social relations as possible majors. He mentioned that a professor named Roger Brown worked in language. I also distinctly recall him trying to remember the name of a professor at MIT, who wrote books about the Vietnam war but who also worked on language. I felt that through the combined study of psychology and linguistics I would find out how children learned language, and that I would be able to dovetail this knowledge into my business career in Japan.

The first course I took in the area of language development was taught by

Donald Olivier. There I was exposed to, among other things, a preprint of Roger Brown's *A First Language*. As an impressionable undergraduate, the feeling of privilege in getting a sneak preview to a yet-to-be-published book (by a Harvard professor) was overwhelming. I read every word carefully, and, as I later found out is true of almost everything that Roger has written, I felt that I had learned not just the information contents of the study described, but a style of thinking and writing as well. In my mind, I reenacted (many times over) the course of the study and the analyses that he and his students had performed.

An opportunity to apply what I had learned from the preprint arrived shortly. For my course project for Don Olivier, I collected spontaneous speech samples from my very own subject. My subject, like Adam, Eve, and Sarah, had the same task ahead of her, namely to learn English. However, unlike Roger's prototypes, my subject (named Uguisu) was 5 years old and was a native speaker of Japanese (the daughter of a visiting scholar family from Japan). I wrote a brief paper for the course, describing the first few samples of her English.

With the school year coming to a close and with Uguisu's English rapidly progressing, I approached Don Olivier for suggestions about how to continue collecting data from my second-language learner. As a student with no money to buy tapes, I wondered whether the department had resources to lend me some tapes. To my amazement, he offered to introduce me to Roger Brown, who might be able to help. I was a bit intimidated by the suggestion because he only existed in my mind as a preprint, which was a comfortable distance. A few days later I received a phone call from a man identifying himself as Roger Brown. He sounded like what I had expected from the preprint. I made an appointment to see him.

On the day of the appointment, I was nervous. His secretary, the unforgettable (late) Esther Sorocka, must have sensed this in me, and she managed to calm me down. By the time I was introduced to Roger Brown, I was ready with my demands. I wanted some cassette tapes and possibly the use of a good quality tape recorder. To my surprise one of the first things he offered was to pay me as a research assistant to continue collecting the data. I had not expected this as within the realm of possibilities. I was stunned but recovered in time to accept the kind offer (but not sufficiently recovered to demand my tapes). After the appointment, I immediately proceeded to resign from my two part-time jobs as a gardener and as a restaurant bus boy. This was the launching of my career in developmental psycholinguistic research. The heat of the excitement of research masked all vestiges of my original goal, of starting an English school in Japan.

The remainder of my undergraduate career was spent following Uguisu and writing up the findings under Roger's guidance (in addition to the support provided by my other mentor, Jill de Villiers, who was then a graduate student). I was tutored through his legendary longhand comments on my papers, comments that addressed not just content but issues of expository style as well. I remember particularly well his advice on how to add dramatic flair, even to the most bland results I obtained.

For graduate school I chose the path of least resistance and remained in the lively, nurturant, safe environment created by Roger at Harvard. I collaborated on some work on first-language acquisition of English with Jill de Villiers and Helen Tager-Flusberg. Although I enjoyed every minute of my work with Jill and Helen, I must admit that working on English L1 acquisition left me unfulfilled in the sense that I was not realizing the full potential of my knowledge of two languages. For example, we were struggling with some hypotheses about English relative clauses (de Villiers, Tager-Flusberg, Hakuta, & Cohen, 1979; Sheldon, 1974), but it was apparent that the competing hypotheses were confounded in English. It occurred to me that Japanese would nicely disentangle such problems. Much of my original research during graduate school thus took me down the road of Japanese L1 acquisition (Hakuta, 1981, 1982a), an effort that Roger categorically applauded. This move did have its drawbacks, such as the fact that I found myself spending a lot of time in graduate school explaining the structure of Japanese to my colleagues and teachers. I succeeded in putting practically the entire faculty to sleep during my dissertation oral examinations. In the United States, there is a certain advantage to the line, "Take any language, say, English. . . ."

For me personally, the legacy of Roger Brown is best captured by his infinitely expansive mind. From his prototypes, Adam, Eve, and Sarah, I created variants: second-language learners and learners of Japanese. He welcomed both of these with open arms (in a way that I suspect he would not have encouraged the cloning of Adam, Eve, and Sarah). As his student, I do not feel constrained to stay within the boundaries of a methodology or area of research in order to obtain his approval. Roger's own research and writings reflect this freedom. To paraphrase, everything from the albino mouse to the American soldier is fair game, as long as it is interesting and informative.

My major change in research emphasis since obtaining my doctorate and taking a job at Yale might be summarized in the following way. The content has shifted, from a specific behavior (language) varying over subjects, to a specific class of subjects (bilinguals) varying over a range of behaviors. I have become interested in creating an integrated picture of bilinguals that is not limited to their linguistic capabilities. How is bilingualism used as a label for political status? What is the cognitive state of a bilingual? What are the social conditions that are overlayed with bilingualism? I am trying to make a case for the problem of bilingualism as an agenda for psychological research; where better a place than in a volume that celebrates the career of a renaissance psychologist?

The importance of understanding the bilingual for society (I hereafter refer both to individuals in the process of becoming bilingual and to those who have achieved some degree of stability in their bilingualism collectively as "bilingual"; "sec-

ond-language learner'' is used for the first group where the distinction is important) is apparent from some simple demographic figures. One estimate in the
United States finds that there were 1,723,000 children between the ages of 5 and
14 enrolled in various instructional programs who were classified as having
"Limited English Proficiency" in 1978 (O'Malley, 1978). If you add to this
number the children who are proficient in English but who nevertheless speak
another language at home, the total grows to 3,097,000. Long-term forecasts
suggest substantial increases in these numbers in the future (Oxford et al., 1980).
Children aside, the number of adult immigrants to the United States is expected to
increase. All these men, women, and children can be considered at risk of unfair
treatment by a generally monolingual American society through, for example,
inadequate educational or employment opportunities.

Bilingualism is hardly a recent phenomenon in the United States (Kloss,
1977), but it has become a prominent issue in the past 20 years through the
combined emergence of ethnic pride and of growing concern that children who
did not speak English at home were lagging behind in school. Various remedies
to the latter problem included "bilingual education" (a misnomer in the sense
that almost all such programs in the United States aim not at maintaining the
child's native language, but rather at assisting in the transition to instruction
conducted solely in English), about which there are more myths and beliefs than
reliable facts. We lack such basic information as how children actually learn
English in these programs, what determines whether they maintain or lose their
first language, and how effective the programs actually are. The extreme tenta-
tiveness of our knowledge is revealed in the vulnerability of bilingual education
policy to arguments by critics whose primary merit appears to be a gift for
rhetoric (Epstein, 1977; Rodriguez, 1982). I say this not as an advocate of
bilingual education (which I am), but rather as a research psychologist frustrated
by the lack of a knowledge base from which to address the issues that the debate
over bilingualism raises.

Bilingualism as an issue is of course not restricted to the United States. The
''guestworker'' situation in Europe has reached explosive proportions. There are
currently an estimated 14 to 15 million such immigrants in Western Europe (Rist,
1979). In West Germany and France, more than 10% of the labor force consists
of foreign workers, mostly from countries in the Mediterranean region. Contrary
to popular belief, primarily for economic reasons these workers have little pros-
pect of returning to their native country. They often bring their families with
them, and the educational problems of their children are a major concern. There
are now 5 million immigrant children in the industrialized Western European
countries (Skutnabb-Kangas, 1978). An estimate for UNESCO by Skutnabb-
Kangas (1978) suggests that "a third of the young European population in the
year 2000 is going to have immigrant background" (p. 228).

To these we must add the mass emigrations produced by war and political upheaval in Southeast Asia and the widely established norms of societal multi-lingualism in much of the world. In much of East Africa, for example, Swahili is the common language that permits communication and some degree of political unity among speakers of a large number of local languages, whereas the colonial language (English) is still used for many official government purposes, such as high court proceedings (Harries, 1976; O'Barr & O'Barr, 1976, pp. 31–136; Polome & Hill, 1980).

The facts just cited serve two purposes. First, they show concretely that bilingualism is a significant social issue. Second, they show that the phenomenon of bilingualism engages a substantial proportion of the population of humans to whom we as psychologists should address our theory and research.

Rather than belabor the question of social relevance, I make the case that the very process of conducting research on bilingualism can shed light on basic issues in psychology. Moreover, this process can lead researchers to an appreciation of the breadth and variety of human behavior, thus helping remedy the prevailing specialization and narrowness in psychology.

The first section that follows provides a brief historical account of the status of research with bilingual subjects in American psychology. In the second section, I focus on trends in developmental psycholinguistics and speculate on the theoretical status of second-language learners in that context. In the third section, evidence is presented to suggest that second-language acquisition in both adults and children is strikingly similar to first-language acquisition. In the fourth section, I suggest some ways in which various specialties might benefit from the inclusion of bilingual subjects in their research. I conclude by arguing that research focused on bilingualism can lead to a more integrated social science.

THE POLITICAL STATUS OF THE BILINGUAL SUBJECT

Tracy Kendler (1950) discusses a statute in Hawaii, passed in 1943, prohibiting the teaching of "foreign" languages (i.e., languages other than English) to children under the age of 10. The statute was based on the belief that "the study and persistent use of foreign languages by children of average intelligence in their early . . . years definitely detract from their ability to understand and assimilate their normal studies in the English language [and] may and do, in many cases, cause serious emotional disturbances, conflicts and maladjustments" (p. 505).

Indeed, many American studies in the early 1900s did obtain results that, on their face, suggested that bilingualism had evil consequences. Typically, such studies compared a group of "bilingual" children with a group of "mono-lingual" children on some psychometric tests of intelligence. The failure of these studies to control for such obvious variables as socioeconomic level and the true "bilinguality" of the children (one study used the child's last name as an indicator of bilingualism!) has made these results difficult to interpret (see Diaz, 1983, for a thorough review). Furthermore, most of the tests were administered in English and were designed for testing monolingual, English-speaking Americans, whereas most of the "bilingual" subjects were children of recent immigrants. Although most current researchers consider these early studies unusable, the findings were consonant enough with prevailing beliefs for their implications to be synthesized and discussed in other social sciences, such as sociology (Shibutani & Kwan, 1965, p. 529).

As these studies suggest, for American psychologists bilingualism has been an issue only in relation to lower socioeconomic groups with educational problems, and so the study of bilingualism was (and by and large still is) associated with remedial efforts. By contrast, the Canadian approach to the study of bilingual children is striking and instructive. Whereas in the United States the problem was to educate minority-language children in the majority language (English), the Canadian problem was to help children of the majority culture (English) achieve functional skills in an increasingly powerful minority language (French). From the conflict perspective in sociology, one can interpret the Canadian situation as an attempt by the majority group to maintain its status in a politically explosive situation by learning the language of the minority (Bratt-Paulston, 1980).

The Canadian work in bilingual education is relatively well known (although frequently misinterpreted) in this country. The Canadian findings, unlike their American analogues, paint a bright and optimistic picture of bilingualism, and in general these findings are supported by recent research conducted with higher scientific standards than the early American efforts (Lambert & Tucker, 1972). One study (Peal & Lambert, 1962) concluded that bilingualism did not interfere with intellectual development but, to the contrary, seemed to be positively related to a general "cognitive flexibility," reflected in a variety of verbal and nonverbal tests that require mental manipulation of a stimulus field. Study of bilingualism has been a respectable and theoretically profitable enterprise in Canadian psychological circles.

Quite frequently, I hear comments like the following: "The Canadian researchers have taken a strong interest in bilingualism because they are faced with the problem." True, Canada has an official policy of bilingualism, but that alone does not explain the research interest. Rather, most researchers in both the United States and Canada are of middle- and upper class origin, and Canadian researchers are tuned in to bilingualism, in my opinion, because it is a problem for their *own* social class. Canadian researchers are confronted with the problem even in their own homes, as their children attempt to struggle with bilingualism (see Lambert, 1967, p. 93, for a point he makes using his daughter as an example). For American researchers, bilingualism is the problem of a social class for whom they have little understanding.

THE THEORETICAL STATUS OF THE BILINGUAL

Social biases aside, there were other confounding reasons why the bilingual individual was of little interest to the American psychologist. Here, I focus on the issue of language acquisition, a research topic to which second-language (L2) acquisition and bilingualism are very germane. There were two reasons that in turn functioned to dispel interest in looking at the second-language learner to understand the human capacity for language.

The standard history of interest in language acquisition in children goes something like this. Up through Chomsky's (1957) revolution in linguistics, studies of language development in children were of two kinds: studies that were intent on establishing age-norms for various "countable" aspects of language, such as vocabulary; and studies that were somewhat eclectic diaries of children's language development, mostly of the researcher's own child (including one by Charles Darwin published in 1877). American psychology under the heavy influence of behaviorism considered verbal behavior no different than other behaviors, one that could be measured and accounted for by familiar variables like response strength and contiguity.

Because the learning of the first language (L1) consisted of forming a set of "habits," the second-language learner had to overcome the first-language habits. Where the two languages differed (grammatically, phonologically, and so forth), difficulties would be encountered, and this was seen to be the major obstacle for the second-language learner. In this sense, L2 learning was very unlike L1 learning. Although L2 learning would be worthwhile studying in its own right for pedagogical purposes, there was no reason why it should yield insights into the nature of L1 learning.

When Chomsky convincingly rejected the simplistic view of language as something like a Markovian process, claiming that it was innate in human beings (a "mental organ"), things changed. The "habit" reason for excluding L2 learners no longer being tenable, biology came into the picture. Most notably, it appeared in the form of Eric Lenneberg's synthesis (1967), and the biological analogy was adopted into some descriptions of children's language. Brown and Bellugi-Klima (1964) wrote: "the very intricate simultaneous differentiation and integration that constitutes the evolution of the noun phrase (in children) is more reminiscent of the biological development of an embryo than it is of the acquisition of a conditional reflex" (p. 150). If language acquisition is considered a biological process bounded by maturational factors (the upper bound being at puberty), the implication is that L2 acquisition would involve a different process. Lenneberg claimed, for example, that a second language is learned by resorting to the language skills acquired in childhood (p. 176).

For the social reasons outlined in the first section of this chapter and the theoretical considerations (the habit account and the maturational account) mentioned here, the L2 learner elicited little interest among psychologists. Most data on L2 learning come from research conducted by applied linguists interested in teaching, but their findings suggest that psycholinguists would do well to study the L2 learner, perhaps with improvements in research methodology.

Is the Second-Language Learner So Different?

Roger Brown (1973a) proposed that the errors made by adult L2 learners be compared with those made by child L1 learners. He did so while suggesting that second-language acquisition among adults might be subject to more traditional learning processes than the seemingly "automatic" acquisition of a first language by children.

The answers to his question already existed, but not in a literature traditionally read by psychologists. An active subfield of applied linguistics is "error analysis," in which the systematic deviations from target language norms observed in the learner are classified by their hypothesized source (Corder, 1967, 1971). One robust finding from this area, which spans errors made by adults as well as children, and in both formal and informal learning environments, is that the kinds of errors made by L2 learners are strikingly similar to those reported for L1 children. The most common errors are those of simplification, such as omission of noun and verb inflections, and overregularization, e.g., using the regular past-tense ending in English for irregular verbs (Dulay & Burt, 1973, 1974; Duskova, 1969; Politzer & Ramirez, 1973).

The discovery that the overwhelming majority of errors are shared by L1 and L2 learners led to the abandonment of an almost axiomatic belief of applied linguists, stated by Charles Ferguson, that "one of the major problems in the learning of a second language is the interference caused by the structural differences between the native language of the learner and the second language" (Preface to Stockwell, Bowen, & Martin, 1965; p. v), an approach called *contrastive analysis*. Errors of transfer from the native language, whereas extremely interesting in their own right, turned out to be quite infrequent. Rather, regardless of one's native language, L2 acquisition seemed to proceed in its own systematic way.

This conclusion was supported both by studies pointing to similarities in error types and by studies that compared the overall patterns of development, such as specific structures that were analyzed in detail. In addition, even the dissimilarities did not appear to derive from negative transfer from the native language. For example, a number of studies now exist that look at the "order of acquisition" of grammatical morphemes, generally following the procedures set by Brown (1973b) for L1 learners. The general conclusion of these studies is that the order for L2 learners is different from that of L1 learners, but that it is the same for L2 learners of different native-language backgrounds. In addition, the same order is observed for both child and adult L2 learners. This matrix of findings suggests that, whereas L2 acquisition may not always recapitulate the exact sequence of L1 acquisition, the process in large part excludes interference from the native language.

To assert the similarities between L1 and L2 acquisition is not to claim they are identical. Nor do I mean to imply that there is no transfer from the native language. Transfer errors, when found, are extremely interesting and useful for theory building (Hakuta & Cancino, 1977). So are some apparent differences in L1 and L2 learners, such as the fact that L2 learners in their initial stages of learning use a large number of "prefabricated" or "formulaic" utterances that have no internal structure but are used in social interaction (Hakuta, 1974; Wong-Fillmore, 1979). A simple example of this is a tourist's memorizing a sentence from a phrase book ("Can you tell me where the station is?") without understanding what the individual words mean. These prefabrications are also used by L1 learners (Clark, 1974), but less extensively than by L2 learners. This difference suggests that there are social-context differences in the two processes, which may prove to be important. Nevertheless, the end products are the same. Both sets of learners must crack the linguistic code of their target language (Macnamara, 1976).

Lenneberg's (1967) somewhat offhand remark, that "automatic acquisition from mere exposure to a given language seems to disappear (after puberty)" (p. 176) must be rejected. At present, the evidence is overwhelming that there are no *categorical* changes in the capacity for L2 learning at puberty, which would be predicted by a maturational argument. Rather, although there appears to be a gradual decline in ultimate attainment with increasing age, the decline appears to be linear (Oyama, 1976, 1978; Patkowski, 1980). In addition, there is some evidence indicating that older children and adults learn a second language at a faster rate, with the possible exception of accent, than younger children (Snow & Hoefnagel-Hohle, 1978; Krashen, Long, & Scarcella, 1979), although the evidence is inevitably confounded with age-related changes in test-taking ability (see Hakuta, 1983). Also, the critical-period hypothesis leaves unexplained the similarities, such as in the kinds of errors made, that are in fact found between prepubescent and postpubescent second-language learners.

Taken together, recent findings suggest that there are many parallels between L1 and L2 acquisition, and that the best working hypothesis is that the two processes are similar in most respects, a view espoused by a number of researchers (Dulay & Burt, 1974; Ervin-Tripp, 1974; Macnamara, 1976). This is a remarkable conclusion if one believes (as most people do) that the cognitive systems of children and adults are different. It is not as surprising if one believes that language acquisition is relatively autonomous from the general conceptual system. In any event, the study of the second-language learner will highlight important issues in developmental psycholinguistics.

In the remainder of this chapter, I discuss some implications that including the L2 learner in the pool of legitimate subjects for psychological research will have for various domains of the general discipline. These suggestions are intended only to open various lines of inquiry, not to exhaust them.

DEVELOPMENTAL PSYCHOLOGY

A major endeavor of developmental psychology is to arrive at age-independent descriptions of change in particular domains of mind and behavior; that is, one hopes to characterize development not in terms of a particular child's age, but rather in terms of the kinds of changes in different processes that take place over time. Piaget's description of the development of symbolic activities into logicomathematical structures is a good example.

One problem in achieving such descriptions without regard to age is that, in the developing child, many of the relevant variables are correlated with age. There are age-related changes in memory, perception, conceptual structure, social cognition, and language, to mention but a few. When it comes time for explanation, it is easy to attribute the observed changes in a particular domain to any of these variables. I have in mind such controversies as the debate between Chomskyan and Piagetian views on the nature of the relationship between language and general cognitive development (Piatelli-Palmarini, 1980). Within developmental psycholinguistics, this controversy is reflected in the numerous attempts in the 1970s to explain away language acquisition on the basis of cognitive development (Beilin, 1976; Cromer, 1974; Macnamara, 1972; Slobin, 1973).

An advantage of looking at second-language learners is that one can look at language acquisition apart from cognitive development. If we find in the cognitively mature L2 learner the same kinds of things we find in L1 learners, it becomes difficult to attribute the findings to cognitive development alone. At the same time, we will probably find dissimilarities in the L2 data that support the cognitive development hypothesis. As examples of the first possibility, there is evidence suggesting that L2 learners process passives (Ervin-Tripp, 1974), interrogatives (Ravem, 1968), relative clauses (Gass & Ard, 1980), and complex complementizer structures (d'Anglejan & Tucker, 1975) in much the same way as L1 children. In Ervin-Tripp's study, subjects were English-speaking children learning French in France. Ravem's was a case study of his 5-year-old Norwegian-speaking son learning English. Gass and Ard's study involved adults of various native-language backgrounds enrolled in English-language courses at the University of Michigan. D'Anglejan and Tucker looked at Francophone military personnel attending an English language course at an army base. In my opinion, these are widely different groups from which a consistent pattern of results has emerged.

The second possibility, that we can attribute many L1 findings to cognitive development, is illustrated by Lightbown's (1977) analysis of the semantic relations expressed in the early stages of L2 acquisition in children. She found that they were not limited to the kinds of relations reported in L1 children (outlined by Bloom, 1970, and summarized in Brown, 1973b, including meanings such as agent–action, attribute–entity, and possessor–possessed), which suggests that L1 children are limited by their cognitive repertoire. In addition, there are good indications that the emergence of sentence coordination (propositions joined by conjunctions such as *and, because,* and *if*) in L1 children is constrained by conceptual or processing-capacity limitations (Bloom, Lahey, Hood, Lifter, & Fiess, 1980): Such structures appear in the earliest stages of L2 acquisition (Hakuta, 1982b).

The number of studies is still quite limited (see Hatch, 1978, for a collection of major studies), but they suffice to indicate that studying the L2 learner will help us separate the respective roles of cognitive developmental factors and linguistically unique factors in the acquisition of language.

A stirring of interest in bilingualism might also enliven some new areas in the emerging study of developmental psychology from the life-span perspective. Carol Ryff (personal communication) points out that many of the older subjects she has interviewed in her own studies are bilingual. Because of the successive waves of immigration to the United States, the same would probably be true of most samples of elderly Americans, yet Ryff notes that bilingualism is a term unfamiliar to life-span psychologists. Because changes in the linguistic circumstances of an individual are related in many cases to other major life changes, some problems addressed by life-span psychologists might be productively articulated in terms of language acquisition as an anchor point in a life history; this would of course be more relevant in some populations than in others. Correlations of language with life change may involve immigration to a culture speaking a different language, marriage to a spouse whose native language is different (see Sorenson, 1967 for an anthropological account of a culture where this is the norm), and offspring who bring home a second language, as in the case of Hispanic children in the United States who bring home English as they become more dominant in that language through schools. These instances would sharply delineate issues such as adjustment to changes primarily beyond one's control, shared values with one's intimates, and the intrusion by society into family dynamics. Because language is symbolic of an individual's identity (Guiora, Brannon, & Dull, 1972; Nida, 1971), there are rather broad implications for the study of humans from the life-course perspective. Conversely, the study of second-language acquisition can gain perspective from typological frameworks being developed by life-span psychologists for life events, where events are classified by properties such as the degree of correlation with age and the expected probability of their occurrence (Brim & Ryff, 1980).

COGNITIVE PSYCHOLOGY

The current trend in cognitive psychology, unlikely to diminish for some time, is information representation and information processing. Recent theories suggest a useful distinction between automatic and controlled processing in attentional and perceptual learning mechanisms (Schneider & Shiffrin, 1977; Shiffrin & Schneider, 1977), which fits well with intuitions about second-language acquisition (McLaughlin, Rossman, & McLeod, 1983); that is, certain tasks and abilities in processing a second language can be seen as involving differential levels of automaticity. In addition, more advanced levels of proficiency in the language should be associated with increased automaticity in processing. For example, McLaughlin et al. report a study by Hatch, Polin, and Part (1970) in which native and non-native speakers of English (all university-level students) were asked to cross out specific letters in a text. As expected, there were differences in the detection of the letters in function and content words among the native speakers, with more errors in the (relatively automatic) function words. However, there were no differences in the two classes of words for non-native speakers. McLaughlin et al. also refer to unpublished studies in which *greater* proficiency in a second language is associated with *lesser* ability to detect changes in the form (but not the meaning) of the sentences (Rossman, 1981; Wolfe, 1981).

These results suggest interesting studies that might be conducted with L2 learners, mapping out the covariation between proficiency in the second language and areas of language showing automaticity. The information that can be obtained from such research is analogous to what might be obtained were such research possible with young children acquiring their native language; namely, one hopes to uncover the bedrock of linguistic components that can predict language comprehension and production. The advantage here is that adults are much better subjects for the kinds of tasks that cognitive psychologists require than are children who have weaker motivation, a shorter attention span, and so forth.

Inclusion of the second-language learner in the company of legitimate subjects might illuminate another area of cognitive psychology (leaning more toward the "cognitive science" end of the spectrum), which is the application of learnability theory (e.g., Wexler & Culicover, 1980) to language acquisition (Pinker, 1979, in press). This approach is rather theory heavy, attempting to formally derive the properties of language (typically English) and relate these to the properties that would be required on the part of the learner in order for the language to be learnable. Many of the critical tests of the theories are based on supposed linguistic constraints that are for all practical purposes untestable with children (see attempts to look for evidence of formal linguistic constraints using children as subjects in Tavakolian, 1981). Such testing can be done with L2-learning adults, and on the basis of reasonable assumptions about the similarity of subject populations, results can be related to L1 acquisition.

Partly in response to Neisser's (1976) call for ecological validity, cognitive psychology has in recent years begun a quest for relevance, as shown by the publicly expressed interests in such applied issues as memory processes in the aged by mainstream researchers (e.g., Craik, 1977, 1983). As can be seen in Craik's work, such interests may even lead to "mainstream" insights, such as support for the notion that one should look at memory not as a sequential series of processes, but rather as the differential recruitment of various capacities that depend quite heavily on situational demands. Cognitive psychology would do well to consider the benefits of studying the second-language learner, the more so because "language" as a complex skill is relatively well defined and certainly more ecologically valid than random digits, consonants, and dot patterns.

SOCIAL AND PERSONALITY PSYCHOLOGY

Owing much to Kurt Lewin, American social psychology has been responsive to the values of society, as reflected in studies of ethnocentrism, stereotyping, race relations, and even international conflict resolution. Investigation of personality and social psychological variables in second-language learning would be of great importance, especially in controverting the misguided belief in a biologically based critical period for second-language acquisition (with the possible exception of accent). It is in these variables, not biological maturation, that we will find the most useful explanations of the differential capacity for second-language acquisition.

One exciting area that can be explored in the second-language learner is the relationship among personality, attitudes, and behavior. In Canada, much interesting work has been done by Robert Gardner and Wallace Lambert (1972) to assess the relationship between attitudes of English-speaking high school students toward speakers of the target language (French) and the extent to which they learn the second language. They have shown in a series of studies, with some replications in the United States with English-speaking high school students, that there is a low but stable correlation (usually somewhere between .30 and .40) between responses on attitudinal scales and performance in measures of various aspects of the second language.

Moreover, in most cases the correlation between second-language learning and attitude is statistically independent of the correlation (around .40) found between second-language performance and measures of language aptitude, such as the Modern Language Aptitude Test (Carroll & Sapon, 1959), which correlates highly with standard tests of general verbal intelligence. Other individual difference variables, such as those studied by personality psychologists, have received limited attention although the results that have been reported look promising. For example, Naiman, Frohlich, and Stern (1975) report significant correlations between cognitive style variables and differential ability in foreign-language learning in high school students. It may turn out that second-language learners provide an ideal laboratory population in which to study the relative contributions of social and personality variables as predictors of behavior.

One reason for this is the robustness of the behavior in question, namely language. William Labov (1966) showed a number of years ago how strong a social marker language is. One can practically reconstruct the social stratification of a city from language data alone. The point of relevance here is that degree of second-language acquisition (and there is considerable variation across individuals) is easily and reliably measured and reflects and varies predictably with a rather broad range of social interactional contexts. Sociolinguistic research (see Fishman, Cooper, & Ma, 1971) has uncovered differential language use by functional social domains, such as home, work, and religion. Such sociological categories might be useful to the social psychologist.

CROSS-CULTURAL PSYCHOLOGY

Many would not consider ''cross-cultural psychology'' to be a traditional area of study, but I include it to underscore what is perhaps the most important contribution the study of second-language learners would make to psychology: It will of necessity force on us a cross-cultural psychology.

The obvious reason is that second-language learners are necessarily becoming bicultural (to varying extents), and an account of their repertoire of behavior will include how they handle and manage two cultural ''systems.'' As a psycholinguist, I can testify that American psycholinguists act almost as if English were the only language in existence. Properties about ''language'' are posited on the basis of the study of English speakers alone. Similar arguments can be made for other areas of psychology; my only point here is that the second-language learner, by virtue of forcing a consideration of cross-cultural issues, will keep us honest in limiting our generalizations to the appropriate population.

INTERDISCIPLINARY PROSPECTS

The research activities of social scientists might be broadly classified as either ''theory-driven'' or ''subject-driven'' work. This simpleminded distinction is meant to point up the ways research topics are chosen, with the choice depending on whether the researcher's main emphasis is on theory testing and elaboration or on understanding a population that is of special interest for practical or personal reasons. The choice of subjects in theory-driven research is largely determined by a convenience criterion, be it control of extraneous factors (pure genetic strains in laboratory animals), easy availability (college sophomores in an introductory psychology course), or the performance of ''critical tests'' of specific hypotheses (using an established experimental paradigm with abnormal subjects, such as aphasics). This is in contrast to subject-driven research, where one tries to relate a specific subject population to whatever relevant theories are available to provide insightful accounts of interesting subject characteristics. Research on the second-language learner and bilingual falls in the latter category.

Measured in terms of academic prestige, theory-driven research wins. This is because theory-driven research generally is associated with "pure" research, subject-driven with "applied." At this point in the history of the social sciences, however, it seems more important to judge the value of research on the basis of its ability to integrate different areas of work. Compartmentalization and specialization (even within the subdomains of psychology) have led to minitheories explaining phenomena that at best may generalize to situations outside the laboratory, but that have scant hope of proving relevant to other minitheories. Because it is beyond our imagination how a theoretically tight system of the social sciences might be achieved (encompassing emotional and cognitive processes within an individual within multiple levels of social structure within macropolitical structures), a theoretical midwife is needed, which arrives in the form of subject-driven research.

The study of second-language learners, in individual psychological processes and in sociological and political ones (Fishman's seminal works should be consulted here), can be seen as a special case of such subject-driven research. Eclectic attempts to account for the multifaceted aspects of bilingualism may not directly lead to an integrated theoretical perspective (which is why it is a midwife), but it will help set the stage for the dissolution of the artificial boundaries created by the specialization of psychology.

In concluding, I suggest a few integrative questions that could be answered by applying ourselves to second-language learners and bilinguals. References to some relevant (though not necessarily integrative) works are cited.

1. How does bilingualism affect cognitive functioning quantitatively and qualitatively, and does the effect vary with individual difference variables (e.g., age, "intelligence"), and with group variables (e.g., societal values placed on bilingualism; Cummins, 1976; Hakuta & Diaz, in press; Lambert, 1978; Peal & Lambert, 1962)?

2. How are the two languages of the bilingual related to the social-interactional domains in which they are differentially used? How are they integrated within the cognitive system of the individual (Albert & Obler, 1978; Ervin & Osgood, 1954)? On the societal level, how are the two languages influenced by the political processes frequently reflected in language boundaries (Blom & Gumperz, 1972; Fishman, 1978; Hymes, 1972; O'Barr & O'Barr, 1976; Schermerhorn, 1970)?

3. How is the human capacity to acquire language related to adult develop-

ment and aging? Is the change in capacity best seen as the result of gradual cognitive decrements, such as loss of memory capacities, or as the result of affective/social changes in the course of the human life span (Krashen, Scarcella, & Long, 1982; Schumann, 1975)?

4. How do linguistic structures interact in the mind of the bilingual? Can these effects be understood using linguistic models from language typology and universals (e.g., Comrie, 1981; Greenberg, 1978), in such a way that the psychological reality of linguistic parameters can be verified (Hakuta, in press)?

Each set of questions offers a focus for the interaction of different social science domains. The answers will require the recruitment of knowledge and methodology from the areas of psychology mentioned in this chapter, and additionally, from anthropology, sociology, political science, and linguistics. I do not hesitate to make such a bold statement that advocates a form of (subject-)guided eclecticism, in part, because as a role model Roger Brown has shown me that it is the questions you ask that matter, not particular methodologies constrained by such formalities as dean's categories and professional associations. And in the case of bilingualism, you end up having to go all over the place.

ACKNOWLEDGMENTS

Much of the discussion contained in this chapter was conceptualized during my year as a Fellow at the Center for Advanced Study in the Behavioral Sciences, Stanford, California. I would like to acknowledge support from the Exxon Education Foundation, the Alfred P. Sloan Foundation, and the Spencer Foundation during the fellowship year. Preparation of the manuscript was supported in part by NIE-G-81-0123 from the National Institute of Education to the author. Many colleagues provided thoughtful comments on this manuscript, including Muriel Bell, Lois Bloom, Fergus Craik, Nancy Goodban, Carl Kaestle, David Kenny, David Leary, Carol Ryff, Nancy Stein, Harold Stevenson, and Jim Stigler.

REFERENCES

Albert, M., & Obler, L. (1978). *The bilingual brain*. New York: Academic Press.
Beilin, H. (1976). *The cognitive basis of language development*. New York: Academic Press.
Blom, J., & Gumperz, J. (1972). Social meaning in linguistic structures: code-switching in Norway. In J. Gumperz & D. Hymes (Eds.), *Directions in sociolinguistics*. New York: Holt, Rinehart, & Winston.
Bloom, L. (1970). *Language development: Form and function in emerging grammars*. Cambridge, MA: MIT Press.
Bloom, L., Lahey, M., Hood, L., Lifter, K., & Fiess, K. (1980). Complex sentences: Acquisition of syntactic connectives and the semantic relations they encode. *Journal of Child Language, 7,* 235–262.

Bratt-Paulston, C. (1980). *Bilingual education: Theories and issues.* Rowley, MA: Newbury House Publishers.

Brim, O., & Ryff, C. (1980). On properties of life events. In P. Baltes & O. Brim (Eds.), *Life-span development and behavior* (Vol. 3). New York: Academic Press.

Brown, R. (1973a). Development of the first language in the human species. *American Psychologist, 28,* 97–102.

Brown, R. (1973b). *A first language.* Cambridge, MA: Harvard University Press.

Brown, R., & Bellugi-Klima, U. (1964). Three processes in the child's acquisition of syntax. *Harvard Educational Review, 34,* 133–151.

The Carroll-Sapon Modern Language Aptitude Test (MLAT). (1959). New York: Psychological Corporation.

Chomsky, N. (1957). *Syntactic structures.* The Hague: Mouton.

Clark, R. (1974). Performing without competence. *Journal of Child Language, 1,* 1–10.

Comrie, B. (1981). *Language universals and linguistic typology.* Chicago: University of Chicago Press.

Corder, S. P. (1967). The significance of learners' errors. *International Review of Applied Linguistics, 5,* 161–170.

Corder, S. P. (1971). Idiosyncratic dialects and error analysis. *International Review of Applied Linguistics, 9,* 147–160.

Craik, F. I. M. (1977). Age differences in human memory. In J. E. Birren & K. W. Schaie (Eds.), *Handbook of the psychology of aging.* New York: Van Nostrand Reinhold.

Craik, F. I. M. (1983). Age differences in remembering. In N. Butters & L. Squire (Eds.), *The neuropsychology of memory.* New York: The Guilford Press.

Cromer, R. (1974). The development of language and cognition: The cognition hypothesis. In B. Foss (Ed.), *New perspectives in child development.* Harmondsworth, England: Penguin Books.

Cummins, J. (1976). The influence of bilingualism on cognitive growth: A synthesis of research findings and explanatory hypothesis. *Working Papers on Bilingualism, 9,* 1–43.

d'Anglejan, A., & Tucker, G. R. (1975). The acquisition of complex English structures by adult learners. *Language Learning, 25,* 281–296.

Darwin, C. (1877). A biographical sketch of an infant. *Mind, 2,* 292–294.

de Villiers, J., Tager Flusberg, H., Hakuta, K., & Cohen, M. (1979). Children's comprehension of relative clauses. *Journal of Psycholinguistic Research, 8,* 499–518.

Diaz, R. (1983). Thought and two languages: The impact of bilingualism on cognitive development. *Review of Research in Education, 10,* 23–54.

Dulay, H., & Burt, M. (1973). Should we teach children syntax? *Language Learning, 23,* 245–258.

Dulay, H., & Burt, M. (1974). Natural sequences in child second-language acquisition. *Language Learning, 24,* 37–53.

Duskova, L. (1969). On sources of errors in foreign languages. *International Review of Applied Linguistics, 7,* 11–36.

Epstein, N. (1979). *Language, ethnicity, and the schools.* Washington, DC: Institute of Educational Leadership.

Ervin-Tripp, S. (1974). Is second-language learning like the first? *TESOL Quarterly, 8,* 111–127.

Ervin, S., & Osgood, C. (1954). Second-language learning and bilingualism. *Journal of Abnormal and Social Psychology, 49,* 139–146.

Fishman, J. (1966). *Language loyalty in the United States.* The Hague: Mouton.

Fishman, J. (Ed.). (1978). *Advances in the study of societal multilingualism.* The Hague: Mouton.

Fishman, J., Cooper, R., & Ma, R. (1971). *Bilingualism in the barrio.* Bloomington: Indiana University Research Center for the Language Sciences.

Gardner, R., & Lambert, W. E. (1972). *Attitudes and motivation in second-language learning.* Rowley, MA: Newbury House Publishers.

Gass, S., & Ard, J. (1980, March). *L2 data: Their relevance of language universals.* Paper presented to the Teachers of English to Speakers of Other Languages Convention, San Francisco.

Greenberg, J. (Ed.). (1978). *Universals of human language* (Vols. 1–4). Stanford, CA: Stanford University Press.

Guiora, A. Z., Brannon, R., & Dull, C. (1972). Empathy and second language learning. *Language Learning, 22,* 111–130.

Hakuta, K. (1974). Prefabricated patterns and the emergence of structure in second language acquisition. *Language Learning, 24,* 287–297.

Hakuta, K. (1981). Grammatical description versus configurational arrangement in language acquisition: The case of relative clauses in Japanese. *Cognition, 9,* 197–236.

Hakuta, K. (1982a). Interaction between particles and word order in the comprehension and production of simple sentences in Japanese children. *Developmental Psychology, 18,* 62–76.

Hakuta, K. (1982b, June 25–26). *The second language learner in the context of the study of language acquisition.* Paper presented at the Society for Research in Child Development Conference on Bilingualism and Childhood Development, New York University.

Hakuta, K. (1983). English language acquisition by speakers of Asian languages. In M. Chu Chang (Ed.), *Comparative research in bilingual education.* New York: Teachers College Press.

Hakuta, K. (in press). In what ways are language universals psychologically real? In W. Rutherford & R. Scarcella (Eds.), *Typological studies in language, Vol. 6: Language universals and second-language acquisition.* Amsterdam: John Benjamins.

Hakuta, K., & Cancino, H. (1977). Trends in second-language-acquisition research. *Harvard Educational Review, 47,* 294–316.

Hakuta, K., & Diaz, R. (in press). The relationship between degree of bilingualism and cognitive ability: A critical discussion and some new longitudinal data. In K. E. Nelson (Ed.), *Children's language* (Vol. 5). Hillsdale, NJ: Lawrence Erlbaum Associates.

Harries, L. (1976). The nationalization of Swahili in Kenya. *Language in Society, 5,* 153–164.

Hatch, E. (Ed.). (1978). *Second-language acquisition: A book of readings.* Rowley, MA: Newbury House Publishers.

Hatch, E., Polin, P., & Part, S. (1970). *Acoustic scanning or syntactic processing.* Paper presented at the Western Psychological Association, San Francisco.

Hymes, D. (1972). Models of the interaction of language and social life. In J. Gumperz & D. Hymes (Eds.), *Directions in sociolinguistics.* New York: Holt, Rinehart, & Winston.

Kendler, T. (1950). Contributions of the psychologist to constitutional law. *American Psychologist, 5,* 505–510.

Kloss, H. (1977). *The American bilingual tradition.* Rowley, MA: Newbury House Publishers.

Krashen, S., Long, M., & Scarcella, R. (1979). Accounting for child–adult differences in second-language rate and attainment. *TESOL Quarterly, 13,* 573–582.

Krashen, S., Scarcella, R., & Long, M. (Eds.). (1982). *Child–adult differences in second-language acquisition.* Rowley, MA: Newbury House Publishers.

Labov, W. (1966). *The social stratification of English in New York City.* Washington, DC: Center for Applied Linguistics.

Lambert, W. E. (1967). A social psychology of bilingualism. *Journal of Social Issues, 23,* 91–109.

Lambert, W. E. (1978). Some cognitive and sociocultural consequences of being bilingual. In J. Alatis (Ed.), *International dimensions of bilingual education.* Washington, DC: Georgetown University Press.

Lambert, W. E., & Tucker, G. R. (1972). *Bilingual education of children: The St. Lambert Experiment.* Rowley, MA: Newbury House Publishers.

Lenneberg, E. (1967). *Biological foundations of language.* New York: Wiley.

Leopold, W. (1939). *Speech development of a bilingual child* (Vol. I). Chicago: Northwestern University Press.

Lightbown, P. (1977, June). *French L2 learners: What they're talking about.* Paper presented at the First Los Angeles Second Language Research Forum, UCLA.

Macnamara, J. (1972). Cognitive basis of language learning in infants. *Psychological Review, 79,* 1–14.

Macnamara, J. (1976). Comparison between first- and second-language learning. *Die Neueren Sprachen, 2,* 175–188.

McLaughlin, B., Rossman, T., & McLeod, B. (1983). *Second-language learning: An information-processing perspective.* Unpublished manuscript, Department of Psychology, University of California, Santa Cruz.

Naiman, N., Frohlich, M., & Stern, H. H. (1975, December). *The good language learner.* Modern Language Centre, The Ontario Institute for Studies in Education.

Neisser, U. (1976). *Cognition and reality.* San Francisco: W. H. Freeman.

Nida, E. (1971). Sociopsychological problems in language mastery and retention. In P. Pinsleur & T. Quinn (Eds.), *The psychology of second language learning.* Cambridge, England: Cambridge University Press.

O'Barr, W., & O'Barr, J. (Eds.). (1976). *Language and politics.* The Hague: Mouton.

O'Malley, J. M. (1978). *Children's English and services study.* Rosslyn, VA: InterAmerica Research Associates.

Oxford, R., Pol, L., Lopez, D., Stupp, P., Peng, S., & Gendell, M. (1980, October). *Projections of non-English language background and limited English proficiency persons in the United States to the year 2000.* National Center for Education Statistics (U. S. Department of Education) Contract OE 300-79-0737 to InterAmerica Research Associates.

Oyama, S. (1976). A sensitive period for the acquisition of a nonnative phonological system. *Journal of Psycholinguistic Research, 5,* 261–285.

Oyama, S. (1978). The sensitive period and comprehension of speech. *Working Papers on Bilingualism, 16,* 1–17.

Peal, E., & Lambert, W. E. (1962). The relation of bilingualism to intelligence. *Psychological Monographs, 76,* 1–23.

Piatelli-Palmarini, M. (Ed.). (1980). *Language and learning: The debate between Jean Piaget and Noam Chomsky.* Cambridge, MA: Harvard University Press.

Pinker, S. (1979). Formal models of language learning. *Cognition, 7,* 217–283.

Pinker, S. (in press). Language learnability and children's language: A multi-faceted approach. In K. E. Nelson (Ed.), *Children's language* (Vol. 5). Hillsdale, NJ: Erlbaum Associates.

Politzer, R., & Ramirez, Lawrence A. (1973). An error analysis of the spoken English of Mexican-American pupils in a bilingual school and a monolingual school. *Language Learning, 23,* 39–61.

Polome, E., & Hill, C. (1980). *Language in Tanzania.* Oxford: Oxford University Press.

Ravem, R. (1968). Language acquisition in a second-language environment. *International Review of Applied Linguistics, 6,* 175–185.

Rist, R. (1979). Migration and marginality: Guestworkers in Germany and France. *Daedalus.*

Rodriguez, R. (1982). Hunger of memory: The education of Richard Rodriguez. Boston: Godine.

Rossman, T. (1981). *The nature of linguistic processing in reading a second language.* Unpublished masters thesis, Concordia University, Montreal.

Schermerhorn, R. (1970). *Comparative ethnic relations: A framework for theory and research.* Chicago: University of Chicago Press.

Schneider, W., & Shiffrin, R. (1977). Controlled and automatic human information processing: I. Detection, search, and attention. *Psychological Review, 84,* 1–66.

Schumann, J. (1975). Affective factors and the problem of age in second-language acquisition. *Language Learning, 25,* 209–235.

Sheldon, A. (1974). The role of parallel function in the acquisition of relative clauses in English. *Journal of Verbal Learning and Verbal Behavior, 13,* 272–281.

Shibutani, T., & Kwan, K. (1965). *Ethnic stratification: A comparative approach.* New York: Macmillan.

Shiffrin, R., & Schneider, W. (1977). Controlled and automatic human information processing. II. Perceptual learning, automatic attending, and a general theory. *Psychological Review, 84,* 127–190.

Skutnabb-Kangas, T. (1978). Semilingualism and the education of minority children as a means of reproducing the caste of assembly line workers. In N. Dittmar, H. Haberland, T. Skutnabb-Kangas, & Ulf Teleman (Eds.), *Papers from the First Scandinavian-German Symposium on the language of immigrant workers and their children.* Roskilde, Denmark: Roskilde University.

Slobin, D. I. (1973). Cognitive prerequisites for the development of grammar. In C. A. Ferguson & D. I. Slobin (Eds.), *Studies in child language development.* New York: Holt, Rinehart, & Winston.

Snow, C., & Hoefnagel-Hohle, M. (1978). The critical period for language acquisition: Evidence from second-language learning. *Child Development, 49,* 1114–1128.

Sorensen, A. P. (1967). Multilingualism in the Northwest Amazon. *American Anthropologist, 69,* 670–684.

Stockwell, R., Bowen, D., & Martin, J. (1965). *The grammatical structures of English and Spanish.* Chicago: Univesity of Chicago Press.

Tavakolian, S. (Ed.). (1981). *Language acquisition and linguistic theory.* Cambridge, MA: MIT Press.

Wexler, K., & Culicover, P. (1980). *Formal principles of language acquisition.* Cambridge, MA: MIT Press.

Wolfe, S. (1981). *Bilingualism: One or two conceptual systems.* Unpublished masters thesis, San Francisco State University.

Wong-Fillmore, L. (1979). Individual differences in second-language acquisition. In C. Fillmore, D. Kempler, & W. Wang (Eds.), *Individual differences in language ability and language behavior.* New York: Academic Press.

15 Language and the Evolution of Identity and Self-Concept

Lerita M. Coleman
University of Tennessee

> *"In spite of the fact that language acts as a socializing and uniforming force, it is at the same time the most potent known factor for the growth of individuality"*
>
> —Sapir 1951, p. 7.

Social psychologists interested in language and nonverbal communication are increasing as the discipline moves toward integrating these topics into studies of more traditional social psychological areas (e.g., identity formation and change, socialization, group processes, social cognition, and development of the self). My exposure to and fascination with language are due to the influence and careful guidance of Roger Brown. Roger's early scholarly inquiries in social psychology reflect his astute insights about language; his perceptions of how language acts as agent of social stratification, social change, and socialization. His initial work also is indicative of his formal training in social psychology. Although Roger has devoted his recent research to developmental psycholinguistics, his influence on my studies of social psychology has been substantial. In many ways, my goals in studying social psychology and language have been similar to those of most psycholinguists: to understand the relation between language and development.

I have always sensed that there was a connection between who I am and how I express myself. I realized that how people interact with me, the language and topics they select, what they choose to disclose or not disclose, and how they express themselves when interacting with me communicates something to me about who I am and, more specifically, who I am relative to them. I have

319

observed the progressive modifications in language as my social status has changed from undergraduate to professor. Similarly, I have noted the contrast between comments I receive from strangers who react solely to my physical appearance with the responses of people who have been introduced to "Dr. Coleman."

These observations intimated to me that language is instrumental in the development and maintenance of identity and self-concept by facilitating life-cycle transitions: moving people like myself from infancy to childhood, from adolescence to young adulthood, from student to "professional." Further, I noticed that language was not acting alone but in concert with other communicative channels such as facial expressions, gestures, and kinesics, on my part as well as on others to reveal to me an identity and a self.

Like most researchers, I was driven in part by intellectual curiosity to understand how social psychological phenomena like language and nonverbal communication have made me a product of my African and American heritages while concurrently creating a unique individual. How does language shape identity and assist in sculpturing a self? Is the process a single, continuous one, or are there a variety of ways in which language interacts with identity and self-concept? Given what seems to be the inherent socializing power of language, how does individuality arise? These were the primary questions that piqued my interest in language and social psychology and continue to stimulate my desire to learn more.

Of the many topics within the general area of social psychology and language, I believe a review of pronoun use and address forms, language and assimilation, the social psychology of second-language learning, as well as a review of some segments of my own research on marking social distance in discourse best exemplify the role of language in the development of identity and self-concept. Although the social psychology of language contains a wealth of subject matters, these topics provide many examples of the potency of language in personal development and suggest two models. One model focuses on the socializing function of language through social interactions, and the other model centers on the creation and expression of different identities and selves in different languages and dialects. In addition, these models offer some ideas for expanding the scope of language and social psychology research.

Identity and self-concept are sometimes used interchangeably in social psychological studies, although many researchers differentiate the two. Frequently, identity is conceptualized as what we acquire and integrate into the self from various social roles. Self-concept captures more of one's personal thoughts and feelings about identity, and in a way the two interact to give the self its own form and uniqueness (Vallacher, 1980). Identity represents the definitional component and self-concept reflects the evaluative component of the individual.

The development of identity and self-concept is an active, ongoing social process involving the intertwining of our own thoughts, feelings, and behaviors with those of others (Jones et al., 1984; Scheirer & Carver, 1980). Some aspects of this process are emphasized more than others—that is, some people rely on outside assessments to define their identity. Still others are more self-accepting and look more internally than externally for self-validation. Communicative exchange though, language in particular, serves as an important mediator in the construction of identity and self-concept.

Unfortunately, not much is directly known about how language affects identity and self-concept. There are two general questions to be answered in research of this kind: The first concerns the role that language plays in developing and shaping identity and self-concept; the second question focuses on how identity and self-concept are displayed in language. The study of language as an expression of identity has been well documented by linguists, social psychologists, sociologists, and anthropologists. Much of our present knowledge about language and identity is derived from an array of studies ranging from experiments on the systematic switching of languages, dialects, and codes to studies of language attitudes and verbal art forms (Giles & St Clair, 1979; Gumperz & Hymes, 1972; Scherer & Giles, 1979). A review of that burgeoning literature is of course beyond the scope of this chapter.

Perhaps, though, the most intriguing knowledge that we have gained from the present literature on language and social psychology is that language and language use, operating through ascribed and achieved roles, mirrors the structure of societies and cultures. Language is what is shared by members of society but also differentiates individuals into smaller social units (e.g., ethnic or regional groups) and allows for individual self-expression.

PRONOUN USE AND ADDRESS FORMS

Our scholarly pursuits are not always linear nor is my presentation of them here. One of my first intellectual discoveries in language and social psychology, however, was of the early work of Roger Brown on the marking of power, status, and solidarity through pronominal use and address forms (Brown & Ford, 1961; Brown & Gilman, 1960). One purpose of these seminal studies was to apply semantic analysis to the study of social structure. Evidence from this work and subsequent studies reveals that the ways in which people address each other within a society reflect social stratification and act to signal social change (Bates & Benigni, 1975; Friedrich, 1972; Leeds-Hurtwitz, 1980; Paulston, 1975). Early European societies, as Brown and Gilman point out, were characterized by rigid class stratification based on birthright, and it was in these and other similarly structured societies where the power and status semantic was clearly delineated and operationalized.

Both the formality that accompanies the use of "vous," for example, denoting the lack of intimacy and the asymmetrical uses of "tu" between social classes or age groups, reinforced the notion of interpersonal distance, power, and control. The use of pronouns, particularly nonreciprocal pronouns, provided the first clue to understanding who you were (e.g., group membership and identification) and where you were located within the societal structure. As Brown and Gilman (1960) noted: "A child learns what to say to each kind of person. What he learns in each case depends on the groups in which he has membership" (pp. 257–271).

In America, where espoused societal attitudes create at least the appearance of less social stratification and the sense that social mobility is less rigidly tied to birthright, the dimensions of power and status are more subtly coded in the language as address forms. The linguistic expression of social stratification through the reciprocal and nonreciprocal use of titles and last names (T + LN), first names (FN), last names (LN), multiple names (MN), or nicknames (NN) points to the emphasis on achieved status relative to ascribed status in the United States. Occupation and age are the best elicitors of linguistic status markers even though occupation often supercedes age. Within professional contexts, when the elder is of lower status, however, the asymmetrical use of address forms has been characterized as uncomfortable (Slobin, Miller, & Porter, 1968).

Forms of address are most effective, then, in sustaining power by telling the superior person and the subordinate person concurrently who is in power or who should remain at a distance. We can control and exert power over others through the ways in which we address them. In using "tu" instead of "vous" or FN instead of T + LN, a speaker can address and treat a subordinate like a child or servant, thus demonstrating to the speaker and the addressee who has the power and status (Brown & Gilman, 1960). The asymmetrical use of address forms also has been cogently exemplified in the historical accounts of social interactions between blacks and whites in the United States, where ascribed status (race) supplanted all claims to a more respectful address form based on occupation (Ervin-Tripp, 1972). Even today many whites display their unease in dealing with blacks of higher status by frequently choosing to use FN rather than T + LN.

Of greater significance, however, are the social relationships within which all these interchanges occur. The power of language, like identity, is tied to social roles or role relationships. Address forms are not best predicted by the social or physical attributes of either the speaker or the addressee but by the social relationship between them. A peasant woman is not a peasant to everyone, nor are blacks necessarily subordinate to other blacks. Even in the most liberal and democratic societies, however, dominance hierarchies abound as signaled in the language of address (Paulston, 1975). Address forms and pronoun use were and continue to be the most expedient manner in which to set and reinforce one's identity as powerful or powerless and one's sense of self as worthy or unworthy.

Some noted exceptions to the marking of status with language, especially when affective states intercede to alter the components of the social situation, are represented by the solidarity dimension of semantic analysis (Ervin-Tripp, 1972; Friedrich, 1972). Occasionally, by violating the norms associated with pronoun usage, one can temporarily erase the barriers of social status and power to express emotions and camaraderie. Paulston (1975), in her analysis of Swedish pronominal usage, observes that hospital patients exchange pronouns of solidarity as they realize that disease and death exempt no one, striking both the rich and poor. Thus, the use of address forms, status, and solidarity markers act to establish identity and self-concept by creating social parameters.

Communicative practices like the use of address forms are very ingrained in social communities and suggest that identity and self-concept are intricately tied to them. Anecdotal evidence demonstrates the eruption of near-riot conditions during the establishment or alteration of certain address forms (Bates & Benigni, 1975; Bauman, 1981; Friedrich, 1972). The Quakers met with great resistance, often enduring beatings and imprisonment, when they introduced "thou" and "thee" as common address forms (Bauman, 1981). Similar expressions of emotional outrage occurred within universities' communities when students were allowed to use solidarity markers with professors (Bates & Benigni, 1975; Peng, 1974).

Taken together, these studies on pronoun use and address forms strongly suggest that language influences the establishment of identity and self-concept in status-role relationships. Through the most pervasive or salient role (e.g., gender, race, age, status), each person exchanges specific forms of address with a higher or lower status other. These address forms communicate an initial and basic identity as a superior or inferior person. In some cultures, the designation of group membership and identity is tied more to ascribed status (birthright), whereas in other cultures achieved status is the greater determinant of address forms. In certain societies, the interrelationships are more complex. A working-class woman, for example, can become a factory supervisor or a well-known union organizer and still feel a sense of shame for being "working class," or, say, Hispanic, or a woman; feelings derived from and reinforced by the (FN) form of address used by superiors. Regrettably, most studies in this area have focused on identifying address forms and pronouns use in various cultures rather than systematically exploring the links between them and identity and self-concept. Comparative studies of pronominal usage and address forms, though, may yield some greater understanding of the universal propensities toward social stratification and its impact on identity and self-concept. Of particular interest would be an examination of the historical and environmental conditions leading to more egalitarian or stratified address forms.

After perusing the literature on address forms and pronoun use, I wondered if there were other ways to establish social distance with language. Self-disclosures, for example, have been identified as a linguistic indicator of social distance (Slobin et al., 1968). In fact, as I began to read more about language and social psychology, the research on dialect and code switching in particular, it became increasingly clear that language acts as a signaling system or cue in much the same way as some nonverbal channels (e.g., facial expressions, tone of voice, proxemics) (Dundes, Leach, & Özkök, 1972). Modifications to language, though, seem to occur at a number of levels (e.g., lexical, topic selection, grammatical and syntactical complexity) to mark social relationships, to express expectations, and to communicate information about who we are and how we might evaluate ourselves.

As a social psychologist, I specifically wanted to know more about the role of language in the psychological development of individuals. What happens to the identity and self-concept of stigmatized or lower status adults who frequently are ignored or spoken to in a condescending manner? Is it through language that the "expectations" in the self-fulfilling prophecy are communicated?

Communication Styles Research

I did not initiate my research on communication styles with a conscious aware-ness of these questions and ideas. I had arrived at Harvard for graduate school eager to pursue my interests in nonverbal communication, and I had the good fortune to meet and work with a then-fellow graduate student, Bella DePaulo. During my early graduate years at Harvard, Bella and I discovered that we had similar interests in language and nonverbal communication. Bella was particu-larly fascinated with the composition, uses, and functions of baby talk (BT).

Baby talk was intriguing to us as social psychologists because it is a speech style that is not solely directed to infants and young children but has been known to be used in communication with the sick, the elderly, pets, plants, and ex-changes between lovers (Brown, 1977; Caporael, 1981; Caporael, Lukaszewski, & Culbertson, 1983; Culbertson & Caporael, 1983; Ferguson, 1975, 1977; Snow & Ferguson, 1977). We were curious about other kinds of special speech styles and whether they were similar or different from baby talk (DePaulo & Coleman, 1981). We decided to explore two other speech styles with what we reasoned to be salient and discernable characteristics: speech directed toward foreigners and speech directed toward mentally retarded adults. We set up, in the traditional social psychological fashion, a controlled laboratory experiment in which we videotaped and recorded 80 women getting acquainted and subsequently explain-ing to a 5–7-year-old child, a foreign student, a mentally retarded adult, or a college student how to complete two simple tasks.

These initial explorations, inspired and supported by Roger Brown, led to an abundance of data.[1] From this research on communication styles, we have learned about the similarities and differences in the modifications in speech (e.g., simplified vocabulary, repetitions) that people make when interacting with members of particular social groups. People tend to hyperexplain (e.g., "Pick up a yellow block, yellow like the sun, a block with four sides") to mentally

---

[1]During this time both Harry Levin and Catherine Snow were taking sabbatical years at Harvard. Their presence and counsel also served as a catalyst for this research.

retarded adults, for example, but fail to include the paralinguistic modifications like high pitch and exaggerated intonation often found in speech addressed to young children (Coleman, 1980; DePaulo & Coleman, 1986). In subsequent research conducted by my graduate students and me, we are exploring how these modifications in communication may foster or impede task performance and affect self-esteem.

Marking Social Distance with Speech

One segment of this data set, though, offers another illustration of the way language shapes identity and self-concept through the marking of social distance. The process is similar to the influence that pronouns and address forms have on establishing status differentials or camaraderie. Various conversational cues can alert the interactants to the nature of social distance with language. To summarize, greater numbers of self-disclosures were present in the conversations between two college student peers; use of slang and jargon occurred more frequently between college students and less frequently with foreign students and mentally retarded adults, and personal or intimate questions characterized the discourse of the college student–child dyads. Further, there were fewer topic shifts in the conversations with the mentally retarded adults, illustrating the common practice of restricting conversations with stigmatized people to safe topics (e.g., weather, task-oriented functions). The total number of words and the total time of the interaction also demonstrated that college students conversed more with their peers and conversed less with mentally retarded adults (Coleman, 1983).

The conversational characteristics of these interactions were also intriguing because they pointed to a number of issues pertaining to language, identity, and self-concept. One issue centers on the formation and maintenance of identity or self-concept among mentally retarded and other stigmatized people (Goffman, 1963). Does the choice by a speaker to use a modified linguistic style or the lack of communication lead to the development of a negative identity or distorted sense of self in stigmatized individuals? Unfortunately, the potential of deleterious effects of language addressed to stigmatized individuals is supported by sociolinguistic research and literature on the social psychology of stigma.

One sociolinguistic study illustrates the role of language in the stigmatization process. Relative to the speech to normal children, communication to children with physical disabilities (not mental) are their status role or social relationship (e.g., superior–subordinate, equals, friends) and are more likely to characterize the conversations with special groups like children, mentally retarded adults, foreign students, and college students. Approximately 5 minutes of unstructured conversations in the getting-acquainted sessions of the previously described experiment provided an excellent source for this discourse analysis.

Once again, I relied on the early studies of power, status, and solidarity to guide my hypotheses. I envisioned the marking of social distance as being mapped onto a set of categories and ordered along a continuum.[2] In this paradigm, speech characteristics representing solidarity would be located on one end of the continuum and extreme politeness or avoidance (i.e., behavior to terminate the interaction) would be located on the other. Talking to children in this context, I hypothesized, would require a special use (or nonuse) of solidarity markers (e.g., fewer self-disclosures on the part of the adult speaker but more intimate questions asked of the children). I hypothesized that more markers of apprehension or avoidance would characterize the conversations with mentally retarded adults. Foreign students presented another special case, in that college student speakers were expected to be polite but the conversations would lack explicit expressions of camaraderie. I analyzed the data for several items that might represent markers of solidarity, politeness, and apprehension. Included in the items reported here are self-disclosures, use of slang/jargon, number of personal questions, topic shifts, total number of words, and total time of the interaction.

The preliminary results provide some clear evidence of marking social distance with language. To summarize, greater numbers of self-disclosures were present in the conversations between two college student peers; use of slang and jargon occurred more frequently between college students and less frequently with foreign students and mentally retarded adults and personal or intimate questions characterized the discourse of the college student-child dyads. Further, there were fewer topic shifts in the conversations with the mentally retarded adults, illustrating the common practice of restricting conversations with stigmatized people to safe topics (e.g., weather, task-oriented functions). The total number of words and the total time of the interaction also demonstrated that college students coversed more with their peers and conversed less with mentally retarded adults (Colemen, 1983).

The conversational characteristics of these interactions were also intriguing because they pointed to a number of issues pertaining to language, identity, and self-concept. One issue centers on the formation and maintenance of identity or self-concept among mentally retarded and other stigmatized people (Goffman, 1963). Does the choice by a speaker to use a modified linguistic style or the lack of communication lead to the development of a negative identity or distorted

---

[2]I later discovered some discussion of what sociolinguists term *communicative distance*. Various words, expressions, or linguistic devices representing social and physical proximity establish a communicative distance that speakers and listeners adhere to (Peng, 1974). In applying the concept of communicative distance to ethnocentric speech characterizing ingroup/outgroup exchanges, Lukens (1969) categorizes the communication of a speaker into three groups: indifference—insensitivity to cultural or social difference; avoidance—a decrease or limit in the amount of interaction; and disparagement—expressed overt hostility. Although these models of speech and social distance focus on different types of communicative situations, they are remarkably similar to mine and suggest that there may be other categories located along the continuum.

sense of self in stigmatized individuals? Unfortunately, the potential of deleterious effects of language addressed to stigmatized individuals is supported by sociolinguistic research and literature on the social psychology of stigma.

One sociolinguistic study illustrates the role of language in the stigmatization process. Relative to the speech to normal children, communication to children with physical disabilities (not mental) are often skewed and distorted (Edelsky & Rosegrant, 1981). There are three major ways in which the communication to physically disabled children is deviant: (1) interactions are predominately initiated and terminated by others—the disabled children are not allowed to terminate or say when *they* are finished; (2) the speech often lacks specificity and is age inappropriate; (3) all the input during a particular speech event is centered on the functions of the event. During dinner conversation, for example, all discourse directed at the disabled child focuses only on the dinner process, thus prohibiting the child from participating in all aspects of the event, including jokes, current events, and other comments. In "normal" discourse, by contrast, children learn a wealth of information as well as a number of sociolinguistic rules, thereby enhancing their "communicative competence" while learning the language (Edelsky, 1978). These results appear to parallel my findings in studies with mentally retarded adults.

Moreover, these distorted modes of communication mirror our current perceptions about how a stigmatized person interacts with the world (Edelsky & Rosegrant, 1981). Given limited exposure to the mentally retarded or other stigmatized people, we do not perceive them as leading "normal" lives or possessing similar attitudes, expectations, and aspirations. In our conversations with them, we often fail to inquire about jobs, family, or friends, and indeed we terminate conversations with them early and abruptly.

From a different perspective, the research on the social psychology of stigma verifies these conclusions. "Hidden metaphors that affect expectations" correspond to notions about stigma and direct communication to stigmatized people (Jones et al., 1984). These researchers also delineate a number of self-presentational styles containing systematic modifications in the communication directed to stigmatized people. The "child among the adult" script, for example, includes characteristics such as condescension, talking to others as if the stigmatized person is absent, and belittling the requests of stigmatized people. Stigmatized roles like those of the mentally retarded, mentally ill, and sometimes alcoholics and drug addicts carry with them the perception of child-like dependency or passivity that elicits a speech style. There are other scripts: the sick script, the moral deviate script, and the ex-con script, which represent the speaker's conception or feelings about each of these stigmas. The communication is most pernicious when the stigmatized, and nonstigmatized parties do not share the same information and expectations about the stigma. Affective responses are often negative, if not patronizing, and can become internalized leading to self-stigmatization (Jones et al., 1984).

This research and my continuing investigations of language and stigma made me cognizant of the power of language. The exiling of stigmatized individuals with language often is not warranted by their physical or social limitations. Moreover, avoidance or minimal conversations disrupt social interaction; interaction that is vital to identity and self-concept.

Model One-Symbolic Interactionism

The work on address forms, marking social distance and stigma, suggests one model depicting the socializing function of language. The formation and maintenance of identity and self-concept is a continual process, initiated and reinforced with language. Like a feedback loop, or Piaget's concept of assimilation and accommodation in cognitive development, language appears to play an active role in the dynamic evolution of identity and self-concept. This model, represented by the symbolic interactionism approach in sociology, notes that the primary function of language—vocal gestures, as George Herbert Mead refers to them—is to create a self and an identity that is a product of society and the individual (Mead, 1936). Through the exchanges of language and similar communicative symbols, individuals come to internalize and reflect society. The impact language has on identity and self-concept may vary to the extent that listeners are sensitive to the speech addressed to them and consider it to be an evaluation of them (Giles, 1979).

Symbolic interactionism, therefore, appears to explain how we come to incorporate the positive or negative assessments of others into our self-definitions and self-evaluations. There are numerous ways in which to test a set of hypotheses stemming from this model. Instances of address form and pronoun use during periods of role incongruency or role transition could provide a topic for future exploration. Empirical studies of new professionals (e.g., medical residents, new Ph.D.'s) or children of varying social backgrounds, for example, also may help to delineate how pronouns and address forms act to shape change in identity and self-concept.

In addition, research on stigma offers another way to study symbolic interactionism. Given the recent gains in equal access and opportunity on the part of stigmatized groups, daily exposure to stigmas is increasing and perceptions of stigmas, at least certain stigmas, are changing (Jones et al., 1984). It is unclear how these changes will affect communication to the stigmatized if the basic assumptions regarding stigmatized people (e.g., source of moral or physical contamination) remain the same. A stigmatized role is an engulfing one and thereby acts as a filter, restricting the information and sociolinguistic features exchanged during an interaction. The communication to stigmatized people represents a special case of the symbolic interactionism process—an extreme example of how people respond to and reinforce most roles with a particular form of language. Salient roles like gender, race, and social status often determine the linguistic nature of the initial social exchange and set the tone for subsequent interactions. From these ongoing social interchanges, we gain a sense of identity and self.

Language and Assimilation

My interest in language and stigmas led me to inquire about other ways in which language figures into the formation and maintenance of identity and self-concept. Did language influence the developing self in other ways, ways that were just as interactive but focused more on individual self-expression? Studies of language and assimilation offer examples of identity change and the development of new selves in immigrants and other individuals in the midst of changing cultures or social environments.

Initially, immigrants are in a marginal situation as they must decide to what degree they want to identify with their new life. This identification process is often marked by language selection (Herman, 1968). The extent to which an immigrant abandons the native or former language often corresponds to the extent to which he or she wants to assimilate and identify as a member of the new culture. New and unfamiliar languages can restrict full expression, and many immigrants report that they do not feel like their old selves or real selves when speaking in the new language (Herman, 1968). Learning a new language includes acquiring a new culture—a culture of different feelings and perceptions of reality. To fully absorb another culture, one must also develop another identity and, in part, develop a new self. Language facilitates and mediates the assimilation process by socializing immigrants into a new culture. Language can also impose a barrier to assimilation.

One of the more famous and often-cited examples of the links among language, identity, and the self is from a study of Japanese female immigrants who described themselves and their life-styles very differently, depending on whether they were speaking Japanese or English (Ervin-Tripp, 1968). There are examples of language as a mediator of self-expression in other cultures as well (Laitin, 1977). Different languages at least for bilingual and multilingual speakers appear to reflect different experiences and aspects of identity and self-concept. The "real self" or core self may be tied to the mother tongue in such a way that feelings, personal disclosures, or displays of the inner self and personality are best expressed in one's native language.

There are other instances, analogous to immigrating to a new country, in which we must develop a new "self" or an identity to accompany the requisite forms of expression in the new social situation. One example is commonly experienced by many black and bilingual children in the educational process. Even in the college years, the predominantly white classroom was indeed foreign territory for me and my black peers. There was also an alien ambience attached to the professorial style and to many of the exchanges between white students and professors. It seemed as if they were communicating in some code, or foreign language, that I, emerging from a black working-class background, had not heard.

Initially, I felt uncomfortable either assuming this new linguistic style as my own or expressing myself in my customary manner (e.g., with portions of black dialect). In the process of developing an "intellectual self," I felt as if I was losing something, some part of my cultural identity. I wondered if my fellow black students, whom I had observed dialect switching, suffered from the same inner conflicts.

As an undergraduate, my fascination with this sociolinguistic/social psychological phenomenon inspired me to study American dialects and to focus on black dialects as an undergraduate.[3] Through my studies, I gained an appreciation for Black English as a form of self-expression that I had been taught to be ashamed of, and I was able finally to relinquish a negative component of my self-concept that told me that my mother tongue epitomized ignorance.

I soon learned from my studies that, owing to racial segregation or blacks' needs to survive in a hostile environment, many components of Black English, including several lexical items, are foreign to most whites (Dalby, 1972; Johnson, 1972). Further, I noted that Black English and the nonverbal communication of Afro–American culture is inherently affective; they convey a level of affect that is absent from the Standard Dialect (Cooke, 1972; Kochman, 1972, 1981). Yet, communicating as an ethnic group member presents a continual dilemma: a choice between communication that reflects one's cultural experiences and real self and the Standard Dialect, which is more prestigious and socially acceptable (Giles, 1979; Giles & Saint-Jacques, 1979).

Studies of sociolinguistic differences in ethnic groups and my own personal experiences also have helped me to understand why so many children from various ethnic groups tend to have difficulty in school. Starting school for them is analogous to moving to a foreign country. As "immigrants" these children must develop a new identity—a different self—to learn and adapt to reading, writing, and speaking the Standard Dialect. The black cultural style, for example, represents a component of the self that virtually must be abandoned on entering school. If this transition is not made successfully, it can result in the emergence of a negative self or a negative component of the "academic identity or self-concept." This negative self-definition or evaluation associated with school and learning may inhibit intellectual development further.

Some studies on the social psychology of second-language learning support

---

[3]One of my first research projects was an investigation of the paralinguistic features of what "sounds" black and who (e.g., black females, black males, white males, and white females) are best at decoding them (Coleman, 1976). This study was conducted for a nonverbal course taught by Dane Archer at University of California, Santa Cruz. Dane, a former student of Roger Brown, encouraged me to apply to the social psychology program at Harvard where I later attended. In essence, I was a "grandstudent" of Roger who later became a "Roger Brown student" in my own right.

this scenario regarding the links among language, identity, and the development of self-concept in ethnic minority children. Research has shown that an encouraging social milieu is vital to the successful learning of a second language. In addition, students must identify with members of the dominant cultural or linguistic group and acquire some of their subtle behaviors (Fanon, 1967; Gardner, 1979; Lambert, 1972). In essence, this research implies that in order to fully master a new language or dialect students must want to be like members of the culture that the language or dialect represents. Gardner (1979) has developed a model that he terms the *additive/subtractive dichotomy* of learning a second language. Learning a second language can be additive and enriching for ethnic children, by offering them access to power and social mobility in a predominately Standard-English-speaking society, or subtractive, "contributing to the loss of identity by orienting the child away from his or her own cultural background toward another imposed one." Gardner considers that second-language learning involves more than the educational experience of mastering vocabulary, grammar, and syntax and includes an affective component (e.g., feelings about the reasons for language learning, attitudes about the culture), which can facilitate or interfere with the acquisition of language.

Given that in the United States and Canada low status is attached to the languages, dialects, and communication styles of minority groups, children who come from homes where these languages and dialects are the primary forms of expression may develop an anomie about school or about the part of their identity or self-concept that becomes associated with learning. Maxine Hong Kingston (1977) poignantly describes the silence of Chinese children in San Francisco, for example, who on entering school experience the degradation of being ostracized for not knowing how to express themselves in Standard English.

Model Two-Developing Selves Through Language Learning

A second model, then, representing the role of language in the development of self-concept and identity focuses on the social psychology of second-language learning. Mastering another language or dialect compels one to internalize the values, attitudes, and perceptions of the linguistic community and incorporate them into an evolving identity and self. Whether the learning of the new language is an "additive" or "subtractive" experience—that is, whether it enhances or undermines one's current identity—may predict positive or negative changes in self-concept. Learning to communicate in Standard English, for example, may require children and adults from linguistic backgrounds with affectively charged languages or dialects to distance themselves from their real feelings or real selves. Fanon (1967) discusses this issue with regard to French and dialect-speaking blacks. He states: "Every dialect is a way of thinking. . . . And the fact that a newly returned Negro adopts a language different from that of the group into which he was born is evidence for a dislocation, a separation.'' (p. 25) Feeling negative about the real self or developing new selves to accommodate the Standard Dialect or national language is not unique to English but appears to be a process occurring in a number of languages. Longitudinal studies of native and non-native Standard English speakers will reveal if such conflicts exist and how they become reconciled.[4]

Future Research

Admittedly, some readers may find this review is only suggestive of the links among language, self-concept, and identity. Although a tremendous amount of work on language and identity has been conducted by European and Canadian social psychologists, one major gap in the present literature is the lack of systematic, empirical studies. Thus, in addition to the further empirical verification of the ideas presented here, a number of topics in social psychology (e.g., social cognition, interpersonal relations, attitudes) are quite appropriate for linguistic analysis. Language and affect as well as language and cognition, in particular, are two research areas that could broaden our knowledge about language, identity, and self-concept.

It is clear that the primary emotions are expressed in all cultures (Ekman, 1971) but are combined in different ways so that labels for emotional expressions sometimes are not translatable from one language to another. It also appears that some languages are structured to facilitate more affective expression than others. Some languages have been described as eliciting great passion or emotional expression (e.g., Italian, Spanish), whereas others appear to inhibit emotional expression (e.g., Japanese, German). Some cultures through their languages may allow for greater expression of individuality and the ''self.'' Comparative studies of languages, then, will provide clues or explanations as to why people feel and think differently in first and second languages.

Research on language and affect raises other questions about feeling and thinking in various forms of language. Is it easier, for example, to express emotions in the verbal or written forms of a language? Writing involves a form of self-expression in the formal Standard Dialect whereas speaking includes colloquialisms, regional pronunciations, and special dialect features. Writing places constraints on self-expression; the freedom gained in oral expression is gradually lost in the written translation. This dichotomy between speaking and writing suggests that feeling and thinking may interact with the mode of communication.

---

[4]It is indeed intriguing and a poignant comment on the sociopolitical atmosphere in the United States that, unlike Canada, Standard English does not contain a term like *Francophones* to describe those whose native tongue is not English. Every term to describe people (e.g., non-native speakers, non-English speakers) is negative, reflecting the strong emphasis and value placed on mastering Standard English in America.

Further, I would hypothesize that the relationship between feeling and thinking may operate differently in people for whom speaking and writing is a continuous process (i.e., native speakers of Standard English) than in those for whom speaking and writing is a discontinuous process (e.g., non-native speakers of Standard English). Experimental research in this area might include a replication of the Ervin-Tripp (1968) study with immigrant women. The study would incorporate written and verbal response conditions in the native and non-native language, in addition to including a control group of Standard English speakers. Another study could extend Laitin's (1977) work on self-descriptions in native and non-native languages to include speaking and writing conditions. Such experiments should expand our present knowledge of the role language plays in affect and cognition as well as in identity and self-concept.

Language also creates visual images or thoughts that may indirectly determine identity and self-concept (MacKay, 1980; MacKay & Fulkerson, 1979; Moulton, Robinson, & Elias, 1978). What kind of feelings and attitudes are stimulated by words or phrases such as "terrorist," or "patriot," or "freedom fighter?" What do we see when a sentence contains only the pronoun "he" instead of "he/she?" Do we visualize something different when we read of policewomen instead of policemen or chairperson instead of chairman? Some recent research suggests that the way in which language is presented may figure importantly in conceptions about identity and self-concept as well as in gender-role development (Hyde, 1984). There are numerous empirical studies that could be conducted to demonstrate that not only do words lead to different images, but they may influence what we envision to be the possibilities or potential for ourselves and others. In essence, identity and self-concept are, in part, structured by the thoughts or visual images created through the printed or spoken word. The printed word—in the media, in schoolbooks, in literature—creates images that we have for our possible identities or future selves. The systematic manipulation of what people read may in fact elicit more positive or negative views of one's identity or self-concept. Longitudinal studies might best assess the long-term effects of language in its literary form on the transformation of identity and self-concept.

CONCLUSION

Our growing knowledge of language can provide us with a better understanding of not only the formation and change of identity and self-concept, but of the vital role language plays in social, cognitive, and affective development across the life-span and in various cultures. Research on how people communicate to children, to the sick, to foreigners, and to the elderly, for example, suggests that modifications in language accompany most life-cycle transitions and reinforce our identification with each new role. Verbal exchanges constantly tell us who we are and how we should evaluate who we are.

It is indeed difficult to discuss the effects language has on social and cognitive development without some consideration of the sociopolitical context in which verbal exchanges occur. Taking the sociopolitical atmosphere into account suggests that lower status individuals or people with less power in society may be more susceptible to the influence of language and communication than higher status individuals who control and often determine the language style that is spoken and valued. Communication, then, based on automatic and stereotypical responses to certain devalued social roles may define and keep low-status individuals in their place by reinforcing a negative identity (Jones et al., 1984). At some point the process becomes self-perpetuating as one's negative or positive identity becomes a central component of one's self-concept.

There are individual differences in linguistic expression, identity, and self-concept and there are a number of explanations for them. Despite the language and communication we share, no two people express themselves in exactly the same manner, thus allowing individuality to evolve from language as well. Language allows the societal or cultural identity and self to coexist with the personal identity and self albeit not always peacefully. Through the shaping of identity and self-concept, language creates an individual.

In another vein, self-acceptance may be a useful term to describe people who have developed the inner strength to resist the labels and expectations encoded in certain linguistic styles. Other approaches to lessening the daily attacks on one's identity and self-concept are offered by Jones et al. (1984). They include controlling one's own identity and self-concept by changing reference groups so that the verbal reinforcement is more supportive. Turning to others who share and appreciate our language or dialect, for example, may help to redefine the central attribute of the self from negative to positive. Others may expand the internal personal self through introspection and learn to depend on the internal, rather than external, voice.

Finally, a number of researchers have begun to discuss the benefits of multiple roles, multiple selves, and multiple identities (Gergen, 1971; Jones et al., 1984; Markus & Nurius, 1986). People having a variety of roles are less likely to allow critical comments to affect their overall identity because they can redirect their attention to another role, another aspect of the self. Enacting a number of roles also makes a variety of options available for self-expression in different languages, dialects, or codes. Personally, I have found all these processes very useful.

In summary, the present research review lends itself readily to two hypothesized models of the effects of language on identity and self-concept. First, social categories (e.g., race, gender, status, age) are clearly tied to the language and nonverbal communication we convey and receive. People can communicate intimacy or avoidance, emphasize egalitarianism or status differentials, and convey respect or disrespect through language. Thus, in social interactions, identity and self-concept are affected by the responses of others and our evaluations of those responses. Acquiring an identity and self-concept through language represents a classic dialectic: a way to understand how others feel about us or what we are doing, and concurrently an opportunity for us to consciously reflect and shape our own unique personality or self (Williams, 1972). At the individual level, language operates like proprioceptive feedback, just as facial muscles provide information about emotional states. Listening to the ways we express ourselves—the use of a specific language or dialect, lexical items or phrases— gives us some insight into ourselves and how we perceive the world. Symbolic interactionism best represents this model of the way language molds identity and self-concept.

The second hypothesized model of language and self-concept is also linked to the way we express ourselves, particularly whether or not we speak in a manner that is culturally valued. In both its written and verbal forms, language is such an important channel for thinking and feeling, for expressing the self and identity. To abandon one's native form of expression may require the denial of a central and salient component of the self. Writing languages, for example, usually requires using the standard form—the linguistic form of the dominant social group. In learning to write, non-native speakers but not Standard English speakers must develop a different self. This process may require these speakers to differentiate one part of the self like the "academic" or "intellectual" self from other parts of the self. In contrast, learning to write for Standard English speakers appears to be more continuous, eliminating the need to dissociate one part of the self from another.

I would hypothesize that teaching a child a new language or dialect, yet also teaching that child that his or her original culture with its special language and dialect is good and valuable, might alter this early creation of a negative identity and self-concept. Black, Hispanic, and Asian children, as well as working-class children, are rarely taught there is anything positive or beautiful about their natural forms of expression and therefore are not taught to respect themselves; to respect a self and identity inextricably tied to their earliest forms of expression. Consequently, one reason why Asian children often turn to the sciences rather than to the humanities, and Black, Hispanic, and working-class children turn away from academics completely may be these early communicative difficulties. The dilemma between comfortable self-expression and the social mobility tied to mastery of the national language continues to be a major source of personal conflict. Although learning Standard English is society's attempt to make us all part of American culture, this model suggests that the role language plays in the cognitive and affective development may be far more complex for non-native English speakers than psychologists and educators ever imagined. One challenge for them will be to understand this process and to understand how successful individuals are able to move beyond such obstacles.

Clearly, there are many influences on the development of identity and self-concept. Many of these influences are communicated, however, directly or indirectly, by language. Certainly there are alternatives to the two models presented here. They are designed to be provocative rather than definitive. I want to stimulate more research in a field terribly neglected by own discipline: experimental social psychology.

Finally, this chapter chronicles a portion of the development of a social psychologist whose changing identity and self has accompanied her continual investigation of the links among language, culture, and the individual. Like many other researchers, I must acknowledge the important role that my own social background and personal experiences have played in shaping my research interests. In addition, special mentors like Roger Brown have been instrumental in helping me to uncover the dormant "intellectual self"; an identity and self that over time has been challenged, negated, exiled, and resurrected; a self that wants to grow, expand, and realize its full potential. His greatest gift to me in my development as a language researcher has been the gift of himself as a model of academic excellence. Through our verbal exchanges he created a positive identity and encouraged in me a sustained belief in my individuality, in my real self.

ACKNOWLEDGMENTS

The author wishes to acknowledge the helpful comments of Bella DePaulo, Hazel Markus, and the invaluable assistance of Dorothy Walker and Cathy Jenkins in preparing this chapter.

REFERENCES

Bates, E., & Benigni, L. (1975). Rules of address in Italy: A sociological survey. *Language in Society, 4,* 271–288.

Bauman, R. (1981). Christ respects no man's person: The plain language of the early Quakers and the rhetoric of impoliteness. *Sociolinguistic Working Paper No. 88,* Austin, TX: Southwest Educational Laboratory.

Brown, R. (1977). Introduction. In C. E. Snow & C. A. Ferguson (Eds.), *Talking to children.* Cambridge, England: Cambridge University Press.

Brown, R., & Ford, M. (1961). Address in American English. *Journal of Abnormal and Social Psychology, 62,* 375–385.

Brown, R., & Gilman, A. (1960). The pronouns of power and solidarity. In T.Sebeok (Ed.), *Style in language* (pp. 253–276). New York: Wiley.

Caporael, L. (1981). The paralanguage of caregiving: Baby talk to the institutionalized aged. *Journal of Personality and Social Psychology, 40,* 876–884.

Caporael, L. R., Lukaszewski, M., & Culbertson, G. H. (1983). Secondary baby talk: Judgments by institutionalized elderly and their caregivers. *Journal of Personality and Social Psychology, 44,* 746–754.

Coleman, L. (1976). Racial decoding and status differentiation: Who hears what? *Journal of Black Psychology, 3,* 31–37.

Coleman, L. (1980). *Changes in speech due to the characteristics of the listener.* Unpublished doctoral dissertation, Harvard University.

Coleman, L. (1983, July). *Social cognitions about group membership: Marking social distance in speech.* Paper presented at the Second International Conference on Language and Social Psychology, Bristol, England.

Cooke, B. G. (1972). Non-verbal communication among Afro–Americans: An initial classification. In T. Kochman (Ed.), *Rappin' and stylin' out* (pp. 32–64). Chicago: University of Illinois Press.

Culbertson, G. H., & Caporael, L. R. (1983). Baby talk speech to the elderly: Complexity and content of messages. *Personality and Social Psychology Bulletin, 9,* 305–312.

Dalby, D. (1972). The African element in American English. In T. Kochman (Ed.), *Rappin' and stylin' out—Communication in urban Black America* (pp. 170–188). Chicago: University Press.

DePaulo, B., & Coleman, L. (1981). Evidence for the specialness of the "baby talk" register. *Language and Speech, 24,* 223–231.

DePaulo, B., & Coleman, L. (1986). Talking to children, foreigners, and retarded adults. *Journal of Personality and Social Psychology, 51,* 945–959.

Dundes, A., Leach, J. W., & Özkök, B. (1972). The strategy of Turkish boy's verbal dueling rhymes. In J. J. Gumperz, & D. Hymes (Eds.), *Directions in sociolinguistics* (pp. 130–160). New York: Holt, Rinehart, & Winston.

Edelsky, C. (1978). "Teaching" oral language. *Language Arts, 55,* 291–296.

Edelsky, C., & Rosegrant, T. (1981). Interactions with handicapped children: Who's handicapped? *Sociolinguistic Working Paper No. 92,* Austin, TX: Southwest Educational Laboratory.

Ekman, P. (1971). Universals and cultural differences in facial expressions of emotions. *Nebraska Symposium on Motivation, 207–283.*

Ervin-Tripp, S. (1968). An analysis of the interaction of language, topic and listener. In J. A. Fishman (Ed.), *Readings in the sociology of language* (pp. 191–211). The Hague: Mouton.

Ervin-Tripp, S. (1972). On sociolinguistic rules: Alteration and cooccurrence. In J. Gumperz & D. Hymes (Eds.), *Directions in sociolinguistics* (pp. 213–250). New York: Holt, Rinehart.

Fanon, F. (1967). *Black skins, white masks.* New York: Grove.

Ferguson, C. A. (1964). Baby talk in six languages. *American Anthropologist, 66,* 103–114.

Ferguson, C. A. (1975). Toward a characterization of English foreigner talk. *Anthropological Linguistics, 17,* 1–14.

Ferguson, C. A. (1977). Baby talk as a simplified register. In C. E. Snow & C. A. Ferguson (Eds.), *Talking to children* (pp. 219–236). Cambridge, England: Cambridge University Press.

Friedrich, P. (1972). Social context and semantic feature: The Russia pronominal usage. In J. J. Gumperz & D. Hymes (Eds.), *Directions in sociolinguistics* (pp. 270–300). New York: Holt, Rinehart, & Winston.

Gardner, R. C. (1979). Social psychological aspects of second-language acquisition. In H. Giles & R. St. Clair, *Language and social psychology* (pp. 193–220). Baltimore: University Park Press.

Gergen, K. J. (1971). *The concept of self.* New York: Holt, Rinehart.

Giles, H. (1979). Ethnicity markers in speech. In K. R. Scherer & H. Giles (Eds.), *Social markers in speech* (pp. 251–289). Cambridge, England: Cambridge University Press.

Giles, H., & Saint-Jacques, B. (Eds.). (1979). *Language and ethnic relations.* New York: Pergamon Press.

Giles, H., & St. Clair, R. (Eds.). (1979). *Language and social psychology.* Baltimore: University Park Press.

Goffman, E. (1963). *Stigma.* Englewood Cliffs, NJ: Prentice-Hall.

Gumperz, J. J., & Hymes, D. (Eds.). (1972). *Directions in sociolinguistics.* New York: Holt, Rinehart.

Hallervell, A. J. (1955). *Culture and experience.* Philadelphia: University of Pennsylvania Press.

Herman, S. R. (1968). Explorations in the social psychology of language choice. In J. Fishman (Ed.), *Readings in the sociology of language.* The Hague: Mouton.

Hyde, J. S. (1984). Children's understanding of sexist language. *Developmental Psychology, 20,* 697–706.

Johnson, K. (1972). The vocabulary of race. In T. Kochman (Ed.), *Rappin and stylin out—Communication in urban Black America* (pp. 170–188). Chicago: University of Illinois Press.

Jones, E. E., Farina, A., Hastorf, A. A., Markus, H., Miller, D., & Scott, R. A. (1984). *Social stigma—The psychology of marked relationships.* New York: W. H. Freeman.

Kingston, M. H. (1977). *Woman warrior: Memoir of a girlhood among ghosts.* New York: Random.

Kochman, T. (Ed.). (1972). *Rappin' and stylin' out: Communication in urban Black America.* Chicago: University of Illinois Press.

Kochman, T. (1981). *Black and white styles in conflict.* Chicago: University of Chicago Press.

Laitin, D. D. (1977). *Politics, language and thought. The Somali experience.* Chicago: University of Chicago Press.

Lambert, W. E. (1972). *Language, psychology and culture.* Stanford, CA: Stanford University Press.

Leeds-Hurtwitz, W. (1980). The use and analysis of uncommon forms of address: A business example. *Working Papers in Sociolinguistics No. 80.* Austin, TX: Southwest Educational Development Laboratory.

Lukens, J. (1979). Interethnic conflict and communicative distance. In H. Giles & B. Saint-Jacque (Eds.), *Language and ethnic relations* (pp. 143–158). New York: Pergamon Press.

Mackay, D. G. (1980). Psychology, prescriptive grammar, and the pronoun problem. *American Psychologist, 35,* 444–449.

Mackay, D. G., & Fulkerson, D. (1979). On the comprehension and production of pronouns. *Journal of Verbal Learning and Verbal Behavior, 18,* 661–673.

Markus, H., & Nurius, P. (1986). Possible selves. *American Psychologist, 41,* 954–969.

Mead, G. H. (1936). The problem of society: How we becomes selves. In M. H. Moore (Ed.), *Movements of thought in the nineteenth century.* Berkeley: University of California Press.

Mitchell-Kernan, C. (1972). Signifying and marking: Two Afro–American's speech acts. In J. J. Gumperz & D. Hymes (Eds.), *Directions in sociolinguistics* (pp. 161–179). New York: Holt, Rinehart.

Moulton, J., Robinson, G. M., & Elias, C. (1978). Psychology in action: Sex bias in language use: "Neutral" pronouns that aren't. *American Psychologist, 33,* 1032–1036.

Paulston, C. B. (1975). Forms of address in Swedish: Social class semantics and a changing system. *Language in Society, 5,* 359–386.

Peng, F. C. (1974). Communicative distance. *Language Science, 31,* 32–38.

Sapir, E. (1951). Language. In D. G. Mandelbaum (Ed.), *Selected writings of Edward Sapir in language, cultures and personality.* Berkeley: University of California Press.

Scheier, M. F., & Carver, C. S. (1980). Individual differences in self-concept and self-process. In D. M. Wegner & R. R. Vallacher (Eds.), *The self in social psychology* (pp. 229–251). New York: Oxford University Press.

Scherer, K. R., & Giles, H. (Eds.). (1979). *Social markers in speech.* Cambridge, England: Cambridge University Press.

Slobin, D. I., Miller, S. H., & Porter, L. W. (1968). Forms of address and social relations in a business organization. *Journal of Personality and Social Psychology, 8,* 289–293.

Snow, C. E., & Ferguson, C. A. (Eds.). (1977). *Talking to children.* Cambridge, England: Cambridge University Press.

Vallacher, R. (1980). An introduction to self theory. In D. M. Wegner & R. R. Vallacher (Eds.), *The self in social psychology* (pp. 3–30). New York: Oxford University Press.

Williams, T. R. (1972). *Introduction to socialization: Human culture transmitted* (pp. 242–267). St. Louis, MO: Mosley.

16 Learning Poetic Language

David C. Rubin
Duke University

This chapter examines the learning of poetic language in oral traditions as a form of language learning in general. By poetic language all that is meant is a style of language, clearly distinguishable to native speakers, that makes use of the repetition of surface structure for artistic purpose. This style is usually sung and is often accompanied by music, though it need not be. Learning a poetic language that is an oral tradition should not be confused with the rote learning of poems or with the learning of a literate poet's style. Rather, learning a poetic language is similar in many ways to learning a first language. For instance, poetic language, like a first language, is typically learned with only very limited special tutoring. The poetic language learned is often as productive and rule bound as a first language, though the rules are often more restrictive. Moreover, like a first language, poetic language is widespread and varies greatly from one society to another (Finnegan, 1977). Oral traditions using Homeric Greek, Serbo–Croatian, Anglo–Saxon, and English are presented as examples before implications are drawn.

The intellectual history that makes this chapter possible goes back to Harvard several decades before Roger Brown arrived. Milman Parry, Assistant Professor of Classics, wanted to understand Homer. From his textual analysis, it appeared that the *Iliad* and *Odyssey* were products of an oral, rather than a written tradition. To test his thesis Parry needed a living oral tradition with practicing poets who sang epic poems similar to Homer's. As described in a later section, he found and recorded extensively from such a tradition in Yugoslavia (Lord, 1960).

HOMERIC EPIC POETRY

Although we cannot learn much about the way Homer or his contemporaries learned poetic language, Homer is worth considering as the prototype and most studied case of poetic language. The *Iliad* and the *Odyssey* are part of a longer cycle of poems (Lattimore, 1951). At the time of the events described in these cycles, writing was not in common use in Ancient Greece. Extensive scholarship provides strong evidence that the poems were part of an active oral tradition that had existed for centuries before being recorded (Havelock, 1978; Lord, 1960). In such an oral tradition, poems would not be memorized. There was no text to which to compare a memorized version. Rather, the poems would be generated anew at each performance. The performance was the poem.

Much of the evidence for viewing the Homeric epics as instances of an oral tradition comes from analysis of the texts themselves. These analyses are used here to describe one poetic language. The following section describes direct observations of singers in a similar poetic language. The basic finding for all poetic languages described here is that there exists the equivalent of sets of generative rules that operate at different structural levels to allow a poet to compose rapidly and to preserve the content and style of the poems.

The Homeric epics are composed of half-line to line phrases called *formulas*. These allow the poet to fit ideas into metrical constraints. Formulas also raise the level of composition from morphemes to tens of morphemes. Examples of formulas are "rosy fingered dawn" or "the wine blue sea." Lord (1960, p. 143), following the work of Parry, examined a passage from Homer and found that 90% of the half-lines were repeated elsewhere in Homer verbatim or with only minor change; that is, 90% of the sample was formulaic.

Homeric formulas show thrift. There tends to be only one formula for each combination of an idea and a metrical scheme. For instance, if 2 feet of a line about Odysseus remained to be filled, the formula used would be brilliant Odysseus; if 3 feet were needed, resourceful Odysseus; for 3½ feet, long-suffering, brilliant Odysseus. For the same three metrical constraints, Hektor changes from glorious Hektor, to Hektor of the shining helm, to tall Hektor of the shining helm (Lattimore, 1951). The epithet used has nothing to do with the current semantic context. Thus, Aphrodite is laughing when she is complaining, and Achilleus is swift footed when he is sitting.

The formulas are the vocabulary of poetic language. Like the words of a first language, they can have internal structure and be productive. A poetic language learner needs to learn a large stock of such formulas; but in learning these he also learns the names and characteristics of heroes, geography, and other facts of heroic life.

Like the words of a first language, formulas need to be combined in an orderly fashion. In addition to metrical constraints, themes guide the combination of formulas in a poetic language. Because epic poems are series of concrete actions, the themes can be described as scripts (Bower, Black, & Turner, 1979). Heroes are armed in a set sequence (Armstrong, 1958). Pieces of armor can be elaborately described or omitted completely, but the order of the armor mentioned is always greaves, corselet, sword, shield, helmet, and spear, Even when Athena is armed, and her shield is the aegis of Zeus, the sequence is not ignored.

More complex sequences follow similar patterns and allow the story line to advance in regular ways. One favorite theme in all epic poetry is the council scene. This scene allows the poet to introduce characters, to provide the listener with background information by having a character describe actions that occurred outside the poem, and to provide the listener with the social relations among the heroes. Once the council scene theme, or script, is begun, it breaks down into subthemes such as the arrival of a hero (if the council is not already in session) with the accompanying description of horse and armor. Homeric council scenes can be of men or of gods. The same basic outline can be followed allowing the poet to compose rapidly, expand some places, and omit others without confusing his audience.

Levels of themes even more complex and useful in preserving a story line are also learned. Thus, the Homeric poems can be viewed in terms of themes common to most epics, themes such as bride stealing and rescue, a hero's absence and return home in disguise, or a hero's wanderings in and return from the netherworld (Lord, 1960).

The poetic language learner needs to master all levels from the overall plot down to the formula. Listening to examples of return epics, council themes, and heroes being armed, the poetic language learner abstracts patterns and catalogues formulas that fit the thematic patterns and the poetic constraints. In doing this, a special language for a small world is mastered.

The poetic language learned is more constrained than normal language, but, as demonstrated in the sections to follow, it is made of generative rules, rather than rote memorization. Both the constraint and the creativity within that constraint are largely products of human memory and language-learning skills. A separate and important claim is that poetic language developed to make efficient use of human abilities to store and transmit large amounts of cultural knowledge before writing was available for such purposes (Havelock, 1978; Ong, 1976). This claim is important because it raises poetic language from being solely an art form to being an art form that increases the culture's chances for survival.

LEARNING SERBO–CROATIAN EPIC POETRY

Extensive collections of Serbo–Croatian epic poems exist and have been analyzed with respect to their structure. Singers have performed under normal situations, as well as in situations specifically designed to test the singers' abilities (e.g., Lord, 1960).

The structure of the epics is surprisingly like that of Homer, and so, in addition to the musical accompaniment, the singer needs to know: (a) the names of people and places; (b) formulas about these names and such things as heroes and horses; (c) themes or scripts for activities such as arming, battles, council meetings, weddings, and heroes in disguise returning home after long absences; (d) and the higher level themes that are the story lines of the poems. The structure of the poems tells us that the singer must know how to combine these components of the scholar's analysis in a way that appears rule bound.

As with Homer, a textual analysis would indicate that singers have productive rules much like a language user's. The tasks set for the singers by Parry and Lord (Lord, 1960), however, provide direct examples of the rule-bound nature of epic. Consider "The Song of Milman Parry," composed by Milovan Vojicic in 1933 (Lord, 1960, pp. 272–275). Before this song was sung, the tradition contained no songs about visiting professors, ambiguous or otherwise, for the singer to reproduce from rote memory. Yet, a song could be composed without great difficulty using common formulas and themes from the tradition that describes heroes and travel. Thus, we have sequences such as "The ship carries him, the Saturnia the glorious/Constructed of fierce steel;/Nothing can slow its path,/But over the sea it drives away the waves,/as a falcon drives away doves." (p. 272) and "He was there for three white days./When the fourth day dawned,/Professor Milman arose early,/Before daylight and white dawn./He leaped to his light feet/" (p. 274).

An example of Lord and Parry's best singer, Avdo Mededovic, learning a new song provides additional insights into what it is that the poetic language learner must learn (Lord, 1960; Lord & Bynum, 1974). Avdo Mededovic, like Homer, was the best recorded singer in a tradition. In an incidental learning paradigm, a singer sang a song of 2,294 lines that Advo Mededovic had never heard before. When the song was finished, Avdo Mededovic was asked if he could sing the same song. He did, only now the song was 6,313 lines long. The basic story line remained the same, but, to use Lord's description, "the song lengthened, the ornamentation and richness accumulated, and the human touches of character, touches that distinguish Avdo Mededovic from other singers, imparted a depth of feeling that had been missing" (p. 78). Avdo Mededovic's song retold the same story in his own words, much as a subject in a psychology experiment would, the only difference being that his own words were poetic language and his story was a song of high artistic quality. Although the particular words changed, the words added were all from the small world of the tradition; and so the stability of the tradition, if not the stability of the words of a particular telling of a story, was ensured.

Several aspects of this feat are of interest. First, the song was composed without preparation and sung at great speed. There was no time for preparation before the 6,313 lines were sung, and once the song began the rhythm allowed little time for Avdo Mededovic to stop and collect his thoughts. Such a feat implies a well-organized memory and an efficient set of production rules. Second, the song expanded yet remained traditional in style, demonstrating that not just the song heard, but parts of others like it, could be easily and rapidly combined. Third, Avdo Mededovic was not trying to be creative; he believed he was telling a true story just the way he had heard it, though perhaps a little better. To do otherwise would be to distort history.

Like students of language, students of poetic language learned much by studying errors. In the preceding example, Lord pointed out an error that gives some insight into Avdo Mededovic's store of scripts. In the original song the messenger asks to be paid, providing a chance for the singer to demonstrate the hero's poverty and generosity. Avdo Mededovic's script for someone's receiving a letter, a script that is used many times in Serbo–Croatian heroic poetry, consists of the letter's being opened and read and then the head of the assembly asking the reader about the letter's contents. Avdo Mededovic, using this script, forgot about the messenger's request for payment and had to return to it later.

These examples are intended to provide some indication of what the poetic language learner must accomplish. Like the child, however, the poetic language learner cannot state the rules he uses. Although singers will often claim they sing the same song repeatedly word for word, they have no idea of what a word, or even a line, is.

If this is what a singer must know, when does he start and how is he taught? Most of the singers Lord and Parry interviewed began actively trying to learn the tradition in their early adolescence. It is a male tradition, and many of the performances were in coffeehouses open only to men. (See Bartok & Lord, 1951, for songs sung by women.) The young singers, like the child, appear to be given little in the way of special instruction. The most active instruction appears to be having a song repeated. It is not known whether the language to be learned is presented more simply or slowly for beginners, as is often done for children learning a first language.

Lord (1960) postulated the existence of three stages in the learning of poetic language. In the first stage, the novice listens, becoming familiar with the tradition. In the second stage, the novice sings, but without a critical audience. In this stage, the act of singing forces the novice to fit his ideas into the fixed rhythmic pattern of the song. In a sense, the novice is continually testing his own knowledge. In Lord's (1960) words, "He is like a child learning words, or anyone learning a language without a school method; except that the language here being learned is the special language of poetry . . . He had no definite program of study, of course, no sense of learning this or that formula or set of formulas. It is a process of imitation and of assimilation through listening and much practice on one's own" (pp. 22–24). This second stage ends, and the third stage begins when the singer can sing a song for a critical audience. There is still much to learn. The vocabulary of formulas, scripts, and songs increases. The skills of singing, playing, and ornamenting improve. Although there are certainly cohort effects, for Parry and Lord, the older singers were generally the best.

The learning of two singers provides brief case studies. Avdo Mededovic, mentioned in the previous example, was Lord and Parry's most skilled singer. He was an illiterate butcher who started singing when he was 15. His father, a singer, encouraged him and was his first teacher. Later he learned from whom ever he could (Lord & Bynum, 1974). Avdo Mededovic produced 78,000 lines of recorded epic poetry. The longest song was 13,000 lines or approximately 16 hours of singing time. These 78,000 lines, however, are only for the 9 different epic songs that were actually recorded. Avdo Mededovic reported a repertory of 58 epics. Thus, it could be calculated that he knew a total of about 500,000 lines or 600 hours of epics, compared to 27,000 lines in the *Iliad and Odyssey* combined. However, such a calculation would take numbers too seriously. Avdo Mededovic could create lines and, as the example of learning a new song shows, even large segments of ballads at will. With the use of generative rules, the number of lines that could be produced is limited only by how much is sung.

Sulejman Makic, an illiterate woodcutter and farmer, was 50 years old when he talked with Parry (Parry & Lord, 1954). Sulejman Makic reported a repertory of about 30 songs, one for each day of Ramadan, and possibly a few more. When Sulejman Makic was 15, a singer stayed in his house for a year. Sulejman Makic said, "He sang and I listened, until I learned. . . . Yes, he used to instruct me. He would sing it through to me once, and I would sit beside him. Then he would go back and sing it through again, and I would learn it" (pp. 263–264).

Sulejman Makic's report of how he would learn a new song provides an example of the constructive process at work, even though any construction was denied by the singer. When asked if he could learn a new song that he heard just once, Sulejman Makic replied, "Yes, I could sing it for you right away the next day" (pp. 265–266). When asked about the delay he replied, "It would stay in my mind. Then I would sing it right away from memory. . . . It has to come to one. One has to think . . . how it goes, and then little by little it comes to him, so that he won't leave anything out. It would be possible right then and there, but one couldn't sing it like that all the way through right away" (p. 266). When asked if he would sing exactly the same song he had heard, he said that he would, and that he would not add nor omit anything. "I would sing it just as I heard it, whatever was worthwhile; what's the good of adding things that didn't happen. One must sing what one heard and exactly as it happened" (p. 266). The verbatim recall Sulejman Makic reported was never observed by Parry or Lord. Sulejman Makic, however, was not bragging. If one does not read, then "exactly the same" is a judgment based on memory. Although the singer is using poetic language in a productive fashion, he will not admit it. If put to the test, Sulejman Makic's performance might have been much like that of Avdo Mededovic— exactly the same, but three times as long as the original.

The learning of Serbo–Croatian epic makes several similarities obvious between first-language learning and poetic-language learning. In both cases of language learning, the learners do not have much insight into either the units and rules being learned or the processes underlying the learning. The learners listen, the learners learn. The language learners do not receive much in the way of specialized instruction. The language learners, nonetheless, learn complex, rule-bound systems that can be used with little effort.

CAEDMON'S POETIC-LANGUAGE LEARNING

The most famous case of an individual's learning a poetic language is both one of the most interesting and, due to its age, one of the most fragmentary. Caedmon was an illiterate cowherd who was employed at the monastery at Whitby around 680 AD. The Venerable Bede (731/1969) provides the description of how Caedmon learned to sing. The relevant parts of the story follow.

It was the custom at feasts that a harp would be passed around and everyone would take turns singing. Although well advanced in age, Caedmon would leave when the harp approached rather than remain and sing. On one such occasion, he went to the stable to mind the animals and to sleep. In his dream, Caedmon was asked to sing about creation, which miraculously he immediately did, singing verses he had never heard. In the morning, he reported his dream and was brought before the abbess and some learned men. There he recited the song he had composed. Caedmon was then read a sacred passage and asked to construct a song from it. Caedmon returned the next morning and repeated the passage in excellent verse. At the abbess' request, Caedmon took monastic vows and was taught sacred history. He learned all he could by listening, "ruminating over it like some clean animal chewing the cud" (Bede, 731/1969, p. 419), and produced excellent verse.

Several observations are clear from the story. First, an oral tradition of singing to the harp existed in Whitby around 670, and all men were expected to be able to take part in the tradition. Second, Caedmon often heard songs, though he was unable or unwilling to sing in public. Third, Caedmon's singing of sacred material was so unusual and of such high quality as to be considered a miracle worthy of note in church history. Fourth, Caedmon's process of composition consisted of listening to a sacred story, often translated into Old English from the Latin, ruminating, and then singing; Caedmon could not write and so had to keep his text in mind while composing.

Bede warned his reader that the translation of verse, including his own translation of *Caedmon's Hymn,* is impossible without changing the original. Old English versions of *Caedmon's Hymn,* however, do exist and provide some further insights into Caedmon's technique of composition. Magoun (1955) found that 15 of the 18 verses of *Caedmon's Hymn* repeat verbatim or with minor changes elsewhere in 30,000 lines of the existing Anglo–Saxon poetical corpus. Fry (1975), in a contrasting analysis, noted that all the half-lines exist in the same corpus if one looks not for verbatim occurrences but rather for productive formulas in which different words of the same general meaning and poetic properties (here meter and alliteration) can be substituted for each other.

The story of *Caedmon's Hymn* is an especially interesting case of learning poetic language, not only because of its antiquity and because it is the only Anglo–Saxon poem that we know from evidence external to the poem itself was orally composed (Fry, 1975), but also because we know the singer composed by rule, not by rote memorization. Caedmon sang a hymn he had never heard before. In fact, he sang in a genre of poetry, sacred poetry sung in traditional Anglo–Saxon style, that was itself novel.

There are some obvious parallels between Caedmon's learning poetic language and Lord's description of how singers of epic learn. First, there is a period in which the singer listens but does not perform. For Caedmon this period was longer than is usual for the singers of epic. Caedmon's embarrassment at not being able to sing at the feast indicated that this period was also longer than was common among Caedmon's peers. The second period of practice without a critical audience was either not present or not recorded for Caedmon except for a single instance in a dream. The slow development was worthwhile. When Caedmon first entered the third stage of true performance, he was already an expert.

The story and the content of the little that remains of Caedmon's singing tells us what Caedmon was learning in his first two stages. He was learning themes from the Christian tradition and poetic language from an Anglo–Saxon oral tradition. The Anglo–Saxon poetic language was from an oral tradition because that was all that existed for Caedmon (Fry, 1975, 1980). Combining these two traditions was made easier because formulas for heroes and gods in the Anglo–Saxon tradition were often well suited for their counterparts in the Christian tradition (Fry, 1975).

It is not clear that Caedmon could ever compose extemporaneously without ruminating; however, this skill should not be expected. Caedmon was combining the themes from one tradition with the language from another, so he was at a disadvantage compared to epic singers for whom certain formulas fall naturally into place in certain thematic contexts. Moreover, even some of Parry and Lord's better singers, such as Sulejam Makic, liked to sleep before returning to sing a new song for the first time. It is clear, however, that both the themes and the language were stored without the use of external memory aids such as writing and that the songs produced, if not composed extemporaneously, were stored in memory until they could be sung to learned men. Caedmon's mastery of Anglo–Saxon poetic language, however, was sufficient to allow him, without the aid of writing, to produce sacred poems with such speed and virtuosity as to have the feat labeled miraculous by the Abbess, her learned men, and the Venerable Bede.

NORTH CAROLINA BALLADS

Ballad singing is a living oral tradition in North Carolina (Belden & Hudson, 1952). Many songs within this tradition can be traced to Child's collection of ballads (1882–1898/1965), which dates back to the seventeenth and eighteenth centuries. Traditional ballads from the English-speaking world have attracted considerable scholarship (e.g., Leach & Coffin, 1961) that provides much information about the structure and transmission of the songs, but less information about how the songs are learned. The ballads usually have from 5 to 20 verses, 4 lines per verse, with lines 2 and 4 rhyming. In North Carolina they are sometimes called *love songs* to distinguish them from religious songs, and, in fact, they are almost all about romance in some way. Even the train and shipwreck songs are set as stories of the death of a loved one.

We have interviewed and recorded local ballad singers. From our initial data some observations are clear. Although the ballads show much less variation from singing to singing than the longer Serbo–Croation epics (Friedman, 1961), they are not repeated verbatim. Rather, ballads are changed from singing to singing with verses modified or substituted, and melodies switched. These changes are far from random. Stronger evidence that ballad singing should be considered a poetic language comes from the ease with which our singers can generate a new ballad of fair quality and traditional style from a newspaper article of a train wreck. Although there are great individual differences in performing this task, we observed four-to-nine-verse ballads generated in the span of 3 to 15 minutes.

All our data to date on the learning of poetic language come from self-report. The singers questioned learned to sing at various ages, but generally singing is learned early—probably simultaneously with first language learning. Not surprisingly then, the main first model is usually an immediate family member, although most of the songs a singer knows as an adult may have been learned from another model. Our singers usually reported not being corrected if they made a mistake or at most receiving a statement like ''This is the way I learned it.'' The singers also reported never practicing per se; unlike the epic singers, the singing itself was their only practice.

Our singers reported that an accomplished singer should be able to learn a new song after hearing it a few times. One singer volunteered that the reason for this was that an accomplished singer already would know most of a new song even before he heard it. Verbatim learning of a new song is expected, though some singers admitted they change songs freely. The expectation of verbatim learning is consistent with the commonly held view among singers that the songs are about true stories and real people their older relatives knew. Such beliefs occur even with songs whose story line dates back hundreds of years. Supporting the emphasis on verbatim learning is the observation by one singer that he recalled learning words that at the time had no meaning to him but were just part of the song.

OBSERVATIONS AND IMPLICATIONS

The acquisition of poetic language in several oral traditions has been described and several parallels with first-language learning have been noted. The following is a list of some of the properties present in both first and poetic language and their learning: (a) Generative rules are learned. These generative rules can produce novel instances that are clearly members of the language; (b) the language learned helps preserve and transmit cultural knowledge (Havelock, 1978; Ong, 1976); (c) speaking in and listening to the language learned appears to be inherently entertaining or reinforcing in that individuals often engage in such behavior without other obvious external reward (Staddon, 1981). From an evolutionary standpoint, this third parallel could follow from the second; (d) the process of learning and what is learned are not available to introspection; that is, rules are followed, but they cannot be stated by the native speakers; (e) most learning occurs without special training beyond the availability of a model, or models, who can be observed producing clear instances of the language. This is not to say that learning is effortless and occurs without practice (Weir, 1962); (f) first language learning is present in all societies. Poetic language learning may have also been present in all societies before literacy (Havelock, 1976). Poetic language is, at a minimum, extremely widespread (Finnegan, 1977), and claims exist that music, a common component of poetic language, is a universal (Serafine, 1983). The list of parallels just given is interesting because it points to similarities that may be true of many other kinds of human learning, and because it might teach us something about each of the domains of language learning considered separately.

Poetic-language learning is the less studied of the two language learnings. It therefore has more to gain initially from the comparison. Although scholars of poetic language know their stimulus material extremely well, they typically have not observed, or have not been able to observe, the behavior of the language user and language learner. In the absence of a solid data base, argument by analogy is helpful, and thanks to Roger Brown and others, there is something worthwhile to which analogies can be drawn. Moreover, in the absence of a solid data base, speculation can run unchecked. From the study of first-language learning, we now know that there are many arguments that are not worth making, classes of theories that are doomed to failure, and other pitfalls too numerous to number. We know of these intellectual paths not worth taking thanks to Roger's students and others in the field. The last 30 years of accumulated knowledge of first-language learning provides a good base from which to study poetic-language learning. The general approaches used by students of first-language learning appear to be more useful than the details of their findings. For instance, a set of generative rules that change with development is an example of a concept that could be adapted for testing in poetic language.

But this volume is directed to students of first-language learning. What can they learn from the scattering of observations presented? Only humans spontaneously learn language, but it is not the case that humans learn only language. Although language learning is unique among species, it may not be unique among human abilities. The main question raised by poetic-language learning is this: What processes does it share with or borrow from first-language learning?; that is, are there general skills available to both kinds of language learning, or alternatively, are there general skills developed in first-language learning that can be used outside of first-language learning? Poetic- and first-language learning have much in common, but the two languages differ enough so that transfer between the two might argue for general skills. For instance, poetic language is not a complete language unto itself but rather is a special form of language used for artistic and mnemonic purposes. Moreover, poetic language is often learned much later than first-language learning and its critical periods.

WHAT ONE CAN LEARN IN THE TIME IT TAKES A CIGAR TO BURN

When I was a graduate student, it appeared that my appointments with Professor Brown were timed by cigar. Shortly after the cigar that was lit when I entered his office was finished, my time would be up. I was glad my mentor puffed long cigars slowly. During that time, I probably learned less about language learning than any of the other contributors to this volume, although I hope this is not obvious from my contribution. I also learned little of Roger's writing style, though I did try. What I hope I learned is an approach to psychology. Allowing for distortions on my part, the approach goes something like this. Find a phenomenon that is interesting for reasons other than the latest fad in psychology and that appears to be amenable to the theories and techniques we have or can develop. Be aware of—but do not be guided by—current theories, the latest statistics, or the research method you just mastered for your last project; rather, let the phenomenon itself determine which theories, statistics, and methods you should use. Sometimes you may notice a phenomenon and begin. Other times a phenomenon of long-time interest will become tractable because of advances in theory or method. In any case, start with a good description of the data that need explanation, a description that does not destroy the phenomenon in the act of quantifying it.

Roger studied language acquisition, an inherently interesting phenomenon that became tractable with advances in linguistics. He described the phenomenon in detail and then went on to analyze and to develop theory. Roger did the same for the tip-of-the-tongue phenomenon and autobiographical memory, two areas in which I have followed him. When he wanted to study sign language, he learned to sign. When he wanted to learn about schizophrenics, he talked to schizophrenics. He observed phenomena as closely as possible and brought to bear all available knowledge. Science advanced because Roger is extremely good at what he does. The advances will be of lasting value because the phenomena studied were not artificially created within psychological theory, but rather were phenomena that any psychology will have to understand.

ACKNOWLEDGMENTS

I wish to thank Albert B. Lord and Wanda T. Wallace for their comments. The North Carolina ballad research is a collaborative effort with Wanda T. Wallace. Support was provided by NSF grant number BNS 8410124.

REFERENCES

Armstrong, J. I. (1958). The arming motif in the Iliad. *American Journal of Philology, 79,* 337–354.

Bartok, B., & Lord, A. B. (1951). *Serbo–Croatian folk songs.* New York: Columbia University Press.

Bede, V. (1969). *Bede's ecclesiastical history of the English people* (B. Colgrave & R. A. B. Mynors, Trans. and Eds.). Oxford: Clarendon Press. (Original work published 731)

Belden, H. M., & Hudson, A. P. (Eds.). (1952). *The Frank C. Brown collection of North Carolina folklore* (Vols. 2–3). Durham, NC: Duke University Press.

Bower, G. H., Black, J. B., & Turner, T. J. (1979). Scripts in memory for text. *Cognitive Psychology, 11,* 117–220.

Child, F. J. (Ed.). (1965). *The English and Scottish popular ballads* (Vol. 1–5). New York: Dover. (Original work published 1882–1898)

Finnegan, R. (1977). *Oral poetry: Its nature, significance, and social context.* Cambridge, MA: Cambridge University Press.

Friedman, A. B. (1961). The formulaic improvision theory of ballad tradition—A counterstatement. *Journal of American Folklore, 74,* 113–115.

Fry, D. K. (1975). Caedmon as a formulaic poet. In J. J. Duggan (Ed.), *Oral literature: Seven essays* (pp. 41–61). Edinburgh: Scottish Academic Press.

Fry, D. K. (1980). *The memory of Caedmon.* Unpublished manuscript, State University of New York at Stony Brook.

Havelock, E. A. (1978). *The Greek concept of justice: From its shadow in Homer to its substance in Plato.* Cambridge, MA: Harvard University Press.

Lattimore, R. (1951). Introduction. In R. Lattimore (Trans.), *The Iliad of Homer* (pp. 11–55). Chicago: University of Chicago Press.

Leach, M., & Coffin, T. P. (1961). *The critics and the ballad.* Carbondale: Southern Illinois University Press.

Lord, A. B. (1960). *The singer of tales.* Cambridge, MA: Harvard University Press.

Lord, A. B., & Bynum, D. E. (1974). *Serbo–Croatian heroic songs* (Vol. 3). Cambridge, MA: Harvard University Press.

Magoun, F. P. (1955). Bede's story of Caedman: The case of history of an Anglo–Saxon oral singer. *Speculumn, 30,* 49–63.

Ong, W. J. (1976). *The presence of the word: Some prolegomena for cultural and religious history.* New Haven, CT: Yale University Press.

Parry, M., & Lord, A. B. (1954). *Serbocroation heroic songs* (Vol. 1). Cambridge, MA: Harvard University Press and Belgrade: Serbian Academy of Sciences.

Serafine, M. L. (1983). Cognition in music. *Cognition, 14,* 119–183.

Staddon, J. E. R. (1981). On a possible relation between cultural transmission and genetical evolution. In P. P. G. Bateson & P. H. Klopfer (Eds.), *Advantages of diversity* (Vol. 4). New York: Plenum.

Weir, R. H. (1962). *Language in the crib.* The Hague: Mouton.

17 Creating a World with Words

Ellen Winner
Boston College and Harvard Project Zero

Howard Gardner
Harvard Project Zero and The Boston Veterans Administration Medical Center

Lisa Silberstein
Christine Meyer
Harvard Project Zero

In 1955, a most unusual book appeared in the United States, one which was to intrigue readers of every stripe. Written by the Russian emigre, Vladimir Nabokov, *Lolita* told the story of an aging scholar, Humbert Humbert, who fell madly in love with a 12-year-old "nymphet" (later to become his stepdaughter). To the surprise of nearly everyone—most of all, perhaps to the many publishers who had rejected the manuscript—the novel became a best seller and, eventually, a widely acclaimed movie. Nabokov was able henceforth to devote himself full time to writing, and the term *Lolita* entered the English language.

Lolita is anything but a transparent piece of fiction. To begin with, two fictional worlds are created—that of the narrator (who relates a story "secondhand") and that of the characters. The reader is also confronted with three narrative voices—that of the author, the narrator, and the protagonist. The reader faces the difficult tasks of distinguishing the various worlds and voices and organizing the relationships among them.

The bound volume begins with an introduction by a man named John Ray, Jr., Ph.D., who tells us that he was asked by Humbert Humbert's lawyer to prepare this memoir of the deceased Humbert Humbert for publication. Ray assures us that the characters in the memoir are not fictional but real. The only "fiction," we are told, is that the names of the characters have been altered in order to preserve the characters' privacy. As evidence for the nonfictional status of the characters, Ray leaks to us what has happened to the characters since the memoirs were written. Ray also separates himself from the characters in the memoir by apologizing for the publication of such a shocking "case history."

Following Ray's tantalizing introduction comes the main body of the novel, which tells the story of the tormented relationship between Lolita and Humbert. This tale is told in the first person by Humbert, but occasionally Ray intrudes (also in the first person) to remind us of his role as editor. For instance, Ray is apt to remind us that a name used by Humbert is not the person's "real" name. Humbert also interrupts his story in order to refer to himself in the third person, or in order to carry on a dialogue with the reader. "Imagine me," he implores his reader. "I shall not exist if you do not imagine me."

In current editions, the memoirs are followed by an afterword by Nabokov, dated November 12, 1956. Here, Nabokov explains why he wrote the novel and airs his own thoughts about its success. He declares his sympathy with the reader's task of making sense of this morass. "After doing my impersonation of suave John Ray, the character in *Lolita* who pens the Foreword, any comments coming straight from me may strike one—may strike me, in fact—as an impersonation of Vladimir Nabokov talking about his own book." In other words, the reader may not be quite sure whether the afterword is a real or a fictional account. We have been played with so much by this point that such uncertainty is to be expected. Nonetheless, as Humbert says in his memoirs, "Every game has its rules," and sophisticated readers ultimately know to take the afterword as real, even as they know to take the foreword as fictional.

Surprising as it was that this labyrinthine novel became a best seller, it was perhaps even more surprising that it was reviewed in *Contemporary Psychology*, the sober American book review journal for the field of academic psychology. But a young psychologist, Roger Brown, was much taken with Nabokov's achievement and was able to convince the editor, E. G. Boring, to allow him to review the book in the pages of the journal (Brown, 1970).

In rereading Roger Brown's review a quarter of a century after it appeared, one instantly recognizes the voice of the remarkable scholar being honored in these pages. There is the feeling of excitement about a phenomenon—in this case, a work of literary art—which Roger Brown enthusiastically communicates to the reader. There is the capacity to enter sympathetically into the world of others—the world of the author Nabokov, and the worlds of his many intriguing characters. Roger Brown pays tribute to Nabokov's incomparable ability to give the "reader the impression of participation in a consciousness not ordinarily his own." There is the uncanny knack of discovering significant psychological questions lurking in human activities and then hitting on a means by which these questions can be attacked. Roger Brown sees *Lolita* as an "experiment in achieving psychological effects through the use of printed language." He illustrates this technique with many examples of how Humbert Humbert's strange mind is conveyed by particularly apt metaphors. As a single illustration, Humbert's obsessive lust is revealed by his description of "a sudden discharge of coins" from a telephone, rather than, for instance, "a *shower* of coins." And there is, as ever, Roger Brown's subtle sensitivity to the world of experience, conveyed in prose that is elegant, engaging, precise.

Roger Brown also demonstrated intellectual prescience in this review. Rejecting the dominant behaviorist psychological dogmas of the time, he argued that the reader of *Lolita* is not passively placed in Humbert's state of mind but is rather an inherently active participant. As he points out, the reader must continually work out the rich verbal play—the puns, anagrams, allusions, and metaphors. Constructive activity is the royal road to Humbert's exotic consciousness. We see in Roger Brown's stance an anticipation of the cognitive revolution that was shortly to sweep psychology and that he has done so much both to stimulate and to humanize. His piece on *Lolita* also harbors a hope that psychology might one day be able to illuminate human artistic endeavors.

FICTIONAL WORLDS

To make sense of a novel like *Lolita*, the reader is well advised to be in possession of all his wits. But which of the wits would seem to be particularly important in apprehending a work of fiction? We might isolate at least two related candidates for this role. The first is the ability to respect the integrity of fictional worlds. *Lolita* is a novel that contains nested worlds, or frames of reference: the world of Nabokov in the afterword, the world of Ray in the foreword and in his constant intrusions in the main body of the text, and the world of Humbert and Lolita. The worlds of Humbert and Lolita and of Ray are nested within the world of Nabokov, because they are imagined by Nabokov. And the worlds of Humbert and Lolita are nested within the world of Ray, because Ray narrates the story of Humbert and Lolita. The reader must recognize that these nested worlds normally do not interact; that is, Ray cannot interact directly with the characters he is describing, Humbert and Lolita; and Nabokov cannot interact directly with either the fictional narrator or the fictional characters. Whereas violations may occur in works of art (e.g., Alfred Hitchcock's cameo appearances in his own movies; Velasquez' appearance as a painter in his own painting), they are to be recognized as violations. It is for this reason that we find them amusing. *Lolita* poses a challenge to the reader precisely because it contains more than the usual number of nested frames of reference.

A second, related ability necessary to make sense of *Lolita* is the recognition that each world can feature its own set of rules. These rules are specified by the author. The author may decide to create one highly realistic, typical world (the world of Ray) and another less plausible, though still realistic world (that of Humbert and Lolita). What matters is that the characters within each world must behave consistently, as governed by a coherent set of rules. In *Lolita* the reader must recognize that the world of Ray is both realistic and normal, whereas that of Humbert and Lolita, although realistic, is at least psychologically abnormal—more like a dream than reality.

Even the experienced reader may sometimes be confused by matters of authorial voice or domains of discourse. Yet readers are usually aware of these entities and have the potential to discriminate among them, given enough time, motivation, and shrewdness. When the reader is a child, however, a different state of affairs may obtain.

It is well known that children are attracted to fictional narratives, that they listen raptly to stories, and that they also create their own imaginary narratives. It is tempting to conclude, as Bruno Bettelheim (1976) has done, that children are especially attuned to the world of fiction—that they have the capacity to make the appropriate discriminations and to apprehend a work of fiction, at least unconsciously, in the way that competent adult readers can. But loving is not understanding, and there is ample reason to consider that, even though children are drawn to the literary experience, they often fail to apprehend the story in a way that would make sense to adults. Although *Lolita* invokes the world of the child, it is hardly a book for children.

At the risk of offending literary and psychoanalytic pursuits, psychologists have interfered with the "natural process" of story telling and story understanding by injecting various experimental conditions into this experience. When such manipulations are performed, they reveal that in many ways young children do not apprehend critical features of literature. We find, for example, that when young children are given stories to complete they do not respect the integrity of a fictional world and the boundary between this world and the "real" world. Rather than creating a set of characters who seem to have a life of their own, these children enter personally into the narrative, interacting directly with the characters they have imagined (Scarlett & Wolf, 1979).

Young children also appear to have difficulty distinguishing between events and characters that are realistic and those that are fantastic (Jaglom & Gardner, 1981). Initially, there is a tendency to construe all portrayed events as being realistic, to be followed a year or two later with a denial that anything presented in the fictional mode is realistic at all. Once again, it is necessary to draw a proper boundary between reality and fantasy, and this achievement takes several years (Morison & Gardner, 1978). To be sure, as in any other area of cognitive development, if the materials are stripped down enough and the mode of response is simplified enough, a higher level of performance can be obtained (e.g., Mandler & Johnson, 1977). But in the nonexperimental world of everyday literary creation and understanding, there is reason to believe that the skills for comprehending fiction develop over a period of many years.

As exemplified by his study of *Lolita*, Roger Brown has always been willing to attack challenging and often unfashionable topics that strike him as interesting and inherently psychological. His review of *Lolita* was certainly adventurous in the 1950s, in the heyday of behaviorism, when most psychologists restricted their studies to far simpler matters and to far simpler organisms. As students of Roger Brown,[1] we were encouraged to do the same—to pursue our interest in the unfashionable and thorny area of the arts, under the auspices of Harvard Project Zero. Much of our work during that period and in the years following has involved studies of children's abilities to appreciate relatively specific features of literature, such as figurative language (e.g., Winner, Wapner, Cicone, & Gardner, 1979), distinctions between realistic and fantasy characters (Morison & Gardner, 1978), and sensitivity to structural aspects of stories (Rosenblatt, Massey, Blank, Gardner, & Winner, 1984). Yet, although these lines of research have been instructive, they fail to illuminate the more general kinds of understanding of literary art that are posed in bold form by a novel such as *Lolita*. We know little about how children apprehend the act of literary imagination and how that apprehension may contrast with that of adults. We know little about children's ability to appreciate that a fictional world originates in and is dictated by the imagination of its author. At the same time, there exists scant evidence on how children sort out the various kinds of worlds that may be included in a work of fiction, and how they appreciate the rules that govern these domains and detect the relationships that obtain among them.

To secure some preliminary information on this set of topics, we recently undertook two studies of the development of literary imagination in young children. Working with Lisa Silberstein, we probed whether children understand that a fictional world is a product of someone's imagination, and that this world exists on another level from the world of the author. Working with Christine Meyer, we examined children's abilities to distinguish among *kinds* of fictional worlds, ones that are highly realistic and ones in which ordinary rules do not hold sway.

Understanding the Act of Literary Imagination

Understanding *Lolita* requires that one discriminate the voices of Ray, Humbert, and Nabokov, and that one recognize that the voices of Ray and Humbert have been imagined by Nabokov. The latter recognition (in turn) calls on an awareness that fantasy (such as a pretend play sequence or a story) originates in someone's mind, and that the imaginer has total control over the imagined events; that is, the imaginer can create a fantasy in which anything goes; the laws of causality may be transgressed, time may flow backwards, gravity may be reversed, and so on. Of course, if the story is to be understood, the imaginer cannot alter rules in an entirely arbitrary and inconsistent fashion; there must be some system in this madness, and ordinarily the imaginer signals this to his audience. Paradoxically,

---

[1]Howard Gardner was a student of Roger Brown in the late 1960s, Ellen Winner in the mid-1970s.

the very child who exercises complete freedom in his own imaginary products (weaving fantasies in which rocks become alive, and people turn into stones) may lack this understanding: Due to egocentrism, or confusion about the process of imagination, he may fail to recognize that other imaginers have this same control over *their* imaginary worlds.

To investigate children's sensitivity to these issues, we presented children with a nonrealistic, fantasy story (defined as a story in which real-world physical laws are violated). In the various conditions of the study, the fantasy story was imagined by the experimenter or by an invisible author. Understanding of the origin of and locus of control over the fantasy story was then assessed by a variety of measures.

There were 120 children, 40 in each group at ages 4, 7, and 10, who participated in this study. A fantasy story relayed the adventures of a family of miniature people (Little Papa, Little Mama, Little Boy, and Little girl) who climb into a picture of a car and proceed to drive the car off the page and then off the table-top on which the pictured car is situated. The plot consisted of the varied efforts of the little family to restore the car to the table: First they try to fly the car on a paper airplane; then they try to pull the car up with a rubber band; and finally they use a paperclip and string as a pulley and succeed. The story ends as the family drives the car back into the picture. This core story was presented in four different conditions, as shown in Table 17.1.

Through a series of questions and tasks, we assessed children's appreciation that the story originated in someone's mind (source of imagination); that the originator of the fantasy was in charge of orchestrating the imagined events and was not constrained by real-world rules (control over imagined events); that realistic fictional characters have a different status from fantasy fictional characters (distinctions among fictional worlds); and that imagination is always a mental process (the child's implicit theory of imagination). For each measure, a coding system was devised to classify the responses given, and 94% interrator reliability was achieved on a subset of the responses by two judges. Chi-square tests were carried out to examine the relationship among response, age, and condition. In what follows we mention only those results that were significant at or below the .05 level.

Source of Imagination.   We investigated two factors that might affect ease of recognition that a fictional world originates in—and is controlled by—someone's mind. The first of these factors was the visibility of the imaginer. In Condition 1, the imaginer is the experimenter and hence is highly visible; in Conditions 3 and 4, the proximate imaginer (Janet) is visible but is not the ultimate imaginer (the author); in Condition 2, the author is invisible. We expected children to find it more difficult to recognize that a fictional world is the product of someone's mind when the imaginer was not visible. The second factor that we examined was the presence or absence of a distinction between the

TABLE 17.1
The Four Conditions of Study 1

Condition 1: Experimenter's Fantasy

Experimenter (E) relates the fantasy; the fantasy is a product
of E's imagination. There is only one narrative voice: that of E.
E and child (C) look at a drawing of a car.
E: "A little family could fit right into this little red
   car. Little Papa would start up the engine....."

Condition 2: Author's Fantasy

E reads fantasy story aloud from an illustrated book. Hence, the
fantasy is a product of an invisible author's imagination, though
this in fact is never stated. There are two narrative voices: that
of E, and that of the author lurking silently in the wings. The
story began as follows:
"A picture of a little red car lay on the desk. A little
family climbed in. Little Papa started up the engine....."

Condition 3: Character's Fantasy: Explicit*

E reads fantasy story aloud from an illustrated book, but the
fantasy story is embedded in a realistic story. The book opens
with a realistic character, Janet, who is told to stay in from
recess and finish her homework. Instead, Janet daydreams and
imagines the story of the little family. Hence, the fantasy is
a product of Janet's imagination, but ultimately both Janet and
the little family originate in the mind of an invisible author.
There are three narrative voices: author, Janet, and E. The
story began as follows:
"Janet, you are to stay in from recess until you finish
your math problems," the teacher told Janet. "You would
have finished like everyone else if you hadn't been drawing
during class. Your picture will stay on my desk until after
school.....Janet looked at her problems. Then she looked at
the teacher's desk. "It's a nice picture of a car, "thought
Janet. "I could have a little Papa and a little Mama in the
front seat.....Little Papa is driving." (The clue that Janet
imagines what follows is the use of the conditional, "I could
have.....").

Condition 4: Character's Fantasy: Implicit*

This condition is identical to Condition 3 with one exception:
There are no clues to signal the shift from Janet's actual world
to the world of her imagination. The story began as in Condition
3 but continued as follows:
"There was the picture of the car that Janet had drawn.
Suddenly, a Little Papa and a Little Mama climb into the
front seat. Little Papa is driving....."

---

* Conditions 3 and 4 reflect the structure of works such as The Wizard of
Oz, as work that takes place, for the most part, in a world imagined by the
fictional character, Dorothy.

imaginer and the teller or narrator of the story. In Condition 1, the imaginer and
teller are one and the same; in Condition 2, the two roles are differentiated: The
experimenter is the narrator but is not the imaginer; in Conditions 3 and 4, the
situation is more complicated: not only are teller and imaginer differentiated, but
there are two imaginers, one ultimate (the author) and one proximate (Janet).
Hence, in these latter conditions Janet stands between the author and the teller:
The experimenter tells the story that Janet imagined, which was ultimately imagined by the author. Because Janet intervenes between imaginer and teller, the

distance between the two is greater in Condition 3 and 4 than in Condition 2. We expected that recognizing the story of the little people as the product of someone's imagination would be more difficult the greater the distance between imaginer and teller.

We asked children to tell us where the little people came from, where their car came from, and, finally, where the story about the little people came from. When adult pilot subjects were asked this question, they readily asserted that all of these came from someone's fantasy or imagination. In contrast, children often gave much more concrete answers. We found that the most important factor affecting comprehension of a fictional world as imagined was the visibility of the imaginer. In Condition 1, in which the imaginer was the experimenter and hence was visible, nearly all children understood the experimenter to be the origin of the fantasy. In Condition 2, in which the imaginer was an invisible author, 4-year-olds rarely invoked someone's imagination as the source of the fantasy. When in Conditions 3 and 4 children cited imagination as the source, they almost always mentioned the visible Janet's imagination rather than that of the invisible author. Thus, were young children faced with the task of making sense of *Lolita*, they might decide (incorrectly) that the story was imagined by the visible narrator, Ray, and they might fail to infer that the source of both Ray's and Humbert's worlds is the mind of the author whose voice is heard in the foreword.

Far less important than the imaginer's visibility was the distance between imaginer and teller. Condition 3 presented a greater distance between imaginer and teller than did Condition 2; yet children in Condition 2 proved far less likely to allude to imagination as the source of the story than did children in Condition 3.

One additional point is worth noting. Even when admitting that the story about the little people was imagined, 25% of the 4- and 7-year-olds (but only 2% of the 10-year-olds) tried to concretize the fantasy creations, suggesting, for instance, that the imaginer pretended that an ant, a crayon, a mouse, or a paper doll was one of the little people. These children thereby revealed their belief that, although imagination is a mental process, it must have a grounding in concrete reality.

Control Over Imagined Events.   Whereas children may recognize a fictional world as coming from someone's imagination, they may yet fail to realize that the author is in full control of the imagined events. There are at least two issues to recognize with respect to the author's control. First, the reader/listener must be aware that the author directs the unfolding of events and therefore can redirect the course at any point. Second, the reader/listener must recognize that the author thus has the freedom to weave a story that does not conform to the "real world." With *Lolita*, for instance, Nabokov has created a story that conforms to the physical laws of the real world but that is psychologically bizarre. In contrast, science fiction stories, or the story of the little people, violate physical rules but not psychological norms.

To assess children's understanding of the author's control over a fictional world, we asked children a series of questions such as, "Why didn't the paper airplane work? Could someone have made it work? How? Could Janet have made it work? How? Could the person who wrote the story have made it work? How?" We expected that young children would fail to grasp that the events were orchestrated at the whim of the imaginer, holding instead that the imaginer was constrained to imagine events conforming to real-world rules. Thus, they would argue that no one could have made the paper plane work because a paper plane is never strong enough to hold up a car. To be sure, children are willing to violate real-world rules in their *own* creations. But when children are asked to reflect on this process when confronted with another's fictional world, we thought they may respond at a less sophisticated level.

The results supported our hypothesis. We found that 10-year-olds were much more likely than younger children to realize that the imaginer could alter the story events merely by changing her mind. For instance, one 10-year-old said, "Of course the author could have made the airplane work, because she made up the story, so she could do anything. She could even have had a big white dog come and eat them all." In contrast, the 4- and 7-year-olds often said there was no way that the imaginer could change the events if this entailed the violation of physical reality. For instance, one 4-year-old said that there was no way for the paper airplane to work, because paper isn't strong enough to hold up a car. The same type of reasoning also led to positive responses, but only among 10-year-olds. For instance, one child said that Janet could have made the airplane work if she had remembered to imagine a motor. In this latter type of response, the child acknowledges that Janet has control over the events but seems to feel that Janet can only offer solutions that would be plausible in the real world.

An unexpected type of misunderstanding was also revealed. Almost half the children at all ages stated that Janet could have made the plane work by intervening physically—she could have risen from her desk and lifted up the plane. Such a solution violates the dividing line between Janet's actual world and her imagined world. There can be no physical interaction between the two worlds—the narrator can talk directly to the audience (as Ray does, in *Lolita*) but never to the characters. As previously mentioned, this kind of boundary violation commonly occurs in the stories that young children themselves produce (Scarlett & Wolf, 1979); that is, children weave fantasy stories and then proceed to interact directly with their imaginary characters, as if reverting from the story domain to the domain of symbolic play. By 5 years of age, however, children consistently respect the boundary between fictional and real worlds in their own stories, allowing their imagined worlds to operate as if they functioned independently of the imaginer. The fact that boundary violations persisted in children as old as 10 in the study under discussion suggests that the child's metaknowledge of the rules of fiction lags far behind their tacit knowledge of those rules.

A further point should be noted. Even 10-year-olds allowed that the imaginer could intervene directly, but they usually "hedged" this claim by pointing out the inconsistency in such control. One ten-year-old said, "Yes, Janet could make the plane work, but she would look pretty funny taking an imaginary car up from the ground and onto the table." Another child in Condition 1 became confused with her response but could not sort out her confusion: "Well, you (the experimenter) could pick up the car onto the paper airplane and then bring them to the table. But wait, there wasn't a real car, so I guess you would put the picture of the car onto the airplane." "Was there really an airplane?" the experimenter asked. "Oh, right," the child replied, "I guess you would make the picture of the car into the paper airplane by folding it."

Status of Fictional Characters.   Competence in the fictional realm requires not only that one recognize that the imaginer has full control, but also that one distinguish among types of fictional worlds. Perhaps the most basic distinction is that between a realistic and a fantasy fictional world. For instance, Nabokov challenges the reader to realize that the world of Humbert Humbert is psychologically bizarre, whereas the world of Ray is entirely normal. Correlatively, in the stories about the little people, full understanding calls on the child to recognize Janet as realistic but the little people as nonrealistic figments of Janet's mind.

We hypothesized that young children would fail to distinguish between the reality status of Janet and the little people, thus revealing a lack of awareness that the little people are not constrained by the rules of the real world. However, we expected that children would more readily recognize the fantasy status of the little people in Conditions 3 and 4: These conditions include both Janet and the little people, thus offering a contrast between types of fictional worlds. Lacking such a contrast (Conditions 1 and 2), children should less readily confer full fantasy status on the little people.

To secure information bearing on these hypotheses, we asked children questions about the characters' physical activities (Can the little people/Janet/eat? Can the little people/Janet/get hurt?) and about temporal changes (Do the little people/Janet/grow old? Does their/her hair grow?). A recognition of the different statuses of realistic and fantasy fictional characters should be associated with attributions of human qualities to Janet but not to the little people. Because the little people operate in a world in which ordinary rules do not operate, it would not be inconsistent to believe that they are immune from the ravages of time, and that they do not function—physically or mentally—like real people. Of course, the most sophisticated belief would entail a recognition that the little people can operate at the human level, but only if the imaginer decides to imagine them in this way.

We found that children of all ages attributed human qualities to Janet. Such a response is appropriate because even though Janet is fictional she operates in a realistic fictional world. Willingness to attribute human qualities to the little people was related to age. As predicted, 4-year-olds were more likely than older children to grant realistic human status to the little people (e.g., "Of course, the little boy will grow old. No one can stay a kid forever.") If older children attributed realistic qualities to the fantasy characters, they acknowledged these characteristics to be dependent on the whims of the imaginer.

Readiness to conceive of the fantasy characters as human was also related to experimental condition, but only for the 10-year-olds. As predicted, children were much less willing to grant human status to the little people when they could be contrasted to Janet than when no such contrast was offered. Although 65% of the 10-year-olds were still willing to grant human qualities to the little people in Conditions 1 and 2, only 12% did so in Conditions 3 and 4. Thus, when fantasy is set against reality as a background, the oldest children differentiated between realistic and fantasy characters (e.g., "Janet will grow old, 'cause she's a real girl, but the little boy is just pretend, so he'll stay the same age"). And only the 10-year-olds offered the most appropriate response: "The little boy will grow old only if Janet imagines that he does."

Unlike the older children, the 4- and 7-year-olds were unaffected by whether the fantasy characters were primary (Conditions 1 and 2) or secondary (Conditions 3 and 4). They failed to distinguish between the characteristics attributable to Janet, as against those attributable to the little people. Moreover, the 4-year-olds entertained the questions from a different frame of reference—as if inside the fantasy world and unaffected by the imaginer. For instance, asked whether the little people's hair grows, the 4-year-olds often gave responses such as, "No, their hair doesn't grow because there aren't scissors little enough to cut it." Thus, as we found with respect to questions about control, for the younger children it is concrete, real-world constraints that govern the fantasy, rather than the imaginer.

The Child's Theory of Imagination.   As the final phase of the interview, a set of questions was posed to elicit children's metaknowledge of imagination. Children were asked: "What do you imagine?" "Why do you imagine?" "What is imagining like?" "Do other people imagine the same things as you or different things?"

To our considerable surprise, these questions yielded responses from the 4-year-olds that were as sophisticated as those of the 10-year-olds. At all ages, children understood imagination to be a private process occurring in the mind and unavailable to public inspection. Thus, responses to direct and general questioning about the process of imagining did not correlate with the ability to understand the specifics of a fictional world. Contrary to the standard developmental sequence, in which metaknowledge lags behind applied knowledge, we found that children's metaknowledge about imagination was in advance of their applied knowledge.

This may occur because imagination is a topic that is often mentioned in ordinary conversation. Moreover, the level of understanding required for a child to define and talk generally about imagination may be simpler than that required to decipher an established imaginary product. It seems noteworthy that children were best able to understand accurately the "live" imagining that occurred in Condition 1—which is most analogous to their own games of pretense and make believe. Thus, whereas children may recognize imagination as a private, mental process, they become confused when the "pretend world" is conveyed as a literary creation.

Taken together, the results of this study suggest three phases in the understanding of imagination. In the first phase, which we call the phase of *realism*, recognition of imagination as the origin of a fictional world is contingent on the imaginer's high visibility or on explicit cues. But even when children do attribute the fantasy to its imaginer, they do not yet perceive the creator as having control over what is created. Rather, the fantasy coexists with reality, sharing an equal rather than subordinate status. Hence, in drawing inferences about fantasy characters, children determine their traits according to the rules of the real world, rather than by virtue of the imaginary status of the characters. A reader at this level could make little sense of *Lolita*. Such a reader would fail to recognize the hand of the invisible Nabokov behind the scenes, originating and controlling the entire sequence of events.

In the second phase, dubbed here the phase of *concrete imagination*, children are far more aware of the imaginer as the origin of the fantasy. However, children do not yet see that the imaginer determines and controls the fantasy simply by thought; they continue to conceive of control in real-world, physical, terms. Children at this level have difficulty envisioning the story as having the potential to have gone in another direction. To them the turn of events was a *fait accompli*, rather than something that emerged in sequence from the creator's imagination. This seems consistent with "concrete operational" thought, in which children have difficulty considering the possibility of two alternatives simultaneously. Confronted with *Lolita*, a reader at this level would recognize that the worlds of Humbert and Ray originate in Nabokov's mind but would fail to realize that Nabokov could in principle have written the story any way that he pleased. Nor is there yet a clear distinction between realistic and nonrealistic fictional worlds. Hence, the distinction in *Lolita* between the ordinary world of Ray and the crazed world of Humbert would not be clearly felt.

Finally, in the third phase, which we call the phase of *imagination mastery*, the fantasy—including all of its subparts and events—is viewed as the creation of the imaginer, and as subordinate to the imaginer. The child realizes that the imaginer has the power to *mentally* alter the course of the fantasy, even in arbitrary and unrealistic ways. In perceiving the imaginary characters, the child becomes cognizant that they exist only in the imaginer's mind, and that the imaginer may do as she will with them. Moreover, at this stage a sharp distinction is made between realistic and nonrealistic fictional worlds. A reader at this level has a better chance of making sense of *Lolita,* distinguishing the various voices and worlds. However, confusions may yet occur. Although children in the third phase distinguish between realistic characters and nonrealistic ones who are not subject to physical real-world laws, yet a finer distinction is called for by *Lolita*—that between a realistic and normal character (Ray) and ones who are realistic yet psychologically aberrant (Humbert, Lolita). This distinction may not be made until the adolescent years, as awareness of more purely psychological issues grows.

To add one final level of nesting to an already complex situation, we asked, "Can the Little People imagine?" A 4-year-old replied, "No, because they only have weeny brains." A 7-year-old responded, "Sure, Little Girl probably likes to pretend she's a mother or stuff." And a 10-year-old laughed at the question, appreciative of the complexity, and stated, "well, if Janet wanted them to imagine, then maybe she would imagine that *they* drew a picture and then they would imagine that there were *littler* People!"

The Rules that Govern Real Versus Fantasy Fictional Worlds

Understanding a fictional world requires that one recognize that world as a product of the author's imagination. It is also important to recognize the kind of world that has been created. We have seen that young children do not easily distinguish between a world created in a realistic piece of fiction and one created in a nonrealistic piece. In a second study, we investigated this challenge more directly by examining the types of rules that children infer to govern a realistic and nonrealistic fictional world. We examined a broad set of issues—do children realize that rule violations can occur only in nonrealistic fiction, do they allow rule violations in any type of world as long as it is a fictional world, or do they remain faithful to reality when constructing fictional worlds? We also examined a subsidiary issue—if and when children permit rule violations in a nonrealistic world, what kind of rules are they most likely to violate?

In a realistic piece of fiction, only events that are plausible and that could occur in the real world may be included. By definition, this constraint does not exist for nonrealistic, fantasy fiction. Not only do physical laws operate in novel ways (Cinderella's coach turns into a pumpkin), but so do moral rules (cruel witches devour children) and social conventions (suitors in fairy tales are asked to perform odious tasks to prove their worth). It is the violation of physical, moral and/or social rules that signals the entrance into a fantasy world. And it is the violation of physical rules that provides the definitive cue: Whereas one can conceive of a realistic work in which social and moral standards operate very differently from ours (e.g., one that takes place in a strange culture), a work in which physical laws operate differently cannot be realistic (at least not until new worlds are discovered in outer space). Hence, although *Lolita* may reveal a world with odd moral and social rules, it is not a surreal novel because physical rules are respected. In this sense, it can be considered a more realistic novel than, for instance, a piece of science fiction.

In sum, our study addressed two questions: (1) When do children demonstrate different expectations about the rules that govern realistic versus fantasy fictional worlds? (2) What types of rule violations—physical, moral, or social—do children recognize as most indicative of a nonrealistic world?

Given the results of our first study, in which we examined attributes ascribed to fantasy figures, we hypothesized that young children would initially fail to distinguish between realistic and nonrealistic fictional worlds. Hence, children should perceive both kinds of worlds as governed by the rules of the "real world." Because young children have been shown to believe that social and moral as well as physical rules are immutable (Lockhart, Abrahams, & Osherson, 1977), young children ought to expect no rule violations of any kind in fictional worlds.

With increasing age, as children become sensitive to the distinction between more and less realistic fiction, they should begin to expect rule violations in fantasy but not realistic fiction. Further, as they become sensitive to the presence of physical rule violations as most indicative of a nonrealistic world, they should expect these rule violations more often than moral or social violations in such fiction.

In order to determine whether children could honor the implicit constraints on each, we constructed an illustrated story that shifted back and forth from a realistic to a fantasy fictional world. Forty-eight children, 16 each at ages 6, 8, and 10, participated. The story was read aloud to each child. The narrative opened in a realistic mode, featuring a character named Sally. The story shifted back and forth from Sally's world to a world that Sally has imagined, located on an island called Aeola. On Aeola, physical, moral, and social rules were shown to operate in the reverse manner from reality. For instance, the sun radiates cold (physical rule violation), lying is considered good (moral rule violation), and one greets another person by turning one's back to him or her (social rule violation). In later parts of the story, children were presented with a situation involving a rule (either in Sally's world or Aeola) and were asked to decide, given three choices, whether the rule operated in a *realistic* manner, a manner *opposite* from reality, or in a manner *unrelated* to real-world functioning. For instance, children were asked to decide whether the rain on Aeola made clothes wet (realistic), dry (opposite), or wrinkled (unrelated). Sometimes these rules were ones that had already been described (assessing sheer recall), whereas at other times the rules were ones that had not been described (assessing whether children had inferred the *principle* that on Aeola rules operate in the reverse, whereas in Sally's world rules operate realistically). For the most part, children were able to recall rules already stated, demonstrating an understanding of the rules as presented in the story. It is with the problem of inferring the principle of rule violation that we are thus concerned here.

Analyses revealed the following pattern of results: First, as expected, the youngest children failed fully to distinguish between fictional worlds. The 6-year-olds often gave real-world responses when questioned about rules in Aeola, revealing that they had not inferred the principle that Aeola was a world in which rules operate strangely. However, children of all ages expected more rule violations on Aeola than in Sally's world, a result that reveals at least a minimal ability to distinguish fictional worlds even among 6-year-olds. With increasing age, children proved more likely to allow rule violations on Aeola.

Contrary to our second hypothesis, children of all ages were more willing to permit moral violations on Aeola than physical or social ones. We speculate that this result occurred because moral rules are often violated both in fiction and in reality (people lie, cheat, and steal, even if these actions are not approved). Moreover, young children often report that, although it is wrong to break moral rules, people often do break such rules (Turiel & Davidson, in press). Physical and social rules present a striking contrast: There is no *possibility* of violating a physical rule in the "real" world, and there is no *motivation* to break a social one. Thus, the fact that children permitted moral rule violations on Aeola suggests that they were treating Aeola as if it were a realistic world.

When questioned about Sally's world, children of all ages incorrectly permitted violations of physical rules. These violations were simply carried over from the world of Aeola. Thus, the children were insensitive to the switch back from a fantasy to a realistic world.

We were surprised at the low level of performance at all ages studied. To determine whether our task was simply insensitive to the ability to distinguish realistic versus fantasy fiction, we administered it to 21 college undergraduates. These subjects had little difficulty; they realized that rules of all kinds were violated on Aeola and allowed more rule violations on Aeola than in Sally's world. However, our previous finding with respect to moral rules was replicated: Adults permitted moral violations in the realistic world in 50% of their responses. We believe that this reflects subjects' (children's as well as adults') theories of human nature—or their accurate perception of our flawed world—rather than an inability to recognize entrance into a realistic fictional world.

This interpretation is buttressed by the types of reasons children gave to justify rule violation responses on Aeola. When explaining physical and social violations, children asserted that on Aeola rules operate differently (e.g., "Because in that country the sun is cold"). But violations of moral rules were justified not by asserting that such violations were the norm in Aeola, but rather in terms of the character's desires (e.g., "He took the bike because he wanted to'') or the situation (e.g., "He took the bike because it was just sitting there"). Thus, in the case of moral laws, children did not seem to realize that an opposite response indicated a rule violation. Rather, they talked about the opposite response as if it were something that could have occurred in the real world.

The finding that the children were most willing to accept violation of moral rules in both episodes diverges from studies showing that children perceive physical laws as least violable, and social laws as most alterable (Lockhart et al., 1977; Nucci & Turiel, 1978). One possible explanation for this discrepancy stems from the fact that, in this study, children were not questioned about the arbitrariness of rules but were instead asked to complete a story involving rules. Even a realistic story may be perceived as operating on a different level from that of reality. Thus, a story task is perhaps inadequate for assessing the ontological status of rules.

Given children's difficulties in sorting out realistic versus nonrealistic fictional worlds, a story constructed on the lines of *Lolita* should prove hopelessly confusing. The reader must distinguish the fictional from the real (i.e., the worlds of Ray and Humbert, on the one hand, and the world of Nabokov in the afterword, on the other); and the reader must also distinguish the two fictional worlds. Although both Ray and Humbert inhabit realistic fictional worlds (people like Humbert certainly do exist outside of fiction), the world of Ray is a normal one, and that of Humbert is abnormal. Because Humbert's world is so psychologically bizarre, the reader must recognize that this is a world closer to dream life than to ordinary waking reality. The reader must be able to recognize that even though physical laws operate realistically in Humbert's world, the world is quite atypical. Moreover, the reader must question whether to take literally all that Humbert reports and must attempt to distinguish between Humbert's actual deeds and deeds acted out only in his fantasy.

The results of our second study help to fill out the three stages involved in understanding the imaginative process sketched earlier. During the preschool and early school years, when children often fail to recognize that a fictional world originates in, and is controlled by, the mind of an invisible author, children also fail to differentiate between kinds of fictional worlds. Presented with a story that shifts back and forth between realistic and fantasy worlds, children remain unaware of the shifts.

During the middle elementary school years, when children readily recognize the imaginer as the source—yet not the ultimate controller—of a story, children begin to distinguish levels of reality characterizing fictional worlds. However, children still remain unwilling to permit many physical rule violations in a nonrealistic work.

At the third level, not yet fully attained by our oldest subjects (10-year-olds), children have become aware that the author can, in principle, do whatever he or she wants. The work originates in an author's mind, it is fully determined by the decisions the author makes, and the author has license to violate any type of real-world rule as long as he or she provides sufficient clues that he or she is creating a fictional world. The author can even mix levels of reality *within* a world, as do Jorge Luis Borges and Gabriel Garcia Marquez. The competent reader will recognize this as a deliberate violation of the traditional distinction between realistic and nonrealistic fiction.

Building a Theory of Literary Understanding

It is well known that Vladimir Nabokov was extremely critical of Freud, fond of punning on Freud's name, as in "Freud-fraud." Nor did Nabokov's denunciation of Freud constitute his only reservation about psychology. Indeed, like many writers, he remained highly skeptical that the experience of the imagination would ever lend itself to psychological analyses. We are under no illusion that we have refuted Nabokov's suspicions. We must concede, at the outset, that our studies cannot pretend to illuminate the subtleties of *Lolita,* or any mature work of art; nor can our studies reveal all the complex mental processes required to enter into and make sense of a fictional world.

How, then, do we evaluate our endeavors? An analogy from Piaget's work may be useful here. In studying a domain, Piaget first considered the highest levels of competence attainable in that domain, sketching out, for instance, the ways in which the adult reasons in the logical, physical, or moral domains. Following this laying out of the territory, he devised tasks to discover the stages through which children passed en route to such developed understanding. In Piaget's view, children's partial understandings can help us to understand the adult endstate better—both what the adult can do, and what limits obtain even for the adult.

When referring to adult competence in understanding a novel such as *Lolita,* we are talking about an ideal, a state difficult to achieve in a single reading. The misunderstandings that children demonstrate along the way, when confronted with much simpler stories, can help us to identify the understandings that adults must eventually achieve, as well as the confusions adults may experience when confronted with complex works. For instance, children's tendency to blur the distinction between realistic and fantasy worlds may be a simpler version of the confusions adults may experience when such levels are mixed within a single fictional world (for example, in *Lolita,* which mixes physical reality and psychological fantasy, or in novels by Borges and Marquez, which introduce violations of physical reality within a seemingly realistic world).

Understanding a complex work of art of course entails much more than making the few basic distinctions considered here. Ultimately, a theory of literary understanding might require a theory of each literary work (e.g., Fish, 1980) or even of each reader (e.g., Holland, 1968); Nabokov's skepticism would thus be vindicated. Nonetheless, we are not willing to rule out the scientific study of literary understanding: We operate on the assumption that there remain some general principles that can be drawn on to explain how individuals ordinarily confront literary texts. What we have studied here are the most basic preliminaries to literary understanding, not sufficient to ensure rich understanding but, quite possibly, the necessary, lean antecedents of such understanding.

We can suggest two facets of literature that may help to bridge the gap between the skills probed in our own preliminary investigations and the skills required for mastering a literary masterpiece. One entails the linguistic aspect of the work—the poetic uses of language that call attention to themselves (Jakobson, 1960), the metaphors, puns, and word plays that figure so richly in *Lolita*, and which Roger Brown elucidated in his review of Nabokov. A second aspect concerns the psychological complexities of fictional characters, alone and in interaction: Humbert's own mind, conscious and unconscious, his intricate relationship to Lolita and her ambivalent relationship to him, and Nabokov's relation to each of his fictional creations. Much of the drama of a great work of art lies in these two areas, areas that we have skirted, but to which Roger Brown called attention in his luminous discussion.

The challenge confronting the analyst who would explain mature literary understanding is to integrate the more elementary aspects of understanding, of the kind investigated here, with such subtle facets as the language of the work and the psychology of its characters. Language and motivation may be relatively straightforward in formulaic works such as dime-store mysteries or airport-rack romances, but they constitute the challenging center of literary masterworks by such authors as James, Chekhov, or Nabokov. For alerting us to this rich repository of psychological puzzles and for encouraging us to believe (contra Nabokov) that it may not be impossible for psychologists to grapple with them, we owe a profound debt to Roger Brown.

ACKNOWLEDGMENTS

The research reported here was supported by grants from the National Science Foundation (BNS 79-24430) and the Spencer Foundation. We are grateful to the following people for their help: Arnold Lanni, Assistant Superintendent, Arlington Public Schools; Mary Murphy, Principal, Dallin School, Arlington; Joan Flanagan, Principal, and Clare O'Connell, Acting Principal, Crosby School, Arlington; Helen Thompson, Director, Soldier's Field Park Children's Center, Cambridge; Marilyn Stoops, Coordinator, Newtowne School, Cambridge; Ellen Krim, Director, Lesley-Ellis Preschool, Cambridge; Hermine Fish, Director, Harvard Law School Child Care Center, Cambridge; Myra Bennett, Director, Harvard Yard Child Care Center, Cambridge; Robert Blaney, Principal, Winn Brook School, Belmont; and the many teachers and students who contributed to this research. We would also like to thank Erin Phelps and Joseph Walters for help in data analysis, Amy Demorest and Fran Ruff for their assistance in the conduct of this research, and Betsy Howard, for the storybook illustrations. Portions of this research were reported at the American Psychological Association Convention, Montreal, September 1980.

REFERENCES

Bettelheim, B. (1976). *The use of enchantment: The meaning and importance of fairy tales.* New York: Knopf.

Brown, R. (1970). A review of V. Nabokov's *Lolita. Psycholinguistics: Selected papers.* New York: The Free Press.

Fish, S. (1980). *Is there a text in this class?* Cambridge, MA: Harvard University Press.

Holland, N. (1968). *The dynamics of literary response.* New York: Oxford University Press.

Jaglom, L., & Gardner, H. (1981). Decoding the worlds of television. *Studies in Visual Communication, 7,* 33–47.

Jakobson, R. (1960). Closing statement: Linguistics and poetics. In T. A. Sebeok (Ed.), *Style in language.* Cambridge, MA: MIT Press.

Lockhart, K., Abrahams, B., & Osherson, D. (1977). Children's understanding of uniformity in the environment. *Child Development, 48,* 1521–1531.

Mandler, J., & Johnson, N. (1977). Remembrance of things parsed: Story structure and recall. *Cognitive Psychology, 9,* 111–151.

Morison, P., & Gardner, H. (1978). Dragons and dinosaurs: How the child distinguishes reality and fantasy. *Child Development, 49,* 642–648.

Nucci, L., & Turiel, E. (1978). Social interactions and the development of social concepts in preschool children. *Child Development, 49,* 400–408.

Rosenblatt, E., Massey, C., Blank, P., Gardner, H., & Winner, E. (1984). *Children's sensitivity to compositional principles in literature.* Unpublished manuscript.

Scarlett, W., & Wolf, D. (1979). When it's only make-believe: The construction of a boundary between fantasy and reality in storytelling. *New Directions for Child Development, 6,* 29–40.

Turiel, E., & Davidson, P. (in press). Heterogeneity, inconsistency and asynchrony in the development of cognitive structures. In I. Levin (Ed.), *Stage and structure.* Norwood, NJ: Ablex.

Winner, E., Wapner, W., Cicone, M., & Gardner, H. (1979). Measures of metaphor. *New Directions for Child Development, 6,* 67–75.

18 Coherences and Categorization: A Historical View

Eleanor Rosch
University of California, Berkeley

Roger Brown has been a widely influential researcher and teacher. We would all agree with that; what then, do we mean by it? The study of intellectual history is the study of coherences, but the meaning of coherence is not entirely clear. Recently, I have argued that to see an event as coherent we must see the eventual outcome to have already been contained in some form in the initial ground of the event, and we must see the happening as just that proper and reasonable means for connecting the ground and outcome—that is, for changing the outcome from its initial to its final form (Rosch, 1984, 1987). Situated in the context of Harvard of the 1950s, 1960s, and 1970s, Roger Brown's qualities of thought—the kinds of questions that he was asking and the style in which he asked and answered them—form part of the ground of the development of all the contributors to this book. That developmental psycholinguistics would not have its present form without Roger Brown is readily apparent. Perhaps less well known is his influence on the study of concepts and categories; this chapter is an attempt to trace some of that influence.

There are three general claims about coherences in ideas that the categorization story illustrates. The first is that a teacher's general intellectual qualities can influence students and thereby appear as attributes of an entire field of inquiry. Second, to the extent that research has a meaning principally within the context of already existing questions and answers in which it is embedded, research that is a contradiction of earlier work effects a true coherence—in other words, contradiction is one of the forms in which grounds may appear in outcomes. Third, concepts can move from one field, one context of questions, to another. In so doing, like human immigrants, they create tensions, and adaptation of both the concept and its new field may result.

The general qualities of Roger Brown's thinking that first attracted me are just those subtle aspects of style that influence generations of students but are hard to trace in attributes of fields of inquiry. When I arrived at Harvard in 1963, having been "cured" of a background in philosophy by taking Wittgenstein's *Philosophical Investigations* (1953) seriously, I wanted my new field to be empirical, but not barbarically so. In a psychology still emerging from behaviorism, the aims of much of the research were not always transparent. Roger Brown's first attractive quality was that he was interested in basic issues (call them philosophical, if you will): how words refer to things; what the nature of abstraction is; how thought is related to language; and so on. Secondly, the way in which he looked at those issues was empirical. Interestingly, it was an empiricism free of the methodological manifesto of any particular school or theory—the kind of approach that could lead naturally to the unprecedented act of studying child speech to answer questions about how humans learn language. Thirdly, those empirically approached questions were inherently interdisciplinary. In Brown's thought, the social world was not something radically separated from individual cognitive processing; rather, issues were formulated from their inception in a combination of cognitive, social, historical, and sometimes biological terms.

Actually Roger Brown had a final quality, perhaps more overarching and influential and less traceable than the others—a sense of wonder. Issues were not cut to procrustean beds: "It goes without saying that the truth may not vote a straight party ticket" (Brown, 1965, p. 114). Like any good artist, his works involved space as well as content—an open ended quality which courted the student's common sense, perhaps wisdom, and certainly participation.

THE CONTEXT OF CATEGORIZATION RESEARCH

It may be a truism that research does not originate in a vacuum. Fields and subfields of inquiry are already divided in a certain way. Each constitutes a context in which questions have already been framed, research conducted, data offered, and conclusions drawn. My own work on categories did *not* originate in learning theory, in concept identification, in formal linguistic semantics, or in semantic memory; it might have taken a very different course had it done so. Rather, my work began by addressing an issue within one of the areas where Roger Brown had pioneered empirical work, that of language and thought.

Empirical issues always involve some controversy, claims not just that the world is one particular way but that it is that way rather than some other. The controversy in the language-and-thought case was that of linguistic relativity and determinism. The linguist Benjamin Whorf had claimed that each language was a metaphysic, both embodying and imposing on a culture a particular world view (Whorf, 1956); thus, our very forms of thought were determined by our language. As evidence he offered tantalizing examples: e.g., the Hopi language in which, he claimed, the major grammatical division was not, as in Standard European Languages, between objects and actions (nouns and verbs)—both of which are coded in Hopi by duration—but, rather, between the two principles of manifest and unmanifest. Literal translations of Hopi into English served to support the view of how oddly the Hopi thought. But was it, in fact, true that the Hopi actually thought differently from us, in ways that we could not imagine, or was it simply a problem of taking too seriously a literal translation of their grammar? Might we not, as Brown (and Mark Twain) pointed out, come to equally sententious but false conclusions considering the metaphysic of Germans from a literal rendering of German into English (Brown, 1958b; Clemens, 1910)? And was this an empirical issue? Could we actually demonstrate any relation at all between some particular forms and categories of a language and some particular aspect of thought? These were the questions that, in part, defined the context of my research.

It turned out that the requirements for a domain where such a demonstration can be satisfactorally performed are fairly exacting. The domain itself must not differ grossly between the two cultures; thus animals, plants, and man-made objects will not do. The domain must be measurable in independent physical units apart from the way it is named in language; thus domains such as feelings or values will not do. The natural languages must differ with respect to the way in which they divide the domain; if the languages are the same in this respect there is nothing to study. And the domain must permit us to obtain, independently of the language, measures of some aspect of cognition, such as perception or memory that can be shown to be a function of the linguistic difference alone.

In light of these demands, Brown and Lenneberg (1954) performed a seminal study using the domain of colors. Color appeared to be an ideal domain on which to do language and thought research: It is a continuous physical variable that can easily be designated by objective measures independent of the color terms in any given language, i.e., the physical aspect of color is the same in every part of the world. On the other hand, many reports by travellers, missionaries, and anthropologists had described differences in the way color names classify the color space. And color discrimination, memory, and classification can be readily measured independently of color names. Thus, what was needed to show an effect of language on cognition was to establish a correlation between some linguistic variable in color naming and some such nonlinguistic cognitive measure.

Reasoning in functional terms, Brown and Lenneberg argued that cultures, perhaps because of differing color ecologies, should differ in the areas of the color space to which they paid the most attention. Culturally important colors should tend to be referred to often in speech, and their names should thus become highly available to members of the culture. Further, available names should have three measurable attributes: they should be shorter (Zipf, 1935, had shown that words used frequently in speech evolve into shorter forms), they should be produced faster, and they should come to have meanings widely agreed on by speakers of the language. For a measure of cognition, Brown and Lenneberg chose recognition memory, i.e., the ability of subjects to recognize a previously viewed color from among an array of colors.

As things turned out, Brown and Lenneberg's research showed that codability of a color (a composite measure of length of name, response latency in naming, and agreement in naming) correlated with recognition memory accuracy, particularly under conditions of delay. A reasonable interpretation (see Krauss, 1968) was that the more codable colors were better remembered specifically because of the greater ease with which they could be linguistically coded and stored in memory. This interpretation was supported and amplified when it was found that a second linguistic variable, viz., communication accuracy (the accuracy with which a name communicated the referent of a color from one individual to another), was found to correlate with memory; and to do so even for arrays of color stimuli of low uniform saturation for which the original measure of codability had failed (Lantz & Stefflre, 1964). Thus, color language was seen to affect memory in that it was the way an individual could communicate with him or herself over time.

It may be noted that this line of research bore the marks of Brown's characteristic qualities of thought. It had its roots in basic issues of the nature of thought and language. It was inherently interdisciplinary; the biology of color vision, linguistics, anthropology, and psychology were all a part of its conception. It was determinedly empirical—graciously allowing that Whorf's most exciting ideas might not be empirical, ingenious means were devised for testing that minimal form of the Whorfian hypothesis that did seem testable. And finally, the variables used were conceived in functional terms.

Color Categorization Reconsidered

This was the form of the field when I argumentatively entered it in 1968. Might there be, I wondered, aspects of cognition, even for colors, that linguistic codes did not affect? This question arose first with regard to the similarity structure of the color space. Given that color names affected accuracy of memory, would they also affect inaccuracy; that is, would color names determine the way colors were confused with each other in memory? The opportunity to do research with a people who had only two basic color names, the Dani of Indonesian New Guinea (K. G. Heider, 1970), and the new technique of multidimensional scaling for analyzing the structure of data spaces, made possible a comparison of confusions in naming and memory for two cultures. Color naming and color recognition memory data were therefore collected from Americans and Dani for a 10-hue by 4-brightness array of Munsell chips. Chips given the same name and chips confused with each other in memory were treated as confusion data and a multidimensional scaling performed on the resultant matrices (Heider & Olivier,

1972). The results showed that, whereas the structure of the color spaces in naming were quite different between Dani and Americans, the scaling solutions for the memory data were remarkably similar. Furthermore, memory confusions were no more likely to be within name boundaries than between them.

This study showed a universal aspect of color cognition and showed it for speakers of two languages with widely divergent color vocabulary. Yet, from the viewpoint of the present chapter, one of the most interesting things about this study is that it has been forgotten. Even the authors seldom refer to it. We might speculate that it had too oblique a relation to the research tradition that gave rise to it. Rather than either extending or contradicting, it limited the very convincing line of argument for relativity which was its context.

The next set of studies on the language and thought issues were more focused. The first, almost trivial, requirement for testing the Whorfian hypothesis—noted earlier—is that there be at least two natural languages whose terminologies with respect to a domain are different. This assumption, which had seemed so obviously met by the domain of colors, was soon challenged by two anthropologists. Berlin and Kay (1969) first looked at the reported diversity of color names linguistically and claimed that there were actually a highly limited number of basic (as opposed to secondary) color terms in any language. Next, using a two-dimensional array of Munsell color chips, they asked speakers of 20 different languages to identify the colors to which the basic color names in their languages referred. The speakers performed two tasks: They marked the boundaries of each of their native language's basic color terms, and they pointed to the chip that they considered the best example of each basic term. As might have been expected from the anthropological literature, there was a great deal of variation in the placement of the boundaries of the terms; surprisingly, however, the choice of best examples of the color terms—Berlin and Kay called them focal colors—was quite similar for the speakers of the 20 different languages.

I first encountered this work (still in manuscript) in a seminar in 1968 at Harvard given by the anthropologist, Roger Keesing, on what was then called *ethnoscience,* and I became very excited. Could it be that these examples of color names, these focal colors, designated areas of the color space that were perceptually (and thus universally) salient, and that it was this perceptual salience that determined both which colors were more memorable and which colors were more codable? Brown and Lenneberg's results applied to English speakers; the reasonable assumption had been that they would have cross-cultural import. Might their findings actually have been an unanticipated by-product of the fact that they had some (universal) focal colors in their array?

Prompted by these questions, my research proceeded in several stages. First, native speakers of a diverse group of languages were asked to name in their language focal and nonfocal color chips. It was found that focal colors were given shorter names and named more rapidly than were nonfocal colors. Thus, color codability itself appeared to be universal (Heider, 1972). For the next step, the Dani were again crucial, and a second and more extended field trip was made to study them. Given only two basic color terms and little elaboration of color language, focal colors were not more codable than nonfocal colors for the Dani. Would focal colors still be more memorable? Both a naming and a recognition memory task were given to American and Dani subjects for focal and nonfocal colors. The results were unequivocal; although the Dani color memory was, as a whole, less accurate than American, both groups' memory was more accurate for the focal than the nonfocal colors (Heider, 1972). Thus, color memory did appear to be a product of something more universal than particular language codes.

At this point, the research began to seem to have implications for the way the color space becomes structured into named categories in languages in the first place. Suppose that there are perceptually salient colors that more readily attract attention and are more easily remembered than other colors. When category names are learned, they tend to become attached first to the salient stimuli; then, by means of the principle of stimulus generalization, they generalize to other, physically similar instances. In this way, these natural prototype colors could become the foci of cognitive organization for categories.

The first test of this line of reasoning examined whether Dani could learn names (i.e., retain color-word pairs in long term memory) for focal colors more easily than for nonfocal colors. This did, in fact, prove to be the case. The definitive test then concerned the structuring of the color space. Here we found that Dani could learn color categories (lean names for a group of color chips) more readily when these were naturally structured, i.e., with the focal color the center of the category, than when they were unnaturally structured, i.e., with the focal chip at the periphery of the category and a nonfocal chip at the center (Rosch, 1973).

Where then did things stand? All this research seemed to turn precisely on its head the earlier findings with respect to language and thought. Rosch (in Heider, 1972) concluded that "far from being a domain well suited to the study of the effects of language on thought, the color space would seem to be a prime example for the influence of underlying perceptual-cognitive factors on the formation and reference of linguistic categories" (p. 20).

Since that time, the semantics of color naming has been related even more closely to the physiology of vision. The four primary basic color terms map closely onto the unique hue points of DeValois' physiological account of color vision (DeValois & Jacobs, 1968). A model of color naming in terms of fuzzy sets has shown how the color space would be logically divided for maximal discrimination for any number of color terms as these enter languages (Kay & McDaniel, 1978). Further, anthropological data have tended to fit this model (Kay, 1981). Indeed, enough was known a decade later for Paul Kay (1981) to begin a talk to the Cognitive Science Society with the statement, "Color is an area in which our ignorance regarding the relation of perception and linguistic meaning is less than total'' (p. 61).

Contradiction and Coherence

The work of the 1970s has been seen as a contradiction of Brown and Lenneberg (1954) and in direct opposition to the relativistic and functional framework in which the Brown and Lenneberg study was conceived. It *is* a contradiction— which is precisely why it is a coherent outcome of the original Brown framework of theorizing. In linguistics a semantic opposite is a pair of terms possessing all semantic markers in common save one (such as day and night, brother and sister); to have meaning, each term of the pair implies the other. The fact is that Heider (1972), in analogous fashion, retained all the theoretically relevant "units" of Brown and Lenneberg but with one flip.

The importance of the overall framework for the impact of any set of studies, and this set in particular, is illustrated by the reception of a talk on cross-cultural work on color, given in the early 1970s by Chad McDaniel to a group of vision scientists at the University of California, Berkeley. There were numerous questions and criticisms as the talk progressed and a general feeling on both sides that communication was not occurring. It was only at the end of the talk that McDaniel got across the point that his topic was color *naming* and, furthermore, that what he was arguing against was the widely held anthropological view that colors were categorized differently and arbitrarily in different cultures. The audience of vision scientists were bemused that anyone could have held such a view and, as a consequence, they were not particularly struck by the reported research. . . . No study can be contradictory without some identity of assumptions, methods, and findings of the field in which it offers such a contradictory finding or conclusion.

Not that the vision scientist should be taken as representing the a priori sensible view with respect to naming. It is not a foregone conclusion for all domains that semantics will follow perception. Function, historically determined language games, or many other hypothesized factors could intervene between perception and language. Even in the domain of color, such factors have not been entirely excluded, and there may still be effects of codability on thought. For example, when an array of colors is formed with all the effects of focality of colors systematically removed, effects of language again seem to emerge (Lucy & Shweder, 1979, although note that this is not the interpretation Lucy and Shweder give of their data). And the relationship between coding accuracy and communication accuracy established in the earlier research has never been challenged. The explanation of this relationship, that memory is the way in which we communicate with ourselves over time, could prove to be an account of consider-

able generative power. However, to my knowledge these lines of partial linguistic effects have not been pursued.

This brings us back to the statement that empirical issues always involve
contradiction and controversy, always involve a claim that the world is one
particular way *rather than* some other way. A dialectical logic appears to govern
our thinking; we act as though truth did vote a straight party ticket. The language–thought issue is reminiscent of other either–or controversies in psychology (are mental images propositional or analog; intelligence due to nature or
nurture?), which also gain greatest impetus when stated in extreme form. This is
a tendency that Newell (1973) has succinctly and critically characterized as,
"You can't play 20 questions with nature and win."

IMPLICATIONS FOR THE STRUCTURE AND PROCESSING OF CATEGORIES IN GENERAL

The work described so far concerned the color space. However, the generality of
its import had to do with the structure and nature of concepts. How was the
transition made?

To begin the story, Rosch was not a contented anthropological field worker.
In fact, especially during the long second sojourn in the Grand Valley of West
Irian New Guinea, I spent a good deal of time wondering why on earth I was in a
place like this spending day after day teaching people names for little color chips.
Eventually, these musings took an intellectual turn—I suppose the logic was
something like "discomfort should be balanced by importance." At any rate, as
I began to mentally review *Words and Things* (Brown, 1958b), various dormant
ideas emerged. When Roger Brown talked there about the meaning aspects of
language, he talked about concepts and their referents—color names were examples of concepts, only thus were they of interest. However, when Brown talked
about concepts and reference, his examples were different things from colors and
his account, in terms of defining and accidental properties of objects, did not
seem to fit color reference. Concept identification research (for example, Bruner,
Goodnow, & Austin, 1956), well embedded in experimental psychology, was
also about concepts, but concepts conceived in that tradition seemed to fit more
with Brown's account of reference than with the color domain. Stimulus generalization seemed appropriate to the color case, but concept identification research
was not done within a generalization paradigm. And Wittgenstein, I recalled,
had talked a great deal about concepts; indeed, he seemed to have argued convincingly that meaning could not be anything like the way it was conceived in
experimental psychology; it need involve neither reference, defining attributes,
nor definitive boundaries. Was it then possible that concepts in general were
structured like colors?

These wonderings took place over an extended period of time. (I think aha! experiences are reserved for temperate climates.) In fact, nothing definite emerged until I returned to the United States in 1970 and regained my proper context of laboratories, a few interested colleagues (Roger Brown among them), and the necessity to write things clearly in introductions to papers. (Health, tuna fish sandwiches, and movies, the absence of which had seemed so momentous in New Guinea, instantly became part of the background.) After a period of what would surely be called incubation by those who believe in it, the process began of operationalizing the extension of the color work to the field of concepts.

An initial question was whether the idea of focal points (best examples, typicality) of a category would apply to semantic categories other than color. Would subjects agree on rating the typicality of members of semantic categories, and, if so, would these ratings predict anything? In the experimental human learning and memory literature, categories had meant clustering in free recall, and this tradition had produced available norms (Battig & Montague, 1969). So the initial categories investigated were semantic superordinates drawn from Battig and Montague. The first experiment (done at Brown University with the help of Richard Millward) showed that subjects did consistently rate typicality and that these ratings predicted reaction times for a categorization task—answering true or false to the statement "A (member) is a (category)" (Rosch, 1973). Working within a somewhat different framework, these results were replicated and extended by Rips, Shoben, and Smith (1973).

The next set of experiments brought the idea of prototypes into the domain of cognitive processing proper. It seemed obvious in the cognitive psychology of those days that categories were represented by a mental code (mental representation), and it seemed greatly exciting to try, by empirical methods, to delicately tease out what the nature of that code might be. Could questions about the nature of abstraction finally be given an answer? Were these codes like images? Did they contain information in a form more general than either words or images? The most appealing methods came from the work of Posner (Posner, Boies, Eichelman, & Taylor, 1969) and Beller (1971), appealing because these did not require any particular a priori processing model. In the basic task a subject is given a pair of stimuli (semantic category members) that he or she must judge as the same if they belonged to the same category. In some conditions the stimuli were word pairs, in others pictures, in another experiment colors. Stimuli varied systematically in their rated goodness of example within their category. On half the trials, the subject was given the name of the category as a prime prior to the appearance of the stimuli. The logic was that a prime could only facilitate a match when it made possible the generation of a mental code that contained within it some of the information needed to make the match.

The basic result both for the colors and for the semantic categories was that the priming facilitated matches for physically identical, good examples of categories but actually hindered matches of poor examples of categories. This suggested that the category name had within it information biased toward typicality. The effect was eliminated when the prime was presented simultaneously with the stimulus, arguing that the prime bore on initial perception rather than on later judgment. Further, for semantic categories the effect was virtually unchanged when mixed trials of words and pictures were used, suggesting that the information from the prime was in a form common to both words and pictures. Varying the time interval between prime and stimulus showed, however, that it took less time to prepare for pictures than for words and suggested that pictures might be closer to the underlying representational form than words. Finally, the interference effect from priming with poor category members was eliminated by long practice for semantic categories but not for color categories, suggesting that color category effects were derived from a nonmanipulable perceptual bias whereas the semantic categories were indeed semantic in character (Rosch, 1975b).

Research on a single issue can come from many traditions. No one brought up in the interdisciplinary broadness of Roger Brown's approach could remain long studying words in isolation; the meanings of words are intimately tied to their uses in sentences. In fact, there have been many attempts in linguistics to define meaning in terms of substitutability of words into sentence frames (e.g., Fodor & Katz, 1964). Taking our next research step, we thus predicted that the probability that a category term could be substituted for its superordinate in a sentence would be a function of typicality. We had subjects generate sentences using superordinates and then substituted category terms at five levels of goodness of example; other subjects rated the naturalness and truth value of the resultant sentences. Results were as predicted. For example, in the sentence "Twenty or so birds often perch on the telephone wires outside my window and twitter in the morning," the term sparrow but not turkey may be substituted to form a sentence that retains its naturalness and truth value (Rosch, 1977).

We also turned to the logic of natural language use of category terms in the form of hedges. Although logic and psychology have treated categories as though membership is an either–or matter, with all members having a full and equal degree of membership, natural languages themselves possess linguistic mechanisms for coding and coping with gradients of membership. Lakoff (1972) calls "hedges" those qualifying terms and phrases such as "almost," "virtually," and "technically," which point to such gradients of membership. Creating sentence frames such as "_____ is virtually _____" we showed that subjects almost invariably prefer to place the poor example in the first spot and the good example in the second; e.g., an off-red color chip is virtually a good red chip, but not vice-versa (Rosch, 1975a). The findings from hedges were then extended to show that, in general, peripheral members of categories with clear prototypes are judged spatially closer to the prototypes than the prototypes are to the peripheral member (Rosch, 1975a; Tversky, 1977, has made an extended argument against the assumption of symmetry in similarity).

The Origins of Category Prototype Structure

Where do prototypes and typicality ordering—revealed through such research—come from? With colors, and the geometric forms and facial expression of emotion to which the color work was first extended (Rosch, 1973), the origin can be argued to be physiological. But what of all the other semantic categories? One of the interesting aspects of extending an idea from one domain into another is that a relevant literature usually already exists. (Coherent events have grounds.) In this instance, there was, in fact, a psychological literature on schema formation.

One obvious hypothesis for prototypes of semantic categories is that they are those objects that have the mean values of the quantifiable attributes of the category. That this can be the case has been demonstrated by two studies, one of artificial categories, the other of natural categories. Reed (1972) showed that for schematic faces, matching to the prototype—where the prototype was defined as a mean—was the most predictive of alternative mathematical models for describing strategies for categorizing new faces. And Rips et al. (1973) demonstrated that animals considered closest to the category name "animal" in a multidimensional scaling solution were just those animals of medium value on the two dimensions that differentiated the animal space (size and predacity). But not all categories have such quantifiable attributes, and there is more to the animal domain than size and predacity. That schemata can be learned for gestalt configurations having no definable attributes had also been demonstrated by Posner, Goldsmith, and Welton (1967). Their subjects learned to classify families of random dot patterns that had been generated by distortions of an initial prototype pattern. With the passage of time they were more accurate in classifying the prototype than other patterns, even when they had not previously seen the prototype pattern.

However, neither means nor gestalt configurations would seem to exhaust the information in prototypes of semantic categories. For years, I had been haunted by Wittgenstein's (1953) criticisms of our ways of thinking about language. Might his account of family resemblances now be used in a positive sense as an actual psychological model to account for prototypes in semantic categories? The concept of family resemblances is actually a very limited part of Wittgenstein's account of language; it does not approach the essence of his "language games" or "forms of life." None the less, it seemed to us that, in as much as objects can be said to possess psychologically identifiable attributes at all, those attributes are related to each other as family resemblances more truly than as defining criteria. To test this Carolyn Mervis and I (Rosch & Mervis, 1975) went about developing a measure of family resemblance. Our hypothesis was that the members of categories that are considered most typical are those having the most attributes in common with other members of the same category and least attributes in common with other categories. In fact, in a series of studies, we found that measures of family resemblance were highly correlated with ratings of typicality for superordinate categories, for basic level categories, and for artificial categories that we constructed with various family resemblance relationships.

Unfortunately—at least from the perspective of research—for categories in natural language there are always multitudes of uncontrolled variables. Critics not happy with the idea of typicality were thus able to quickly pass off typicality effects as due to something else, often item frequency. Accordingly, we proposed to test the structural bases of typicality effects using controlled artificial categories. Three types of artificial categories were constructed: dot patterns, in which typicality was defined as similarity to a prototype pattern in overall configuration; stick figures, in which typicality was defined as closeness to a prototype figure possessing the means of attributes for the category; and letter strings, in which typicality was defined as the degree of family resemblance (overlap of letters) among category members. For all three types of category, we found that structural typicality determined ease of item learning, speed of classification of items after learning, ratings of the typicality of items, order in which items were generated in a production task, and facilitation or inhibition of responses to items in a priming paradigm. This was true both when frequency of items was equated and when rates of learning were equated (Rosch, Simpson, & Miller, 1976).

By 1976 there was an accumulating body of empirical data showing the effects of prototype structure in categories on virtually all the major dependent variables used as measures in psychological research: speed of processing, speed of learning, order and probability of output, effects of advance information on performance, and the logic of natural language use of category terms. The prototype view of categories could not be ignored.

The Immigration of Prototypes

As we have seen, the concept of prototypes and typicality originated in relation to color categories; it came neither from the field of information-processing psychology nor linguistics nor philosophy. However, the concept made claims relevant to those fields. As observed earlier, when a concept moves from one field, one context of questions, to another, it creates tensions. In the present case, prototypes and degree of typicality began as concepts pointing to both our intuitions about the meanings of color terms and other simple semantic categories and to a body of empirical data about them. In relation to the color space, the only theoretical notions that needed to be invoked for a prototype account were perceptual salience, memorability, and stimulus generalization. However, as the concept of typicality entered information-processing psychology, this was not sufficient; information-processing models of the representation of categories and the processing of category information were demanded. As the concept entered linguistics, it was asked to perform the functions of a linguistic theory of semantic meaning; typicality came stated in ordinary language and a formalization was soon suggested for it. And as the concept entered philosophy, it was debated as an account of intension, reference, and natural kind terms.

In information-processing psychology, the concept of prototypes had two kinds of effects. On the one hand, the information-processing approach suggested questions and provided techniques whereby the representation and processing of categories according to the typicality view might be investigated. Using techniques such as priming, and making minimal assumptions about models, Rosch (1975b,c) attempted to extract information about the nature of category representations. The type of conclusions generated by this approach were, however, very general: e.g., that the representation evoked by the category name was more like good examples than poor examples of the category; that it was in a form more general than either words or pictures. On the whole, other information-processing researchers have considered the concept of prototypes and typicality functions underspecified and have provided a variety of more precise models, minimodels, and distinctions to be tested (see Medin & Smith, 1984, Mervis & Rosch, 1981, and Smith & Medin, 1981, for reviews). There have also been formal treatments of the concept of prototypes (Osherson & Smith, 1981). In these ways, the prototype concept began to be assimilated to the information-processing view and to be defined and modeled in various ways compatible with such theorizing.

A second and opposite kind of tension was also provided: The prototype concept challenged the classical view—inherited from the empiricist approach to concept formation (see Mervis & Rosch, 1981)—that concepts should be treated as logical conjunctions of criterial attributes with clear-cut boundaries within which all members had equal degree of membership. Because typicality effects were shown to be so robust and so widespread, cognitive models have been forced to become compatible with them in some fashion, to accommodate to typicality. Thus, any model dealing with concepts must now show how it handles typicality, and models that do this more easily, such as probabilistic and exemplar models, have a conceptual advantage (Medin & Smith, 1984).

When we consider the case of linguistics, there are certain requirements for the functions of a semantic theory: It should account for synonymy and contradiction and should specify how meanings of combinations of words can be derived from their individual meaning. Osherson and Smith (1981) have pointed out that (at least according to their formalization of prototype theory) prototypes could not perform these functions. For example, from knowing the prototypes of "pet" and "fish," we cannot derive the typicality of "pet fish." Responding to this challenge, psychologists are working on extension of the prototype concept so that it can handle such cases (Hampton, 1984). On the other side of the coin, some linguists feel it necessary to incorporate typicality data in their account of meaning (Lakoff, 1982). Again, the process seems to be one of mutual assimilation and accommodation.

In philosophy, the idea of criterial features for categories is at least as old as Aristotle (1941). In its extreme form the concept of prototypes suggests that criteriality is not necessary for the psychology of categorization. Wittgenstein (1953) of course had provided a profound critique of the basis of the criterial view, and in recent years Putnam (1977) has developed an influential noncriterial account of natural kind terms. There has been, in response, argument both in philosophy and psychology that these, or any, noncriterial accounts of concepts are inadequate. For example, in psychology Gleitman (Gleitman, Armstrong, & Gleitman, 1983) argues that because even concepts that should be clear cases of the classical criterial theory (such as odd number) show standard typicality effects, these effects must not be related to the actual meaning of the concept. Kelley and Krueger (1984) provide a summary of recent philosophical arguments that noncriterial accounts do not provide an adequate theory of concepts.

What seems to be going on is that we have two apparently contradictory sets of intuitions about categories. One is that some members of categories are better examples of the category than others and that we can use category terms without knowing either the criteria for membership or the boundaries of the category precisely. It is this intuition that Rosch's prototype view of categories was engendered to capture. The other intuition is that categories have a nature (essence) and defining properties (whether or not one knows them), which determine what objects truly are in the category. It is this latter intuition that has classically determined the logic of categories.

In information-processing psychology, there have been recent efforts to combine the two views by means of two-stage or two-aspect models of categorization. For example, a model may state that we first quickly try to identify an instance as a member of a category by using both defining features if the first stage does not yield a conclusive decision (Smith, Shoben, & Rips, 1974). Alternatively, one may claim that the core meaning of concepts involves defining features but that there is, in addition, an identification procedure associated with the category (Miller & Johnson-Laird, 1976). It is typical of such models that the criterial feature aspect of categories is taken as basic and prototype effects relegated to be the results of "mere" processing heuristics; thus, this ecumenicism actually represents an assimilation of prototypes to the classical view of categories. As yet there have been no combination models in linguistics or philosophy; the reader might wish to try to imagine what such models could look like.

What will happen next to prototypes? The concept has already entered social psychology (McCauley, Stitt, & Segal, 1980), personality (Buss & Craik, 1984; Cantor & Mischel, 1979) and clinical psychology (Cantor, Smith, French, & Mezzich, 1980). It will be interesting to observe what direction of tensions this new immigration will create.

In summary, the claim is that when concepts enter a new context they change and so may the context. This is as much true for concepts about concepts and other "scientific" ideas as for simple concepts. The prototypes story has nicely illustrated this point. (We may be reminded of Wittgenstein's apparently innocent query, "What time is it on the moon?")

The Origins of Categories

There is one more part to the story of Roger Brown's influence on the field of categorization. Where do categories come from in the first place? For the color space, perceptual factors seemed to give a coherent answer. But what of common semantic categories? Why are chairs chairs and a different category from tables or sofas? Why do chairs seem to be truly chairs; that is, why does the "real name" of this object on which I am now sitting seem to be "chair" rather than "piece of furniture," "material object," or "desk chair?" Why does the category of "gray chairs weighing between 1.3 and 2.9 lbs" seem neither basic, coherent, nor likely?

The prevailing view of the origin of categories in anthropology in the early 1970s was extreme cultural relativism. For example, according to Leach (1964), "the physical and social environment of a young child is perceived as a continuum. It does not contain any intrinsically separate 'things'" (p. 34). Whorf (1956) states: "The categories and types that we isolate from the world of phenomena we do not find there because they stare every observer in the face; on the contrary, the world is a kaleidoscopic flux of impressions which has to be organized by our minds" (pp. 212–213). Such a view was mirrored in the kinds of categories used in concept identification research in psychology; they consisted of arbitrary combinations of attributes from arrays in which all combinations of attributes were equally probable (Bruner, Goodnow, & Austin, 1956).

Although Roger Brown also favored a cultural relativism with respect to concepts, his view had an empirical and functional flavor. Contrast with the preceding quotes a statement from Brown (1965) about relativity: "If reality were such as directly to impose itself on the child's mind one would expect it to have imposed itself in that same form on the languages of the world. The ubiquity of linguistic non-equivalence suggests that reality can be variously construed and, therefore, that the child's manipulations and observations are not alone likely to yield the stock of conceptions that prevail in his society" (p. 317). What does determine that stock of conceptions? Brown suggests a partial answer. He addressed the question in terms of the level of abstraction at which mothers name objects for their young children; why do mothers name a dime "dime" rather than "money" or "1942 dime"? The answer he suggested is that mothers name things for their children at just that level of nonlinguistic equivalence at which the thing is commonly used (Brown, 1958a).

As in the case of color categories, Rosch's claims about the origins of semantic categories appear to contradict Brown's position, as well as the general position of cultural relativism. In this case, however, the work is not only closely related but also is not a true contradiction. In the first place the type of question being asked—"Where do categories come from in the first place?"—has a Roger Brown flavor to it; it is inherently interdisciplinary, and it requires some kind of account of functions. However, the account that I came to give in the mid-1970s was biased toward cognitive, rather than social, functionalism: Concepts are most useful if they contain the most information for the least cognitive load. Thus, our preference is to segment the world into categories that are as abstract as possible while carrying the most possible specific information about members of the category. What kind of information is meant? Garner (1974) demonstrated the great gain in information obtained by redundancies of attributes in stimulus spaces. And the anthropologist Berlin (1972) had argued that there is a universal, primary generic level of categorization in plant taxonomies that follows perceived discontinuities in nature. It seemed obvious to us that the perceived attributes of the world did not come as a continuum or as a grid in which all co-occurrences were equally probable. (It is a fact of the perceived world that creatures with feathers also have wings and beaks.) Thus, we proposed that the basic level of categorization is that which maps onto the correlated clusters of attributes in the perceived world.

A series of experiments (Rosch, Mervis, Gray, Johnson, & Boyes-Braem, 1976) demonstrated that, in taxonomies of common concrete nouns in English based on class inclusion, basic object categories were the most inclusive categories: (a) whose members possessed significant numbers of attributes in common as measured by asking subjects to list attributes; (b) for whose members similar motor sequences were invoked when the object was used or interacted with in its usual manner; (c) whose members had similar shapes as measured by a correlation of shape; and (d) whose members could be identified from averaged shapes of members of the class. The measurement of similarity of motor movements was intended to capture function at a microlevel, whereas the measurement of similarity of shape and recognizability of averaged shapes was intended to suggest a basis for cognitive coding of basic objects in a simple image-like format.

The basic level so defined was shown to have implications for many other areas. The basic level was found to be the most abstract level at which priming with the category name significantly improved detection of a picture of an object in visual noise, facilitated reaction time in a same–different judgment task, and speeded identification of the item as a member of its category. Thus, the basic level of categorization appears to have a perceptual priority. Developmentally, 3- and 4-year-olds performed oddity problems and sorted objects at the basic level into adult types of categories—a cognitive feat young children had been judged incapable of performing in previous studies that had used only items from superordinate categories.

With respect to linguistic issues, we found that the basic level was the level at which objects were invariably named by both adults and children in a free naming situation. The development of the use of these names was further examined from archival material—the transcripts of the spontaneous speech of Roger Brown's Sarah (Brown, 1974). Sarah began using basic level words in spontaneous speech long before superordinates or subordinates. Finally, relating to the historical linguistic issue of what categories are coded first in a language, some evidence was presented that American Sign Language, which has a restricted vocabulary for nouns, has single signs almost entirely and exclusively at the basic level. (All these studies are presented in Rosch *et al.*, 1976.) Two follow-up studies using artificial categories have confirmed that basic level effects are a function of the most abstract level at which attributes are clustered (Mervis & Crisafi, 1982; Murphy & Smith, 1982). And several recent studies have extended the basic level idea to categories of scenes (Tversky & Hemenway, 1983) and to events (Cantor, Mischel, & Schwartz, 1982).

The concept of basic level categories as clusters of correlated attributes is not a contradiction of a functional view. Attributes include both forms and functions. In fact, the claim is that function follows form for non-manmade objects, and vice-versa for man-made objects. Recently, Tversky and Hemenway (1984) have suggested that it is at the level of parts of basic level objects that form and function most closely come together. Our claim is that form and function are highly redundant and that it is this very redundancy that makes the basic level so effective for the learning of categories.

Of course, the last word has not been said about the nature and origins of categories. Categorization is, after all, part of the forms of life in which we engage. It is just that kind of broad perspective that Roger Brown's psychology, a social psychology in its widest sense, may someday encompass.

Coherences Again

In talking about the history of ideas, or the influence of a person or school, we are talking about coherences. As I suggested in the introduction, events are seen as coherent if the outcome can be seen as already contained in the ground and the intervening activity seen to be the proper connection between ground and outcome. This notion of coherence is, in fact and altogether appropriately, already presaged in Roger Brown's own (1979) single helix image of historical development.

Usually, a demonstration of coherence and, likewise, of influence relies on showing the similarity of the ground and the outcome. Although this account was oriented toward trying to show the *connections* between grounds and outcomes, I fear I may have done little better than to handwave at some connections and point to some similarities—even though in presenting a first person account I should presumably have privileged access to something or other.

Actually, the one factor of influence about which I am most certain is the one for which no evidence at all can be offered. In preparing to write this chapter I sat down to reread some of Roger Brown's early works and was startled to remember, in an almost sensory manner, why I became and remained a psychologist. That one factor is the sense of wonder in the way Roger Brown sees psychology. Perhaps that is the invisible thread running through the diverse contributions in this volume and the most lasting heritage of Brown's work and teaching.

REFERENCES

Aristotle. (1941). *The basic works of Aristotle*. R. McKeon (Ed.), New York: Random House.

Battig, W. F., & Montague, W. E. (1969). Category norms for verbal items in 56 categories: A replication and extension of the Connecticut category norms. *Journal of Experimental Psychology, 80* (Monograph Supplement 3, Part 2).

Beller, H. K. (1971). Priming: Effects of advance information on matching. *Journal of Experimental Psychology, 87,* 176–182.

Berlin, B. (1972). Speculations on the growth of ethnobotanical nomenclature. *Language in Society, 1,* 51–86.

Berlin, B., & Kay, P. (1969). *Basic color terms: Their universality and evolution.* Berkeley: University of California Press.

Brown, R. (1958a). How shall a thing be called? *Psychological Review, 65,* 14–21.

Brown, R. (1958b). *Words and things.* New York: The Free Press.

Brown, R. (1965). *Social psychology.* New York: The Free Press.

Brown, R. (1974). *A first language.* Cambridge, MA: Harvard University Press.

Brown, R. (1979). Cognitive categories. In R. A. Kasschau & C. N. Cofer (Eds.), *Psychology's second century: Enduring issues.* New York: Praeger.

Brown, R., & Lenneberg, E. (1954). A study in language and cognition. *Journal of Abnormal and Social Psychology, 49,* 454–462.

Bruner, J. S., Goodnow, J. J., & Austin, G. A. (1956). *A study of thinking.* New York: Wiley.

Buss, D. M., & Craik, K. H. (1984). Acts, dispositions, and personality. In B. A. Maher & W. B. Maher (Eds.), *Progress in experimental personality research.* New York: Academic Press.

Cantor, N., & Mischel, W. (1979). Prototypes in person perception. *Advances in Experimental Social Psychology, 12,* 3–52.

Cantor, N., Mischel, W., & Schwartz, J. C. (1982). A prototype analysis of psychological situations. *Cognitive Psychology, 14,* 45–77.

Cantor, N., Smith, E. E., French, R. D., & Mezzich, J. (1980). Psychiatric diagnosis as prototype categorization. *Journal of Abnormal Psychology, 89,* 181–193.

Clemens, S. L. (1910). The horrors of the German language. *In Mark Twain's speeches.* New York: Harper.

DeValois, R. L., & Jacobs, F. H. (1968). Primate color vision. *Science, 162,* 533–540.

Fodor, J. A., & Katz, J. J. (1964). *The structure of language.* Englewood Cliffs, NJ: Prentice-Hall.

Garner, W. R. (1974). *The processing of information and structure.* New York: Wiley.

Gleitman, L. R., Armstrong, L. L., & Gleitman, H. (1983). On doubting the concept 'concept.' In E. Scholnick (Ed.), *New trends in cognitive representation: Challenges to Piaget's theory.* Hillsdale, NJ: Lawrence Erlbaum Associates.

Hampton, J. A. (1984). *A composite prototype model of conceptual conjunction.* Unpublished manuscript, City University of London.

Heider, E. R. (1972). Universals in color naming and memory. *Journal of Experimental Psychology, 93,* 10–20.

Heider, E. R., & Olivier, D. C. (1972). The structure of the color space in naming and memory for two languages. *Cognitive Psychology, 3,* 337–354.

Heider, K. G. (1970). *The Dugum Dani: a Papuan culture in the highlands of West New Guinea.* Chicago: Aldine.

Kay, P. (1981). Color perception and the meaning of color words. In *Proceedings of the third annual conference of the Cognitive Science Society,* Berkeley, 61–64.

Kay, P., & McDaniel, C. K. (1978). The linguistic significance of the meanings of basic color terms. *Language, 54,* 610–646.

Kelley, D., & Krueger, J. (1984). The psychology of abstraction. *Journal for the Theory of Social Behavior, 14,* 43–67.

Krauss, R. M. (1968). Language as a symbolic process in communication: A psychological perspective. *American Scientist, 56,* 263–278.

Lakoff, G. (1972). Hedges: A study in meaning criteria and the logic of fuzzy concepts. *Journal of Philosophical Logic, 2,* 458–508.

Lakoff, G. (1982). Categories and cognitive models. *Berkeley Cognitive Science Report* (No. 2). Berkeley, CA: Institute for Human Learning.

Lantz, D., & Stefflre, V. (1964). Language and cognition and revisited. *Journal of Abnormal and Social Psychology, 69,* 472–481.

Leach, E. (1964). Anthropological aspects of language: Animal categories and verbal abuse. In E. H. Lenneberg (Ed.), *New directions in the study of language.* Cambridge, MA: MIT Press.

Lucy, J. A., & Shweder, R. A. (1979). Whorf and his critics: Linguistic and non-linguistic influences on color memory. *American Anthropologist, 81,* 581–615.

McCauley, C., Stitt, C. L., & Segal, M. (1980). Stereotyping: From prejudice to prediction. *Psychological Bulletin, 87,* 195–208.

Medin, D., & Smith, E. E. (1984). Concepts and concept formation. In M. R. Rosenzweig & L. W. Porter (Eds.), *Annual review of psychology* (Vol. 35). Palo Alto, CA: Annual Reviews.

Mervis, C. B., & Crisafi, M. A. (1982). Order of acquisition of subordinate-, basic-, and superordinate-level categories. *Child Development, 53,* 258–266.

Mervis, C. B., & Rosch, E. (1981). Categorization of natural objects. In M. R. Rosenzweig & L. W. Porter (Eds.), *Annual review of psychology* (Vol. 32). Palo Alto, CA: Annual Reviews.

Miller, G. A., & Johnson-Laird, P. N. (1976). Language and perception. Cambridge, MA: Harvard University Press.

Murphy, G., & Smith, E. E. (1982). Basic level superiority in picture categorization. *Journal of Verbal Learning and Verbal Behavior, 21,* 1–20.

Newell, A. (1973). You can't play 20 questions with nature and win. In W. B. Chase (Ed.), *Visual Information processing.* New York: Academic Press.

Osherson, D., & Smith, E. E. (1981). On the adequacy of prototype theory as a theory of concepts. *Cognition, 9,* 35–58.

Posner, M. I., Boies, S. J., Eichelman, W. H., & Taylor, R. L. (1969). Retention of visual and name codes of single letters. *Journal of Experimental Psychology Monograph, 79* (1).

Posner, M. R., Goldsmith, R., & Welton, K. E. (1967). Perceived distance and the classification of distorted patterns. *Journal of Experimental Psychology, 73,* 23–38.

Putnam, H. (1977). Meaning and reference. In S. P. Schwartz (Ed.), *Naming, necessity and natural kinds.* Ithaca, NY: Cornell University Press.

Reed, S. K. (1972). Pattern recognition and categorization. *Cognitive Psychology, 3,* 382–407.

Rips, L. J., Shoben, E. J., & Smith, E. E. (1973). Semantic distance and the verification of semantic relations. *Journal of Verbal Learning and Verbal Behavior, 12,* 1–20.

Rosch, E. (1973). On the internal structure of perceptual and semantic categories. In T. E. Moore (Ed.), *Cognitive development and the acquisition of language.* New York: Academic Press.

Rosch, E. (1975a). Cognitive reference points. *Cognitive Psychology, 7,* 532–547.

Rosch, E. (1975b). The nature of mental codes for color categories. *Journal of Experimental Psychology: Human Perception and Performance, 1,* 303–322.

Rosch, E. (1977). Human categorization. In N. Warren (Ed.), *Studies in cross-cultural psychology*. London: Academic Press.

Rosch, E. (1984). Towards a general structure of events. *Mathematical Social Sciences, 7,* 205–207.

Rosch, E. (1987). What does the tiny vajra refute? Causality and event structure in Buddhist logic and folk psychology. *Cognitive Science Reports,* Berkeley, CA: Institute for cognitive studies.

Rosch, E., & Mervis, C. B. (1975). Family resemblances: Studies in the internal structure of categories. *Cognitive Psychology, 7,* 573–605.

Rosch, E., Simpson, C., & Miller, R. S. (1976). Structural bases of typicality effects. *Journal of Experimental Psychology: Human Perception and Performance, 2,* 491–502.

Rosch, E., Mervis, C. B., Gray, W. D., Johnson, D. M., & Boyes-Braem, P. (1976). Basic objects in natural categories. *Cognitive Psychology, 8,* 382–439.

Smith, E. E., & Medin, D. L. (1981). *The psychology of conceptual processes*. Cambridge, MA: Harvard University Press.

Smith, E. E., Shoben, E. J., & Rips, L. J. (1974). Structure and process in semantic memory: A featural model for semantic decisions. *Psychological Review, 81,* 214–241.

Tversky, A. (1977). Features of similarity. *Psychological Review, 84,* 327–352.

Tversky, B., & Hemenway, K. (1983). Categories of environmental scenes. *Cognitive Psychology, 15,* 121–149.

Tversky, B., & Hemenway, K. (1984). Objects, parts, and categories. *Journal of Experimental Psychology: General, 113,* 169–193.

Whorf, B. L. (1956). Language, thought, and reality: Selected writings of Benjamin Lee Whorf. J. B. Carroll (Ed.). Cambridge, MA: MIT Press.

Wittgenstein, L. (1953). *Philosophical investigations*. New York: Macmillan.

Zipf, G. K. (1935). *The psycho-biology of language*. Boston: Houghton-Mifflin.

Afterword

Roger Brown
Harvard University

When I had read all the chapters in this book, I dropped my advance plan to comment on the psycholinguistic and developmental issues they raise. Anything I could add would only diminish the evidence that psycholinguistics is a tremendously vital field. The authors of the chapters do not seem to have understood that for a Festschrift one digs out something ancient and unpublishable or else pens a graceful little nothing. Major contributions are not to be expected. Of course, when one is made, it is a really tremendous compliment. These authors have paid me such a compliment, and all that I want to or really feel able to say is "Thank you." Not a thank you to a collectivity because each relation has been completely individual, and as I say the names, I think of the person: "Thank you Dan, Melissa, Jill, Camille, Eric, Steve, Michael, Ursula, Laura, Rick, Helen, Jean, Courtney, Kenji, Rita, Dave, Ellen, Howard, and Eleanor. Thank you for all that I have learned from you and am still learning from you."

Individual impulses do not compound into a successful collective enterprise without a leader, and Frank Kessel has been the leader, the one who took the initiative and followed through. Thank you, especially, Frank. And thanks to Marion (Mrs. Kessel) for getting involved and adding the music.

There is just one question that I might be better positioned to answer than anyone else: How have I come to be blessed with so exceptional a succession of students? Time and place had a lot to do with it. Psycholinguistics has been and is a profound subject, a deep and serious subject, with, nevertheless, an aspect of playfulness, and Harvard is a place that attracts students who respond to this combination of qualities. The teacher's role has been an easy one: to nod encouragement at the better ideas and withhold it for the worser. For these students I have had more than nods to dispense or withhold; I have had strong affection.

The affection is no credit to me. Anyone not determined to deny all frivolous things any role in science would notice that the authors of the chapters in this book are quite unusually attractive persons.

Psycholinguistics has never been institutionalized at Harvard. There has never been a degree program or any power of appointment or even a fixed set of requirements. The authors in this book took degrees in experimental psychology, or social, or developmental; none has a Ph.D. in psycholinguistics. Looking back, I count that as an advantage. It is mainly responsible, I think, for the intellectual spacing of the essays. A well-defined topic in psychology, even so broad and difficult a topic as the acquisition of syntax, seems able to support only a small number of first-rate careers. Nineteen doctoral students doing psycho-linguistics at one university might well find themselves "stacked up," after 30 years, in a holding pattern over one or two American professorships. But the present 19 with their interests in sign language, artistic language, developmental variation, universals of development, language and thought, and bilingualism live in neighboring but not disputed territories. The necessity for each one in his or her training to be something more than a psycholinguist, to do something else in a major way, has, I think, inclined them to discover connections and invent new things.

There is no strand that runs the length of the rope. There is no feature common to all members. They are not a family. But when all were gathered together for a party celebrating this book, you could see that there is a family resemblance.

Appendix

Roger Brown
An Autobiography in the Third Person[1]

Citation: 1971 Distinguished Scientific Contribution Award

Who with the help of Adam and Eve and Sarah has described the course of the child's acquisition of his mother tongue, and thereby enriched the study of language development. His recent research has revived the concern of psychologists with the nature of meaning and with the development of cognition in relation to language. His early research on linguistic relativity clarified this difficult problem for the psychological investigator. The tip-of-the-tongue phenomenon is an excellent example of how the study of everyday experience may inform us about the intricacies of memory. His book *Social Psychology* is an important work and an original approach to a whole branch of psychology. In it he has shown that psychological writing can be witty, literate, and urbane.

Roger William Brown was born April 14, 1925, in Detroit, Michigan. He attended the Detroit public schools, and, when he graduated from Edwin Denby High in 1943, Brown's ambition was to become a novelist of social protest, as much as possible like Upton Sinclair.

[1]Reprinted in part from *American Psychologist,* January, 1972. Copyright 1972 by the American Psychological Association. Reprinted by permission of the publisher and author.

He began his freshman year at the University of Michigan, then was accepted into the Navy V-12 Program and sent first to Oberlin College in Ohio, and then for midshipman's training to Columbia University. He served near the end of World War II, and for some time after, on the U.S.S. Wichita and then on a numbered but unnamed LST (Landing Ship Tank). Once the war had ended, the LST carried food and medical supplies for the United Nations up and down the Yangtze River from Shanghai. Aboard ship, Brown read Watson's *Behaviorism* and thought how he would like to become a psychologist.

Released from the Navy, Brown returned to the University of Michigan where he earned his B.A. in 1948, his M.A. in 1949, and his Ph.D. in 1952. Psychology was burgeoning in those years at Michigan under its brilliant young Chairman, Donald G. Marquis. Brown was given a great many chances to teach as a graduate student, including the experimental laboratory course, courses in sensation and perception, and in history and systems. He remembers as particularly valuable seminars in the philosophy of science with Edward L. Walker in psychology and Charles Stevenson in philosophy, and seminars in theory of literature with Austin Warren. As a graduate student he was identified as a "basic processes" experimentalist, but when it came to thesis time he chose a topic in social psychology, rigidity, and authoritarianism; E. Lowell Kelly was his principal adviser, and Brown remembers with gratitude Professor Kelly's expert help and generosity with his time.

Immediately after finishing his thesis, Brown felt a little bored with, and discouraged about, the ancient and difficult problems of psychology, quite sure that he was not talented enough to be a creative writer, and not at all sure how to put his several interests together. He had a postdoctoral year at Michigan, part of it to include a research seminar with philosophers Charles Stevenson, Paul Henle, and William Frankena, and the linguist Charles Fries. Brown remembers the very evening and talk that made the difference to him. Professor Fries introduced linguistics with a lecture on the phoneme. Brown was enthralled; he had not even known there was a discipline of general linguistics and, as some linguists may have suspected, never had a course in the subject. But the psychology of language became the research interest that has dominated his life. He has always done his wider reading and teaching in social psychology, and that is what became of the Upton Sinclair identification, refreshed in later years by admiration of Gordon Allport.

The first long article Brown wrote on the psychology of language (though not the first published) was "A Stimulus–Response Analysis of Language and Meaning." It is an analysis in terms of classical and instrumental conditioning; Brown learned well his Hilgard and Marquis as a graduate student. It took a year to write the paper, and at the end it occurred to the author that he had not thought of a single experiment he really cared to do. He concluded that, whereas thinking in terms of S and R obviously enabled some people to be very creative, it did not do so for him.

In 1952–1953 he became an instructor at Harvard, joined Jerome Bruner's cognition research project, and was assigned to teach the undergraduate courses in social psychology and in the psychology of language. From 1953 to 1957, he was an assistant professor at Harvard and head tutor (a job that involved administering aspects of the undergraduate program). This was an intellectually exciting time for Brown because the category–attribute–strategy line of thought developed in the cognition project suggested all kinds of fascinating experiments to do in the psychology of language. Jerome Bruner, then as now, had the gift of providing great intellectual stimulus, but also the rarer gift of giving his colleagues the strong sense that psychological problems of great antiquity were on the verge of solution that afternoon by the group there assembled.

In 1957 Harvard let Brown go as it lets most of its assistant professors go, and as he had assumed it would do—though privately hoping not. He suspects today that he did the administrative work of the head tutor so that Harvard would at least feel a twinge of guilt over its ingratitude. He wrote *Words and Things* on a final sabbatical half-year, and in 1957 was appointed associate professor of social psychology at the Massachusetts Institute of Technology and professor in 1960. There he continued to teach Social Psychology, the Psychology of Language, Theories of Personality, Psychology for Industrial Executives, and just about anything he liked. He found the M.I.T. students as stimulating as the Harvard students, and to his surprise, more interested in the supposedly soft topics of psychology than the well-developed scientific topics. They thought of psychology as a needed holiday from calculus and chemistry and were not about to be cheated out of Freud and ESP and race relations by an overdose of psychophysics. Brown saw quite a lot of Noam Chomsky and Morris Halle, and he began to learn generative transformational grammar.

Although always interested in taking a flyer on pronouns of address or questions of literary style (these with the collaboration of Professor Albert Gilman of the Boston University English Department), Brown's research increasingly became concentrated on the child's acquisition of its first language. Having done a number of experiments on very limited aspects of this process, he conceived a desire to study the whole process, naturalistically, on a level of detail that meant working with just a very few children.

Returning to Harvard as professor of social psychology in 1962, Brown also obtained National Institute of Mental Health support for a 5-year study of three children, the three called in the literature Adam, Eve, and Sarah. The work chiefly consisted of the collection, transcription, and linguistic analysis of large samples of spontaneous conversation between mother and child at home. In the first year of the project, there was a concurrent weekly seminar to discuss the children's protocols. When he recalls the membership of that seminar, Brown realizes how exceptional a year it was: Ursula Bellugi, Colin Fraser, Courtney Cazden, Jean Berko Gleason, David McNeil, Dan Slobin, Sam Anderson, Richard Cromer, and Gordon Finley.

Brown's *Social Psychology* was finished in 1965. He knew that it made a combination of topics that was distinctly eccentric for social psychology, including two interminable chapters on language that most teachers who adopted the book have surely skipped. He knew too that there was much "unscientific" use of anecdote and introspection but could not see why a text in social psychology should look like a text in chemistry or physics. The one principle he followed was to write only on things that seriously interested him, and to try to find the level of detail that could engage interest. He thought it very decent of The Free Press to publish *Social Psychology* at all. The success of the book with both teachers and students was both a great surprise and gratification to him. In 1981 the 1965 *Social Psychology* became an official "Citation Classic" largely because of the analysis in the book of the risky shift that became a popular research topic. In 1987 the unrevised first edition is still in print.

The National Institute of Child Health and Human Development generously extended support of the study of Adam, Eve, and Sarah from 5 to 10 years. Brown had not foreseen the labor involved in a detailed study of the linguistic development of even three children. The first round of analysis, which took some years, comprised the writing of five extensively annotated grammars for each child at evenly spaced developmental points. The grammars had to be indeterminate at many points; there is never enough material to settle everything. The result was 15 manuscripts, all 50 pages or more in length, which Brown estimated about half-a-dozen people in the world combined the interest, the knowledge, and the patience to read; nay, not so many as half-a-dozen. He decided that the whole venture had been a vast fishing expedition. It did leave him knowing what things something reliable could be written about and what things one might as well remain silent about. And so he began again—a work intended to be in two volumes. The first volume, *A First Language: The Early Stages,* was published by the Harvard University Press in 1973.

Of *A First Language* Brown says it does not explain how the acquisition of language was possible. But it did establish some empirical generalizations that have held up very well in subsequent research. In 1982 *A First Language* became a "Citation Classic" and in 1987 is in print and still frequently cited.

The planned second volume of *A First Language* that was to cover *The Later Stages* was never written. People used to ask about it but after several years that became embarrassing and developmental psycholinguists came to assume that it never would appear. Why has it not? Data collection had been complete in 1973 and so had data description in the form of unpublished grammars. Brown had an unhappy sabbatical year in which he worked hard on *The Later Stages* but finally had to admit defeat. The detailed analyses of presumptive Stages III, IV, and V did not yield up to Brown, then, any strong generalizations comparable to those of the early stages, and he could see no value in publishing the possibly quite idiosyncratic details available in the unpublished grammars. In addition, linguistic theory was evolving rapidly and Brown, never quick at learning new formalisms, could hardly keep up. Finally, the international data base of acquisition studies had grown apace and it seemed that only a prodigious polyglot, which Brown never was, could hope to think productively on a "human species level" about acquisition. Brown gave up on *The Later Stages* and also regretfully decided that the time was now past when he could effectively initiate research on first-language acquisition. However, greatly gifted students like Jill de Villiers, Helen Tager Flusberg, and Kenji Hakuta kept coming along and initiating on their own.

In 1985 Dan Slobin and his associates accomplished what seemed impossible 10 years earlier: acquisition studies for 16 languages (published in two volumes) and the findings from all effectively integrated. But then, Dan Slobin *is* a prodigious polyglot. Michael Maratsos and Steven Pinker, both very gifted at learning formalisms, are up-to-date on linguistic theory and cognitive psychology and have proposed acquisition theories (different theories) that are more explicit and detailed than one expected to see in this decade. And the protocols of Adam, Eve, and Sarah have been entered into the Child Language Data Exchange System directed by Brian MacWhinney and Catherine Snow and are available to all. It is not easy nowadays to understand events on the frontier of developmental psycholinguistics, but it is clear that the field has an advancing frontier and not just a new shuffle.

In 1967–1970 Roger Brown served as chairman of the Department of Social Relations at Harvard, the last chairman of that department as it happened, because many things came together in those years to cause the sociologists to set up their own independent department and all the varieties of psychologists to come together as the Department of Psychology and Social Relations. As chairman of Social Relations in the late 1960s, Brown had a number of "confrontations," as they used to be called, with angry students over issues now difficult to remember because they were never over the only real issue which was the war in Vietnam. On that one real issue there was almost no student–faculty disagreement in Social Relations, but members continued to fight little substitute wars with one another over courses and curriculum and other such nonsense. From those confrontations Brown remembers only one event—his single shining hour. Hundreds of students had gathered in Harvard's largest auditorium to wave flags and stamp feet over some policy the chairman was bound, by his office, to defend. First came a really abusive harangue to which Brown replied. "I think," he said, "that I make a very unlikely Fascist Pig." Everyone had to admit he did and there was a long laugh that briefly broke the spell of that Theater of the Absurd.

In 1974 Brown published, with his colleague Professor Richard Herrnstein, *Psychology,* which is an introductory textbook with a difference. The book developed out of the authors' collaboration in teaching the introductory course. *Psychology* was praised by most reviewers but adopted by very few teachers. The fact that teachers of psychology did not assign the book meant that students did not read it, and that was a great disappointment to the authors.

In the early 1980s Roger Brown had some very enjoyable research experiences in diverse areas. He will never forget the May and June in which he did about a dozen experiments on emotional meanings in music. The experiments did not much impress the music educators who created the occasion for the work. They would have preferred a generative transformational grammar of music theory, but Brown was not about to "dash the hopes" of a perfect springtime with anything so glum. He admits that the experiments in taping musical passages and testing for affective meanings may have been an excuse for listening to some wonderful music at his favorite time of year and regrets nothing.

"Flashbulb Memories," done in collaboration with James Kulik, is a paper that Brown groups with "The Tip of the Tongue Phenomenon" in that both start from familiar but rather odd psychological phenomena which, being traced to their sources, yield surprising knowledge. "The Psychological Causality Implicit in Language," done with Deborah Fish, felt unique in that it was not just a study but a discovery. No one, they thought, had ever realized that interpersonal verbs (*admire, like, charm*) allocated causality in lawful ways to their logical arguments. It seemed a discovery and not just a study because it represented new knowledge even if that knowledge was not terribly consequential. When Brown and Fish learned that the knowledge was not, in fact, new but had been anticipated by Catherine Garvey and Alfonso Caramazza, it did not matter because they had already had the thrill of feeling themselves to be discoverers.

At the start of his sabbatical year in 1983, Brown began a large undertaking. The success of the 1965 *Social Psychology* and his continuing fascination with the subject matter made him want to try again. He had been teaching the course every year and had worked out ways of presenting about half the content a text must necessarily cover. The sabbatical would provide the unbroken stretch of time needed. But what should such a book be like? Brown knew he had no choice. He could only write one kind of book: selective in content, essayistic and argumentative in style, longwinded by comparison with most texts. In fact, it would have to be an entirely new book, continuous with the first on a deep level, but with many new topics and issues and all new sentences.

What, when it was finished, could such a book be called? One would like to carry over the good will the first edition had won, and so there was good reason to say *Social Psychology, 2nd ed.* But *2nd ed.* did not convey the fact that this was an entirely new book. To say "completely revised" would be laughable because any decent text not completely revised after 20 years would be inconceivable. What about *Social Psychology The Second Edition* with every word in the title on the same level, nothing subordinate and nothing superordinate. *Social Psychology* for the things preserved—the style of writing, the deep questions that do not go away, the haunting experiments that are timeless—and *Second Edition* for the new book that it is, the fresh presentation of everything, the recently emerged social issues.

In 1986, the book was published and the suspense—for Brown—is keen. Can a book of this kind succeed today? A rather difficult book, a book that needs to be studied, a book that does not just list findings but develops arguments. And what would success mean? Not just approval from the profession, certainly not just adoptions, but interest—the interest of the present generation of college students.

. . . . . .

Roger Brown was President of the New England Psychological Association in 1965–1966 and of the Division of Personality and Social Psychology of the APA in the same year. In 1971–1972 he served as President of the Eastern Psychological Association. He is a Fellow of the American Academy of Arts and Sciences. In 1969 the University of Michigan gave him its "Outstanding Achievement Award," and in 1970 York University, England, gave him the honorary degree, "Doctor of the University." In 1971 Mr. Brown received the Distinguished Scientific Achievement Award of the American Psychological Association, and in 1972 he was elected to the National Academy of Sciences. In 1973 he was awarded the G. Stanley Hall Prize in Developmental Psychology of the American Psychological Association. In 1980 Bucknell University made him an honorary D.Sci., and in 1983 Northwestern University did the same. In 1980 Roger Brown gave the Katz–Newcomb Lecture in Social Psychology at the University of Michigan, and in 1985 he was awarded the internation prize of the Fondation Fyssen in Paris.

SCIENTIFIC PUBLICATIONS
ROGER BROWN

1953

A determinant of the relationship between rigidity and authoritarianism. *Journal of Abnormal and Social Psychology, 48,* 469–476.

1954

Mass phenomena. In G. Lindzey (Ed.), *Handbook of Social Psychology.* Vol. 2. Cambridge, MA: Addison-Wesley, 833–876.
With E. Lenneberg. A study in language and cognition. *Journal of Abnormal and Social Psychology, 49,* 454–462.

1955

With A. H. Black and A. E. Horowitz. Phonetic symbolism in natural languages. *Journal of Abnormal and Social Psychology, 50,* 388–393.
With D. C. Hildum. Verbal reinforcement and interviewer bias. *Journal of Abnormal and Social Psychology, 53,* 108–111.

1956

Language and categories. In J. S. Bruner, J. Goodnow, & G. A. Austin, *A Study of Thinking*. New York: Wiley, 247–312.

The taxonomy of conferences and their reports. *Contemporary Psychology, 1,* 231–232.

With D. C. Hildum. Expectancy and the perception of syllables. *Language, 32,* 411–419.

1957

Linguistic determinism and the part of speech. *Journal of Abnormal and Social Psychology, 55,* 1–5.

With R. Leiter & D. C. Hildum. Metaphors from music criticism. *Journal of Abnormal and Social Psychology, 54,* 347–352.

Review of G. Herdan, *Language as Choice and Chance. Language, 33,* 170–181.

1958

Words and Things. Glencoe, IL: Free Press.

A stimulus-response analysis of language and meaning. In P. Henle (Ed.), *Language, Thought and Culture.* University of Michigan Press.

How shall a thing be called? *Psychological Review, 65,* 14–21.

The semantics of the English parts-of-speech. *Actes du Quinzieme Congrès International de Psychology.*

With E. Lenneberg. Studies in linguistic relativity. In E. Maccoby, T. Newcomb, & E. Hartley (Eds.), *Readings in Social Psychology.* New York: Holt.

With A. Gilman. Who says "tu" to "whom." *Etc., 15,* 169–174.

Review of C. Osgood, et al., *The Measurement of Meaning. Contemporary Psychology, 3,* 113–115.

1959

With R. Nuttall. Method in phonetic symbolism experiments. *Journal of Abnormal and Social Psychology, 59,* 441–445.

1960

With A. Gilman. The pronouns of power and solidarity. In T. Seboek (Ed.), *Aspects of Style in Language.* Cambridge, MA: MIT Press.

With J. Berko. Psycholinguistic research methods. In P. Mussen (Ed.), *Handbook of Research Methods in Child Psychology.* New York: Wiley.

With J. Berko. Word association and the acquisition of grammar. *Child Development, 31,* 1–14.

Review of A. R. Luria and E. Ia. Yudovich, *Speech and the Development of Mental Processes in the Child. Word, 16,* 125–130.

1961

With M. Ford. Address in American English. *Journal of Abnormal and Social Psychology, 62,* 375–385.

1962

The language of social relationship. *Proceedings of the Sixteenth International Congress of Psychology.* Amsterdam: North Holland, 663–667.

Psychology of speech and language. *Encyclopedia Britannica.*

Models of attitude change. In R. Brown, E. Galanter, E. Hess, & G. Mandler (Eds.), *New Directions in Psychology, I.* New York: Holt, Rinehart, Winston.

1963

With C. Fraser. The acquisition of syntax. In C. N. Cofer & B. Musgrave (Eds.), *Verbal Behavior and Learning.* New York: McGraw-Hill.

With C. Fraser & U. Bellugi. Control of grammar in imitation, comprehension, and production. *Journal of Verbal Learning and Verbal Behavior, 2,* 121–135.

1964

With U. Bellugi (Eds.), The acquisition of language. *Monographs of the Society for Research in Child Development,* Whole No. 92.

With U. Bellugi. Three processes in the child's acquisition of syntax. *Harvard Educational Review, 34,* 133–151.

With C. Fraser & U. Bellugi. Explorations in grammar evaluation. In U. Bellugi & R. Brown (Eds.), The acquisition of language. *Monographs of the Society for Research in Child Development,* Whole No. 92.

The acquisition of language. In D. M. Rioch & E. A. Weinstein (Eds.), *Disorders of Communication.* Baltimore: Williams & Wilkins, 53–61.

Discussion of the conference on transcultural studies in cognition. *American Anthropologist, 66,* No. 3, Part 2, 243–253.

1965

Social Psychology. New York: Free Press.

1966

With A. Gilman. Personality and style in Concord. In M. Simon & T. H. Parsons (Eds.), *Transcendentalism and its Legacy.* University of Michigan Press, 87–122.

With D. McNeill. The "tip of the tongue" phenomenon. *Journal of Verbal Learning and Verbal Behavior, 5,* 325–337.

From codability to coding ability. In J. Bruner (Ed.), *Learning About Learning.* Washington, DC, U.S. Government Printing Office, 185–195.

1968

With C. Cazden & U. Bellugi. The child's grammar from I to III. In J. P. Hill (Ed.), *Minnesota Symposium on Child Psychology* (Vol. 2). Minneapolis: University of Minnesota Press.

The development of Wh questions in child speech. *Journal of Verbal Learning and Verbal Behavior, 7,* 279–290.

Introduction to J. Moffett, *Teaching the Universe of Discourse.* New York: Houghton Mifflin.

Review of F. Smith & G. A. Miller (Eds.), *The Genesis of Language: A Psycholinguistic Approach. Contemporary Psychology, 13,* 59–51.

With C. Cazden & E. Heider. Social class differences in the effectiveness and style of children's coding ability. *Project Literacy Reports,* 1–10.

1970

With others. *Psycholinguistics; Selected Papers.* New York: Free Press.

With C. Hanlon. Derivational complexity and order of acquisition in child speech. In J. R. Hayes (Ed.), *Cognition and the Development of Language.* New York: Wiley, 11–53.

The first sentences of child and chimpanzee. In R. Brown & others, *Psycholinguistics; Selected Papers.* New York: Free Press, 208–231.

Psychology and reading; commentary on Chapters 5 to 10. In H. Levin & J. P. Williams (Eds.), *Basic Studies on Reading.* New York: Basic Books, 164–187.

Introduction to *Cognitive Development in Children; Five Monographs of the Society for Research in Child Development.* Chicago: University of Chicago Press.

1973

A First Language; The Early Stages. Cambridge, MA: Harvard University Press.

Development of the first language in the human species. *American Psychologist, 28,* 97-106.
Schizophrenia, language, and reality. *American Psychologist, 28,* 395–403.

1974

With Richard Herrnstein. *Psychology.* Boston: Little, Brown.

1977

Introduction. To C. E. Snow & C. A. Ferguson (Eds.), *Talking to Children: Language Input and Acquisition.* Cambridge, England: Cambridge University Press.
With J. Kulik. Flashbulb memories. *Cognition, 5* (1), 73–99.
In reply to Peter Schönbach. *Cognition, 5,* 185–187.

1978

A new paradigm of reference. In G. A. Miller & E. Lenneberg (Eds.), *Psychology and Biology of Language and Thought; Essays in Honor of Eric Lenneberg.* New York: Academic Press.
Why are signed languages easier to learn than spoken languages? Part Two. *Bulletin of the American Academy of Arts and Sciences, XXXII,* 25–44.

1979

With J. Kulik. Frustration, attribution of blame, and aggression. *Journal of Experimental and Social Psychology, 15,* 183–194.

1980

The maintenance of conversation. In D. R. Olson (Ed.), *The Social Foundations of Language and Thought.* New York: W. W. Norton, 187–210.

1981

Cognitive categories. In R. A. Kasschau & C. N. Cofer (Eds.), *Psychology's Second Century; Enduring Issues.* New York: Praeger, 188–212.
Music and language. In Music Educators National Conference. *Report of the Ann Arbor Symposium on the Applications of Psychology to the Teaching and Learning of Music,* 233–264.
Symbolic and syntactic capacities. *Philosophical Transactions of the Royal Society,* London. B 292, 197–204. Reprinted in: The Royal Society and British Academy, *The Emergence of Man.*

1982

Piaget's contribution to developmental psycholinguistics. *Archives de Psychologie, 50,* 69–74.

1983

With D. Fish. The psychological causality implicit in language. *Cognition, 14,* 237–273.
With D. Fish. Are there universal schemas of psychological causality? *Archives de Psychologie, 51,* 145–153.

1986

Social Psychology The Second Edition. New York: Free Press.
Linguistic relativity. In S. H. Hulse & B. F. Green, Jr. (Eds.), *100 Years of Psychological Research in America: G. Stanley Hall and the Johns Hopkins Tradition.* Baltimore: Johns Hopkins University Press, 241–276.

Author Biographies

Ursula Bellugi is the Director for the Laboratory for Language and Cognitive Studies at the Salk Institute for Biological Studies. She has a Ph.D. from Harvard University, where Roger Brown was her mentor. For the past 15 years she has been studying the biological foundations of language through the examination of languages in a different modality, the sign languages of deaf people. Her laboratory has produced more than 100 papers and several books on this research, including *The Signs of Language*, published by Harvard University Press in 1979, and a current book called *What the Hands Reveal About the Brain*, to be published by Bradford Books/MIT Press. She collaborates with her husband, Edward S. Klima, in a range of studies that examine the links among language, mind, and brain.

Melissa Bowerman was born in Syracuse, New York, in 1942. The daughter of an anthropologist, she spent her childhood years in Mexico and Spain as well as in the United States. She received a B.A. in Psychology from Stanford in 1964 and a Ph.D. in Social Psychology from Harvard in 1971. From 1970 to 1982 she was in the Bureau of Child Research and the Department of Linguistics at the University of Kansas, Lawrence, and continues to maintain formal ties with the University. She spent 1978–1979 as a fellow at the Netherlands Institute for Advanced Study, Wassenaar, where she was one of an international group of specialists on language acquisition. Since 1982 she has been a member of the scientific staff of the Max Planck Institute for Psycholinguistics in Nijmegen, The Netherlands. Her interests include the acquisition of syntax, morphology, and word meaning, the relationship between language and cognition, the crosslinguistic study of language development, and the relationship between child language and linguistic theory. She has published *Early syntactic development: A crosslinguistic study with special reference to Finnish* (1973) and numerous articles and chapters on language acquisition. On the side, she tends a houseful of children and pets and tries to find time to play chamber music. She hopes she will finish writing about her children's language development before they become old enough to do it themselves.

Roger Brown's "Autobiography in the Third Person" appears in the Appendix.

Courtney Cazden had a B.A. in philosophy from Radcliffe, a year of teacher training at the Bank Street School in New York City, and 9 years of primary grade teaching when she returned to Harvard in 1961 as a doctoral student in Education. During her first semester she took Eric Lenneberg's course in the Psychology of Language (in which Roger Brown was a guest lecturer) and never strayed far from issues of child language and education after that. The following year she joined Brown's research seminar and became the research assistant in charge of "Sarah." Her 1965 doctoral thesis on "Environmental Assistance to the Child's Acquisition of Grammar" was an experimental spin-off from the Brown work. In that year Cazden joined the faculty of the Harvard Graduate School of Education where she is now Professor of Education. Her major research interests are in the development of children's verbal ability in and out of school, and the functions of language in all educational settings. She has been president of both the American Association for Applied Linguistics and the Council of Anthropology and Education, and is a former member of the Executive Board and Council of the American Educational Research Association. Cazden has been a Fellow at the Center for Advanced Study in the Behavioral Sciences. Recent research articles have dealt with contexts for literacy, ethnographic research, instructional practices in bilingual education, and a review of classroom discourse that is being expanded into a book.

Lerita Coleman received her Ph.D. in social psychology from Harvard University in 1980. She is presently an assistant professor in the Department of Psychology at the University of Tennessee, having previously been assistant professor/research scientist in the Department of Psychology and at the Institute for Social Research at the University of Michigan, Ann Arbor. She was a fellow at the Center for Advanced Study in the Behavioral Sciences in 1985–1986. As a social psychologist, her primary interests lie in the area of communication (verbal and nonverbal) and its impact on social/psychological development across the life-span. In addition to her publications in the area of social psychology of communication, her writings include a forthcoming edited volume *The Dilemma of Difference: A Multidisciplinary View of Stigma* (with Gaylene Becker and Stephen Ainlay).

Rick Cromer, who was born and raised in Miami, Florida in the days before concrete had essentially destroyed its tropical beauty, attended Tulane University in New Orleans, where, in 1962, he took his AB in psychology. But he was equally influenced by Tulane's anthropology department where there was much interest in the effects of culture and language on personality and thought. After Tulane, he attended Harvard University and spent his first year as a graduate student helping to collect the data on Adam and Eve as one of Roger Brown's research assistants. In the following years, he also served as a research assistant to Jerry Bruner and as a teaching assistant to George Miller. After obtaining his Ph.D. in 1968 he sailed for England where he took up the post of research psychologist in the Medical Research Council's Developmental Psychology Unit in London; there he came to appreciate the importance of studying impaired populations not only for the obvious reasons of understanding the development and functioning of such individuals, but for the light they shed on normal processing. In the research group now reorganized as the Medical Research Council Cognitive Development Unit, Cromer continues to do research on developmentally aphasic children and has most recently begun to look at the language of hyperverbal, hydrocephalic children. He is currently bringing together and updating his various chapters on the cognition hypothesis, children's strategies during language acquisition, and on language in aphasic, mentally subnormal children, and autistic individuals, to be published as *Language and Cognition in Normal and Handicapped Children,* by Basil Blackwell Publishers.

Jill de Villiers graduated from Reading University, England, in 1969, with a bachelor's degree in psychology. After a year working in Oxford as a research assistant, she entered the graduate program in Experimental Psychology at Harvard, with her husband-to-be, Peter de Villiers. She worked closely with Roger Brown at Harvard on the "later stages" of language development in children, and with Peter made a widely used documentary film on the subject of language development for the Canadian Broadcasting Corporation. After receiving her Ph.D. in 1974, she began teaching on the Harvard faculty and served as a tutor in Lowell House. After 5 years at Harvard, two books (*Early Language* and *Language Acquisition,* Harvard University Press), and a son, the de Villiers accepted posts at Smith College and collaborated on producing a daughter in 1980. As an Associate Professor of Psychology and Philosophy at Smith College, Jill de Villiers continues to contribute to the research literature on language acquisition and is writing a book on biological aspects of language.

Howard Gardner came to Cambridge, Massachusetts in September 1961 and, except for a year spent in London in 1965–1966, has been affiliated with Harvard University ever since. At present, he is Co-Director of Harvard Project Zero, a Research Psychologist at the Boston Veterans Administration Medical Center, and Professor of Neurology at the Boston University School of Medicine. His major research interest is human symbol use: He investigates the development of symbol-using capacities in normal and gifted children and the breakdown of these capacities as the result of damage to the brain. His professional interests in the arts and human development complement his personal engagements with music, travel, and children, most especially Kerith, Jay, and Andrew; and he occasionally discusses work with his wife, Ellen Winner. Among his books are *Art, Mind, and Brain, Frames of Mind, The Mind's New Science,* and *Developmental Psychology,* for which Roger Brown graciously provided a foreword. In 1981 he was awarded a MacArthur Prize Fellowship.

Jean Berko Gleason was one of Roger Brown's first cohort of graduate students and received a joint Ph.D. in linguistics and psychology from Radcliffe College in 1958. Her doctoral dissertation, "The child's learning of English morphology" was published that year in *Word* and has since been reprinted many times, both in English and in other languages. She has published widely in the fields of both language development and aphasia, including a textbook on the development of language and work that won the Editor's Award of the *Journal of Speech and Hearing Research.* She has been a visiting scholar at Stanford and at the Hungarian Academy of Sciences in Budapest, where she has studied language and socialization among the Gypsies. Currently, she is professor of psychology and chairperson of the department at Boston University.

Kenji Hakuta is Professor of Education and Psychology at the University of California, Santa Cruz. He was previously Associate Professor of Psychology at Yale University. He received his B.A. (Psychology and Social Relations) and Ph.D. (Experimental Psychology) from Harvard, both under the watchful eyes of Roger Brown. His current research interests are in the areas of bilingualism and in comparative studies of child development in Japan and the United States. He is author of *Mirror of Language: The Debate on Bilingualism* (Basic Books) and coeditor (with Hiroshi Azuma and Harold Stevenson) of *Kodomo: Child Development and Education in Japan* (W. H. Freeman). In his free time, he enjoys tennis, woodworking, gardening, and sumo wrestling.

Camille Hanlon is a native of New Orleans, Louisiana. She was an undergraduate at the University of Texas and a graduate student at Stanford University, where she completed her doctoral work in psychology in 1964. From 1964 to 1967 she was an assistant professor in the Departments of Psychology and Pediatrics at the University of Iowa. Following the award of a National Institutes of Health Postdoctoral Research Training Fellowship in 1967, she spent a year as a Research Fellow and Lecturer in the Department of Social Relations at Harvard University. Since that time she has taught at Connecticut College, where she is currently a professor in the Department of Child Development. Her major research interests are in language and cognitive development. Time off is likely to be spent in family travel, relaxing with friends, or taking the occasional photograph.

Frank Kessel's undergraduate and early graduate studies in psychology were at the University of Cape Town where he was introduced to Piaget, phenomenological psychology, and much else besides, by Kurt Danziger and others. He then had the good fortune to pursue his interests in cognitive and language development at the University of Minnesota in the late 1960s, when and where "revolution" à la Kuhn was much on the minds of persons such as James Jenkins and John Flavell, while Herbert Feigl's Philosophy of Science Center was close at hand to satisfy that interest. After graduating in 1969—with a language development dissertation—and spending a postdoctoral spell at the University of Alberta's Theoretical Psychology Center, he became involved in international early education efforts, first as Research Director of the Early Learning Centre back in Cape Town and then as Scientific Associate at the Bernard van Leer Foundation in The Hague. Since joining the University of Houston in 1976, he has happily played the role of itinerant impresario, helping to organize and coedit the Psychology Department's "Houston Symposium" series there, and elsewhere staging symposia that have explored varied facets of developmental psychology and the philosophy and history of psychology. His not unrelated affection for the arts has been engaged and enriched by his wife, Marion, a pianist and percussionist now involved in performing-arts management. His childhood passion for sports, dimmed by Bjorn Borg's departure from the world's tennis courts, has been somewhat revived recently by Akeem Olajuwon's unlikely arrival and ascent on Houston's basketball courts.

Michael Maratsos was born in San Francisco in 1945. He received a B.A. at Stanford University and an M.A. and Ph.D. from Harvard University, where he worked with Roger Brown. He has received a Boyd McCandless Award from Division 7 of APA, and an Early Career Award from APA. He is a professor at the Institute of Child Development at the University of Minnesota and has been a visiting professor or fellow at the University of Texas at Austin, the University of California at La Jolla, the Center for Advanced Study in the Behavioral Sciences, the Institute for Advanced Studies at the Hebrew University of Jerusalem, and the East China Normal University of Shanghai. He lives with his wife, Mary Anne Chalkley, two children, Jessica and Paul, and a dog.

Laura Petitto is currently an Assistant Professor in the Department of Psychology at McGill University in Montreal, having travelled the educational and professional path sketched in her contribution to this volume. In addition to language acquisition and sign languages, her interests include disorders in language (e.g., aphasia) and spatial cognition.

Steven Pinker received his B.A. in Psychology from McGill University in 1976 and his Ph.D. in Experimental Psychology from Harvard University in 1979. In 1979–1980 he was a Postdoctoral Fellow at the Center for Cognitive Science at the Massachusetts Institute of Technology. During the next 3 years he was Assistant Professor in three different psychology departments: Harvard in 1980–1981, Stanford in 1981–1982, and MIT in 1982–1983. Since then he has remained at MIT, where he is currently Associate Professor of Psychology and Co-Director of the Center for Cognitive Science. In 1984 he was awarded the Distinguished Scientific Award for an Early Career Contribution to Psychology of the American Psychological Association and delivered the Nijmegen Lectures at the Max-Planck-Institute for Psycholinguistics. Pinker has done research in language acquisition and in visual cognition since he was in graduate school. He recently wrote *Language Learnability and Language Development* (Harvard University Press, 1984) and edited *Visual Cognition* (MIT Press, 1985). He is married to Nancy Etcoff, a clinical psychologist and neuropsychologist, who shares his passion for the Boston Celtics but not for the Montreal Canadiens.

Eleanor Rosch graduated from Reed College in 1963 with a major in philosophy. In the course of doing her honors thesis on Wittgenstein's method in the *Philosophical Investigations,* she was sufficiently influenced to be "cured" of philosophy, and she entered graduate school at Harvard University in clinical psychology. Soon disenchanted with clinical, she then came to work with Roger Brown, doing her dissertation on an aspect of social class differences in language use. As she was completing her dissertation, she first encountered the then-new field of cognitive psychology, which seemed to allow for empirical investigation of some of the kinds of issues that had drawn her to philosophy. She received her Ph.D. in 1969 and spent that year doing field research in West Irian, New Guinea, with her former husband, Karl Heider. The following year was spent at Brown University under the auspices of Lewis Lipsitt and Richard Millward. In 1971 she began teaching in the Psychology Department at the University of California, Berkeley, where she has remained ever since.

David Rubin decided to go to graduate school in social psychology after reading Roger Brown's text. By the time he received his B.S. in physics and psychology from Carnegie–Mellon University in 1968, however, graduate education was no longer an option and he worked instead for 2 years as an Aerospace Engineer for NASA's Electronic Research Center. He then entered the Psychology Department at Harvard and, under Roger Brown's supervision, received his Ph.D. in 1974. The next 4 years were spent in Appleton, Wisconsin, as one-sixth of Lawrence University's Psychology Department. Except for a year's sabbatical at the Medical Research Council's Applied Psychology Unit in Cambridge, England, the rest of his career has been spent at Duke University. Starting with his Ph.D. thesis on memory for prose, Rubin's main research interest has been the attempt to predict which parts of stimuli are recalled under different circumstances. This work ranges from the recall of word lists under laboratory conditions through prose to the recall of material learned outside the laboratory— coins, counting-out rhymes, and even autobiographical memories. The research discussed in this volume, part of a larger effort to understand recall in oral traditions, allows for a synthesis of much of his earlier work.

Dan I. Slobin studied psychology at the University of Michigan (B.A., 1960), where he first encountered psycholinguistics and Roger Brown—through an exciting initiation in reading *Words and Things,* and through a colloquium that Roger gave in Ann Arbor in 1959, showing that the study of child language could reveal something about the highly intelligent character of children's unconscious mental processes. This resonated with Slobin's interests in Freudian psychology, cognition, and anthropology; and he went on to Harvard's Department of Social Relations and Center for Cognitive Studies to work with Roger, Jerome Bruner, George Miller, and Eric Lenneberg, while absorbing the energy and promise of transformational grammar at MIT. He soon fell into experimental and developmental psycholinguistics, supplemented by studies and translations of Soviet psychology. Earning a Ph.D. in 1964, Slobin went to Berkeley's Department of Psychology, where he has remained ever since. His primary concern has been to develop a crosslinguistic approach to the study of child language acquisition, elaborating a system of "operating principles" to account for both universal and language-particular aspects of acquisition. He has carried out investigations of language development in Turkey, Israel, Italy, Yugoslavia, and the United States and has organized a number of crosslinguistic research endeavors. This work can be found in a recent set of volumes edited by Slobin, *The crosslinguistic study of language acquisition* (Lawrence Erlbaum Associates, 1986). Most recently, he has spent a 1984–1985 Guggenheim Fellowship year considering issues of historical language change from the viewpoints of developmental and cognitive psychology and psycholinguistics.

Helen Tager was born, raised, and educated in England. As an undergraduate she studied Psychology at University College London where she became captivated with the field of psycholinguistics. She travelled to Cambridge, Massachusetts in 1973 to study for her doctorate, ready to begin work with Roger Brown. Unfortunately, she had applied and been accepted into the Experimental Psychology program at Harvard, while in the meantime Roger had returned to the Social Psychology program. For a first-year student in the wrong program, it was not so easy to gain entrance to the 12th floor of William James Hall. But fortune was with her, and after 6 months of hard labor studying psychophysics and animal learning, Jill de Villiers came by and casually asked Helen if she would be interested in working as a research assistant on Roger Brown's NSF grant. For several years they worked together, along with Peter de Villiers and

Kenji Hakuta, and Jill taught her everything about child language methodology. She completed her dissertation, finally, in 1978, and then began teaching in the Psychology Department at the University of Massachusetts in Boston. She has been there ever since, working a little on normal language development and a lot on language development in autistic and retarded children. Her full-time teaching position, two children, and husband (who provided her with her hyphenated name in 1974) leave no time for hobbies, but she does try hard to read at least three novels a month, and to watch Masterpiece Theater on Sunday nights!

Eric Wanner is currently President of the Russell Sage Foundation, a Fellow of the New York Institute of the Humanities, and a sometime psycholinguist. Prior to being a Vice President of the Alfred P. Sloan Foundation he previously served as the Behavioral Science Editor at Harvard University Press and as a member of the junior faculty in the Department of Psychology and Social Relations at Harvard, where he received his Ph.D. in 1969. His research has chiefly been concerned with the problems of parsing: how people do it, how computers do it, and how the one might be related to the other. He is the author of one book, *On Remembering, Forgetting and Understanding Sentences* and the co-editor of another, *Language Acquisition* (with Lila Gleitman).

Ellen Winner studied literature at Radcliffe College and painting at Boston's Museum School before becoming a developmental psychologist. Her work in psychology has focused on the development of artistic knowledge in children, with emphasis on the visual and verbal arts. She has carried out psycholinguistic research on children's sensitivity to figurative and fictional language. She received her Ph.D. in 1978 from Harvard University (with Roger Brown as her thesis advisor). She is currently a research associate at Harvard Project Zero and an associate professor of psychology at Boston College. In her book, *Invented Worlds: The Psychology of the Arts,* she returns to her original interest in the arts via the psychology of the arts.

Author Index

Subject Index